A MUTTS TREASURY

BONK!

PATRICK McDONNELL

Andrews McMeel
Publishing, LLC

Kansas City • Sydney • London

Other Books by Patrick McDonnell

Mutts
Cats and Dogs: Mutts II
More Shtuff: Mutts III
Yesh!: Mutts IV
Our Mutts: Five
A Little Look-See: Mutts VI
What Now: Mutts VII
I Want to Be the Kitty: Mutts VIII
Dog-Eared: Mutts IX
Who Let the Cat Out: Mutts X
Everyday Mutts
Animal Friendly
Call of the Wild
Stop and Smell the Roses
Earl & Mooch
Our Little Kat King

Mutts Sundays
Sunday Mornings
Sunday Afternoons
Sunday Evenings

The Best of Mutts

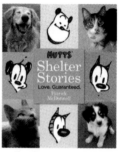

Shelter Stories

Mutts is distributed internationally by King Features Syndicate, Inc. For information, write to King Features Syndicate, Inc., 300 West Fifty-Seventh Street, New York, New York 10019, or visit www.KingFeatures.com.

Bonk! copyright © 2012 by Patrick McDonnell. All rights reserved. Printed in the United States of America. No part of this book may be used or reproduced in any manner whatsoever without written permission except in the case of reprints in the context of reviews. Andrews McMeel Publishing, LLC, an Andrews McMeel Universal company, 1130 Walnut Street, Kansas City, Missouri 64106.

12 13 14 15 16 BAM 10 9 8 7 6 5 4 3 2 1

ISBN: 978-1-4494-2308-7

Library of Congress Control Number: 2012936724

Printed on recycled paper.

Mutts can be found on the Internet at
www.muttscomics.com

Cover design by Jeff Schulz.

ATTENTION: SCHOOLS AND BUSINESSES

Andrews McMeel books are available at quantity discounts with bulk purchase for educational, business, or sales promotional use. For information, please e-mail the Andrews McMeel Publishing Special Sales Department: specialsales@amuniversal.com.

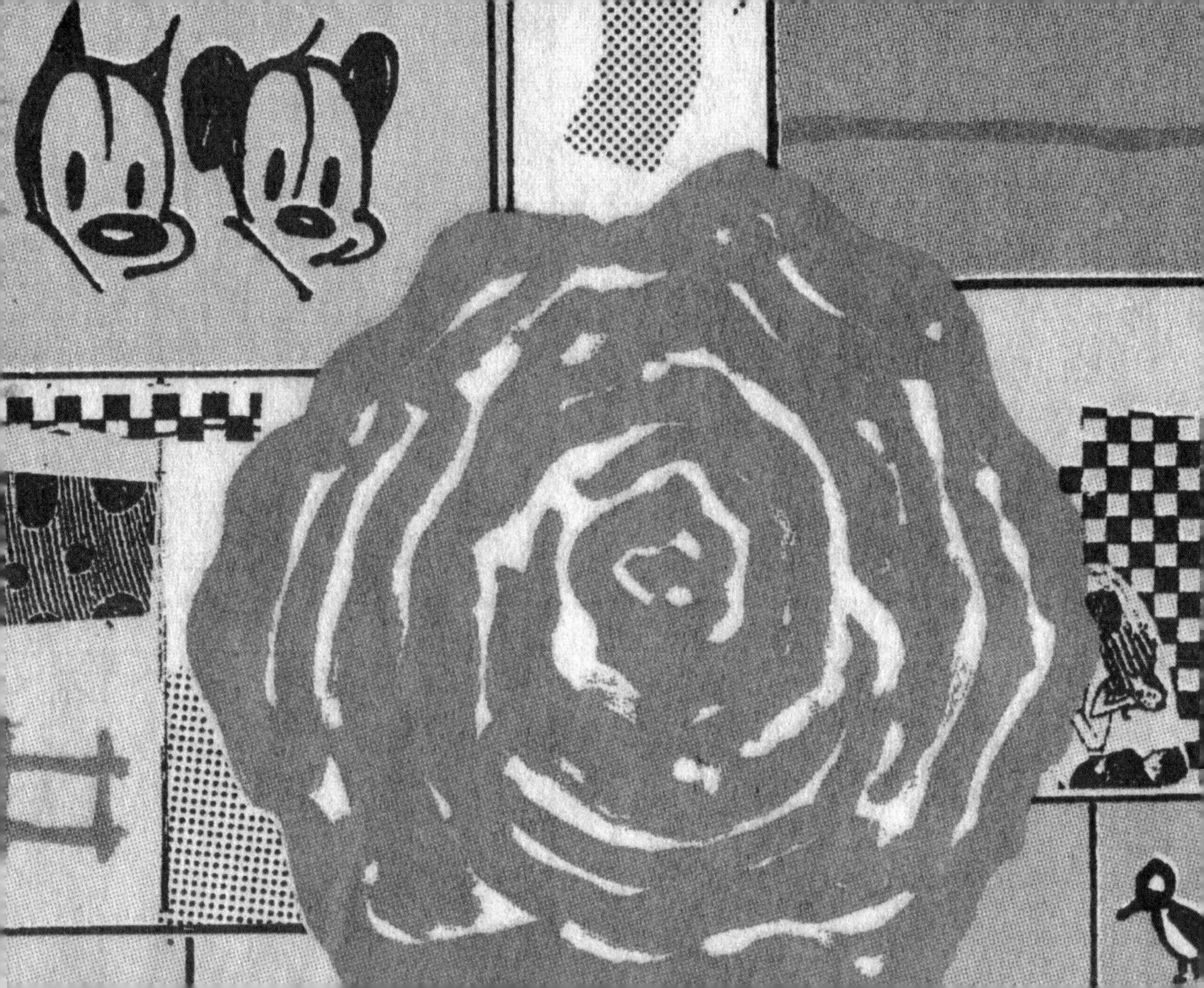

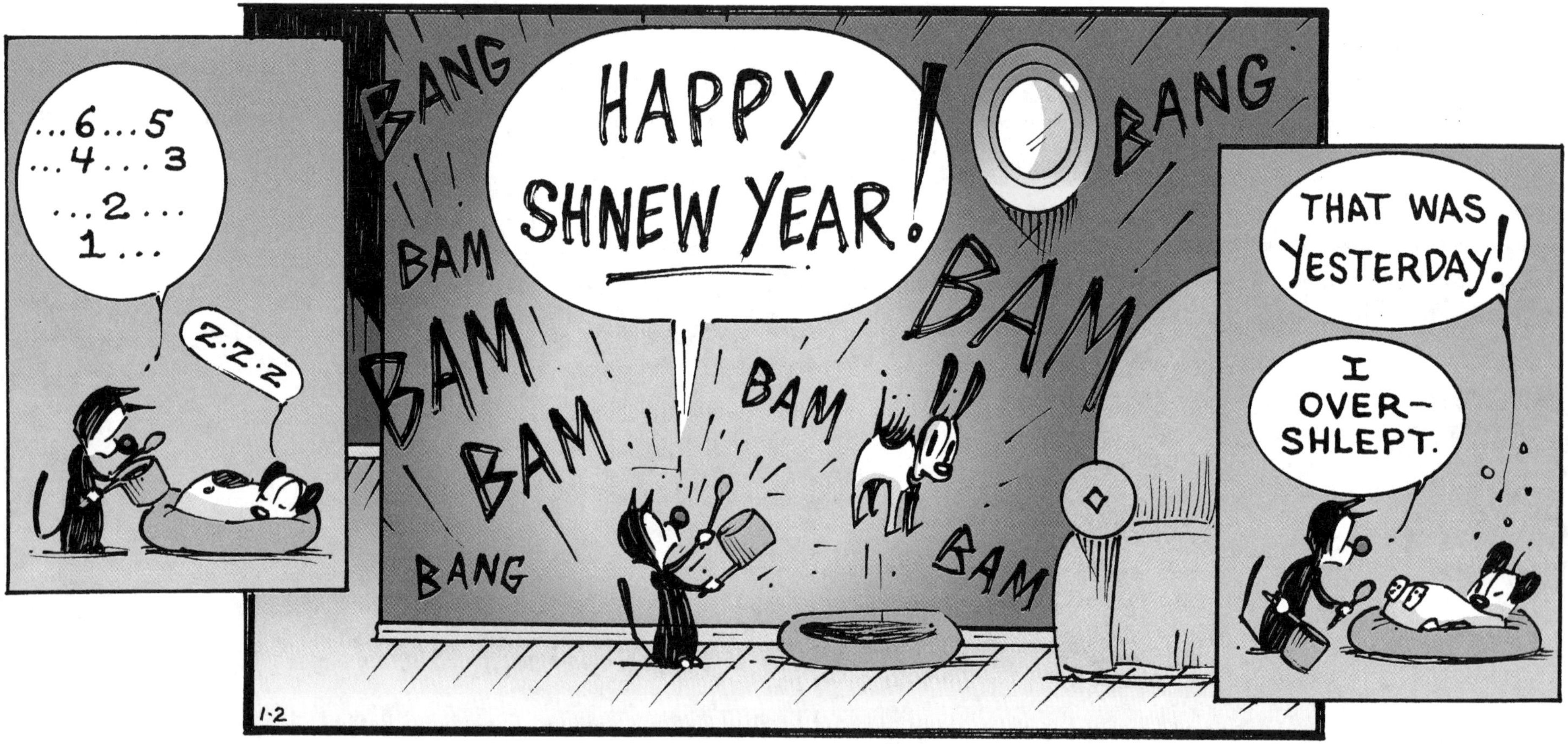
...6...5
...4...3
...2...
1...
Z·Z·Z
BANG
HAPPY SHNEW YEAR!
BANG
BAM
BAM
BAM
BAM
BAM
BAM
BANG
BAM
1·2
THAT WAS YESTERDAY!
I OVER-SHLEPT.

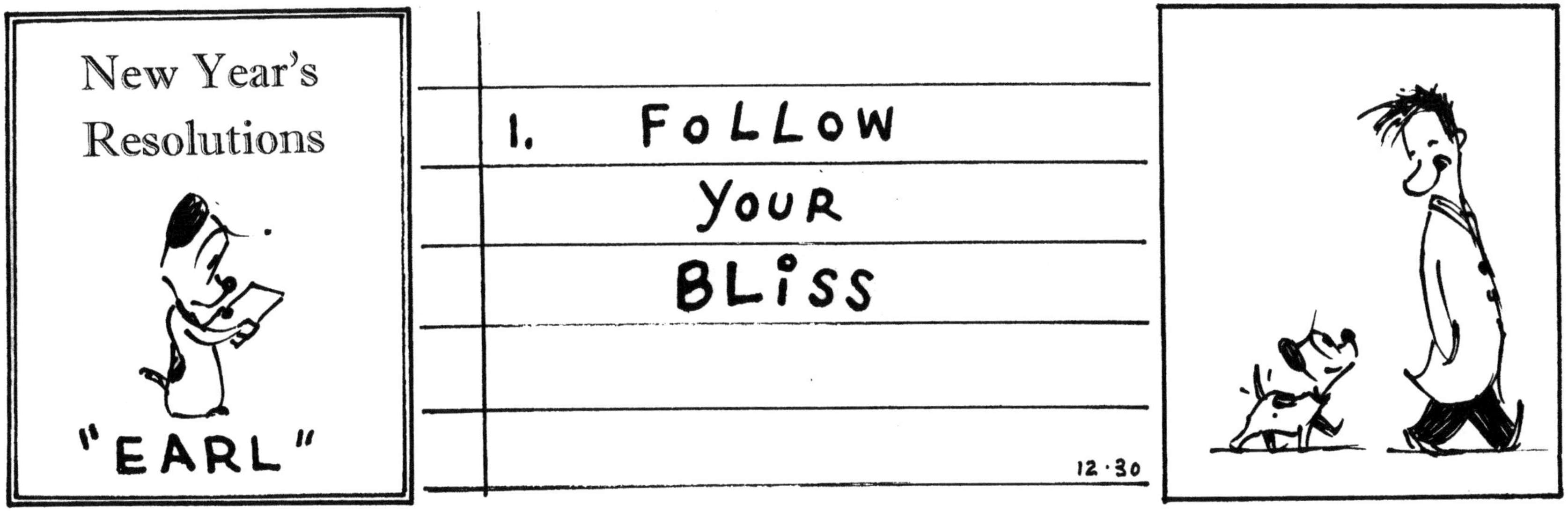
New Year's Resolutions
"EARL"
1. FOLLOW YOUR BLISS
12·30

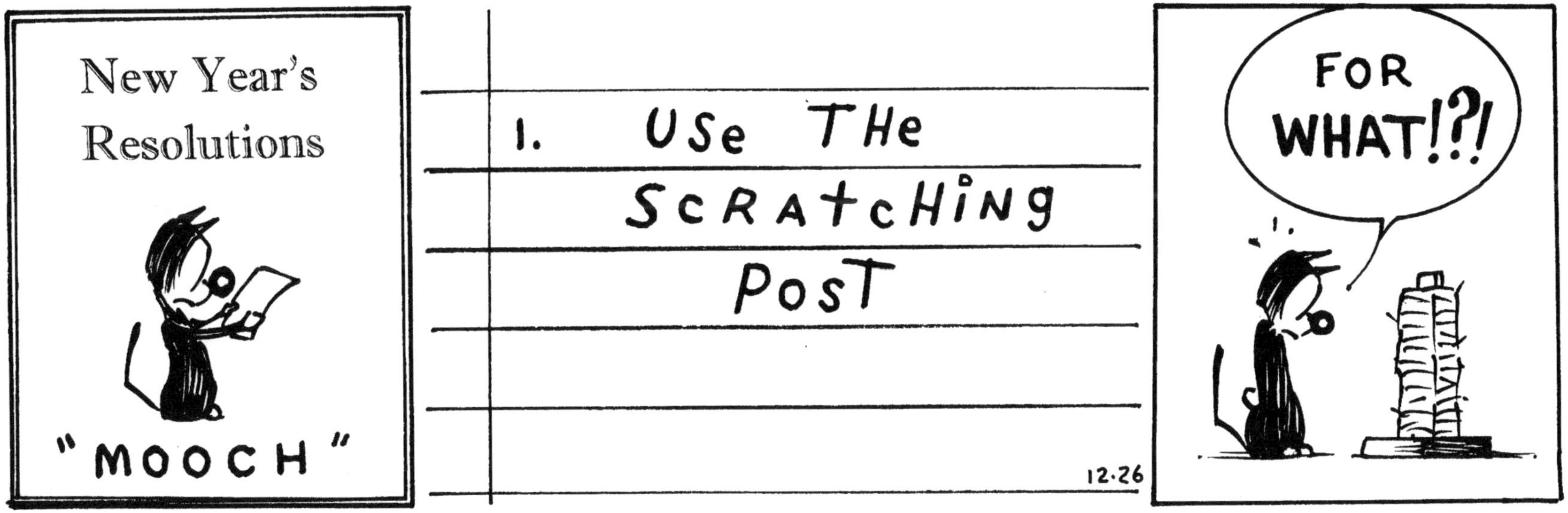
New Year's Resolutions
"MOOCH"
1. USE THE SCRATCHING POST
12·26
FOR WHAT!?!

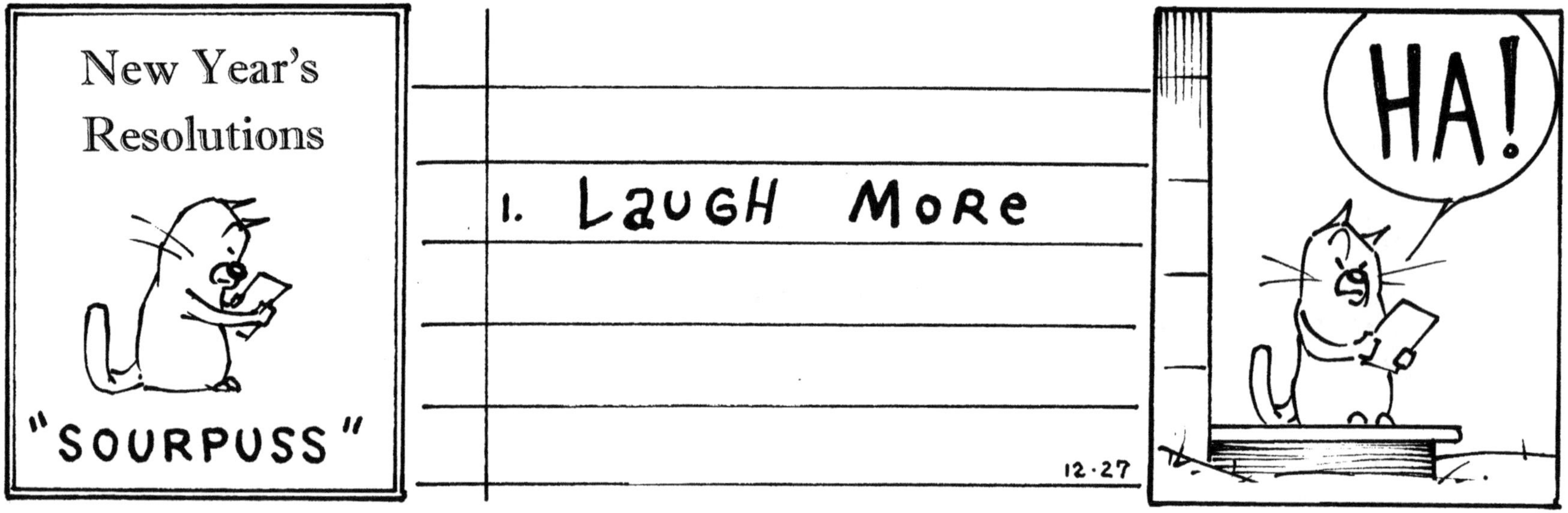
New Year's Resolutions
"SOURPUSS"
1. LAUGH MORE
12·27
HA!

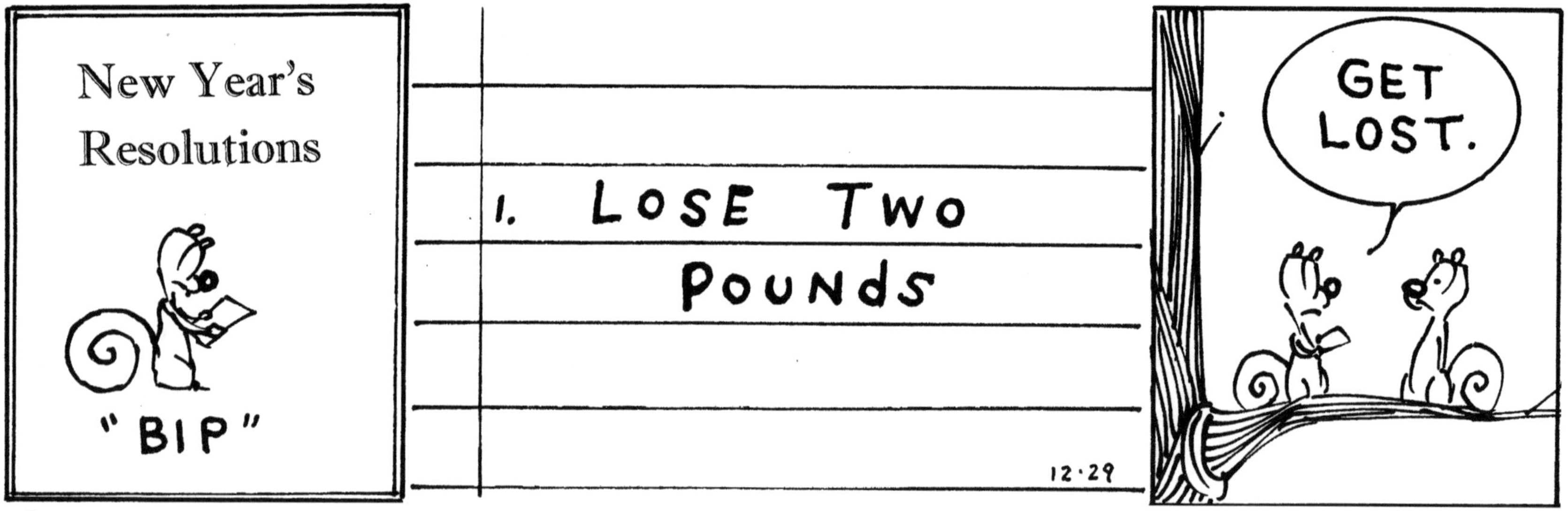
New Year's Resolutions
"BIP"
1. LOSE TWO POUNDS
12·29
GET LOST.

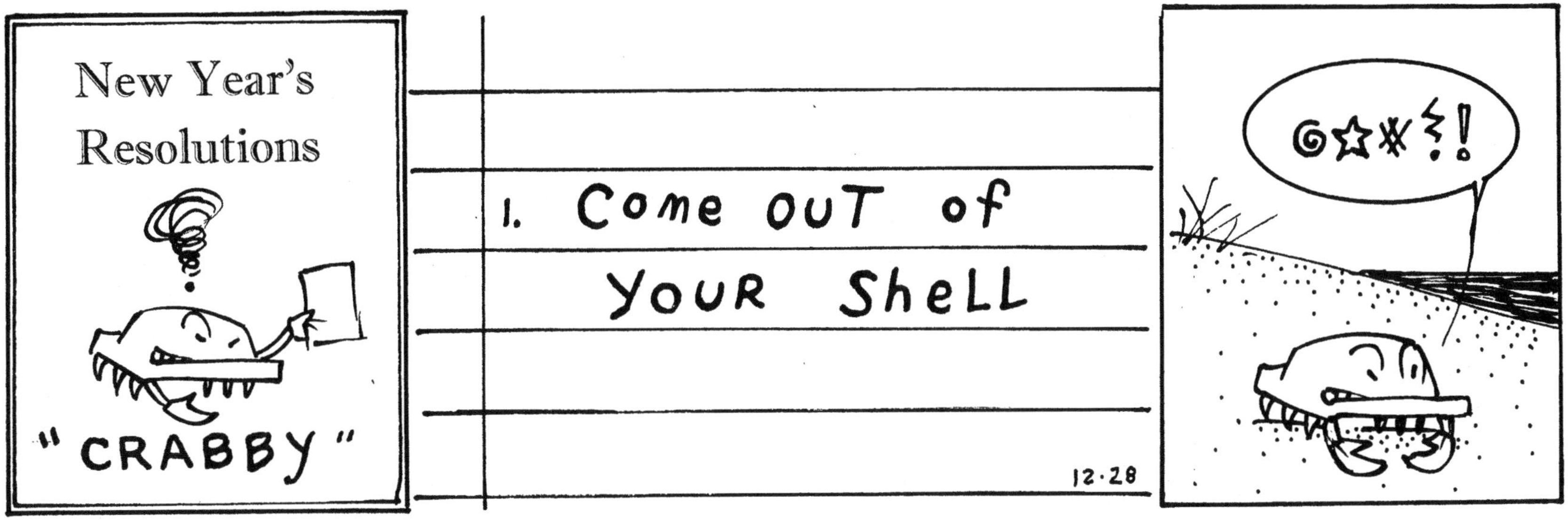
New Year's Resolutions
"CRABBY"
1. Come OUT of YOUR ShELL
12·28
G☆✱ȿ!

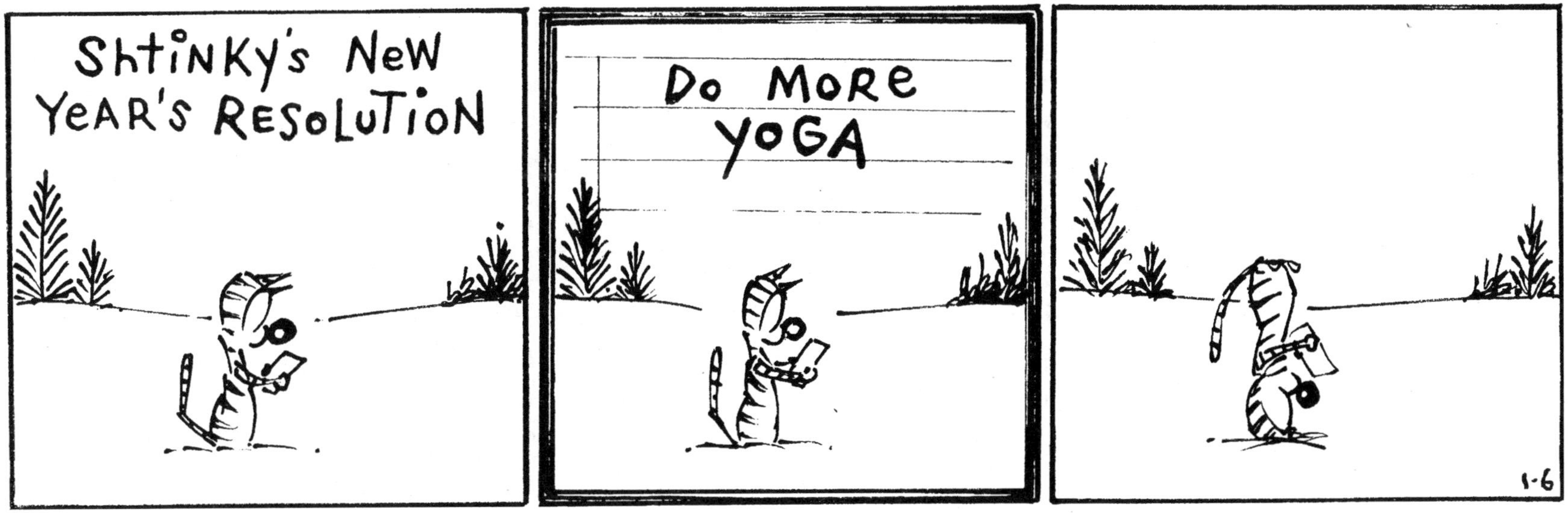
ShtiNKy's New YeAR's ResoLuTioN
Do MoRe YoGA
1-6

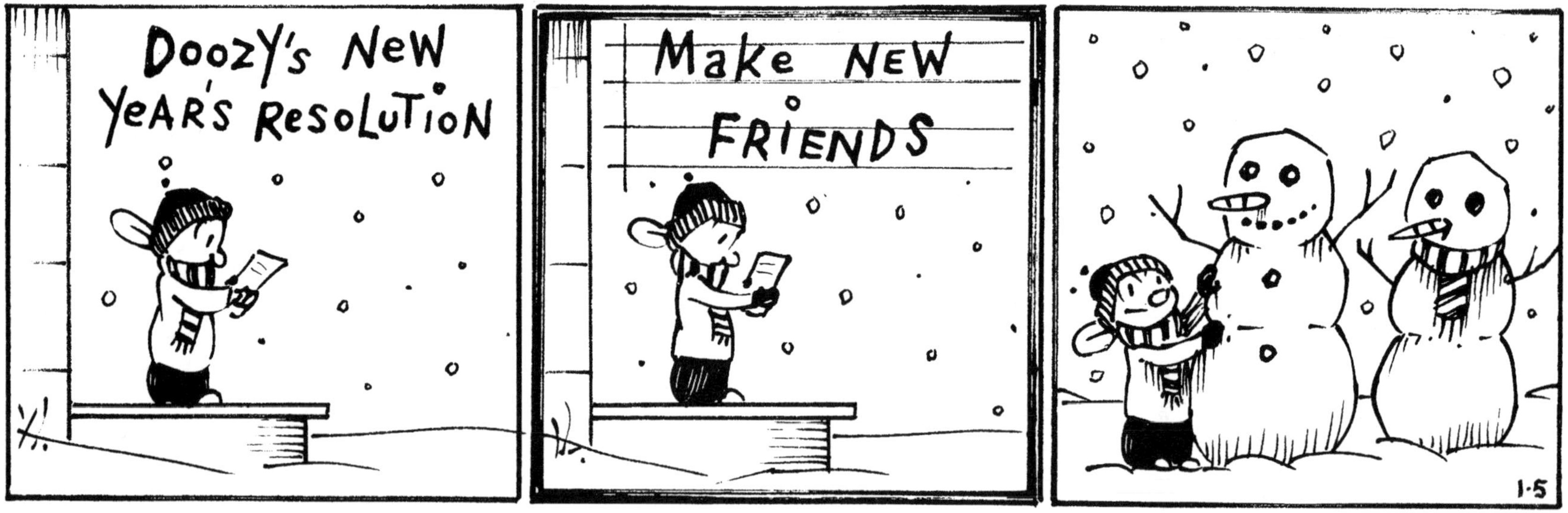
DOOZY'S NEW YEAR'S RESOLUTION
MAKE NEW FRIENDS
1·5

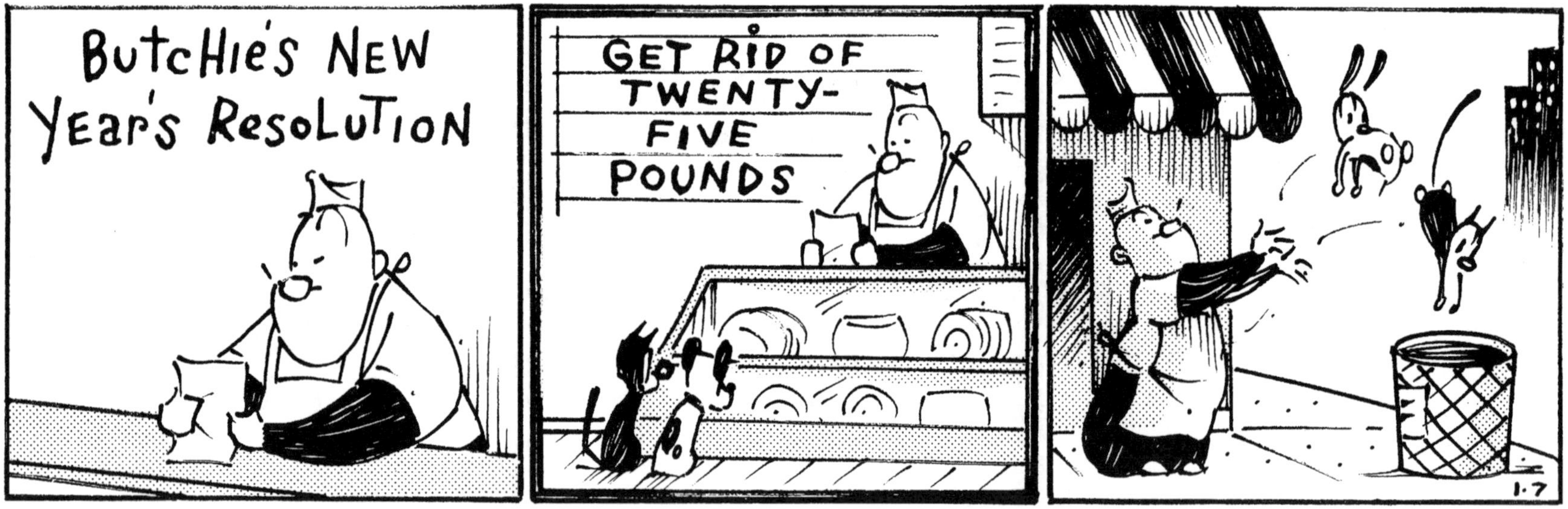
BUTCHIE'S NEW YEAR'S RESOLUTION
GET RID OF TWENTY-FIVE POUNDS
1·7

MUTTS

EARL, I'VE DECIDED TO TRY TO HIBERNATE ALL WINTER!
WHAT FUN!
I'M GOING TO SHLEEP ALL DAY AND ALL NIGHT—ONLY TO GET UP FOR MEALS, SHNACKS AND OCCASIONAL FLIGHTS OF FANCY!
BUT MOOCH
THAT'S WHAT YOU ALWAYS DO!!
IT DID SOUND FAMILIAR.
1·23

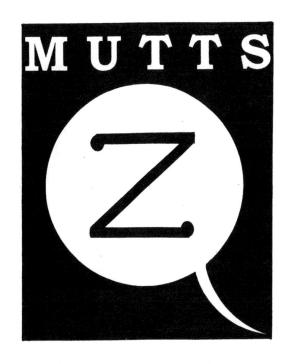

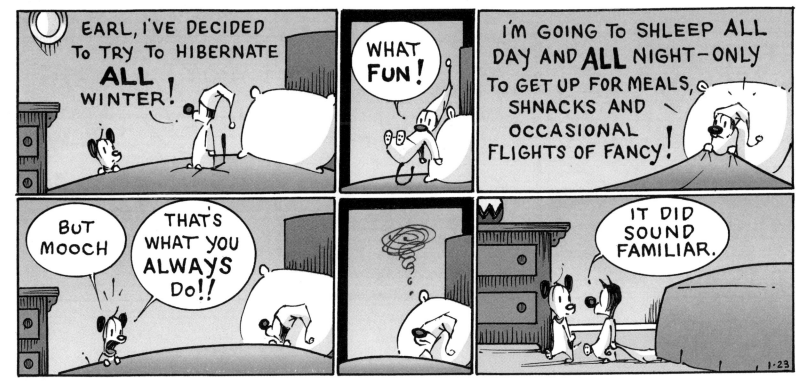

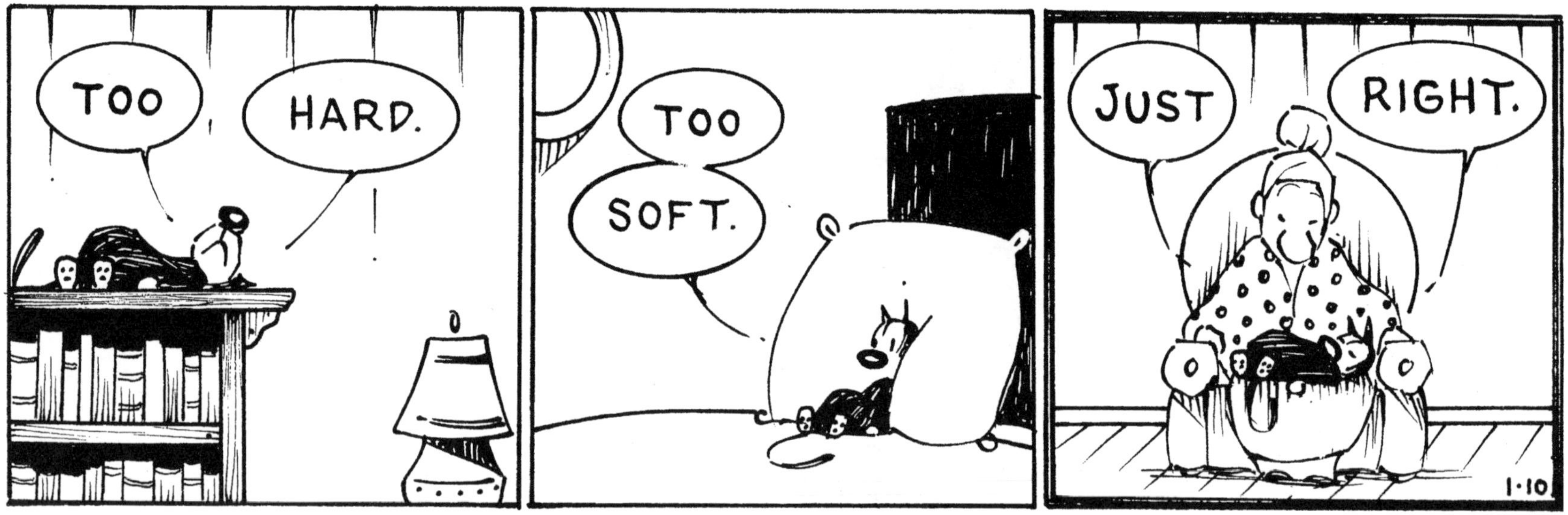
TOO
HARD.
TOO
SOFT.
JUST
RIGHT.
1·10

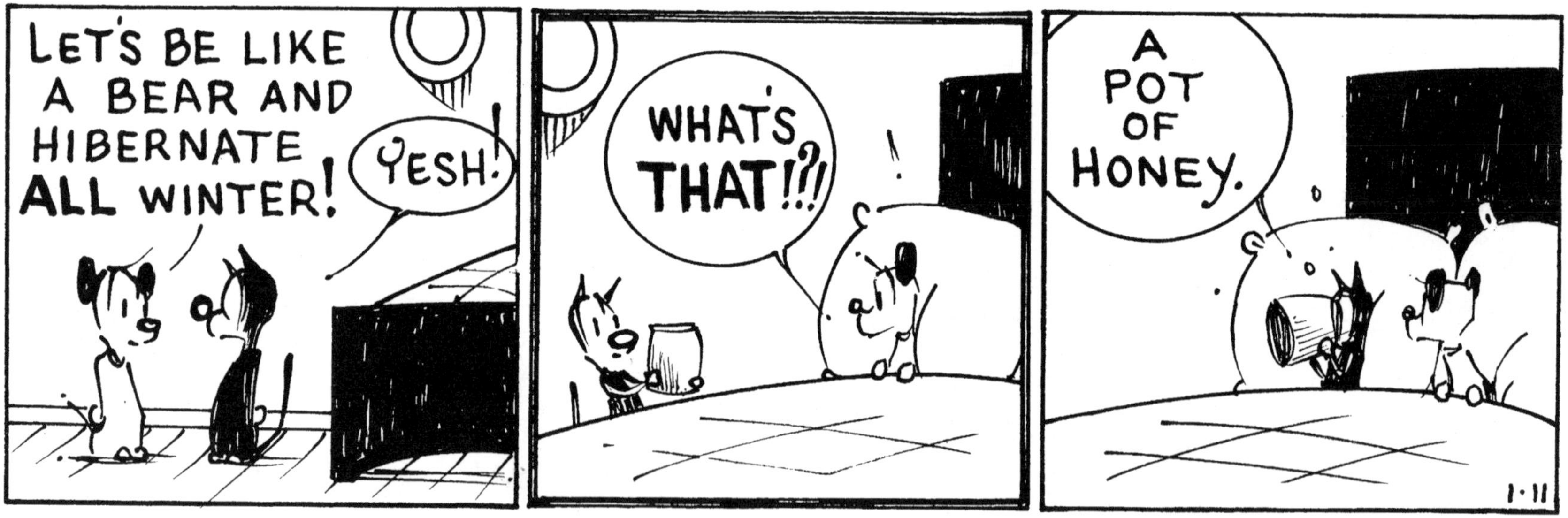
LET'S BE LIKE A BEAR AND HIBERNATE ALL WINTER!
YESH!
WHAT'S THAT!?!
A POT OF HONEY.
1·11

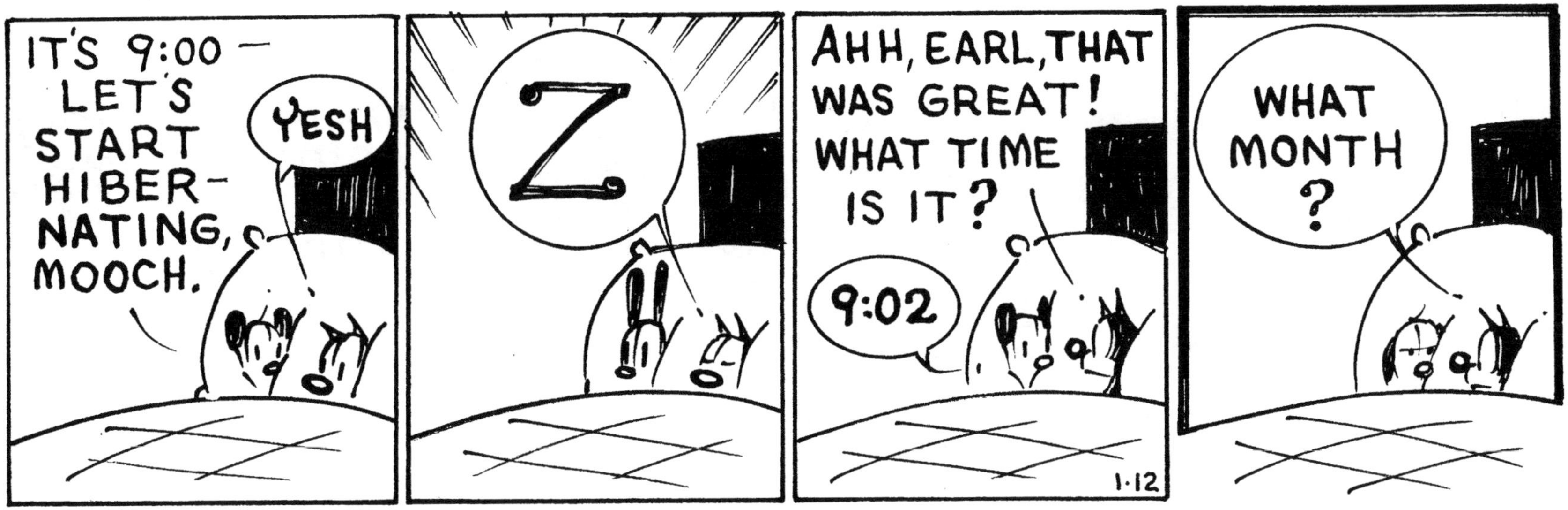
IT'S 9:00 — LET'S START HIBER-NATING, MOOCH.
YESH
Z
AHH, EARL, THAT WAS GREAT! WHAT TIME IS IT?
9:02
WHAT MONTH ?
1·12

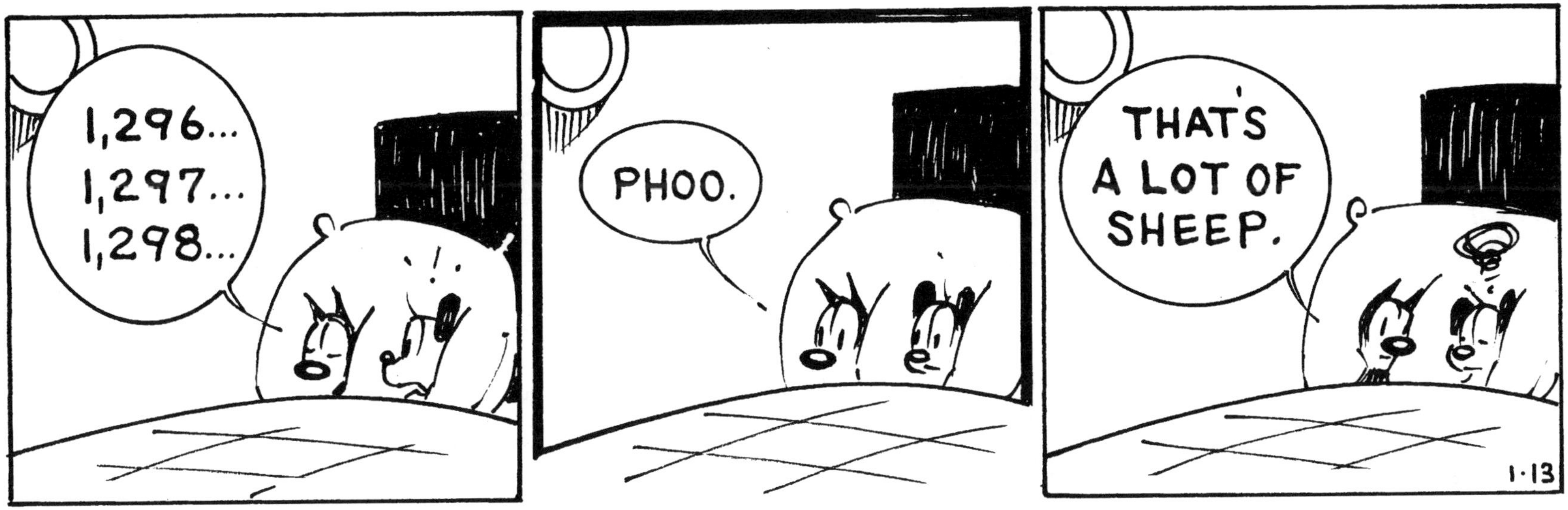
1,296... 1,297... 1,298...
PHOO.
THAT'S A LOT OF SHEEP.
1·13

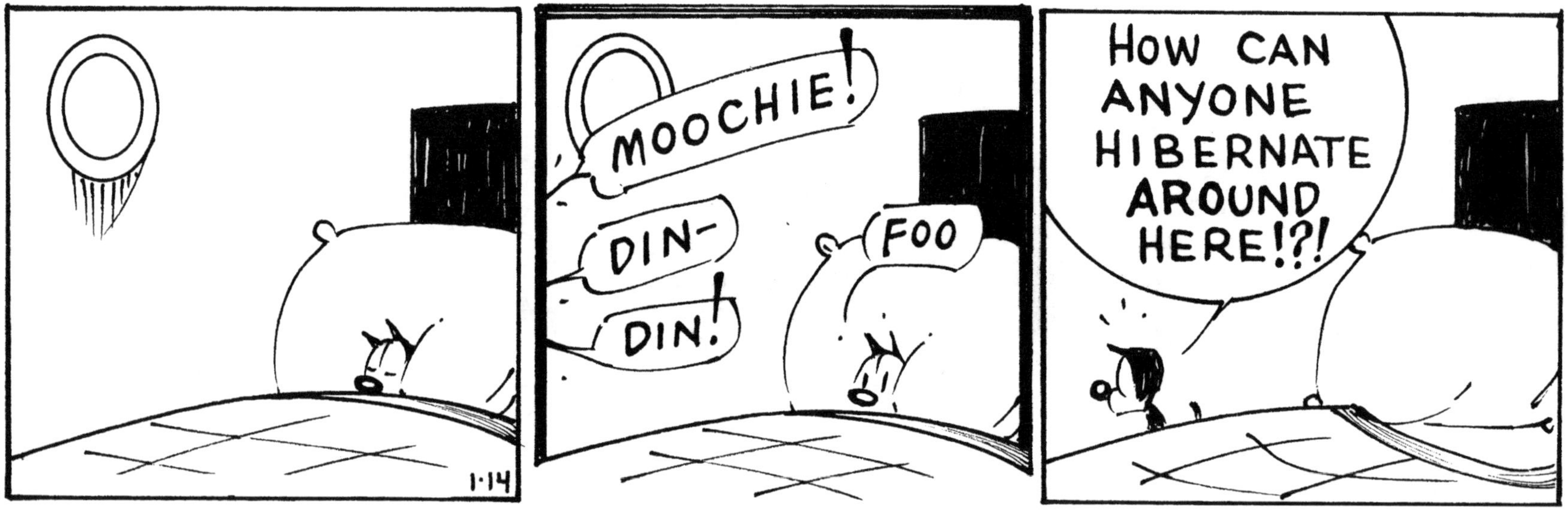
MOOCHIE!
DIN-DIN!
FOO
HOW CAN ANYONE HIBERNATE AROUND HERE!?!
1·14

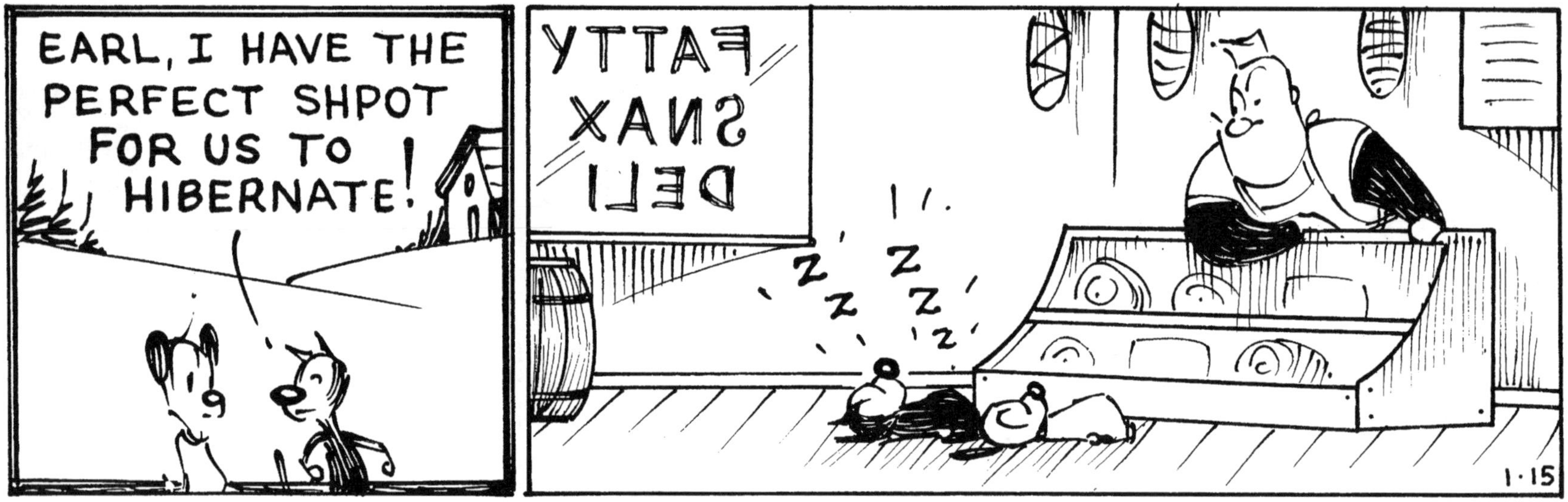
EARL, I HAVE THE PERFECT SHPOT FOR US TO HIBERNATE!
FATTY SNAX DELI
Z Z Z Z Z
1·15

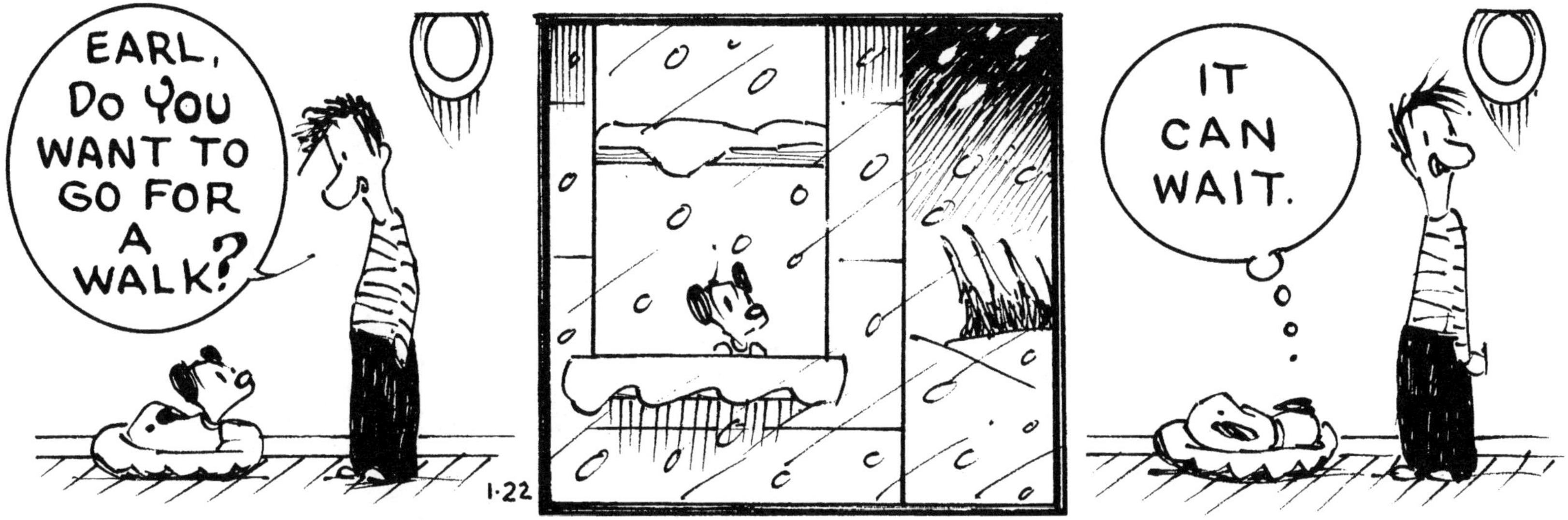
EARL, DO YOU WANT TO GO FOR A WALK?
IT CAN WAIT.
1·22

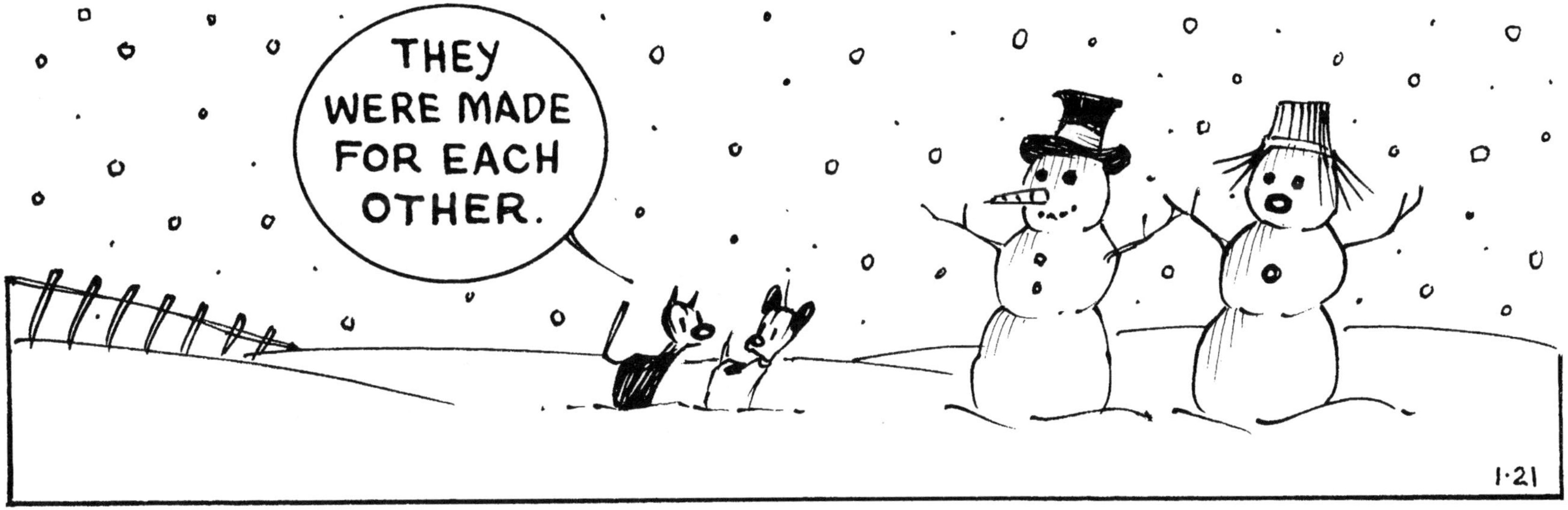
THEY WERE MADE FOR EACH OTHER.
1·21

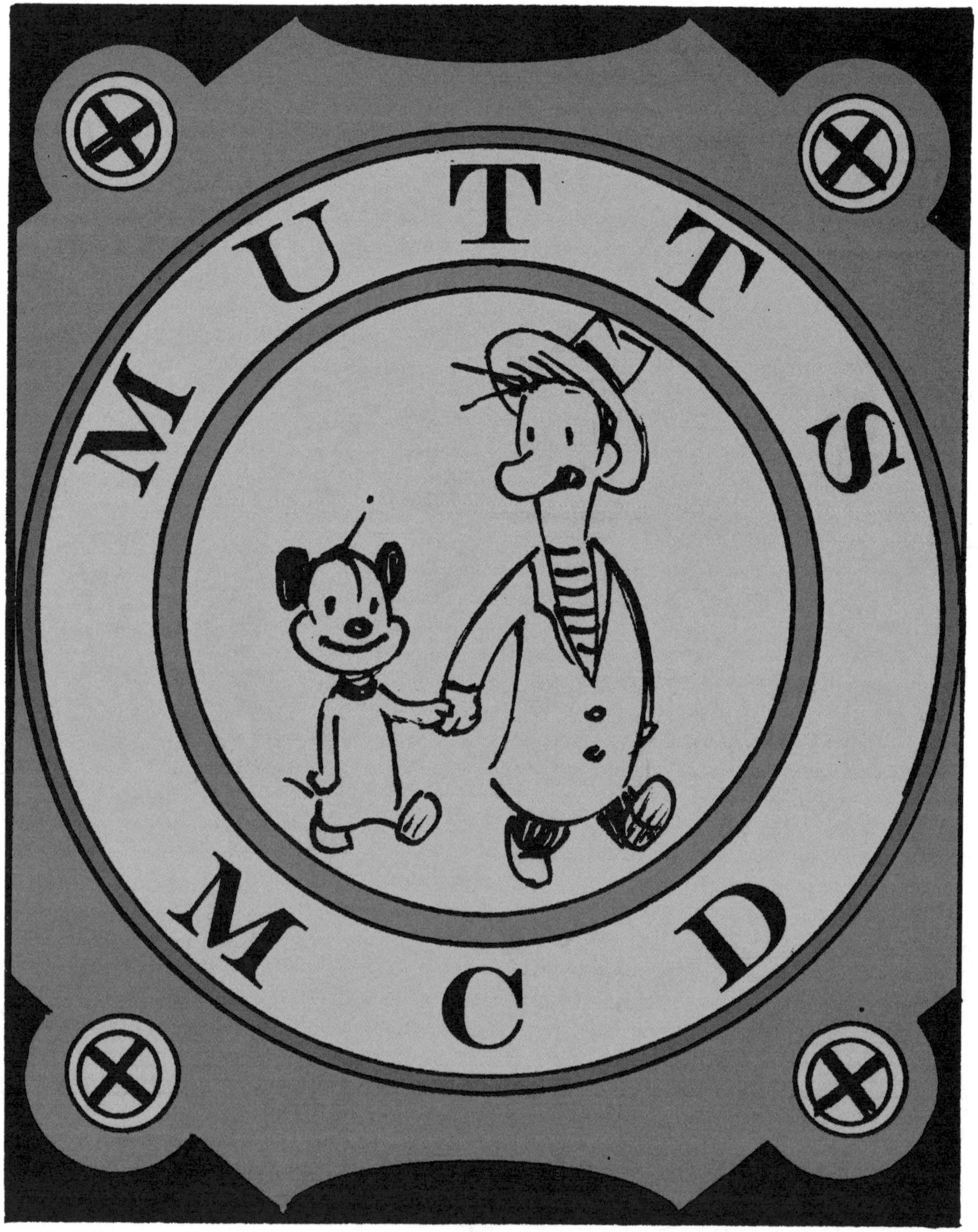
MUTTS
MCD

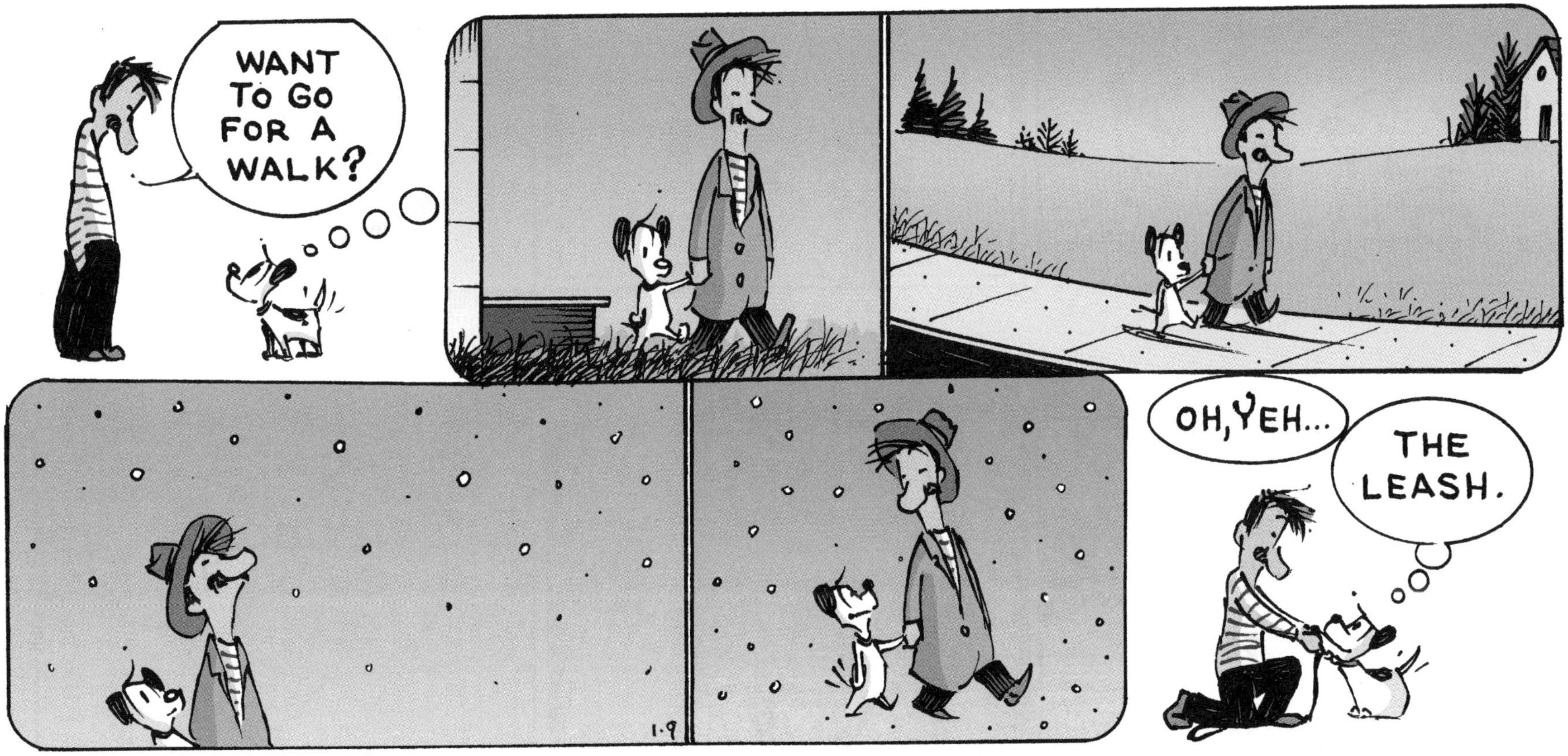
WANT TO GO FOR A WALK?
OH, YEH...
THE LEASH.

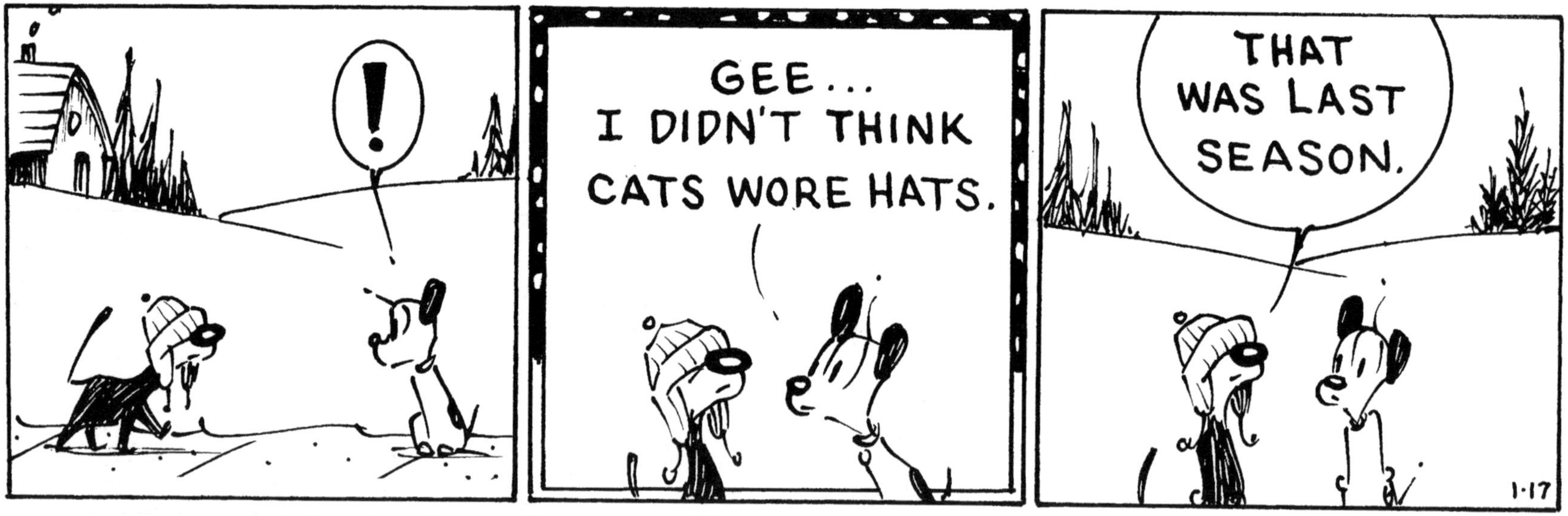
!
GEE... I DIDN'T THINK CATS WORE HATS.
THAT WAS LAST SEASON.
1·17

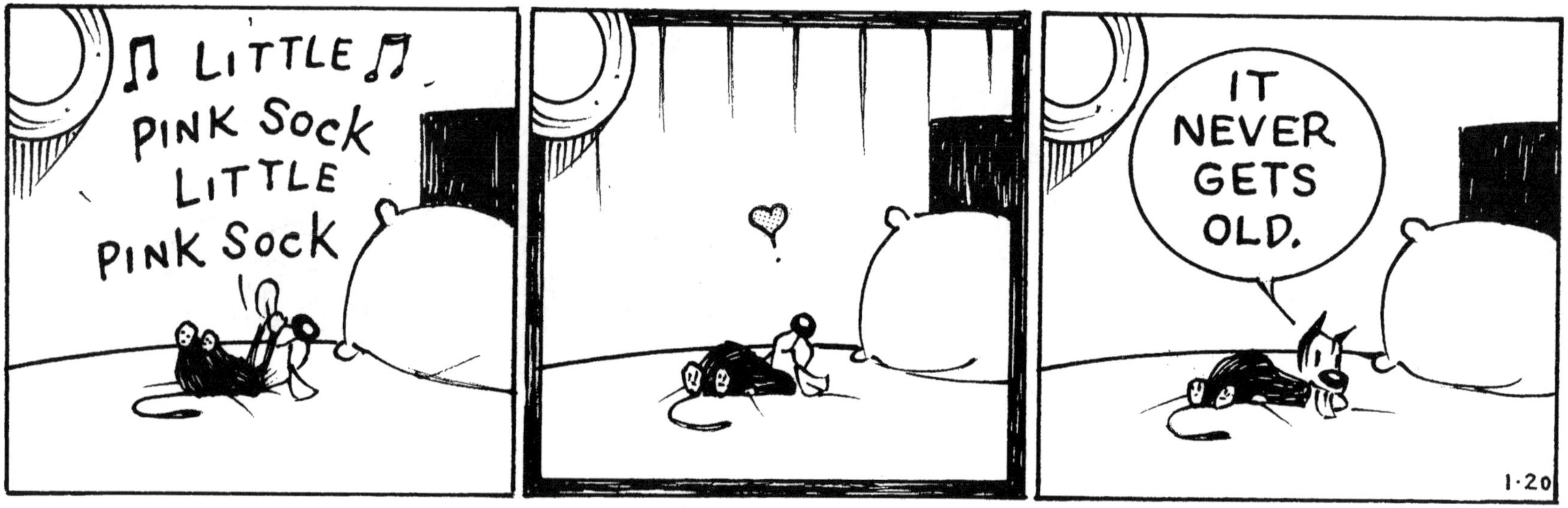
♫ LITTLE ♫ PINK SOCK LITTLE PINK SOCK
IT NEVER GETS OLD.
1·20

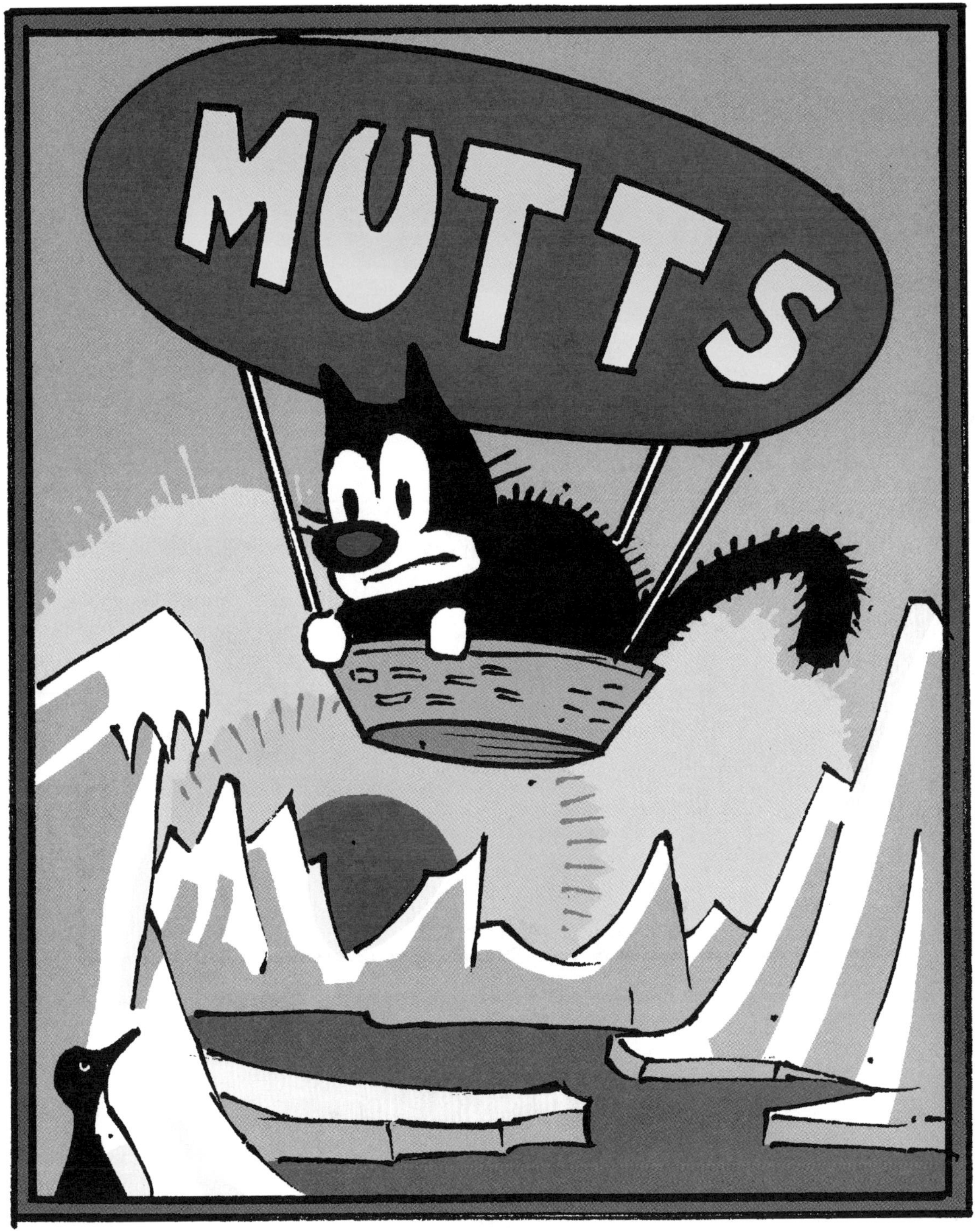
MUTTS

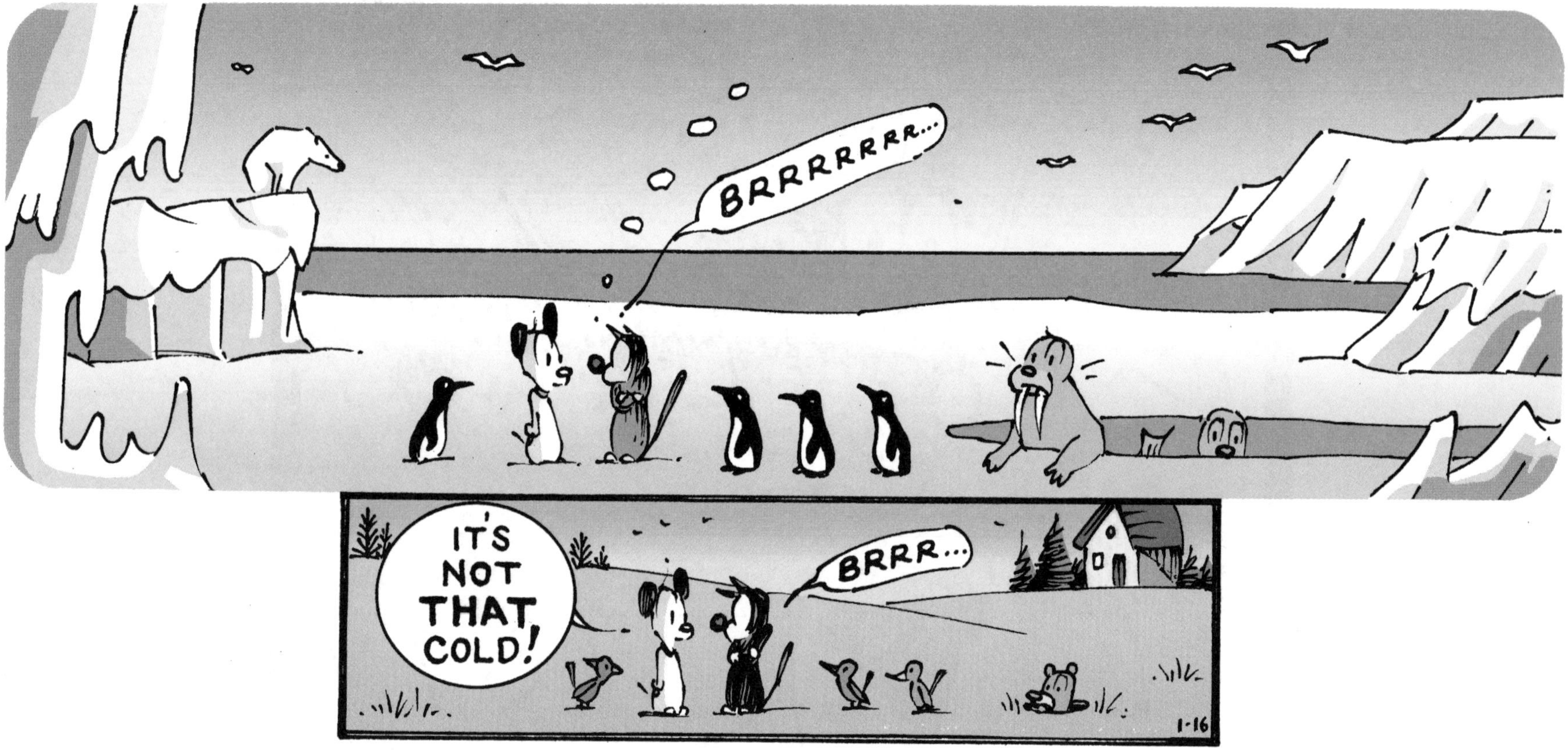
BRRRRRRRR...
IT'S NOT THAT COLD!
BRRR...
1-16

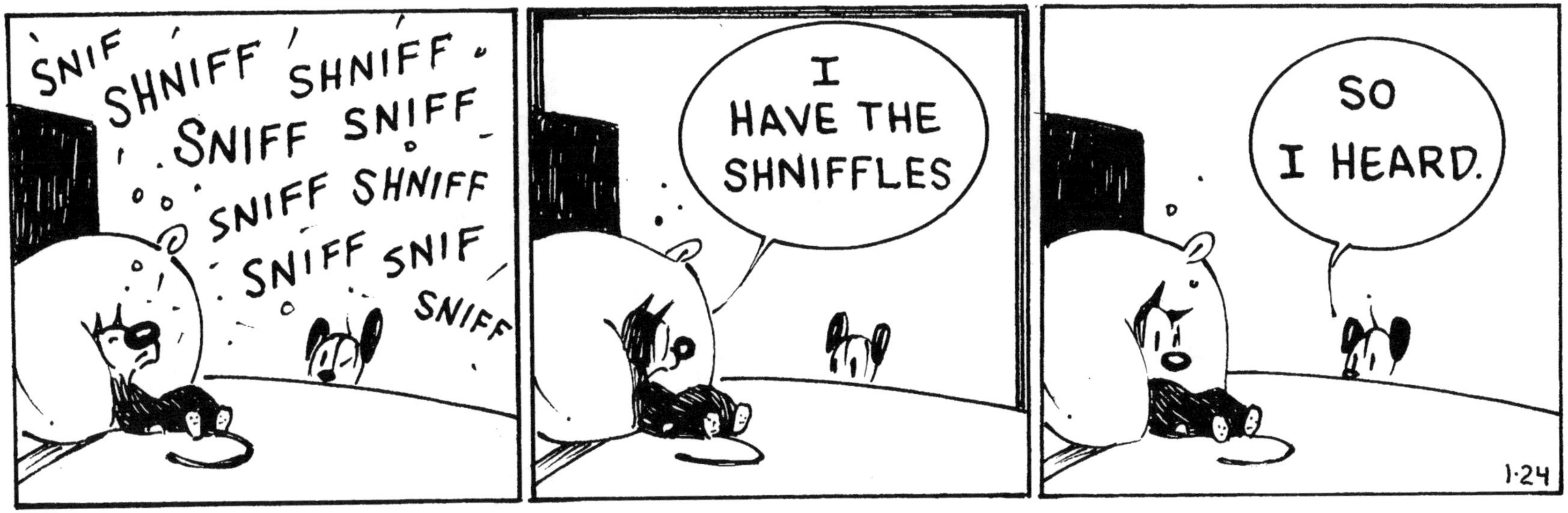
SNIF SHNIFF SHNIFF SNIFF SNIFF SNIFF SHNIFF SNIFF SNIF SNIFF
I HAVE THE SHNIFFLES
SO I HEARD.
1·24

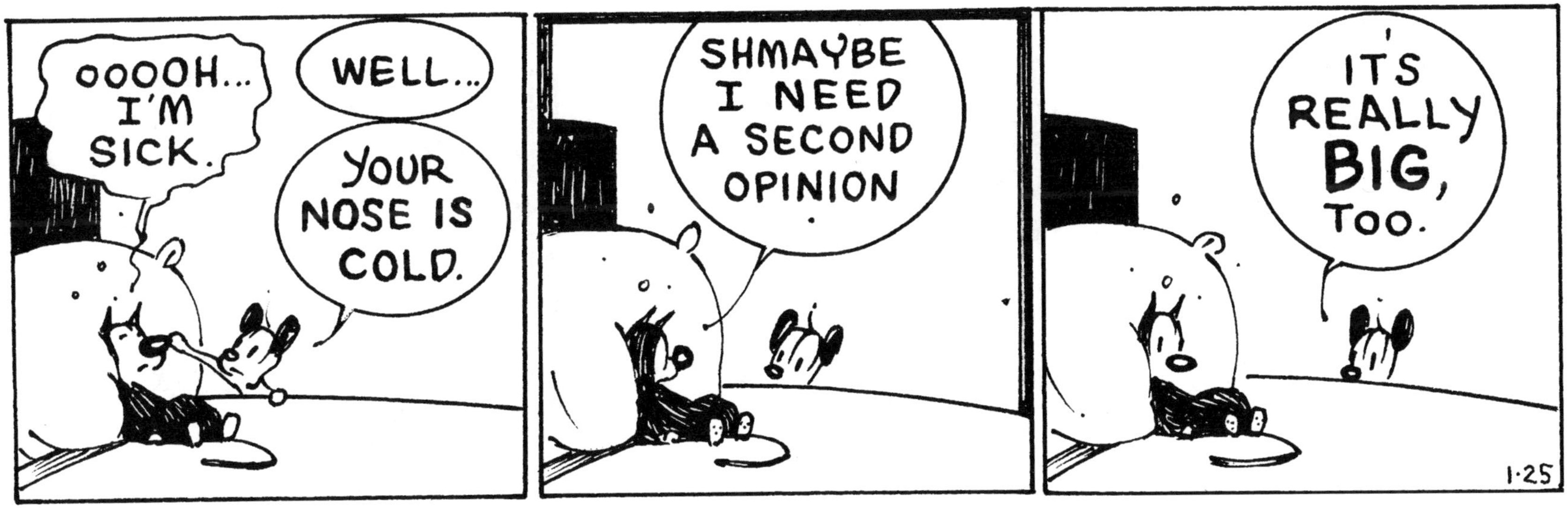
OOOOH... I'M SICK.
WELL...
YOUR NOSE IS COLD.
SHMAYBE I NEED A SECOND OPINION
IT'S REALLY BIG, TOO.
1·25

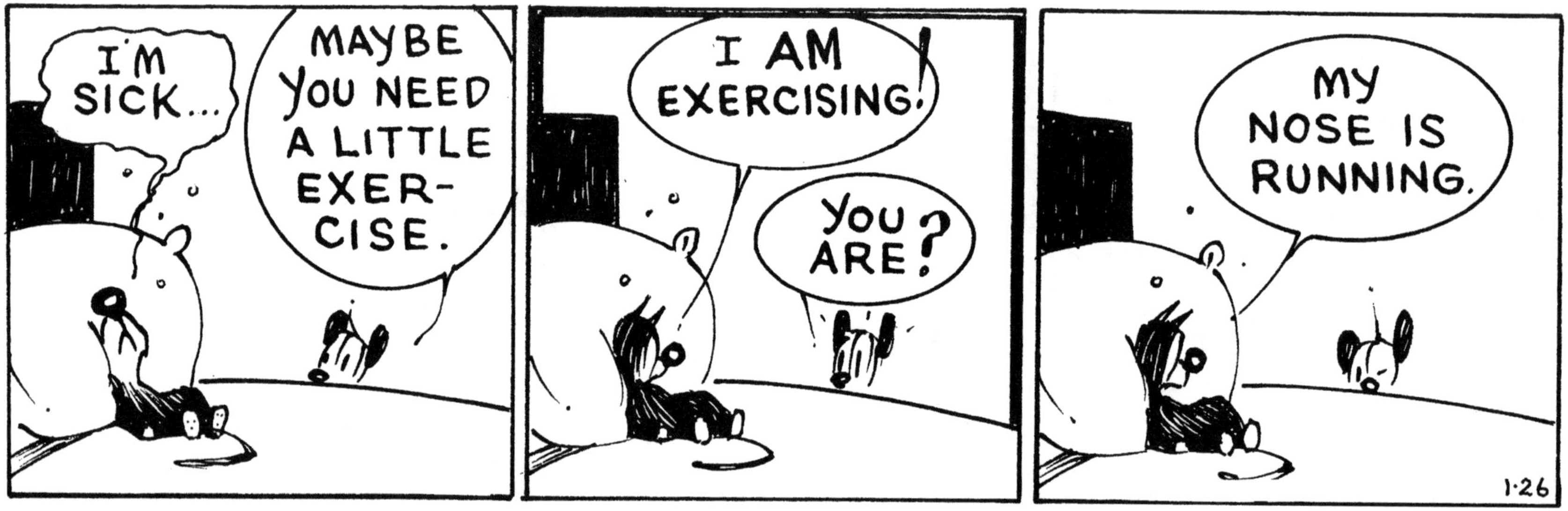
I'M SICK...
MAYBE YOU NEED A LITTLE EXER-CISE.
I AM EXERCISING!
YOU ARE?
MY NOSE IS RUNNING.
1·26

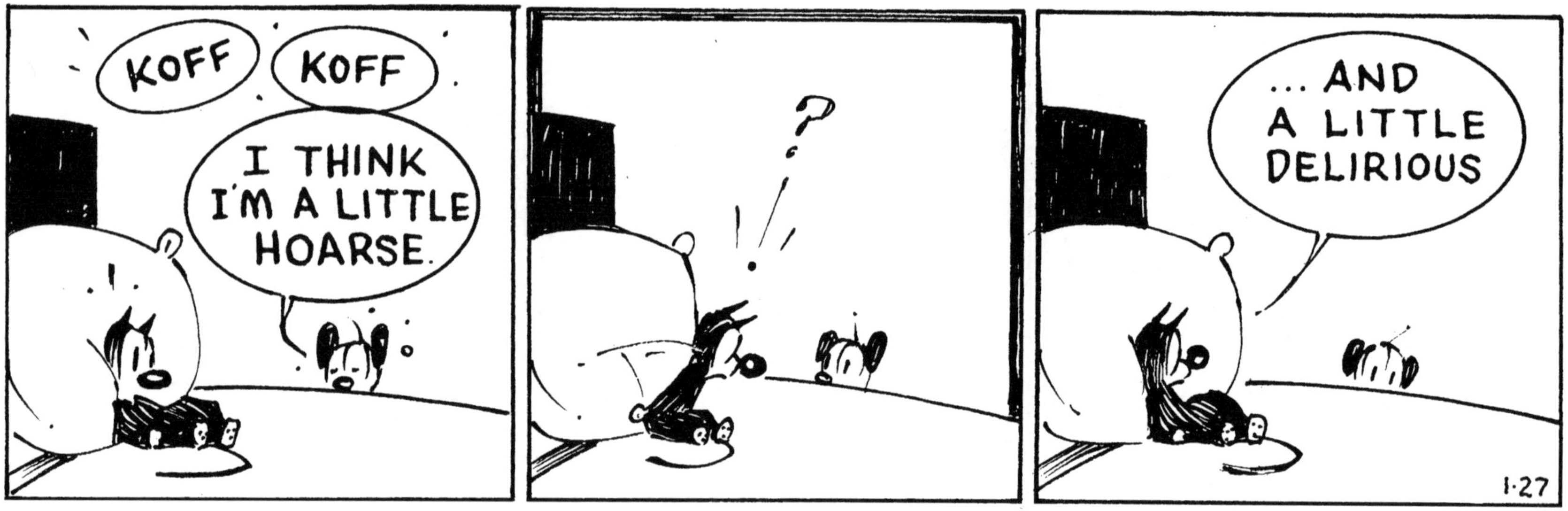
KOFF
KOFF
I THINK I'M A LITTLE HOARSE.
?
... AND A LITTLE DELIRIOUS
1·27

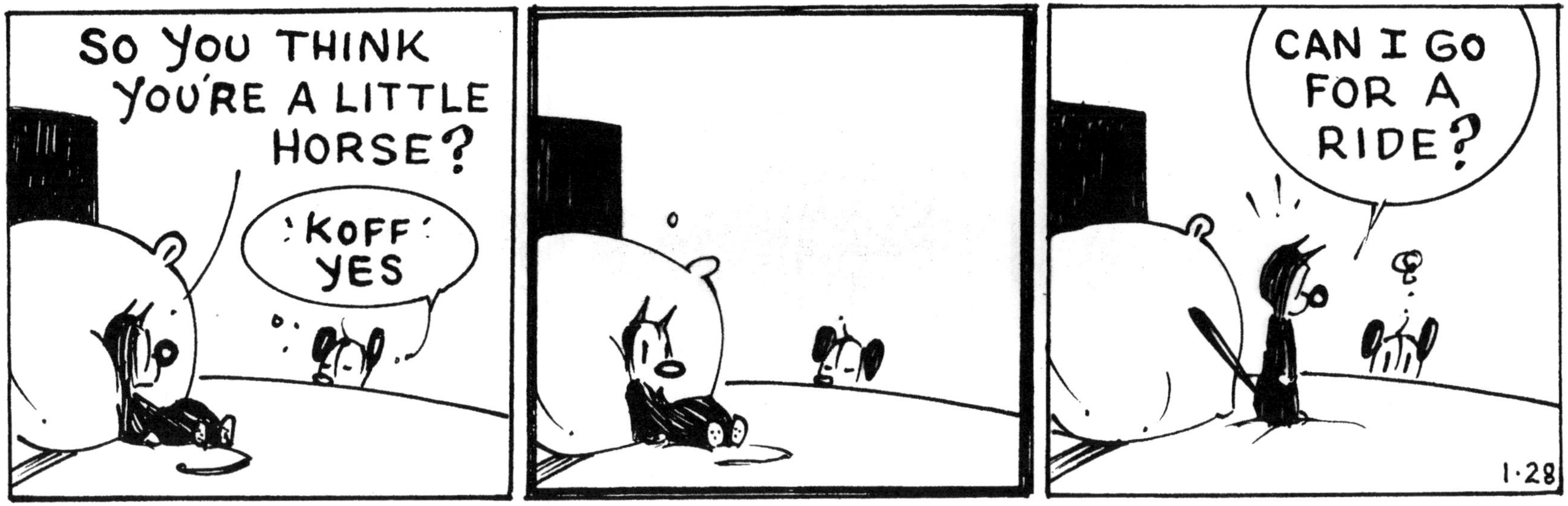
SO YOU THINK YOU'RE A LITTLE HORSE?
KOFF YES
CAN I GO FOR A RIDE?
1·28

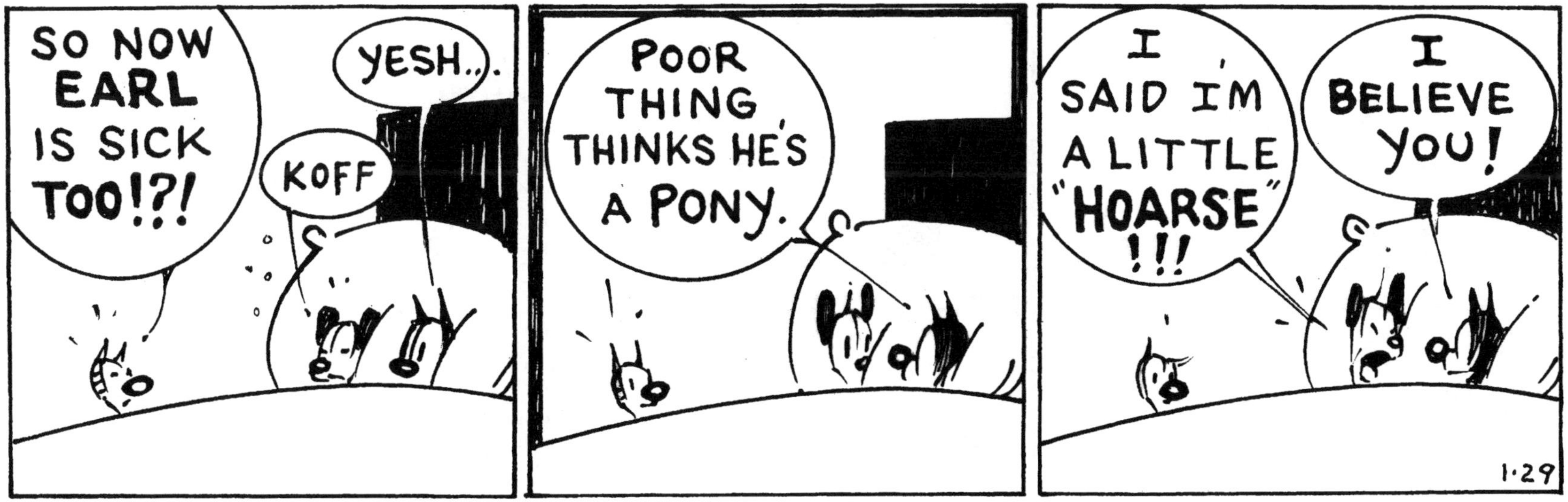
SO NOW EARL IS SICK TOO!?!
YESH...
KOFF
POOR THING THINKS HE'S A PONY.
I SAID I'M A LITTLE "HOARSE" !!!
I BELIEVE YOU!
1·29

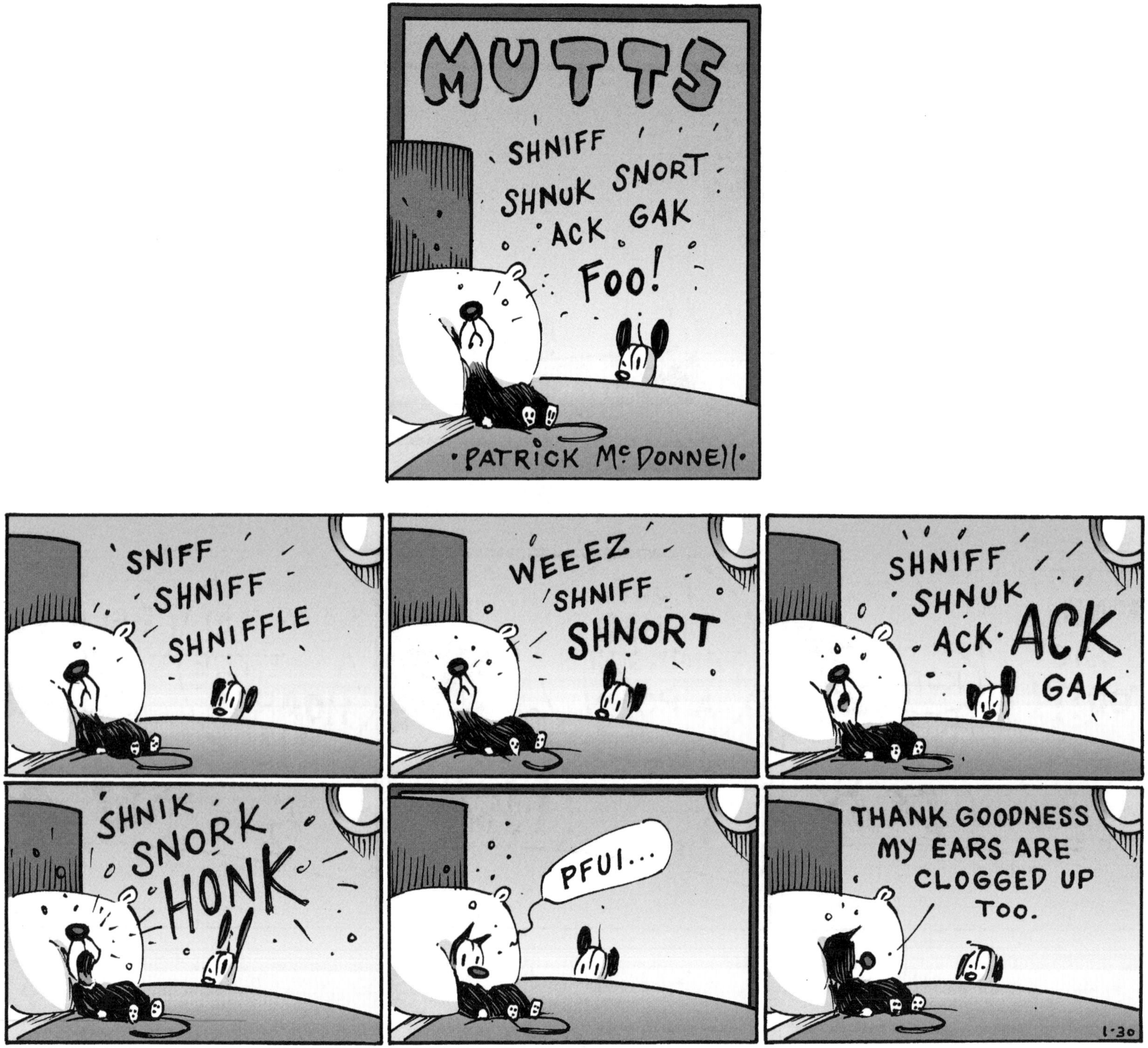
MUTTS
SHNIFF
SHNUK SNORT
ACK GAK
FOO!
PATRICK McDONNELL
SNIFF
SHNIFF
SHNIFFLE
WEEEZ
SHNIFF
SHNORT
SHNIFF
SHNUK
ACK ACK
GAK
SHNIK
SNORK
HONK
PFUI...
THANK GOODNESS MY EARS ARE CLOGGED UP TOO.
1-30

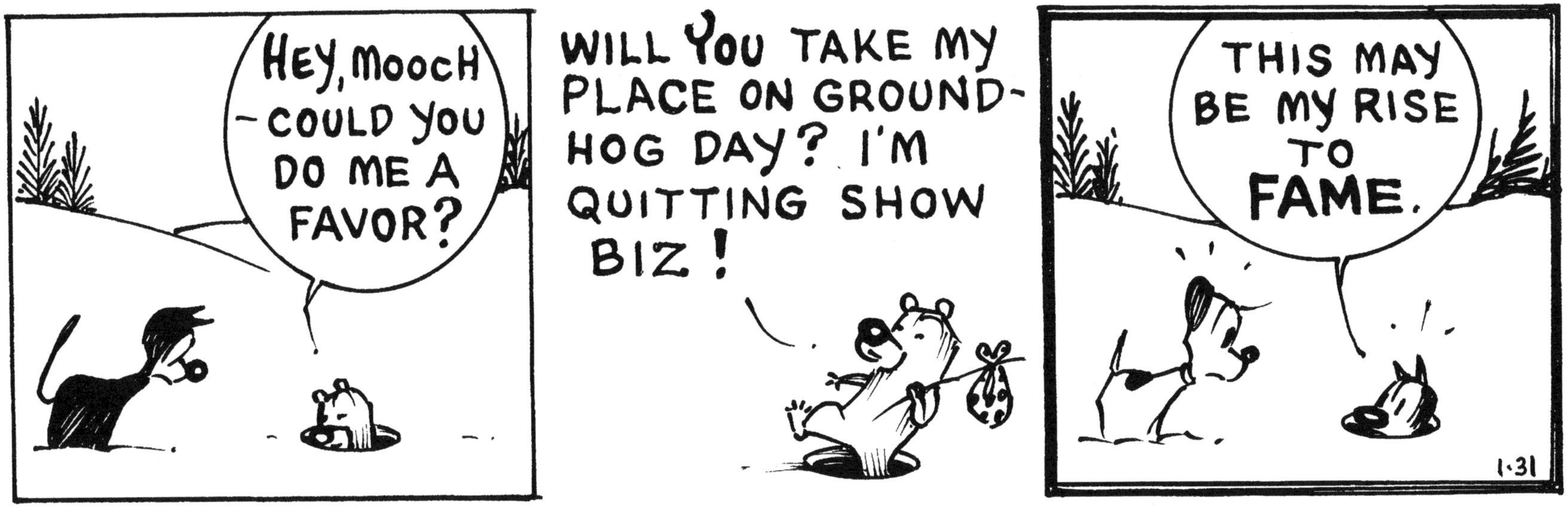
HEY, MOOCH — COULD YOU DO ME A FAVOR?
WILL YOU TAKE MY PLACE ON GROUND-HOG DAY? I'M QUITTING SHOW BIZ!
THIS MAY BE MY RISE TO FAME.
1·31

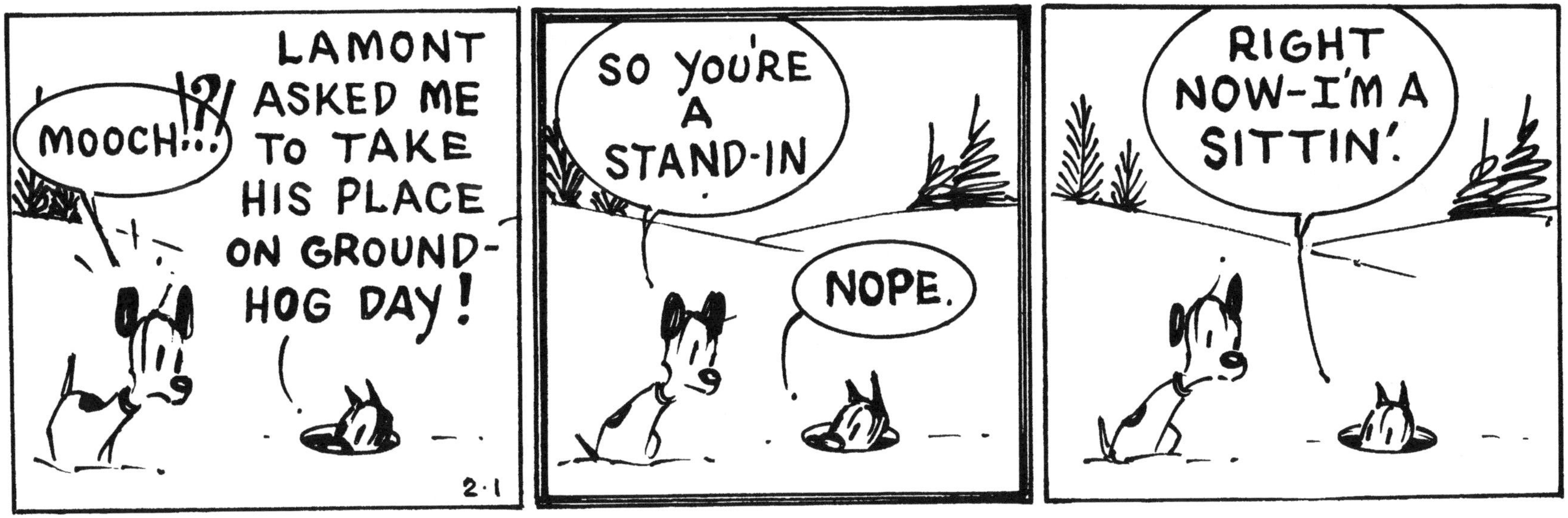
MOOCH!?!
LAMONT ASKED ME TO TAKE HIS PLACE ON GROUND-HOG DAY!
2·1
SO YOU'RE A STAND-IN
NOPE.
RIGHT NOW—I'M A SITTIN'.

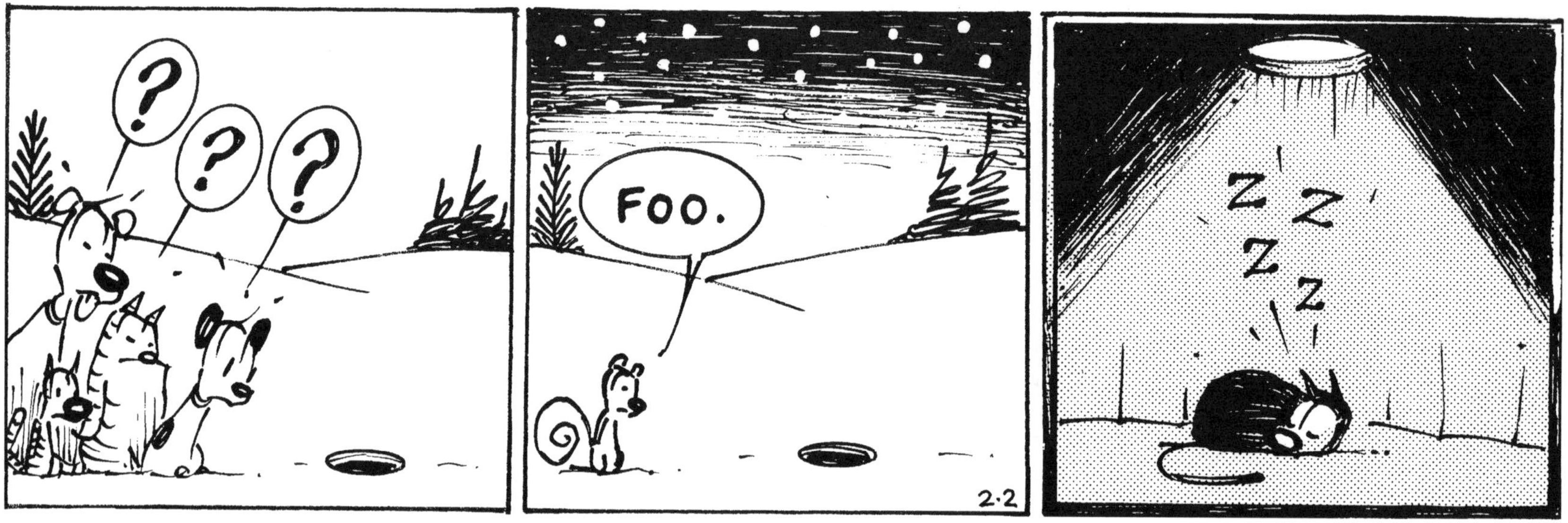
?
?
?
FOO.
2.2
Z Z Z Z

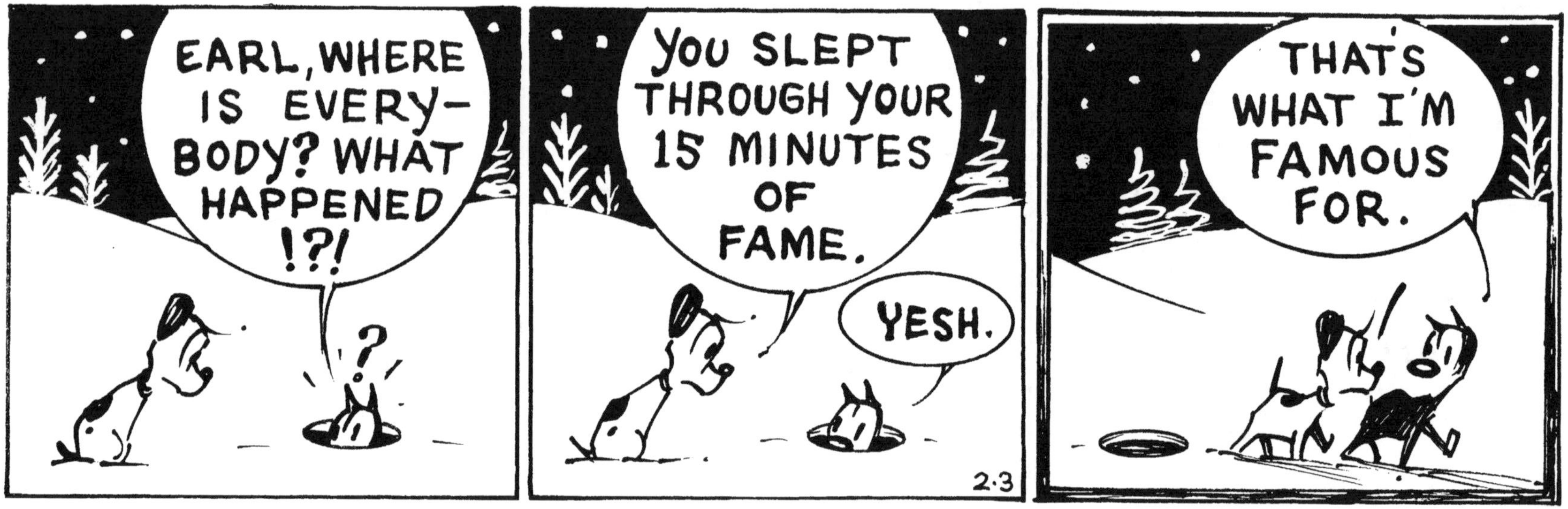
EARL, WHERE IS EVERY-BODY? WHAT HAPPENED !?!
?
YOU SLEPT THROUGH YOUR 15 MINUTES OF FAME.
YESH.
2.3
THAT'S WHAT I'M FAMOUS FOR.

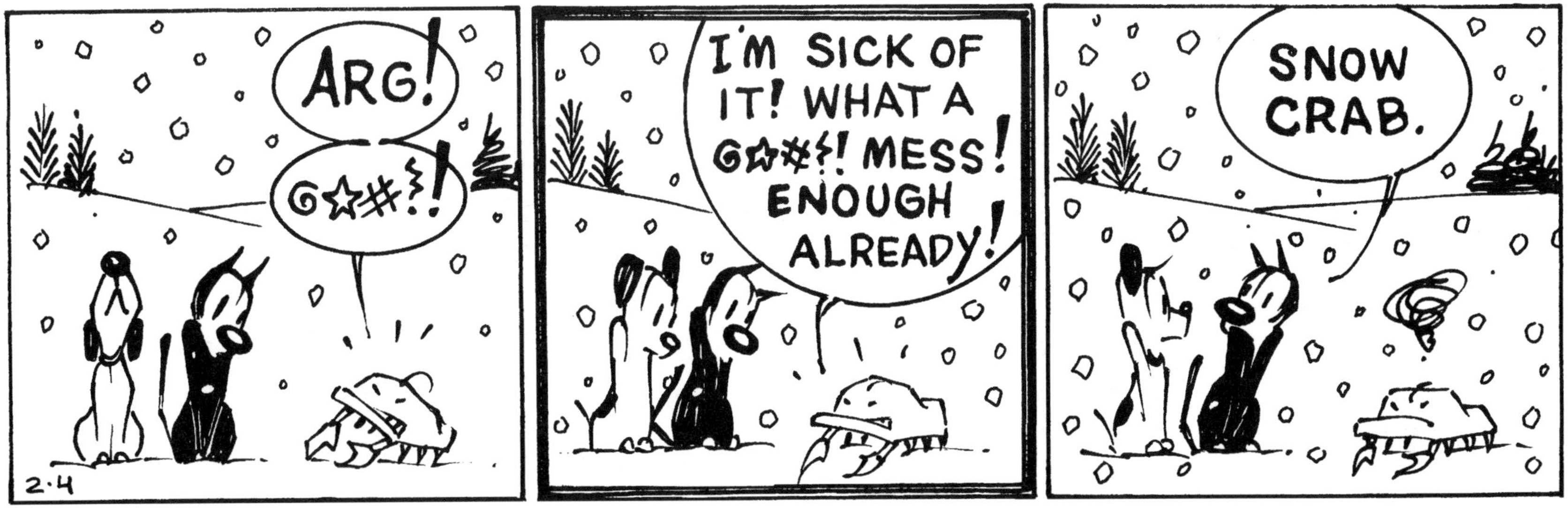
ARG!
@☆#?!
I'M SICK OF IT! WHAT A @☆#?! MESS! ENOUGH ALREADY!
SNOW CRAB.
2·4

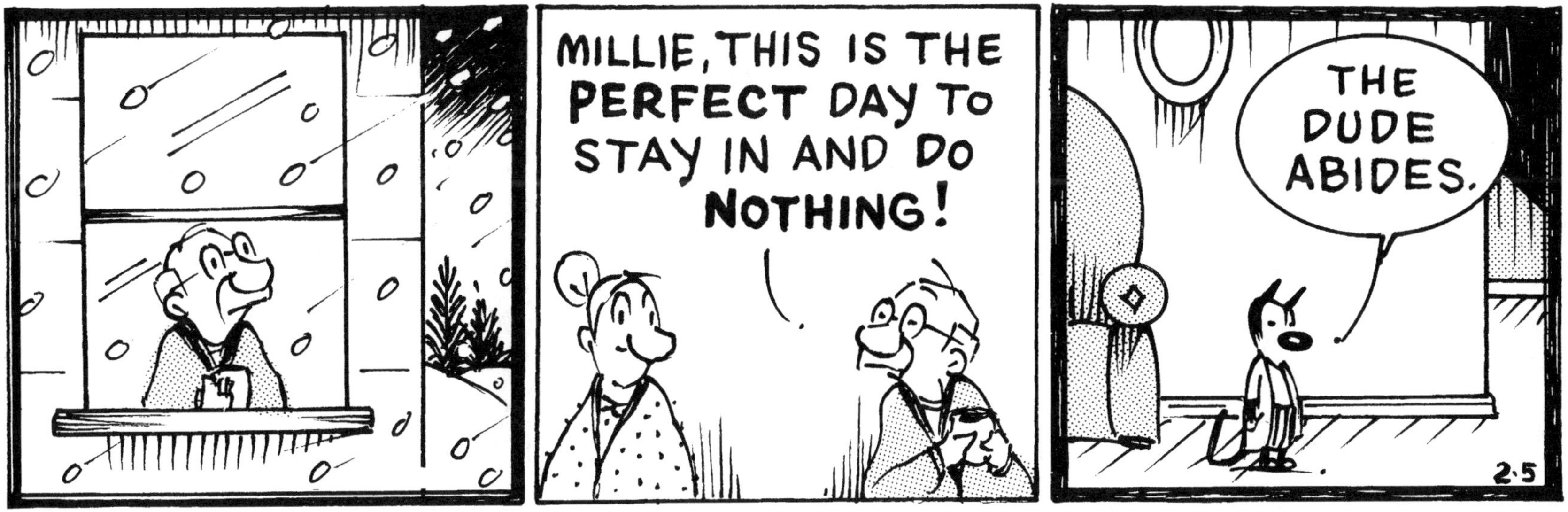
MILLIE, THIS IS THE PERFECT DAY TO STAY IN AND DO NOTHING!
THE DUDE ABIDES.
2·5

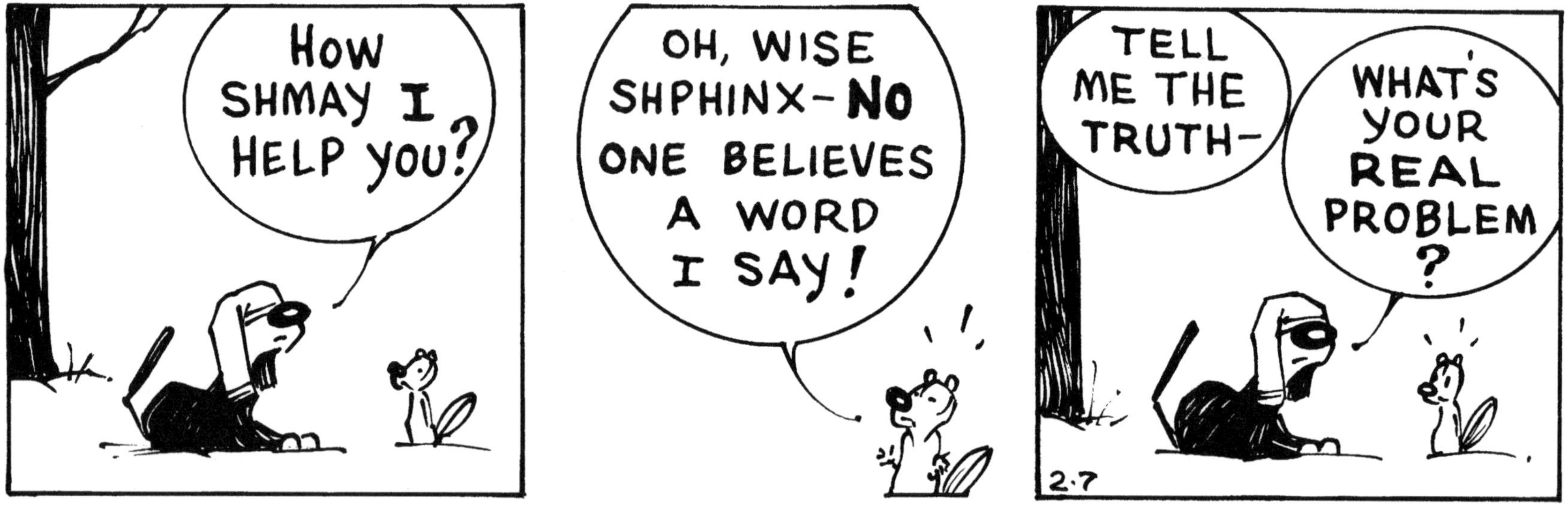
HOW SHMAY I HELP YOU?
OH, WISE SHPHINX–NO ONE BELIEVES A WORD I SAY!
TELL ME THE TRUTH–
WHAT'S YOUR REAL PROBLEM?
2·7

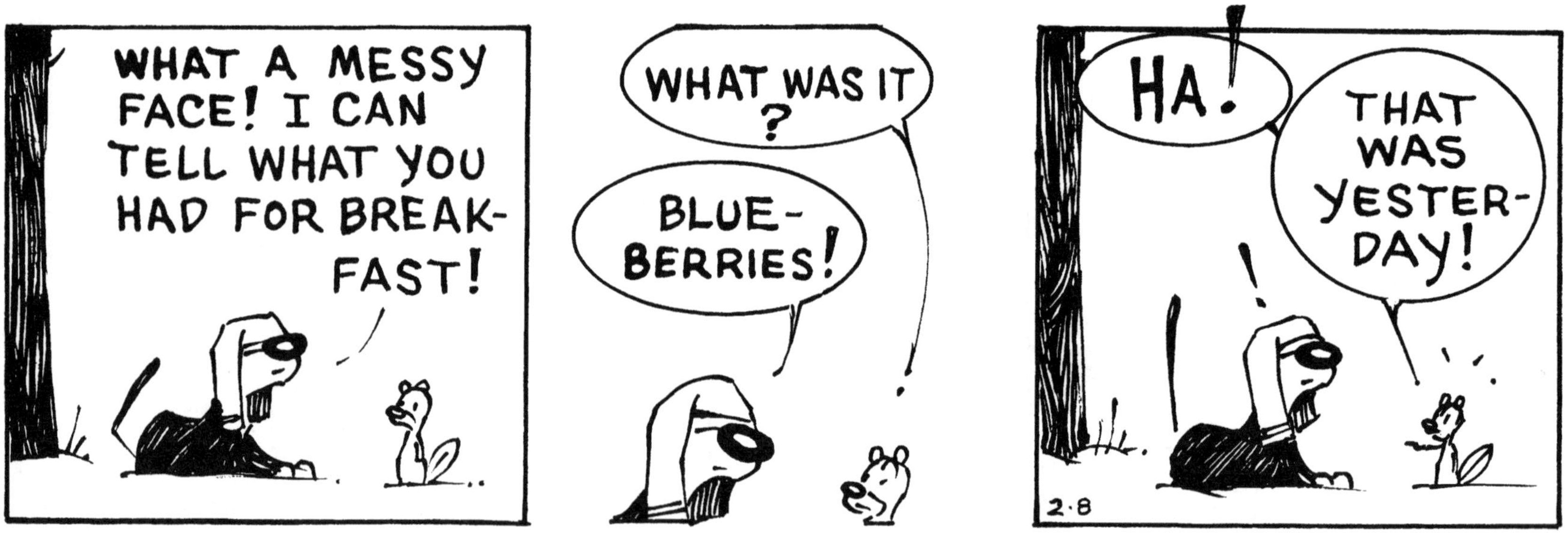
WHAT A MESSY FACE! I CAN TELL WHAT YOU HAD FOR BREAK-FAST!
WHAT WAS IT?
BLUE-BERRIES!
HA!
THAT WAS YESTER-DAY!
2·8

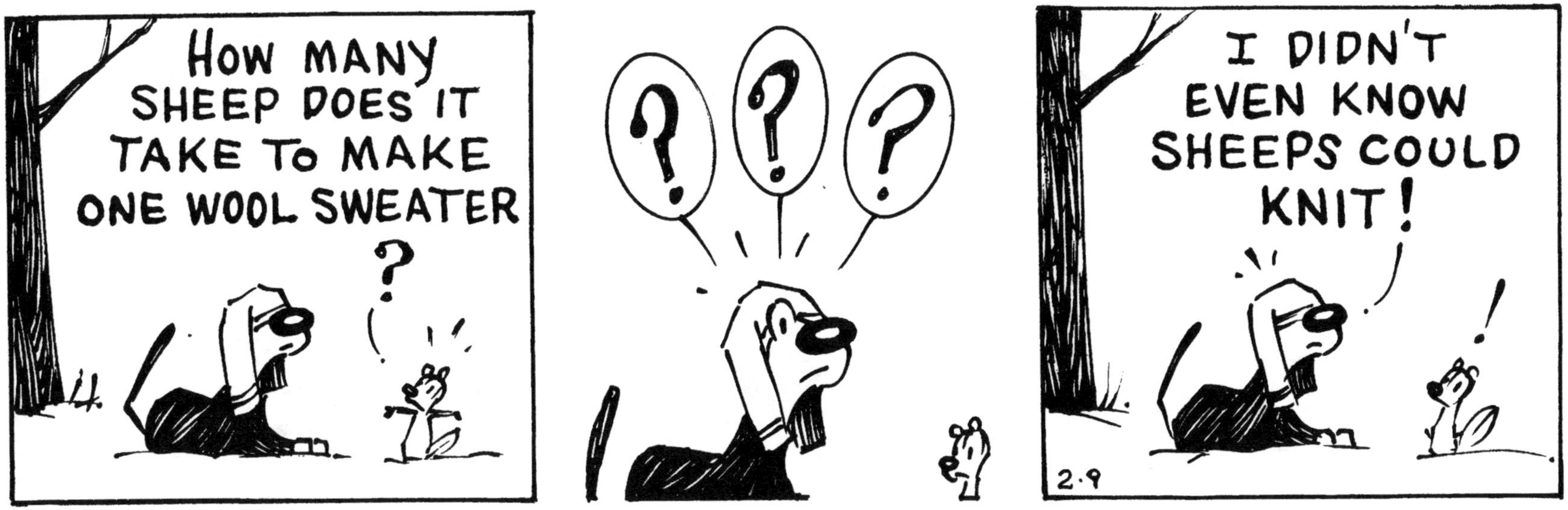
HOW MANY SHEEP DOES IT TAKE TO MAKE ONE WOOL SWEATER
?
???
I DIDN'T EVEN KNOW SHEEPS COULD KNIT!
!
2·9

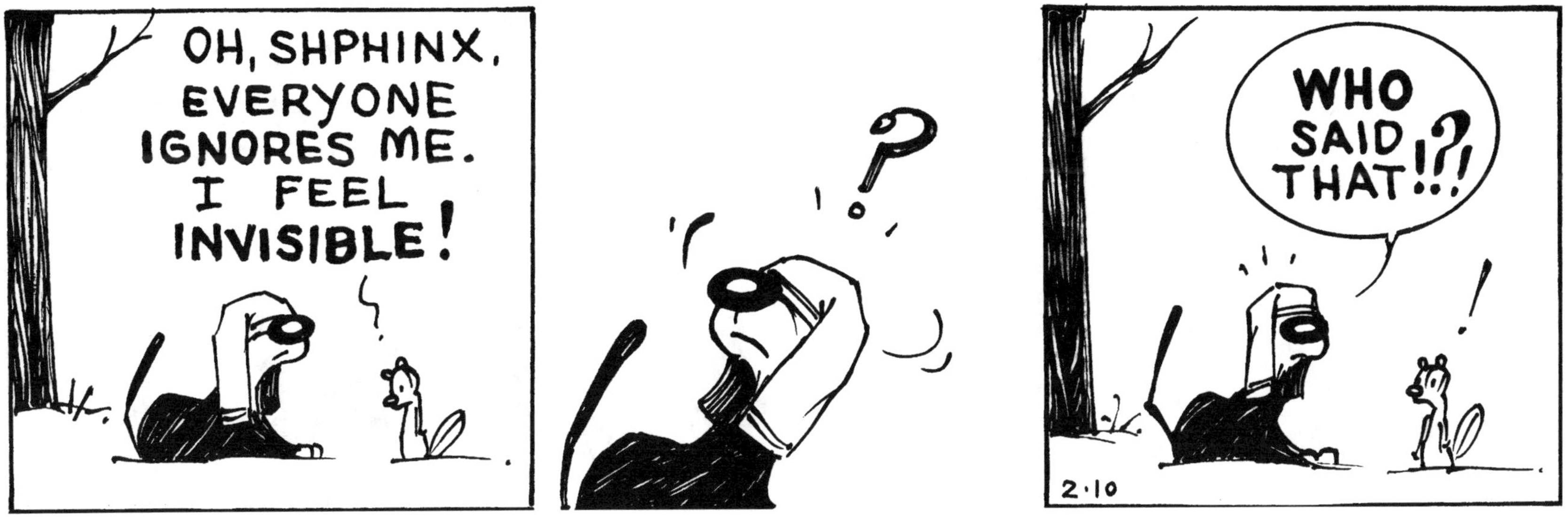
OH, SHPHINX, EVERYONE IGNORES ME. I FEEL INVISIBLE!
?
WHO SAID THAT!?!
!
2·10

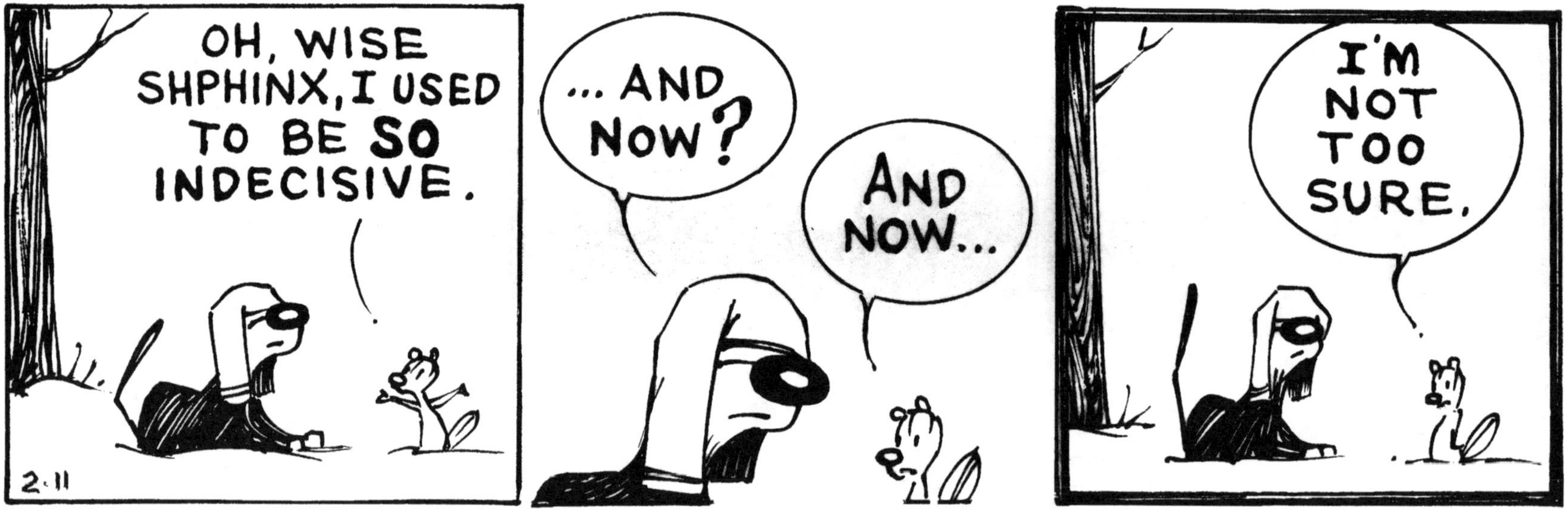
OH, WISE SHPHINX, I USED TO BE SO INDECISIVE.
... AND NOW?
AND NOW...
I'M NOT TOO SURE.
2.11

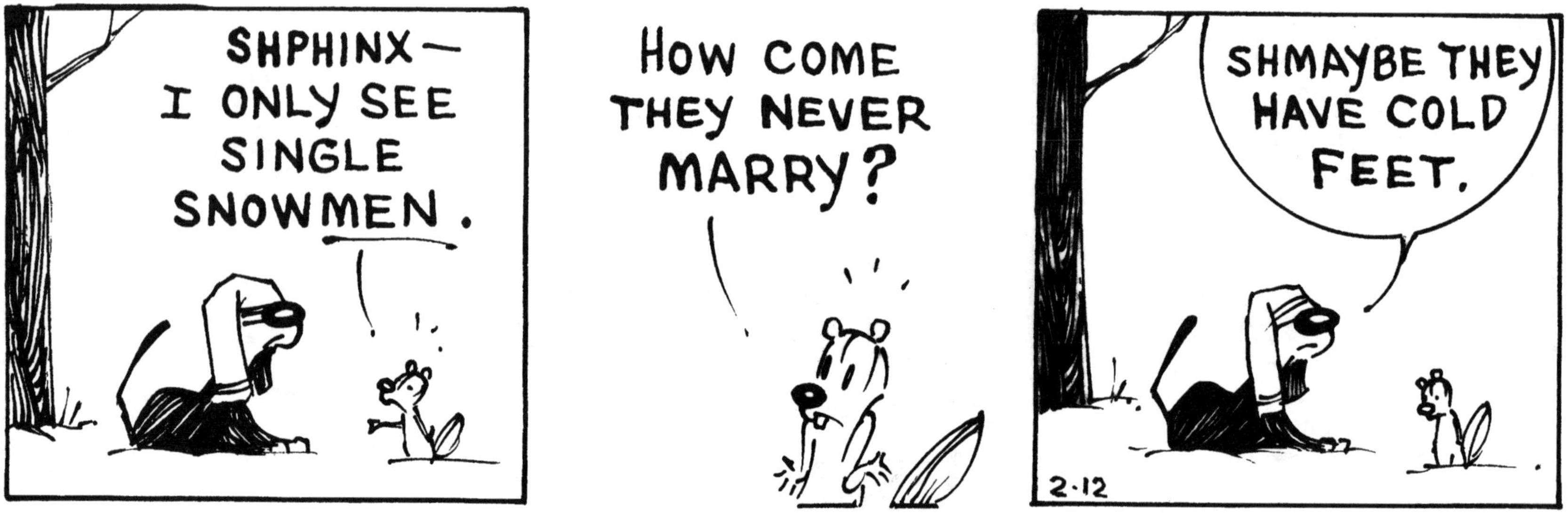
SHPHINX— I ONLY SEE SINGLE SNOWMEN.
HOW COME THEY NEVER MARRY?
SHMAYBE THEY HAVE COLD FEET.
2.12

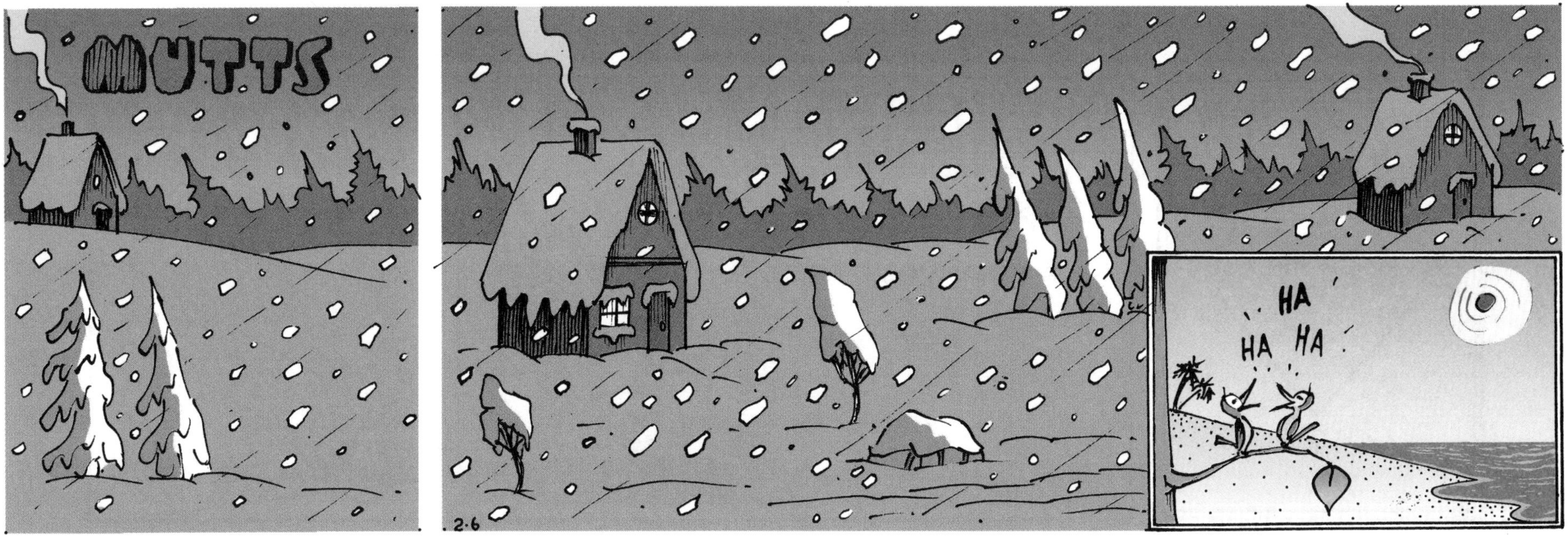
MUTTS
2·6
HA
HA HA

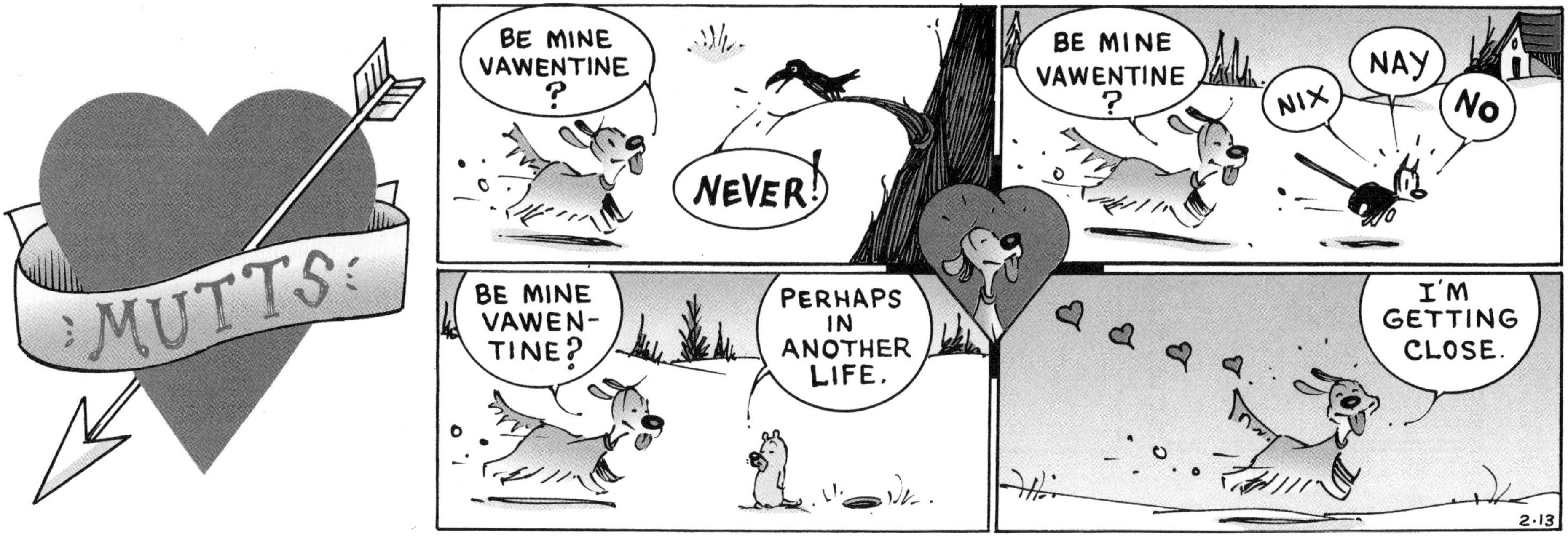
MUTTS
BE MINE VAWENTINE ?
NEVER!
BE MINE VAWENTINE ?
NIX
NAY
NO
BE MINE VAWEN-TINE?
PERHAPS IN ANOTHER LIFE.
I'M GETTING CLOSE.
2·13

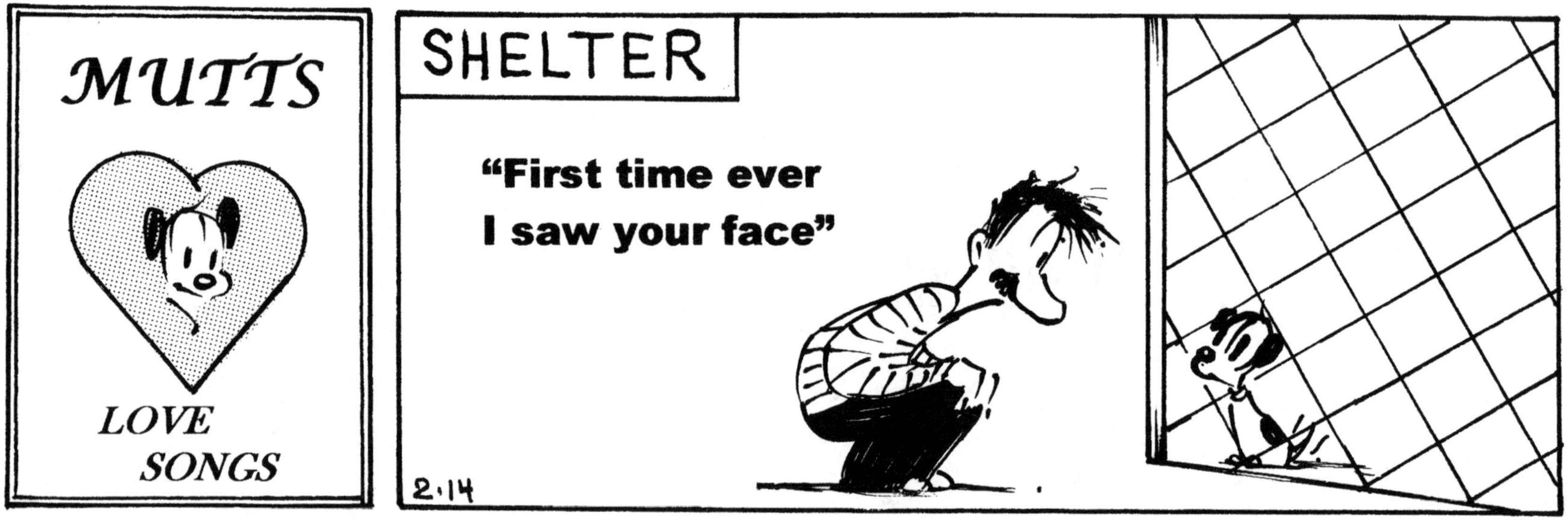
MUTTS
LOVE SONGS
SHELTER
"First time ever I saw your face"
2.14

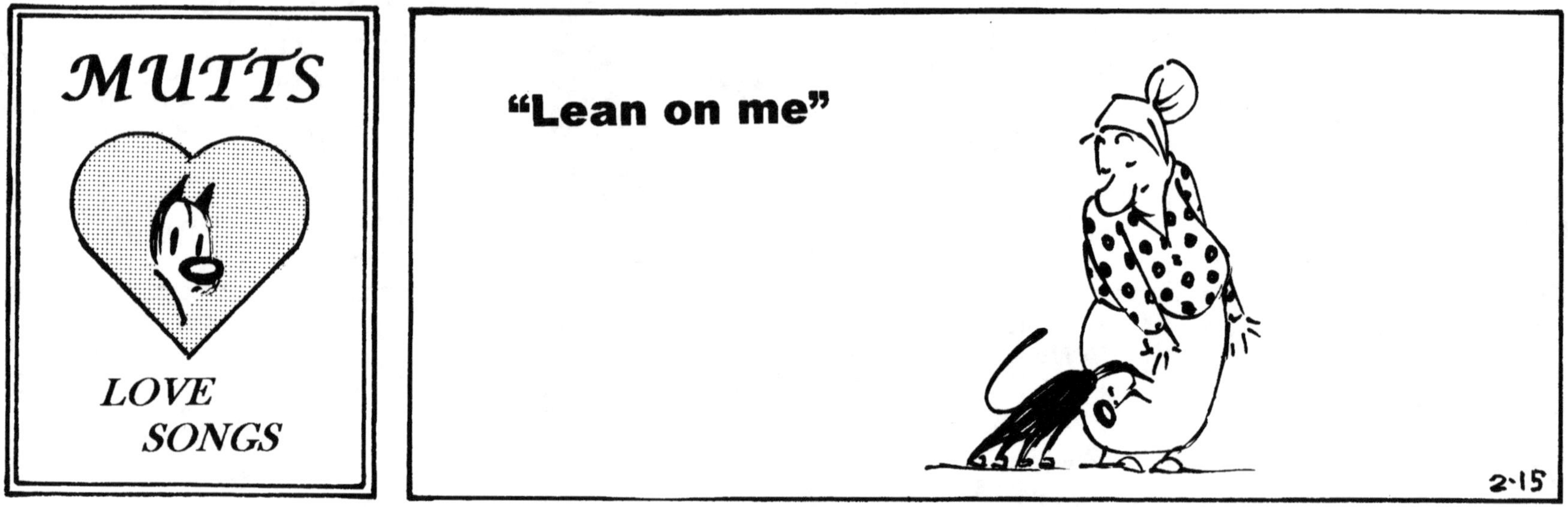
MUTTS
LOVE SONGS
"Lean on me"
2.15

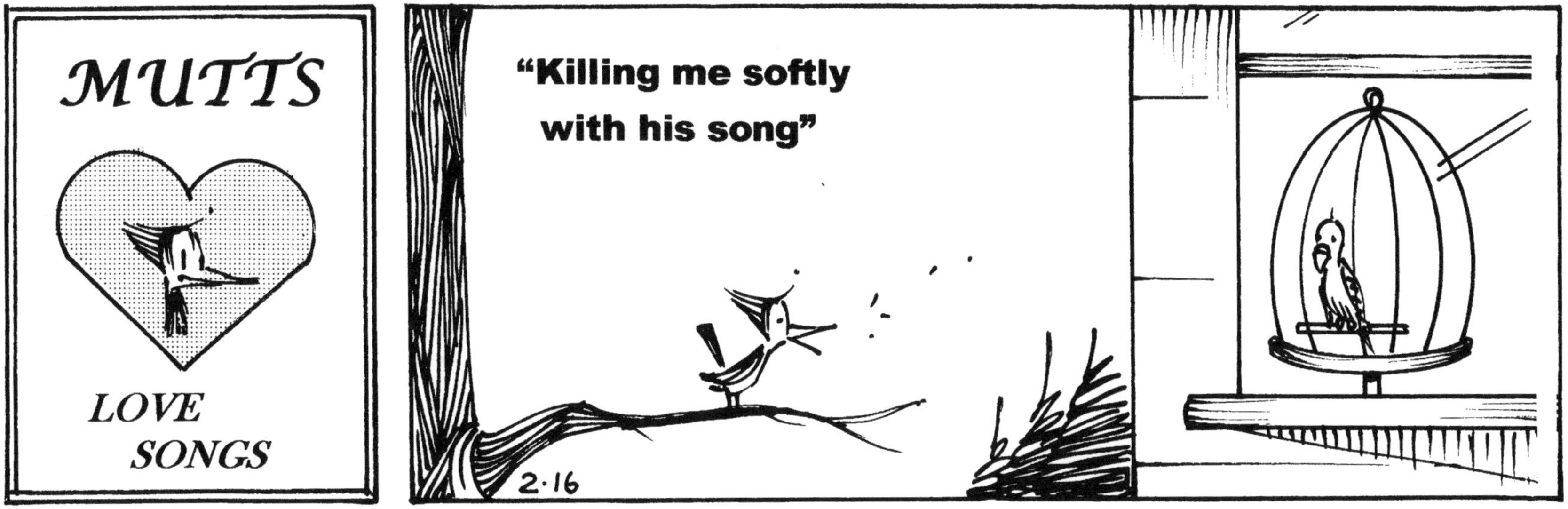
MUTTS
LOVE SONGS
"Killing me softly with his song"
2·16

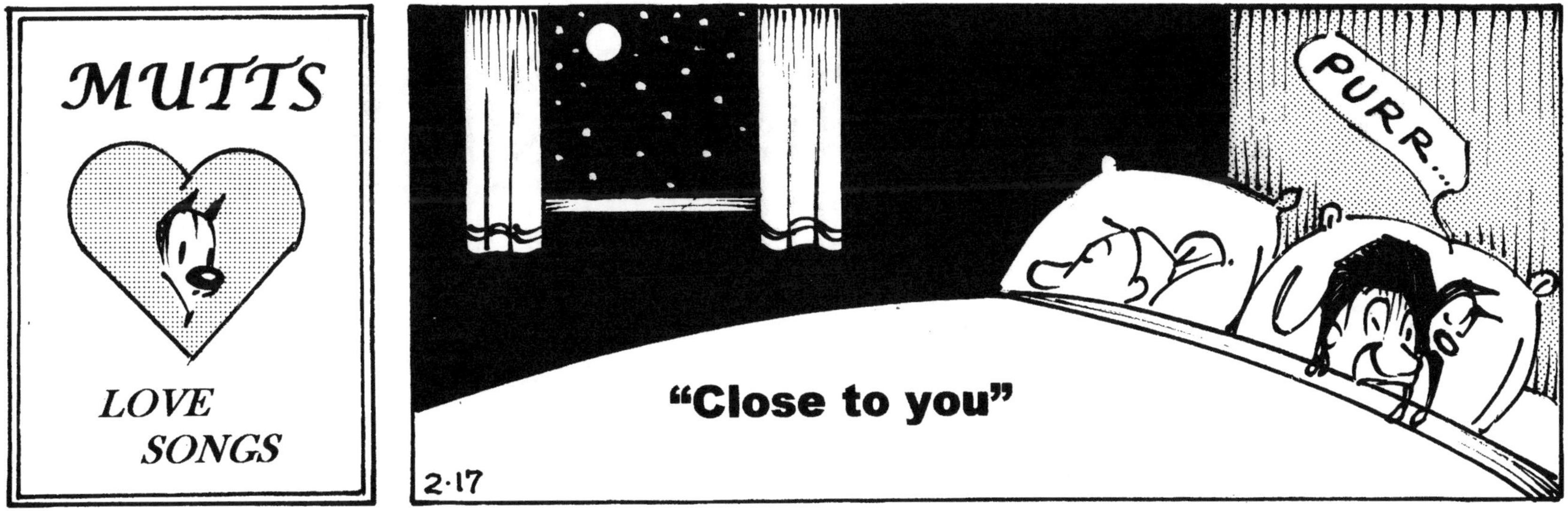
MUTTS
LOVE SONGS
PURR...
"Close to you"
2·17

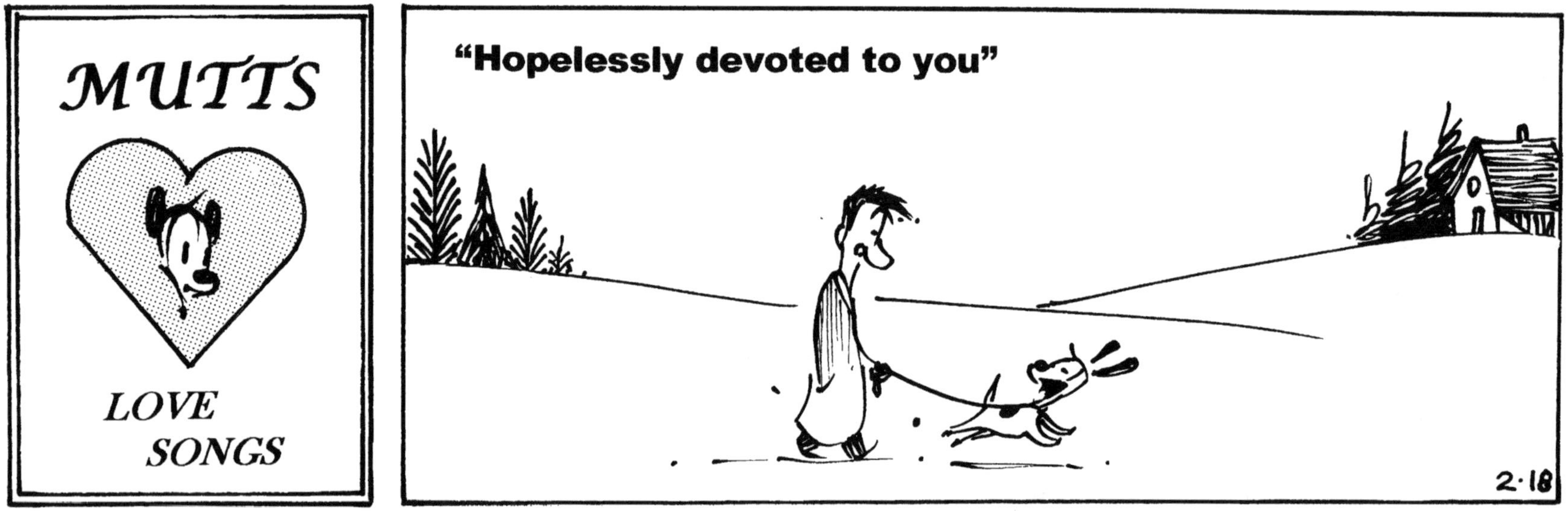
MUTTS
LOVE SONGS
"Hopelessly devoted to you"
2·18

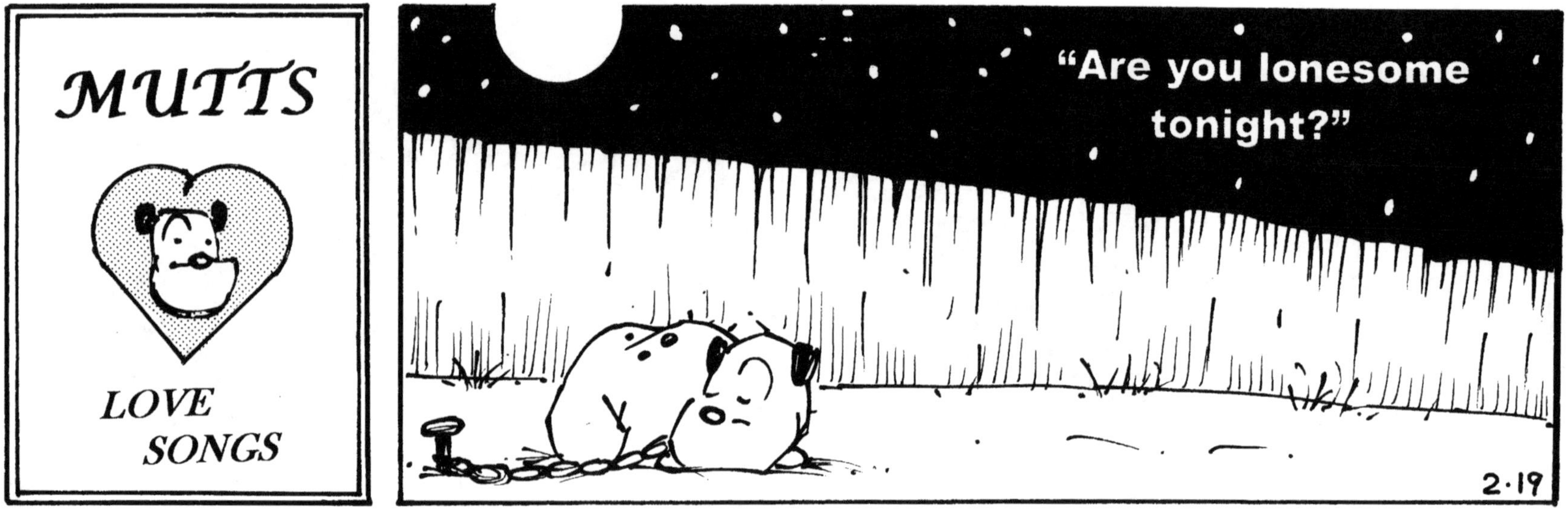
MUTTS
LOVE SONGS
"Are you lonesome tonight?"
2·19

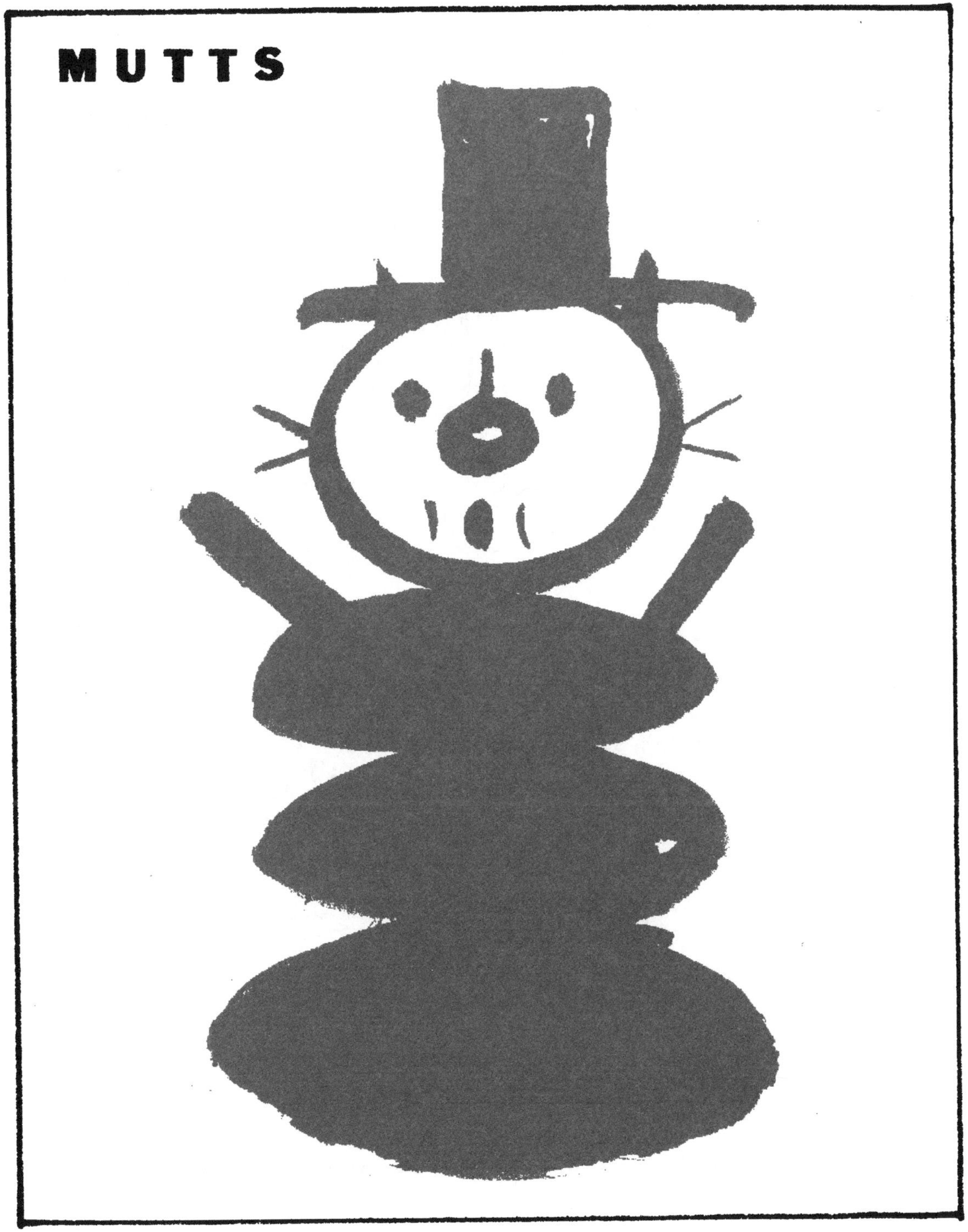
MUTTS

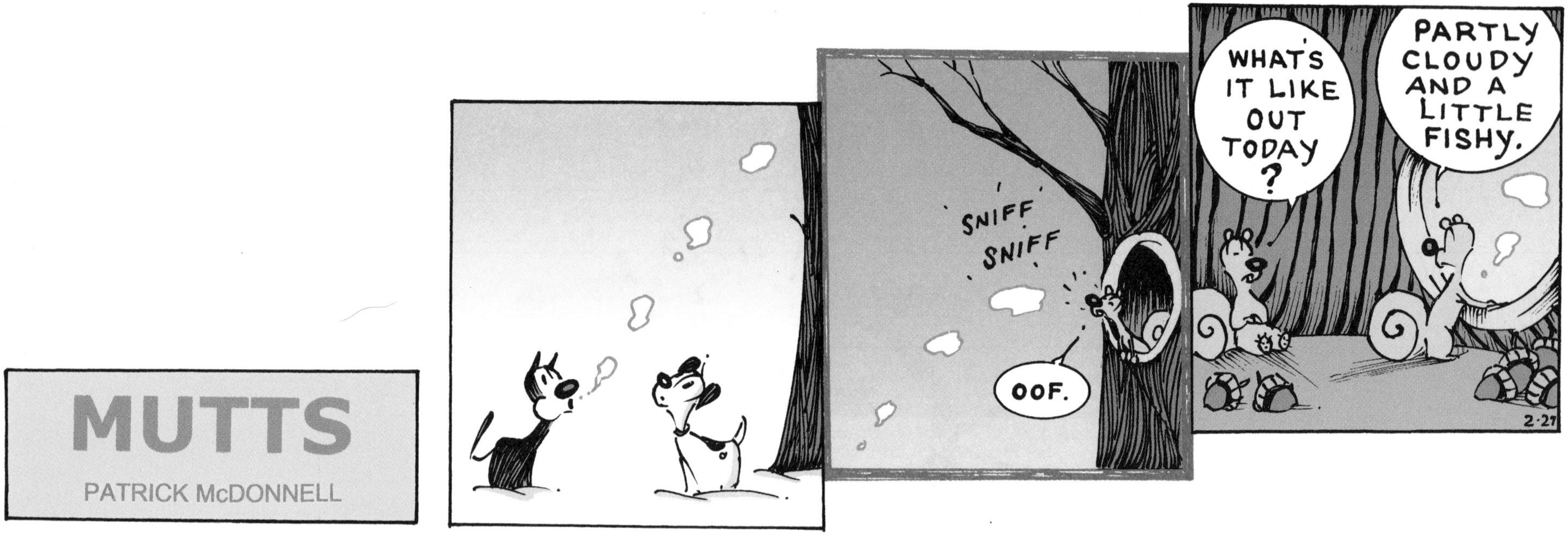
MUTTS
PATRICK McDONNELL
SNIFF SNIFF
OOF.
WHAT'S IT LIKE OUT TODAY?
PARTLY CLOUDY AND A LITTLE FISHY.
2·27

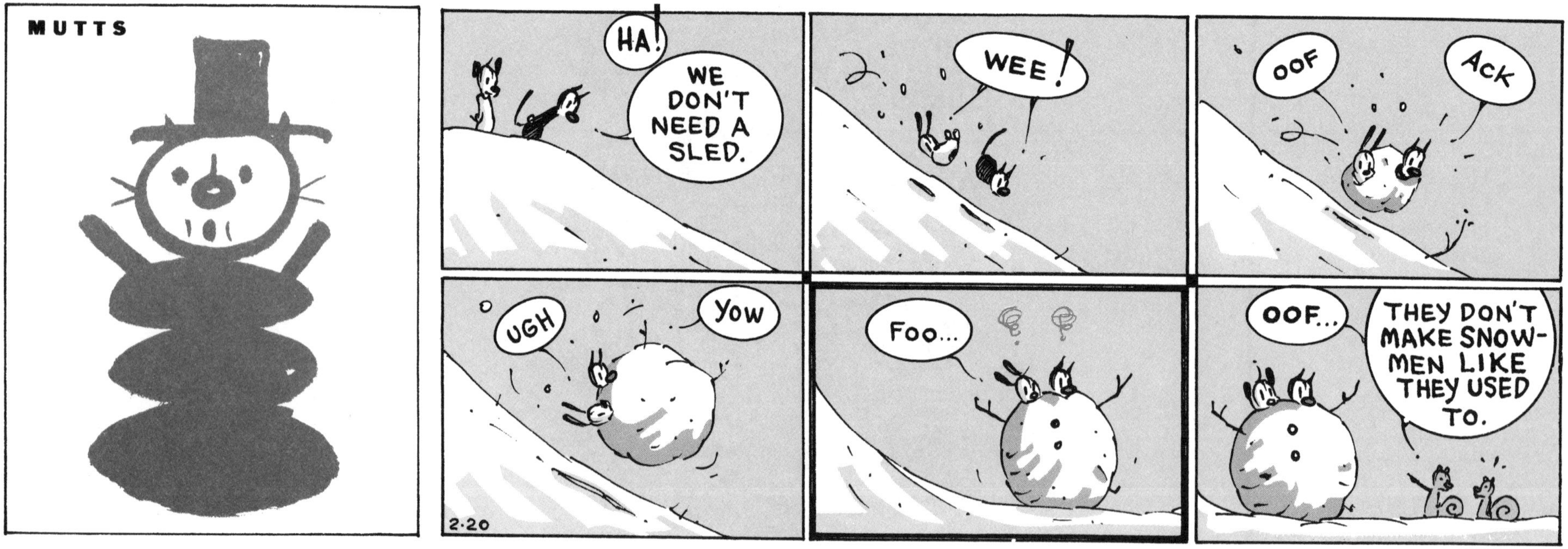
MUTTS
HA!
WE DON'T NEED A SLED.
WEE!
OOF
ACK
UGH
YOW
FOO...
OOF...
THEY DON'T MAKE SNOW-MEN LIKE THEY USED TO.
2·20

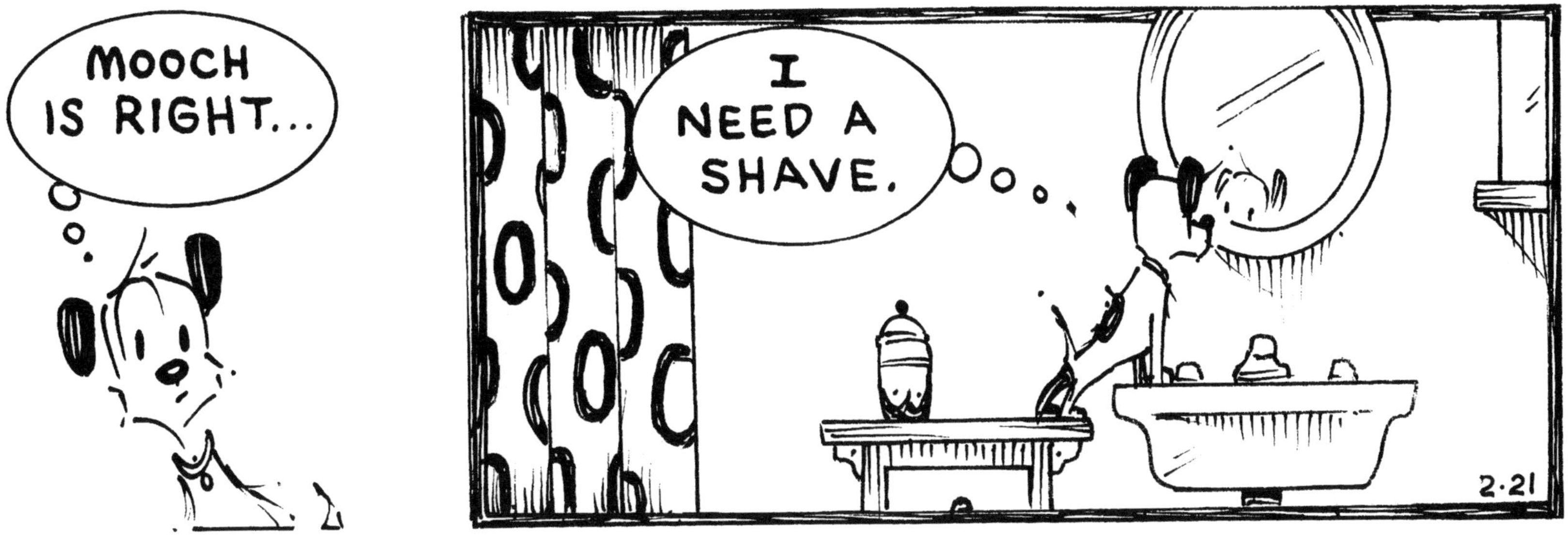
MOOCH IS RIGHT...
I NEED A SHAVE.
2·21

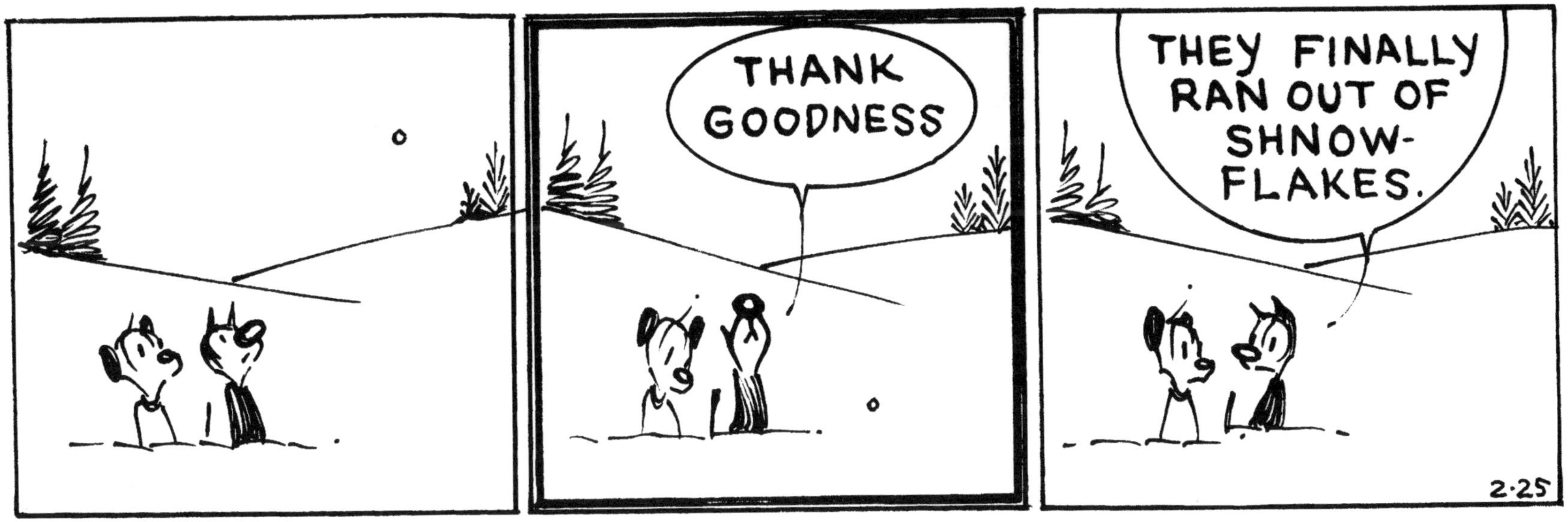
THANK GOODNESS
THEY FINALLY RAN OUT OF SHNOW-FLAKES.
2·25

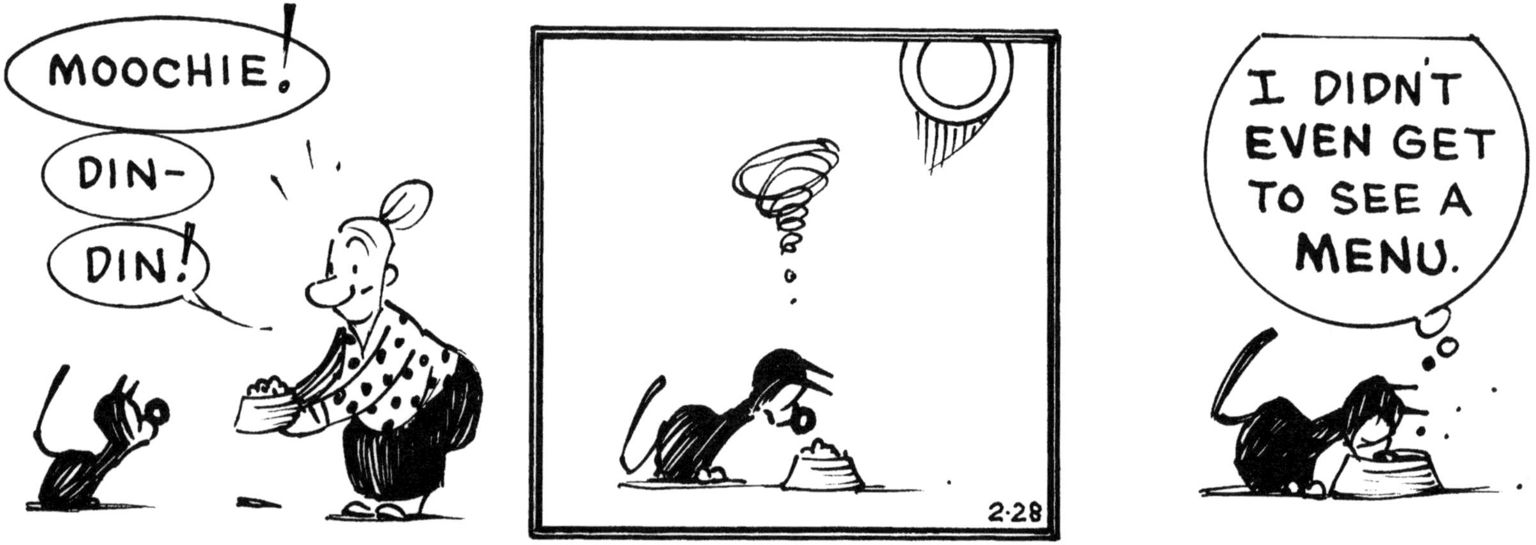
MOOCHIE!
DIN-
DIN!
2·28
I DIDN'T EVEN GET TO SEE A MENU.

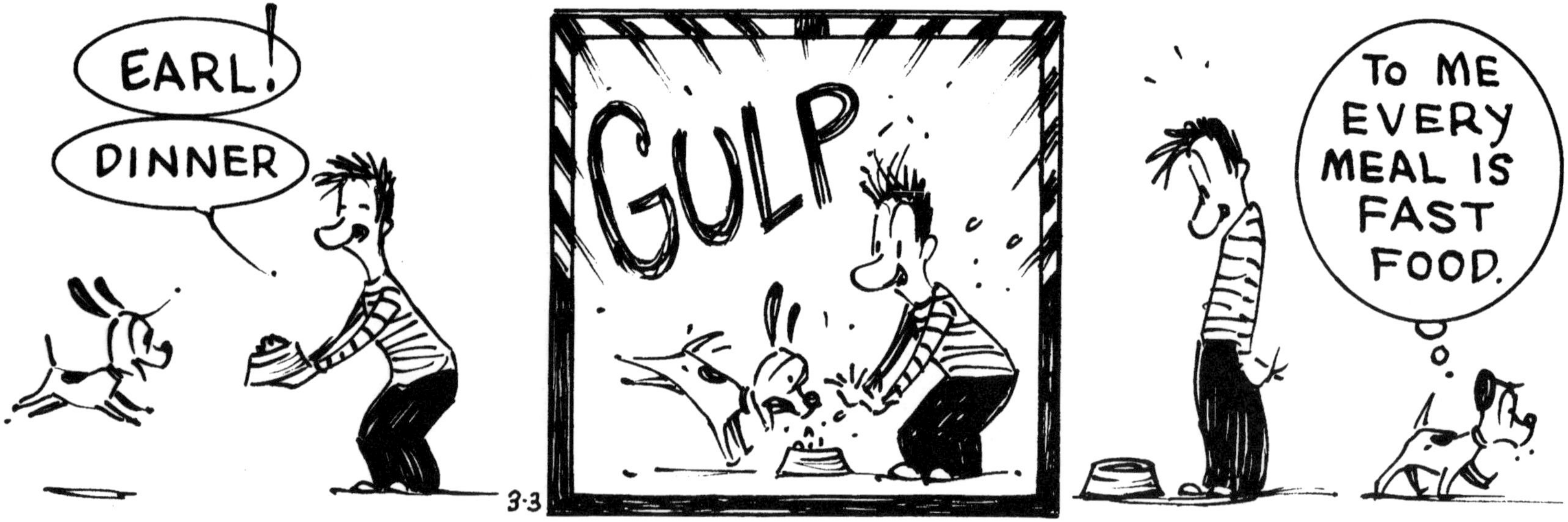
EARL!
DINNER
3·3
GULP
To ME EVERY MEAL IS FAST FOOD.

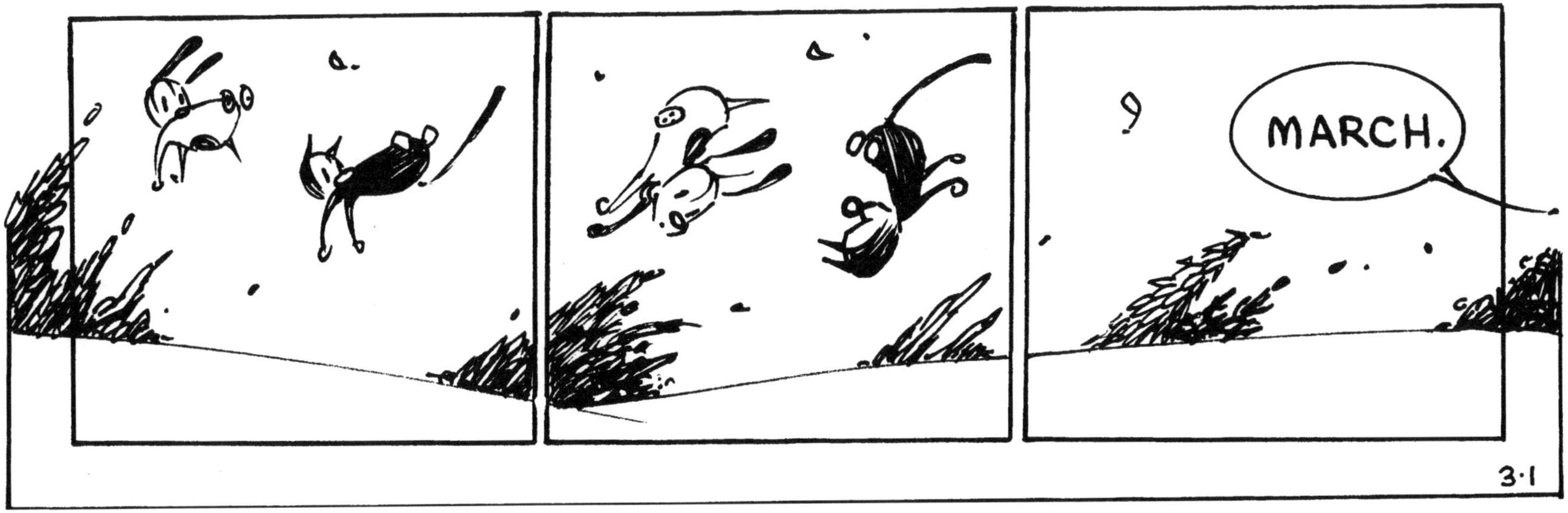
MARCH.
3·1

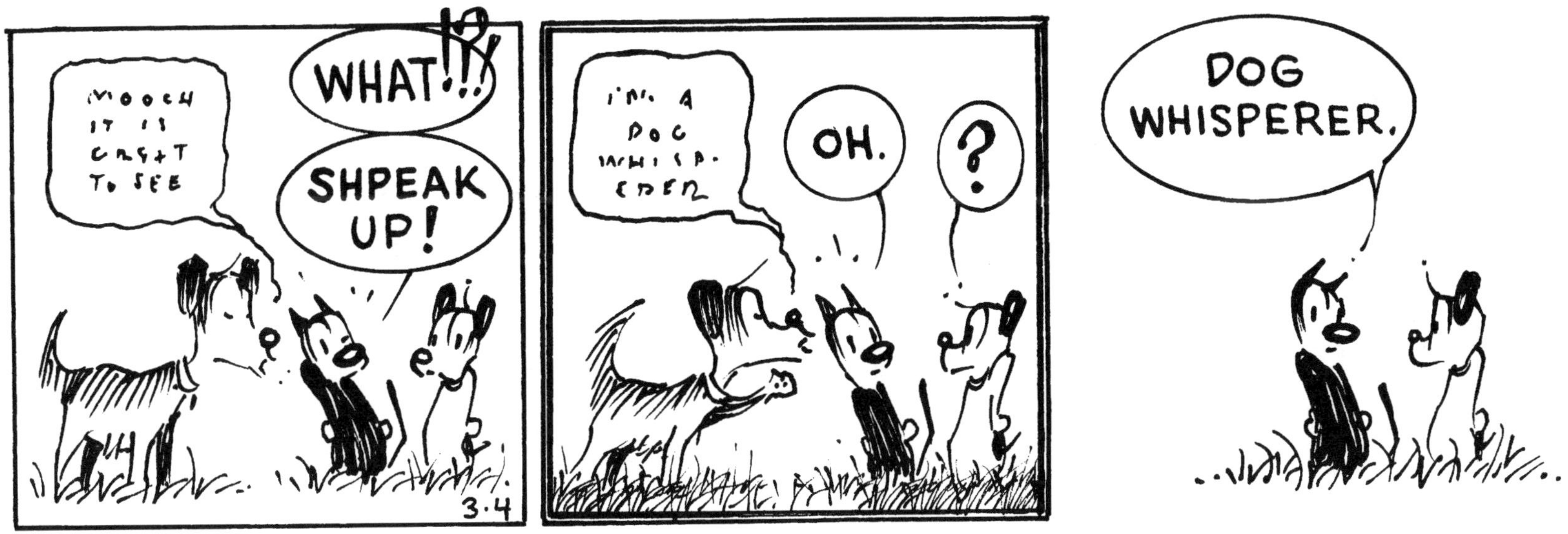
WHAT!!?
SHPEAK UP!
3·4
OH.
?
DOG WHISPERER.

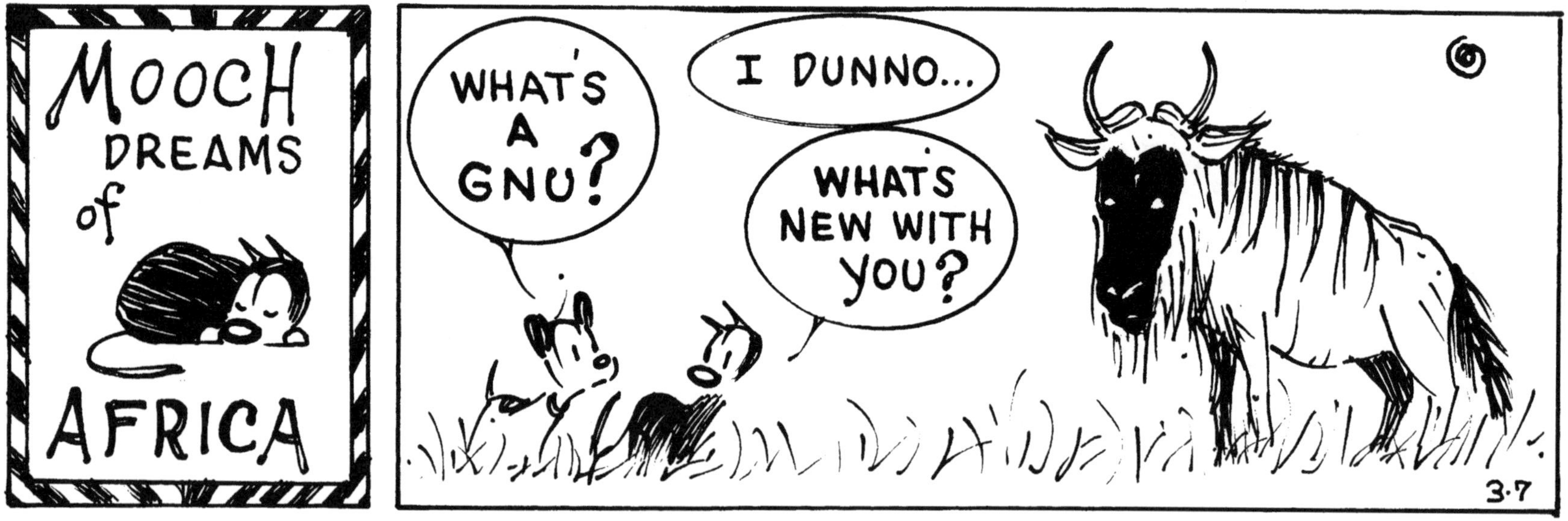
MOOCH DREAMS of AFRICA
WHAT'S A GNU?
I DUNNO...
WHAT'S NEW WITH YOU?
3·7

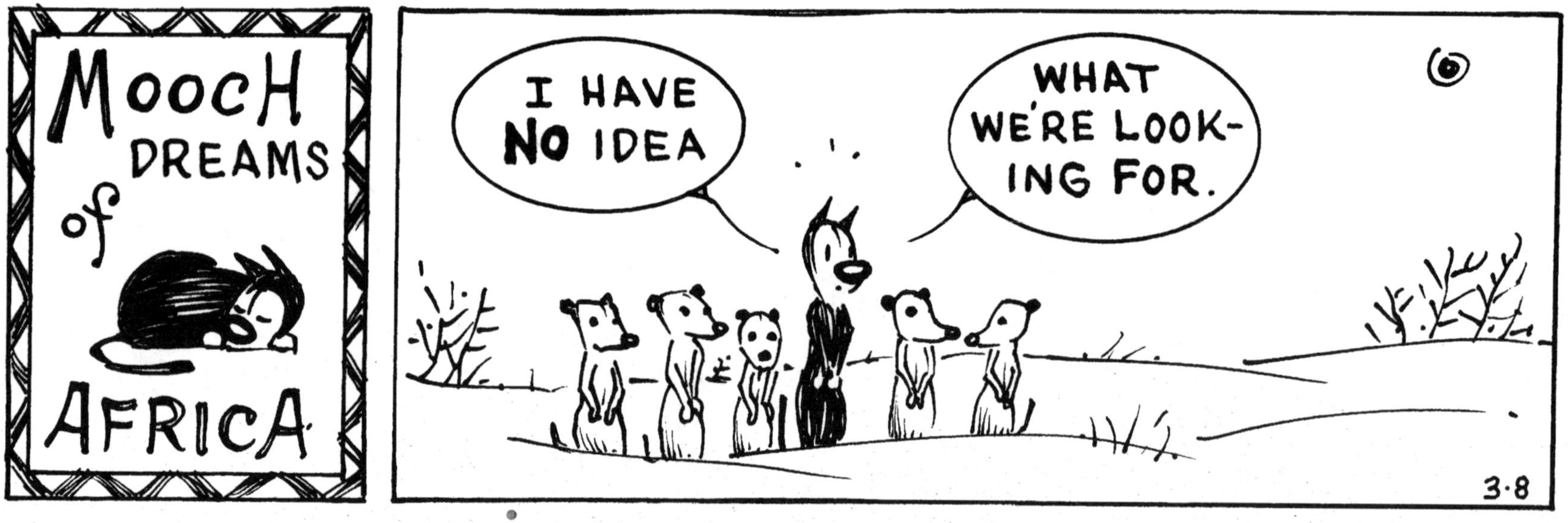
MOOCH DREAMS of AFRICA
I HAVE NO IDEA
WHAT WE'RE LOOKING FOR.
3·8

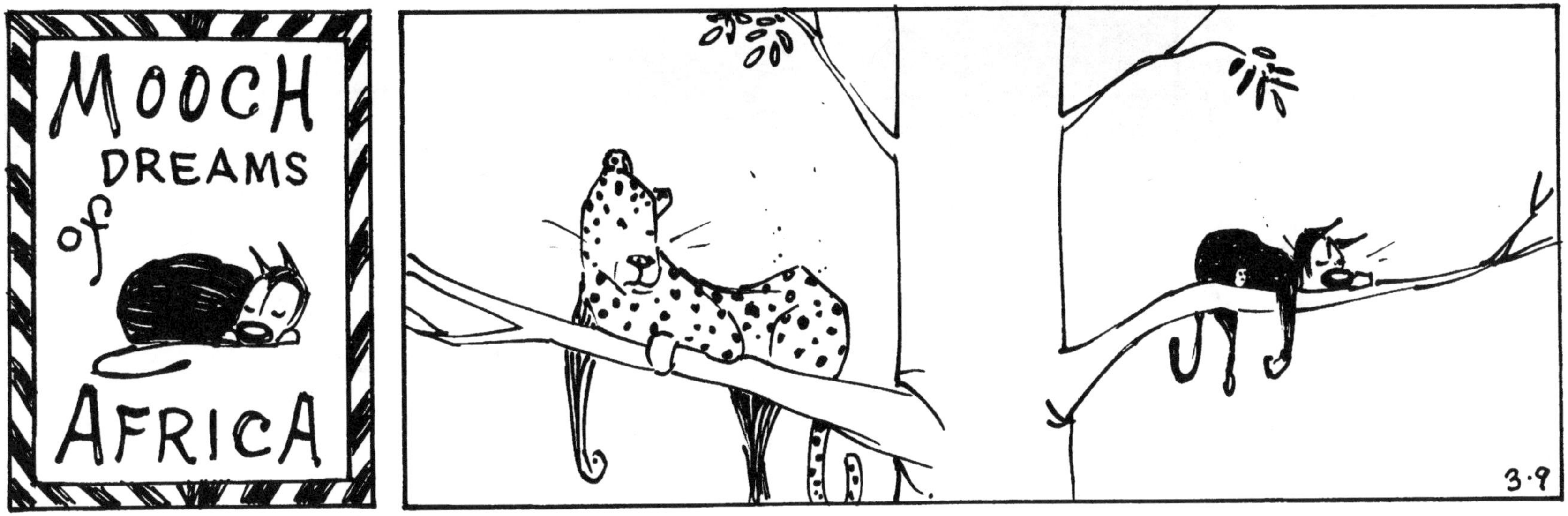
MOOCH DREAMS of AFRICA
3·9

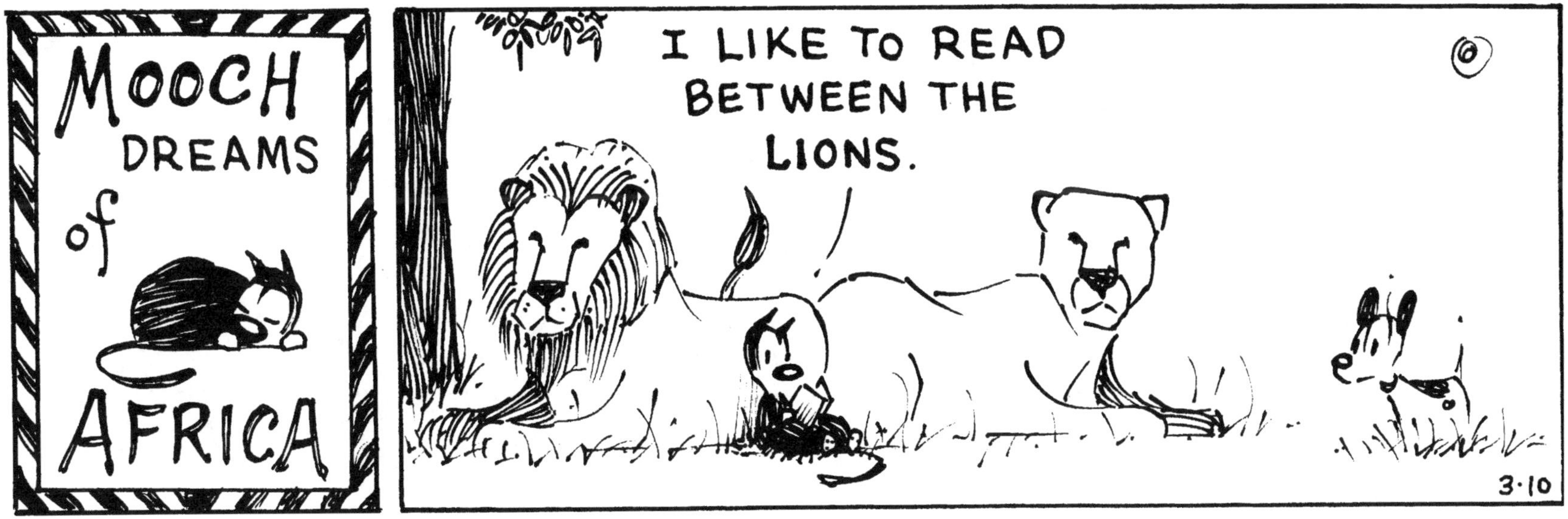
MOOCH DREAMS of AFRICA
I LIKE TO READ BETWEEN THE LIONS.
3·10

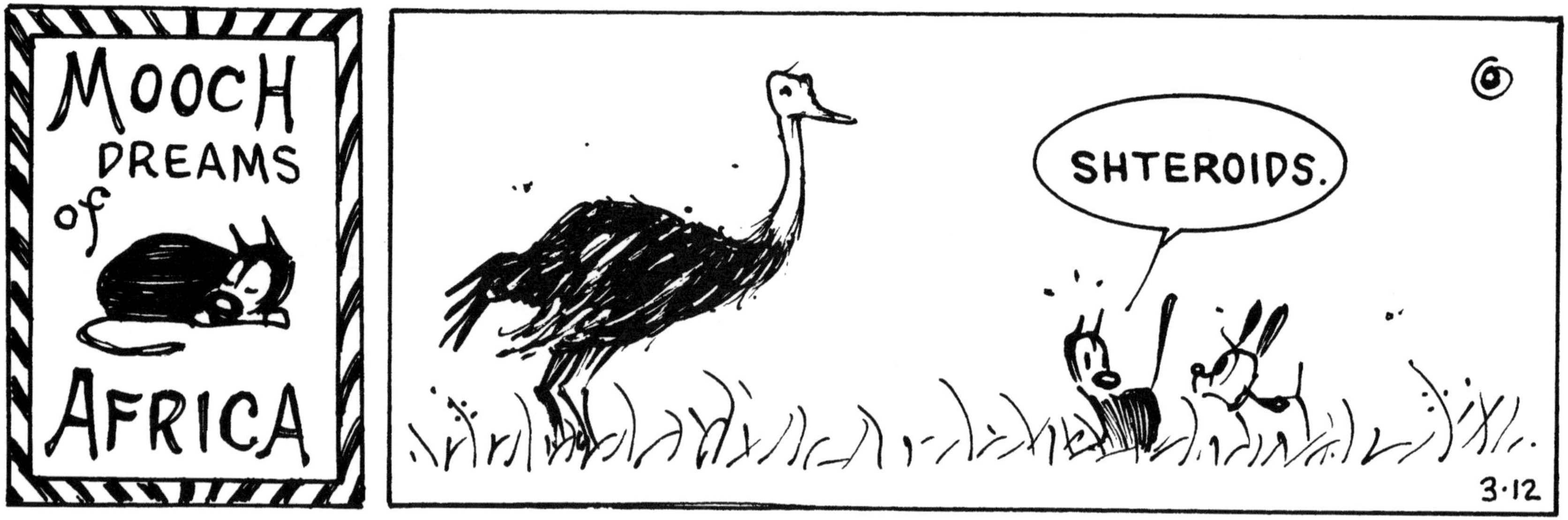
MOOCH DREAMS of AFRICA
SHTEROIDS.
3·12

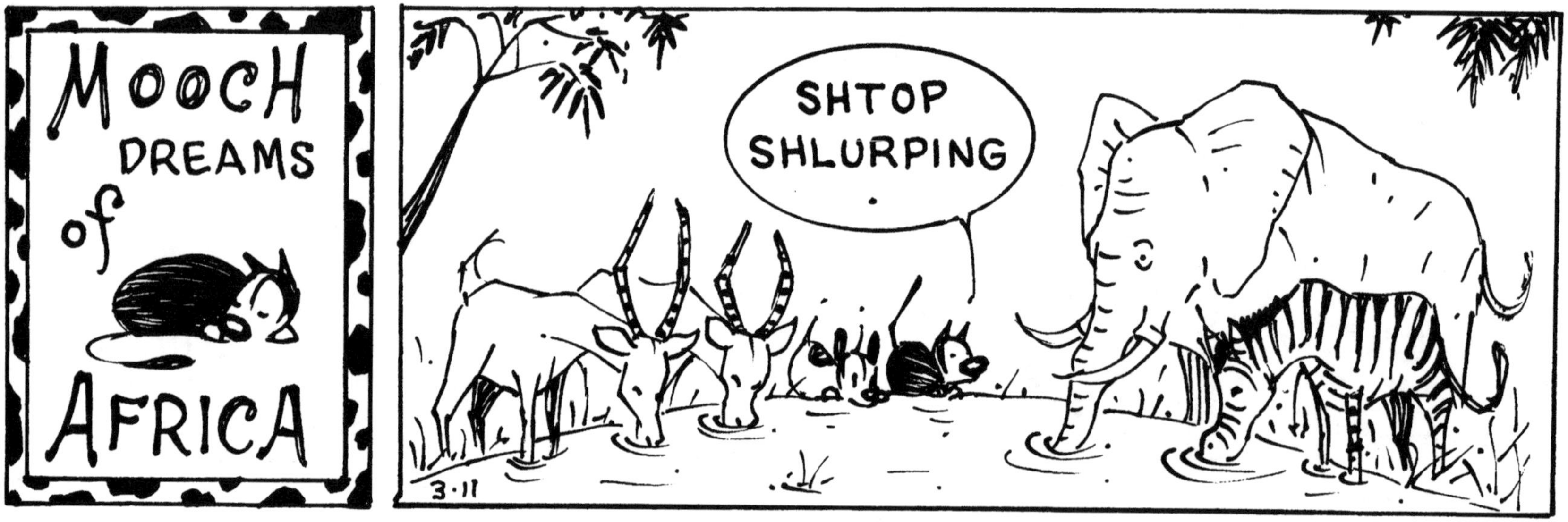
MOOCH DREAMS of AFRICA
SHTOP SHLURPING.
3·11

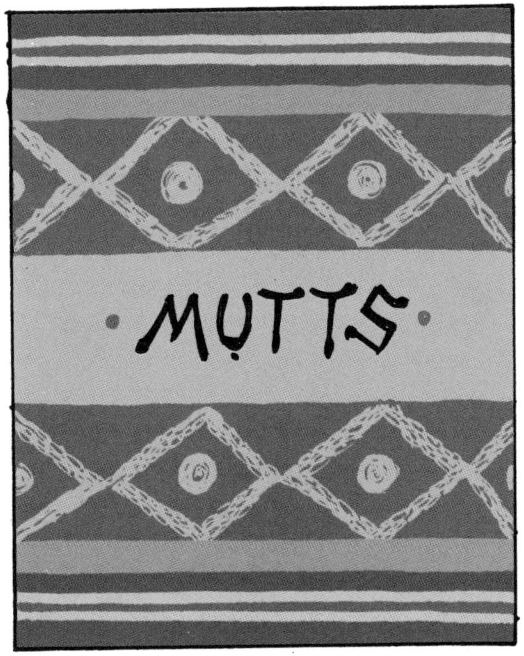
MUTTS

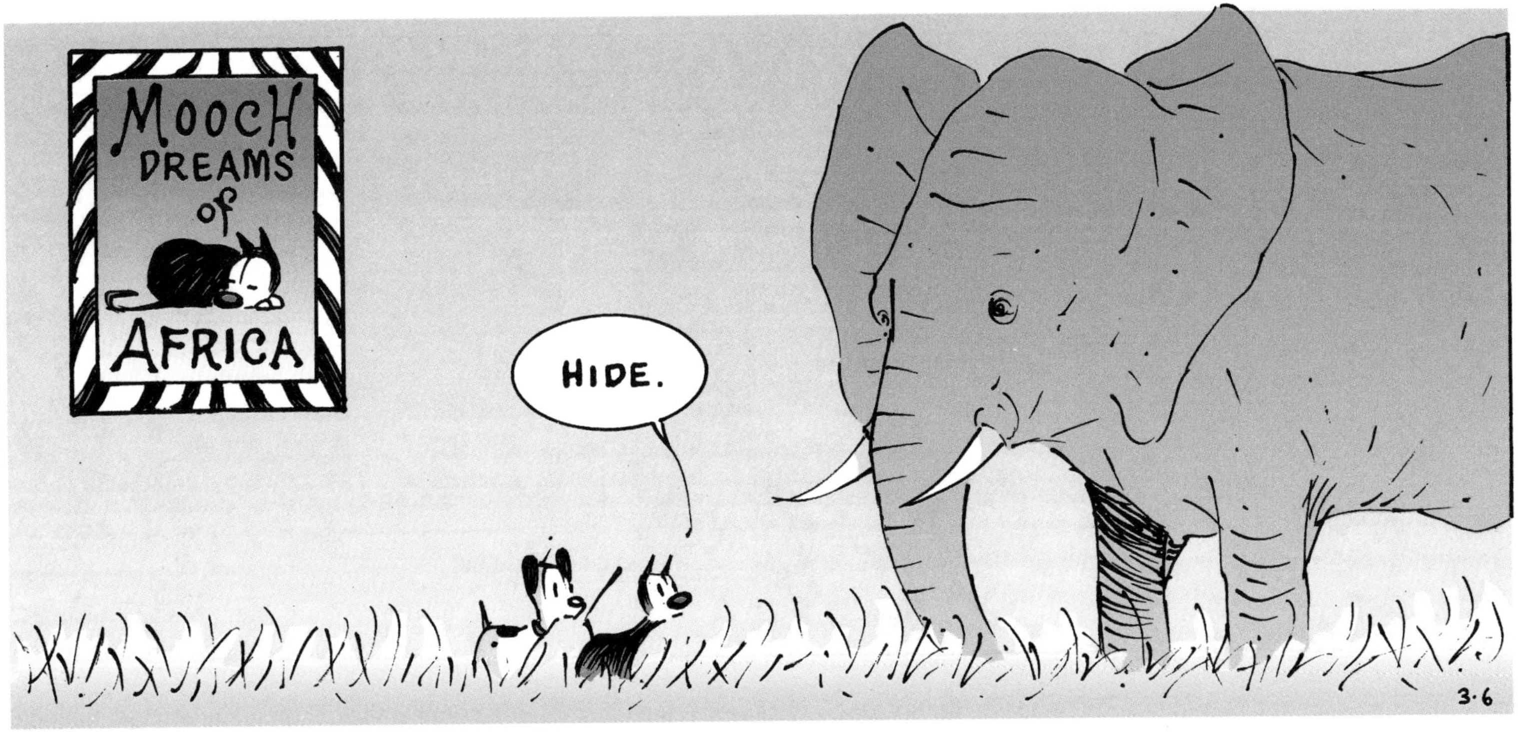
MOOCH DREAMS OF AFRICA
HIDE.
3·6

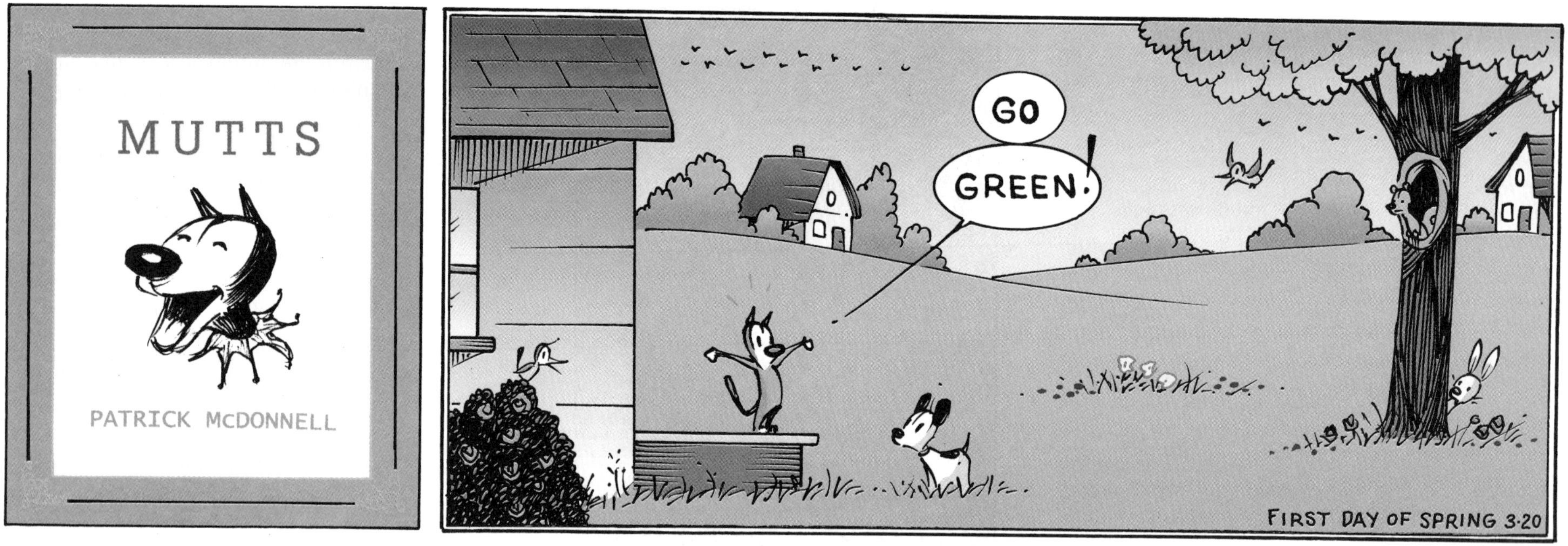
MUTTS
PATRICK McDONNELL
GO GREEN!
FIRST DAY OF SPRING 3·20

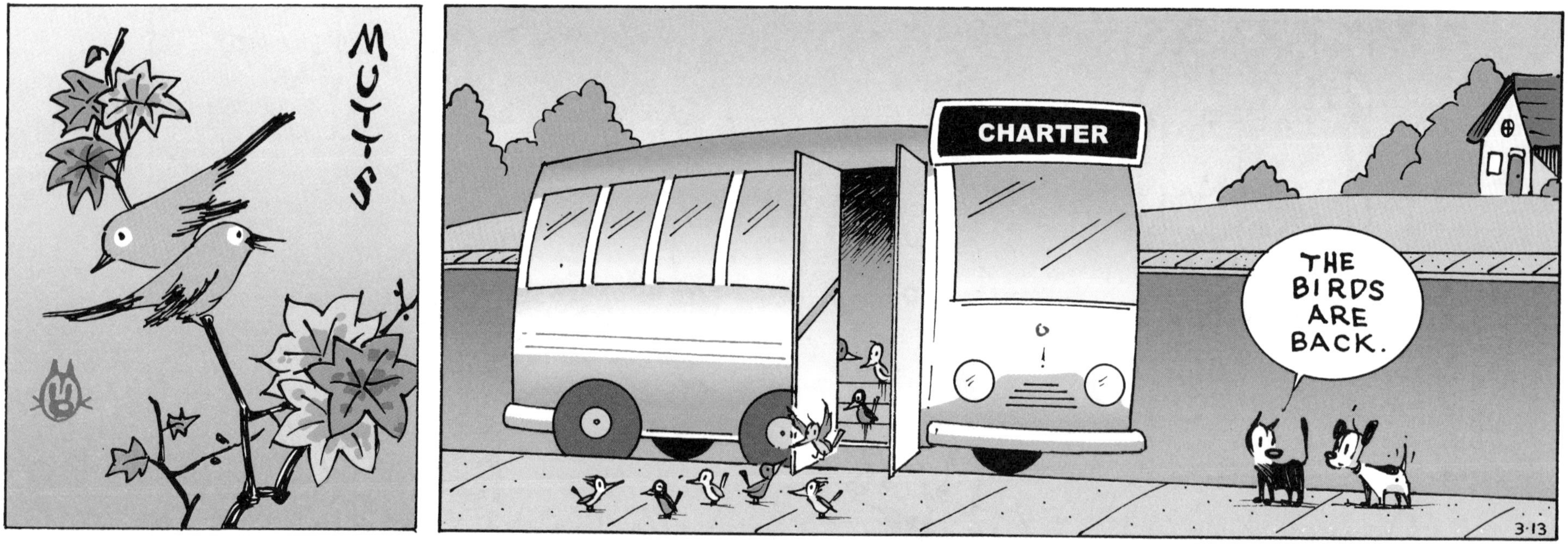
MUTTS
CHARTER
THE BIRDS ARE BACK.
3·13

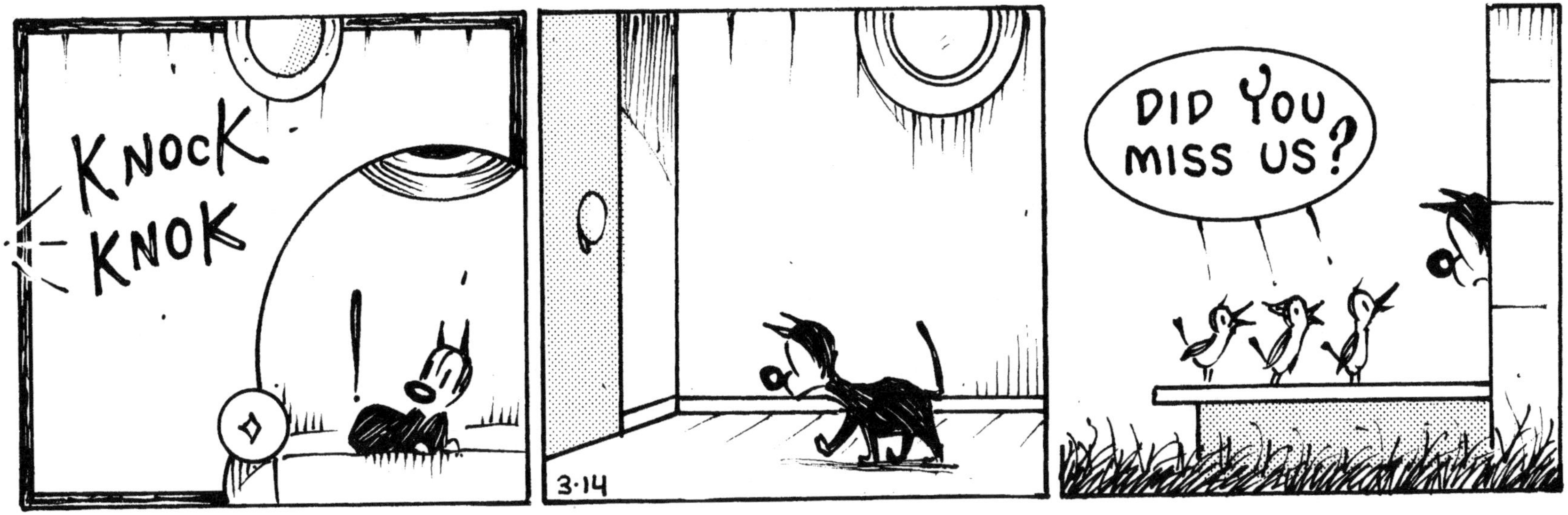
KNOCK
KNOK
!
3·14
DID YOU MISS US?

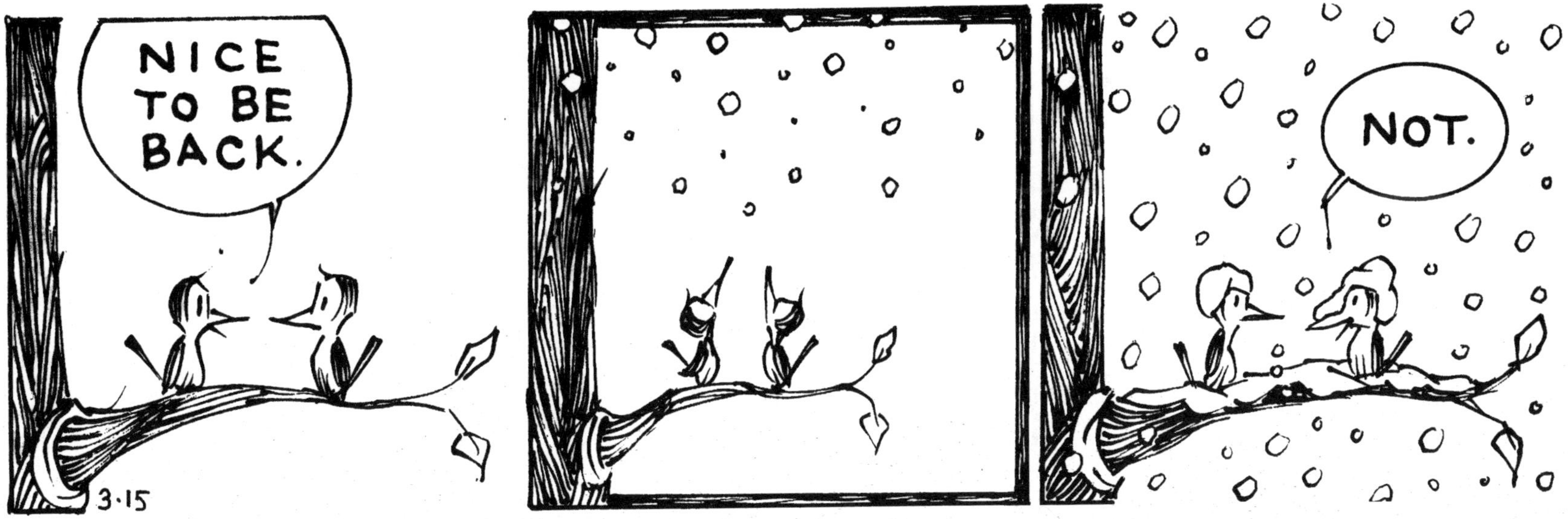
NICE TO BE BACK.
3·15
NOT.

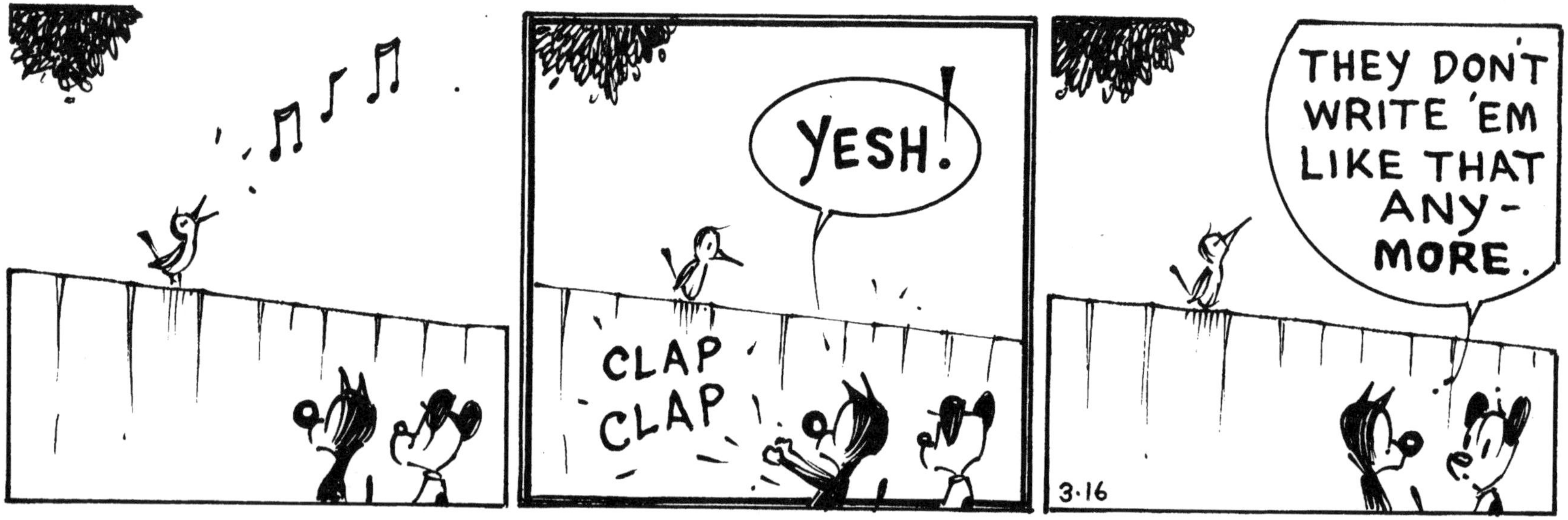
CLAP
CLAP
YESH!
THEY DON'T WRITE 'EM LIKE THAT ANY-MORE.
3·16

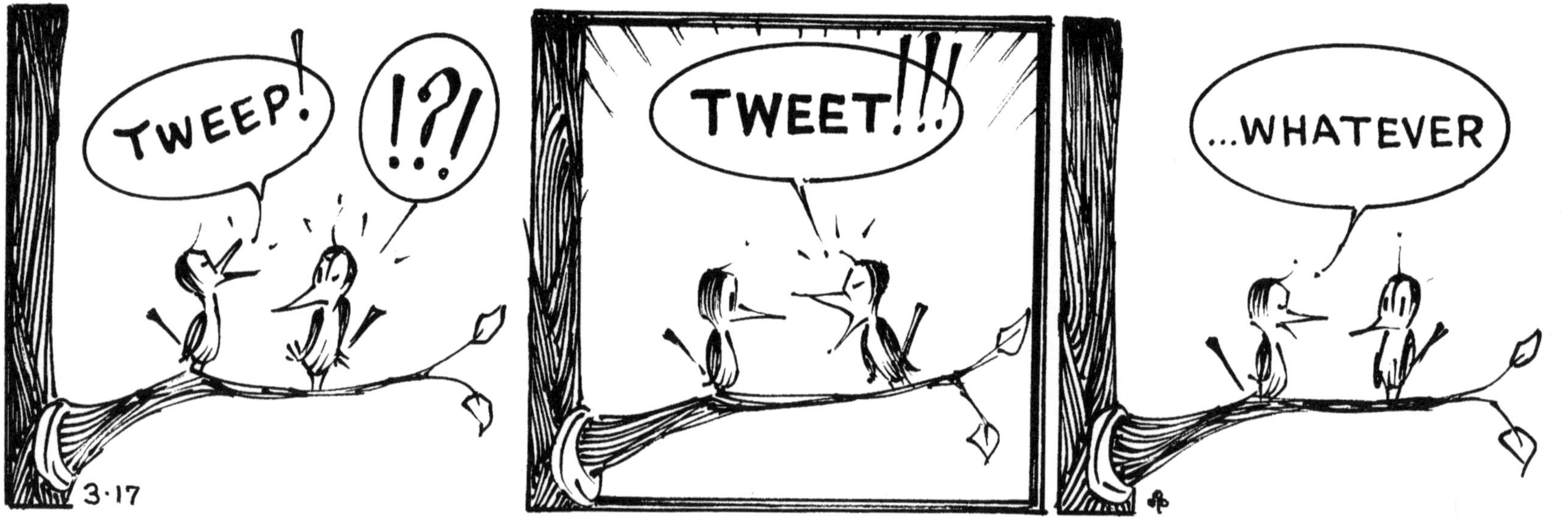
TWEEP!
!?!
3·17
TWEET!!!
...WHATEVER

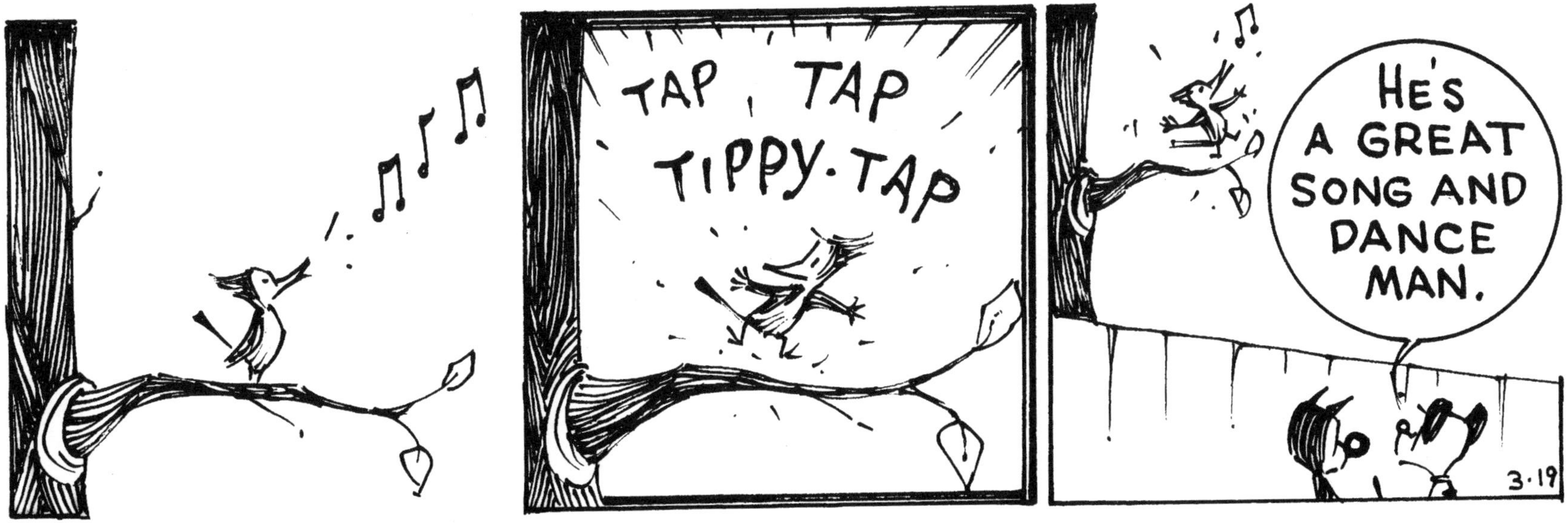
TAP TAP
TIPPY·TAP
HE'S A GREAT SONG AND DANCE MAN.
3·19

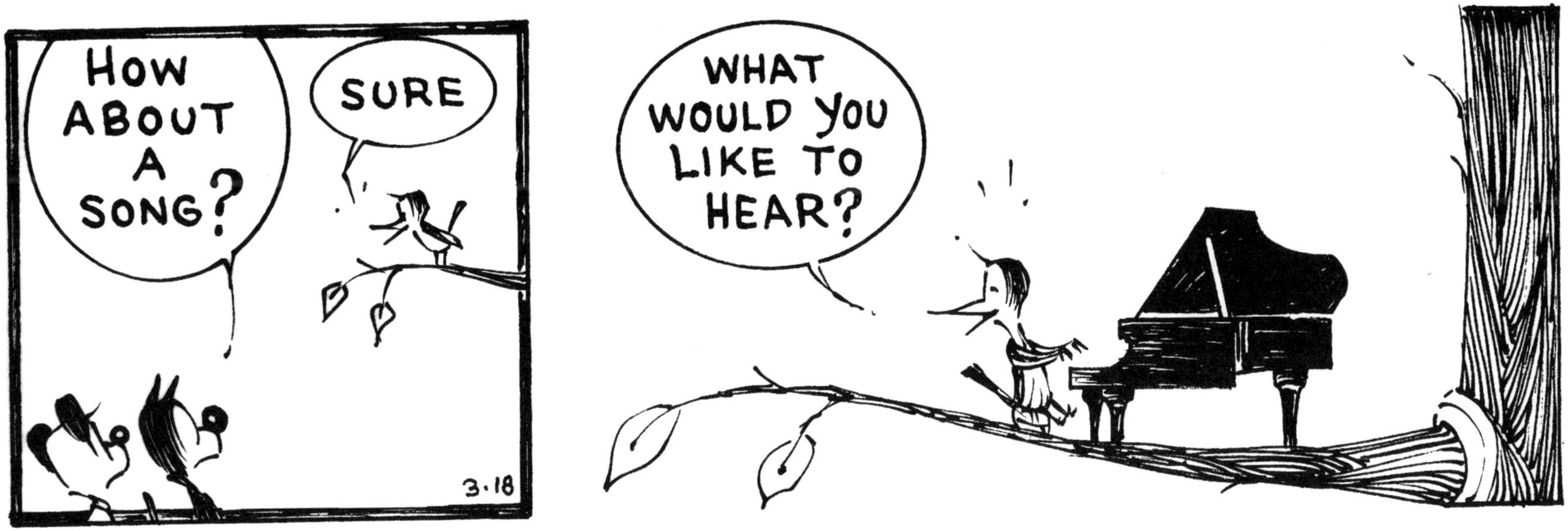
HOW ABOUT A SONG?
SURE
WHAT WOULD YOU LIKE TO HEAR?
3·18

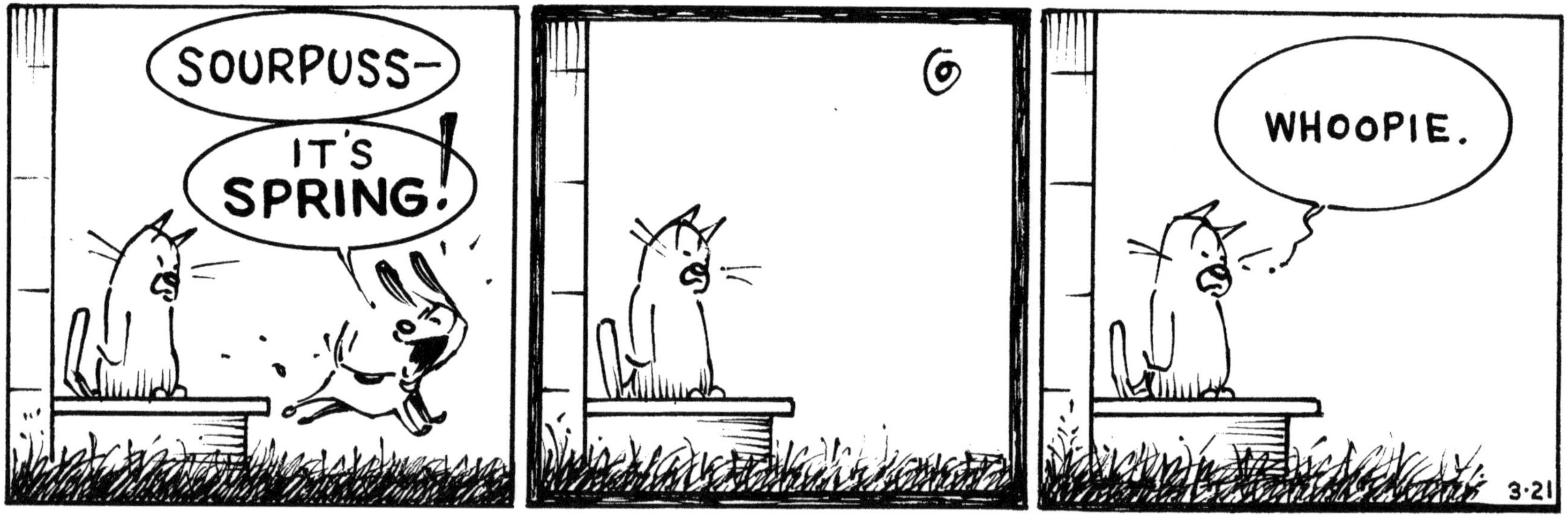
SOURPUSS—
IT'S SPRING!
WHOOPIE.
3·21

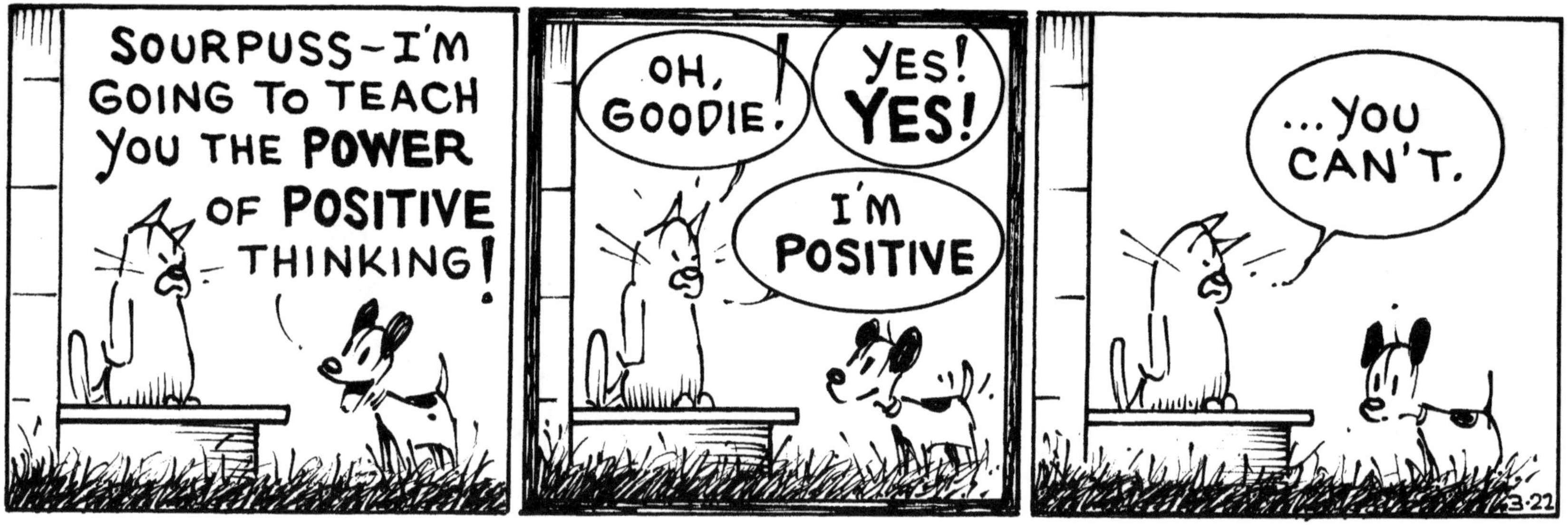
SOURPUSS—I'M GOING TO TEACH YOU THE POWER OF POSITIVE THINKING!
OH, GOODIE!
YES! YES!
I'M POSITIVE
...YOU CAN'T.
3·22

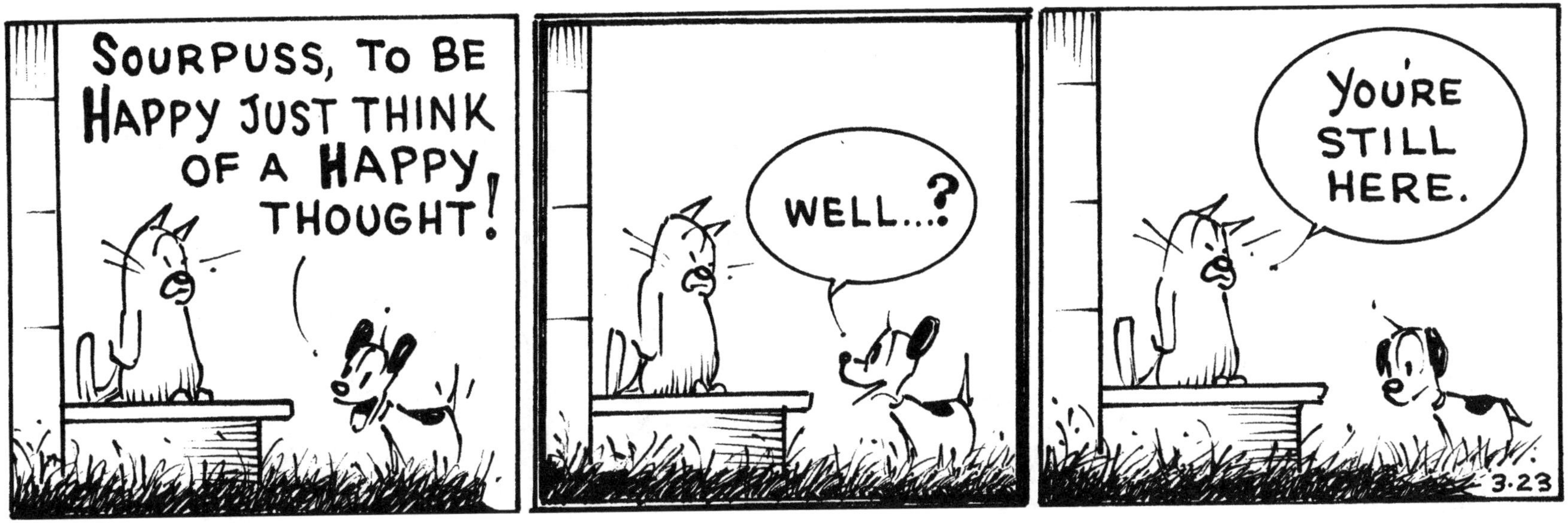
SOURPUSS, TO BE HAPPY JUST THINK OF A HAPPY THOUGHT!
WELL...?
YOU'RE STILL HERE.
3·23

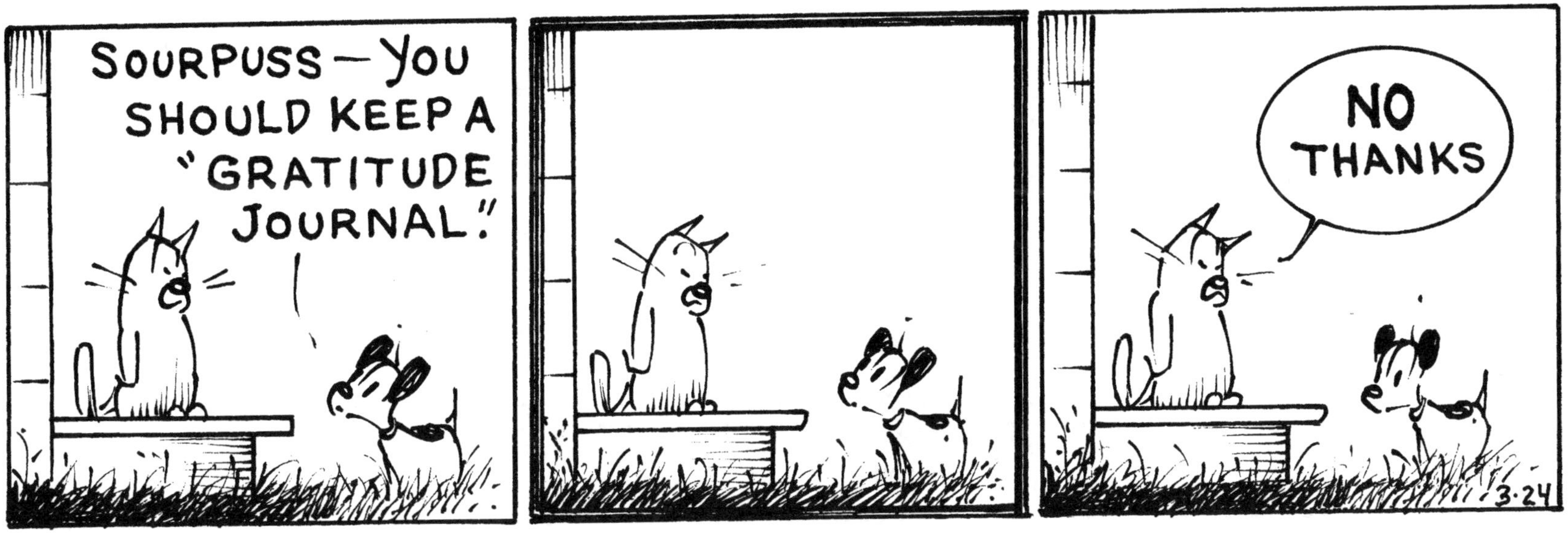
SOURPUSS—YOU SHOULD KEEP A "GRATITUDE JOURNAL."
NO THANKS
3·24

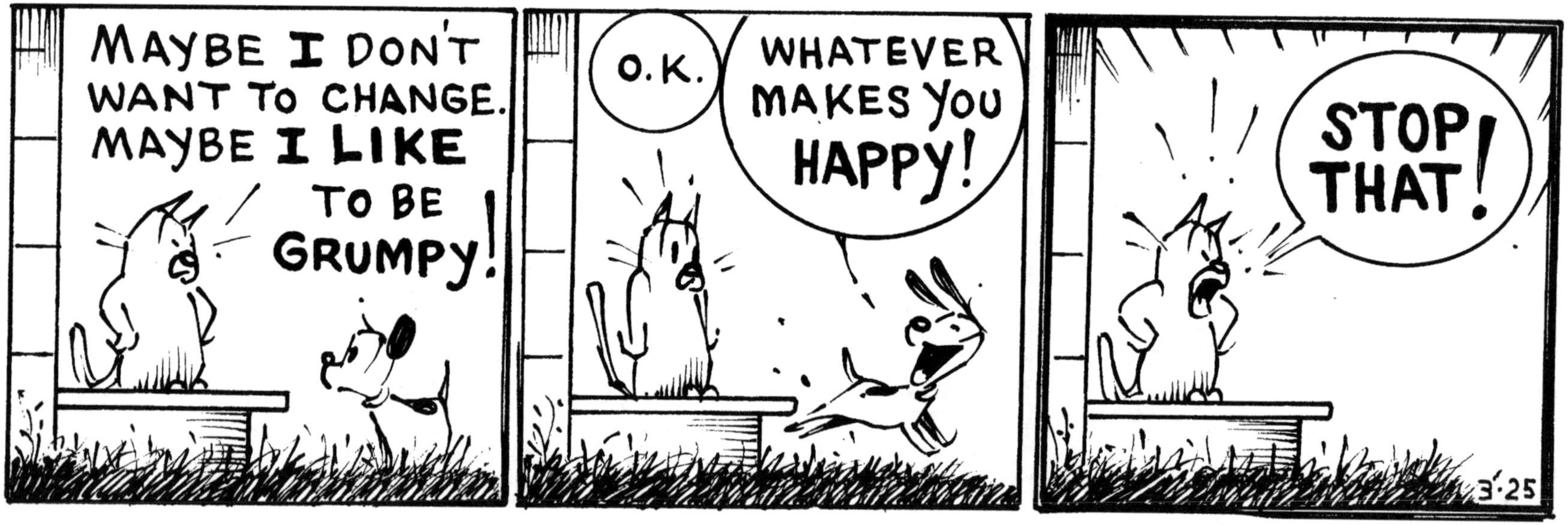
MAYBE I DON'T WANT TO CHANGE. MAYBE I LIKE TO BE GRUMPY!
O.K.
WHATEVER MAKES YOU HAPPY!
STOP THAT!
3·25

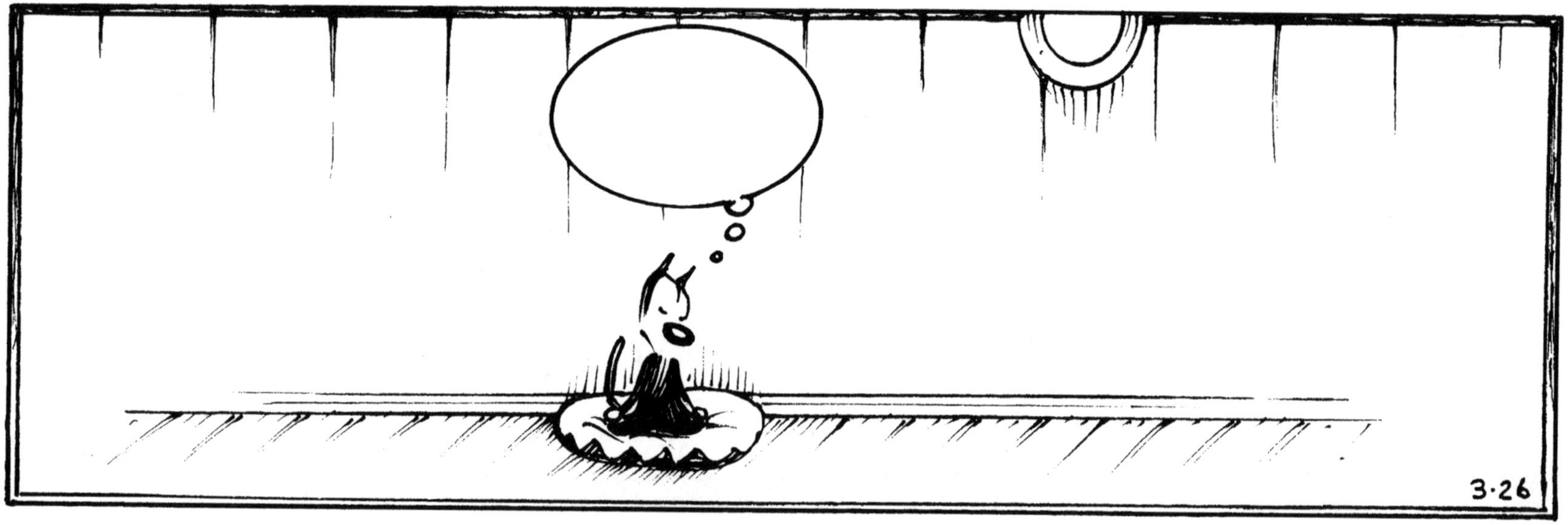
3·26

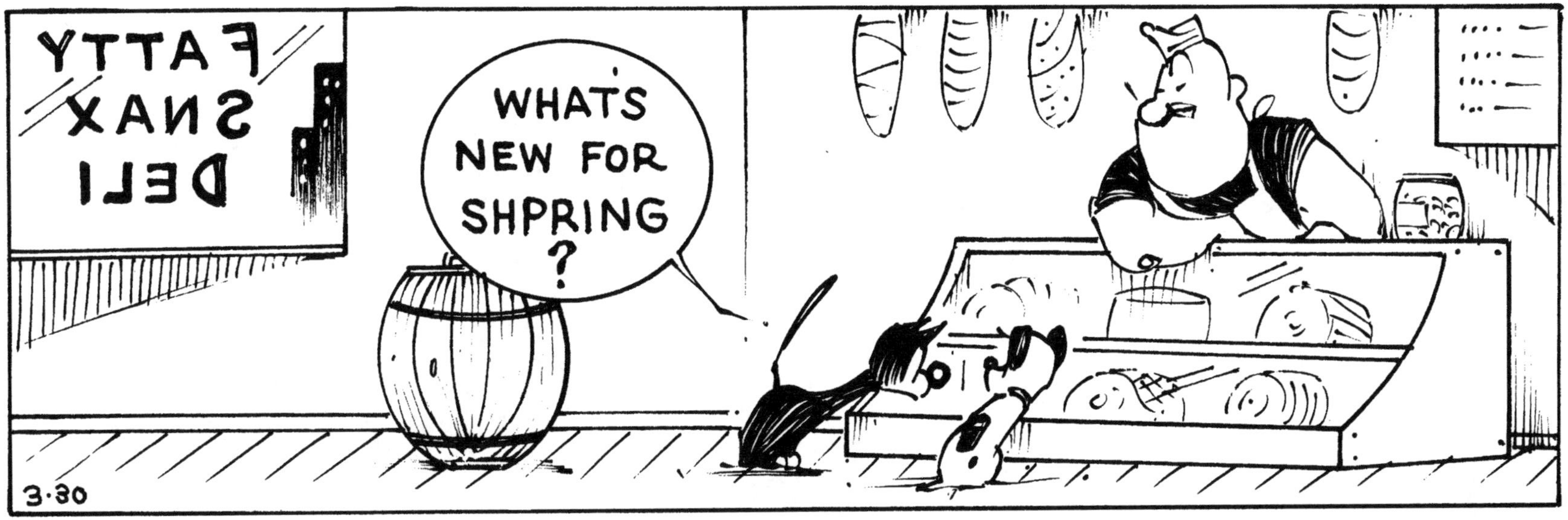
FATTY SNAX DELI
WHAT'S NEW FOR SHPRING?
3·30

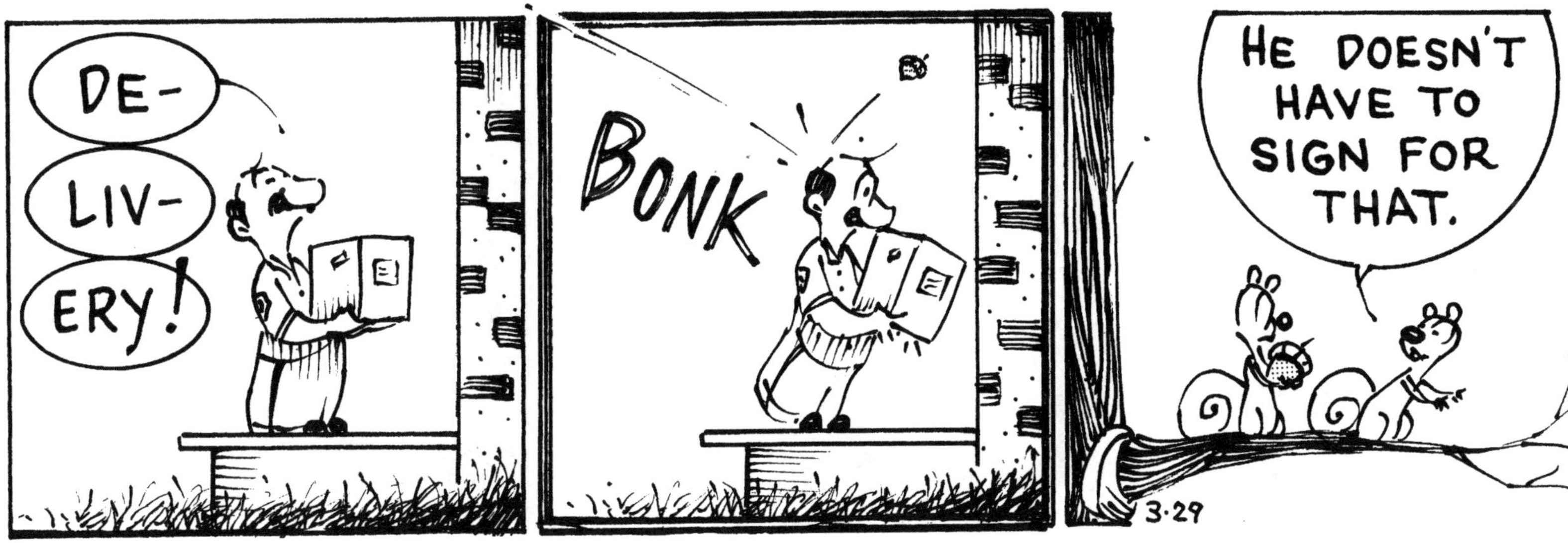
DE- LIV- ERY!
BONK
HE DOESN'T HAVE TO SIGN FOR THAT.
3·29

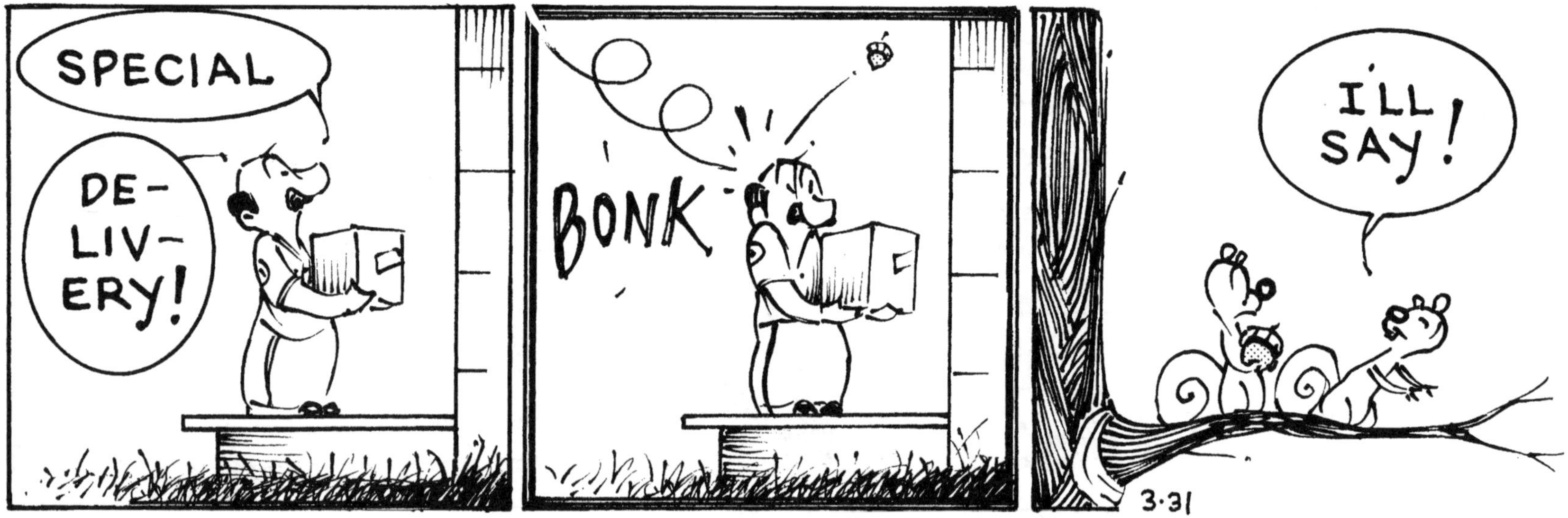
SPECIAL
DE-LIV-ERY!
BONK
I'LL SAY!
3·31

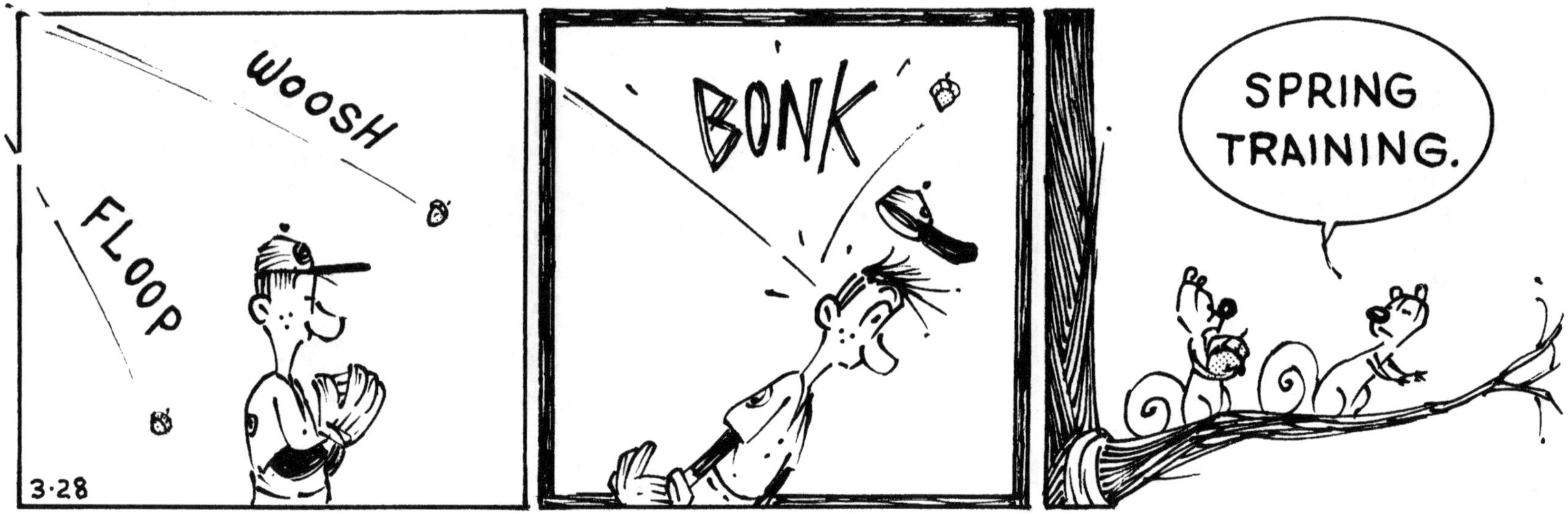
WOOSH
FLOOP
3·28
BONK
SPRING TRAINING.

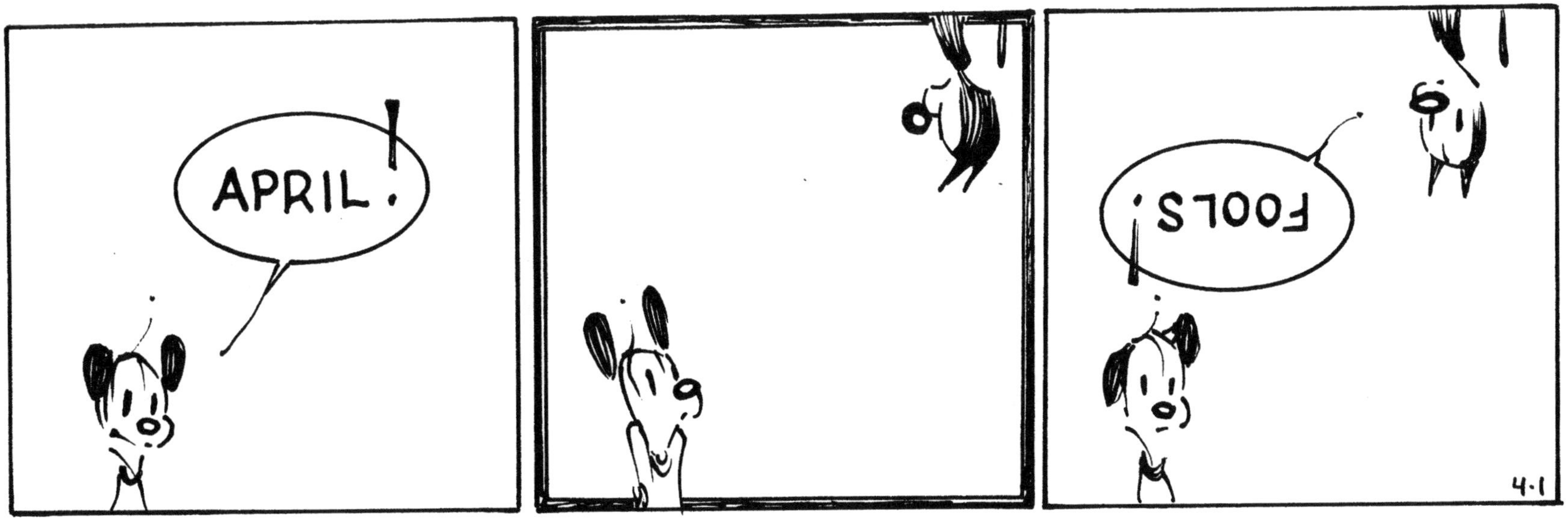
APRIL!
FOOLS!
4·1

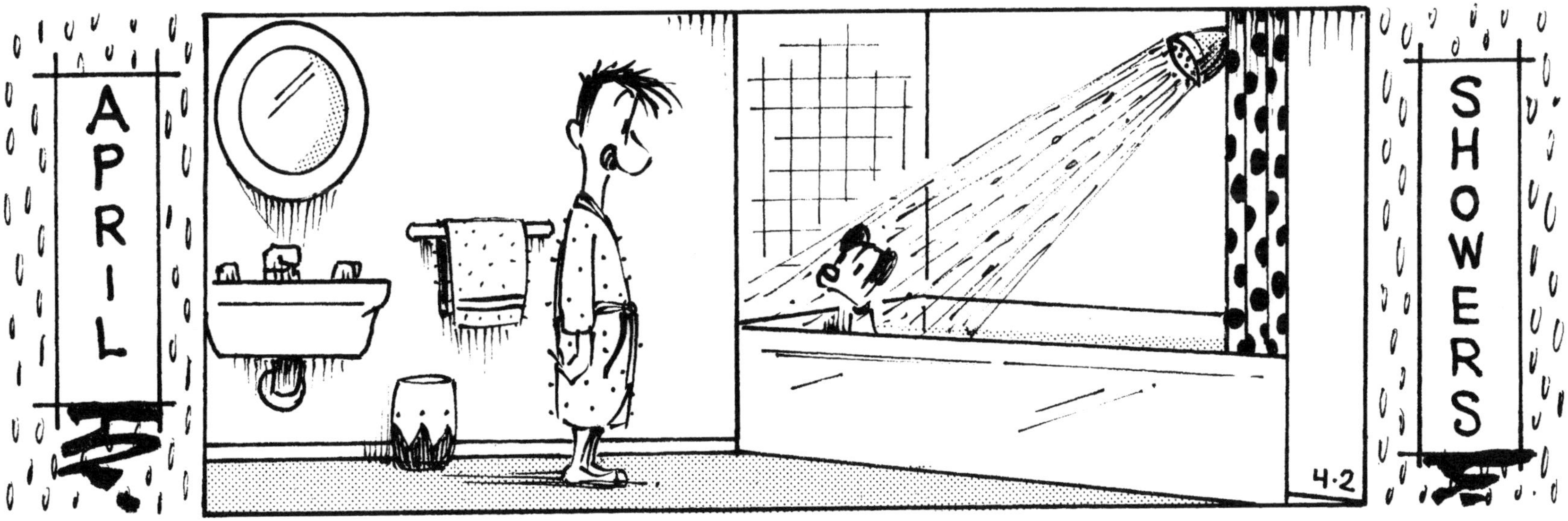
APRIL
4·2
SHOWERS

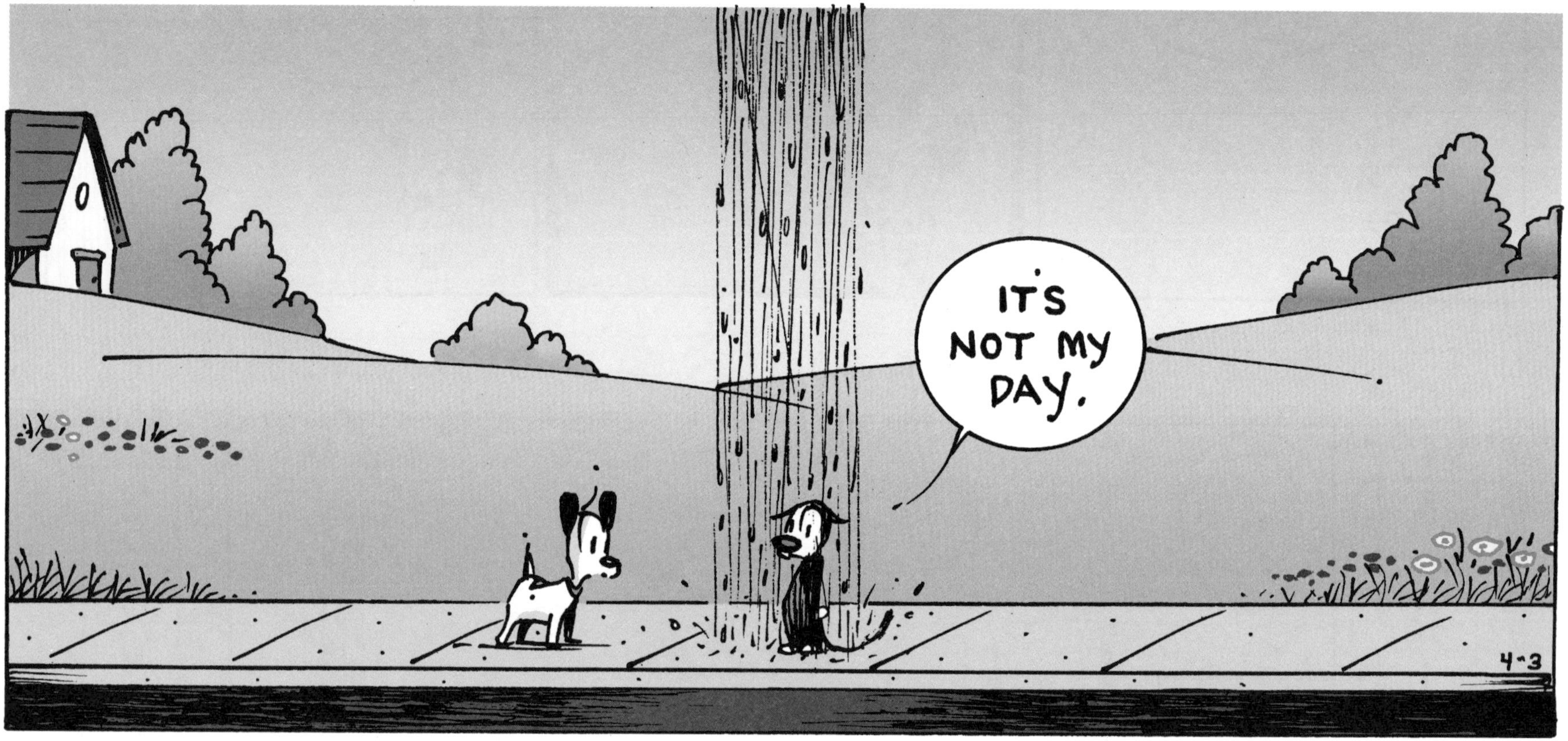
IT'S NOT MY DAY.
4-3

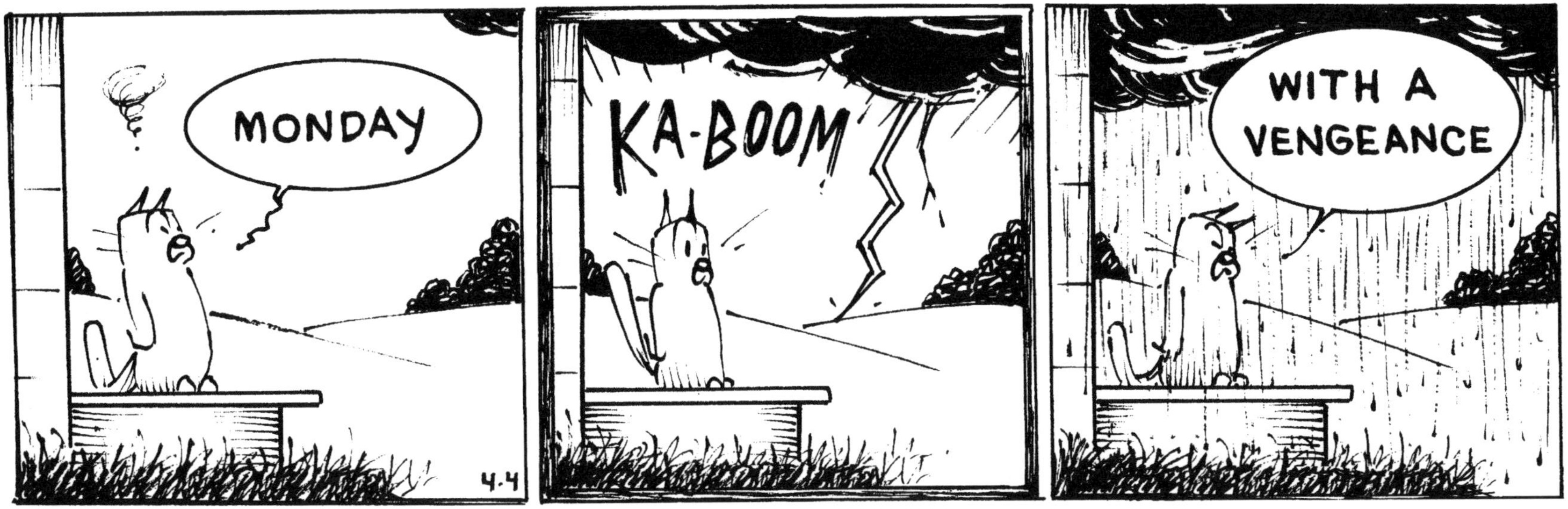
MONDAY
KA-BOOM
WITH A VENGEANCE
4·4

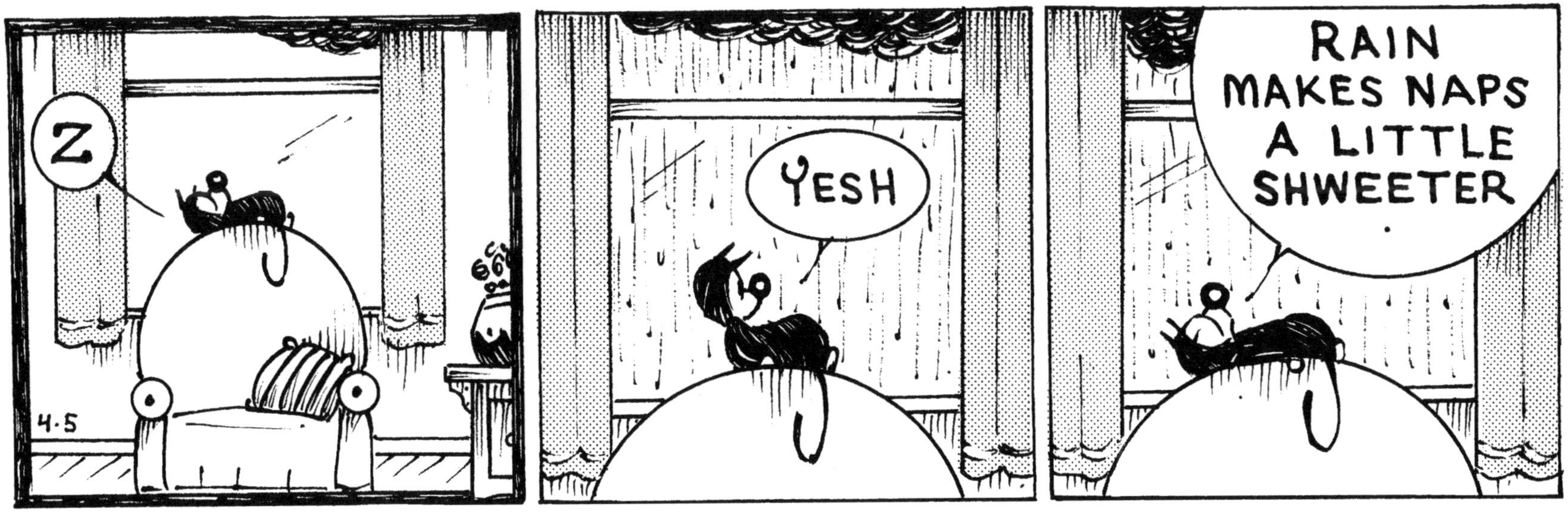
Z
YESH
RAIN MAKES NAPS A LITTLE SHWEETER
4·5

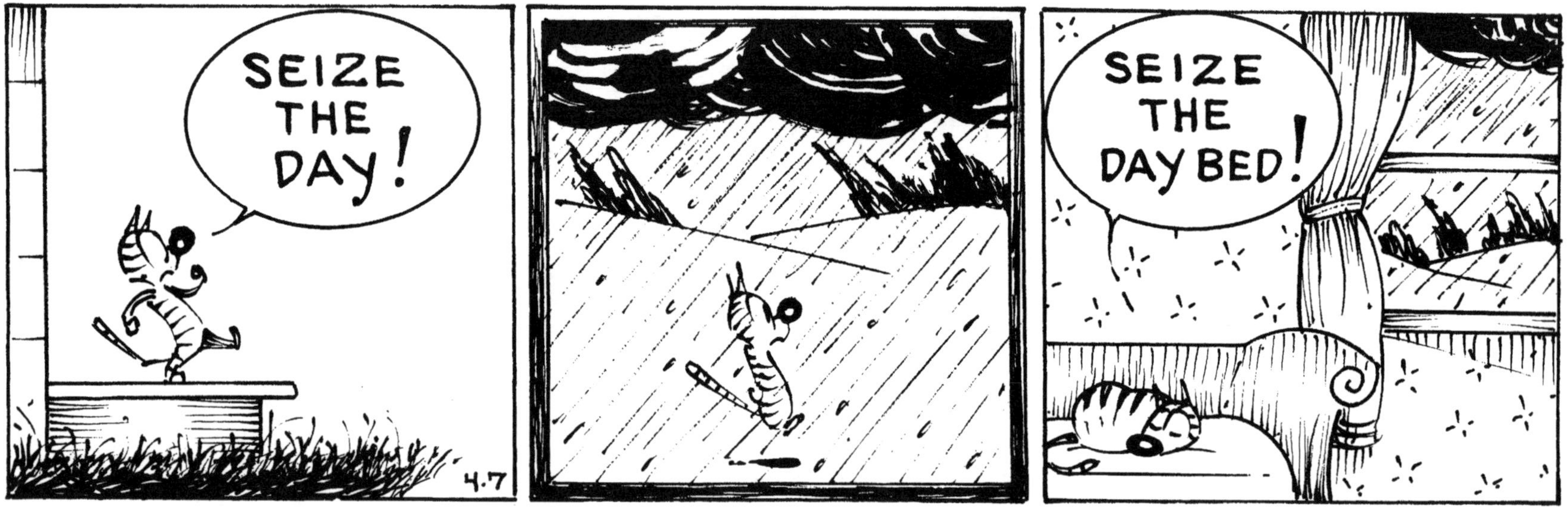
SEIZE THE DAY!
4.7
SEIZE THE DAY BED!

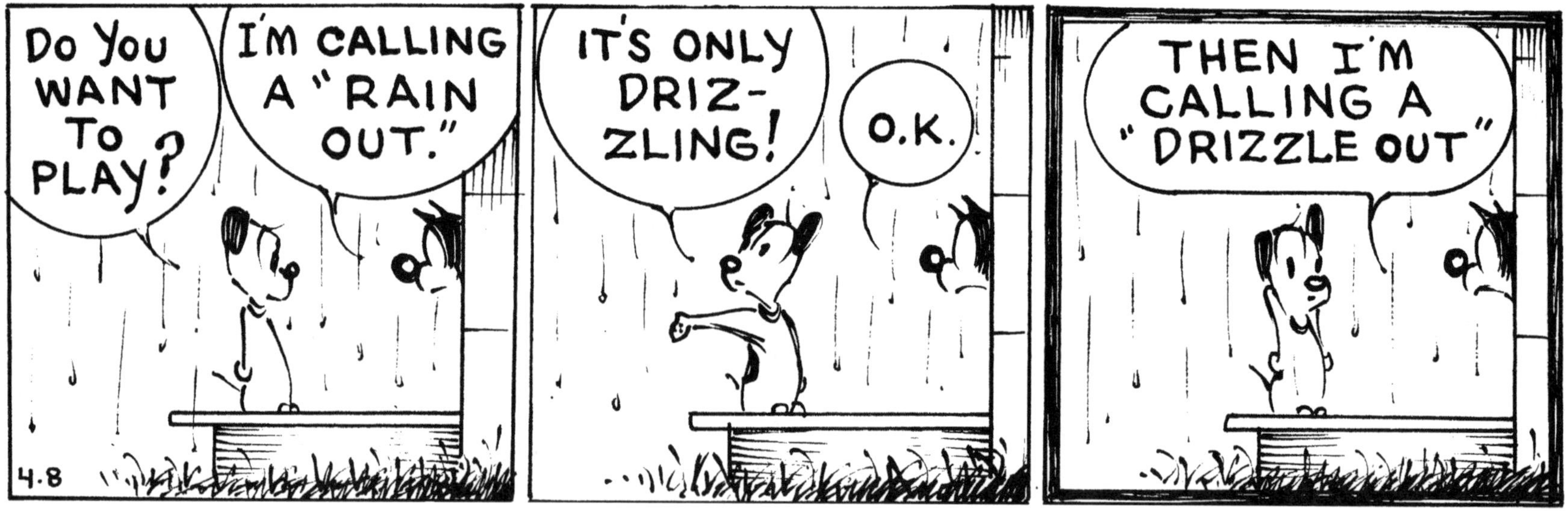
DO YOU WANT TO PLAY?
I'M CALLING A "RAIN OUT."
4.8
IT'S ONLY DRIZ-ZLING!
O.K.
THEN I'M CALLING A "DRIZZLE OUT"

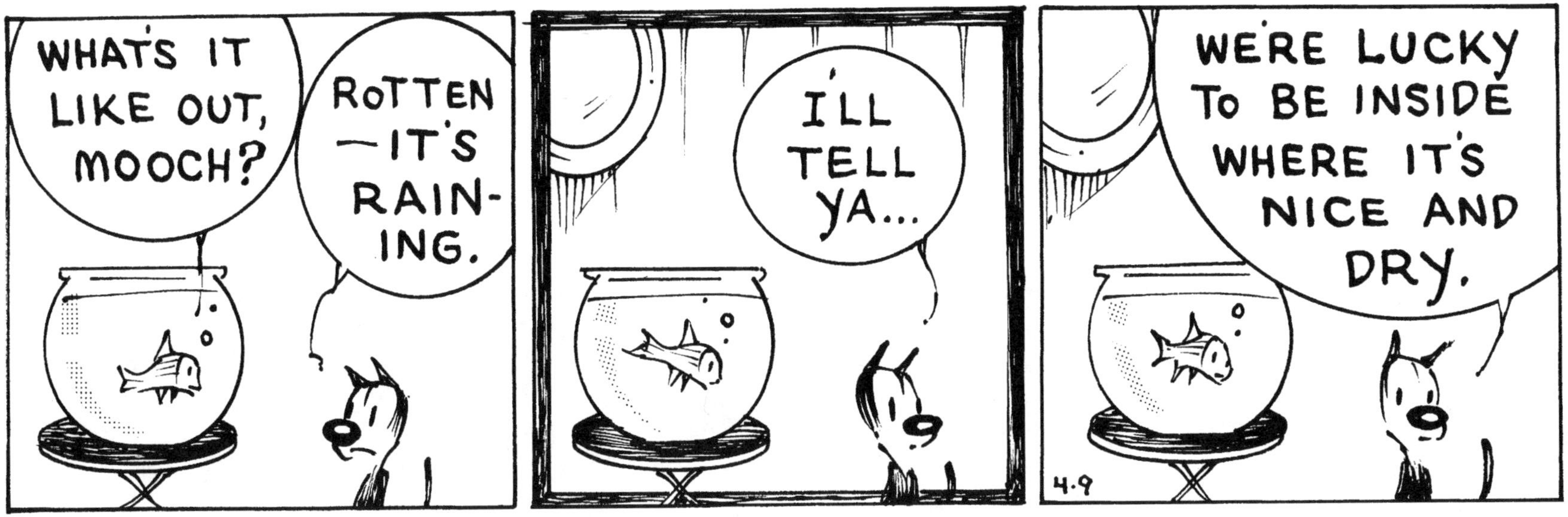
WHAT'S IT LIKE OUT, MOOCH?
ROTTEN —IT'S RAIN-ING.
I'LL TELL YA...
WE'RE LUCKY TO BE INSIDE WHERE IT'S NICE AND DRY.
4·9

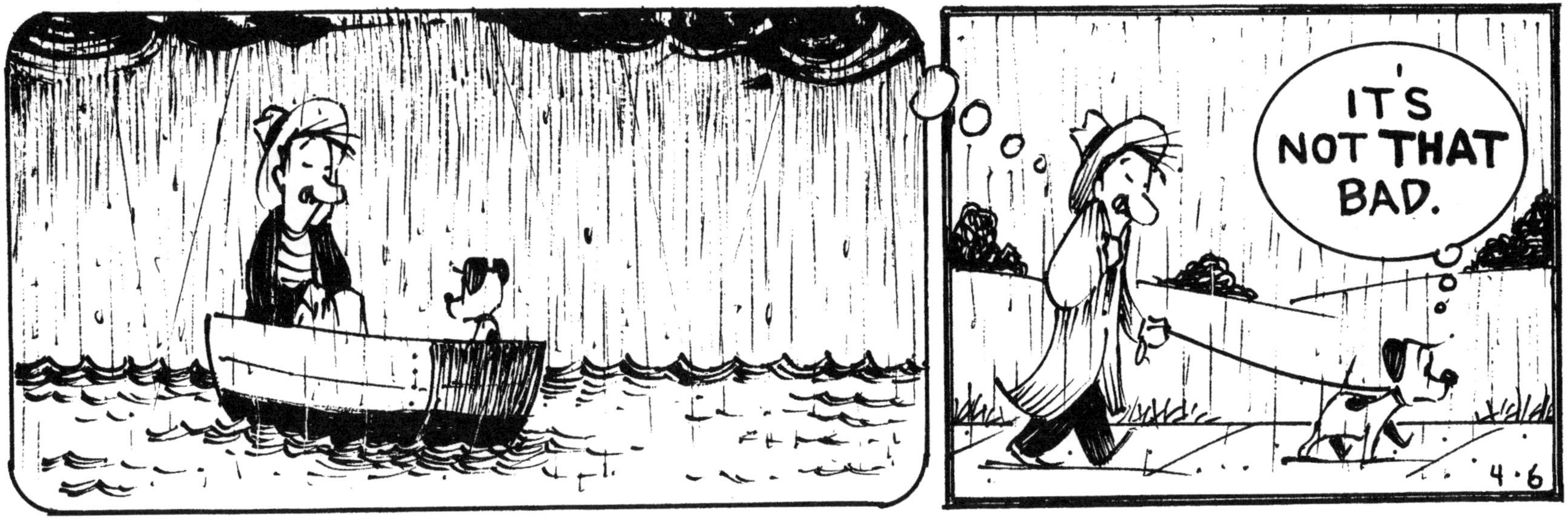
IT'S NOT **THAT** BAD.
4·6

Mutts
Patrick McDonnell
RAIN... RAIN,
GO AWAY...
THIS MUST BE THAT
"SOME OTHER DAY."
4·17

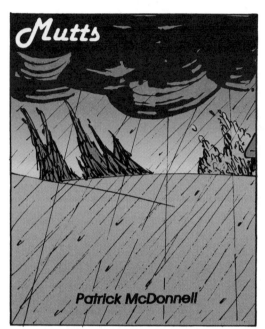

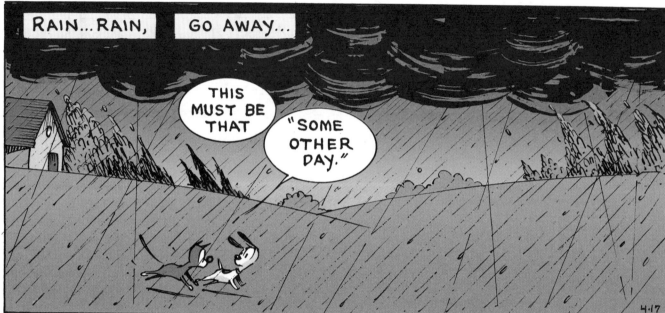

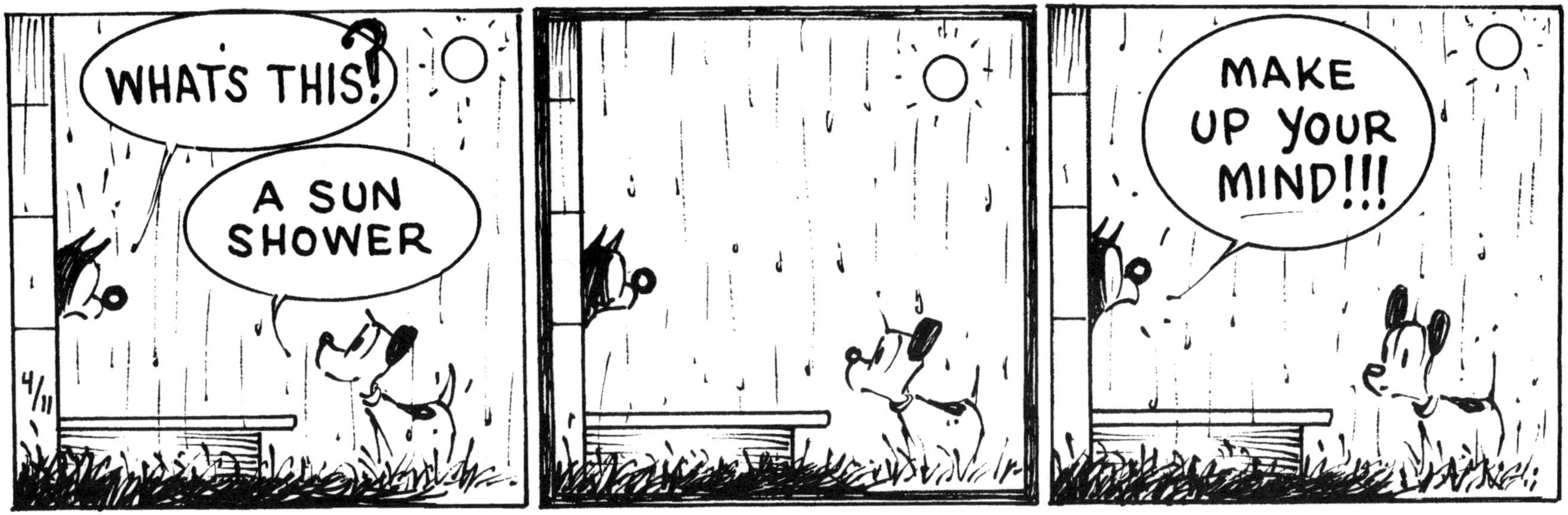
WHAT'S THIS?
A SUN SHOWER
4/11
MAKE UP YOUR MIND!!!

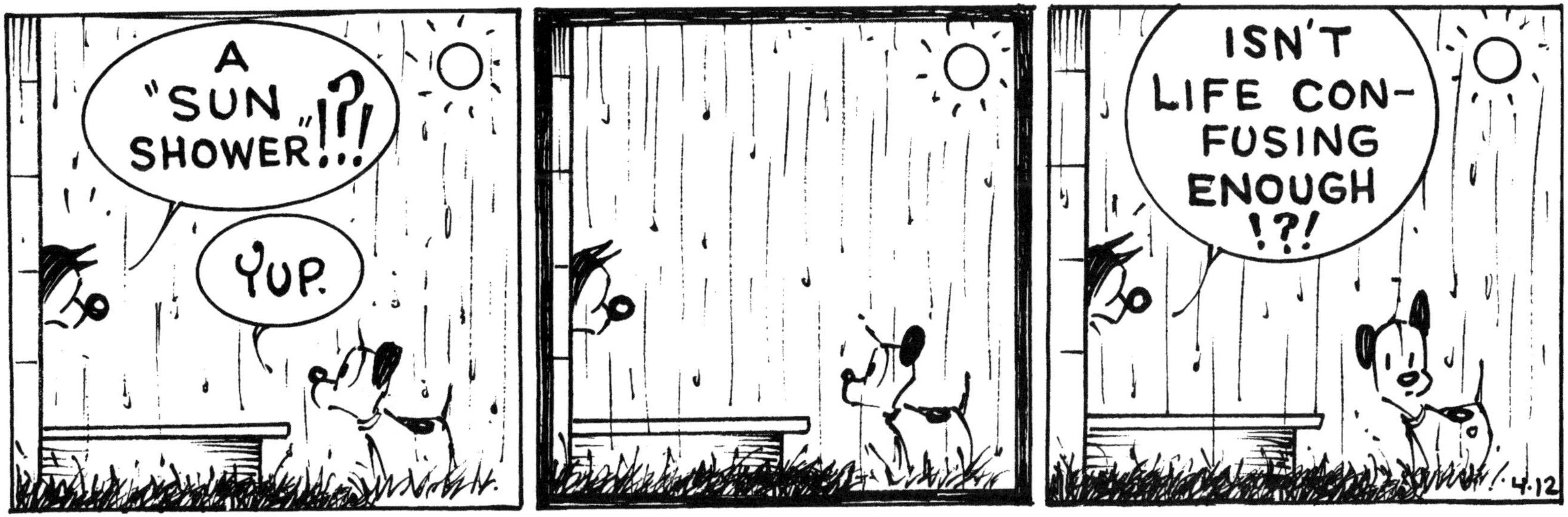
A "SUN SHOWER"!?!
YUP.
ISN'T LIFE CON-FUSING ENOUGH !?!
4.12

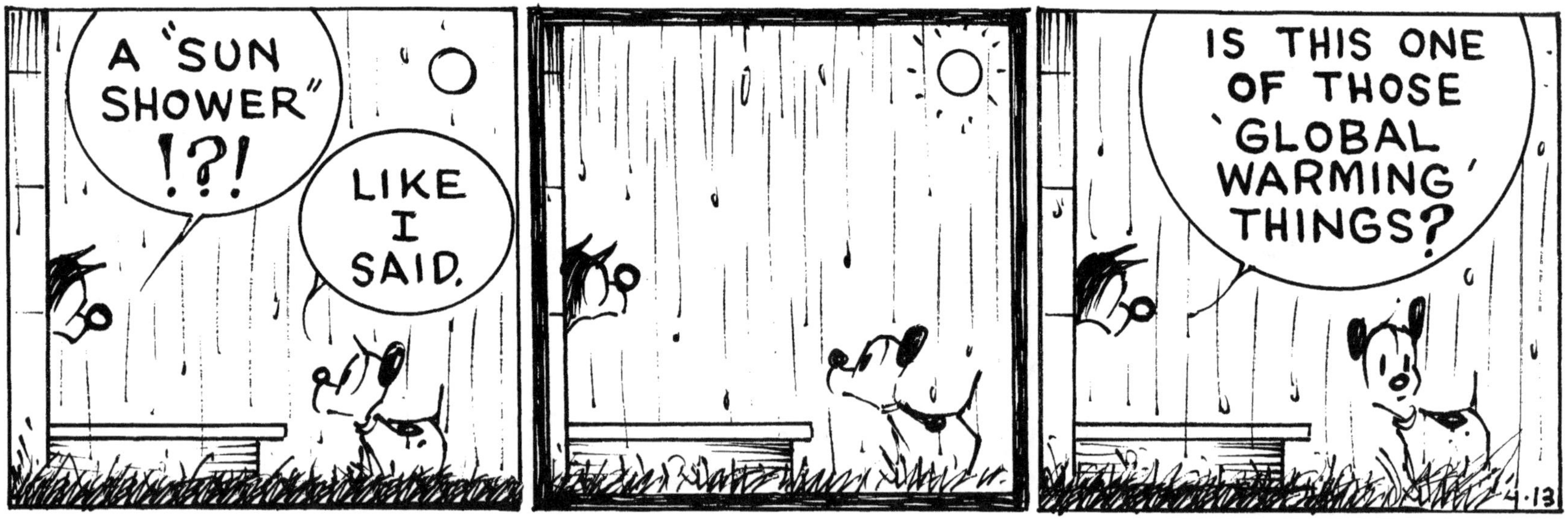
A "SUN SHOWER" !?!
LIKE I SAID.
IS THIS ONE OF THOSE 'GLOBAL WARMING' THINGS?
4·13

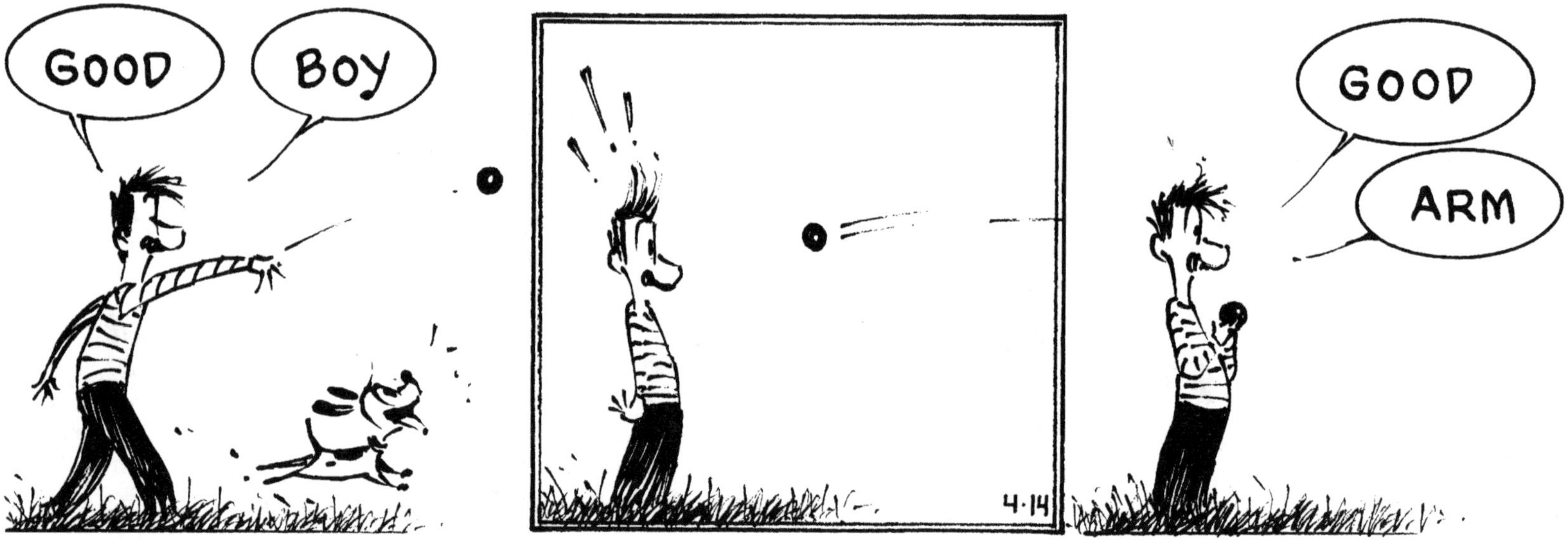
GOOD
BOY
4·14
GOOD
ARM

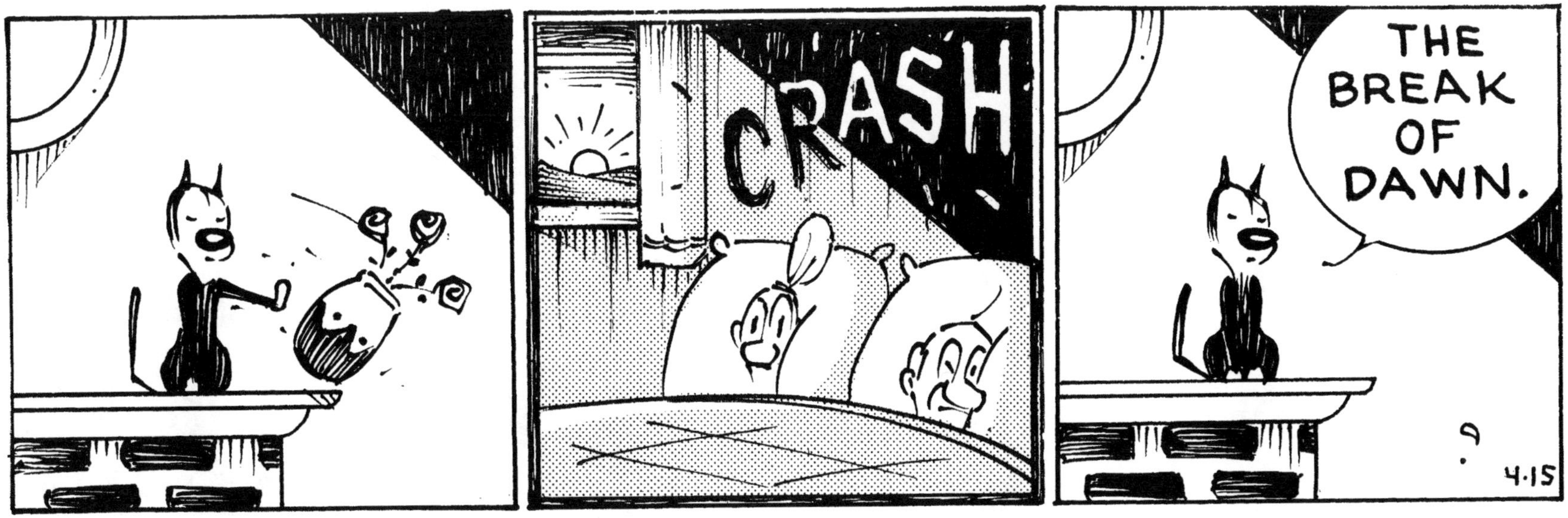
CRASH
THE BREAK OF DAWN.
4·15

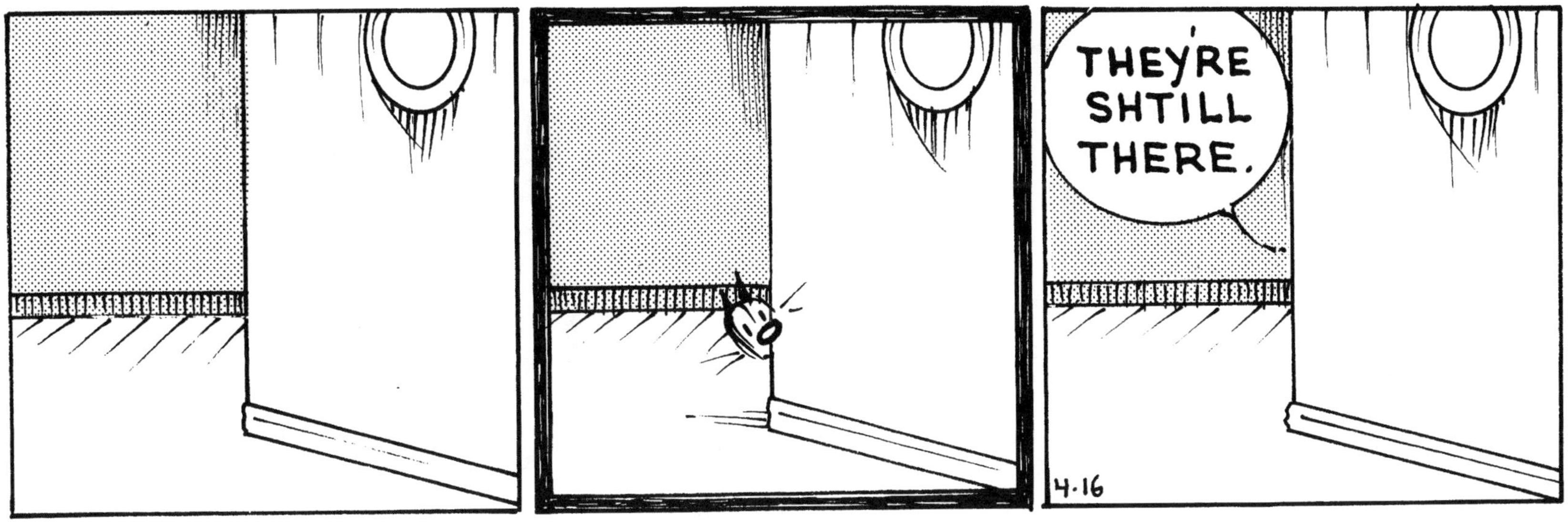
THEY'RE SHTILL THERE.
4·16

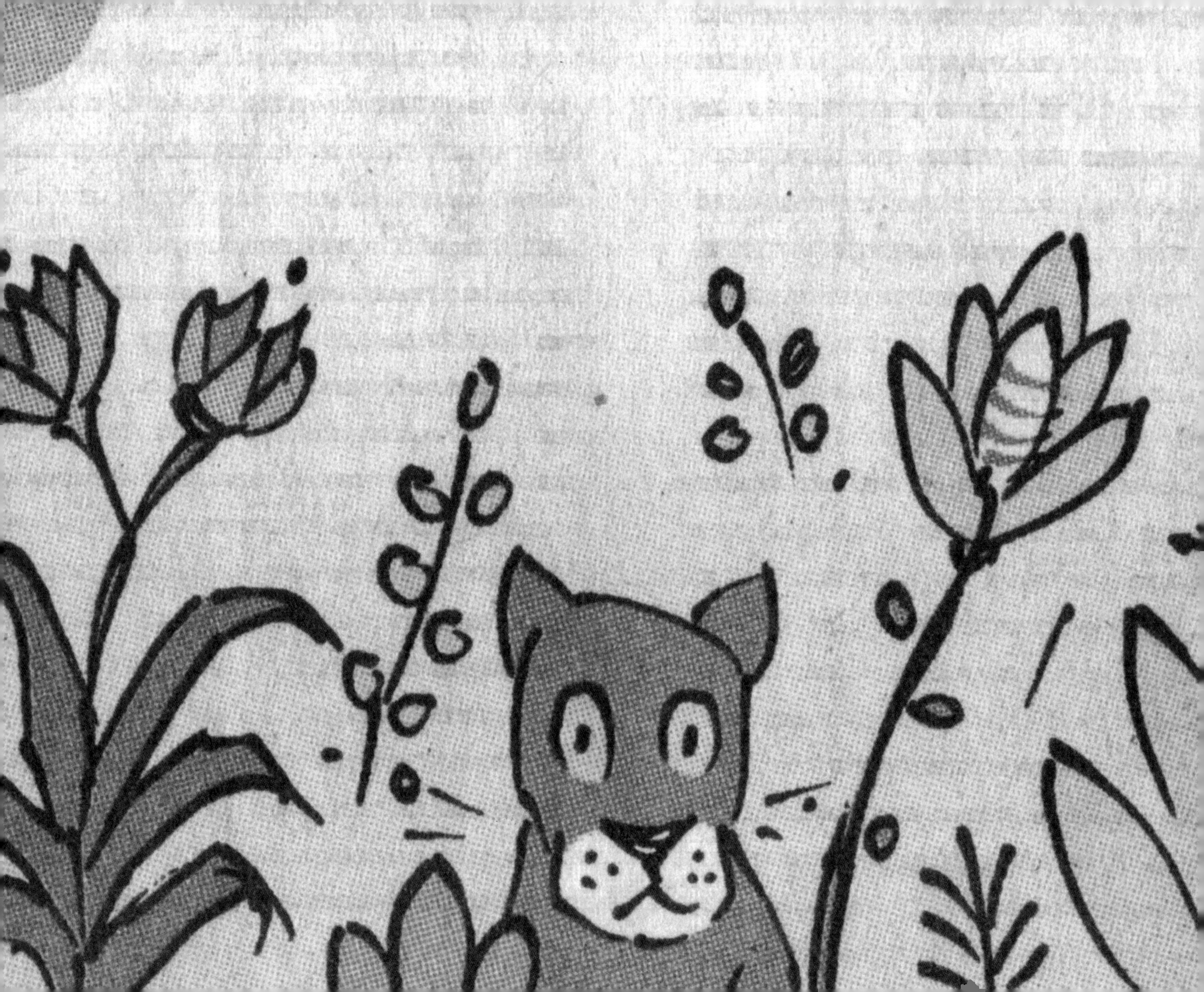

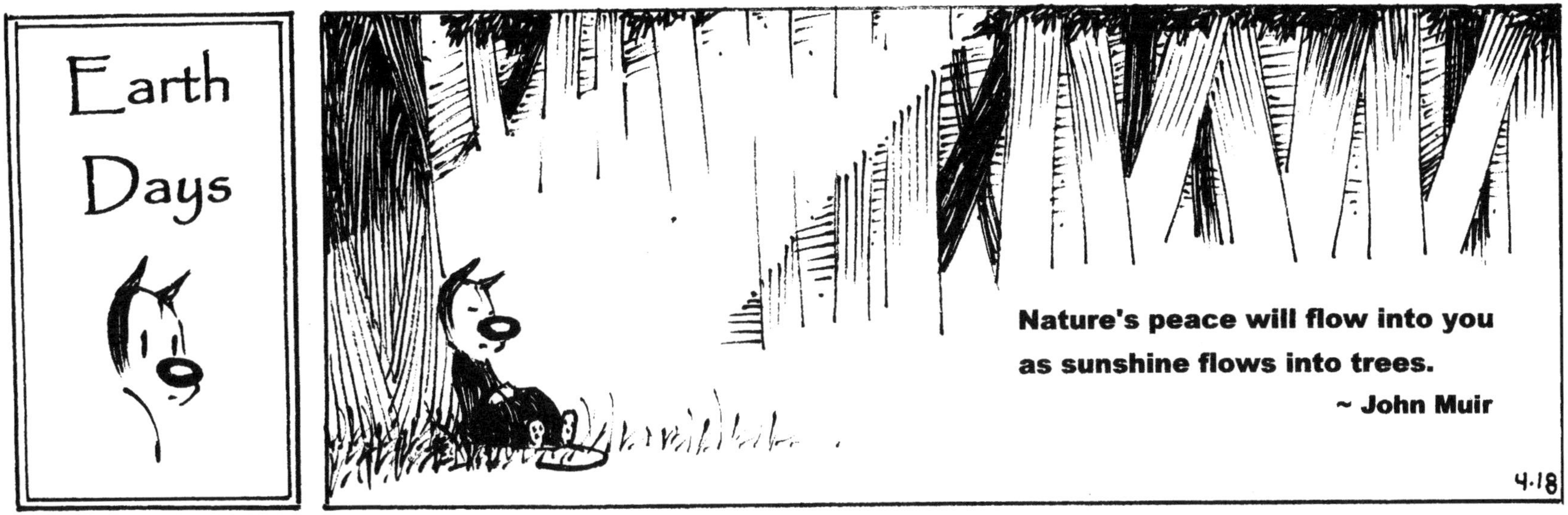
Earth Days
Nature's peace will flow into you
as sunshine flows into trees.
~ John Muir
4.18

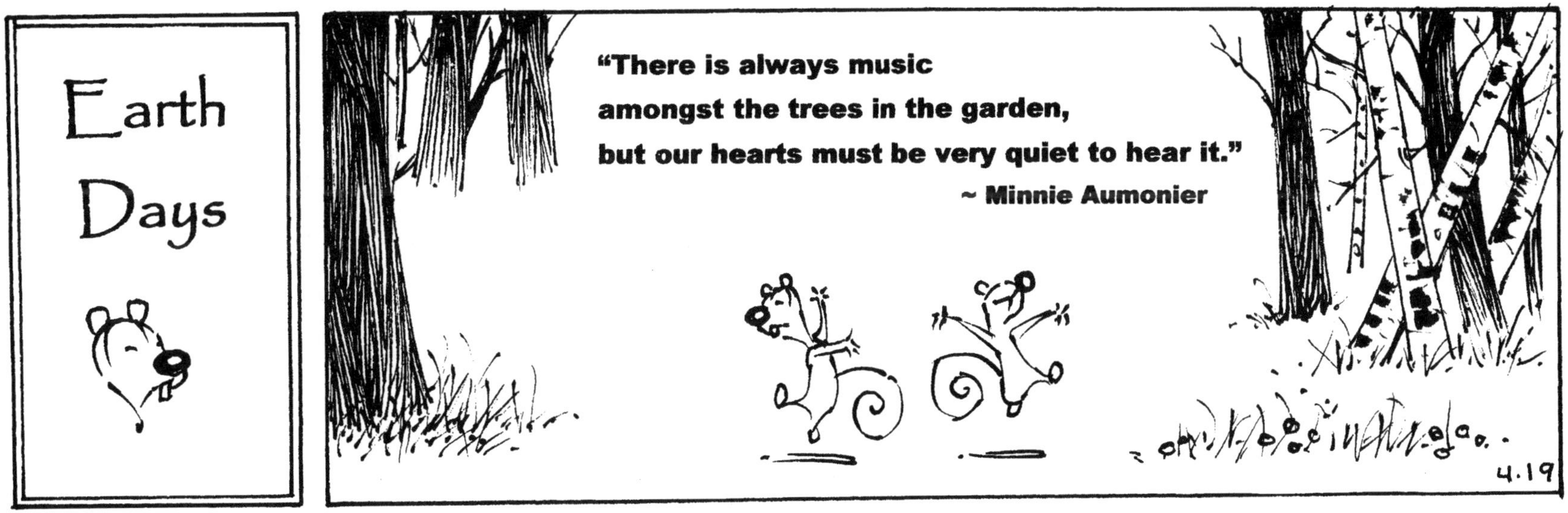
Earth Days
"There is always music
amongst the trees in the garden,
but our hearts must be very quiet to hear it."
~ Minnie Aumonier
4.19

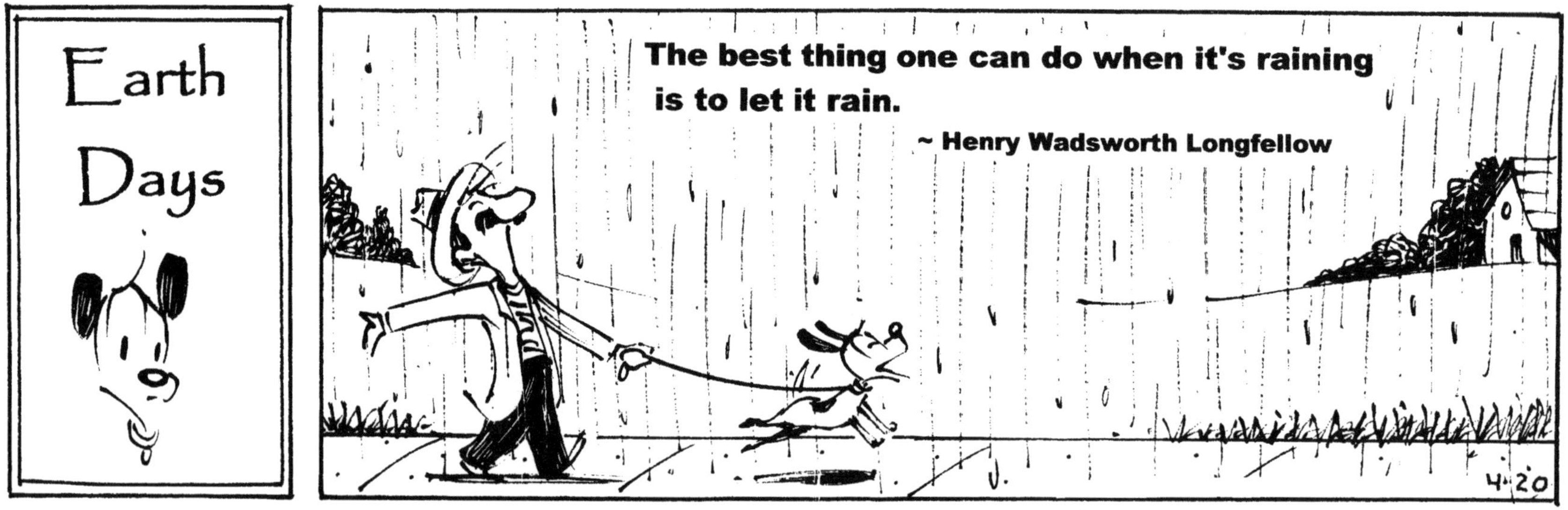
Earth Days
The best thing one can do when it's raining is to let it rain.
~ Henry Wadsworth Longfellow
4·20

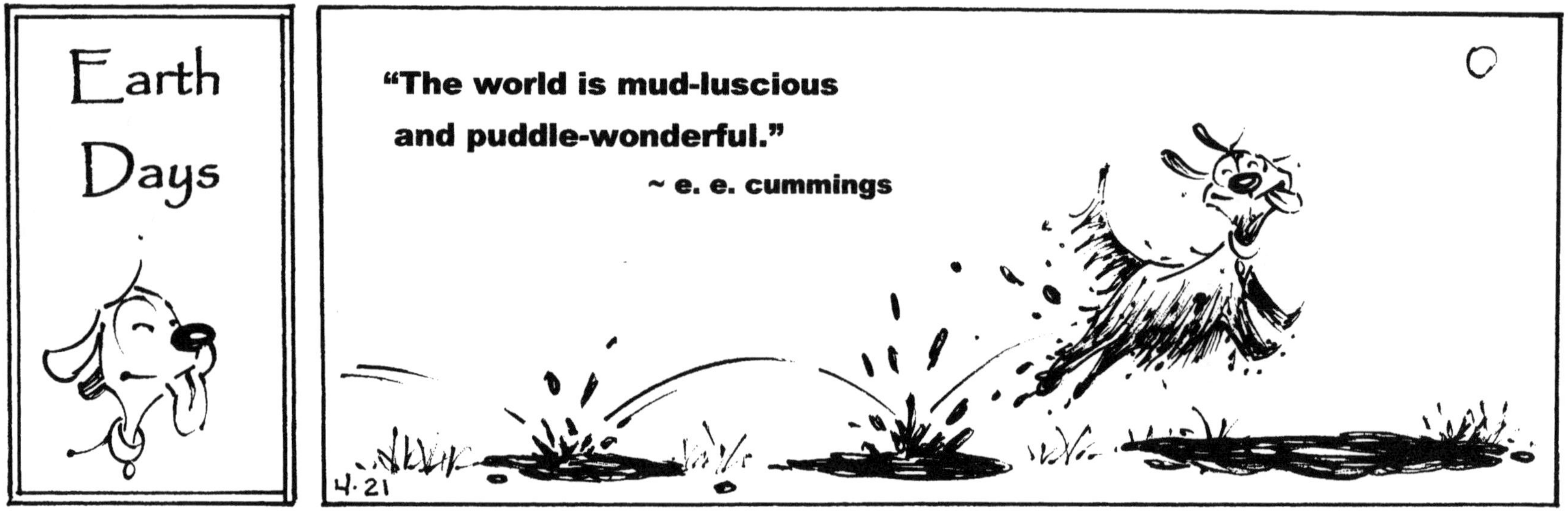
Earth Days
"The world is mud-luscious and puddle-wonderful."
~ e. e. cummings
4·21

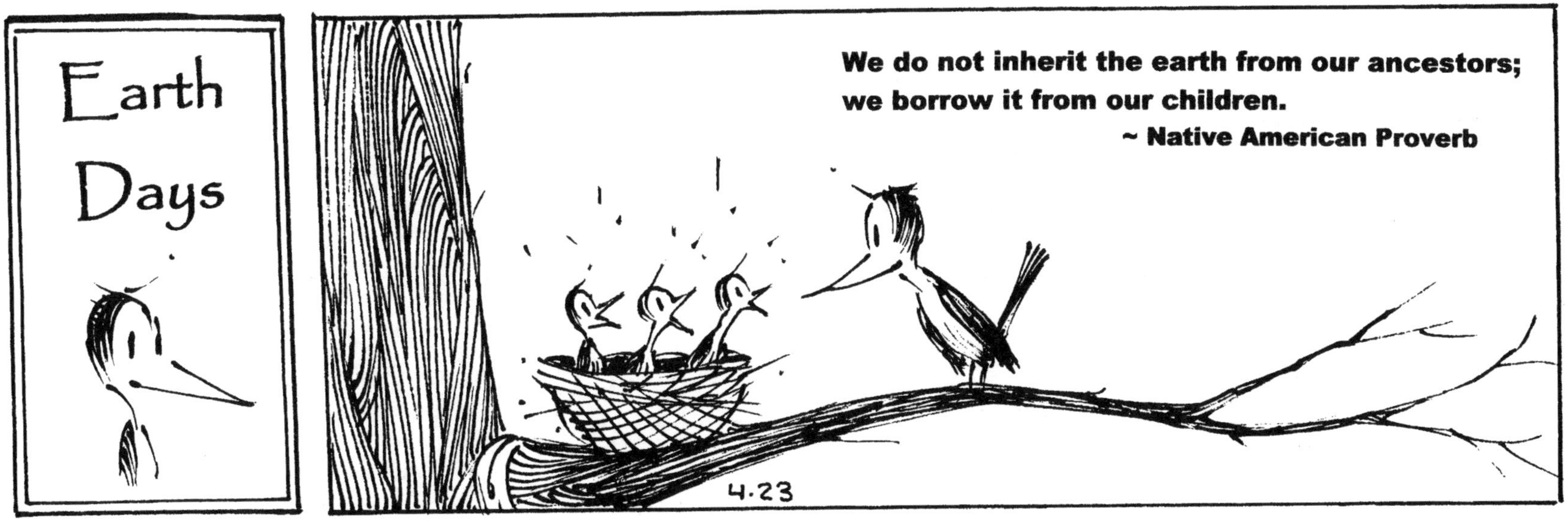
Earth Days
We do not inherit the earth from our ancestors;
we borrow it from our children.
~ Native American Proverb
4.23

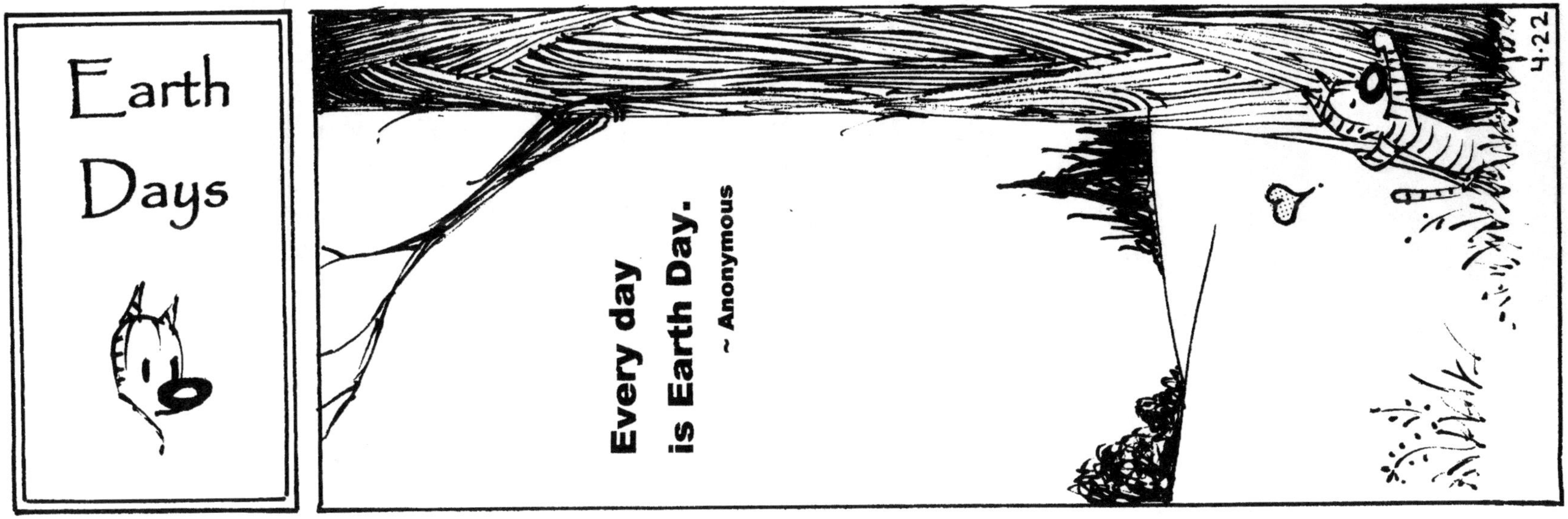
Earth Days
Every day
is Earth Day.
~ Anonymous
4.22

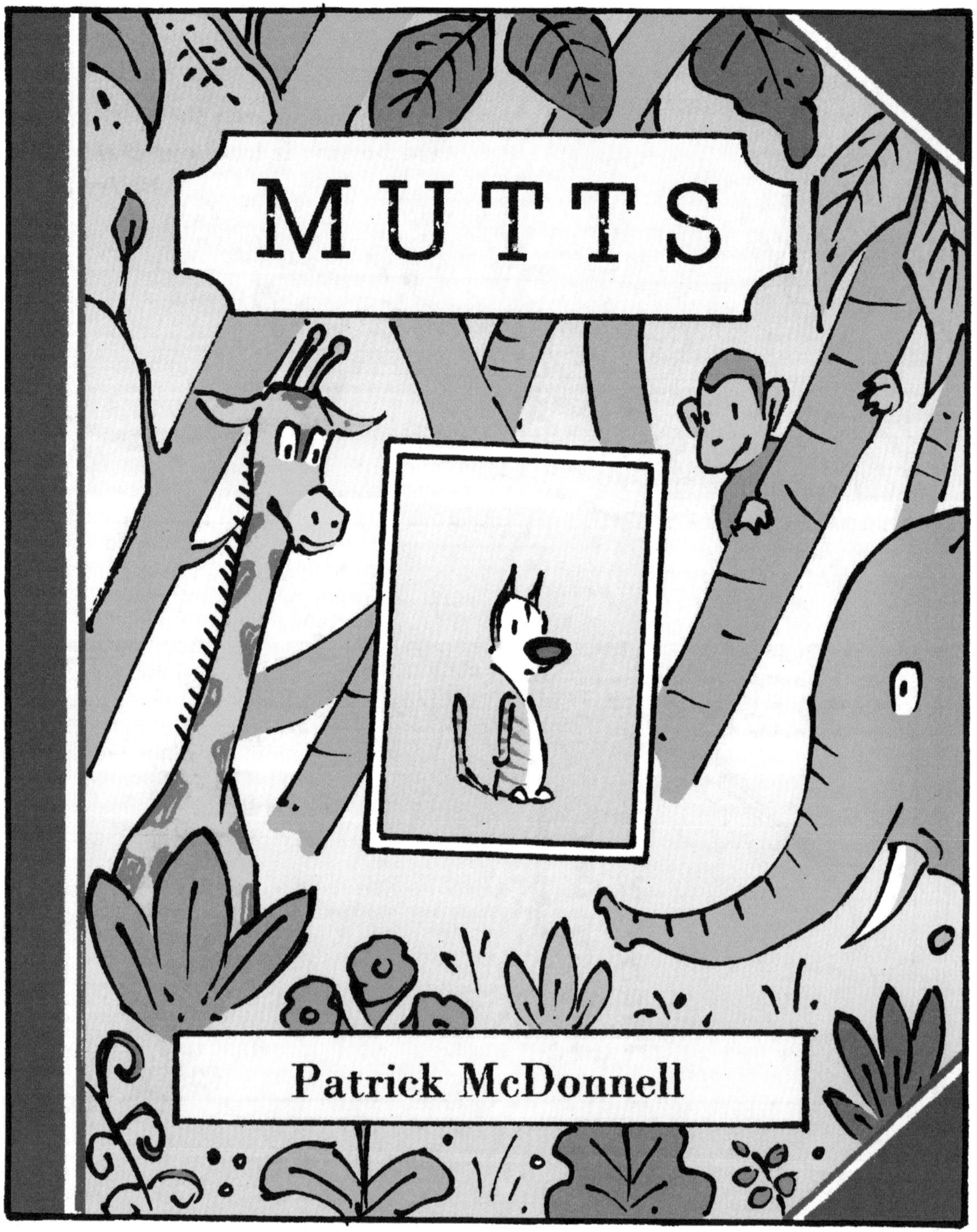
MUTTS
Patrick McDonnell

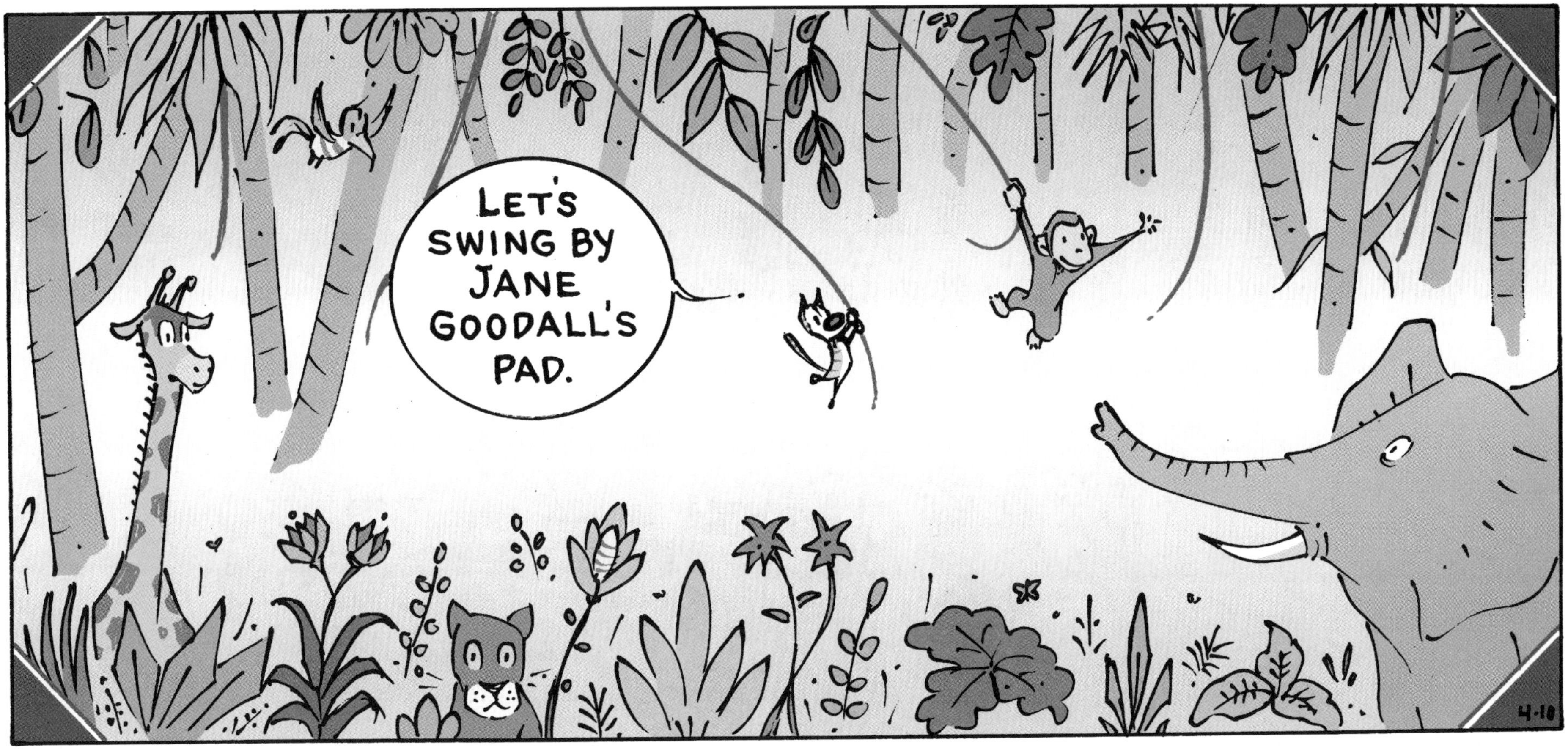
LET'S SWING BY JANE GOODALL'S PAD.
4-10

MUTTS

HEY, MOOCH—

WHAT WERE YOU DOING UP THERE?

4-24

HOLIDAY CHEER!

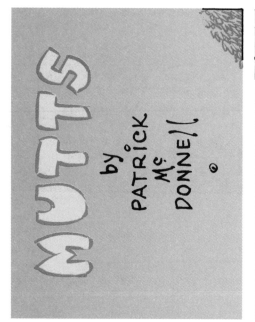

MUTTS by PATRICK M^c DONNELL

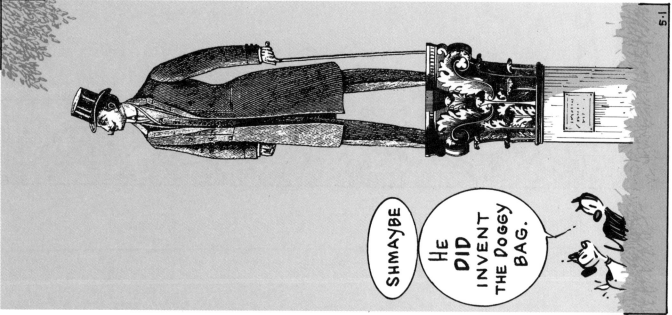

5-1

SHMAYBE

HE DID INVENT THE DOGGY BAG.

66

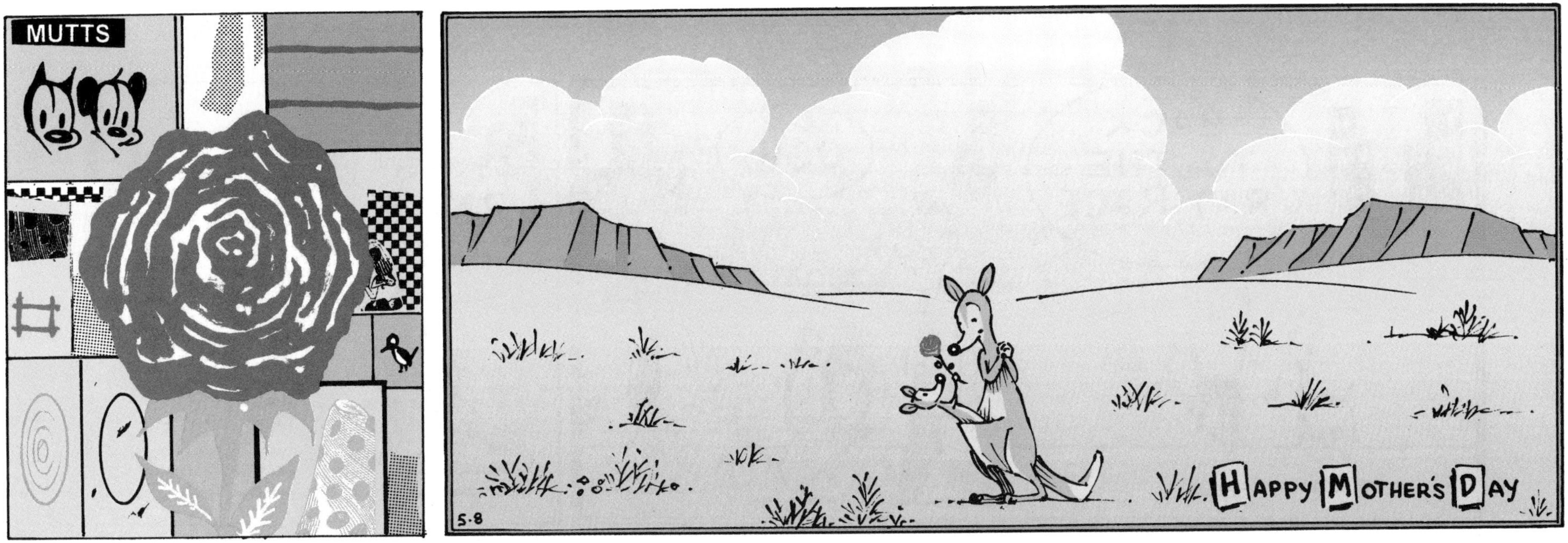
MUTTS
HAPPY MOTHER'S DAY
5·8

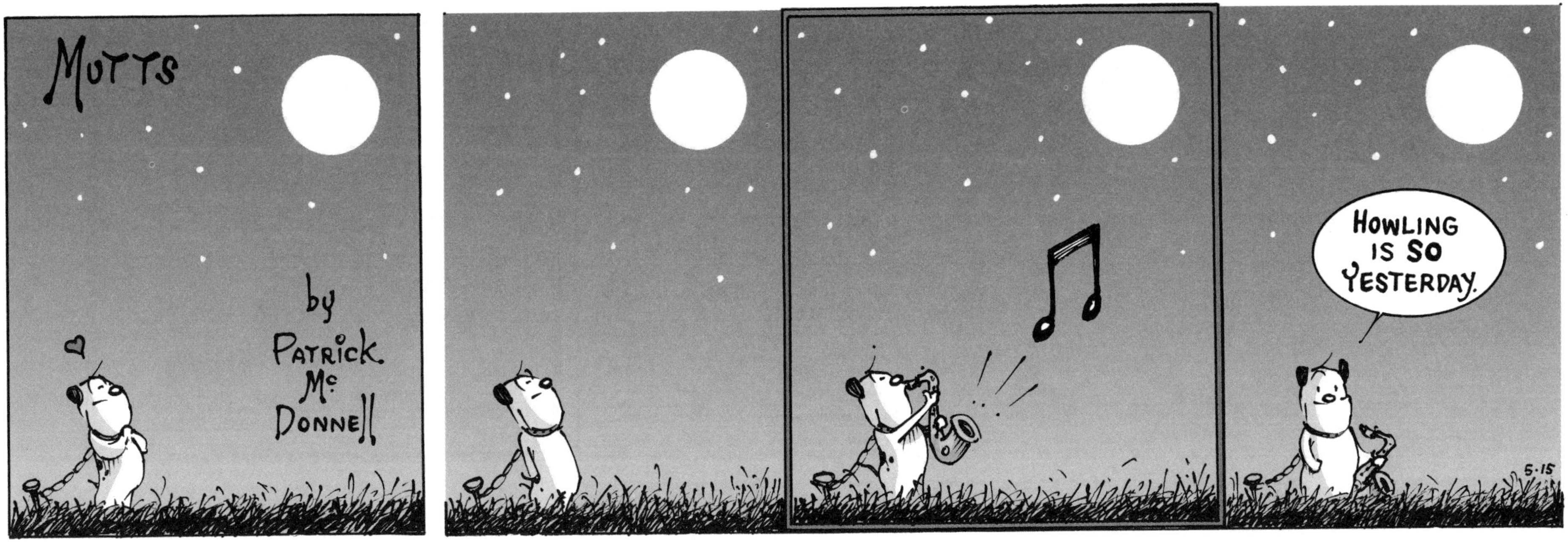
MUTTS
by PATRICK McDONNELL
HOWLING IS SO YESTERDAY.
5·15

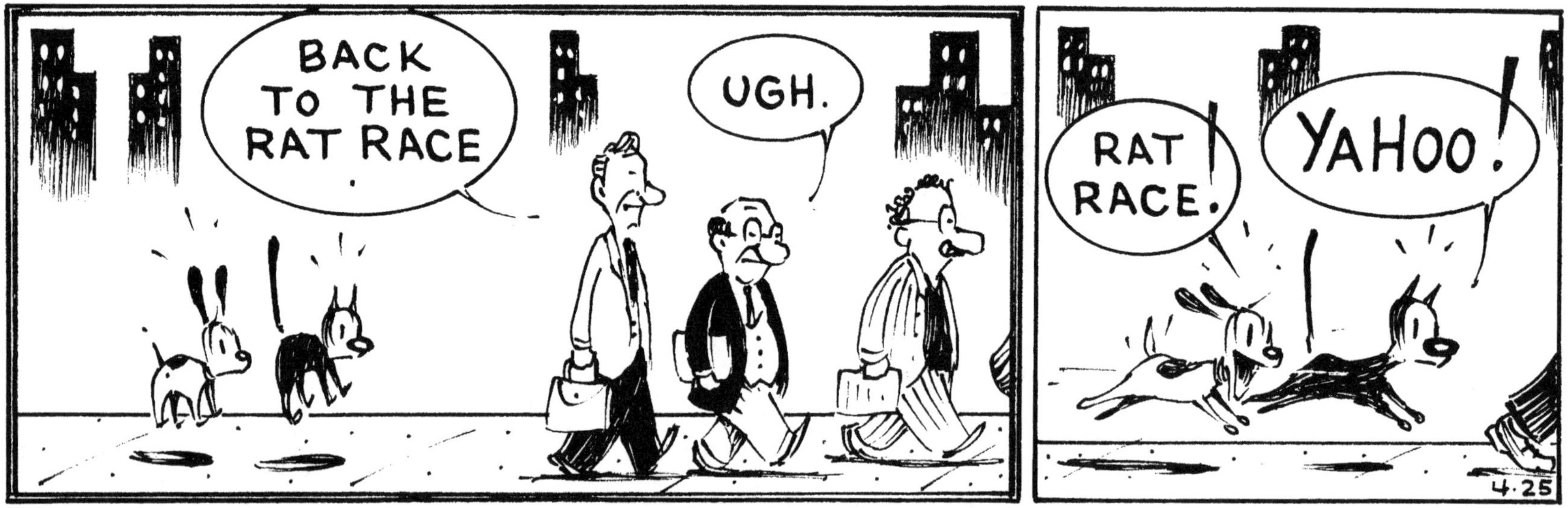
BACK TO THE RAT RACE.
UGH.
RAT RACE.!
YAHOO!
4·25

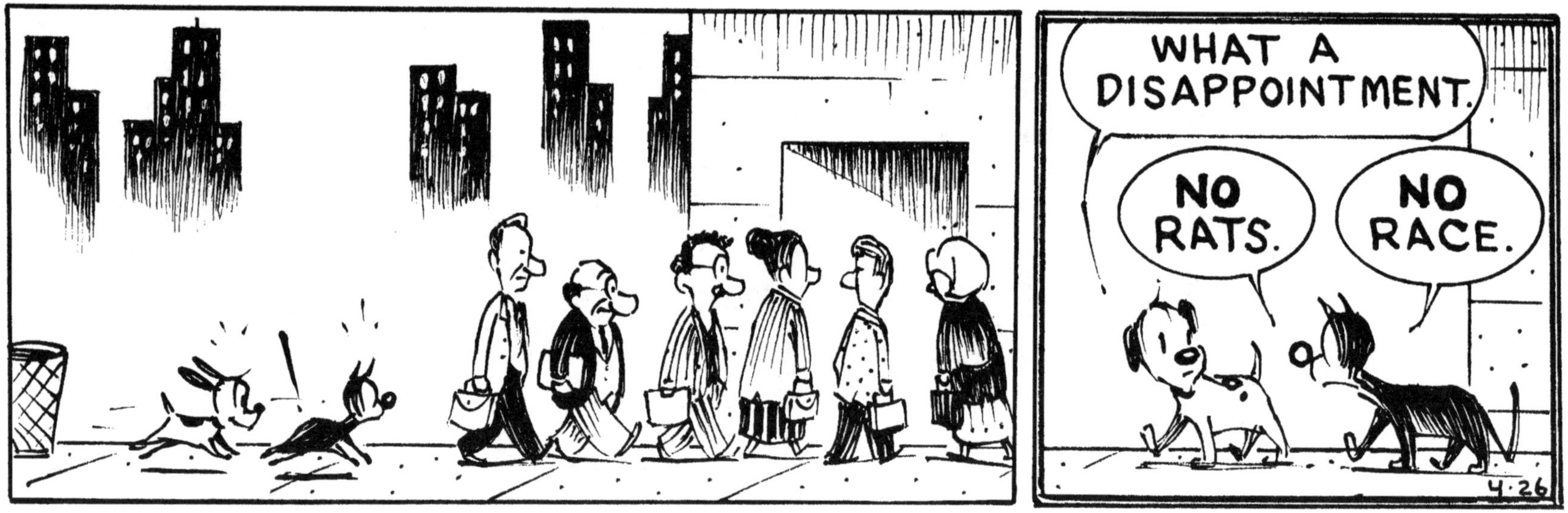
WHAT A DISAPPOINTMENT.
NO RATS.
NO RACE.
4·26

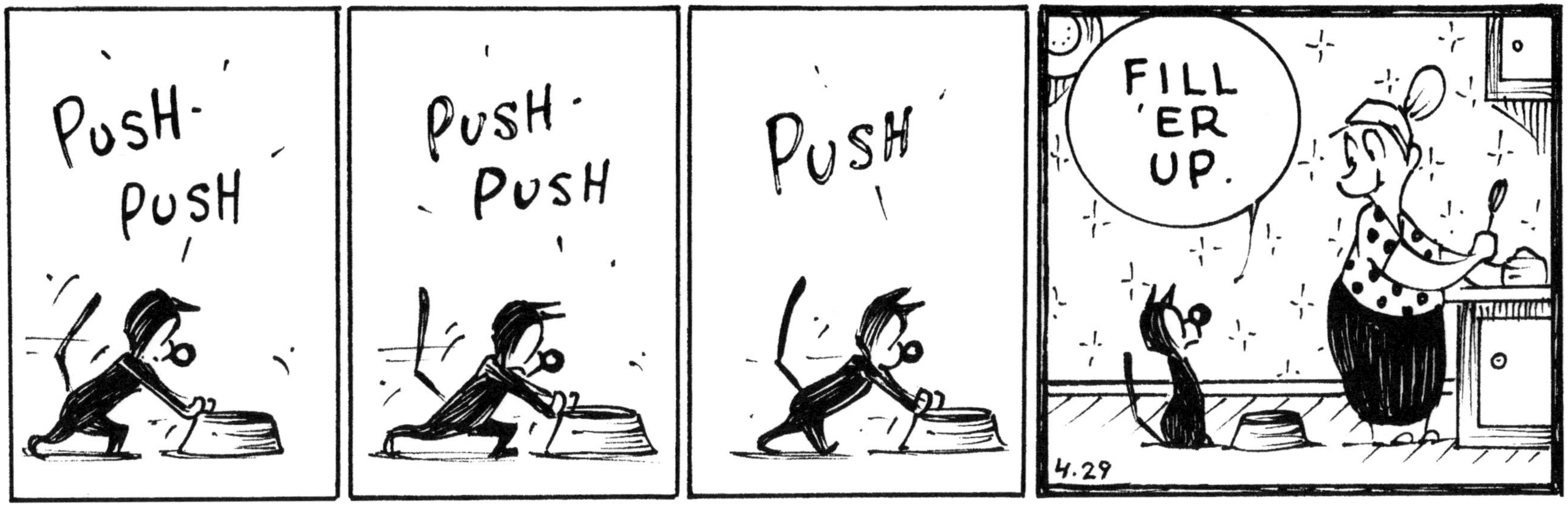
PUSH-
PUSH
PUSH-
PUSH
PUSH
FILL 'ER UP.
4.29

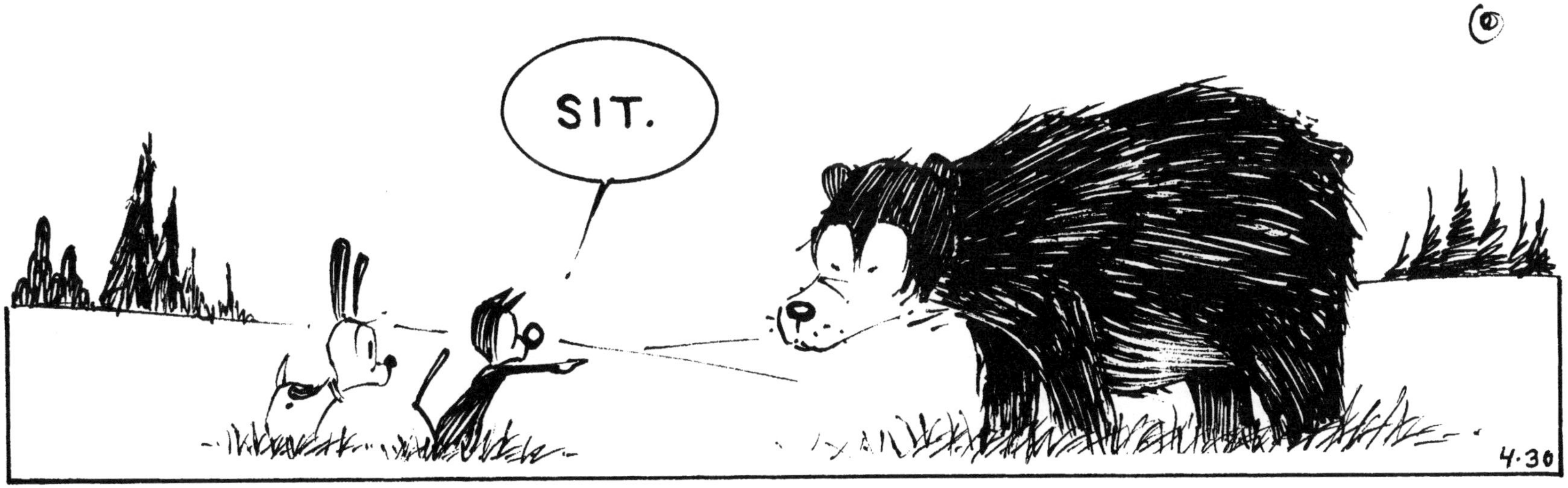
SIT.
4.30

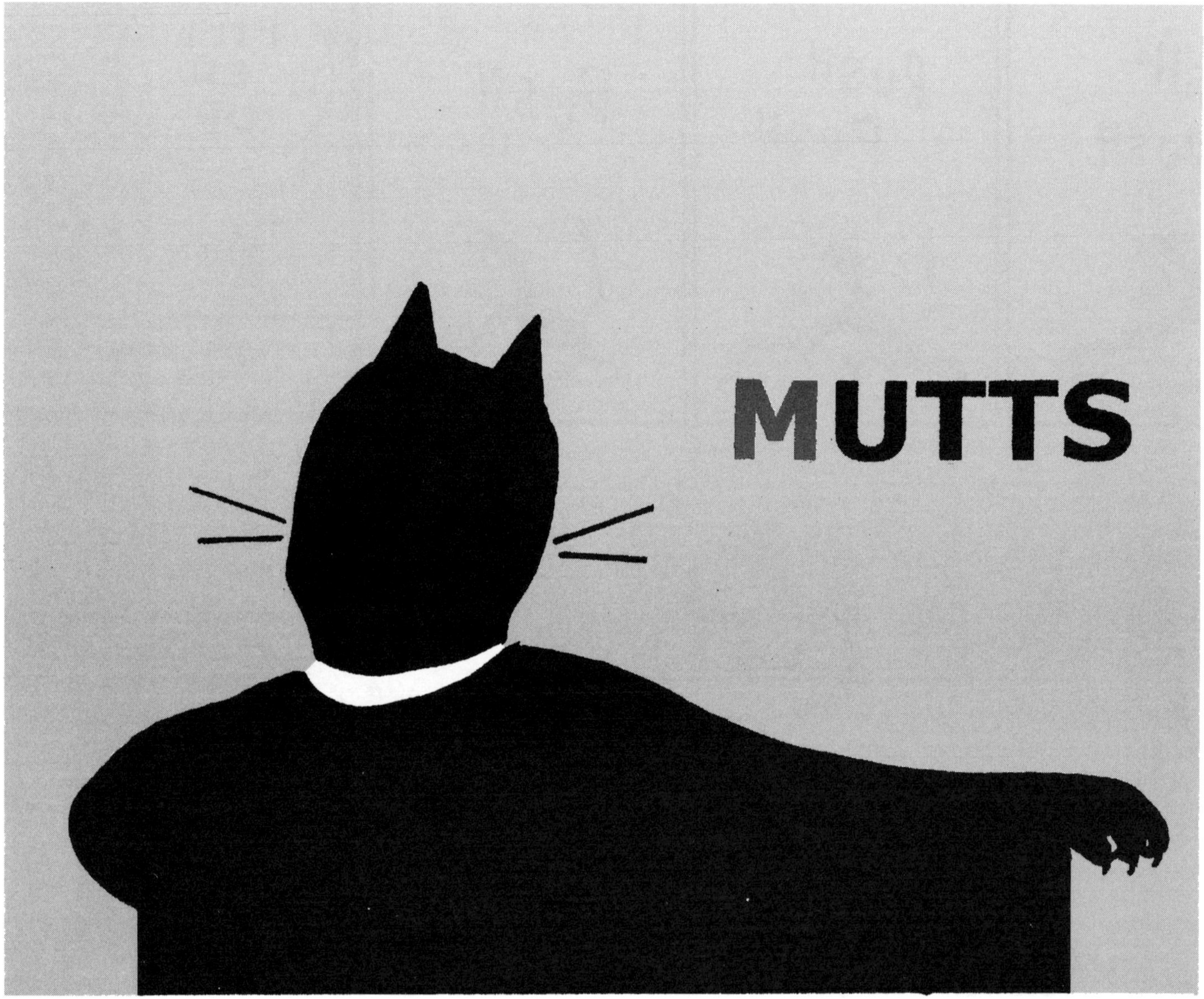
MUTTS

RING
AND SO THE DAY BEGINS
5·22

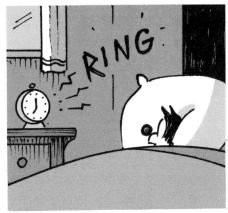

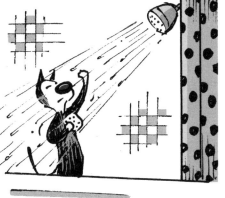

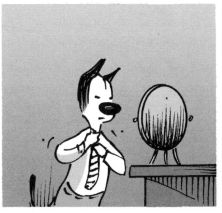

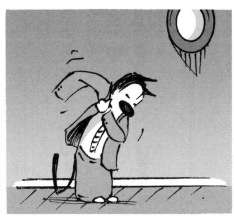

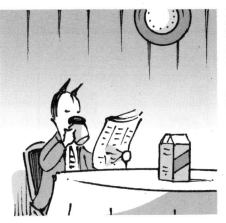

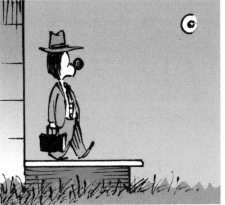

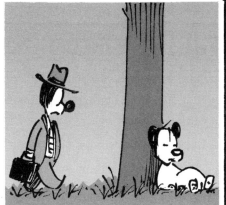

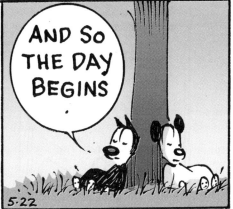

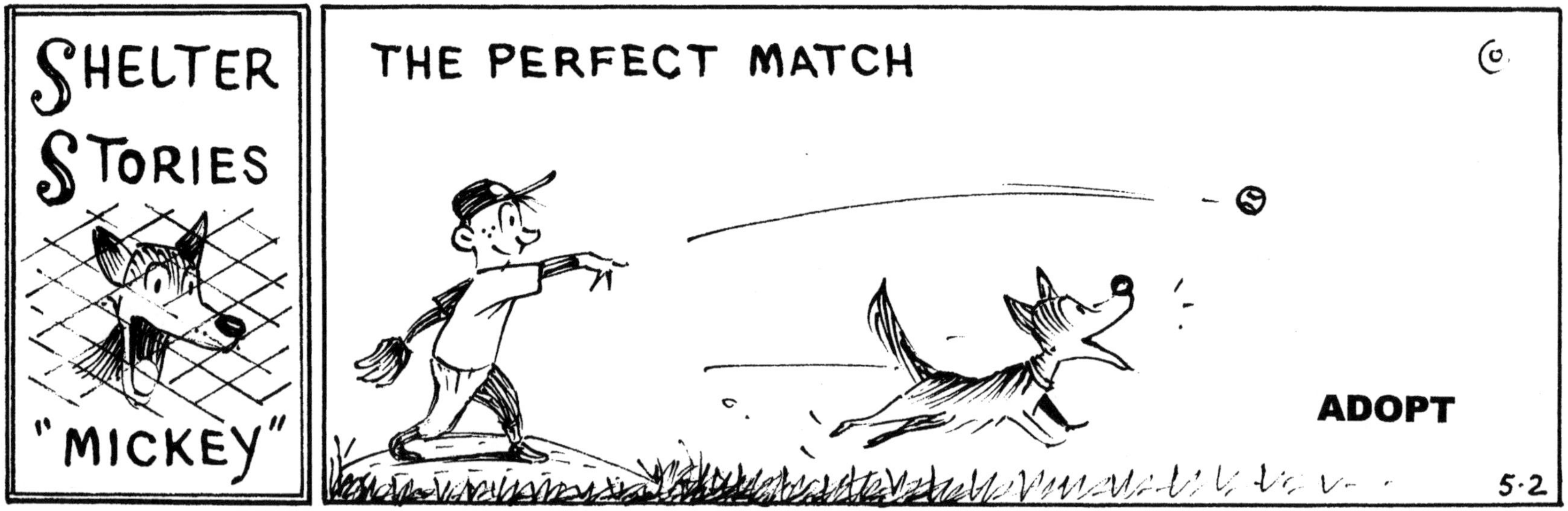
SHELTER STORIES
"MICKEY"
THE PERFECT MATCH
©
ADOPT
5·2

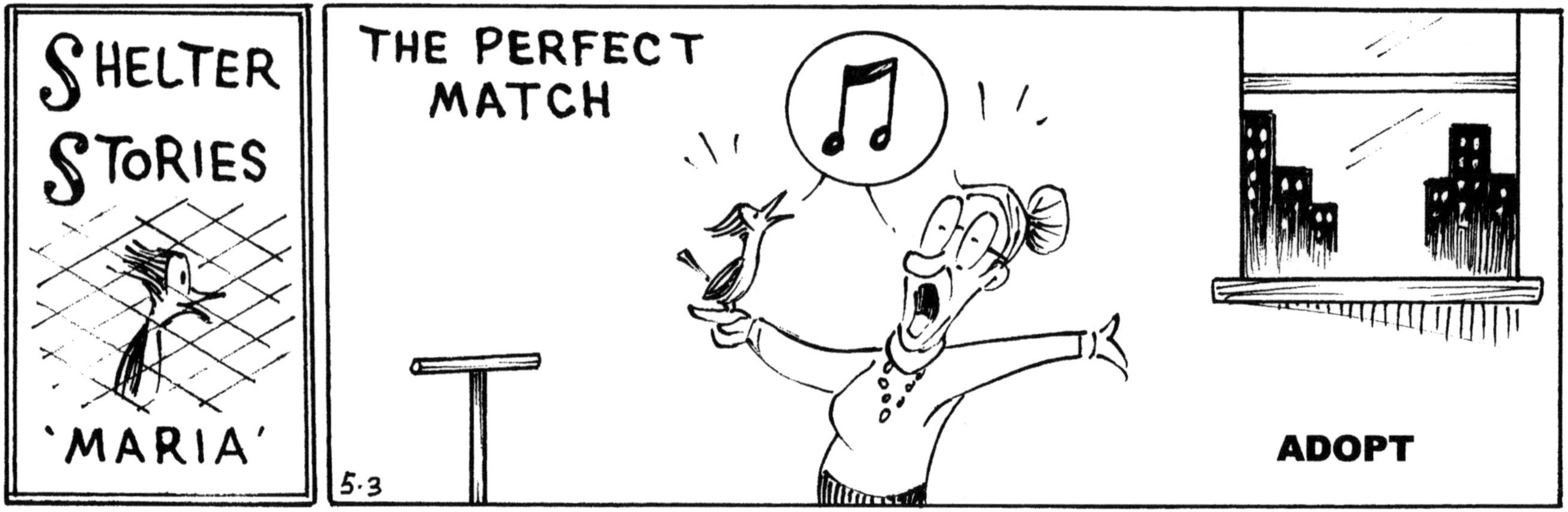
SHELTER STORIES
'MARIA'
THE PERFECT MATCH
ADOPT
5·3

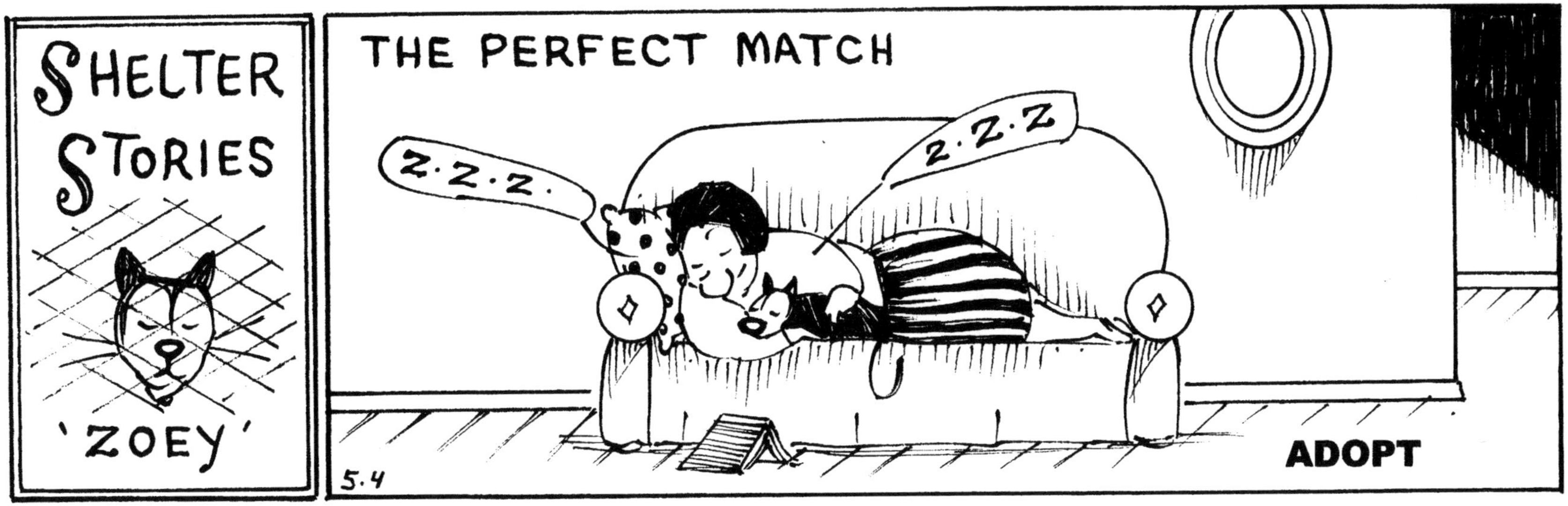
SHELTER STORIES
'ZOEY'
THE PERFECT MATCH
Z·Z·Z
Z·Z·Z
ADOPT
5·4

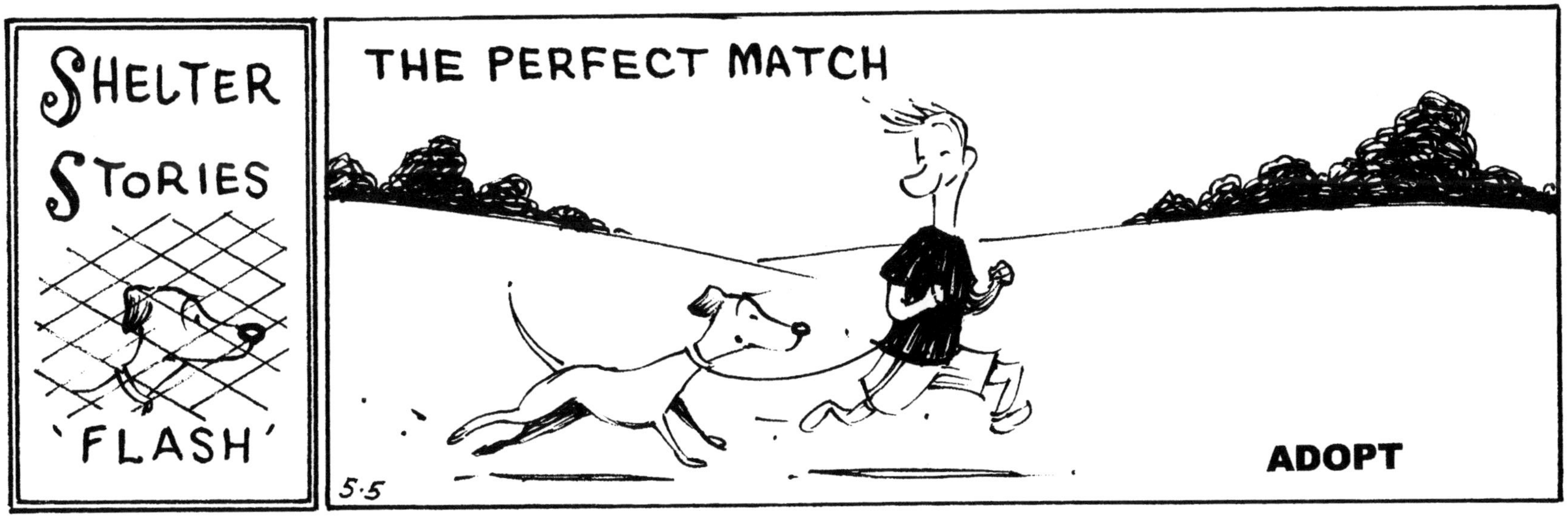
SHELTER STORIES
'FLASH'
THE PERFECT MATCH
ADOPT
5·5

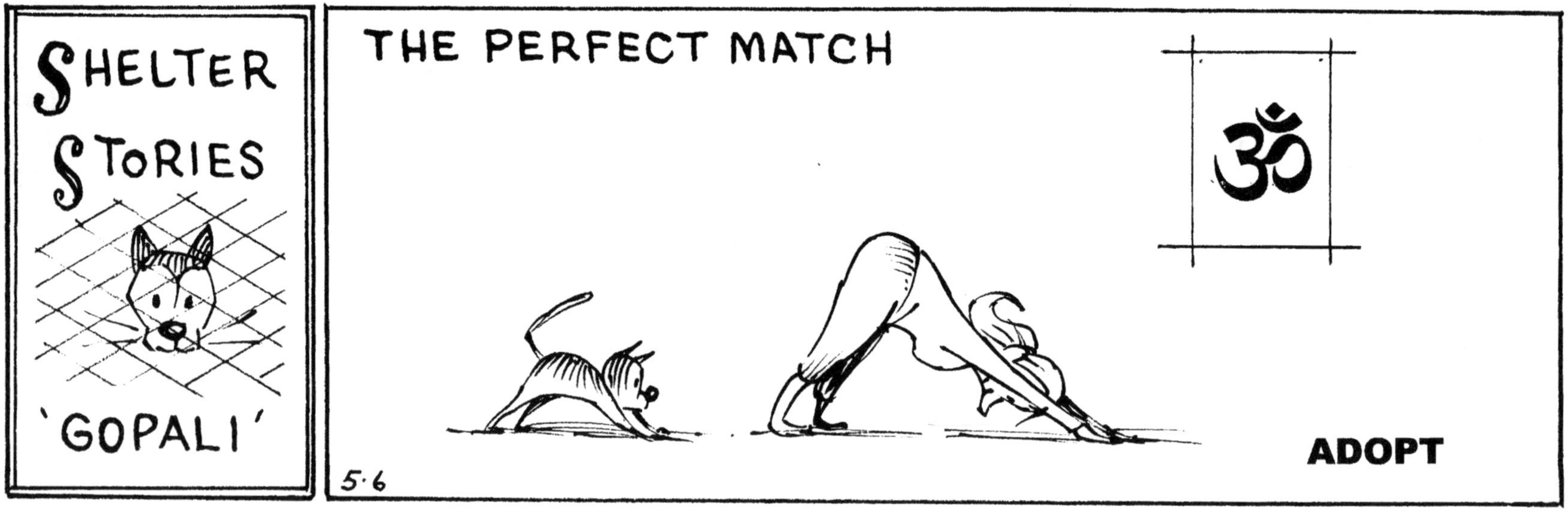
SHELTER STORIES
'GOPALI'
THE PERFECT MATCH
ADOPT
5·6

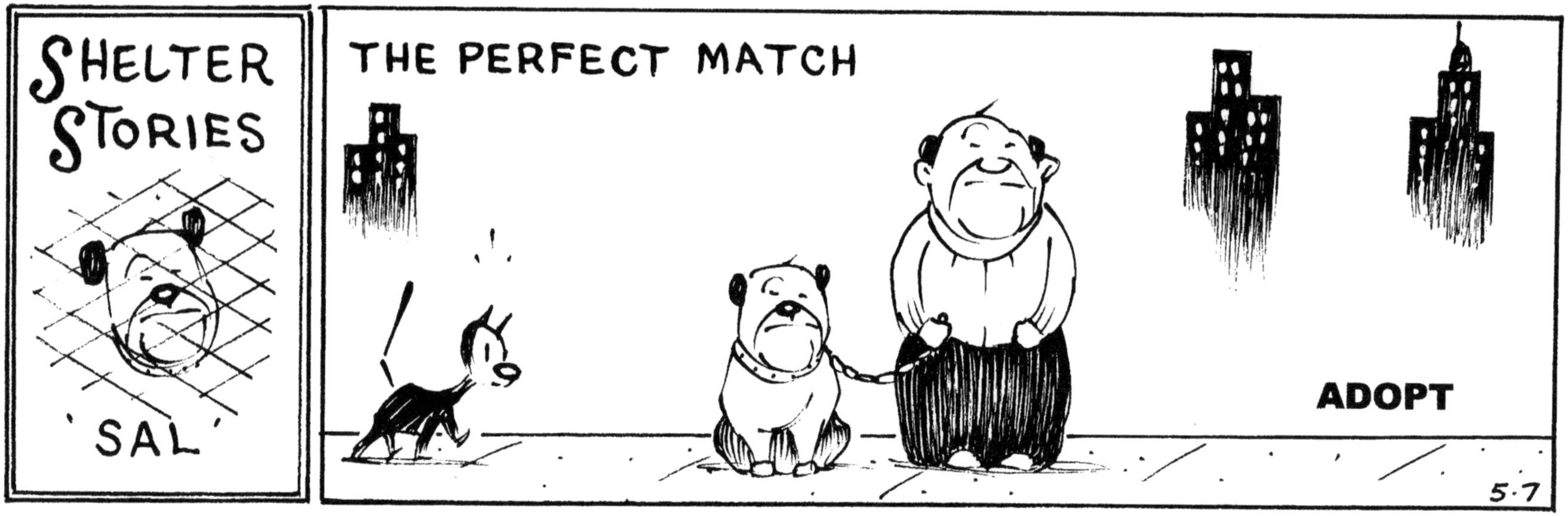
SHELTER STORIES
'SAL'
THE PERFECT MATCH
ADOPT
5·7

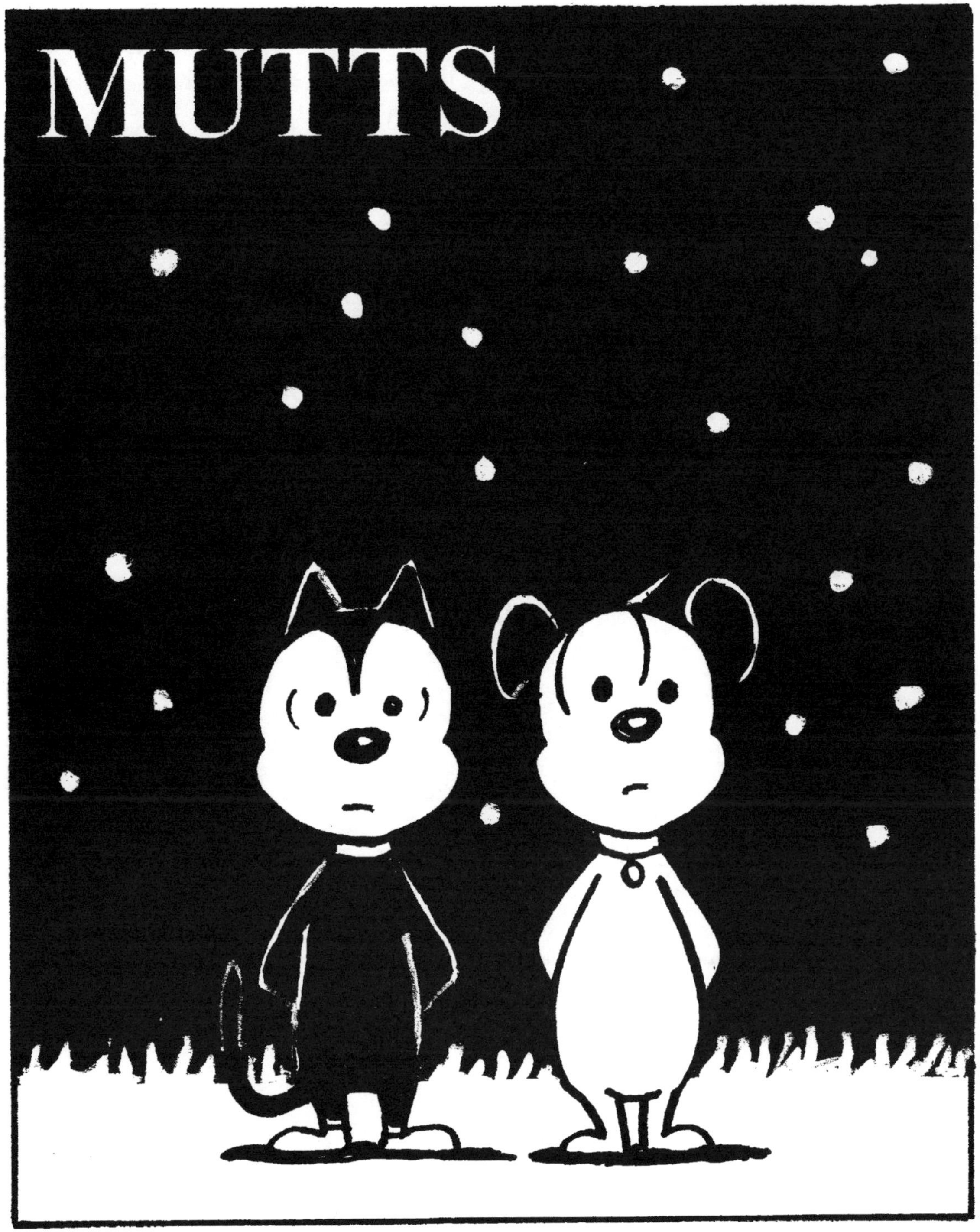
MUTTS

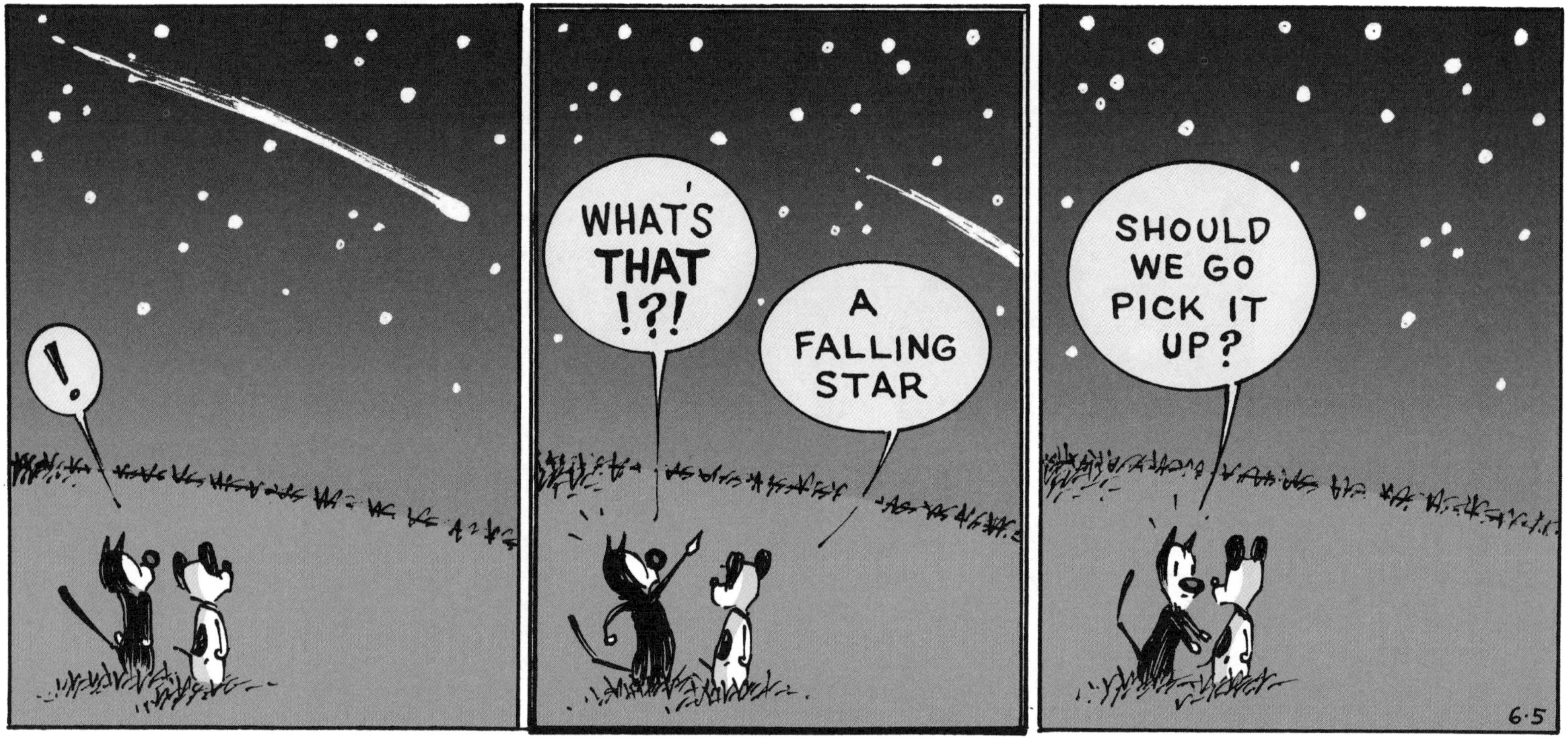
!
WHAT'S THAT !?!
A FALLING STAR
SHOULD WE GO PICK IT UP?
6·5

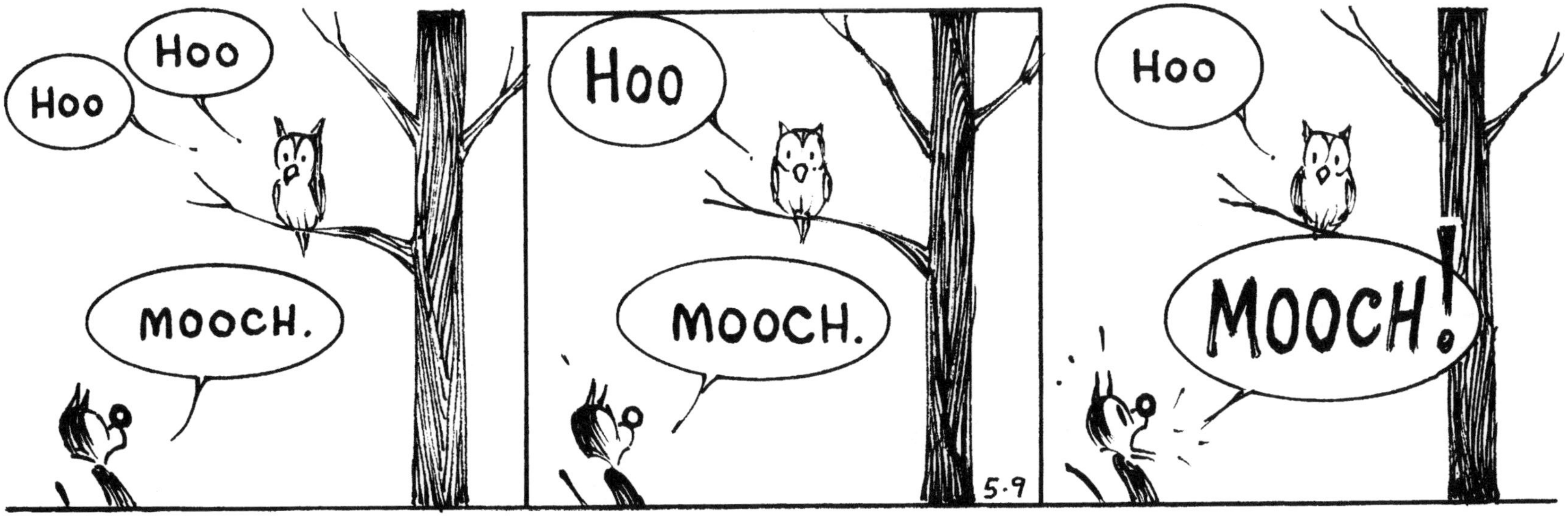
Hoo
Hoo
MOOCH.
Hoo
MOOCH.
5·9
Hoo
MOOCH!

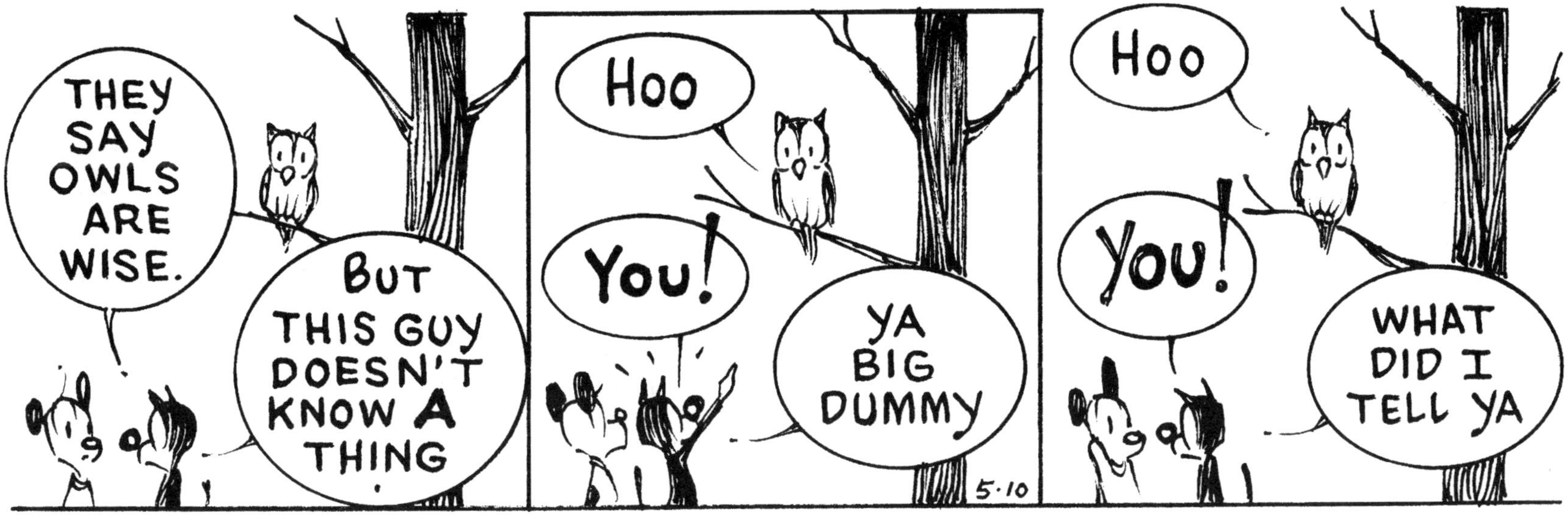
THEY SAY OWLS ARE WISE.
BUT THIS GUY DOESN'T KNOW A THING.
Hoo
YOU!
YA BIG DUMMY
5·10
Hoo
YOU!
WHAT DID I TELL YA

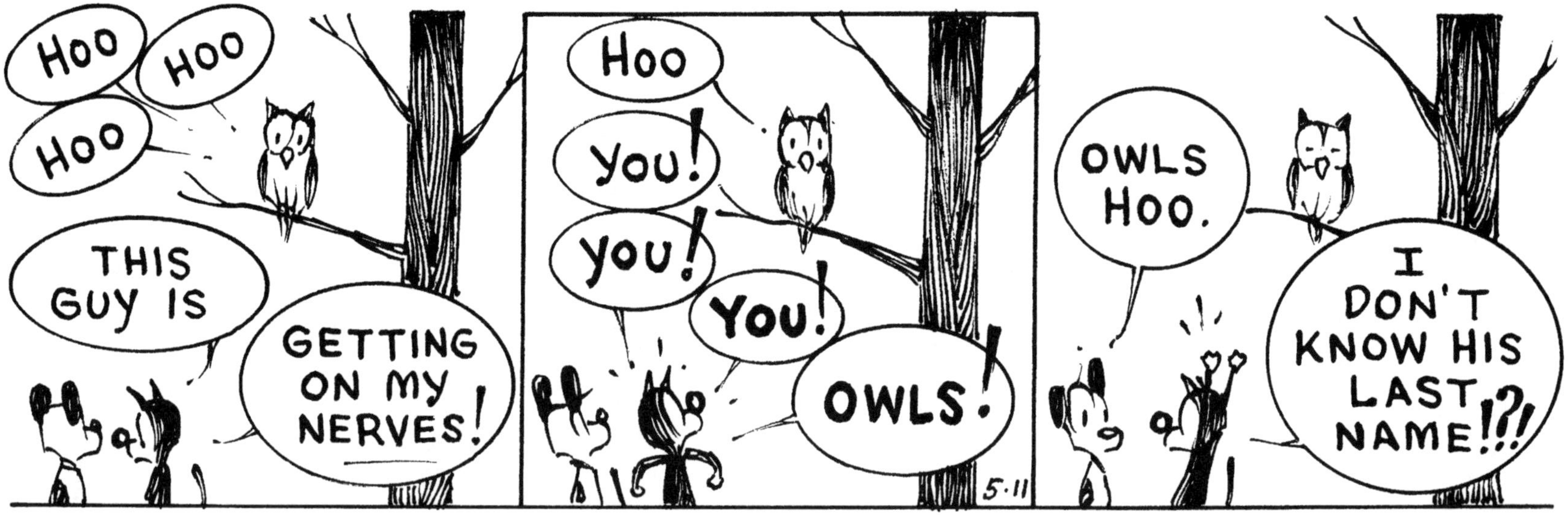
HOO
HOO
HOO
THIS GUY IS
GETTING ON MY NERVES!
HOO
YOU!
YOU!
YOU!
OWLS!
5·11
OWLS HOO.
I DON'T KNOW HIS LAST NAME!?!

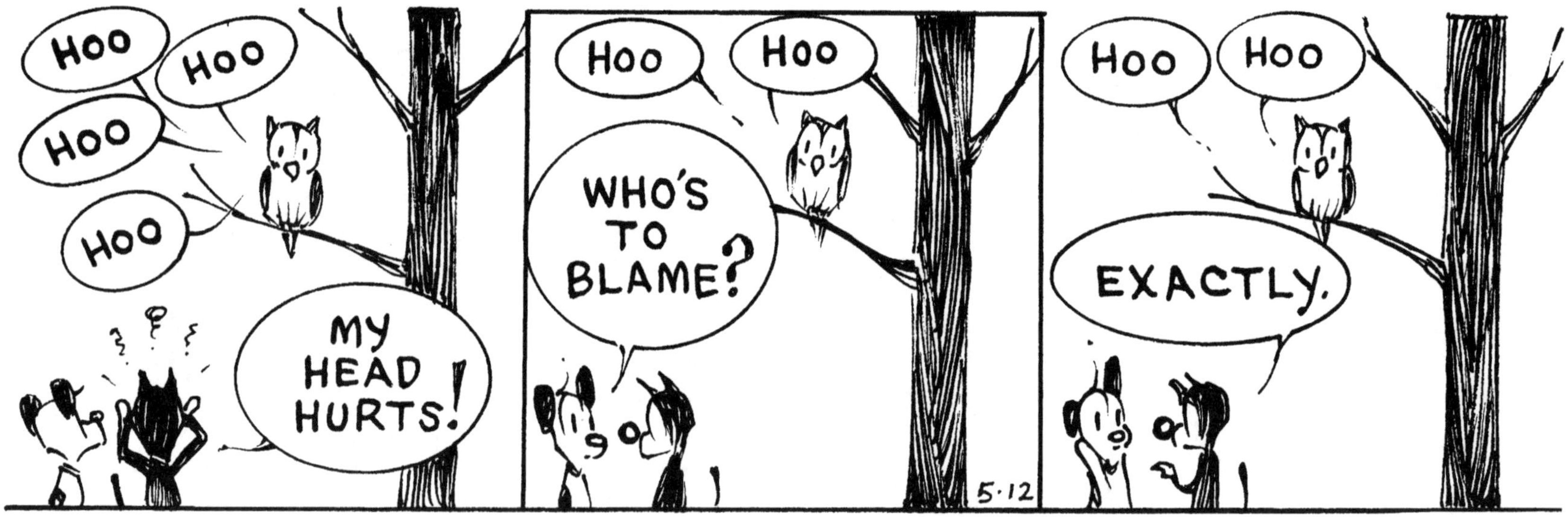
HOO
HOO
HOO
HOO
MY HEAD HURTS!
HOO
HOO
WHO'S TO BLAME?
5·12
HOO
HOO
EXACTLY.

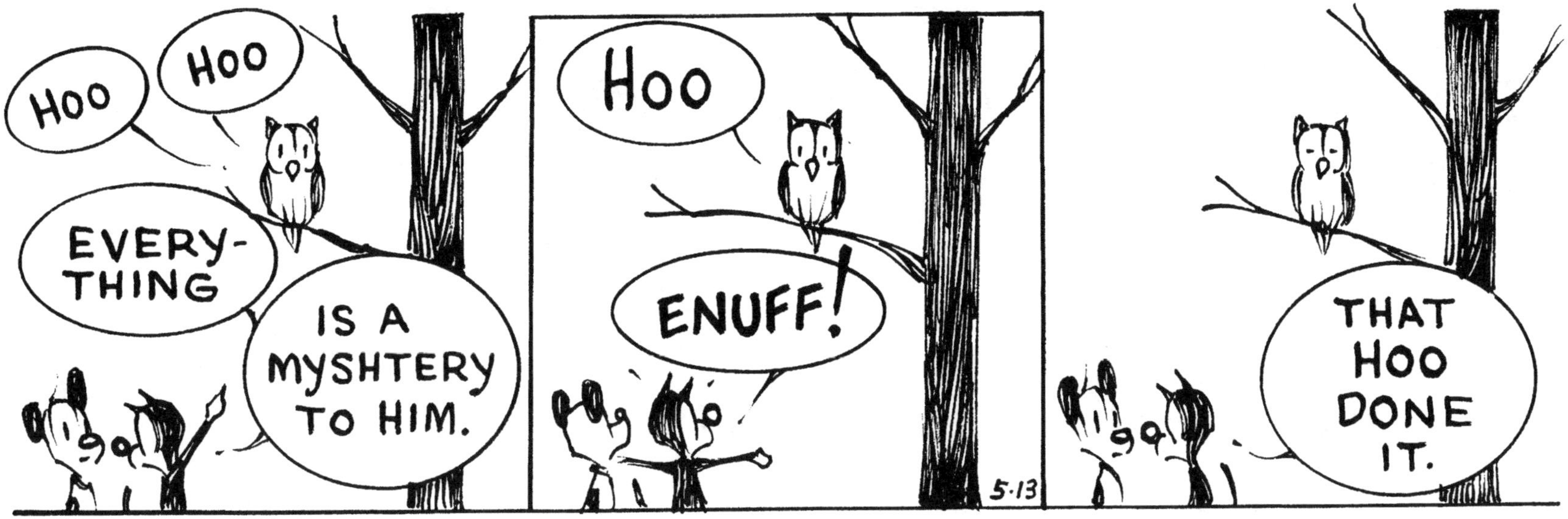
HOO
HOO
EVERY-THING
IS A MYSHTERY TO HIM.
HOO
ENUFF!
THAT HOO DONE IT.
5·13

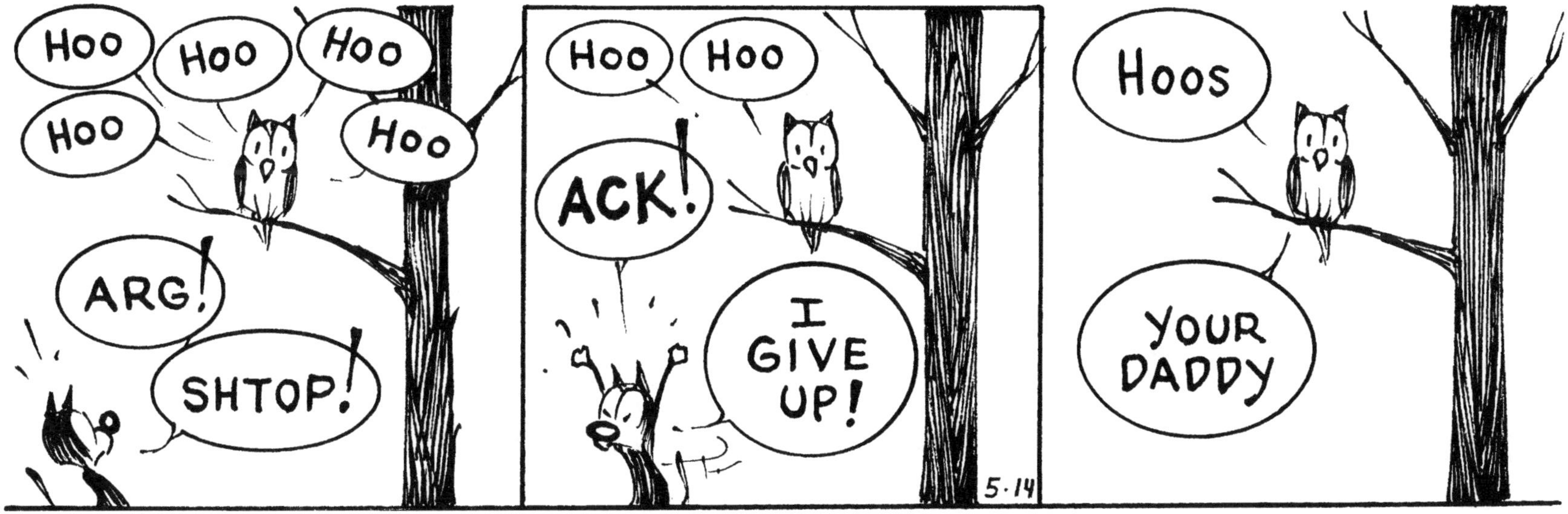
HOO
HOO
HOO
HOO
HOO
ARG!
SHTOP!
HOO
HOO
ACK!
I GIVE UP!
HOOS
YOUR DADDY
5·14

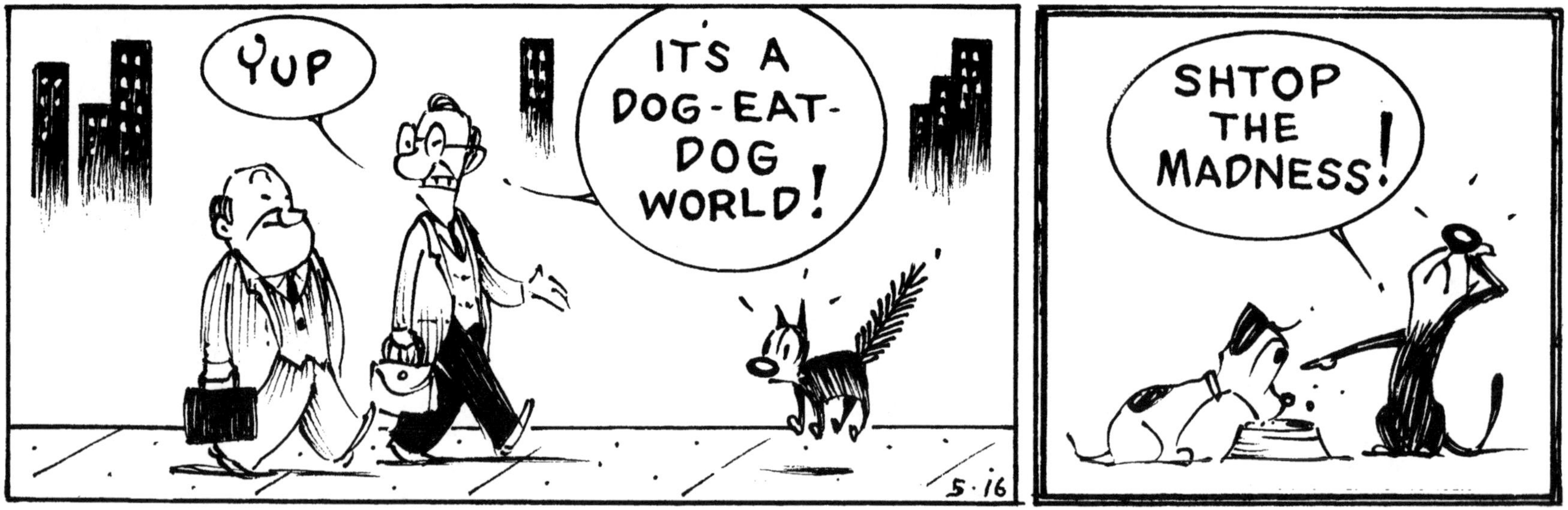
YUP
IT'S A DOG-EAT-DOG WORLD!
SHTOP THE MADNESS!
5·16

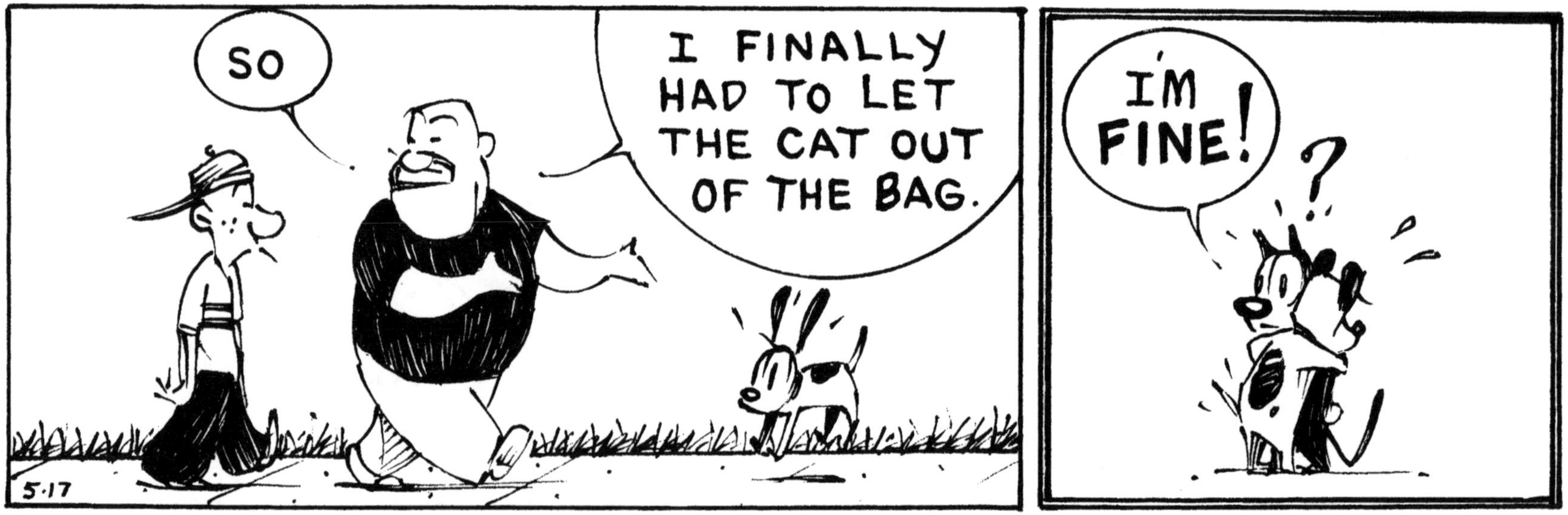
SO
I FINALLY HAD TO LET THE CAT OUT OF THE BAG.
I'M FINE!
?
5·17

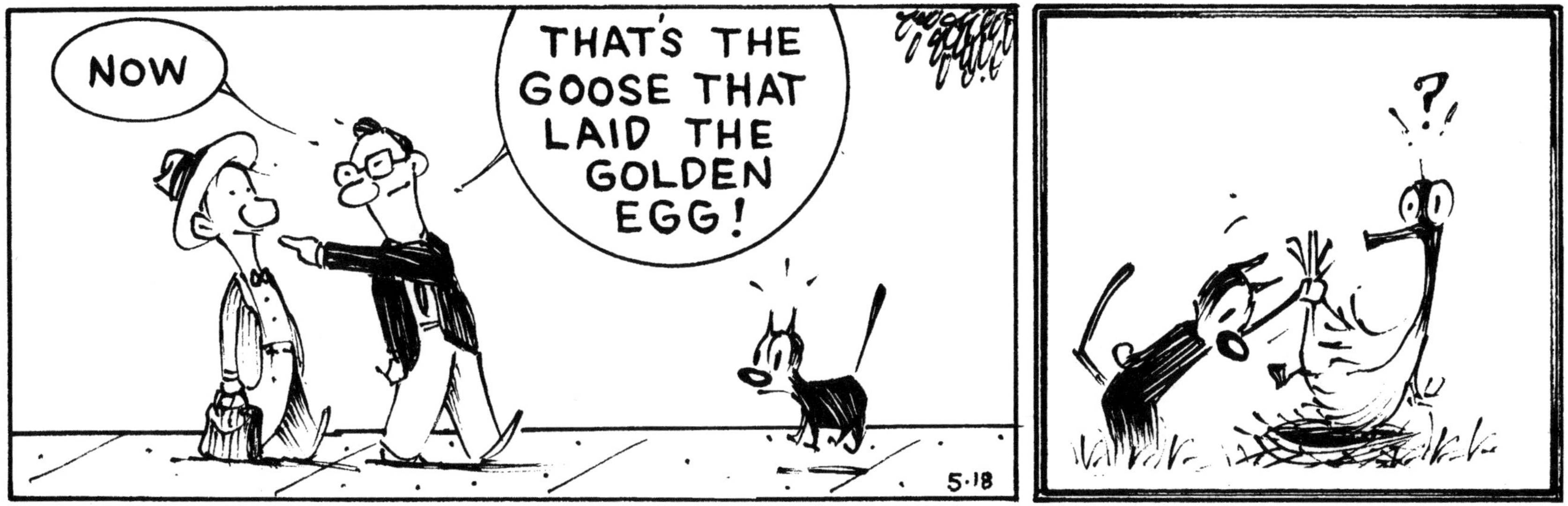
NOW
THAT'S THE GOOSE THAT LAID THE GOLDEN EGG!
?
5·18

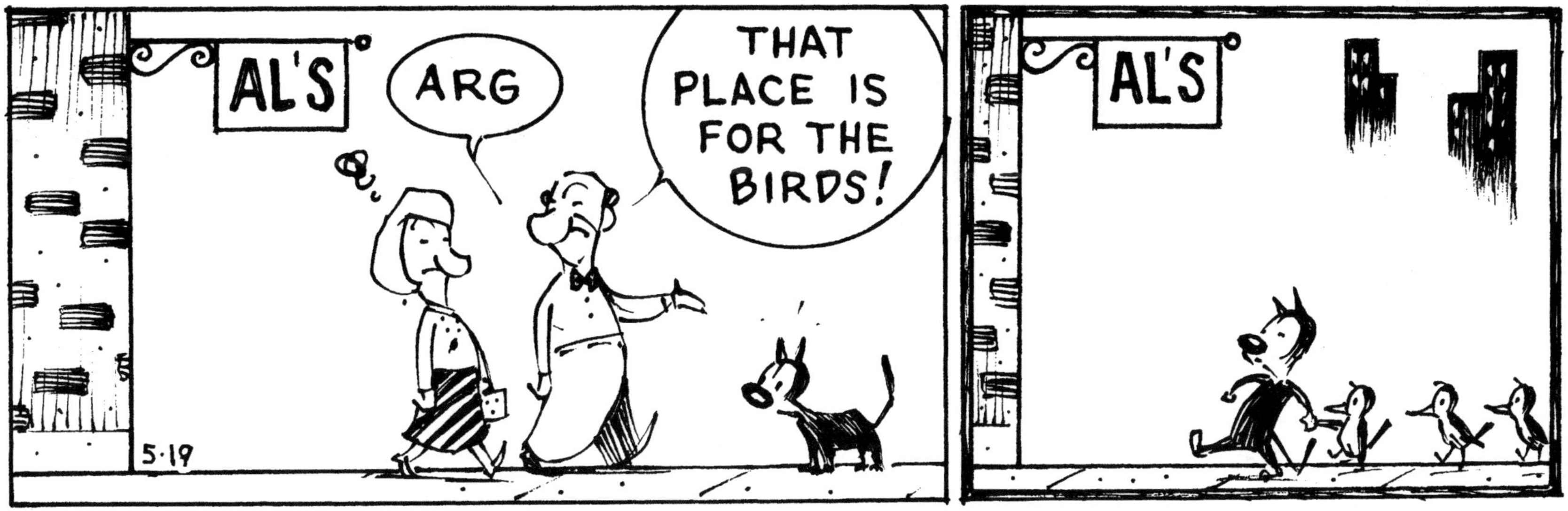
AL'S
ARG
THAT PLACE IS FOR THE BIRDS!
5·19
AL'S

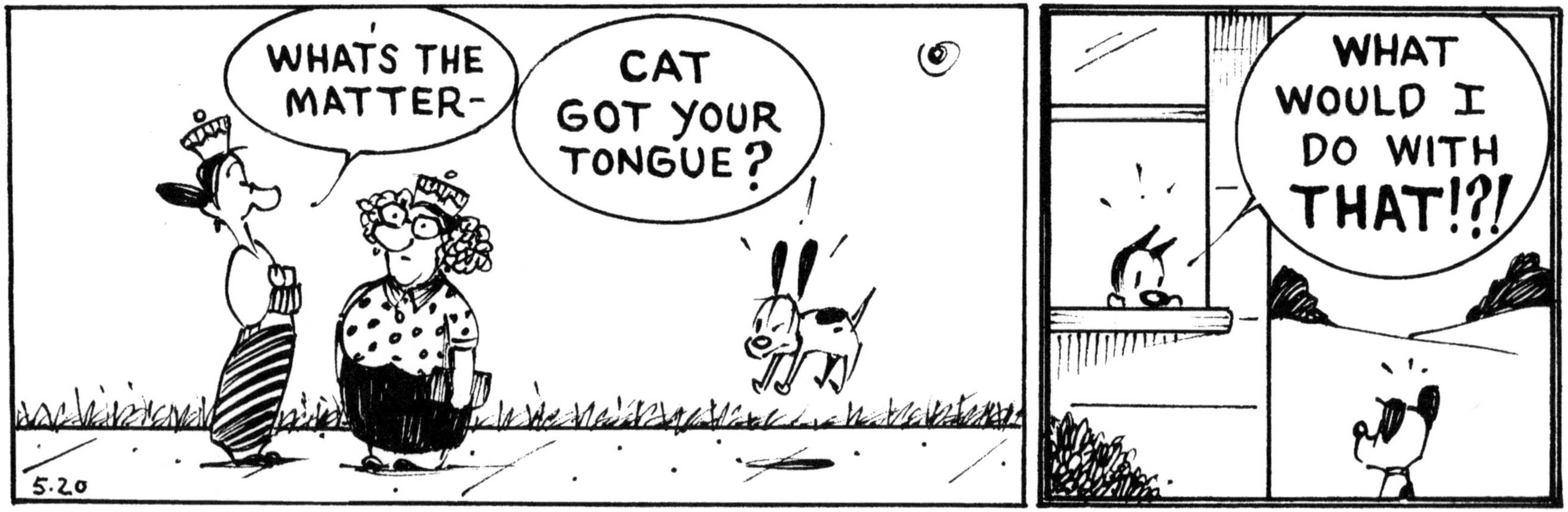
WHAT'S THE MATTER-
CAT GOT YOUR TONGUE?
WHAT WOULD I DO WITH THAT!?!
5.20

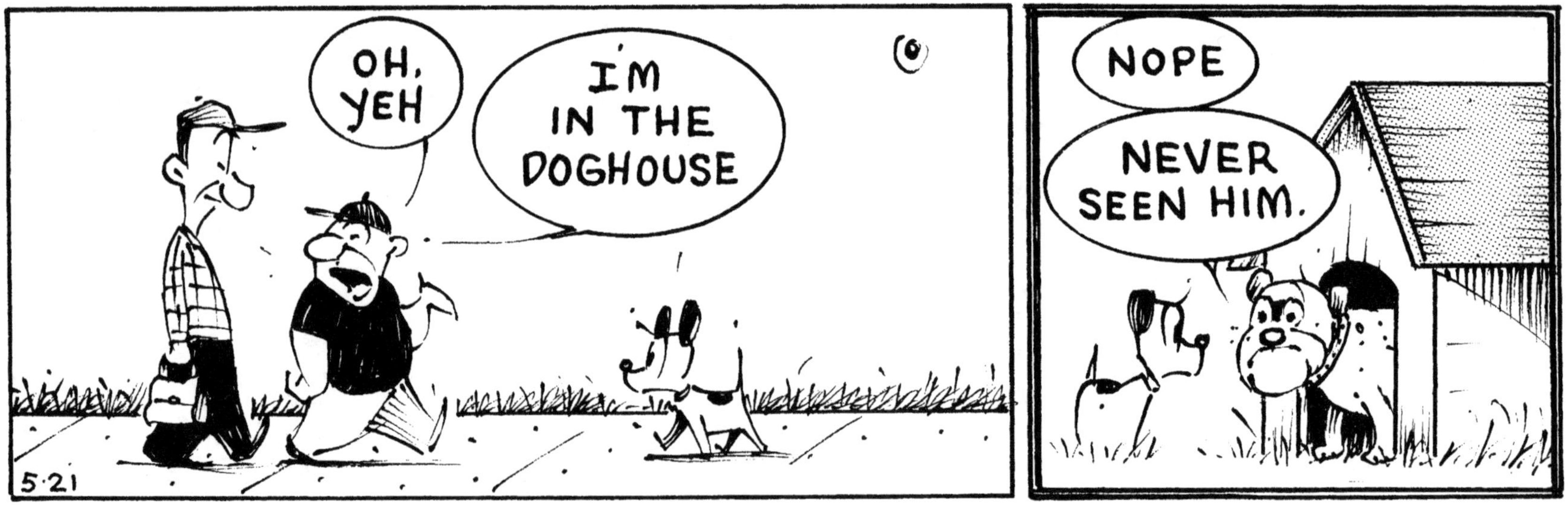
OH, YEH
I'M IN THE DOGHOUSE
NOPE
NEVER SEEN HIM.
5.21

THE LITTLE KAT KING

MUTTS

THE LITTLE KAT KING

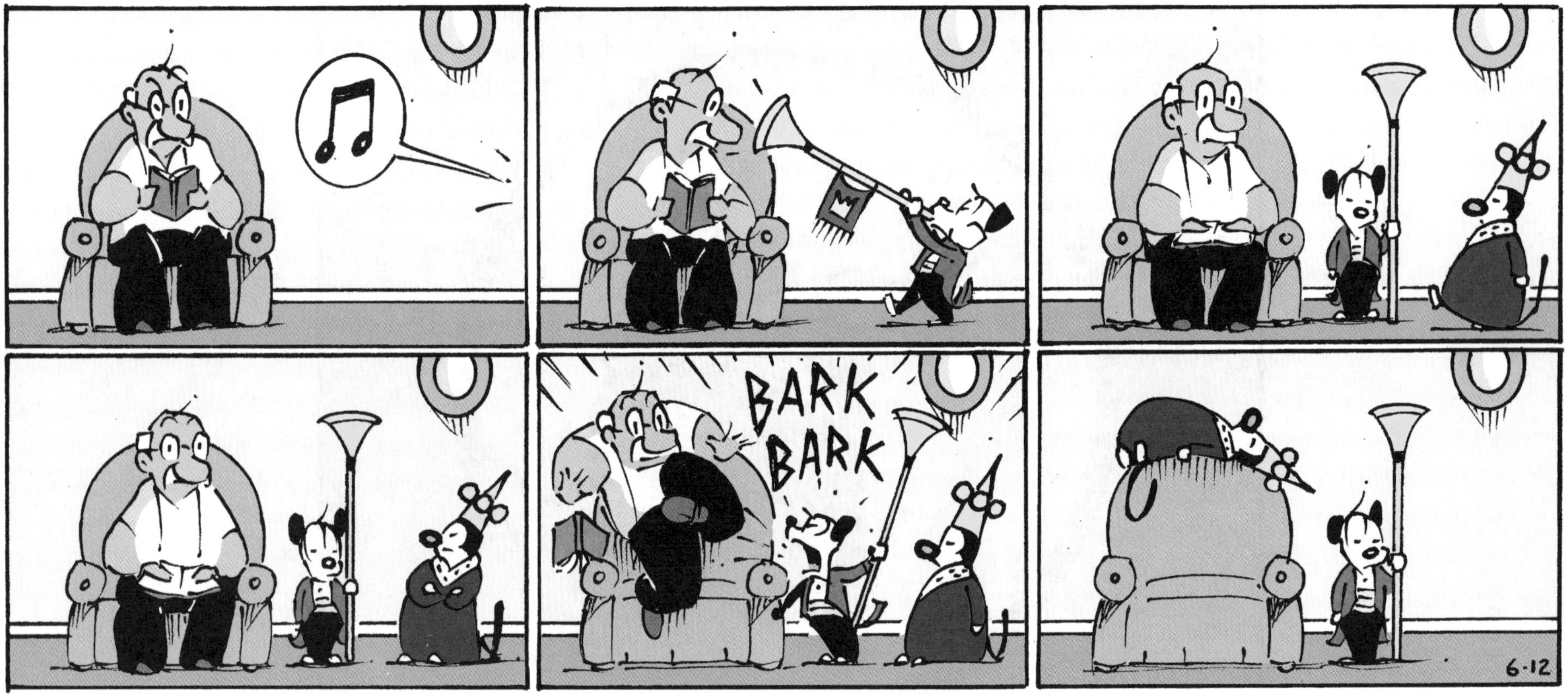
BARK
BARK
6-12

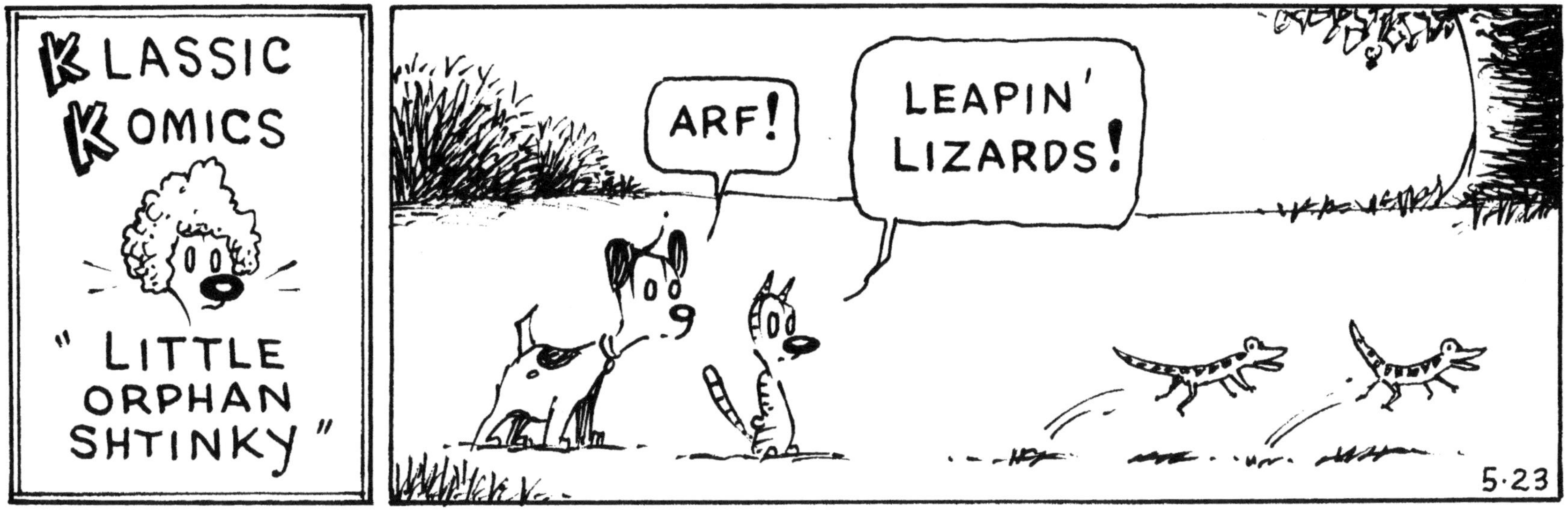
KLASSIC KOMICS
"LITTLE ORPHAN SHTINKY"
ARF!
LEAPIN' LIZARDS!
5·23

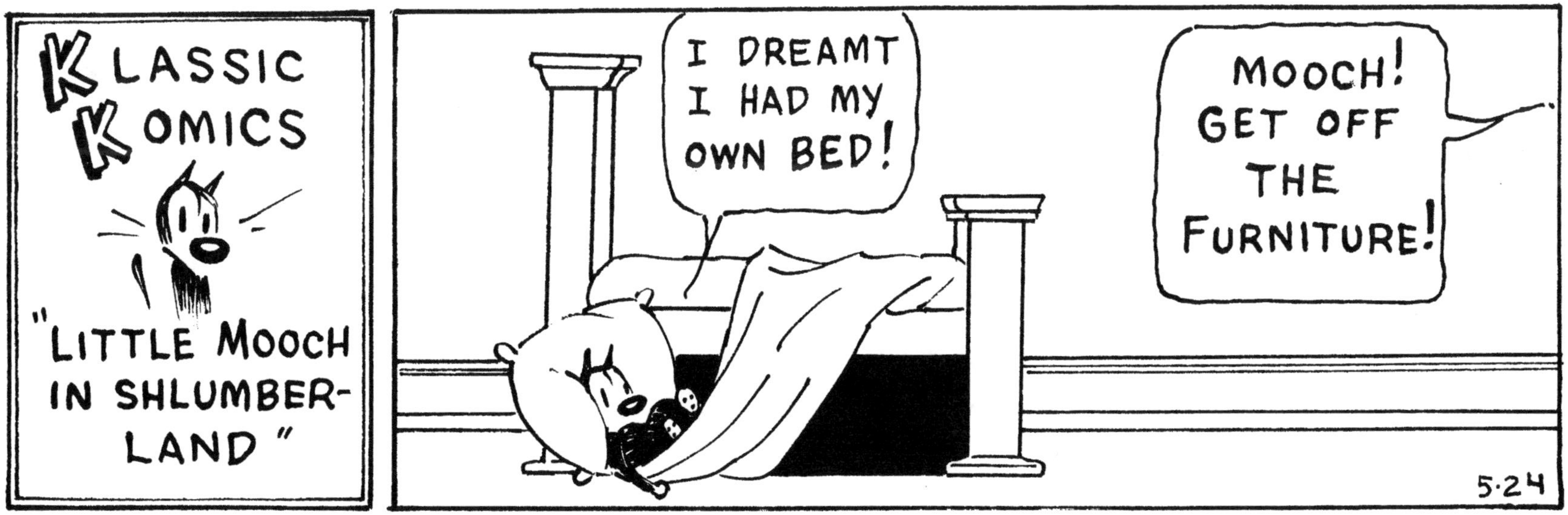
KLASSIC KOMICS
"LITTLE MOOCH IN SHLUMBER-LAND"
I DREAMT I HAD MY OWN BED!
MOOCH! GET OFF THE FURNITURE!
5·24

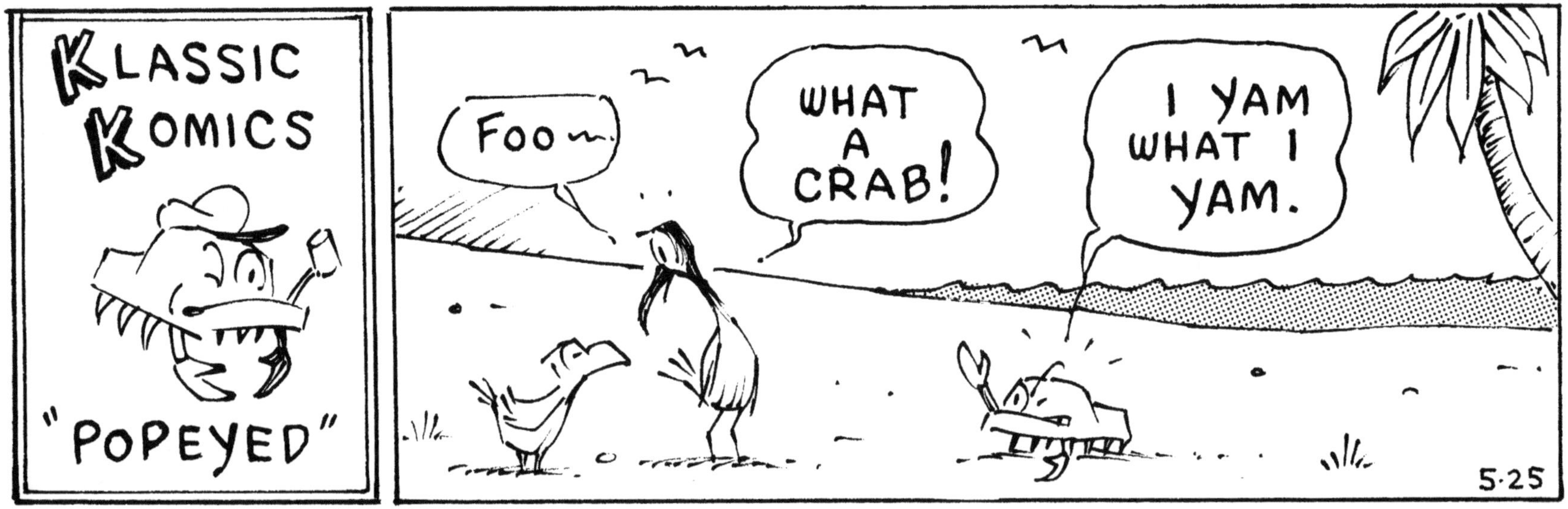
KLASSIC KOMICS
"POPEYED"
FOO~
WHAT A CRAB!
I YAM WHAT I YAM.
5·25

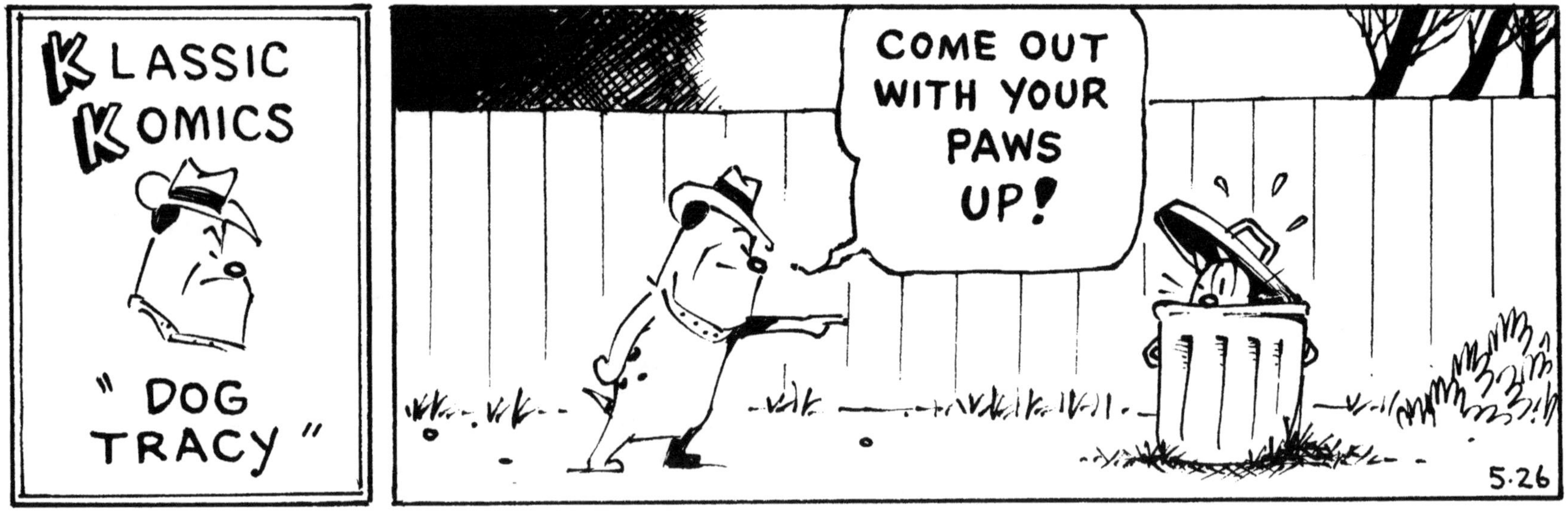
KLASSIC KOMICS
"DOG TRACY"
COME OUT WITH YOUR PAWS UP!
5·26

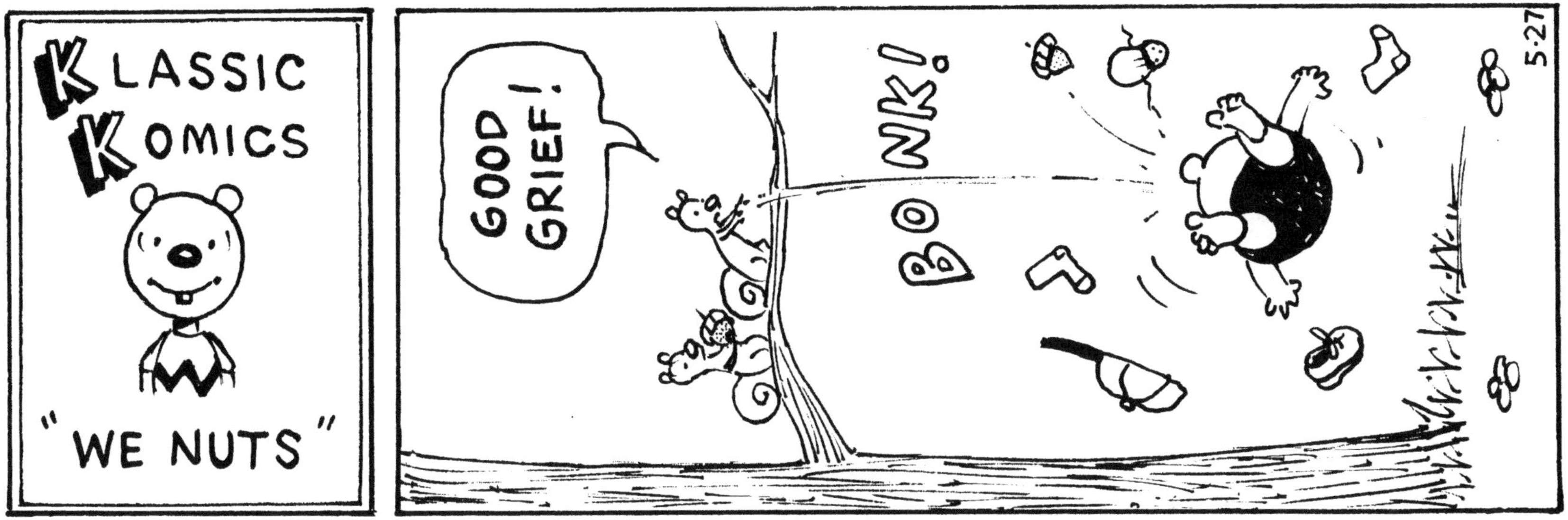
KLASSIC
KOMICS
"WE NUTS"
GOOD GRIEF!
BONK!
5·27

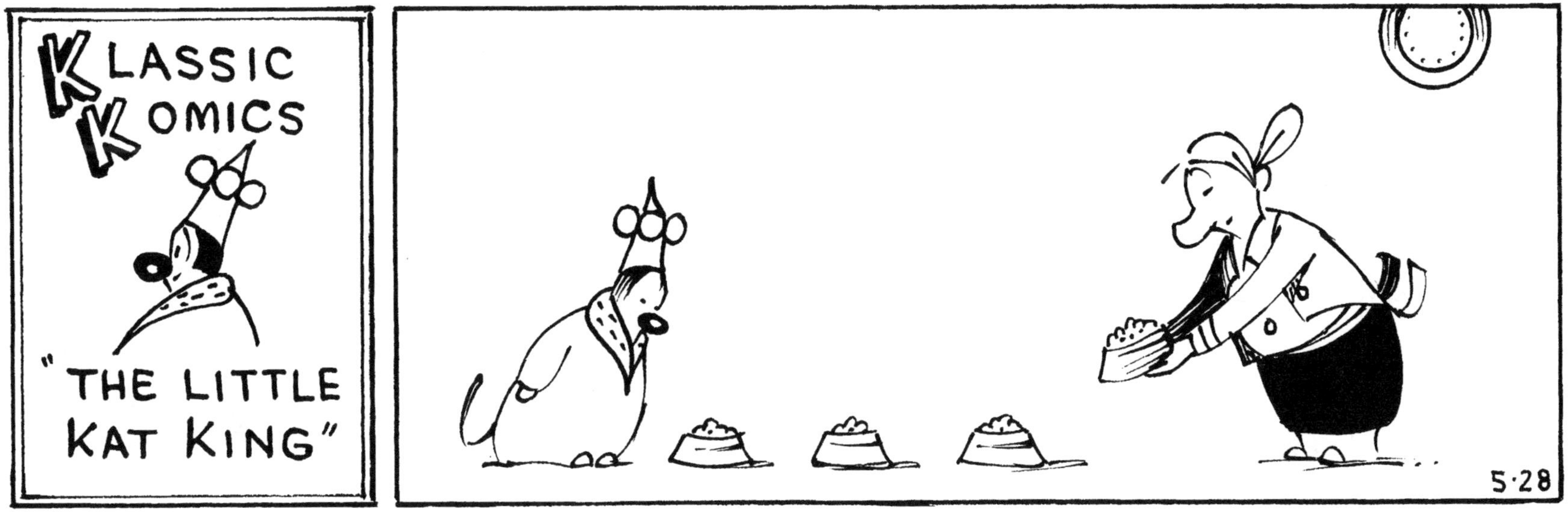
KLASSIC
KOMICS
"THE LITTLE KAT KING"
5·28

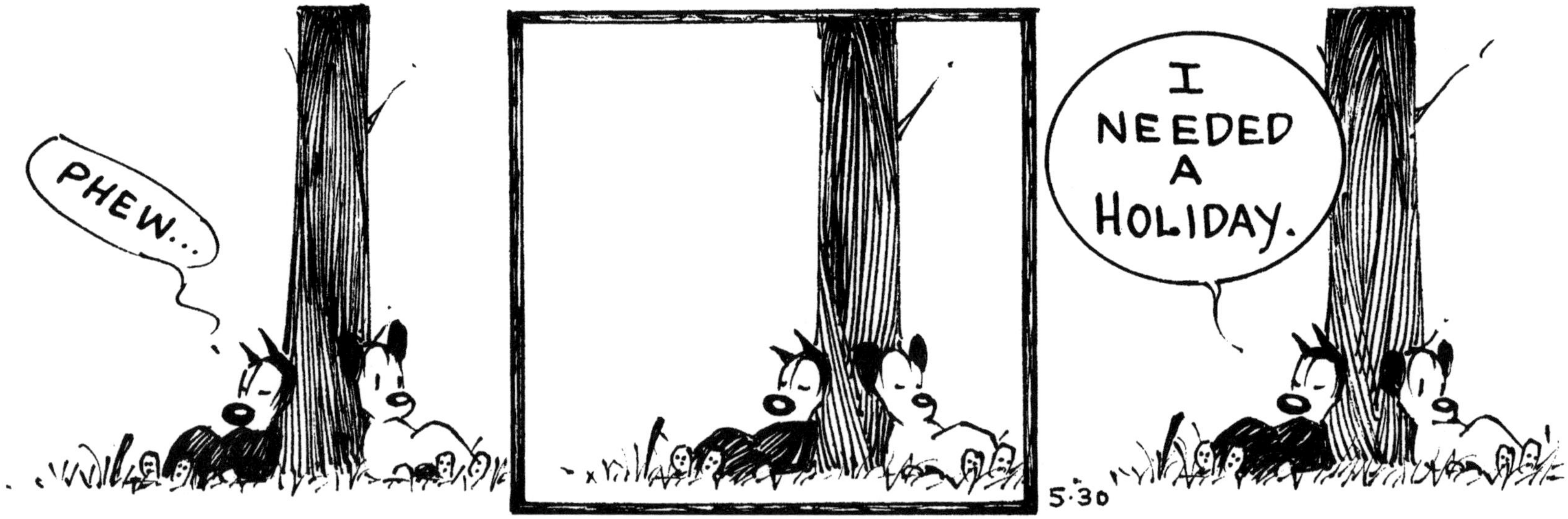
PHEW...
I NEEDED A HOLIDAY.
5·30

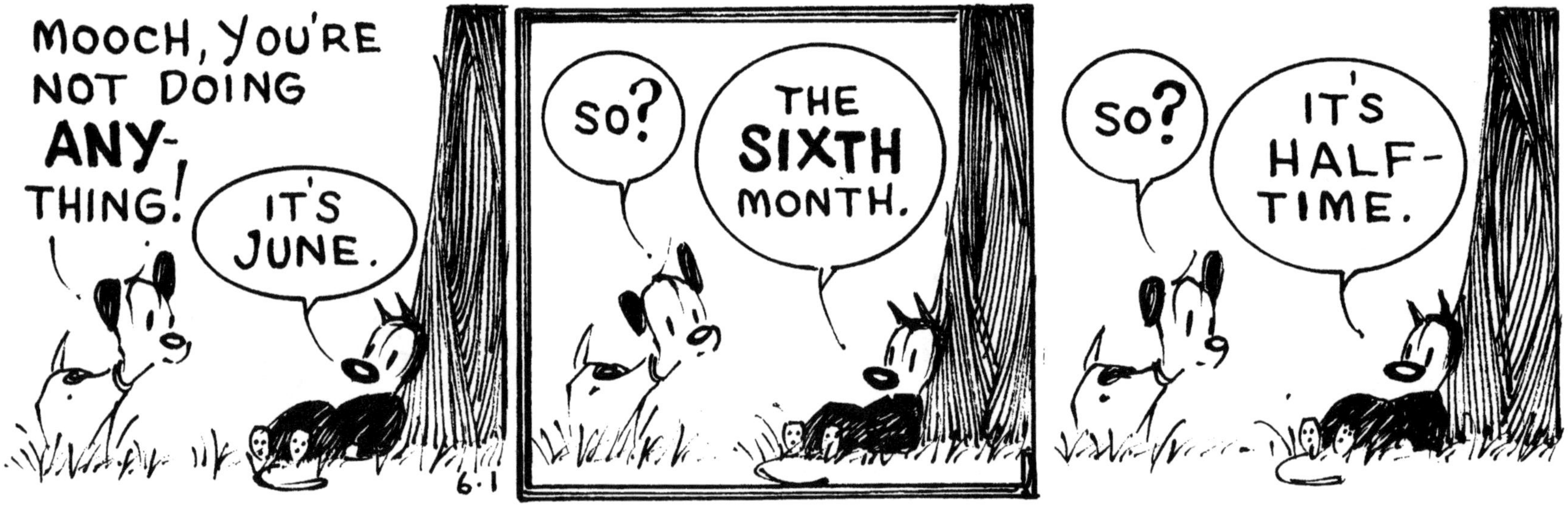
MOOCH, YOU'RE NOT DOING ANY-THING!
IT'S JUNE.
6·1
SO?
THE SIXTH MONTH.
SO?
IT'S HALF-TIME.

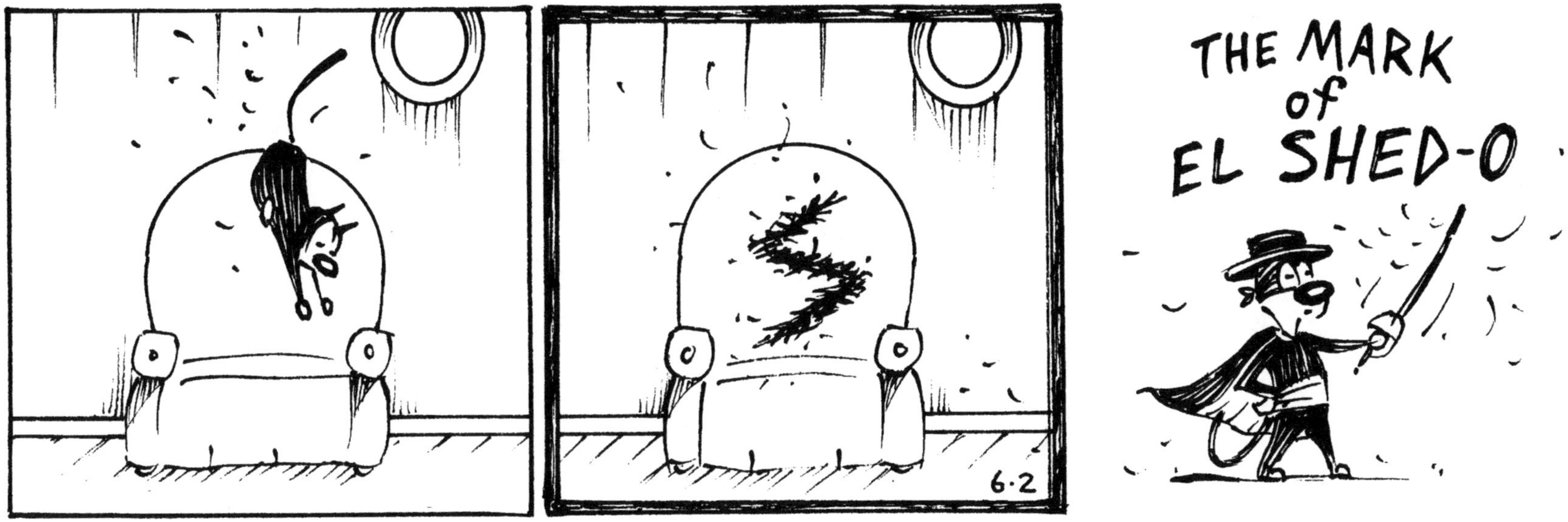
6·2
THE MARK of EL SHED-O

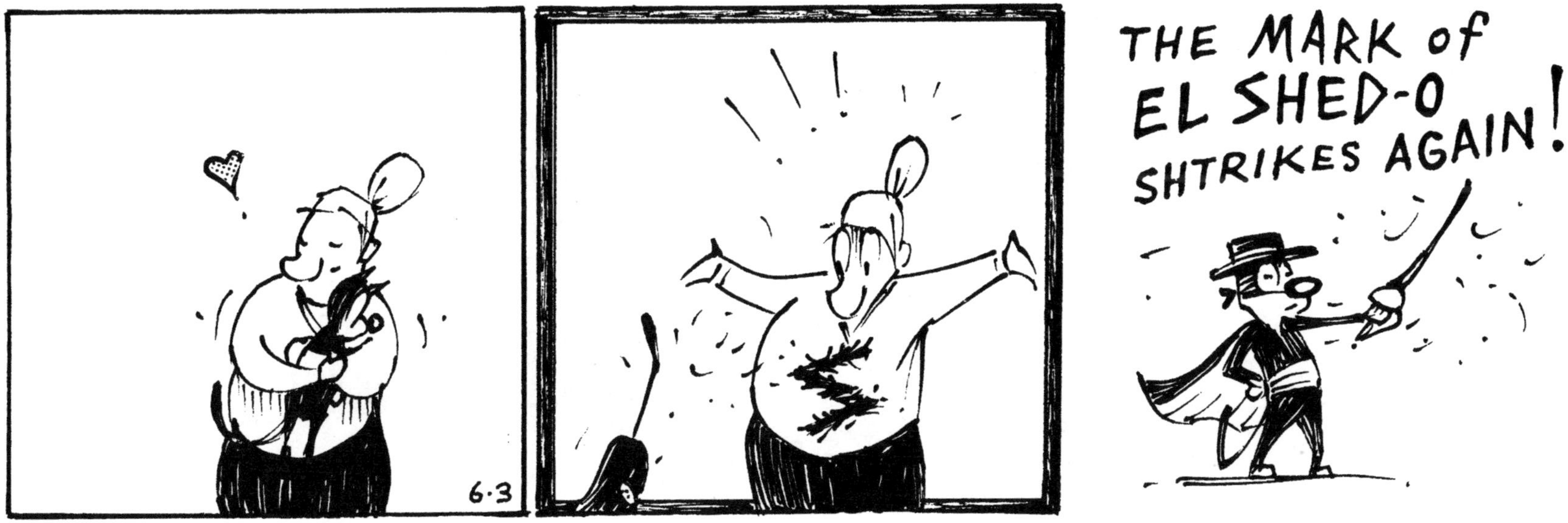
6·3
THE MARK of EL SHED-O SHTRIKES AGAIN!

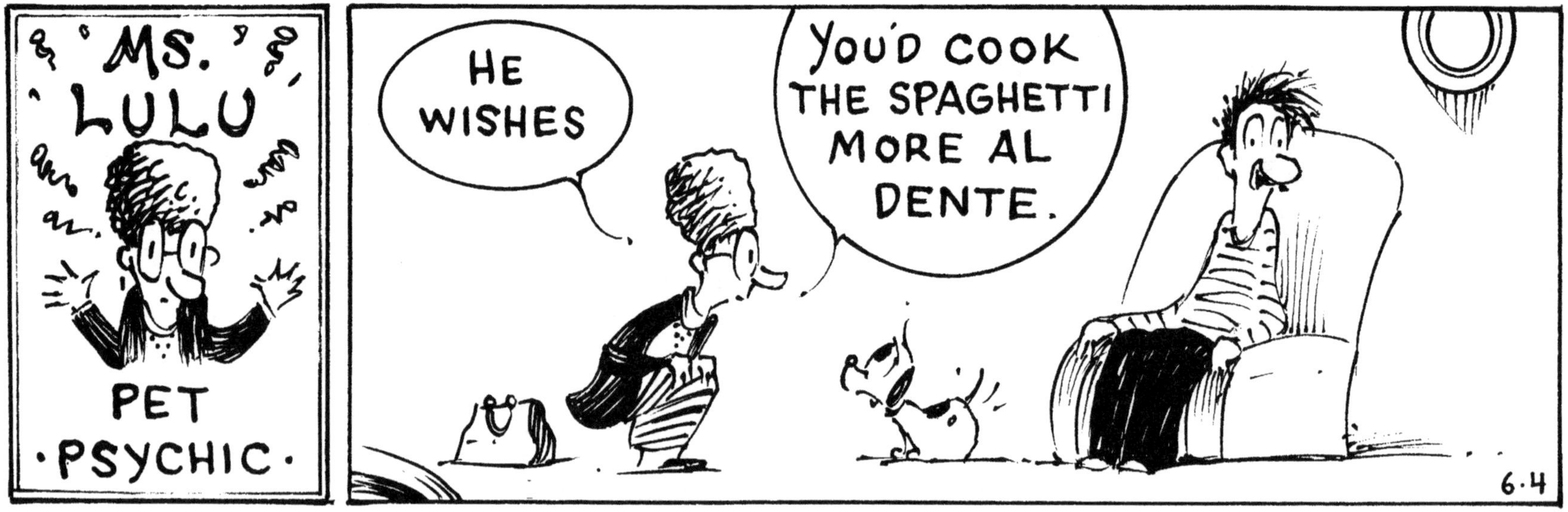
MS. LULU
PET ·PSYCHIC·
HE WISHES
YOU'D COOK THE SPAGHETTI MORE AL DENTE.
6·4

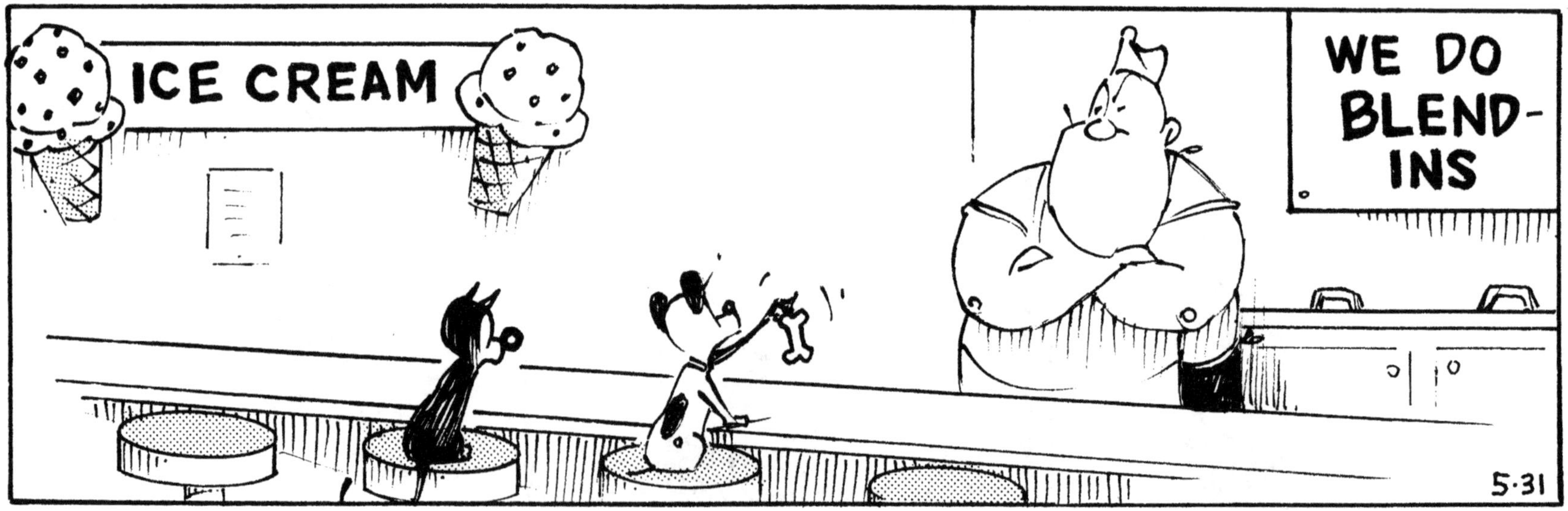
ICE CREAM
WE DO BLEND-INS
5·31

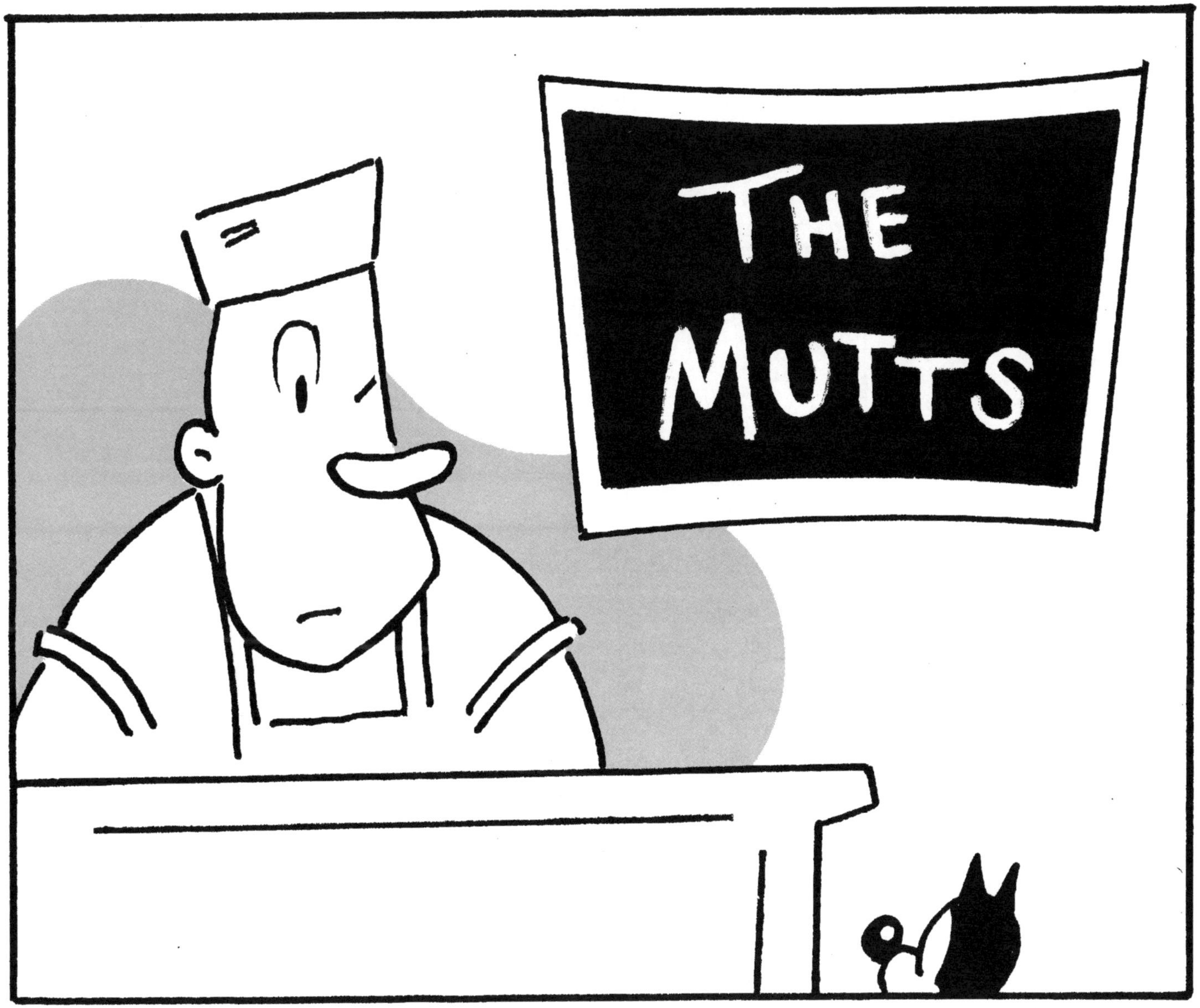
THE MUTTS

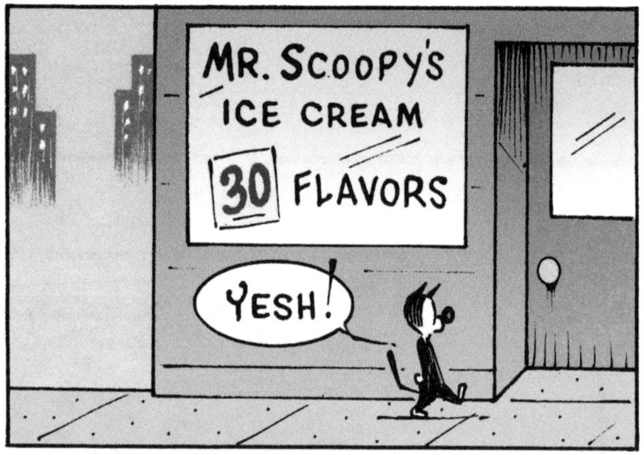
MR. SCOOPY'S
ICE CREAM
30 FLAVORS
YESH!

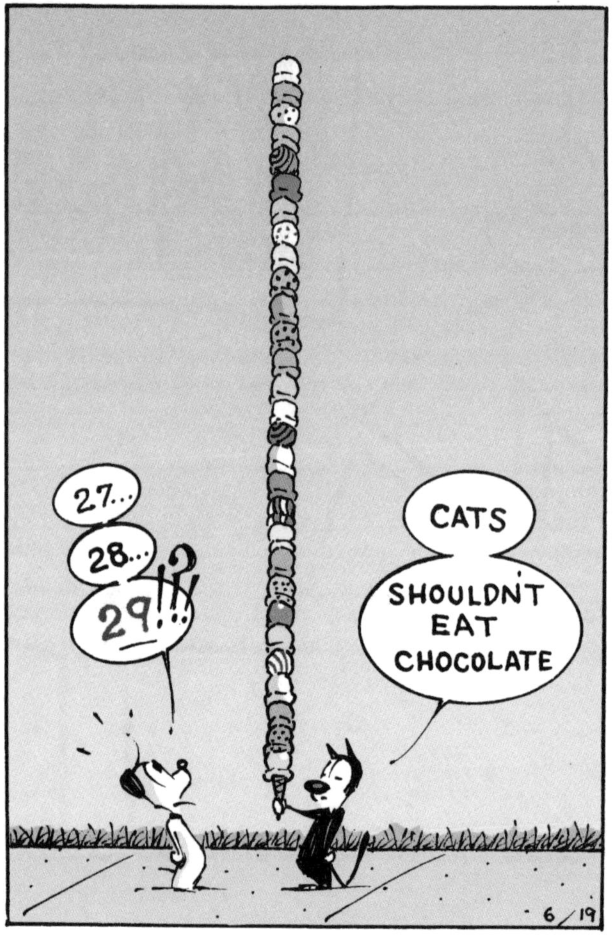
27...
28...
29!!!?
CATS
SHOULDN'T EAT CHOCOLATE
6/19

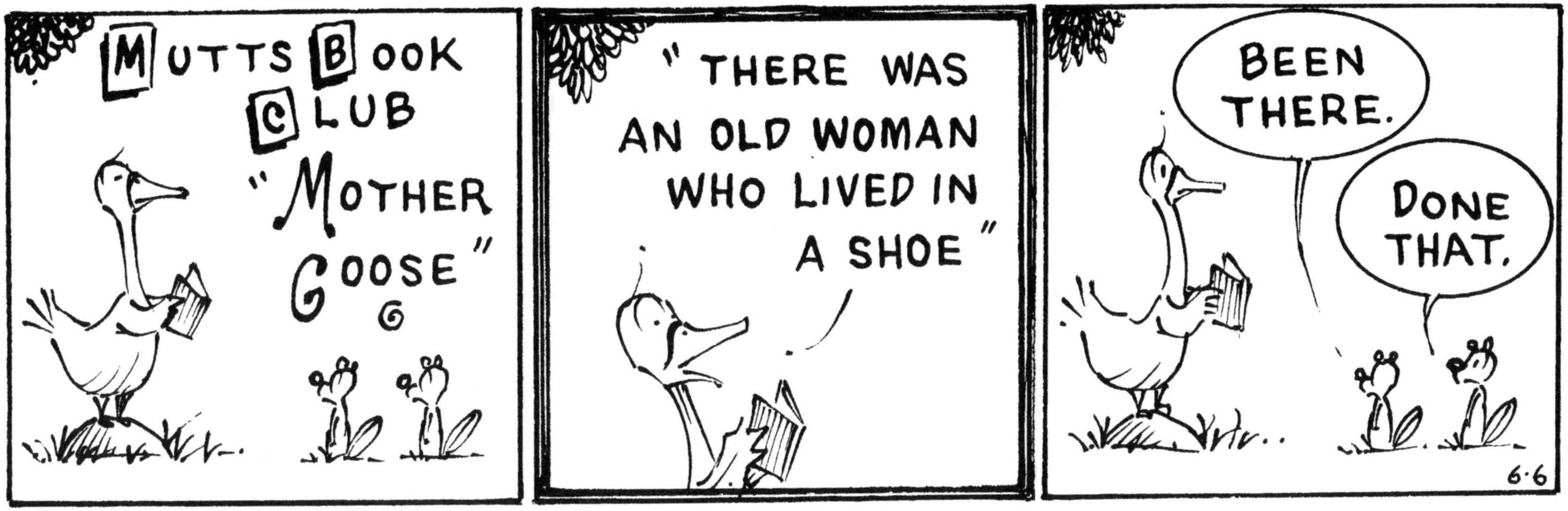
MUTTS BOOK CLUB
"MOTHER GOOSE"
" THERE WAS AN OLD WOMAN WHO LIVED IN A SHOE "
BEEN THERE.
DONE THAT.
6·6

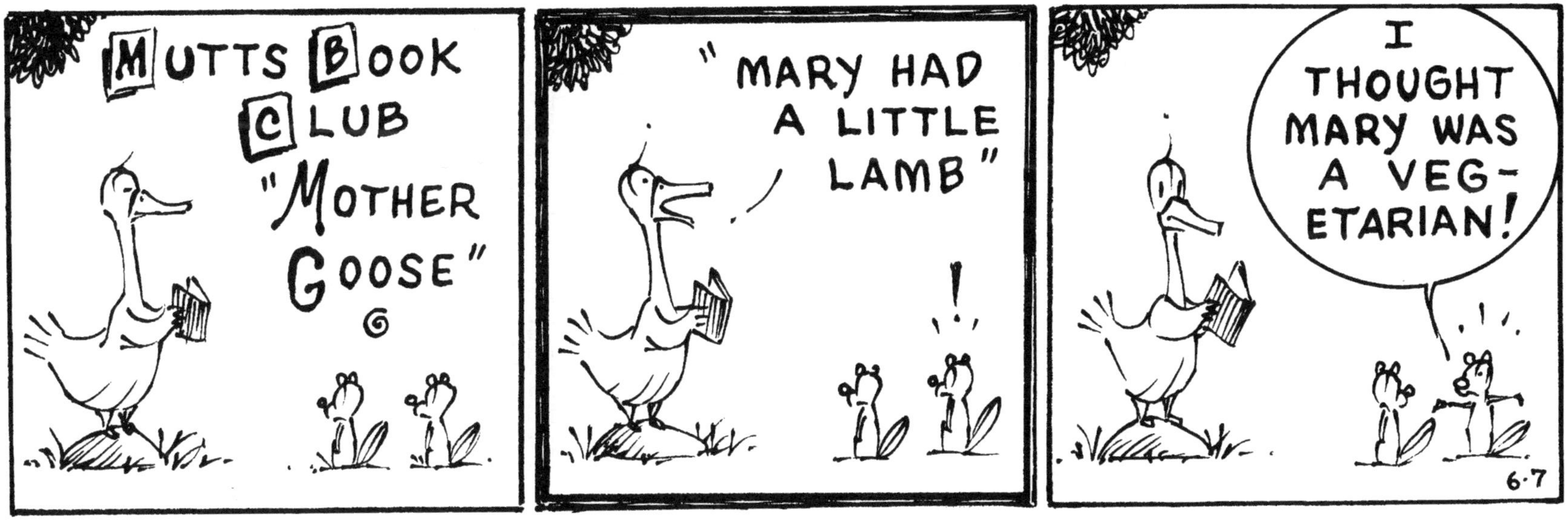
MUTTS BOOK CLUB
"MOTHER GOOSE"
" MARY HAD A LITTLE LAMB "
!
I THOUGHT MARY WAS A VEG-ETARIAN!
6·7

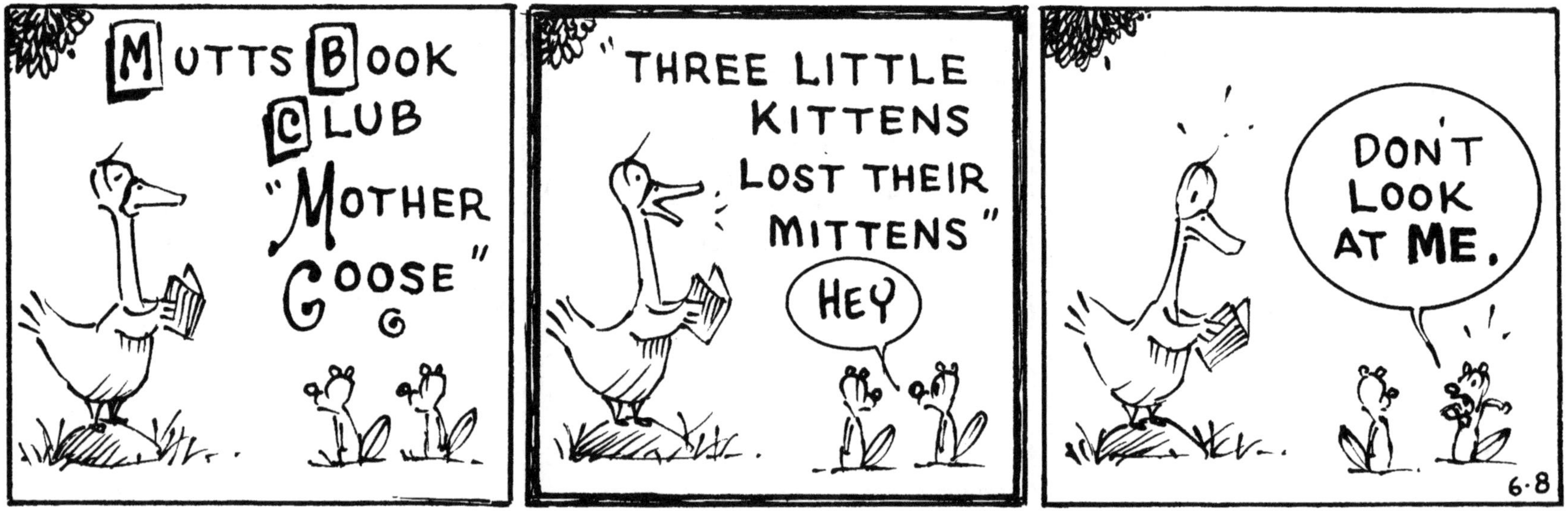
MUTTS BOOK CLUB
"MOTHER GOOSE"
"THREE LITTLE KITTENS LOST THEIR MITTENS"
HEY
DON'T LOOK AT ME.
6·8

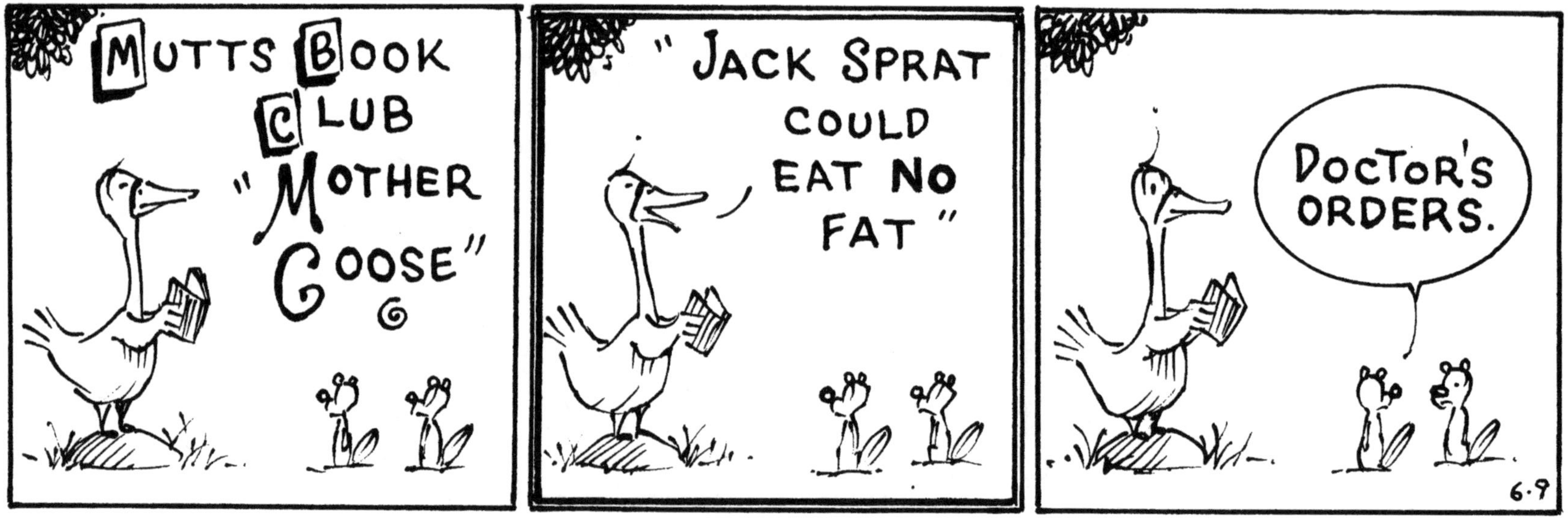
MUTTS BOOK CLUB
"MOTHER GOOSE"
"JACK SPRAT COULD EAT NO FAT"
DOCTOR'S ORDERS.
6·9

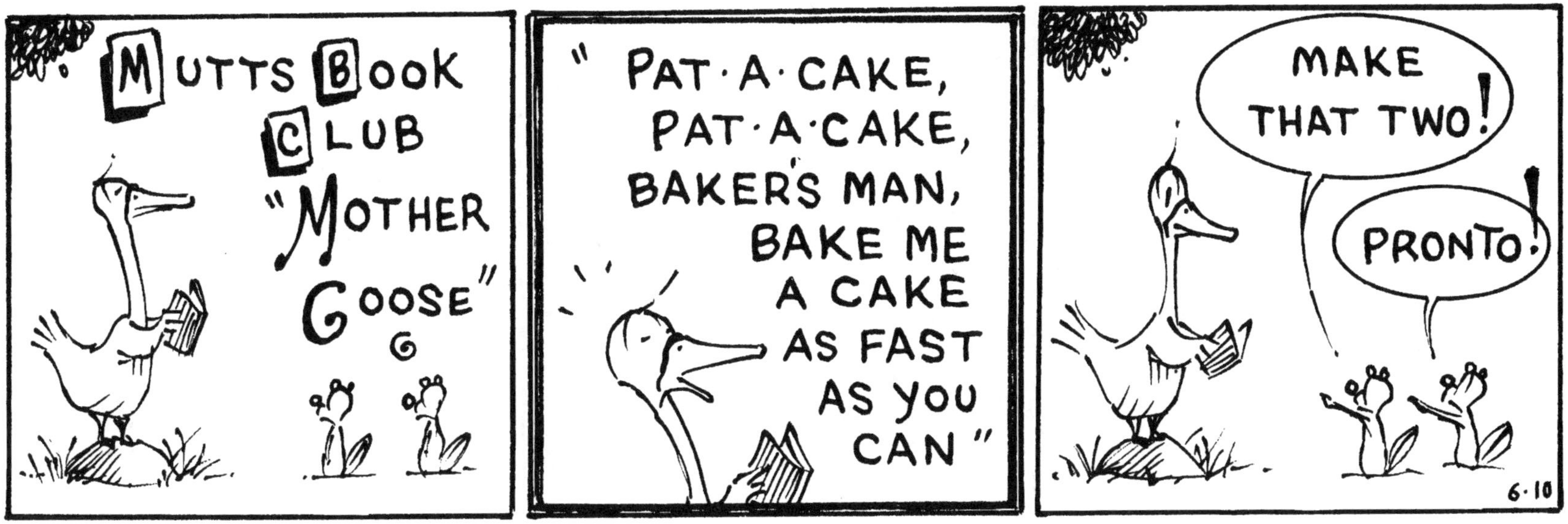
MUTTS BOOK CLUB
"MOTHER GOOSE"
"PAT·A·CAKE, PAT·A·CAKE, BAKER'S MAN, BAKE ME A CAKE AS FAST AS YOU CAN"
MAKE THAT TWO!
PRONTO!
6·10

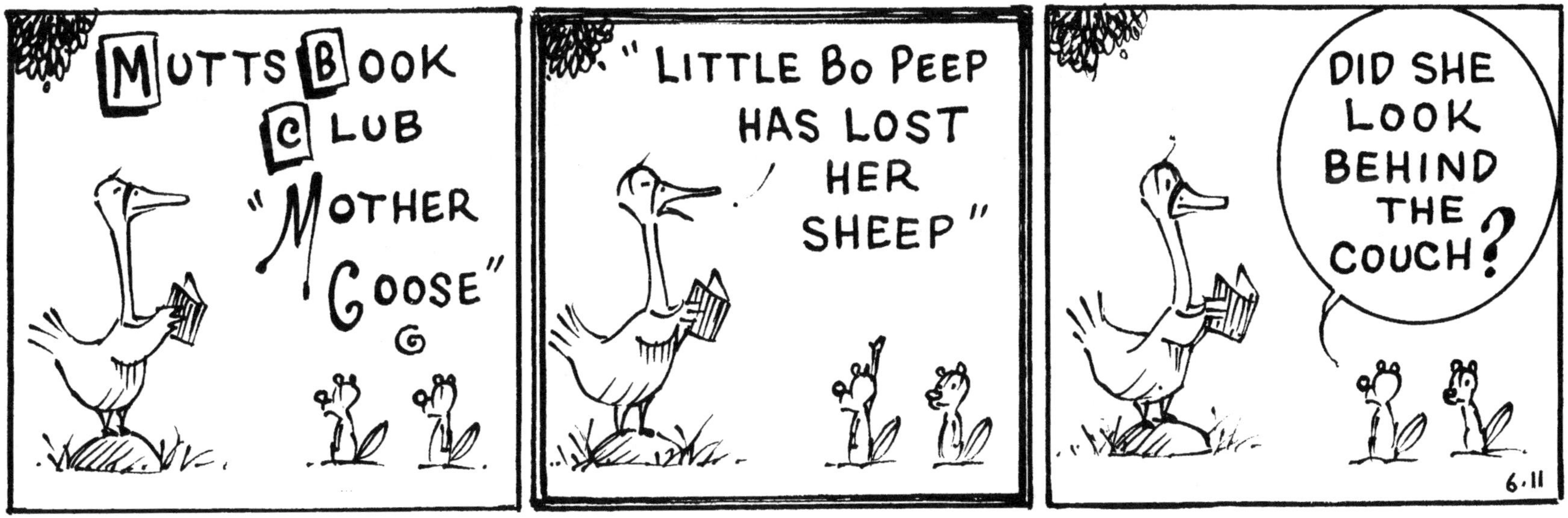
MUTTS BOOK CLUB
"MOTHER GOOSE"
"LITTLE BO PEEP HAS LOST HER SHEEP"
DID SHE LOOK BEHIND THE COUCH?
6·11

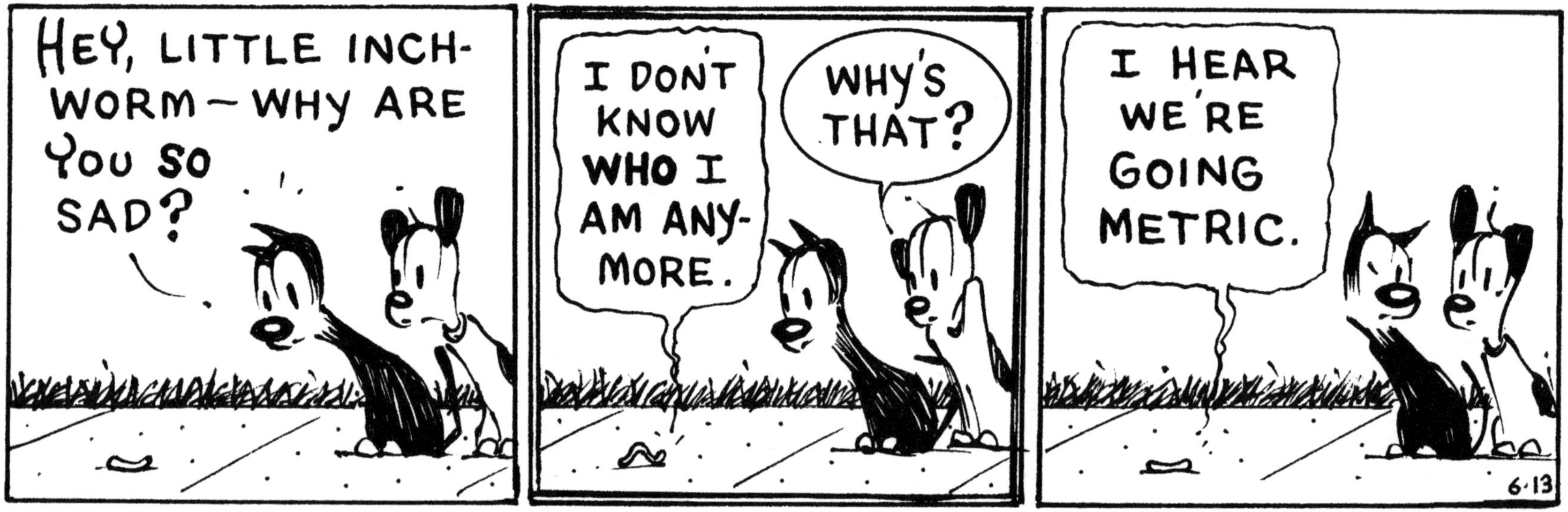
HEY, LITTLE INCH-WORM — WHY ARE YOU SO SAD?
I DON'T KNOW **WHO** I AM ANY-MORE.
WHY'S THAT?
I HEAR WE'RE GOING METRIC.
6·13

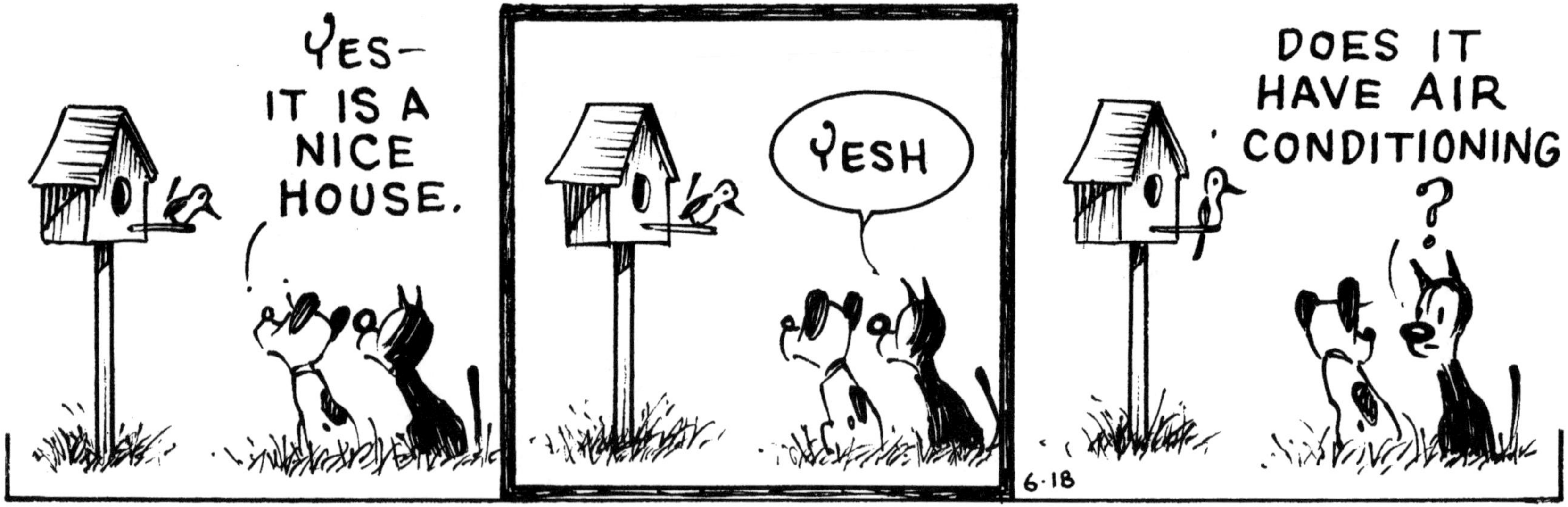
YES — IT IS A NICE HOUSE.
YESH
DOES IT HAVE AIR CONDITIONING?
6·18

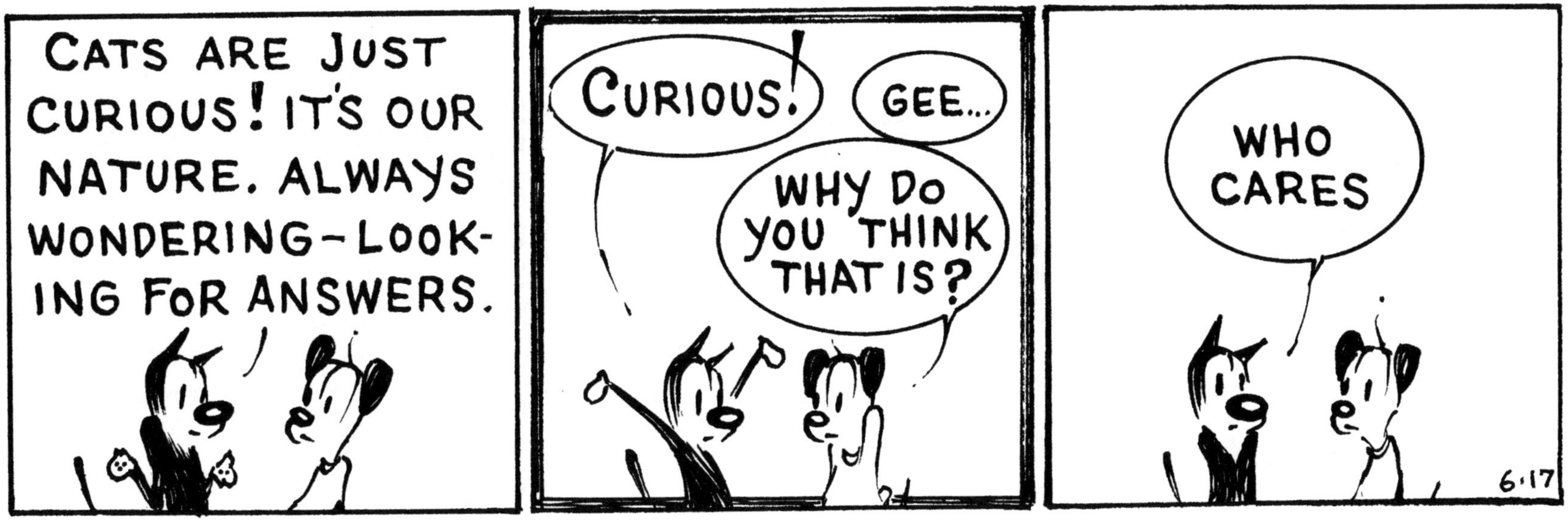
CATS ARE JUST CURIOUS! IT'S OUR NATURE. ALWAYS WONDERING–LOOKING FOR ANSWERS.
CURIOUS!
GEE...
WHY DO YOU THINK THAT IS?
WHO CARES
6·17

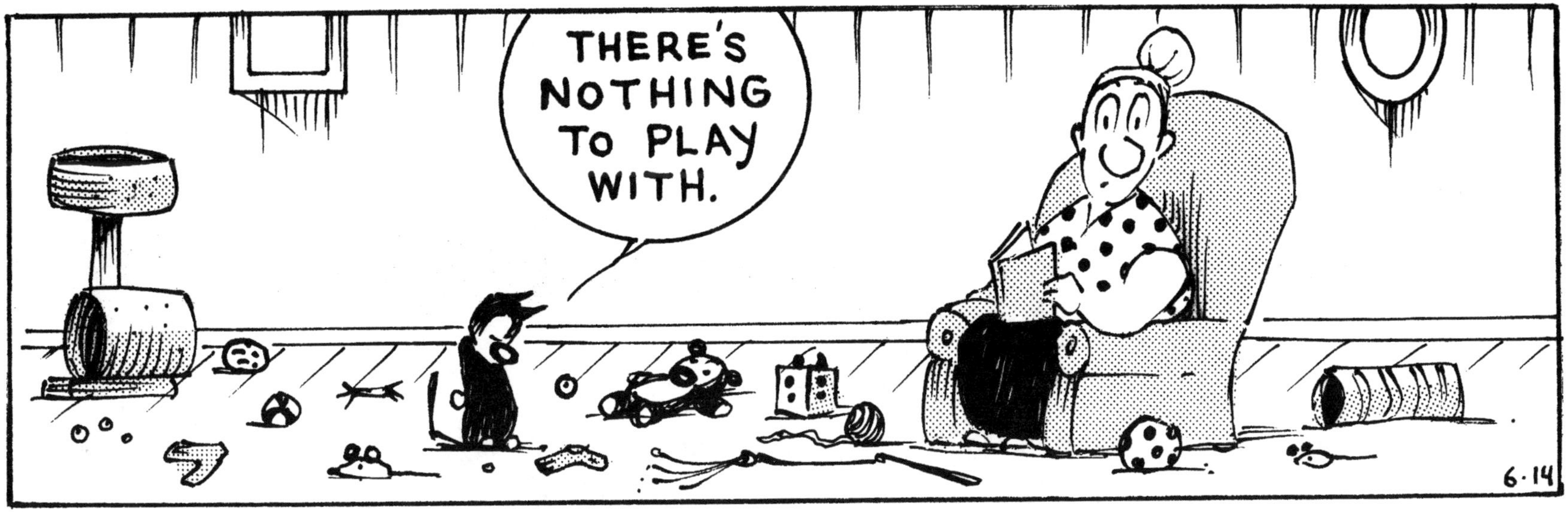
THERE'S NOTHING TO PLAY WITH.
6·14

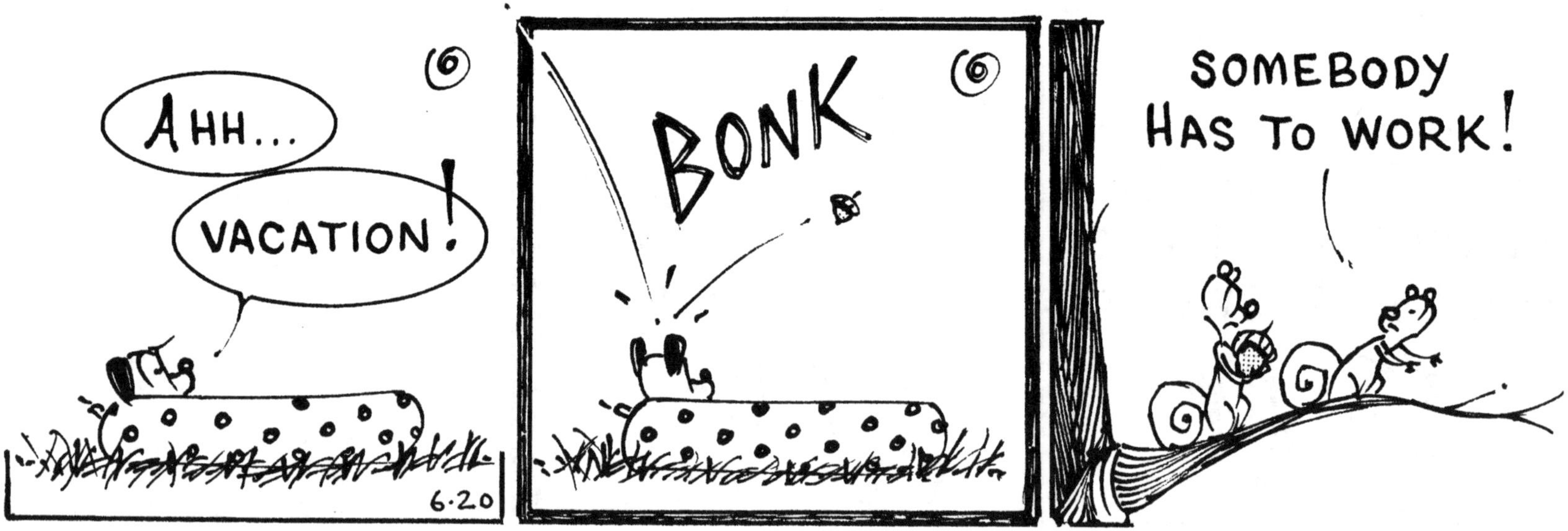
AHH...
VACATION!
BONK
SOMEBODY HAS TO WORK!
6·20

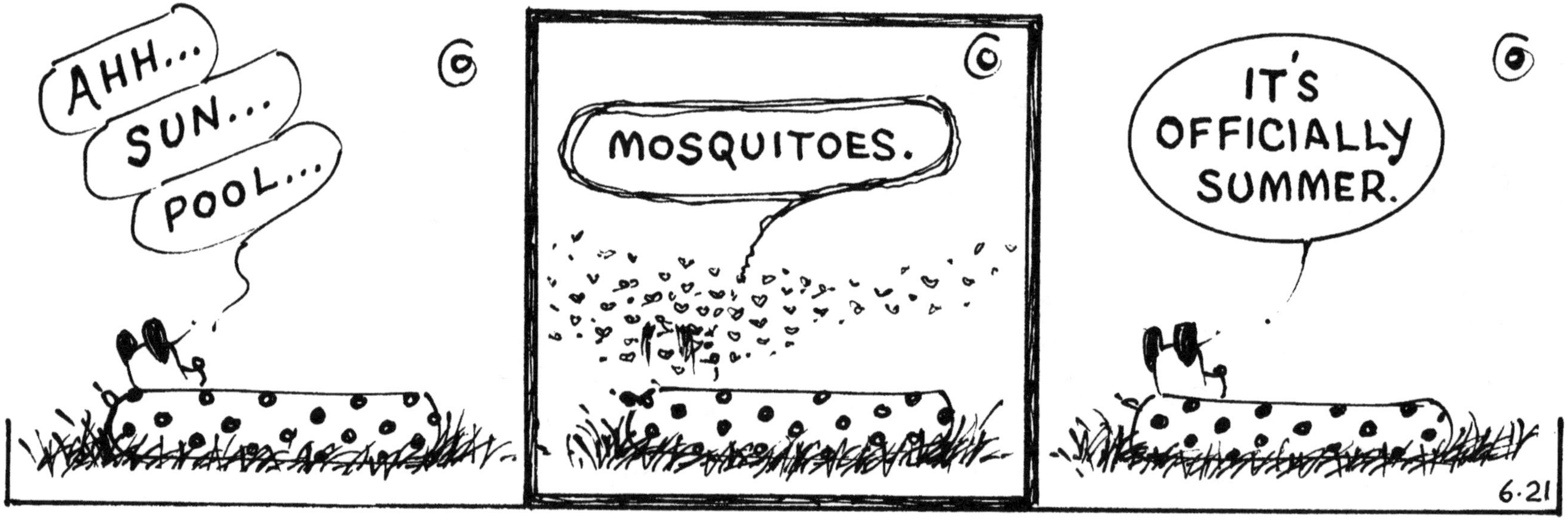
AHH...
SUN...
POOL...
MOSQUITOES.
IT'S OFFICIALLY SUMMER.
6·21

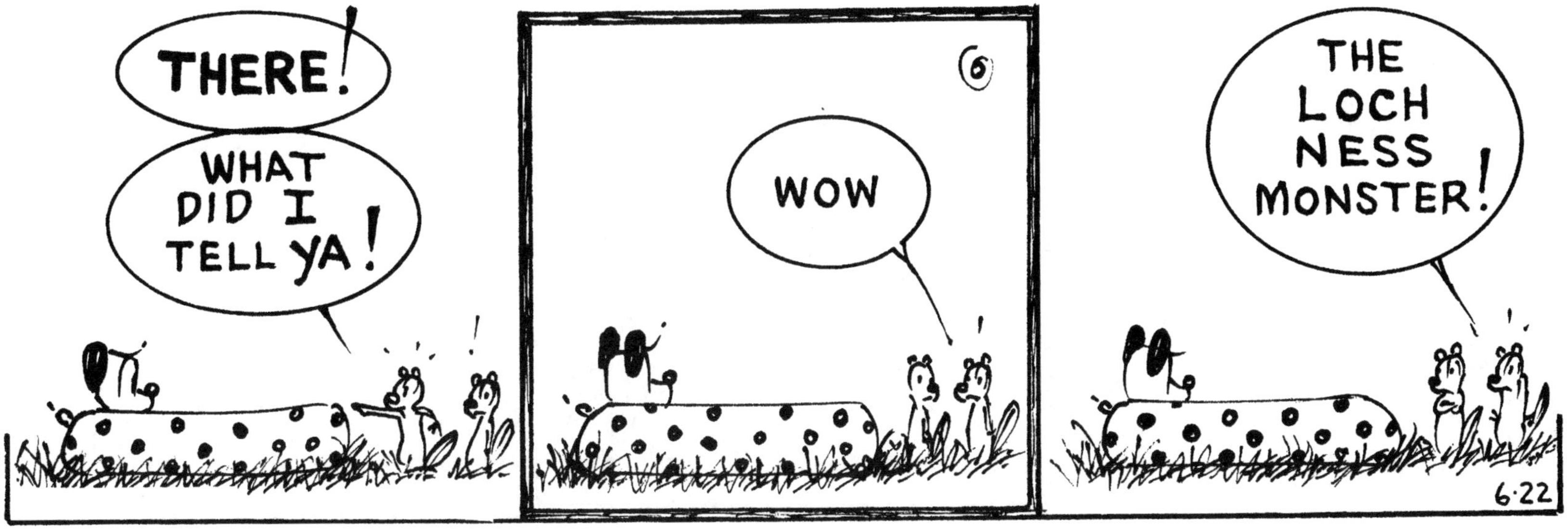
THERE!
WHAT DID I TELL YA!
6
WOW
THE LOCH NESS MONSTER!
6·22

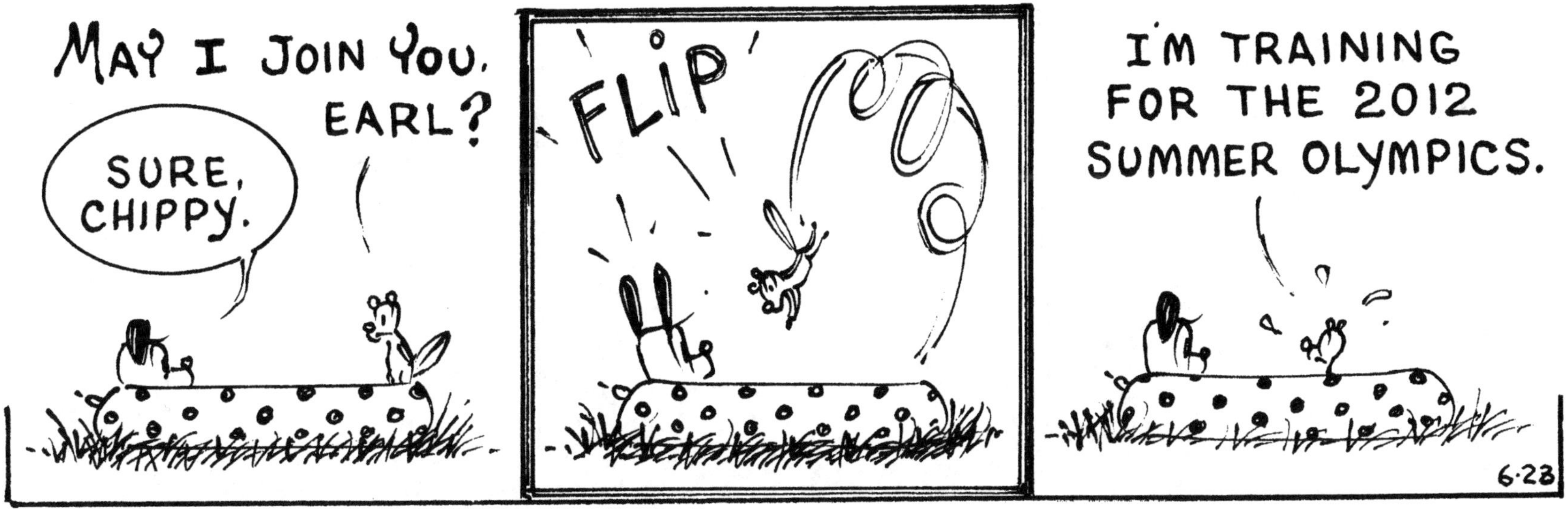
MAY I JOIN YOU, EARL?
SURE, CHIPPY.
FLIP
I'M TRAINING FOR THE 2012 SUMMER OLYMPICS.
6·23

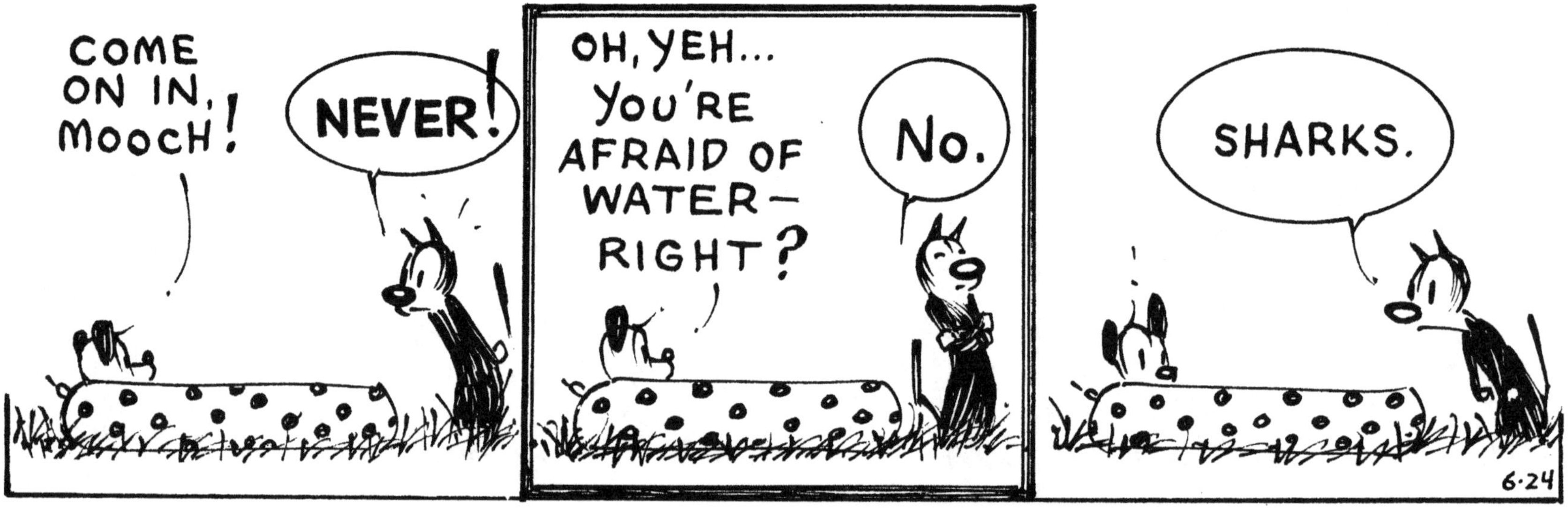
COME ON IN, MOOCH!
NEVER!
OH, YEH... YOU'RE AFRAID OF WATER– RIGHT?
No.
SHARKS.
6·24

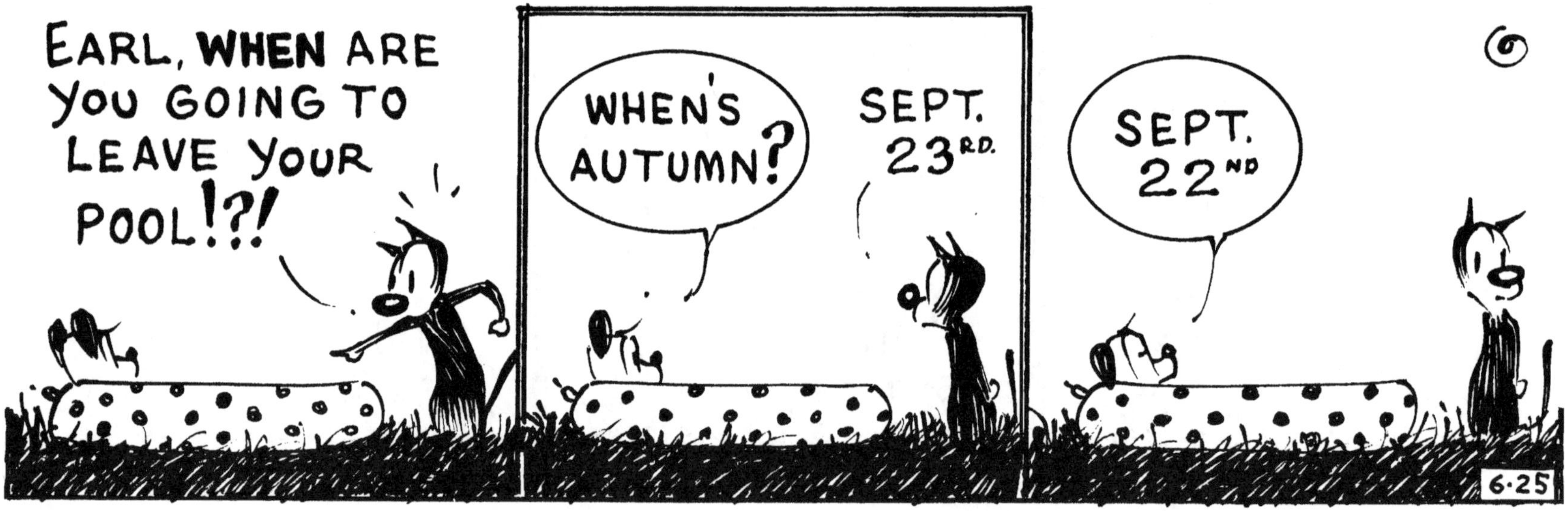
EARL, WHEN ARE YOU GOING TO LEAVE YOUR POOL!?!
WHEN'S AUTUMN?
SEPT. 23RD.
SEPT. 22ND
6·25

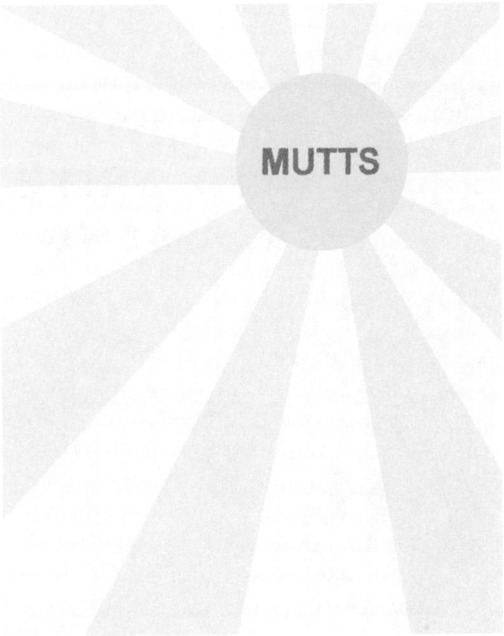
MUTTS

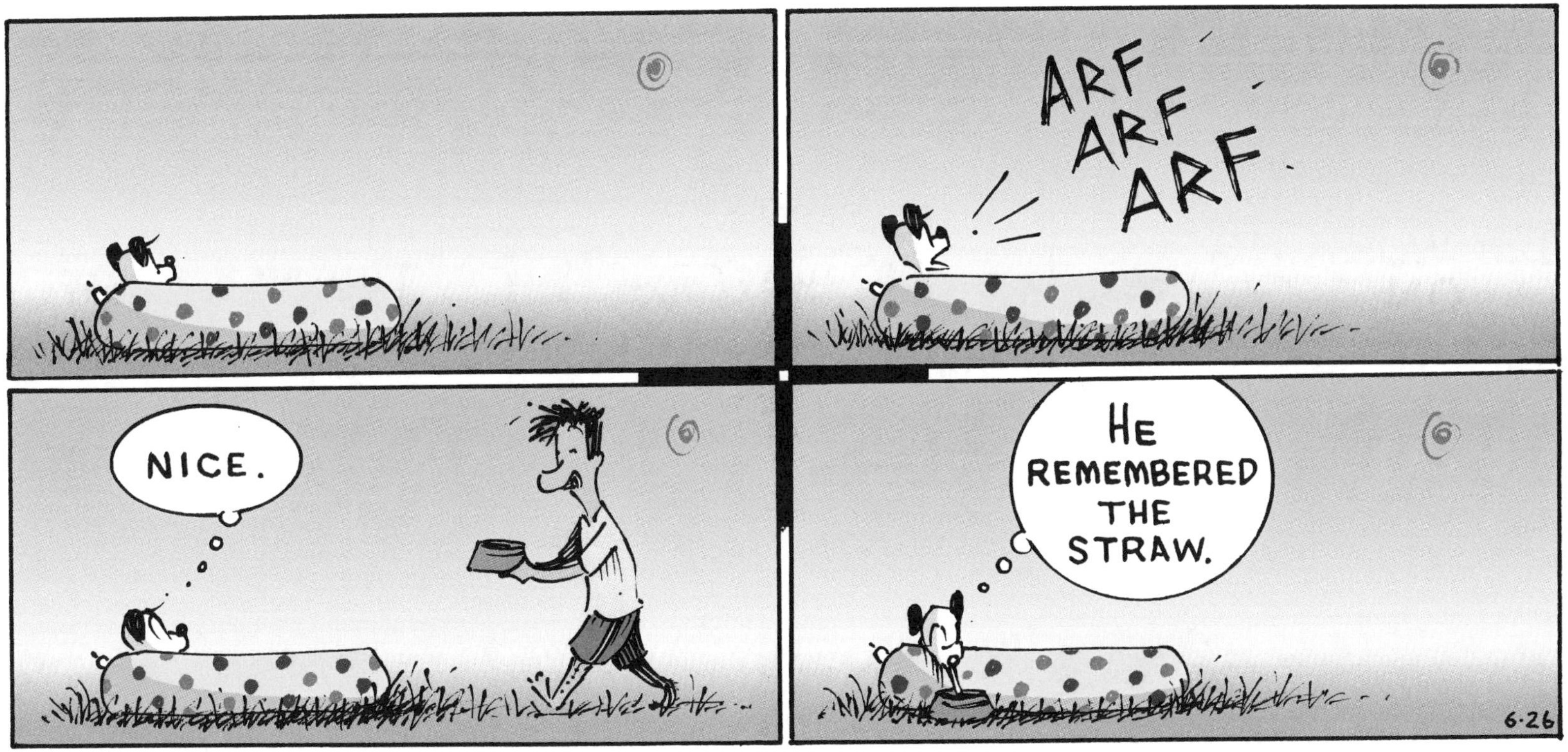
ARF
ARF
ARF
NICE.
HE REMEMBERED THE STRAW.
6·26

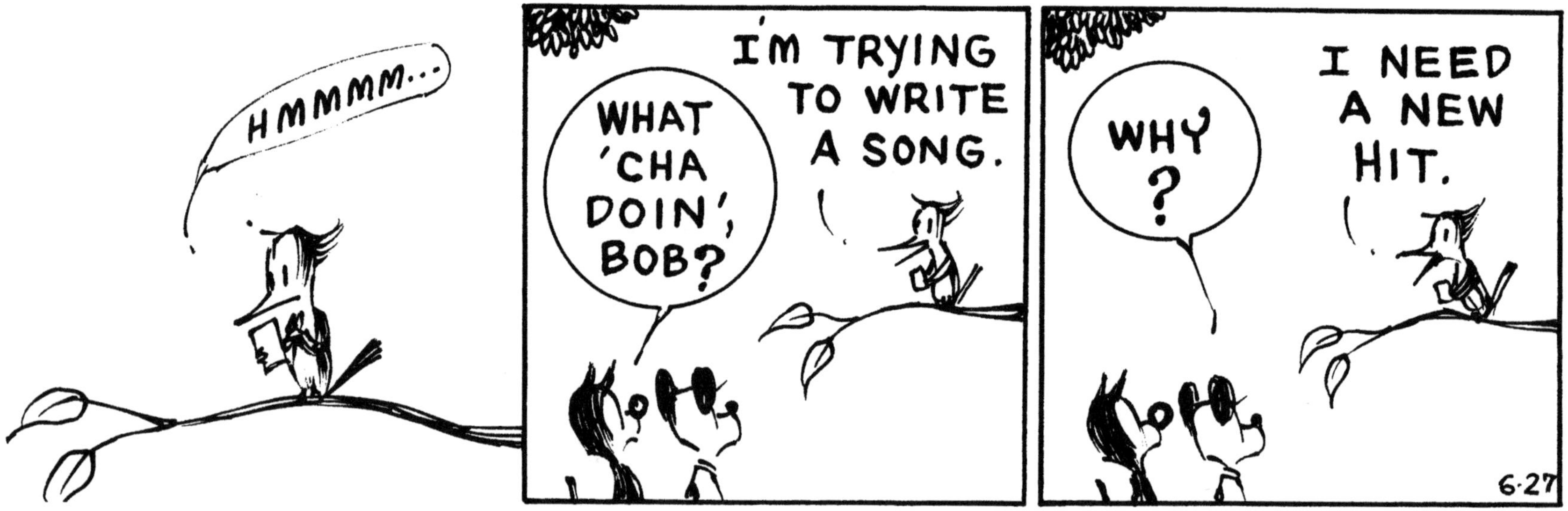
HMMMM...
WHAT 'CHA DOIN', BOB?
I'M TRYING TO WRITE A SONG.
WHY?
I NEED A NEW HIT.
6·27

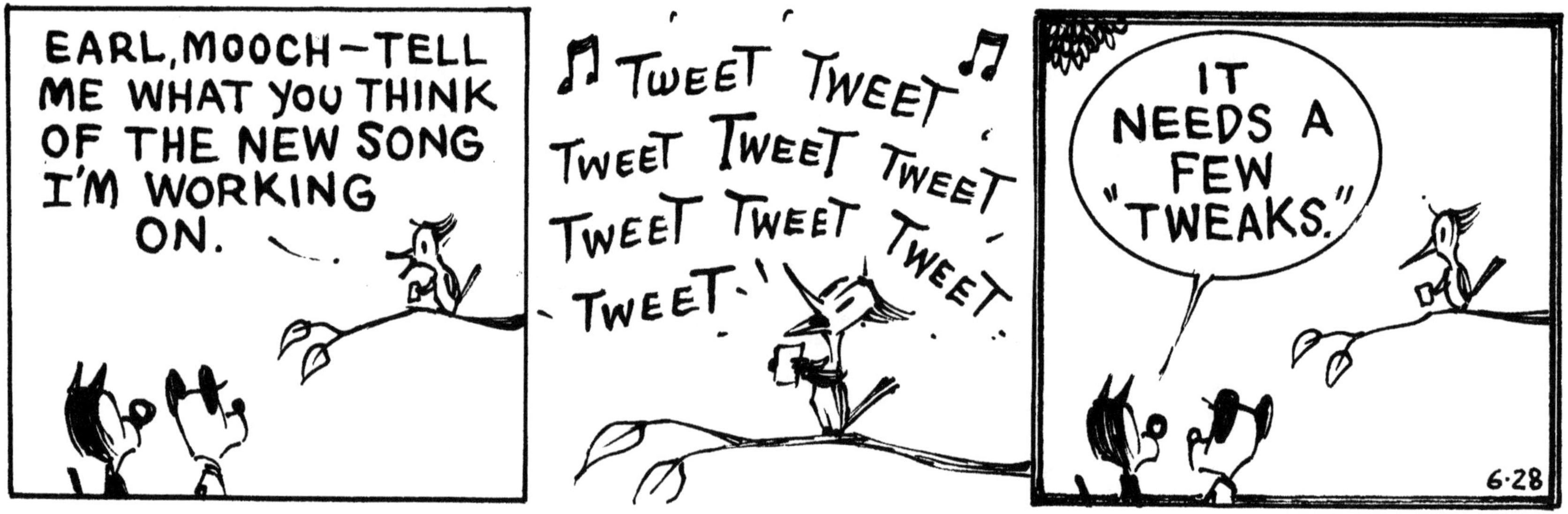
EARL, MOOCH—TELL ME WHAT YOU THINK OF THE NEW SONG I'M WORKING ON.
TWEET TWEET TWEET TWEET TWEET TWEET TWEET TWEET TWEET
IT NEEDS A FEW "TWEAKS."
6·28

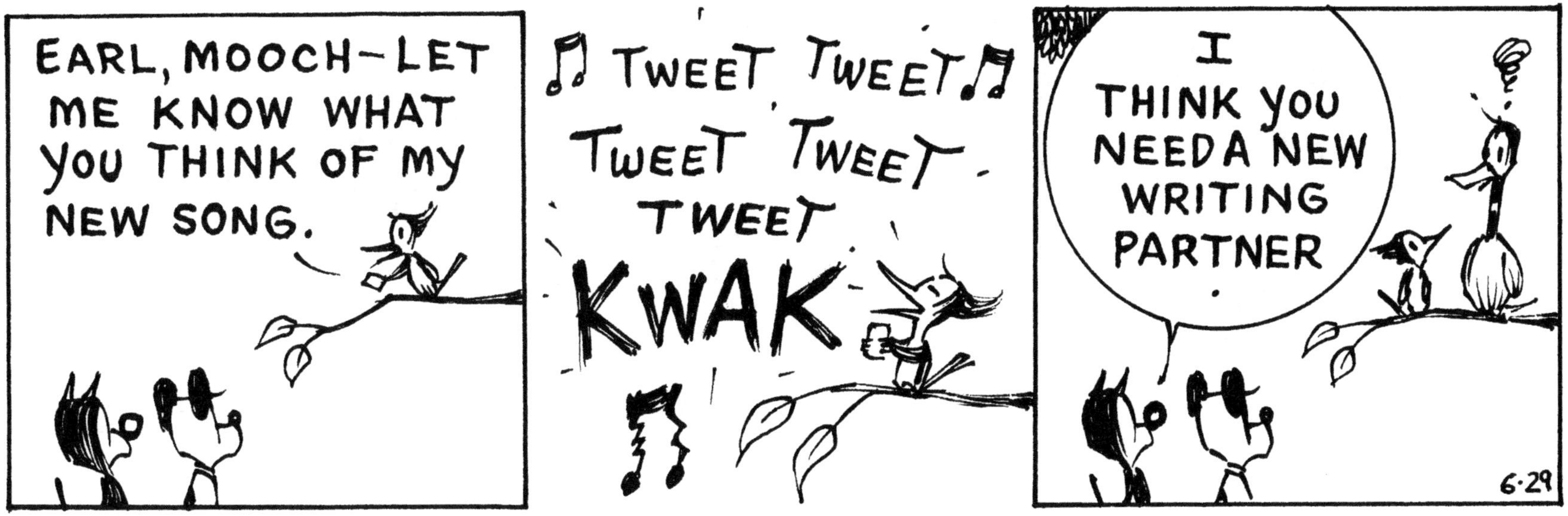
EARL, MOOCH–LET ME KNOW WHAT YOU THINK OF MY NEW SONG.
♫ TWEET TWEET ♫
TWEET TWEET TWEET
KWAK
I THINK YOU NEED A NEW WRITING PARTNER.
6·29

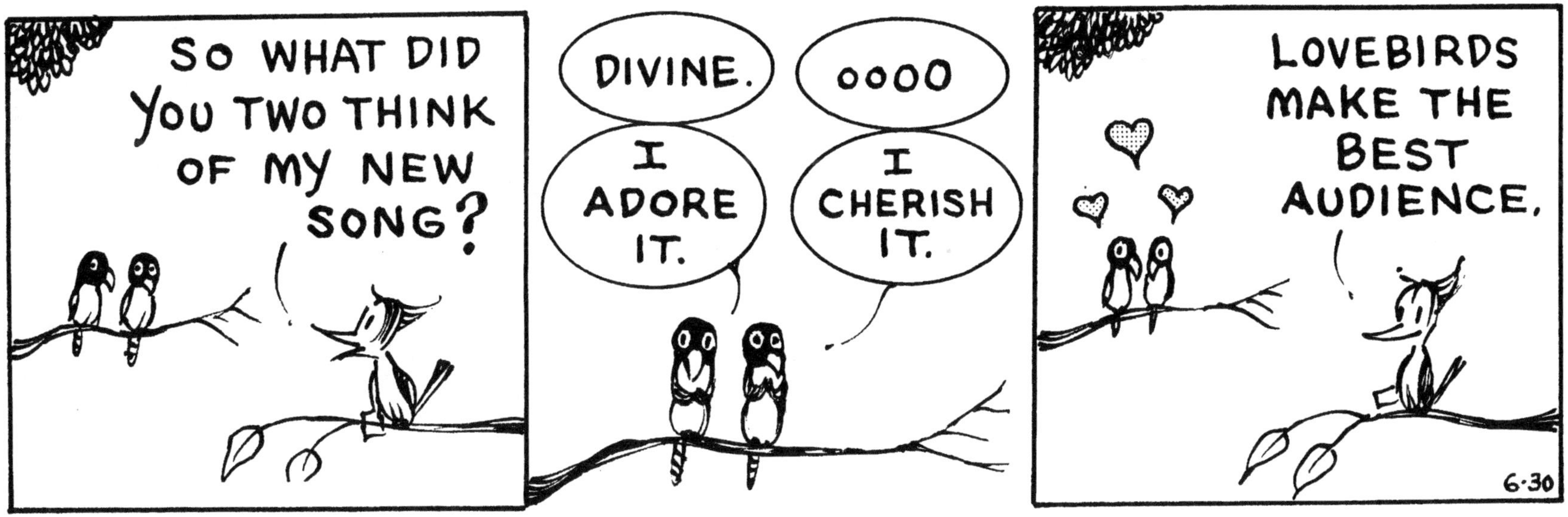
SO WHAT DID YOU TWO THINK OF MY NEW SONG?
DIVINE.
I ADORE IT.
OOOO
I CHERISH IT.
LOVEBIRDS MAKE THE BEST AUDIENCE.
6·30

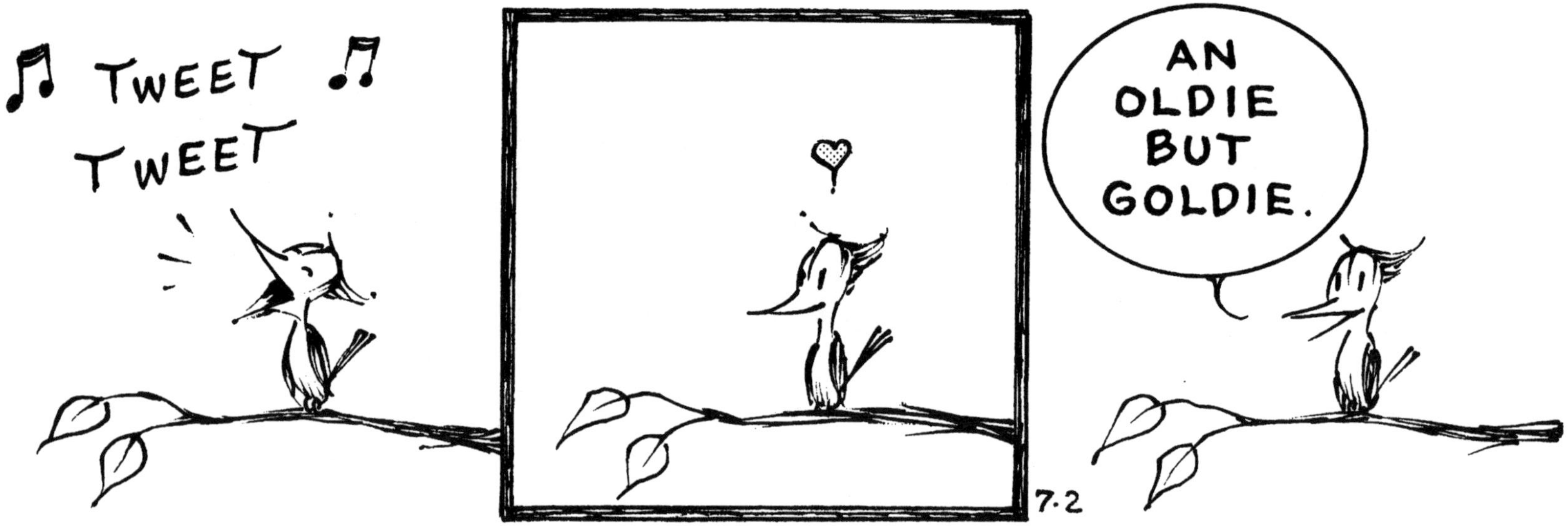
TWEET
TWEET
AN OLDIE BUT GOLDIE.
7.2

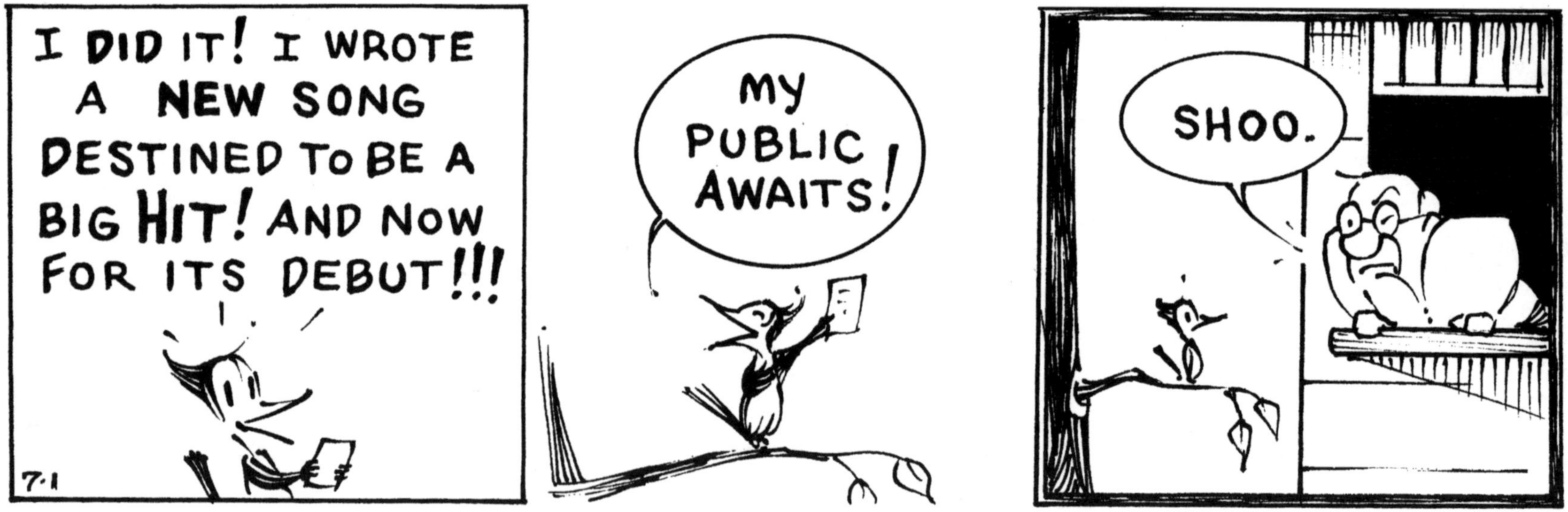
I DID IT! I WROTE A NEW SONG DESTINED TO BE A BIG HIT! AND NOW FOR ITS DEBUT!!!
7.1
MY PUBLIC AWAITS!
SHOO.

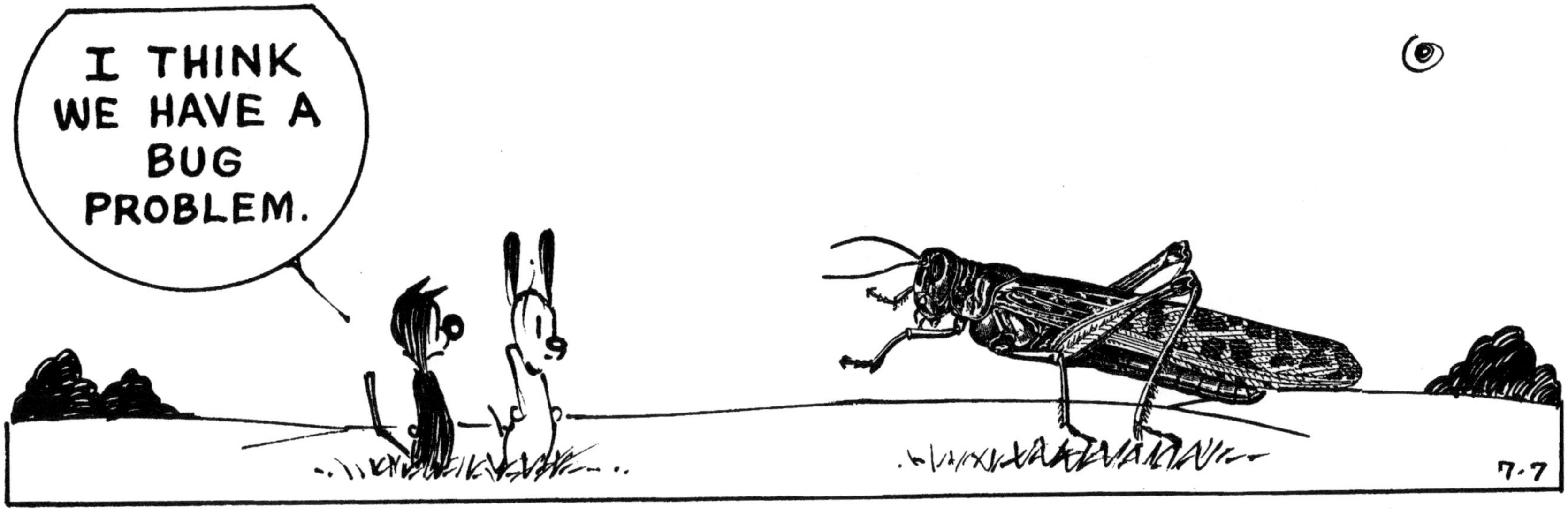
I THINK WE HAVE A BUG PROBLEM.
7·7

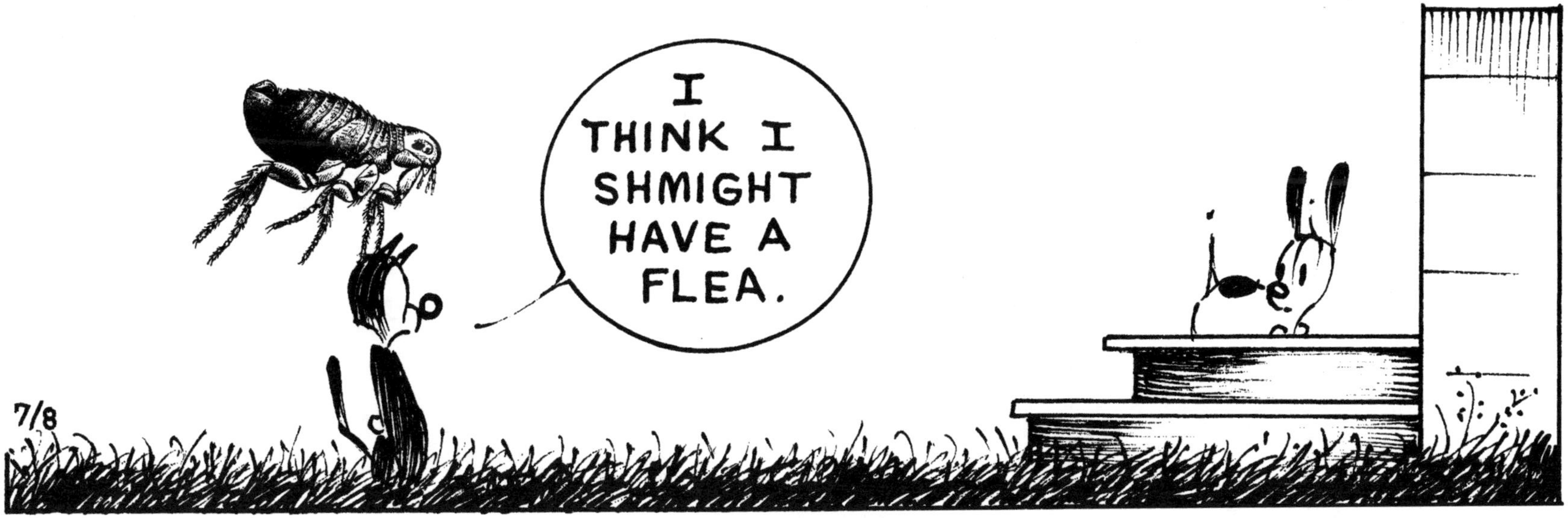
I THINK I SHMIGHT HAVE A FLEA.
7/8

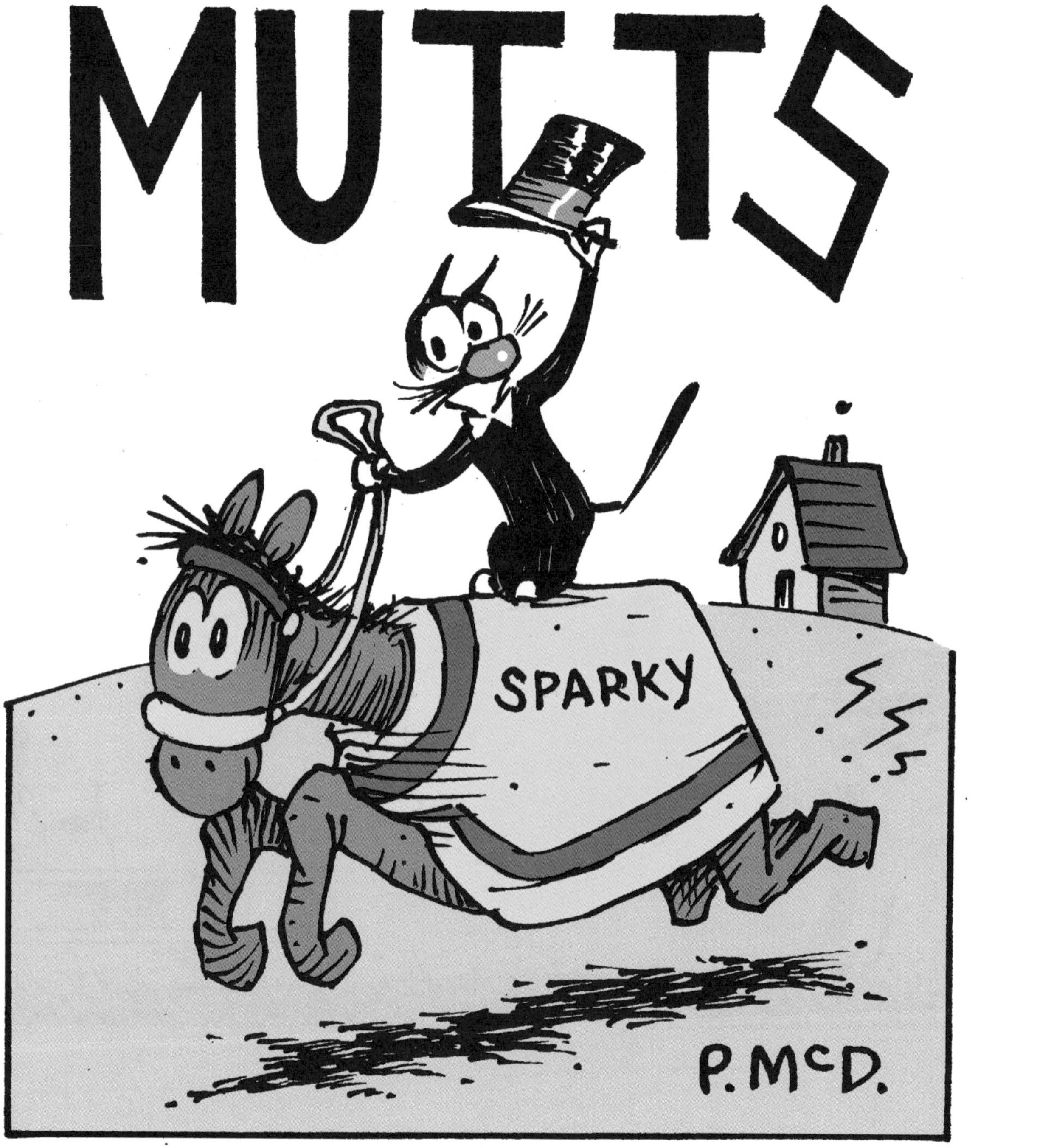
MUTTS
SPARKY
P. McD.

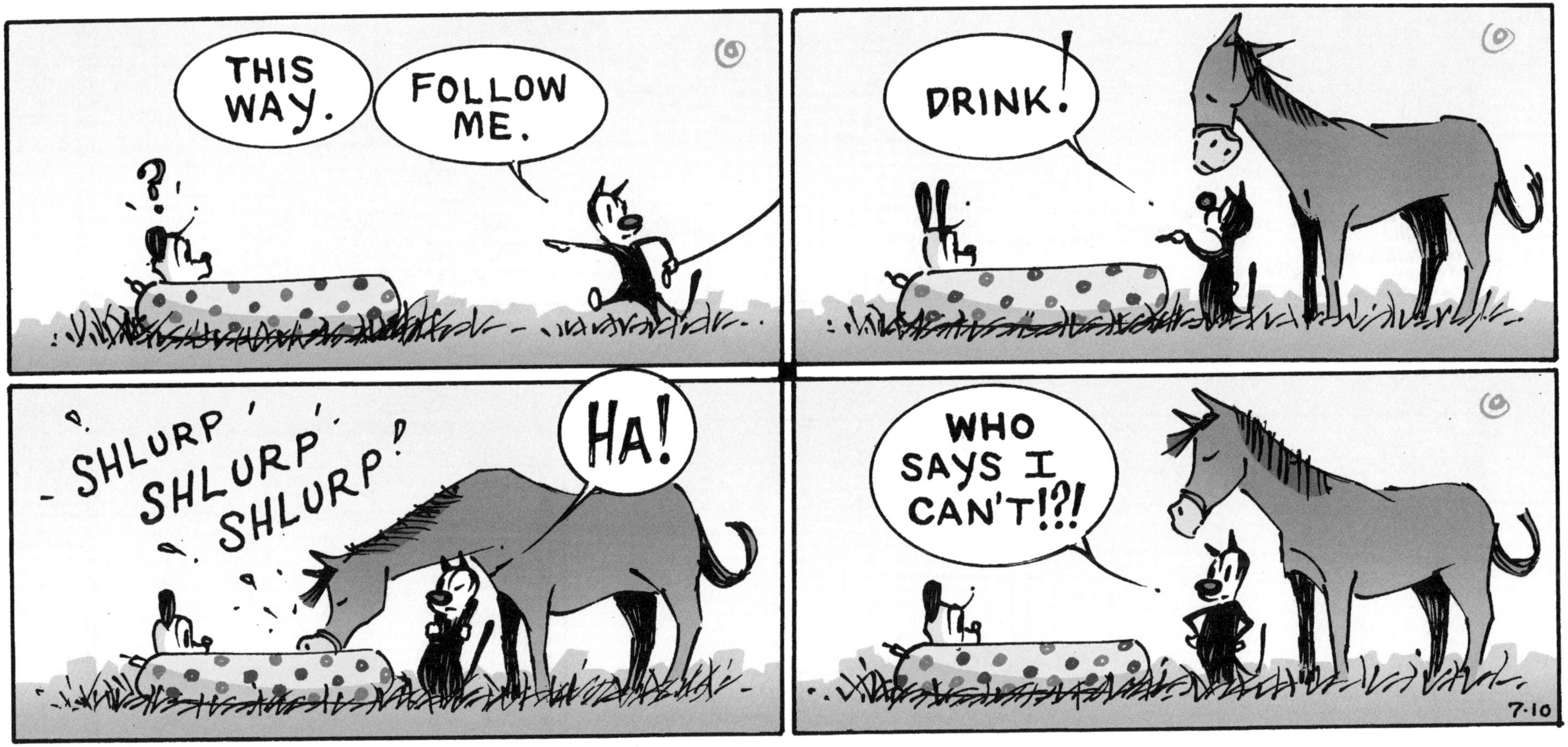
THIS WAY.
FOLLOW ME.
?
DRINK!
SHLURP SHLURP SHLURP!
HA!
WHO SAYS I CAN'T!?!
7·10

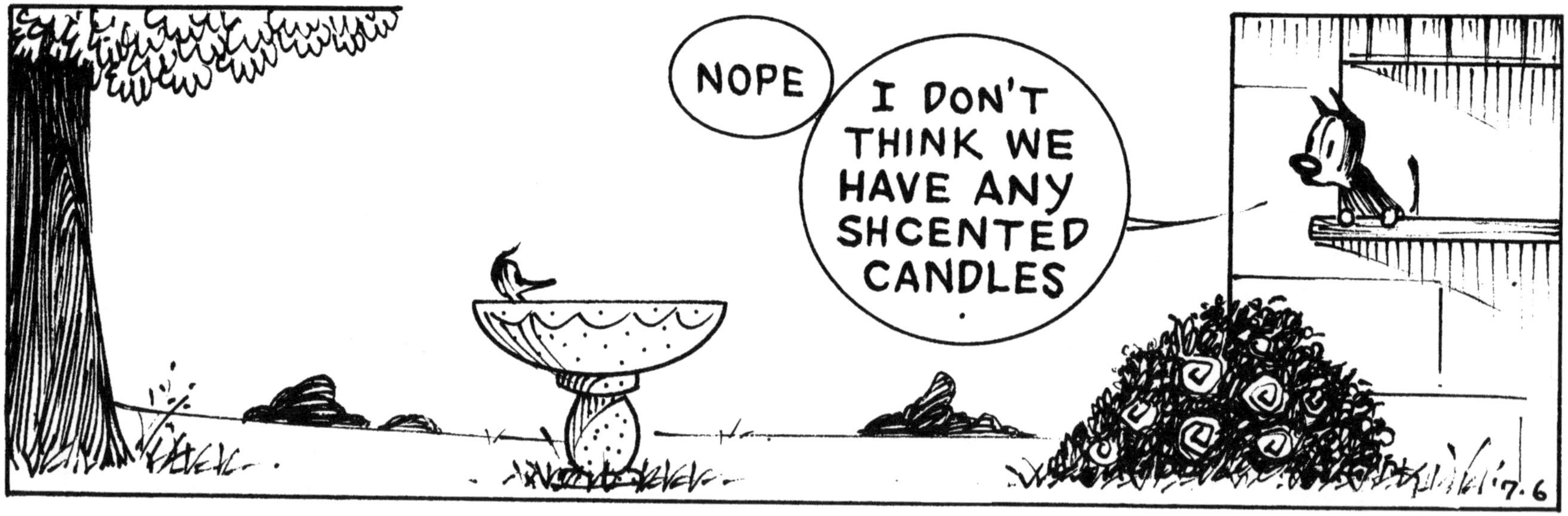
NOPE
I DON'T THINK WE HAVE ANY SHCENTED CANDLES.
7.6

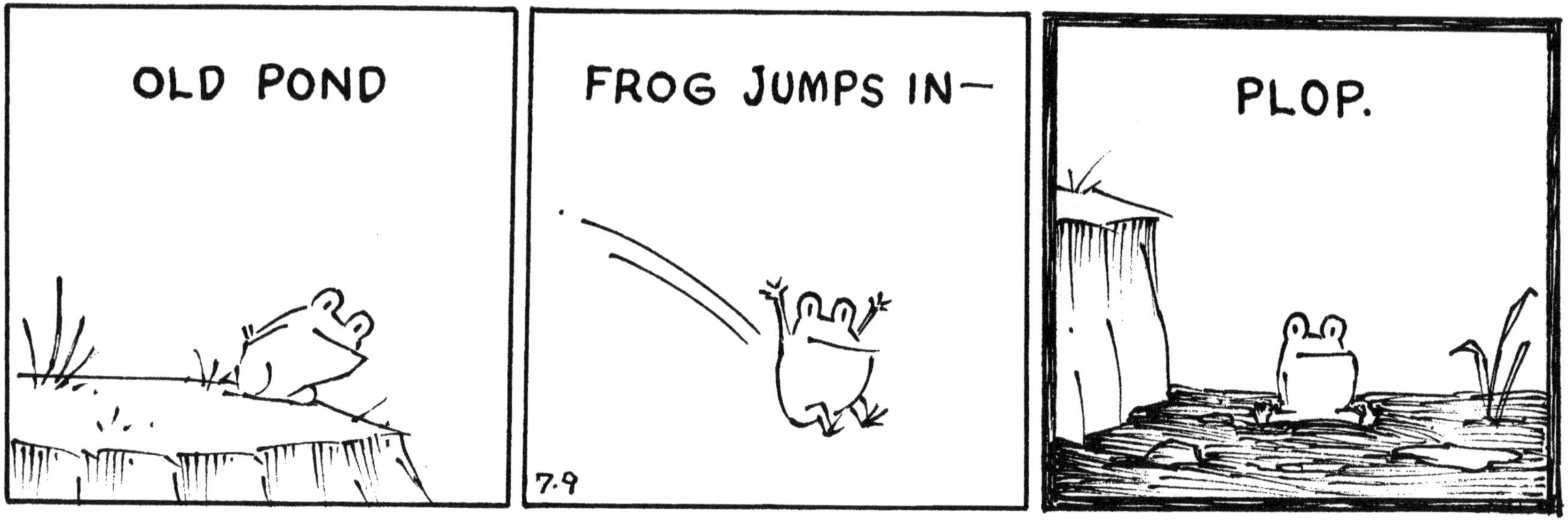
OLD POND
FROG JUMPS IN—
7.9
PLOP.

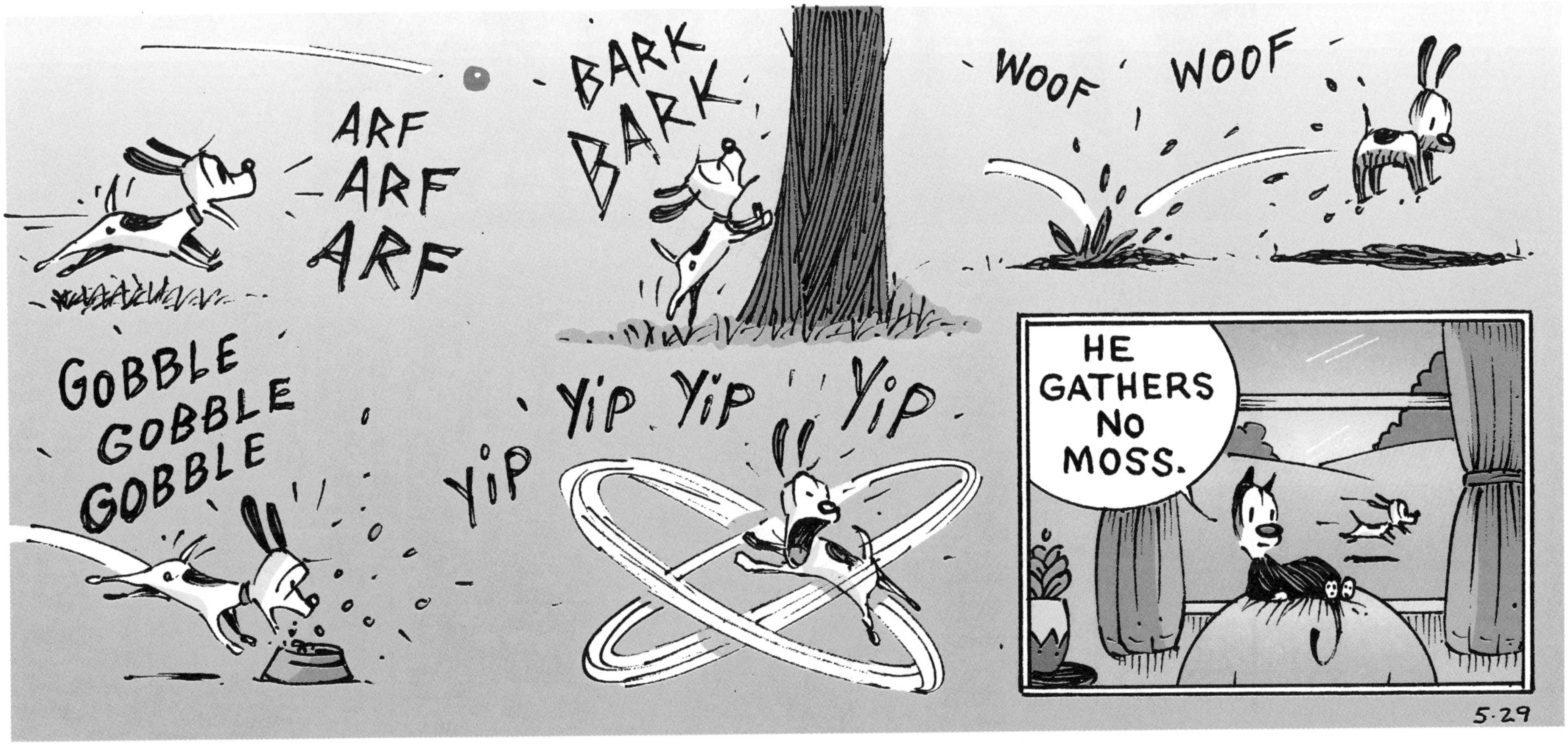
ARF
ARF
ARF
BARK
BARK
WOOF
WOOF
GOBBLE
GOBBLE
GOBBLE
YIP
YIP
YIP
YIP
HE GATHERS NO MOSS.
5·29

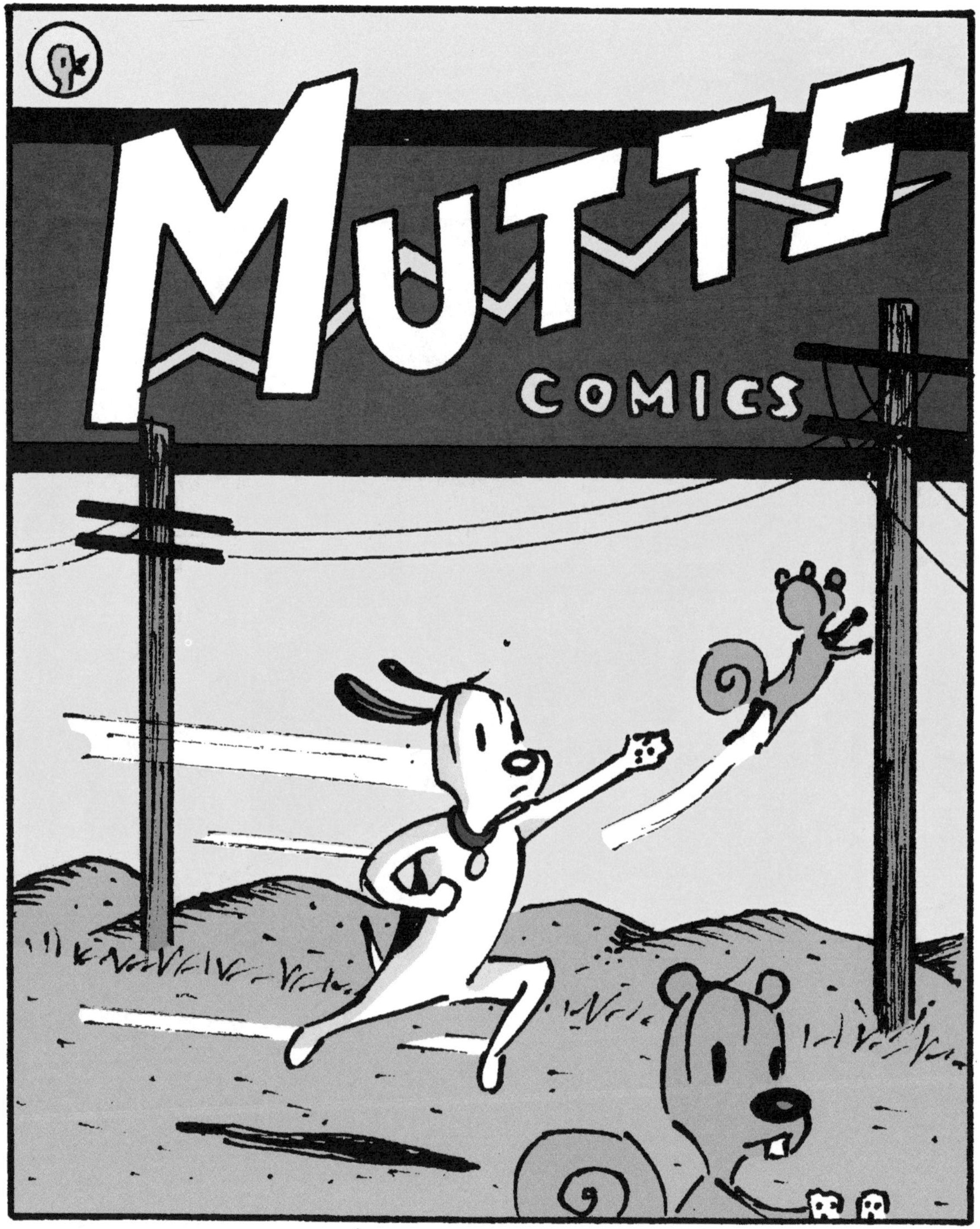
MUTTS
COMICS

COMIC "CONS"
DOCTOR SHTRANGE
HE'S MAKING HIS DRY FOOD
DISAPPEAR!
7.21

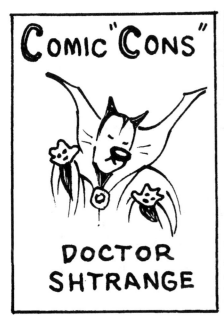

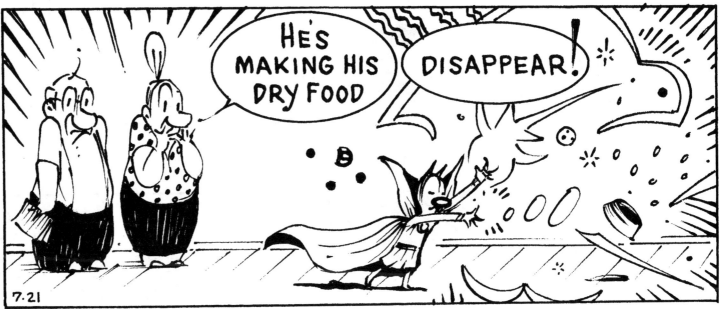

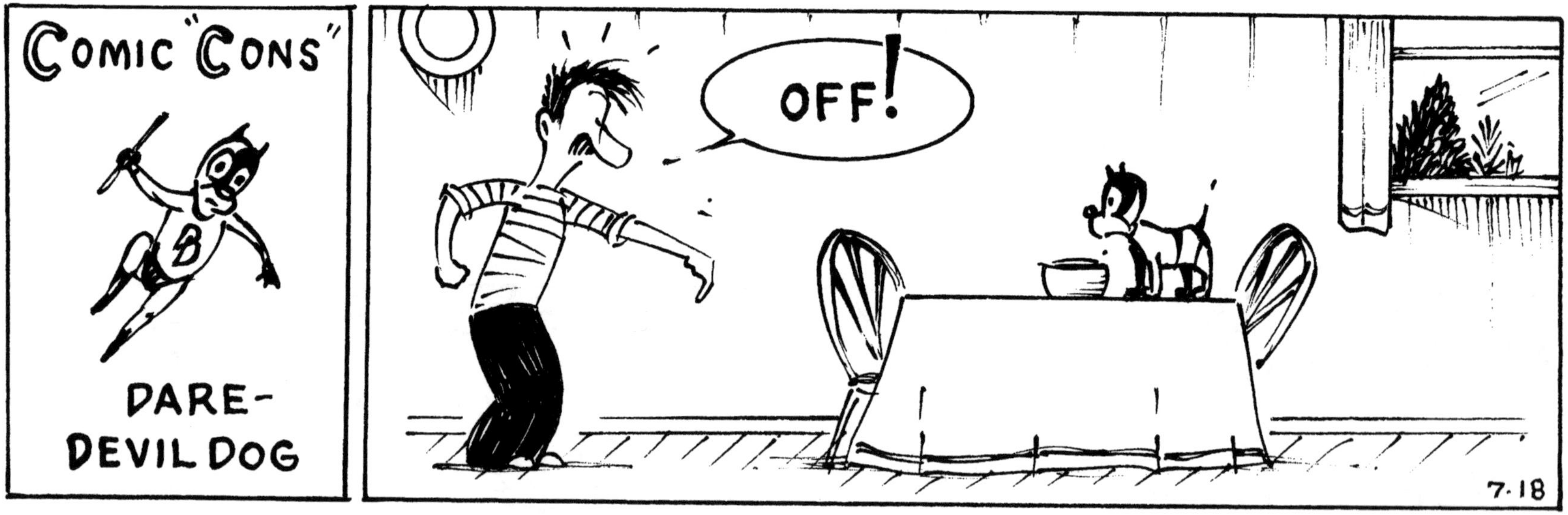
COMIC "CONS"
DARE-DEVIL DOG
OFF!
7-18

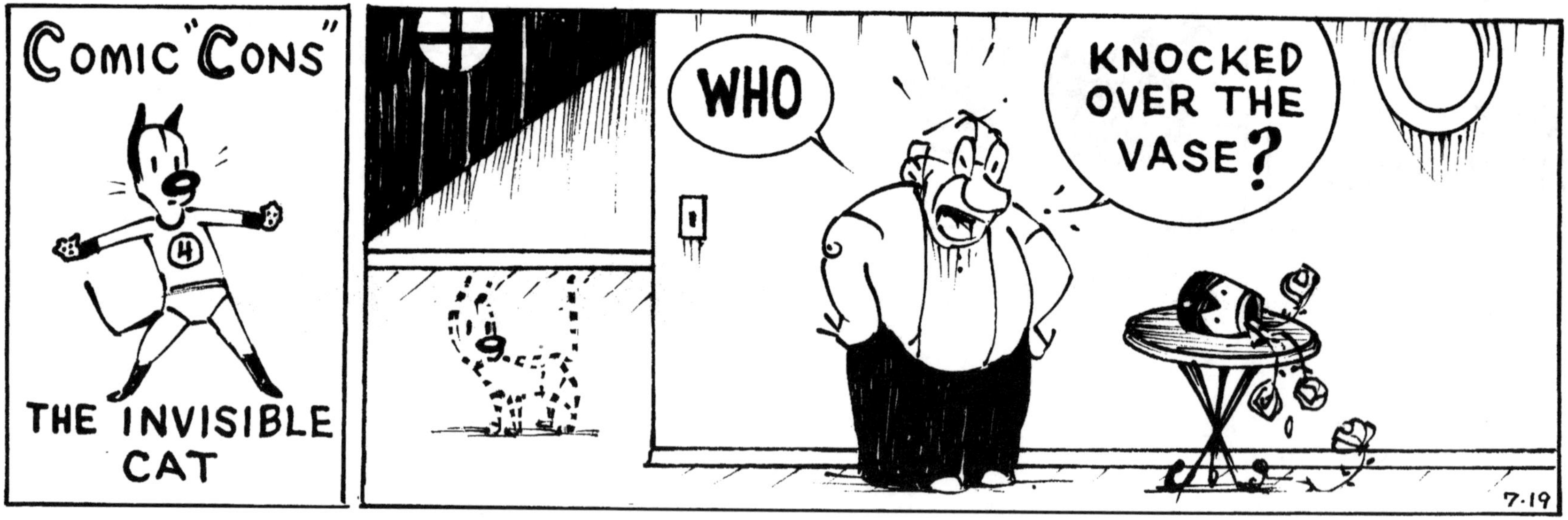
COMIC "CONS"
THE INVISIBLE CAT
WHO
KNOCKED OVER THE VASE?
7-19

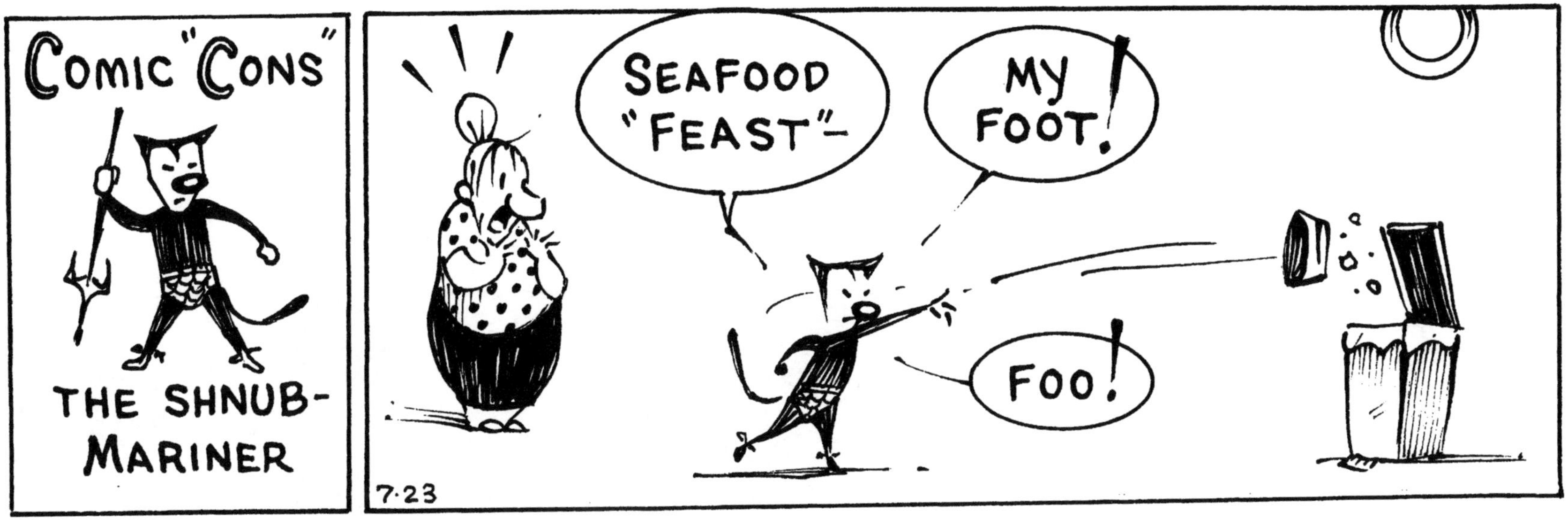
COMIC "CONS"
THE SHNUB-MARINER
SEAFOOD "FEAST"–
MY FOOT!
FOO!
7·23

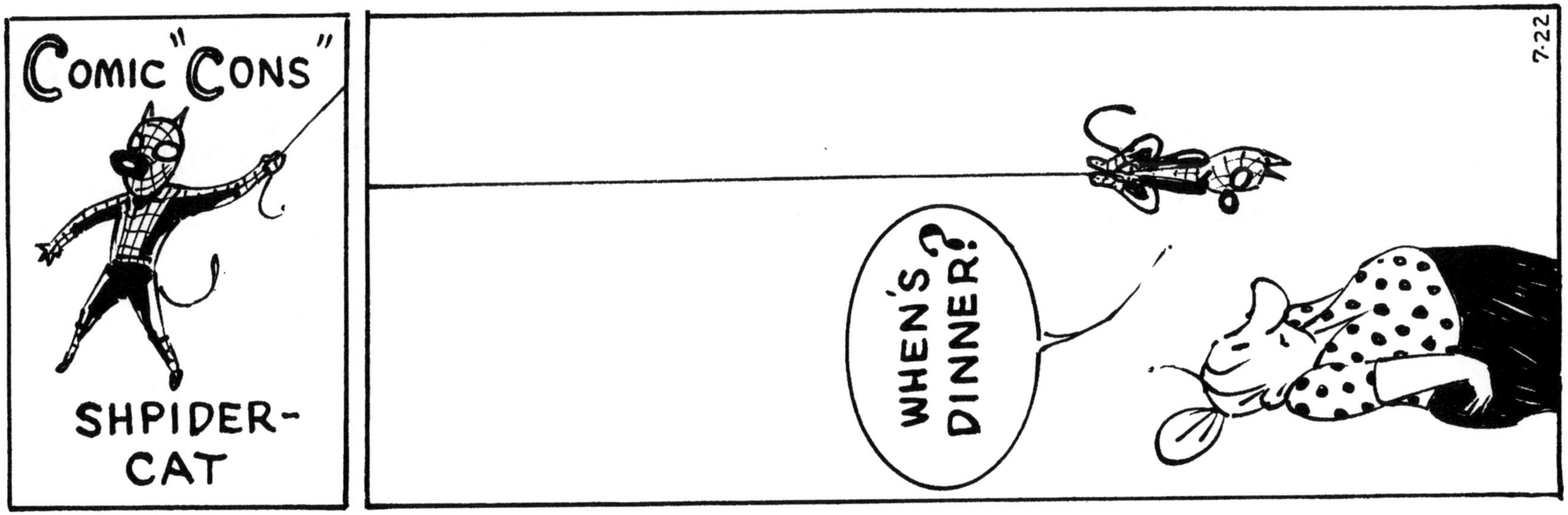
COMIC "CONS"
SHPIDER-CAT
7·22
WHEN'S DINNER?

COMIC "CONS"
THE WATCHER DOG
NOW
I'VE SEEN EVERY-THING.
7·20

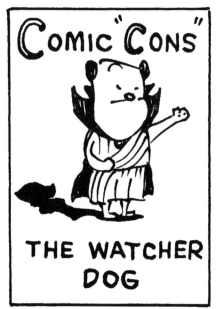

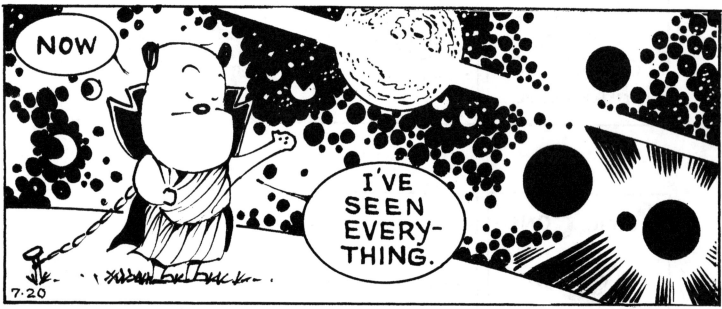

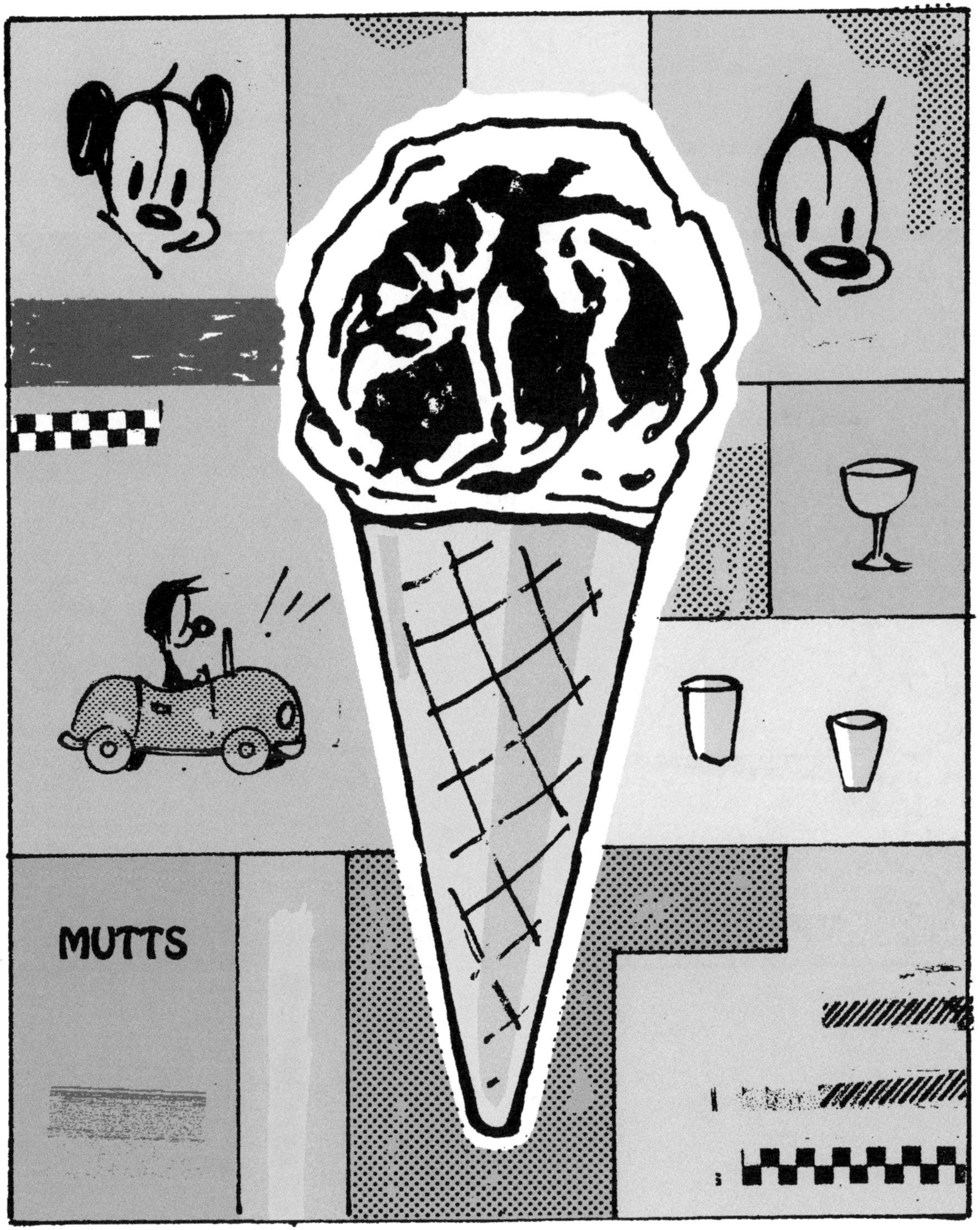
MUTTS

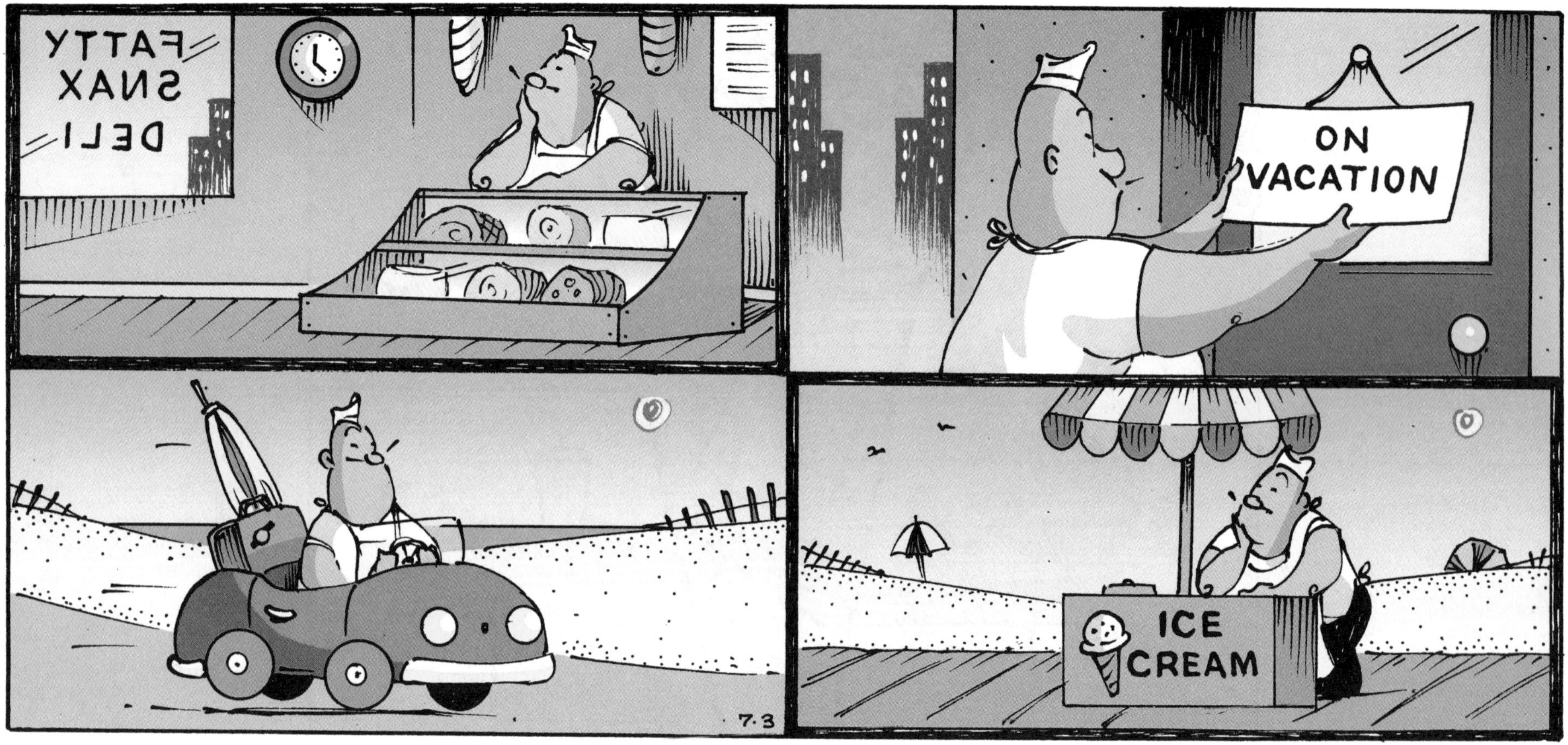
FATTY SNAX DELI
ON VACATION
7-3
ICE CREAM

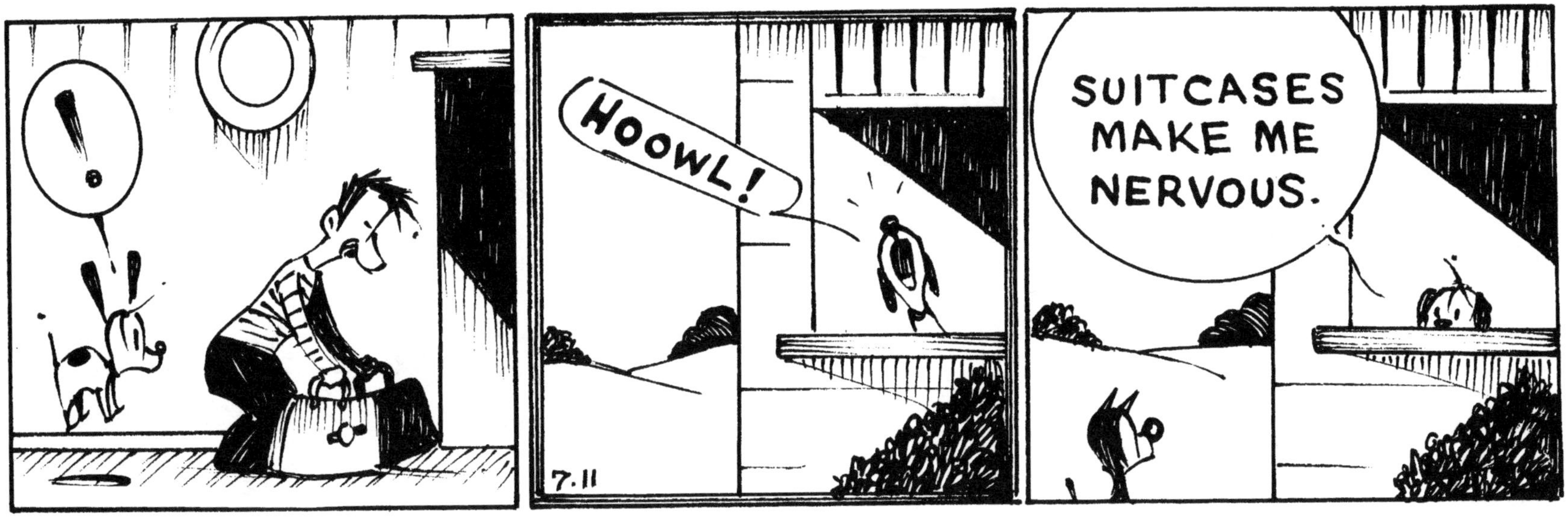
!
HOOWL!
SUITCASES MAKE ME NERVOUS.
7.11

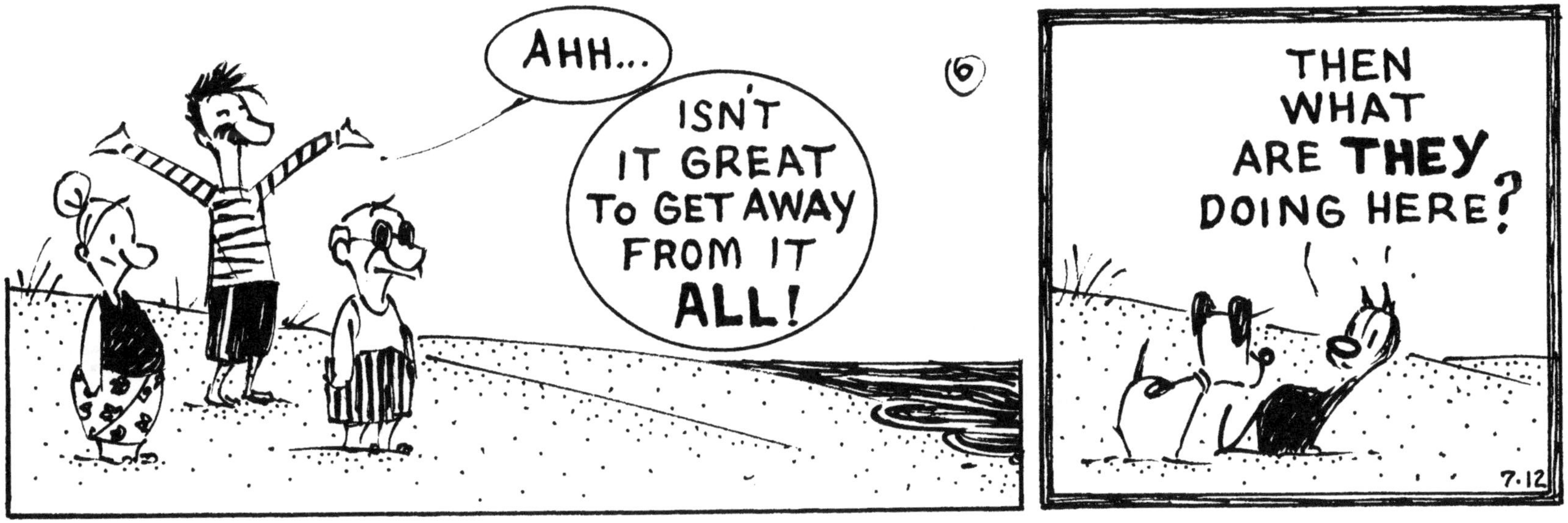
AHH...
ISN'T IT GREAT TO GET AWAY FROM IT ALL!
THEN WHAT ARE THEY DOING HERE?
7.12

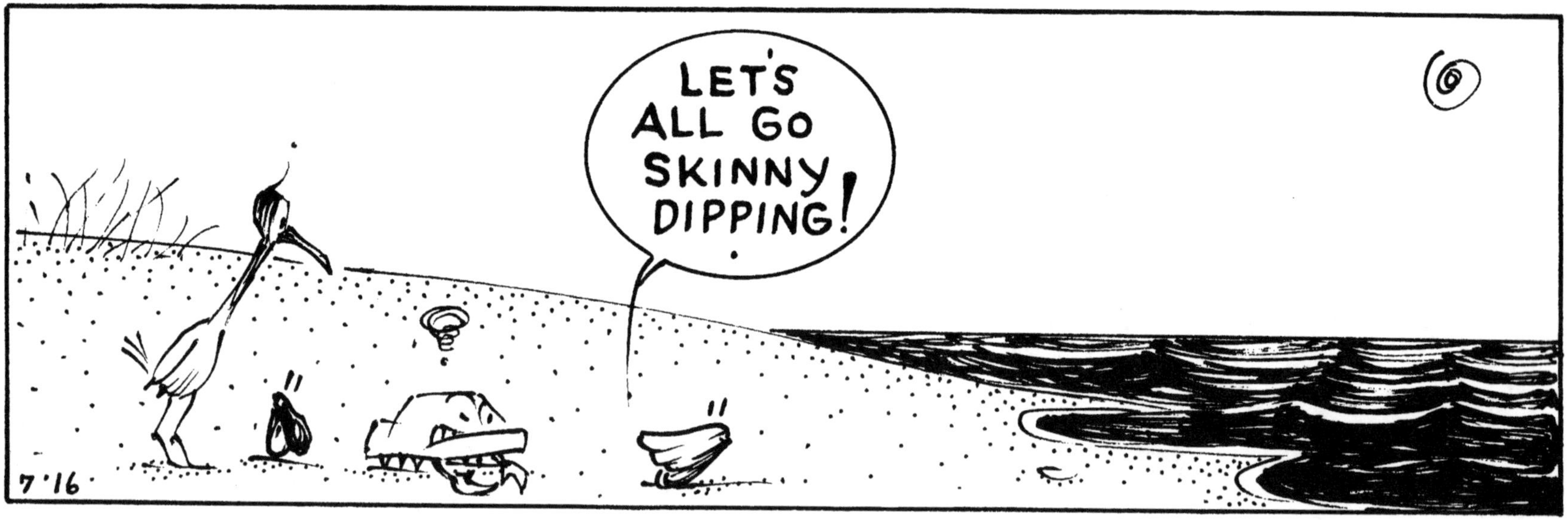
LET'S ALL GO SKINNY DIPPING!
7'16

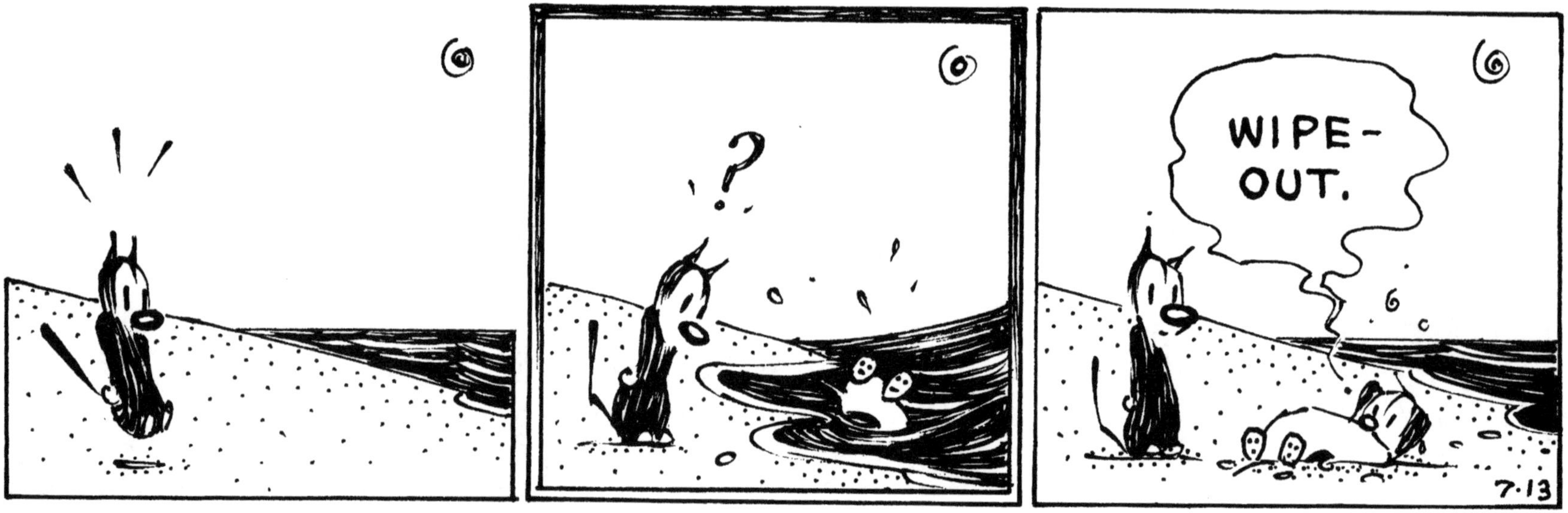
?
WIPE-OUT.
7·13

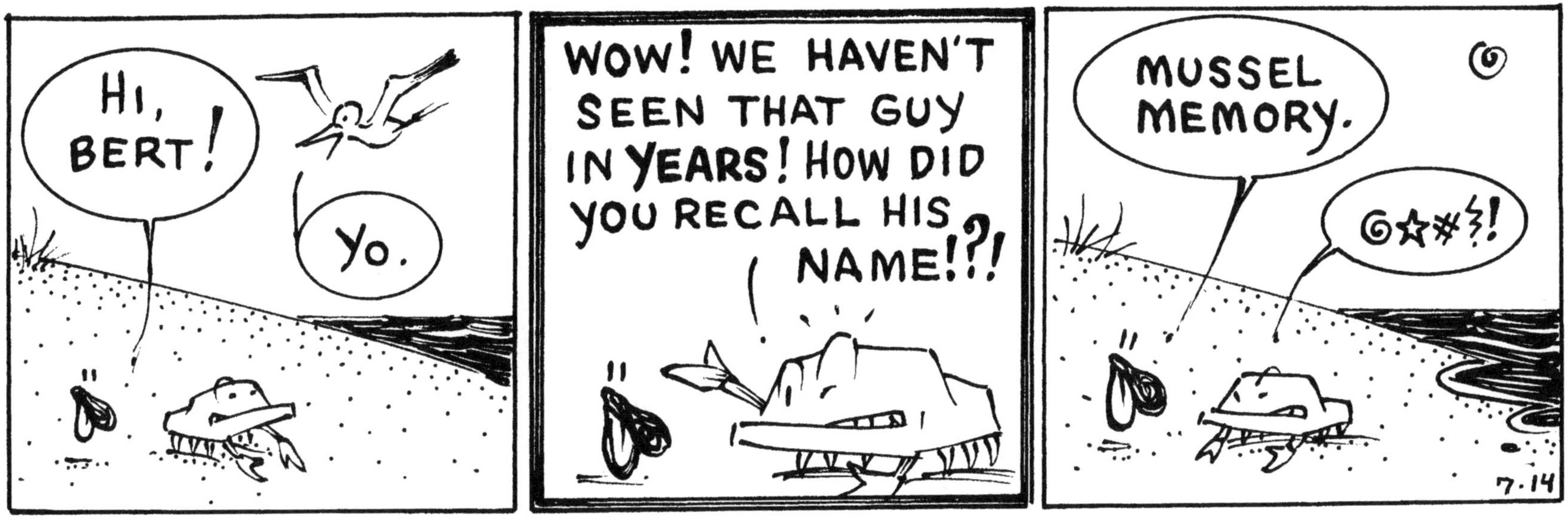
HI, BERT!
YO.
WOW! WE HAVEN'T SEEN THAT GUY IN YEARS! HOW DID YOU RECALL HIS NAME!?!
MUSSEL MEMORY.
7.14

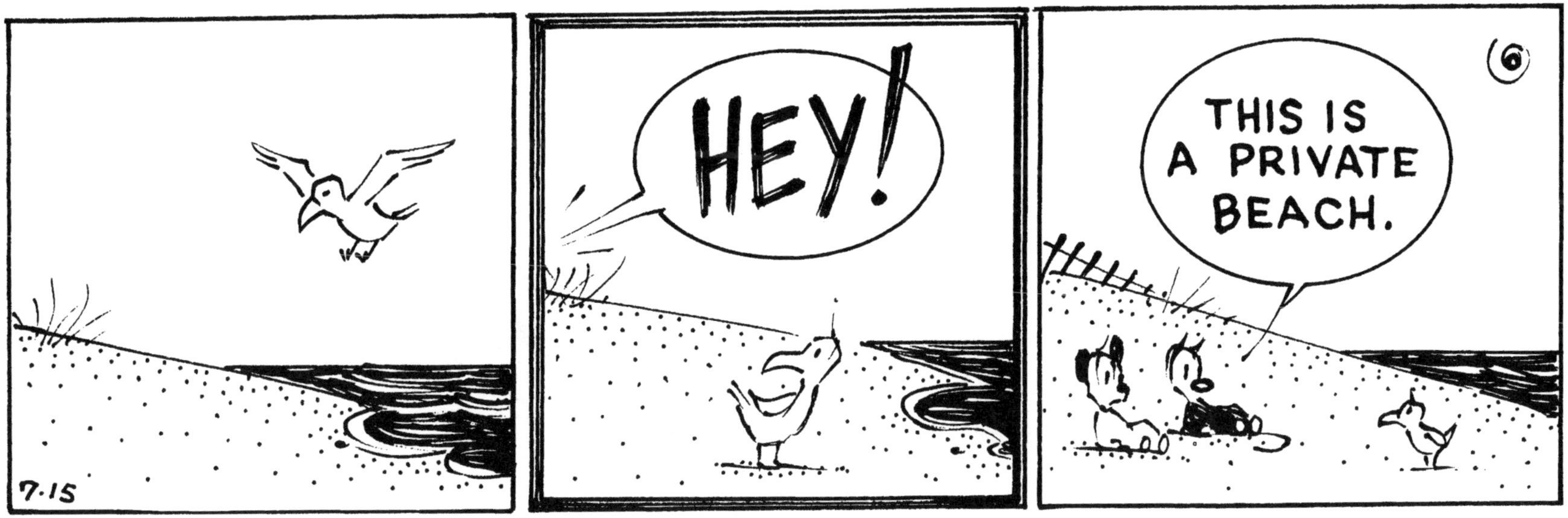
7.15
HEY!
THIS IS A PRIVATE BEACH.

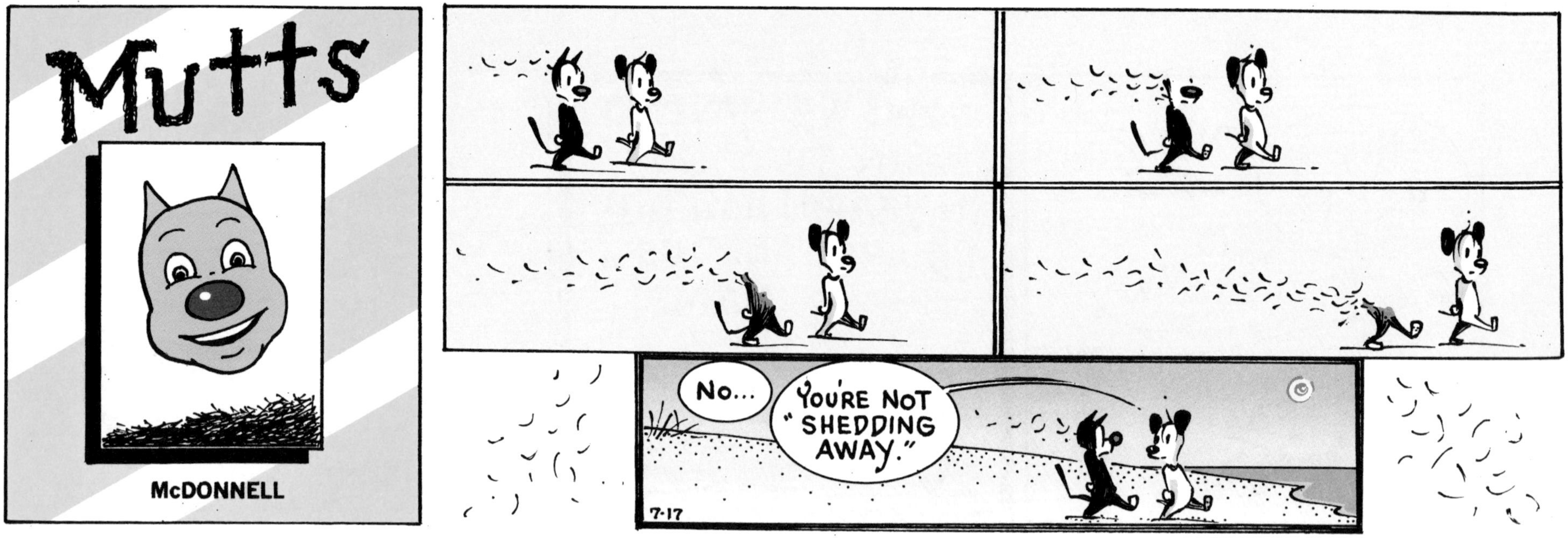
Mutts
McDONNELL
No...
YOU'RE NOT "SHEDDING AWAY."
7·17

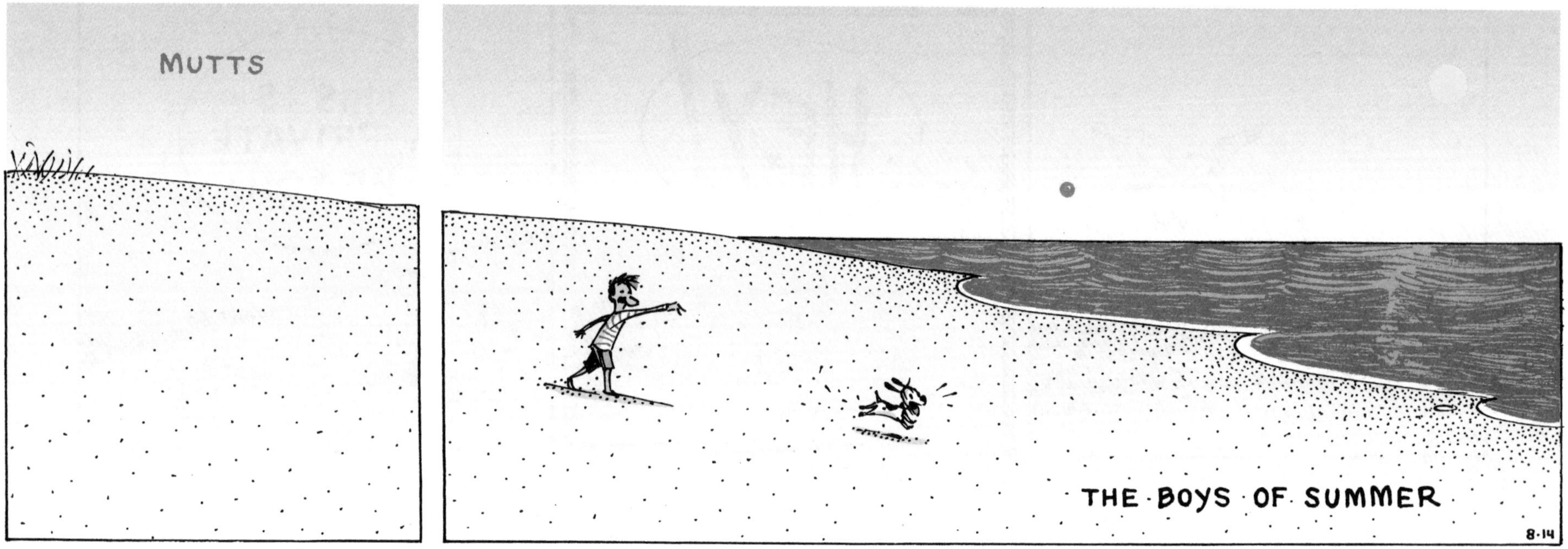
MUTTS
THE · BOYS · OF · SUMMER
8·14

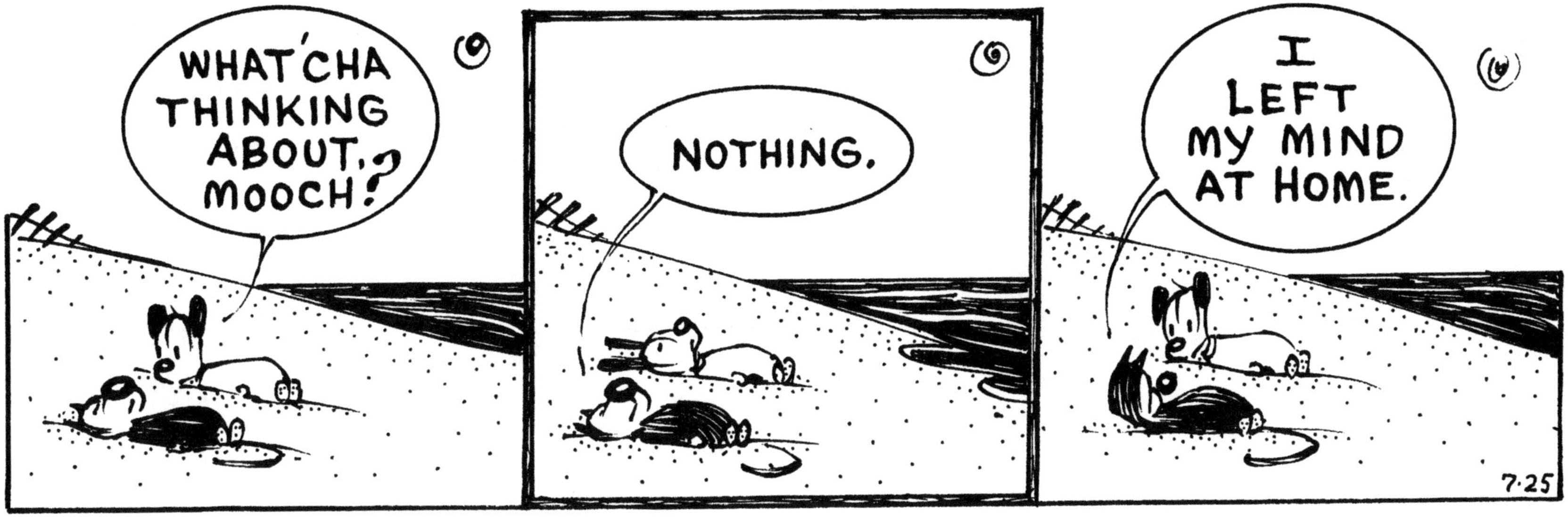
WHAT'CHA THINKING ABOUT, MOOCH?
NOTHING.
I LEFT MY MIND AT HOME.
7·25

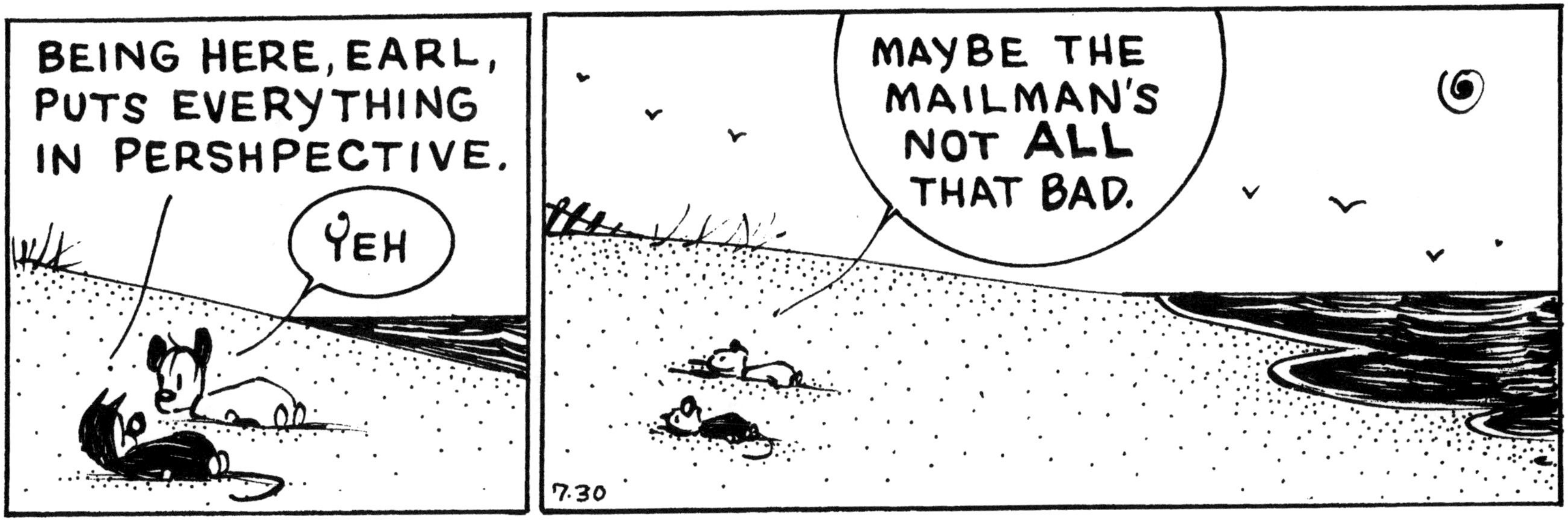
BEING HERE, EARL, PUTS EVERYTHING IN PERSHPECTIVE.
YEH
MAYBE THE MAILMAN'S NOT ALL THAT BAD.
7·30

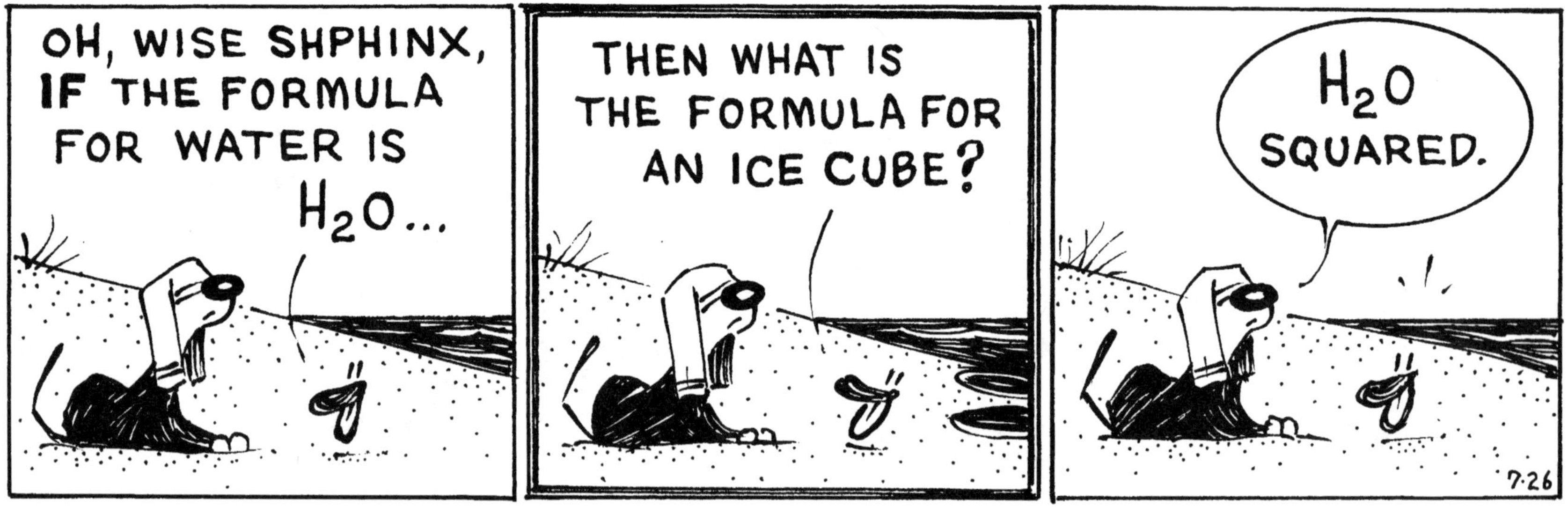
OH, WISE SHPHINX, **IF** THE FORMULA FOR WATER IS H_2O...
THEN WHAT IS THE FORMULA FOR AN ICE CUBE?
H_2O SQUARED.
7·26

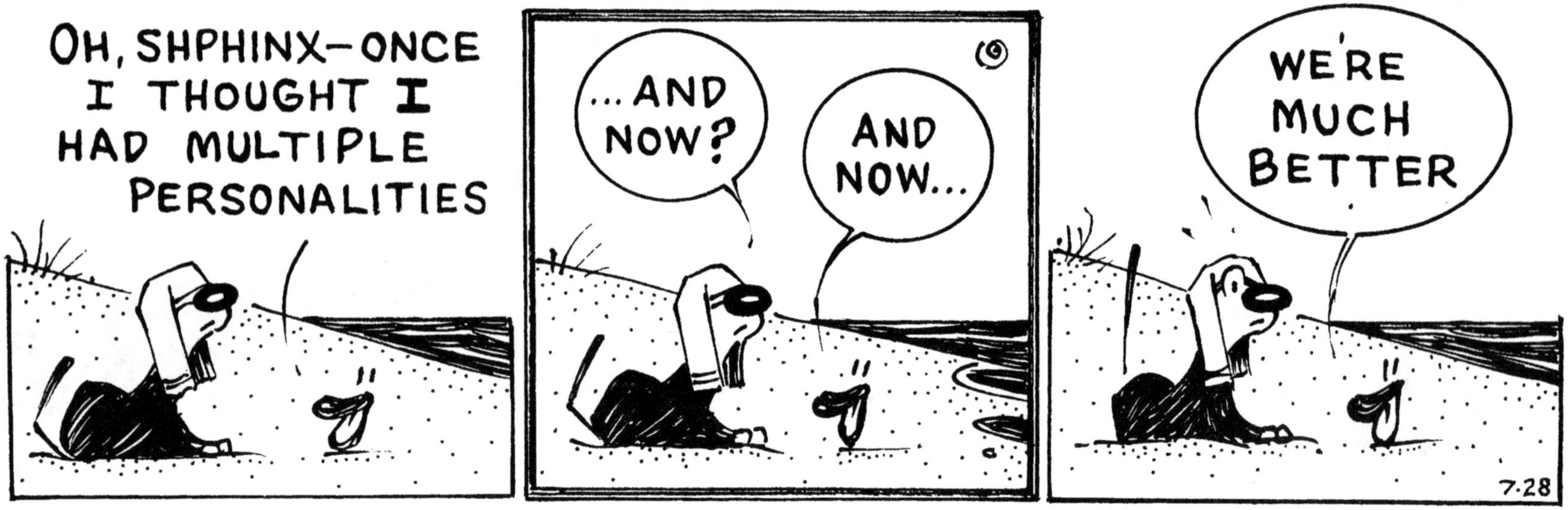
OH, SHPHINX—ONCE I THOUGHT **I** HAD MULTIPLE PERSONALITIES
...AND NOW?
AND NOW...
WE'RE MUCH BETTER
7·28

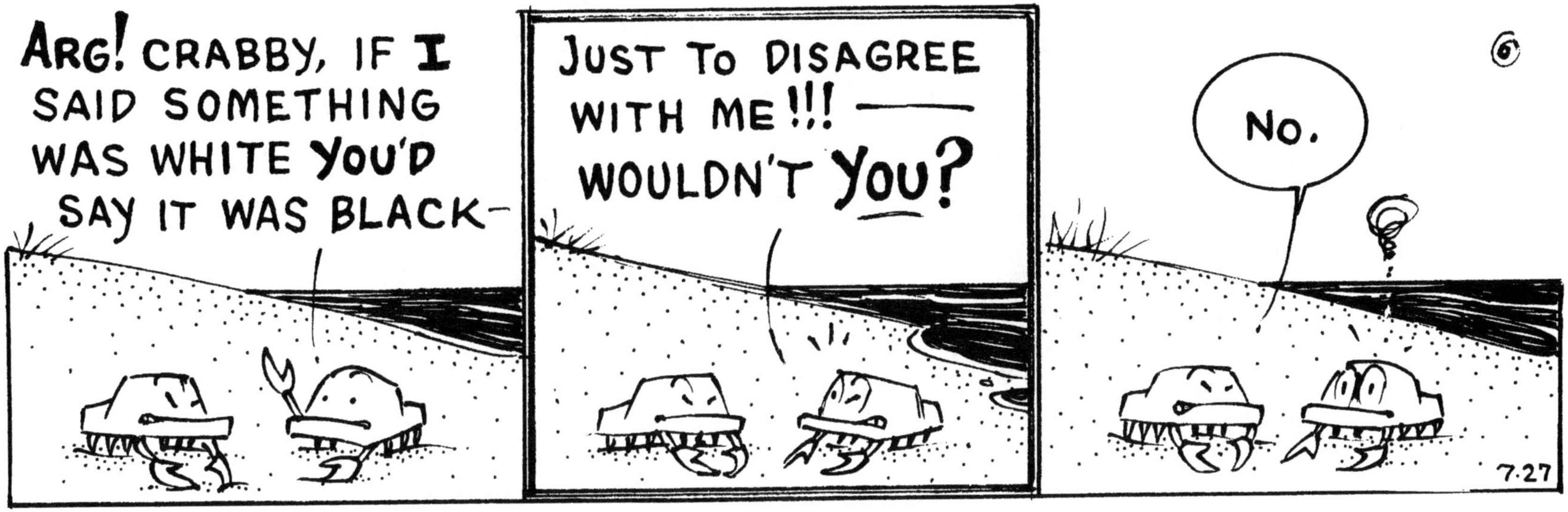
ARG! CRABBY, IF I SAID SOMETHING WAS WHITE YOU'D SAY IT WAS BLACK–
JUST TO DISAGREE WITH ME!!! — WOULDN'T YOU?
NO.
7·27

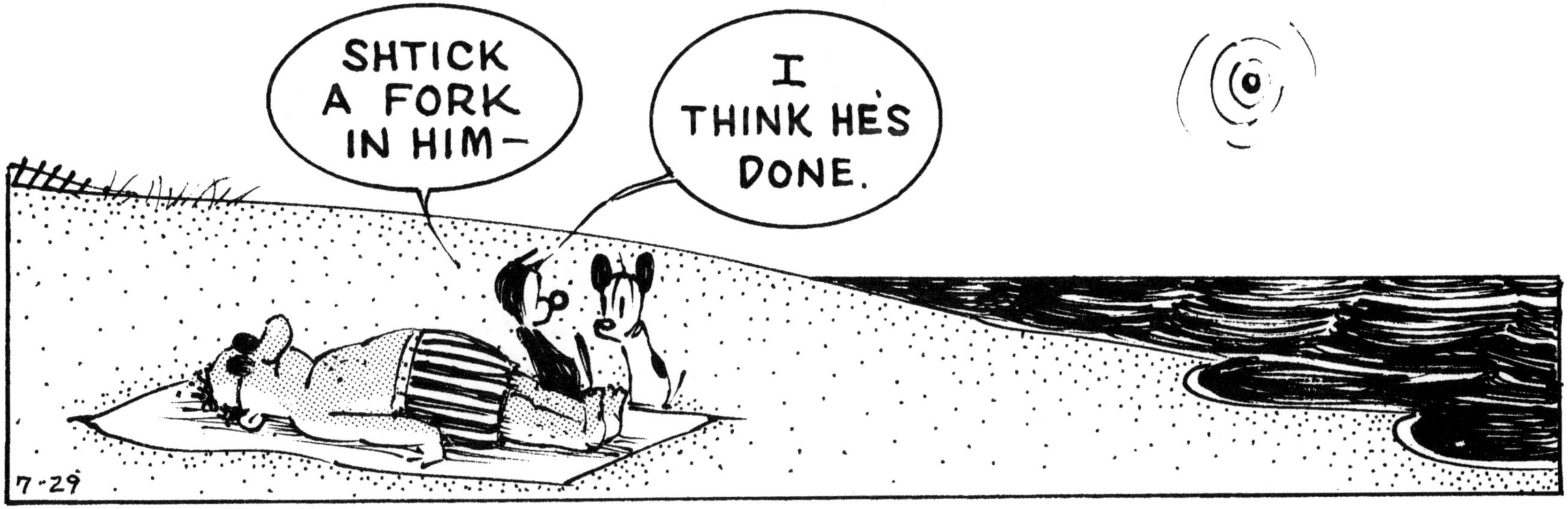
SHTICK A FORK IN HIM–
I THINK HE'S DONE.
7-29

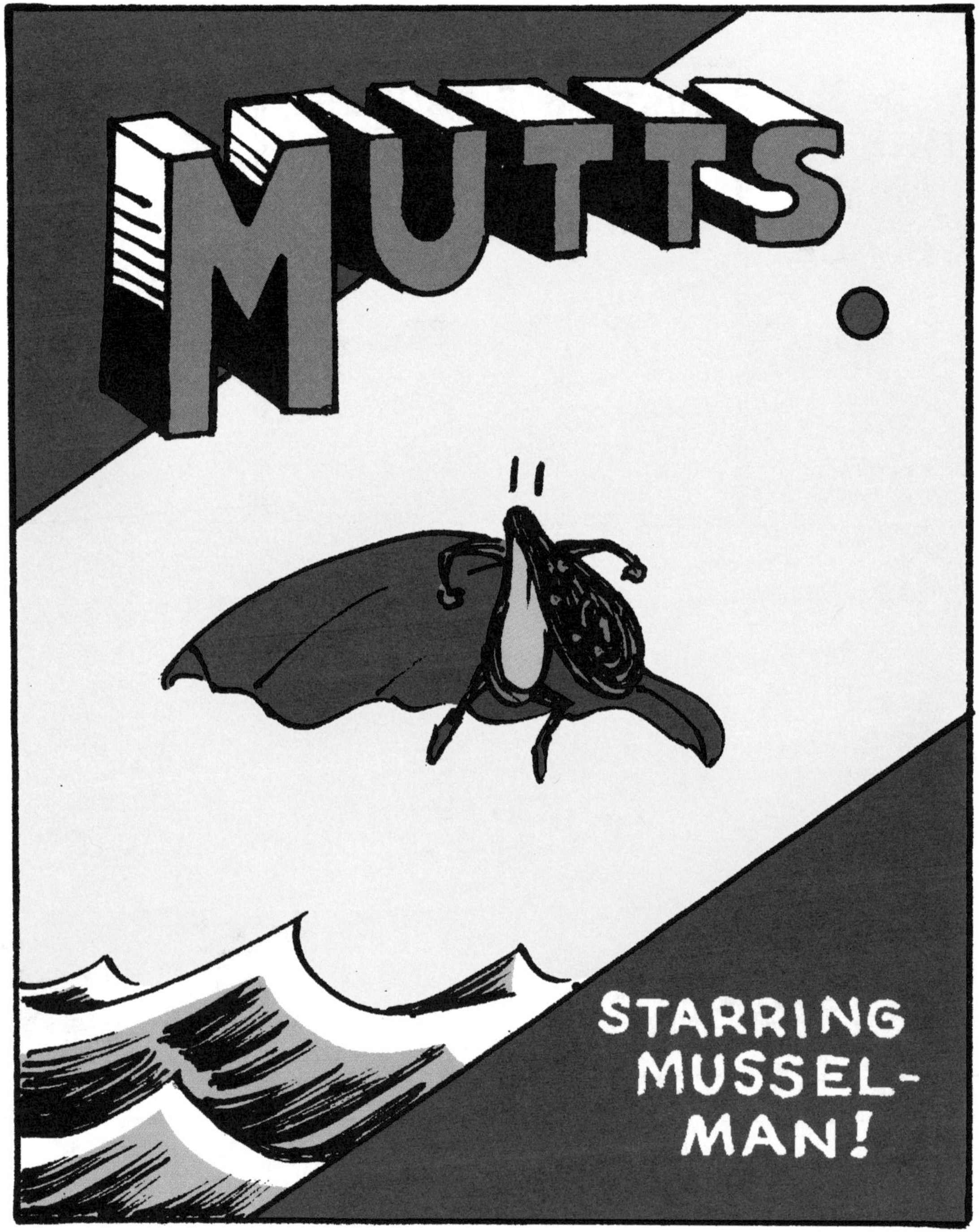
MUTTS.
STARRING MUSSEL-MAN!

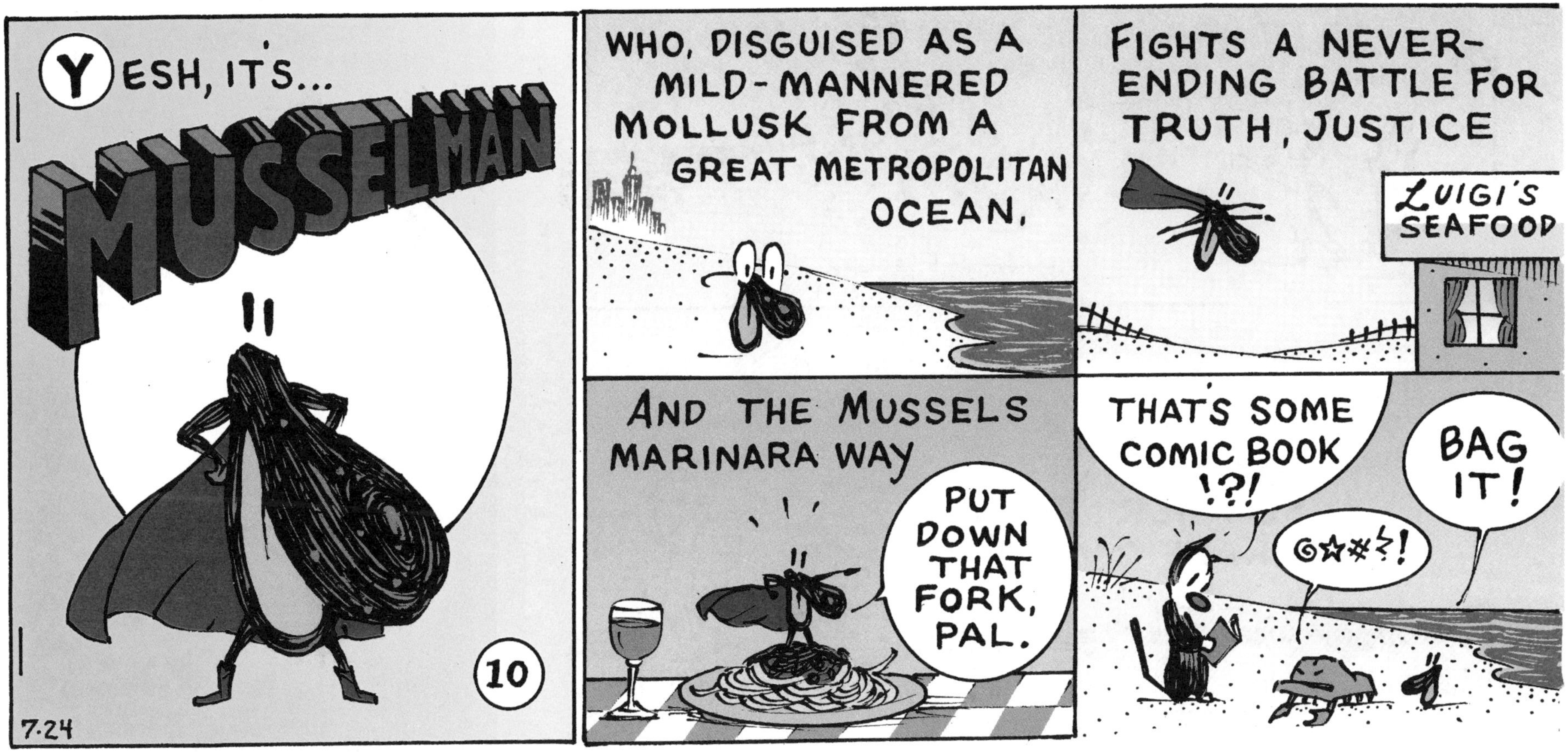
YESH, IT'S...
MUSSELMAN
10
7·24
WHO, DISGUISED AS A MILD-MANNERED MOLLUSK FROM A GREAT METROPOLITAN OCEAN,
FIGHTS A NEVER-ENDING BATTLE FOR TRUTH, JUSTICE
LUIGI'S SEAFOOD
AND THE MUSSELS MARINARA WAY
PUT DOWN THAT FORK, PAL.
THAT'S SOME COMIC BOOK !?!
BAG IT!
©☆#$!

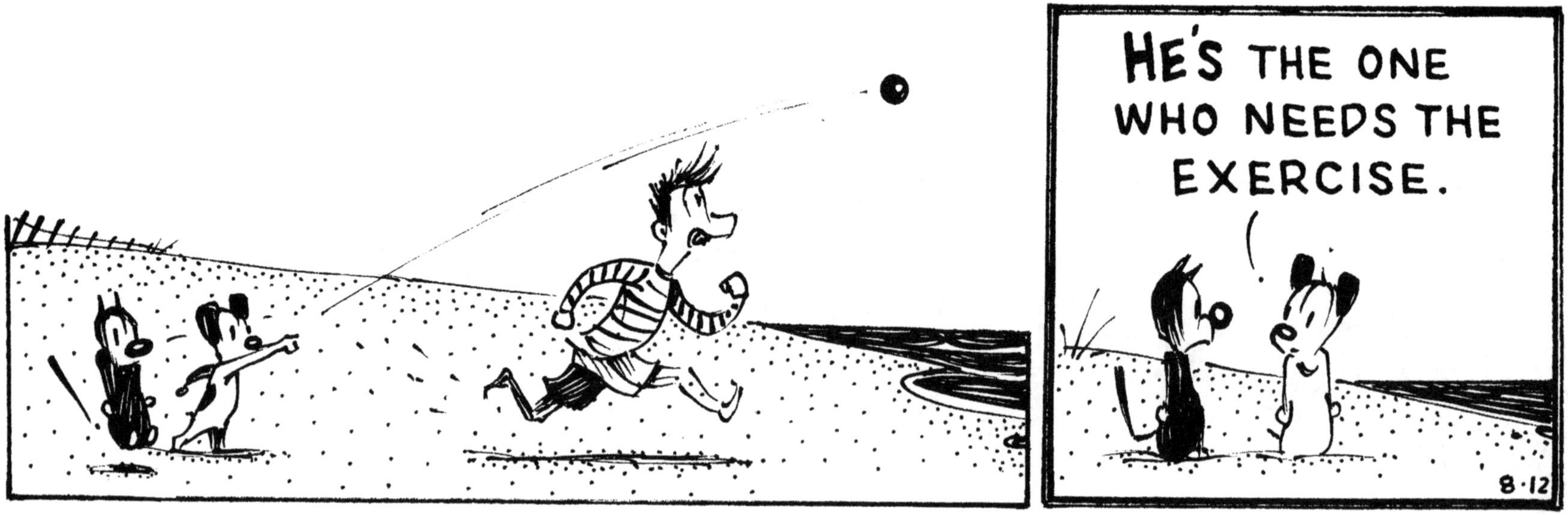
HE'S THE ONE WHO NEEDS THE EXERCISE.
8·12

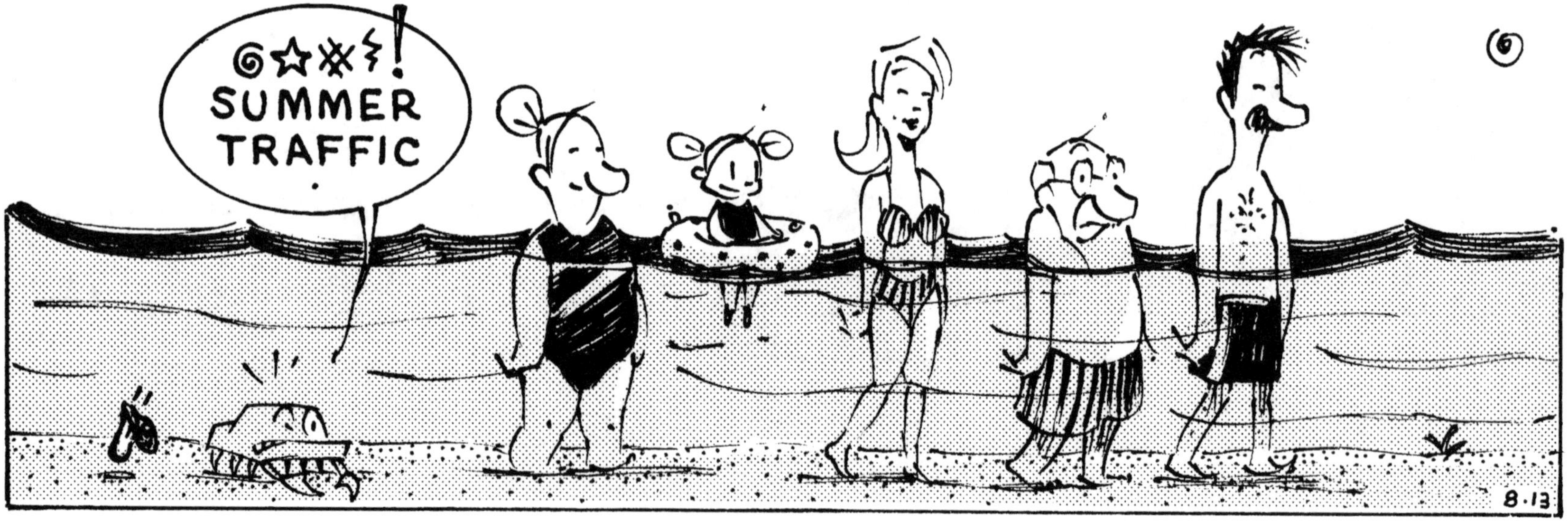
SUMMER TRAFFIC
8·13

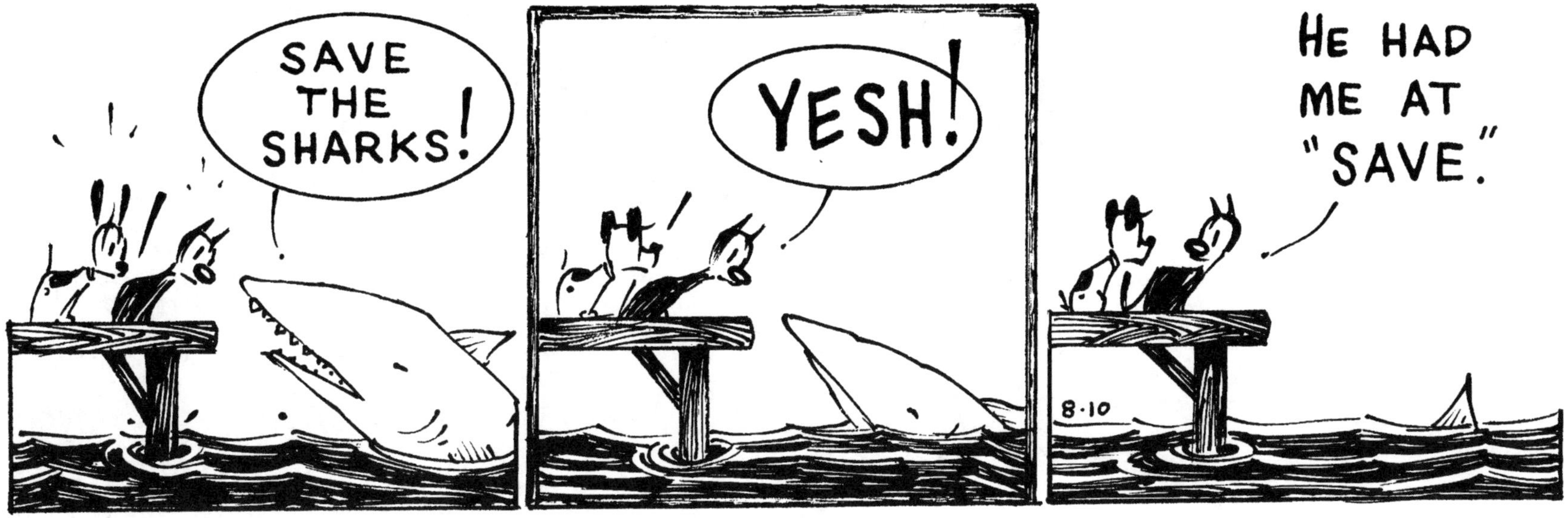
SAVE THE SHARKS!
YESH!
HE HAD ME AT "SAVE."
8·10

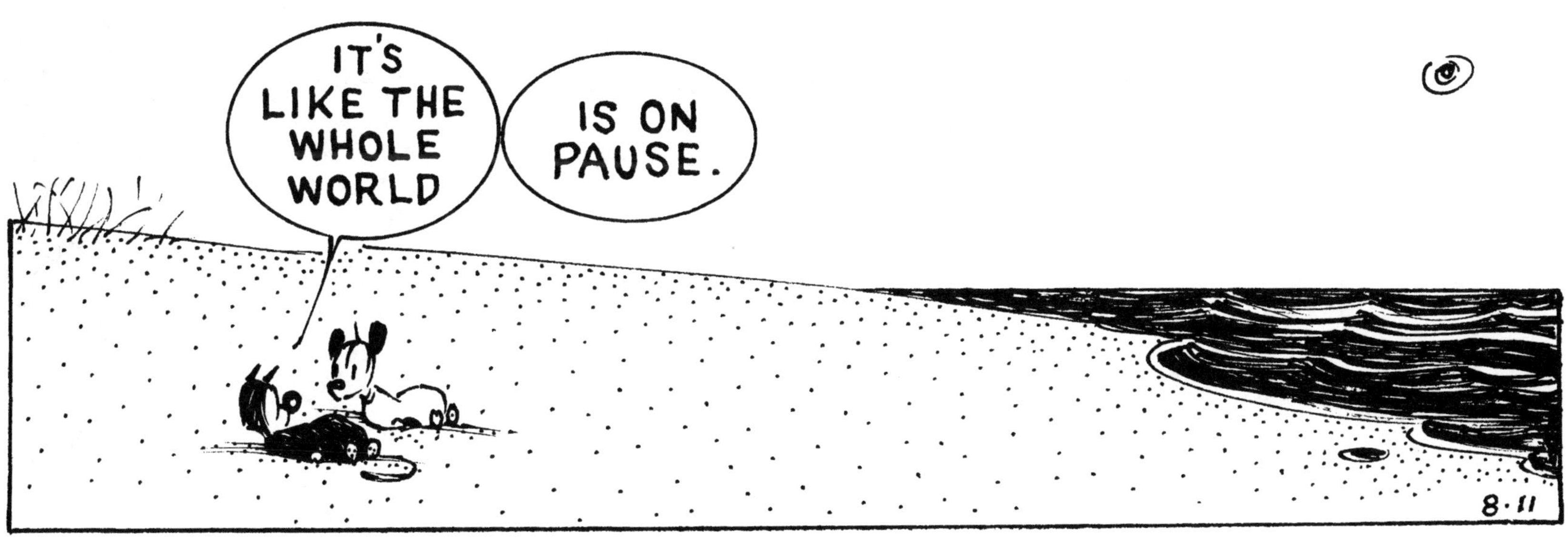
IT'S LIKE THE WHOLE WORLD
IS ON PAUSE.
8·11

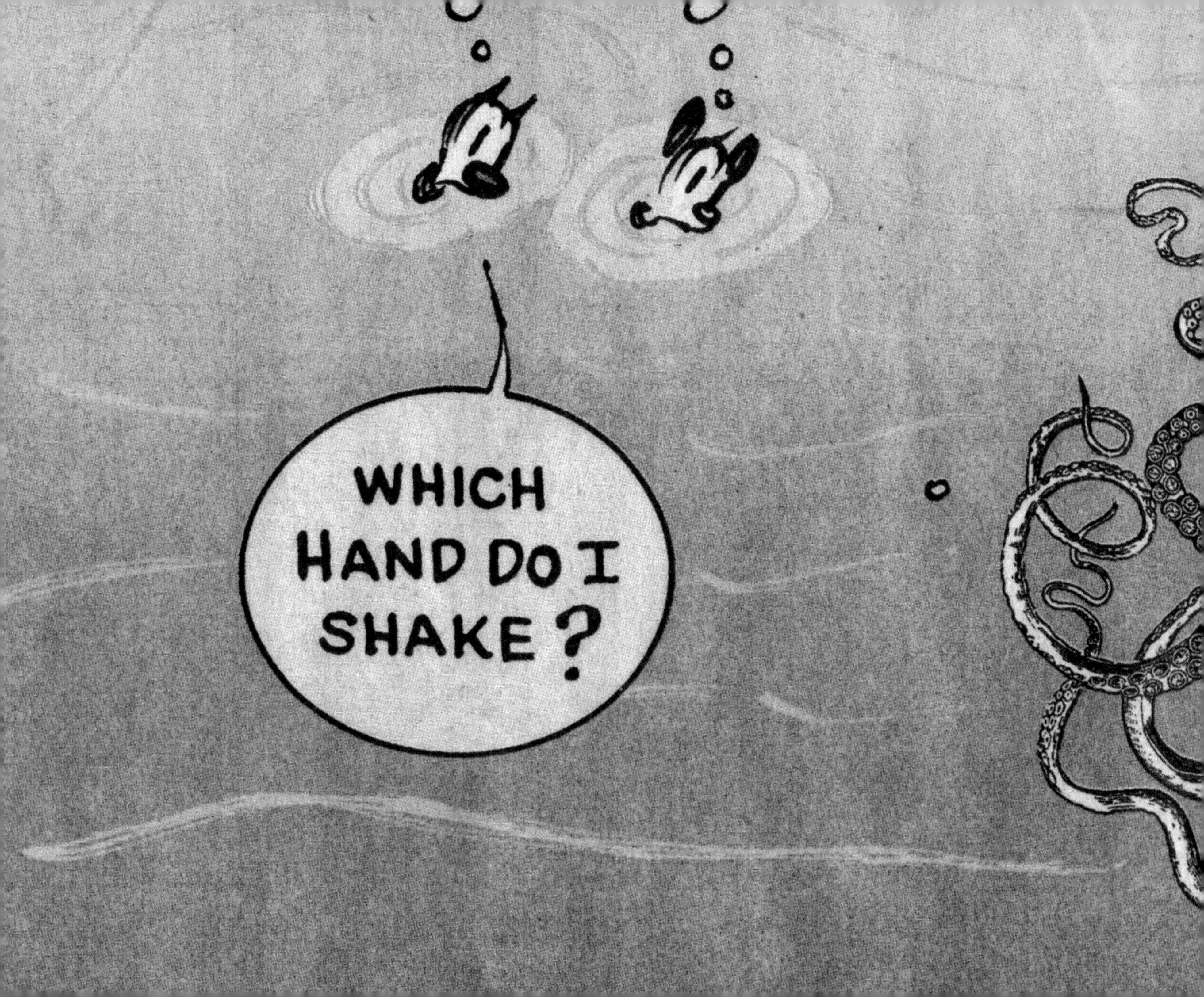
WHICH HAND DO I SHAKE?

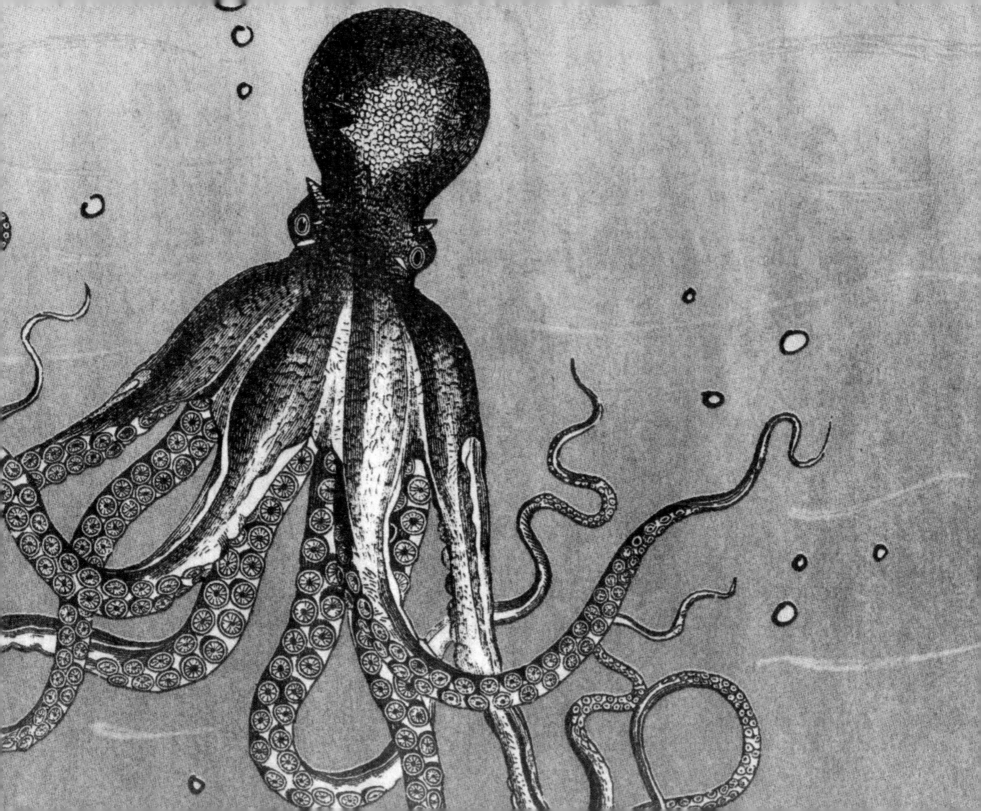

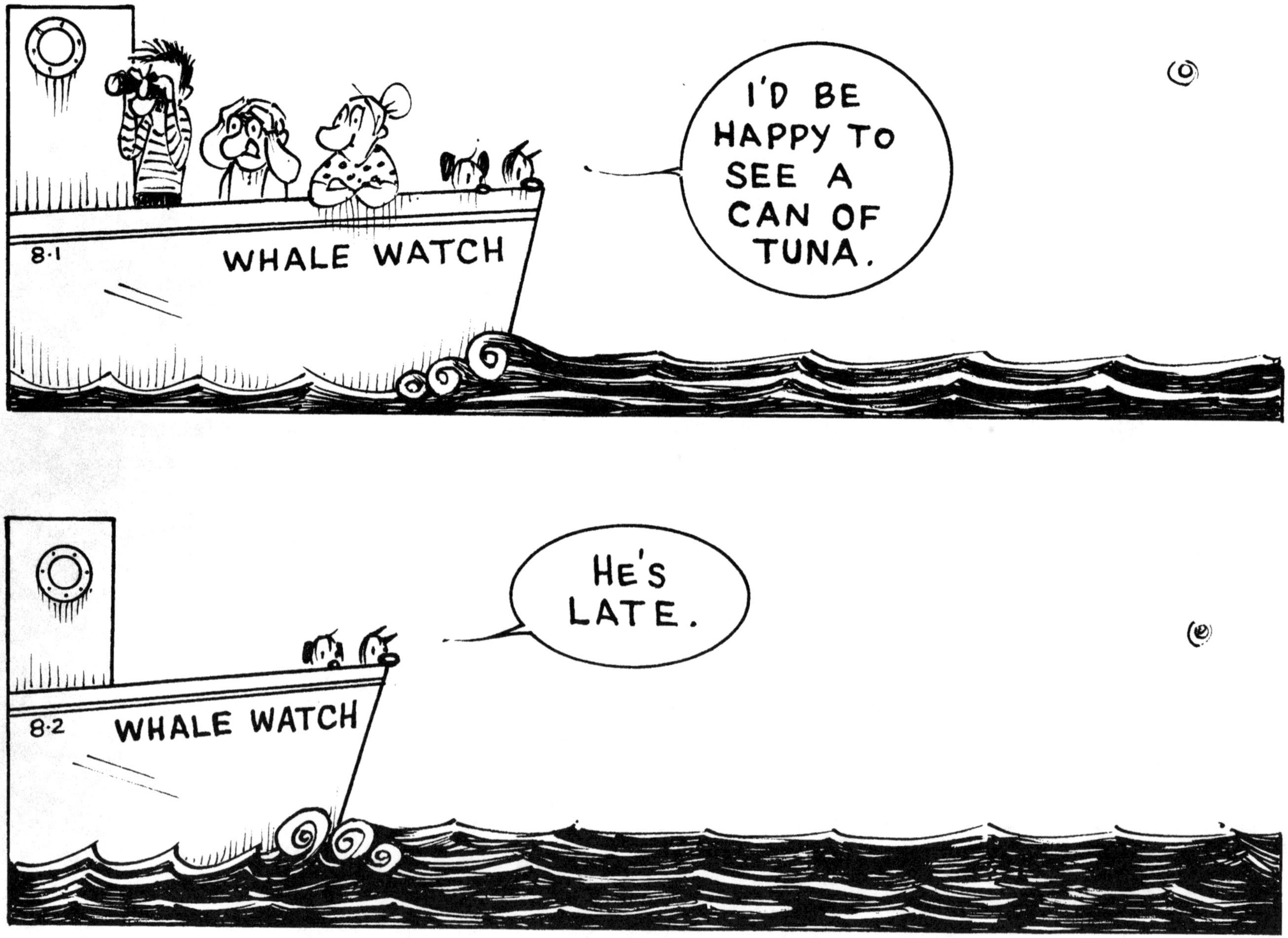
8·1
WHALE WATCH
I'D BE HAPPY TO SEE A CAN OF TUNA.
8·2
WHALE WATCH
HE'S LATE.

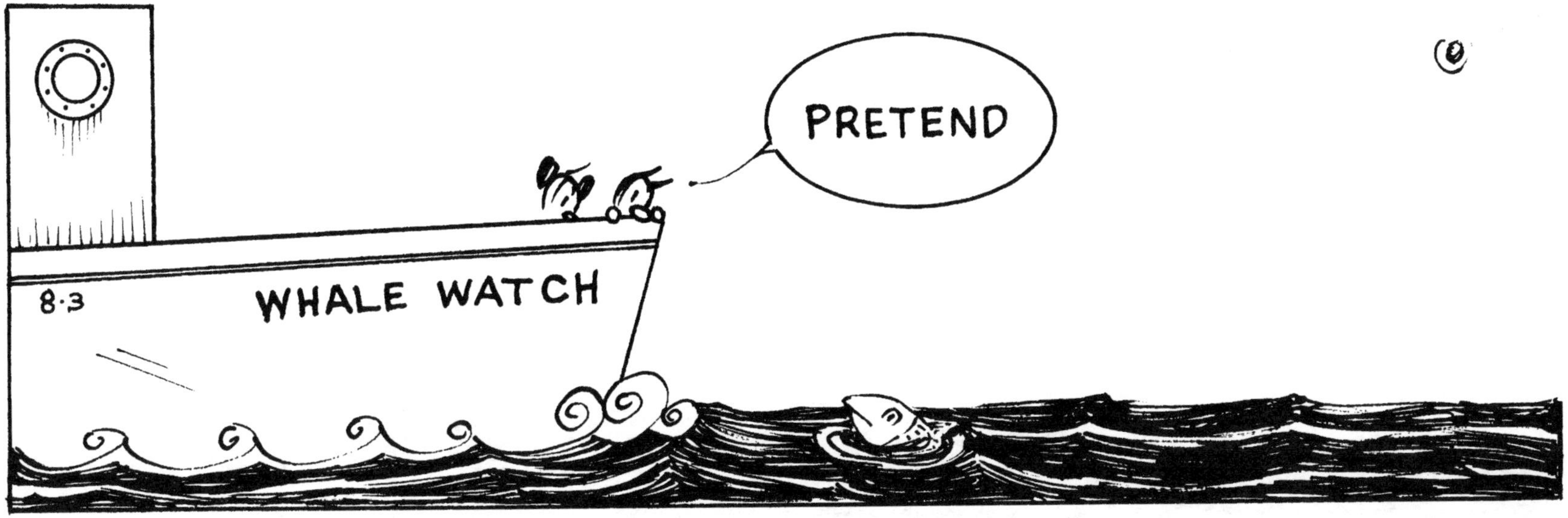
PRETEND
8.3
WHALE WATCH

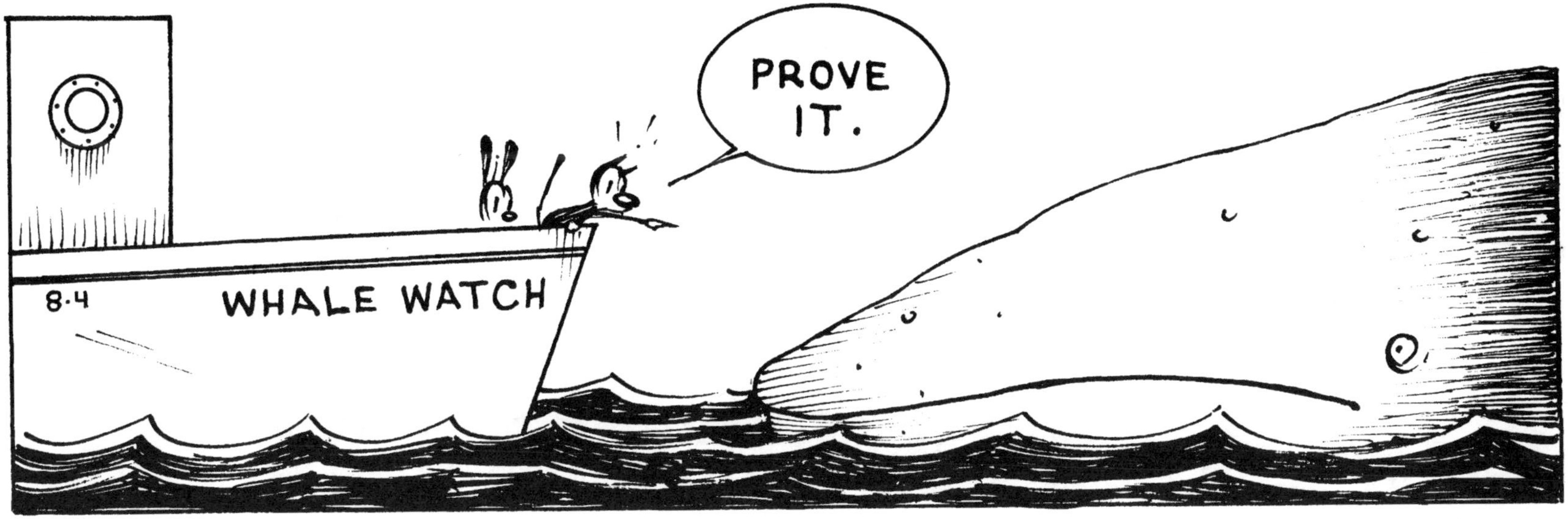
PROVE IT.
8.4
WHALE WATCH

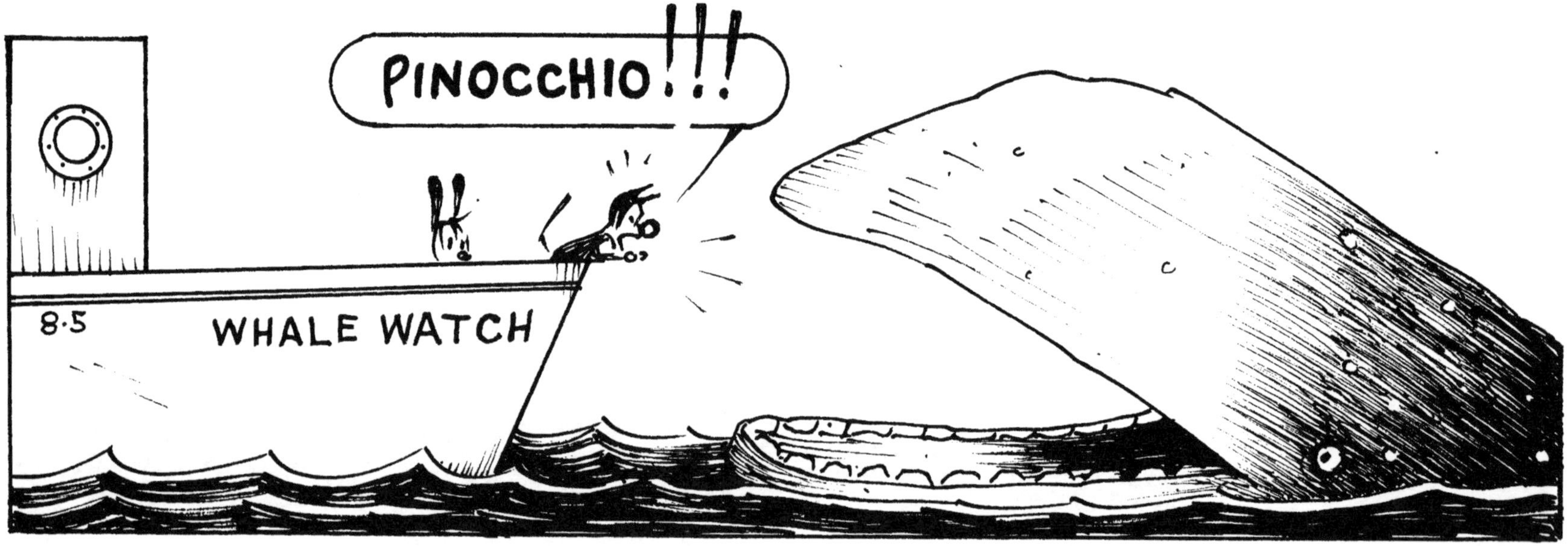
PINOCCHIO!!!
8·5
WHALE WATCH

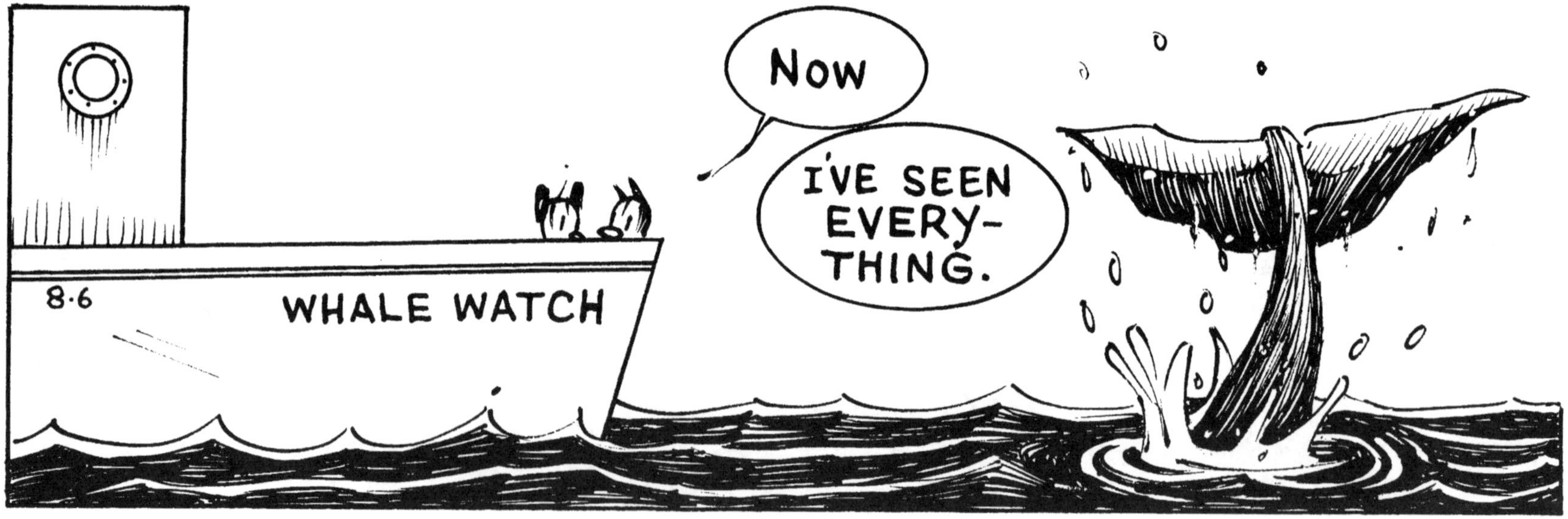
8·6
WHALE WATCH
Now
I'VE SEEN EVERY-THING.

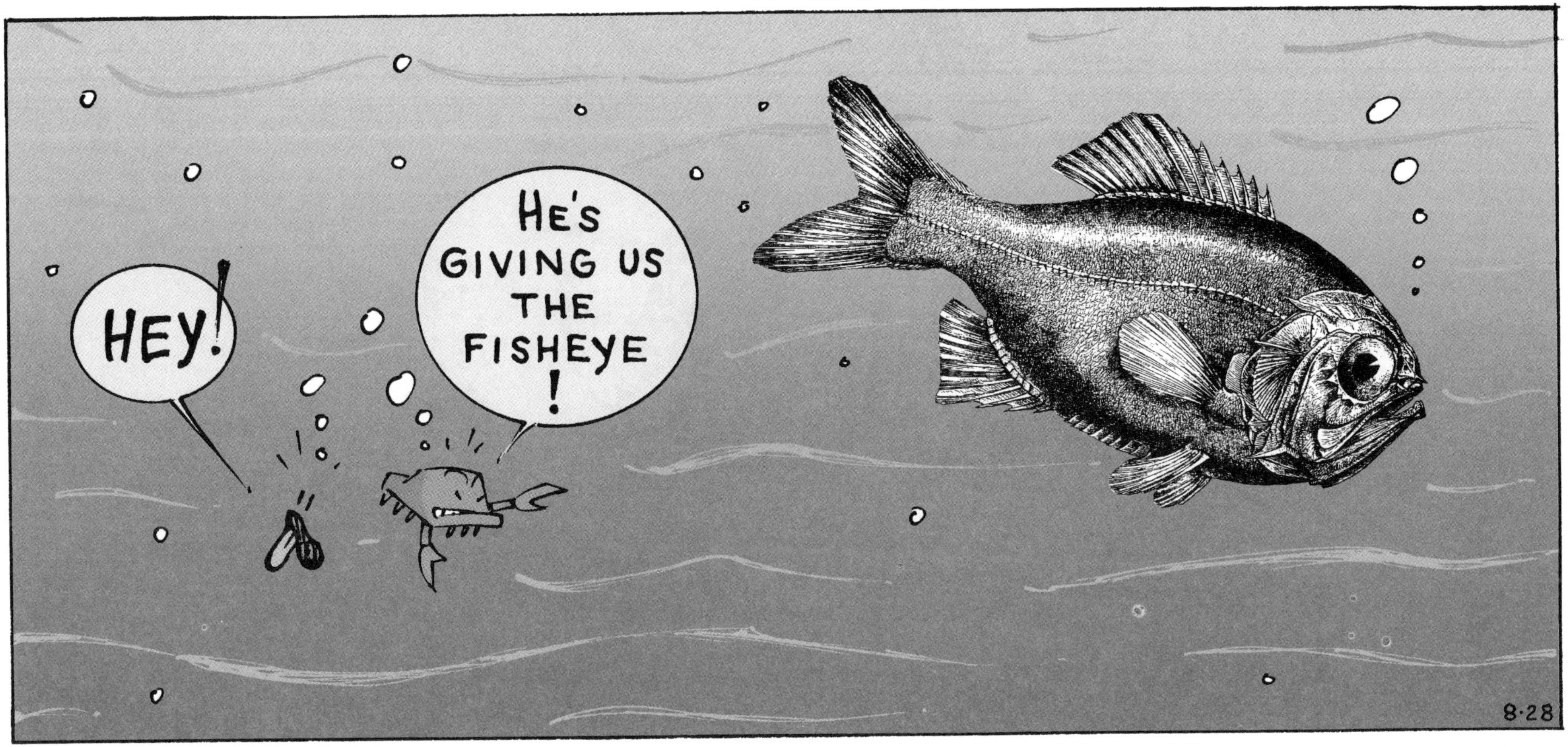
HEY!
HE'S GIVING US THE FISHEYE!
8·28

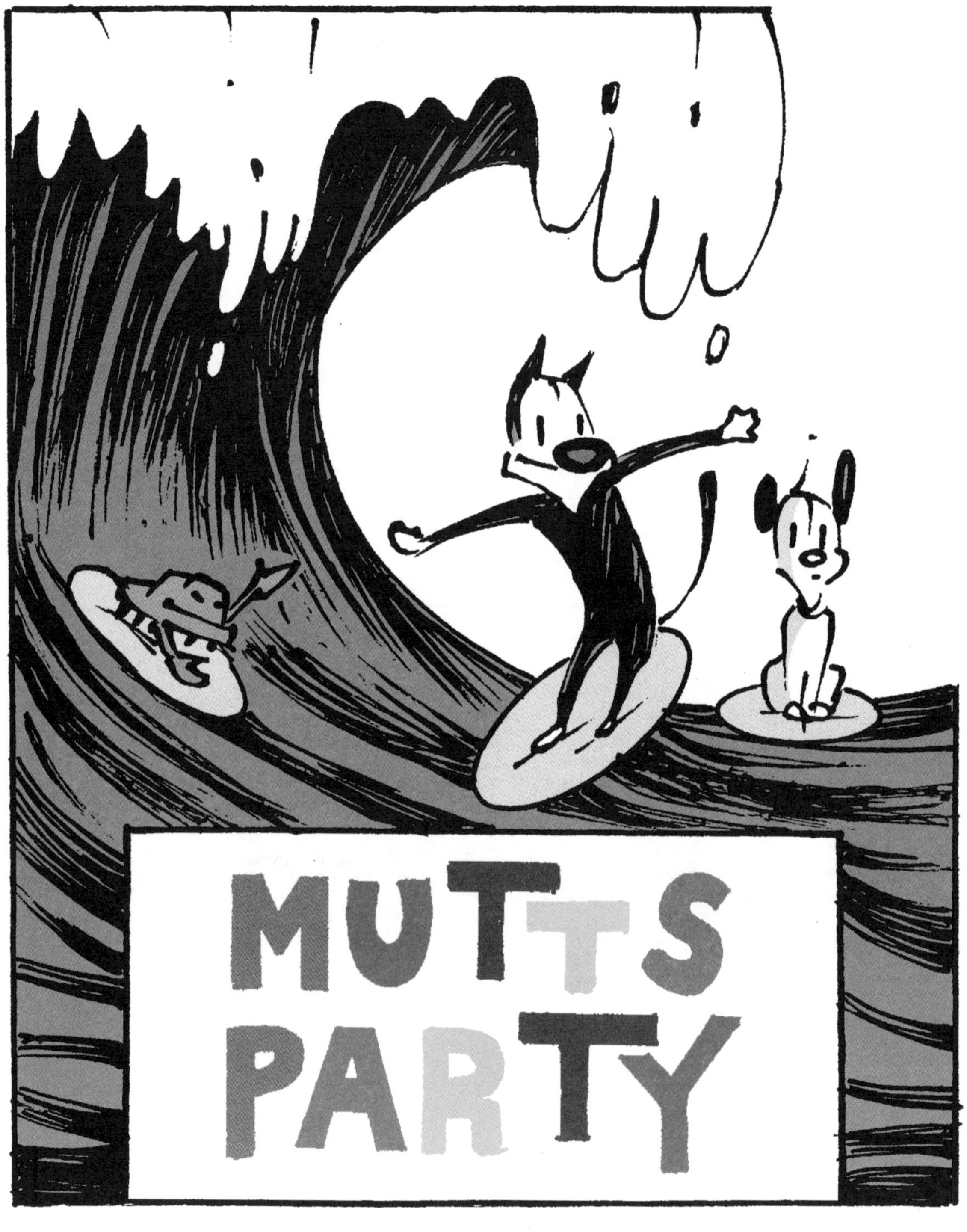
MUTTS
PARTY

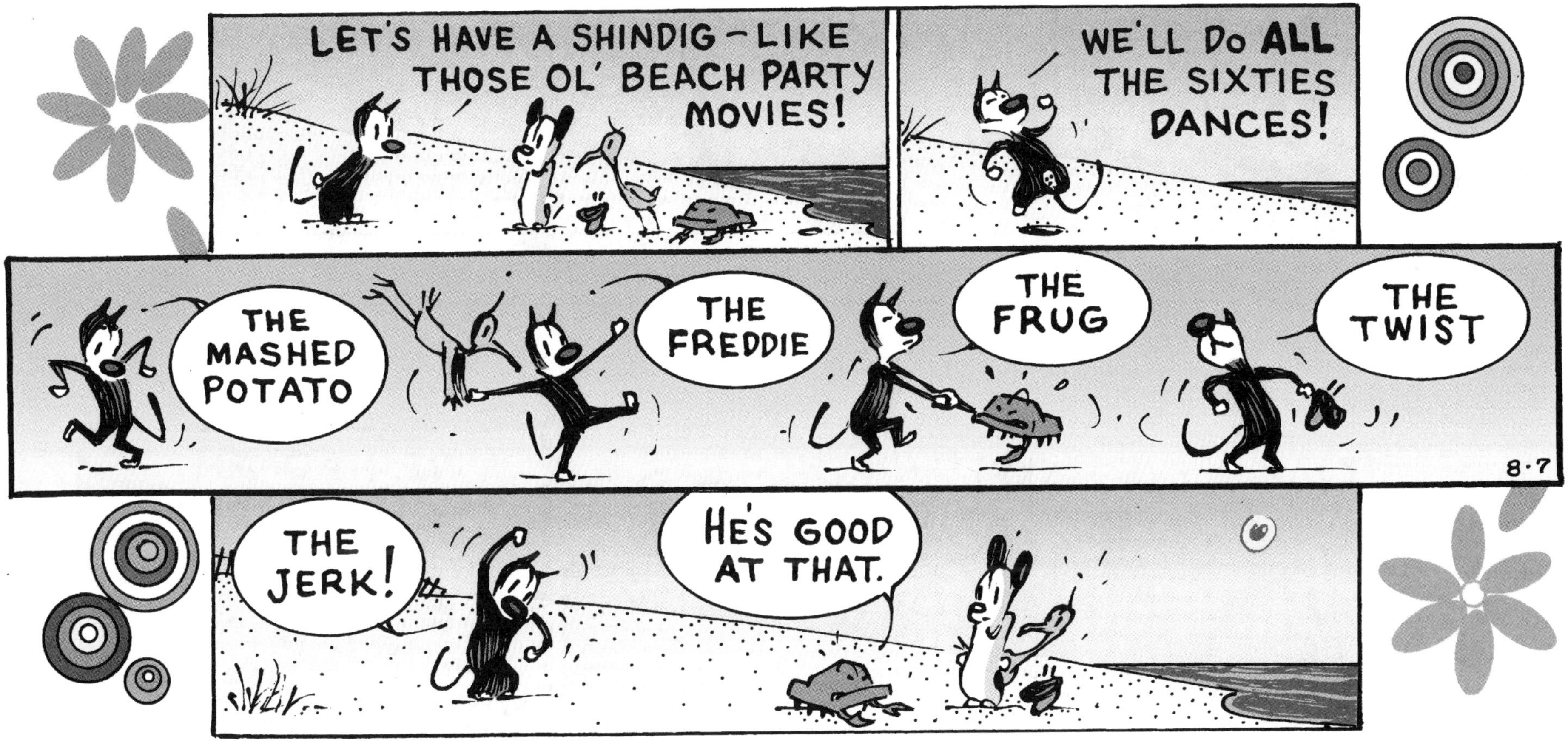

LET'S HAVE A SHINDIG—LIKE THOSE OL' BEACH PARTY MOVIES!
WE'LL DO **ALL** THE SIXTIES DANCES!
THE MASHED POTATO
THE FREDDIE
THE FRUG
THE TWIST
8·7
THE JERK!
HE'S GOOD AT THAT.

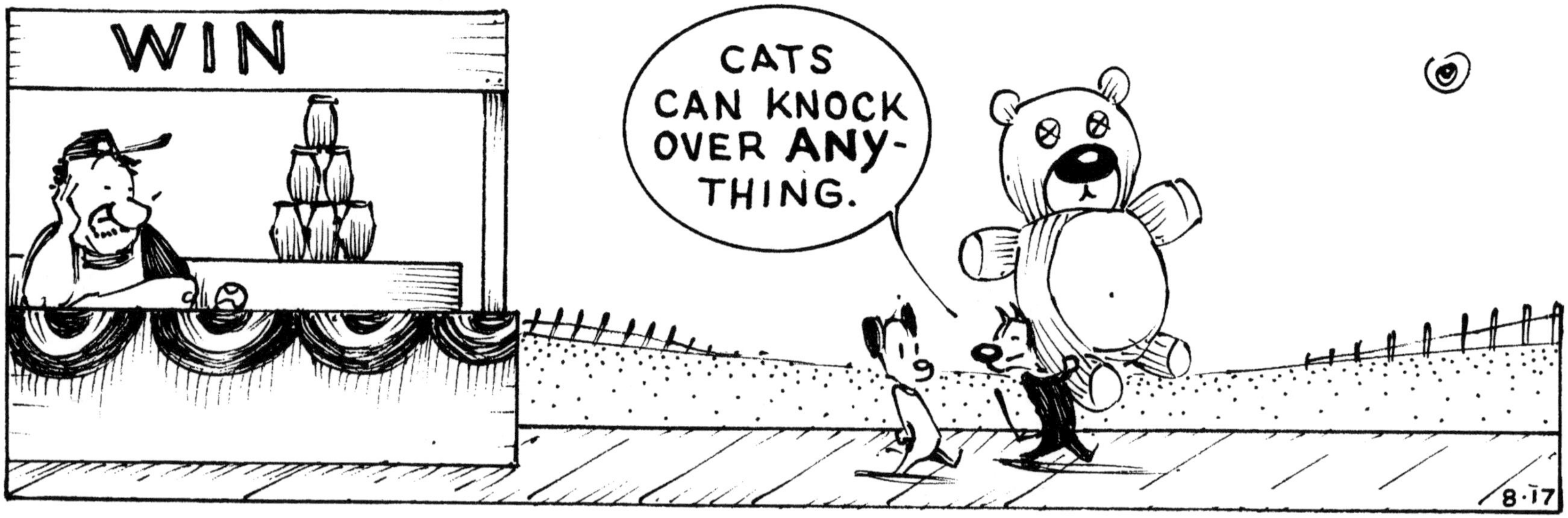
WIN
CATS CAN KNOCK OVER ANY-THING.
8·17

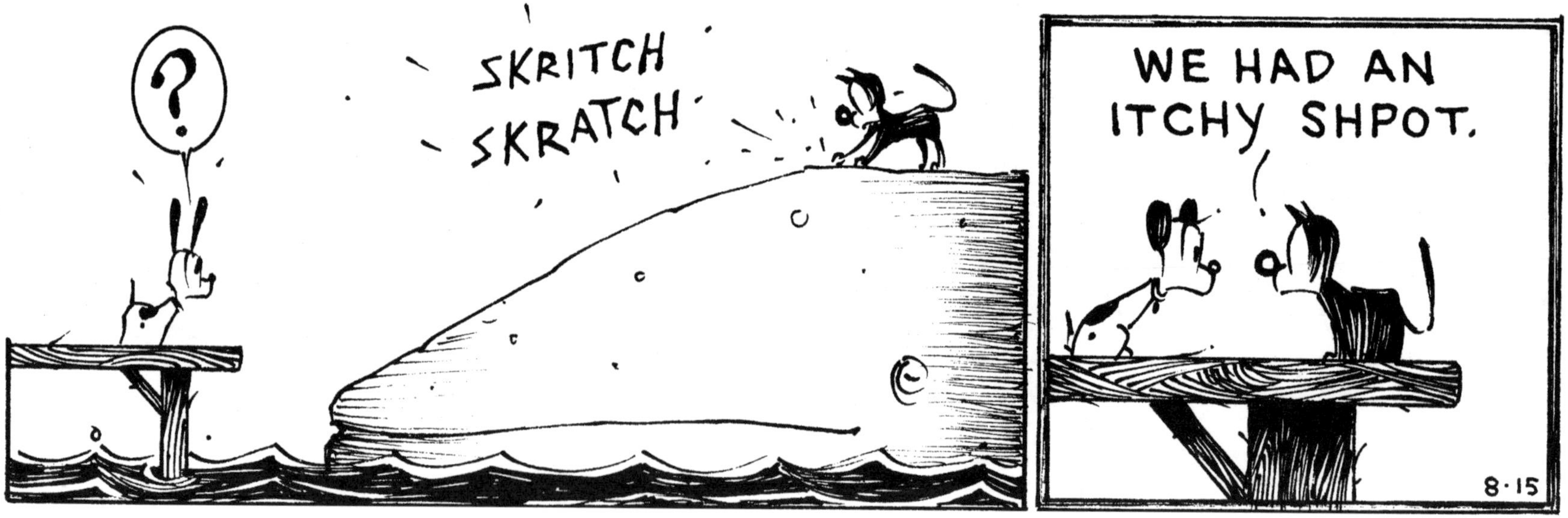
?
SKRITCH SKRATCH
WE HAD AN ITCHY SHPOT.
8·15

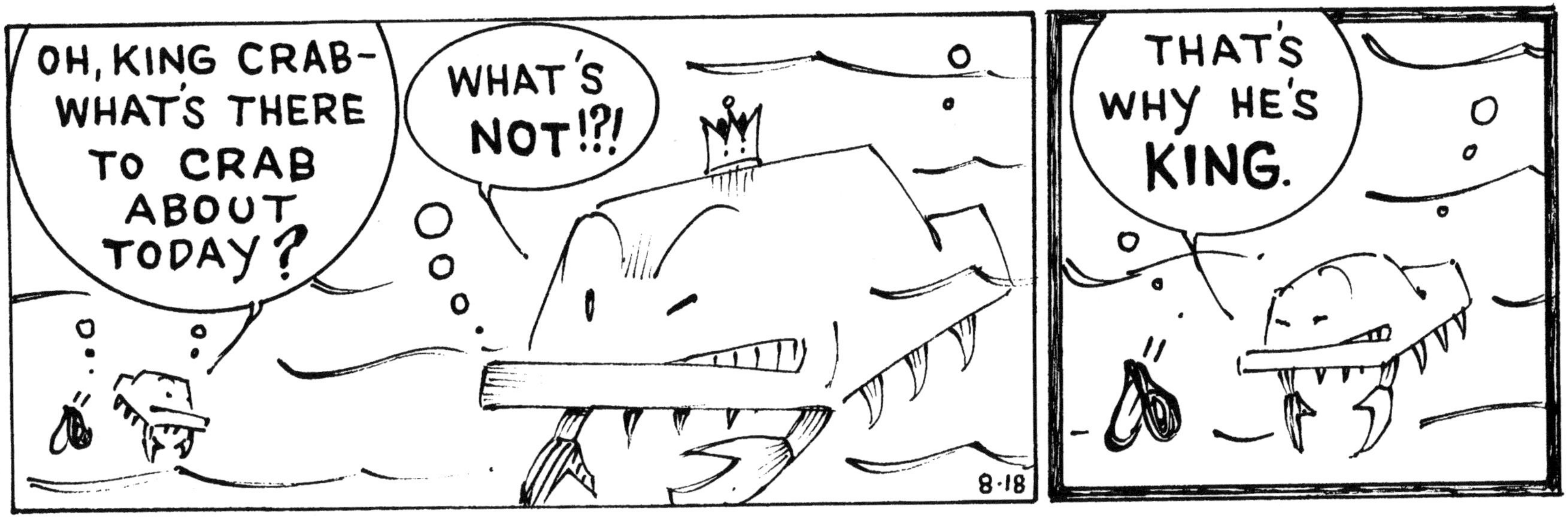
OH, KING CRAB-
WHAT'S THERE
TO CRAB
ABOUT
TODAY?
WHAT'S
NOT!?!
THAT'S
WHY HE'S
KING.
8·18

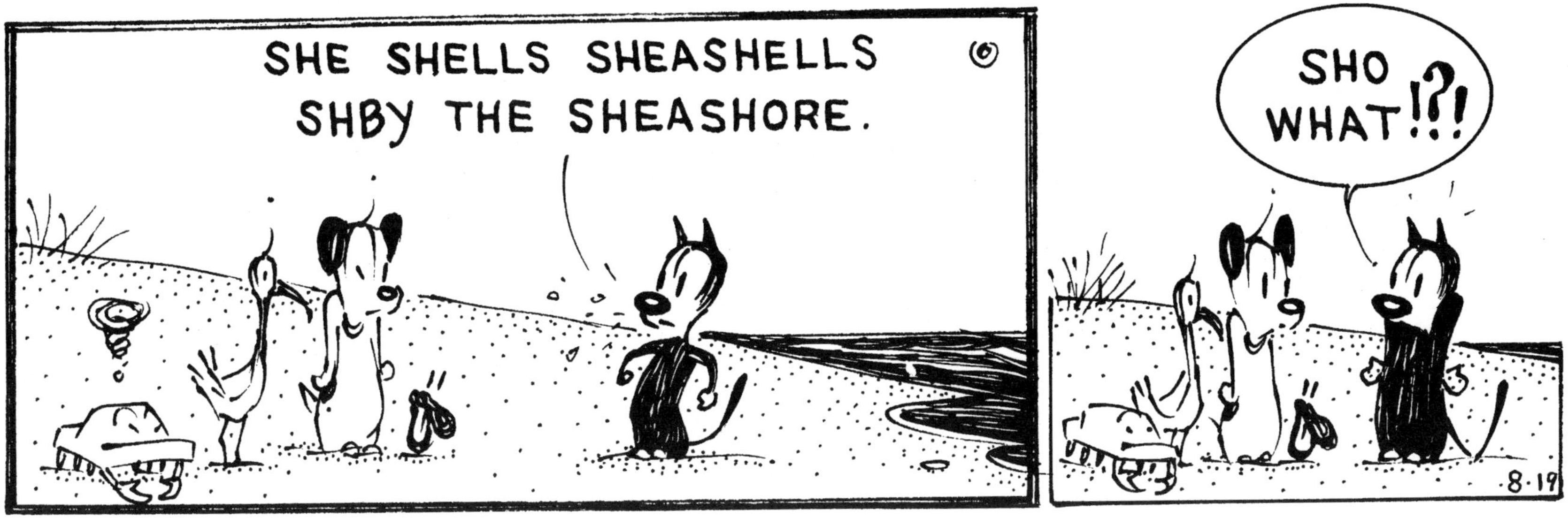
SHE SHELLS SHEASHELLS
SHBY THE SHEASHORE.
SHO
WHAT!?!
8·19

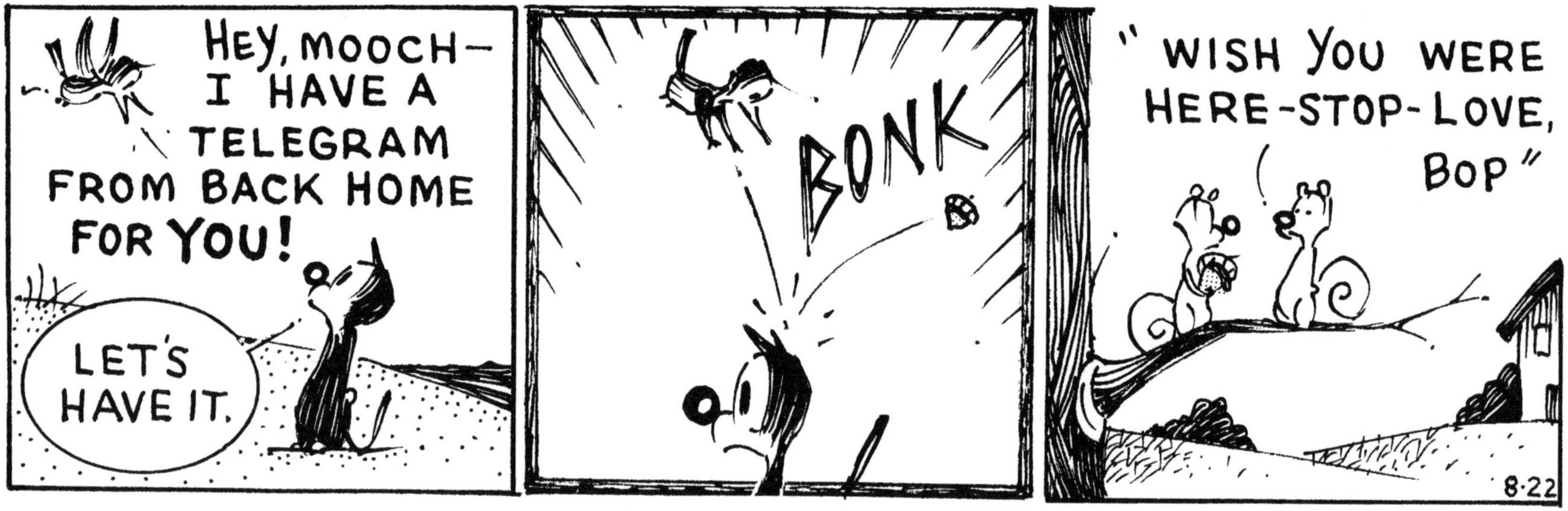
HEY, MOOCH— I HAVE A TELEGRAM FROM BACK HOME FOR YOU!
LET'S HAVE IT.
BONK
"WISH YOU WERE HERE-STOP-LOVE, BOP"
8·22

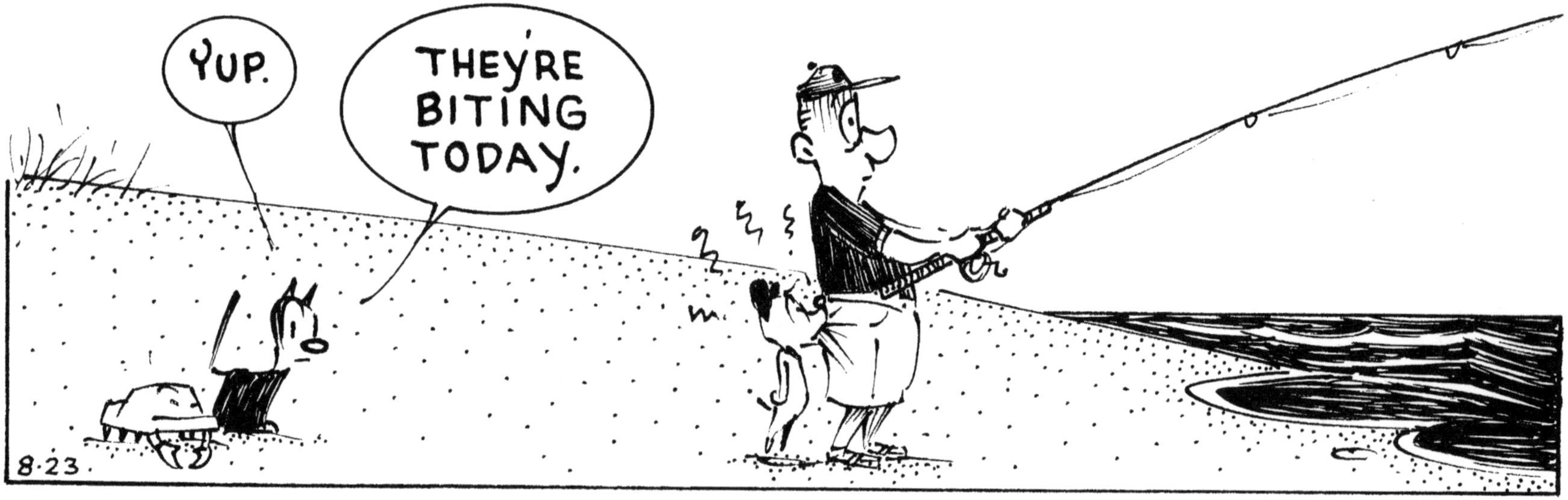
YUP.
THEY'RE BITING TODAY.
8·23

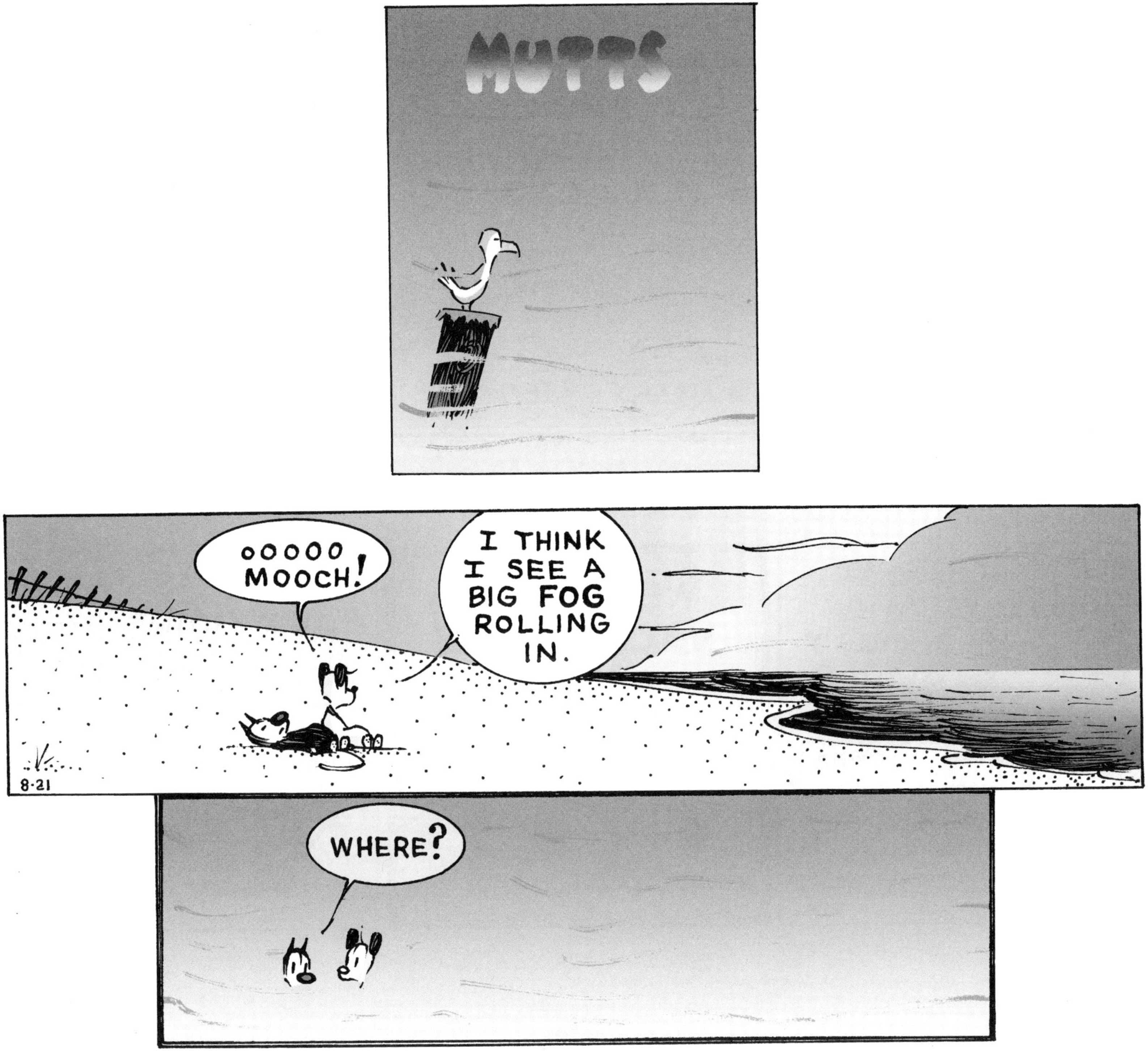
MUTTS
OOOOO MOOCH!
I THINK I SEE A BIG FOG ROLLING IN.
8·21
WHERE?

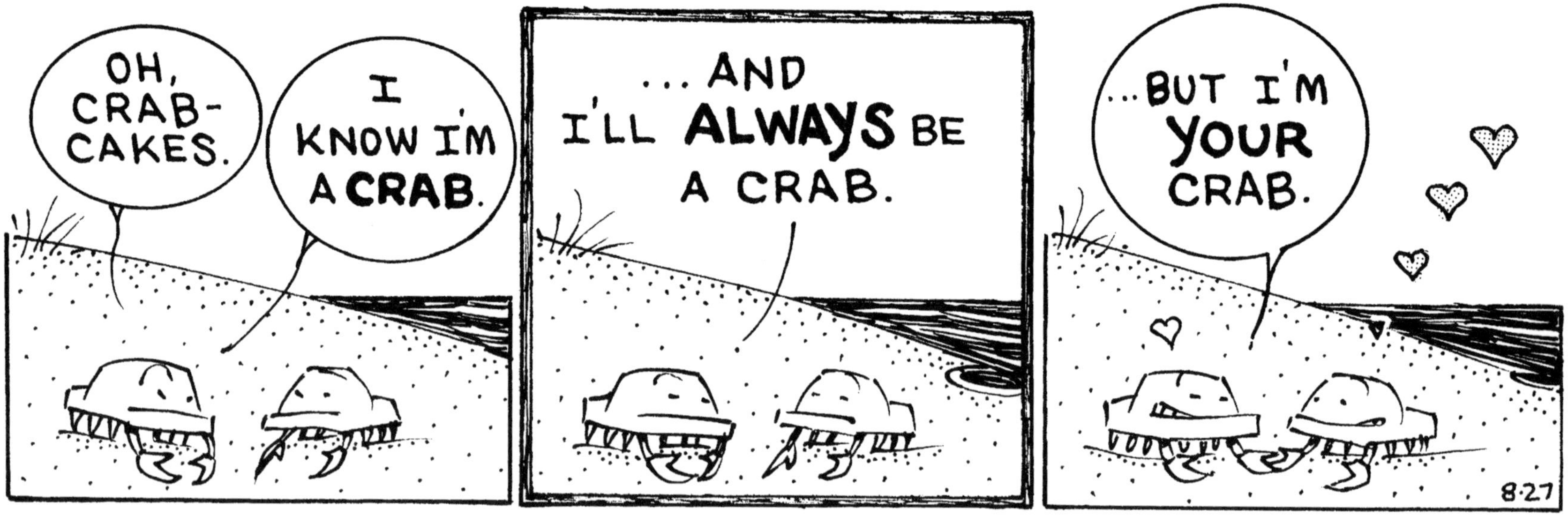
OH, CRAB-CAKES.
I KNOW I'M A CRAB.
...AND I'LL ALWAYS BE A CRAB.
...BUT I'M YOUR CRAB.
8·27

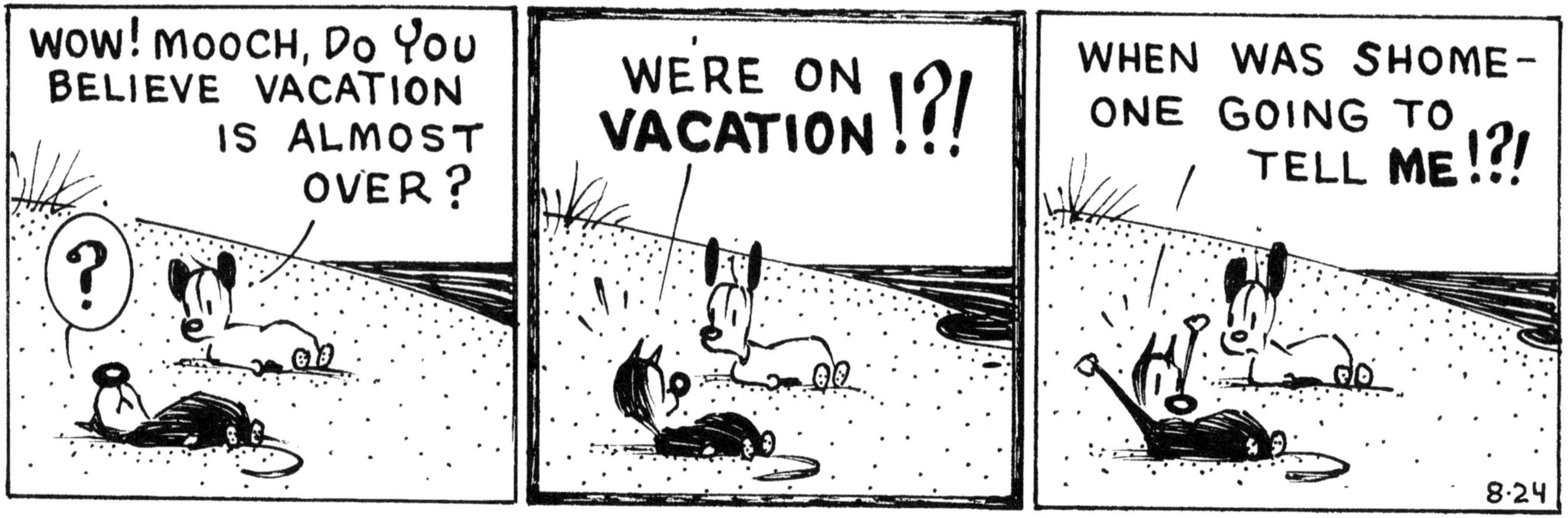
WOW! MOOCH, DO YOU BELIEVE VACATION IS ALMOST OVER?
?
WE'RE ON VACATION!?!
WHEN WAS SHOMEONE GOING TO TELL ME!?!
8·24

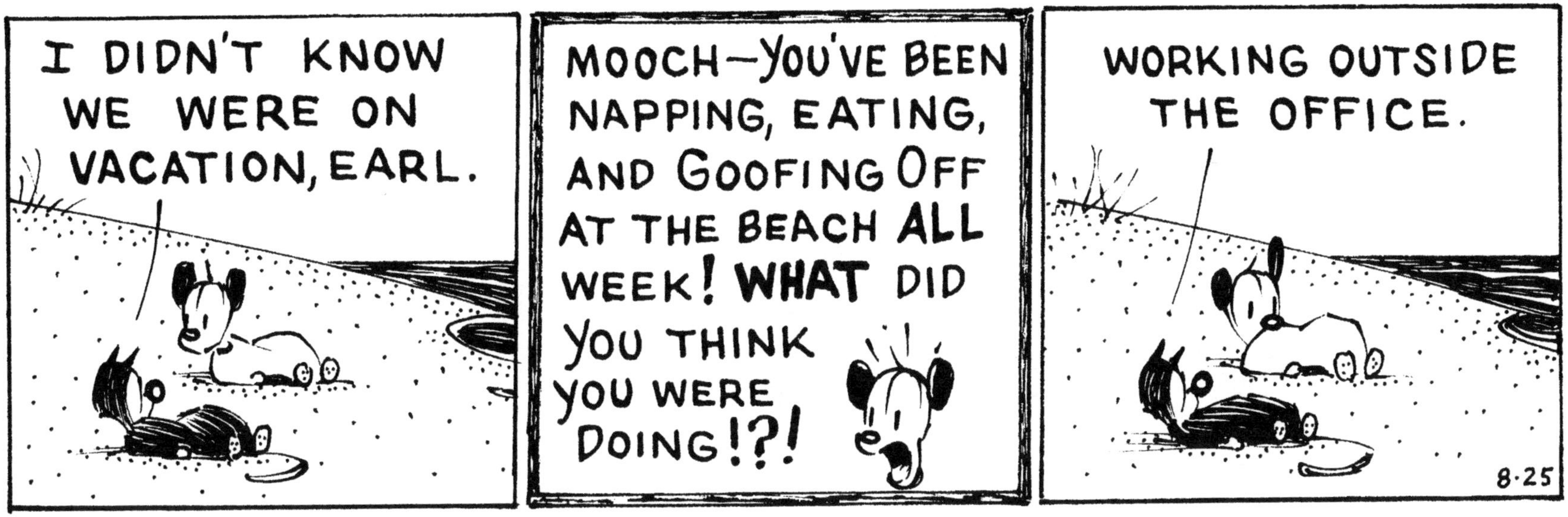
I DIDN'T KNOW WE WERE ON VACATION, EARL.
MOOCH—YOU'VE BEEN NAPPING, EATING, AND GOOFING OFF AT THE BEACH ALL WEEK! WHAT DID YOU THINK YOU WERE DOING!?!
WORKING OUTSIDE THE OFFICE.
8·25

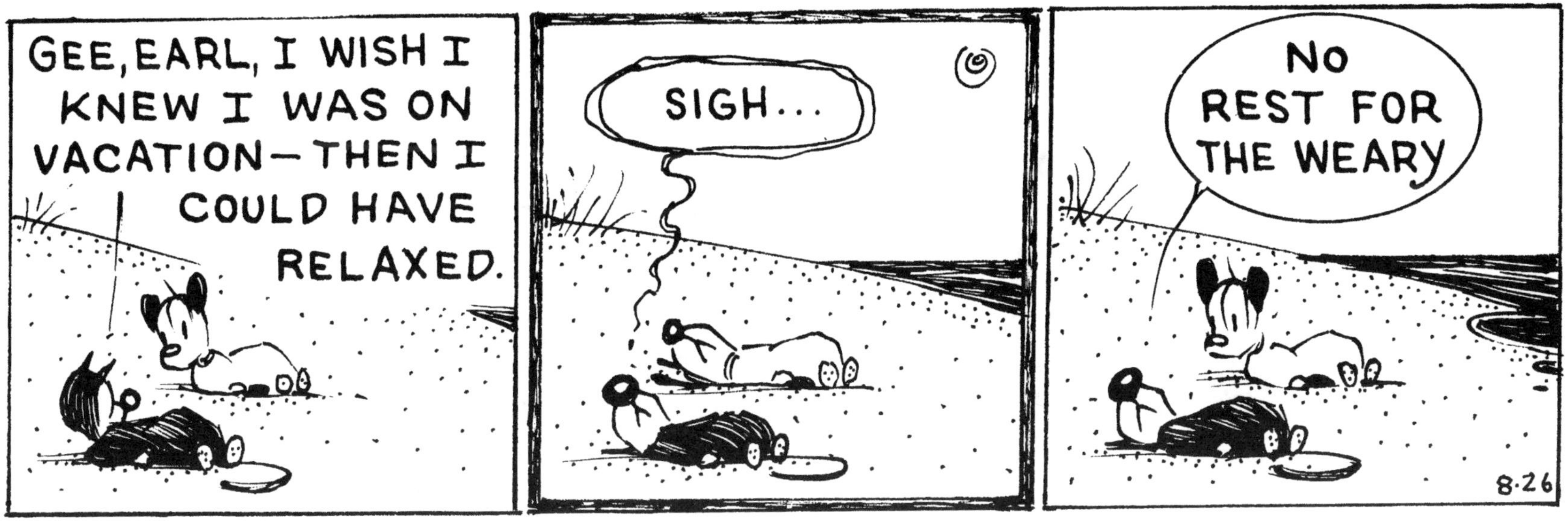
GEE, EARL, I WISH I KNEW I WAS ON VACATION—THEN I COULD HAVE RELAXED.
SIGH...
NO REST FOR THE WEARY
8·26

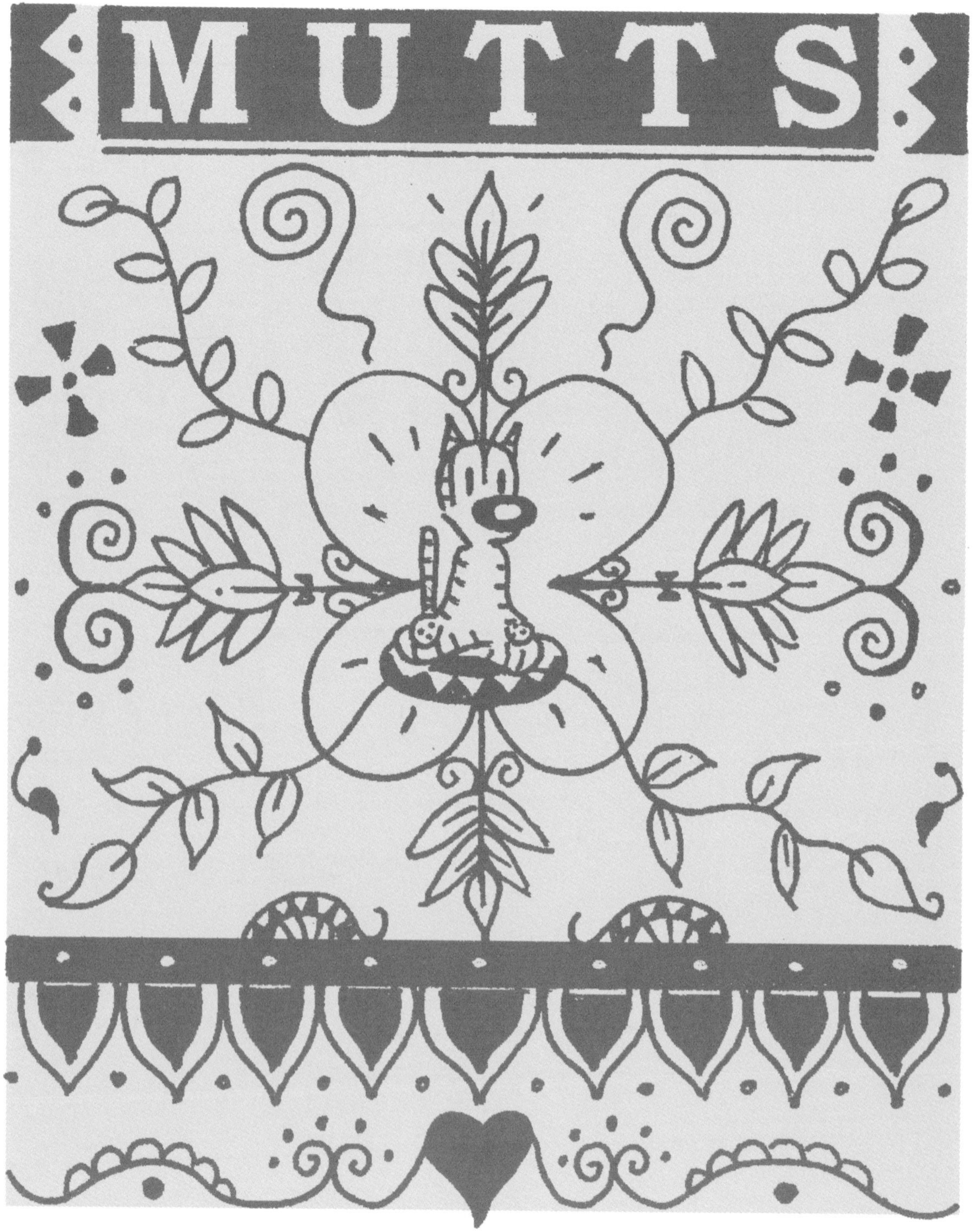
MUTTS

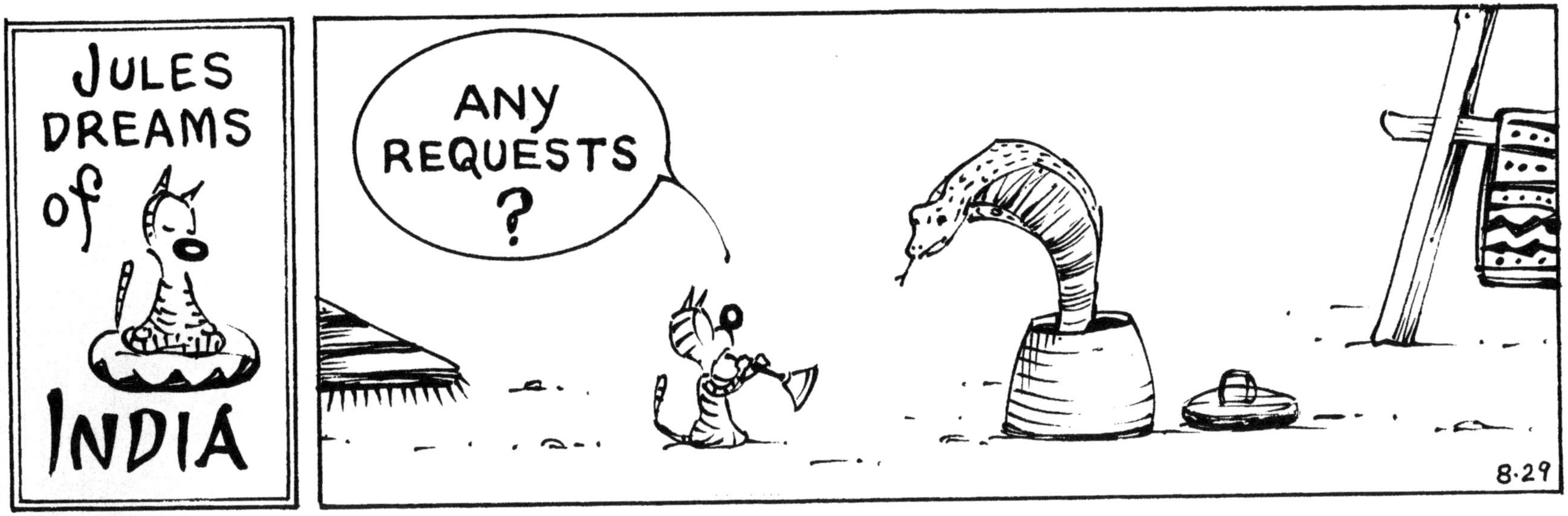
JULES DREAMS of INDIA
ANY REQUESTS ?
8·29

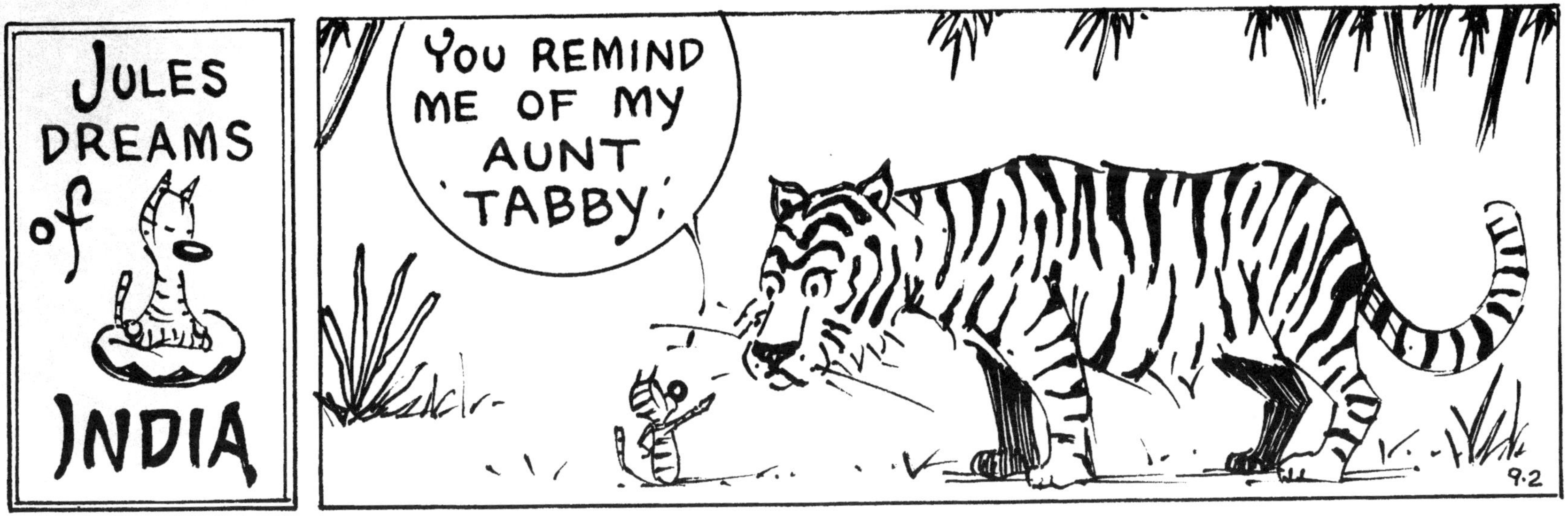
JULES DREAMS of INDIA
YOU REMIND ME OF MY AUNT 'TABBY'
9·2

JULES DREAMS of INDIA
THE BEAR NECESSITIES ARE GETTING PRETTY BARE.
8·31

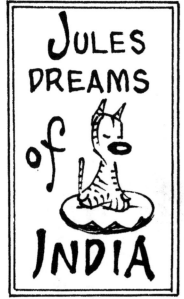

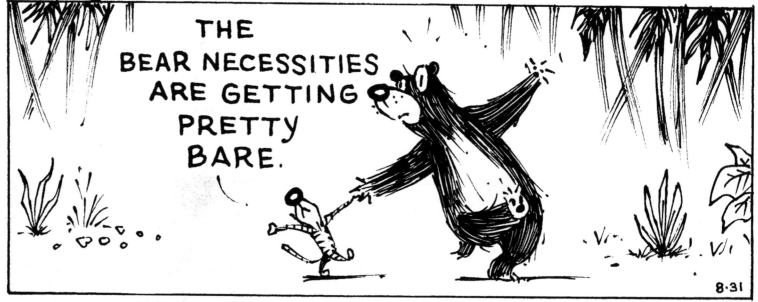

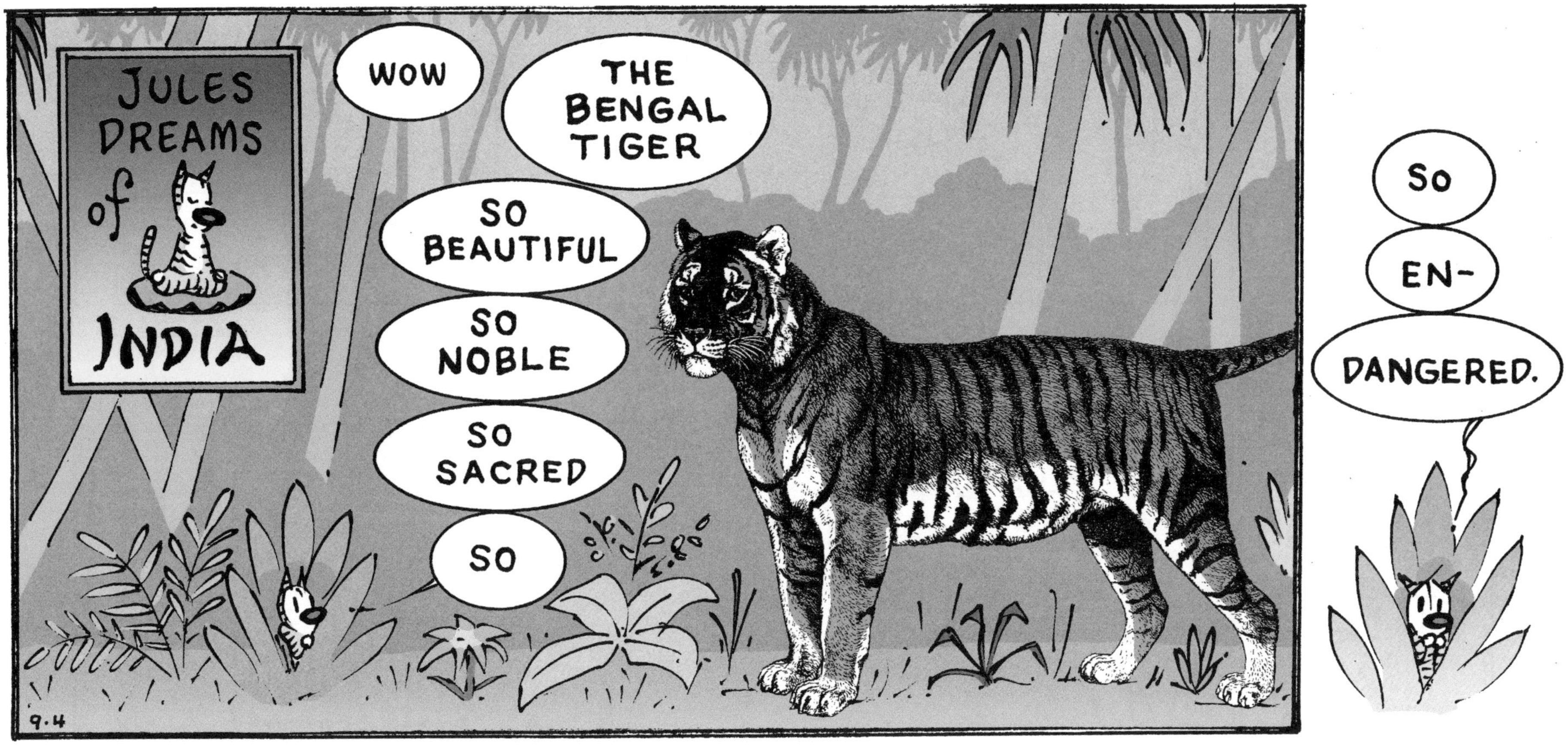
JULES DREAMS of INDIA
WOW
THE BENGAL TIGER
SO BEAUTIFUL
SO NOBLE
SO SACRED
SO
So
EN-
DANGERED.
9.4

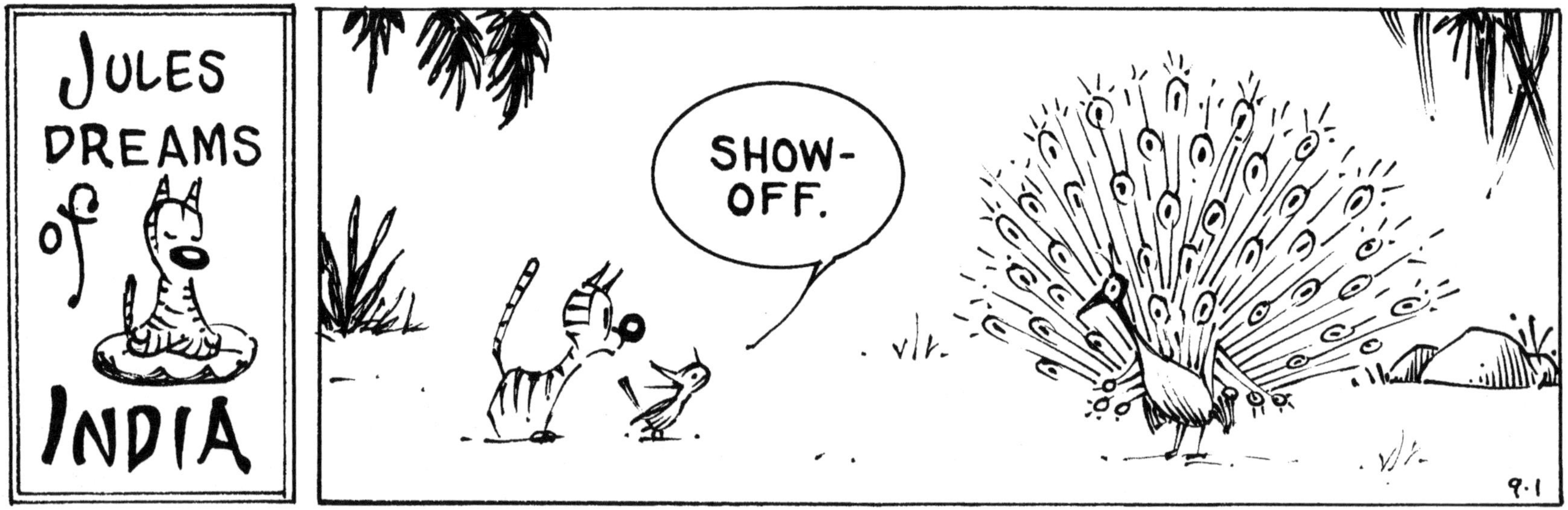
JULES DREAMS of INDIA
SHOW-OFF.
9·1

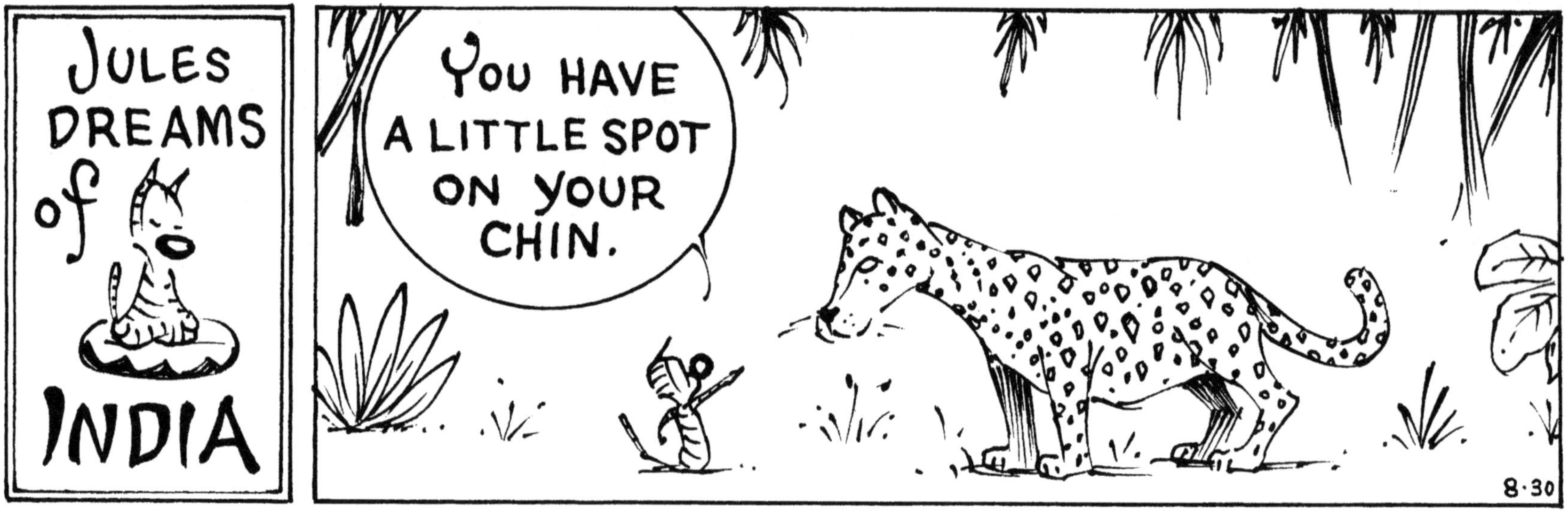
JULES DREAMS of INDIA
YOU HAVE A LITTLE SPOT ON YOUR CHIN.
8·30

JULES DREAMS of INDIA
NAMASTE
9·3

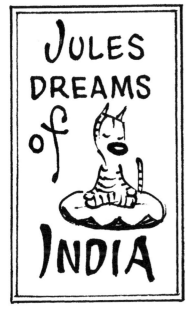

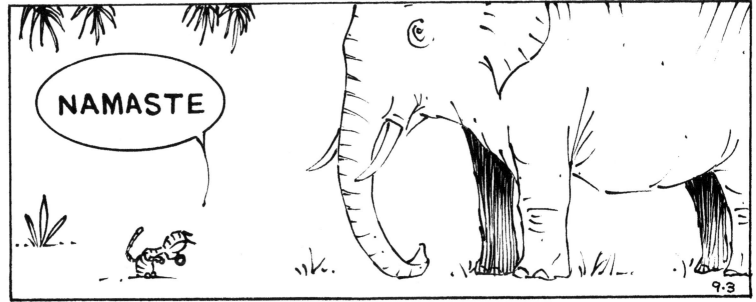

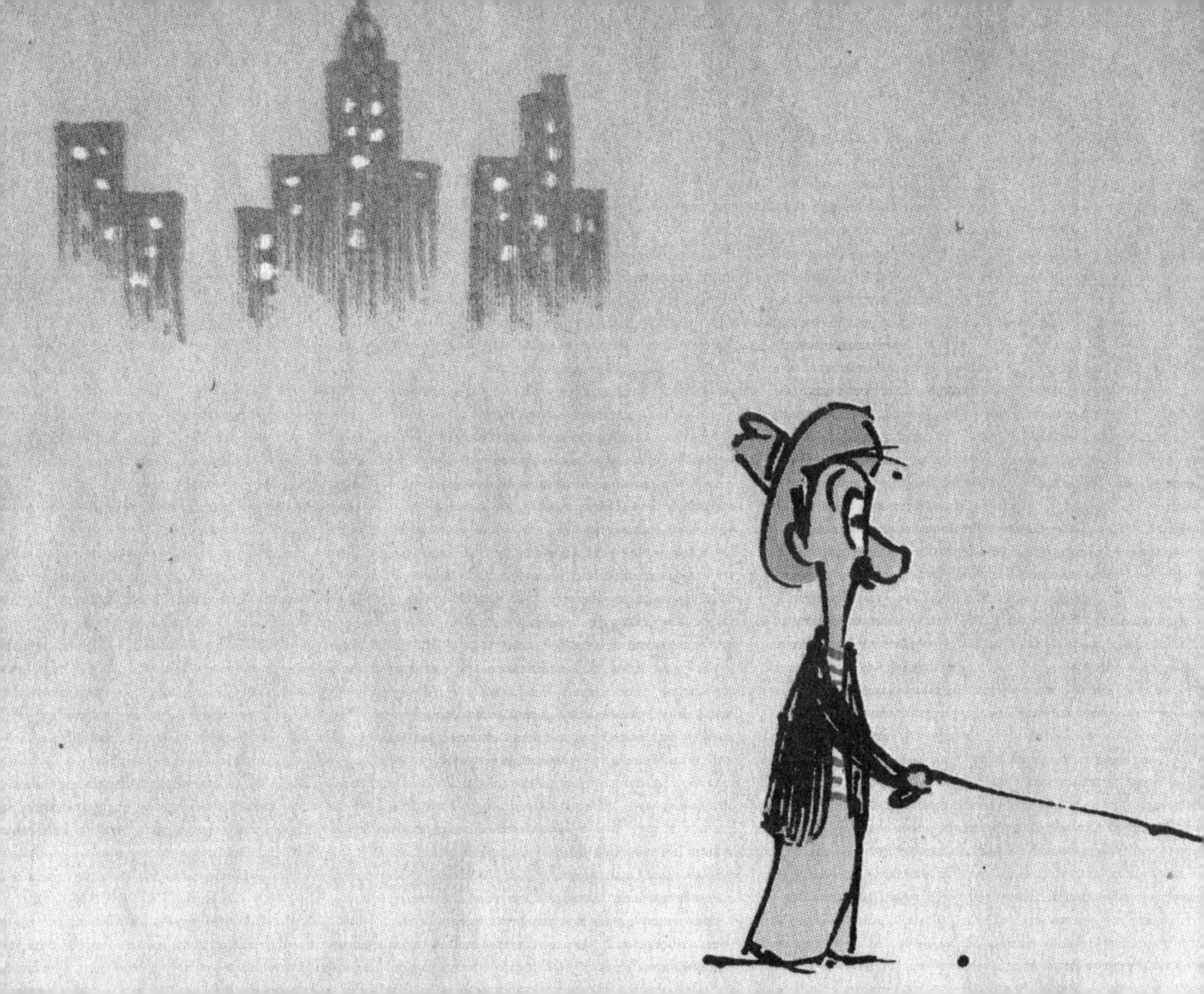

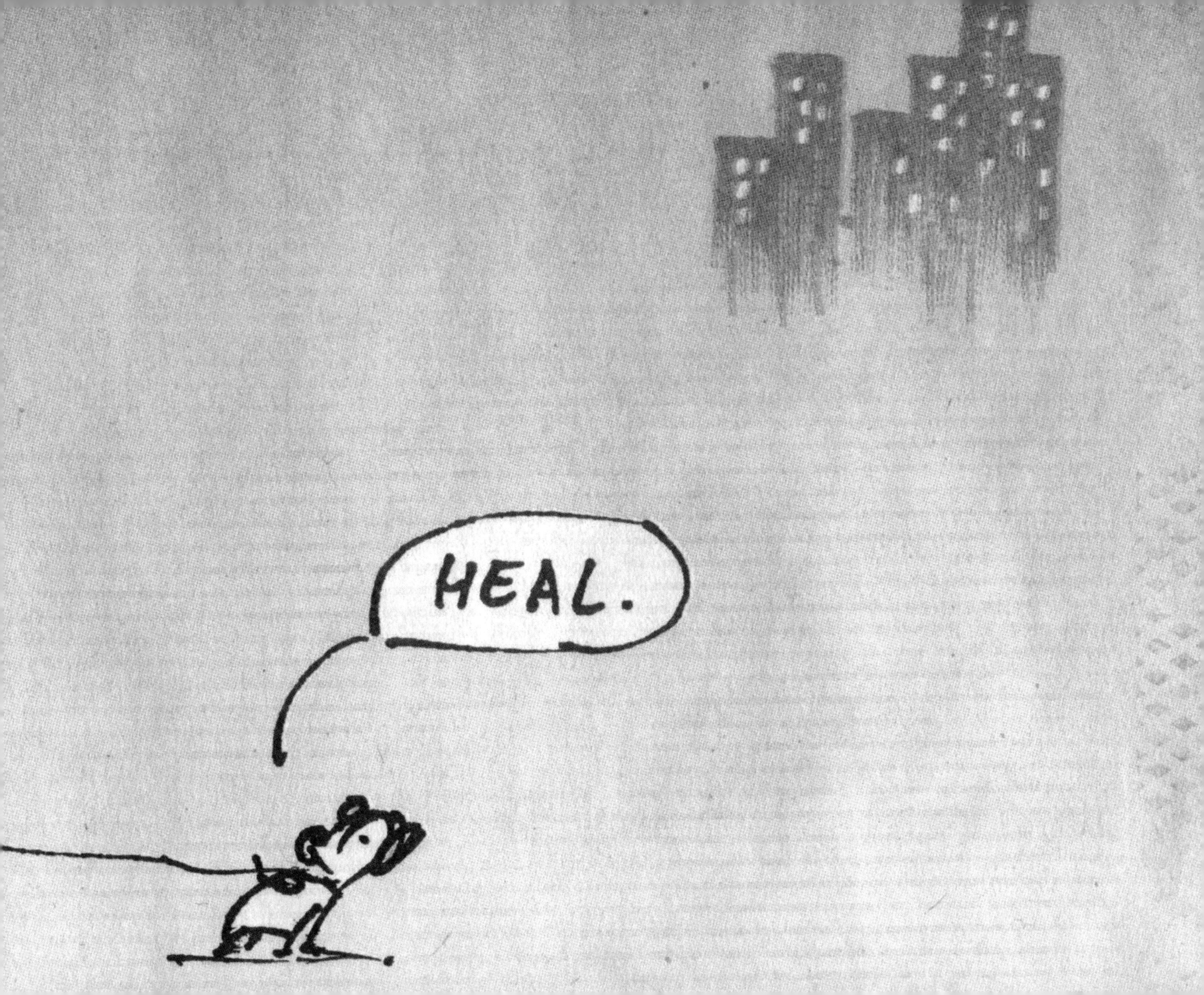
HEAL.

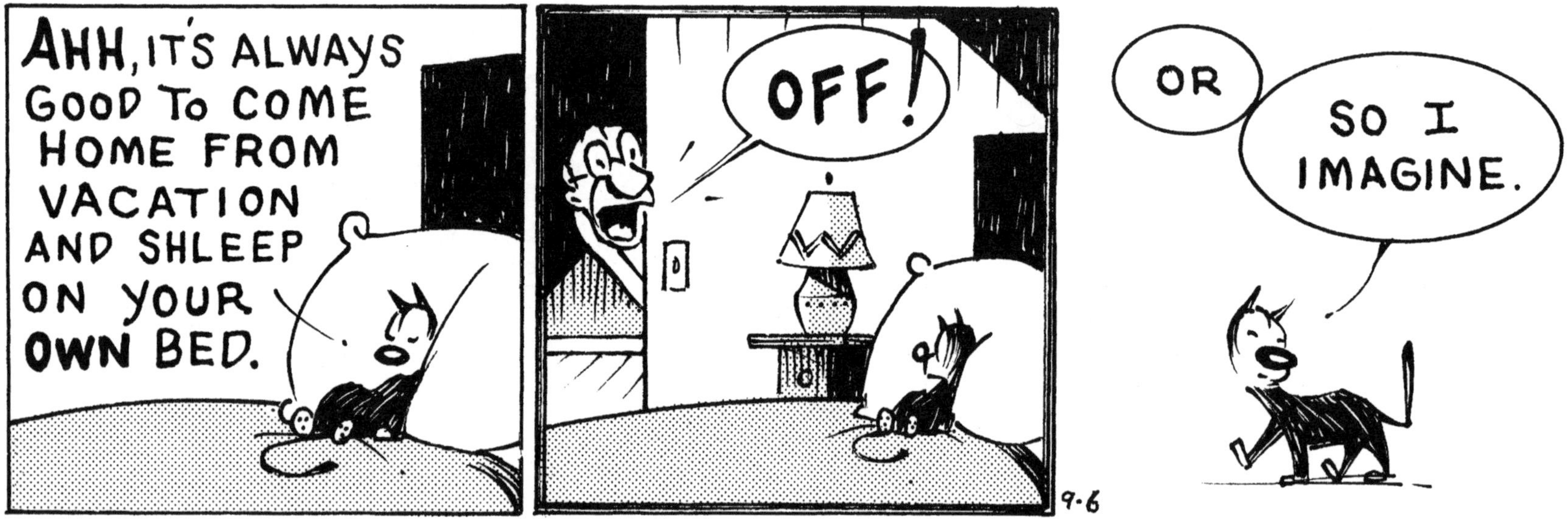
AHH, IT'S ALWAYS GOOD TO COME HOME FROM VACATION AND SHLEEP ON YOUR OWN BED.
OFF!
OR
SO I IMAGINE.
9·6

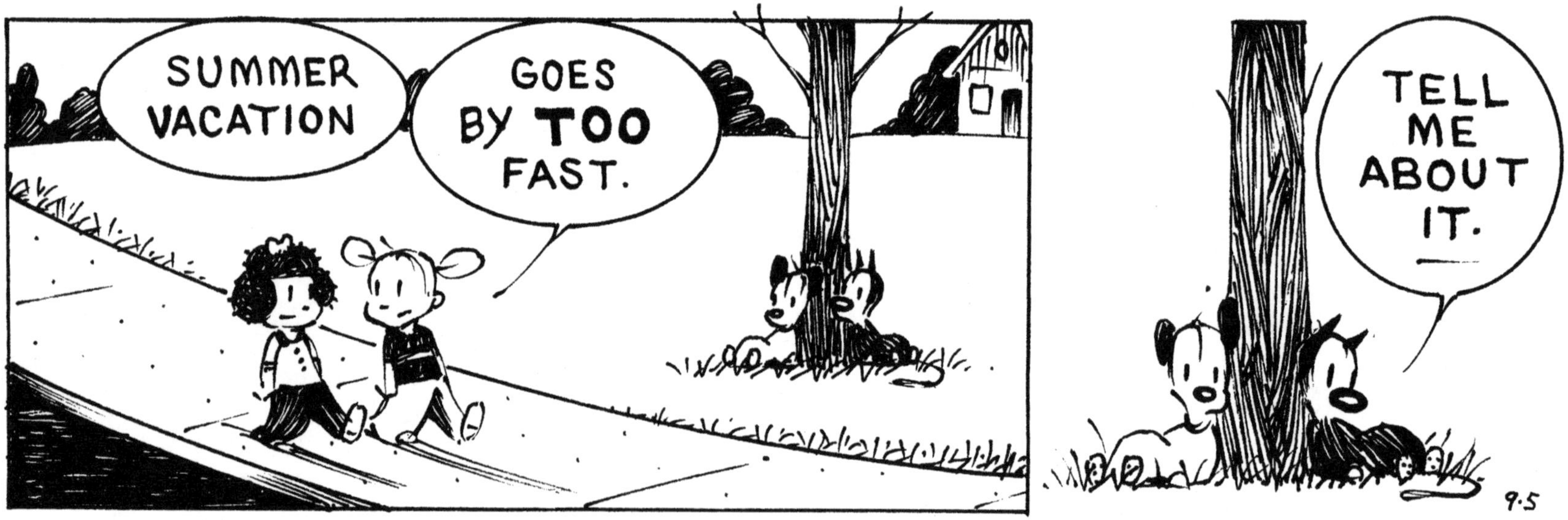
SUMMER VACATION
GOES BY TOO FAST.
TELL ME ABOUT IT.
9·5

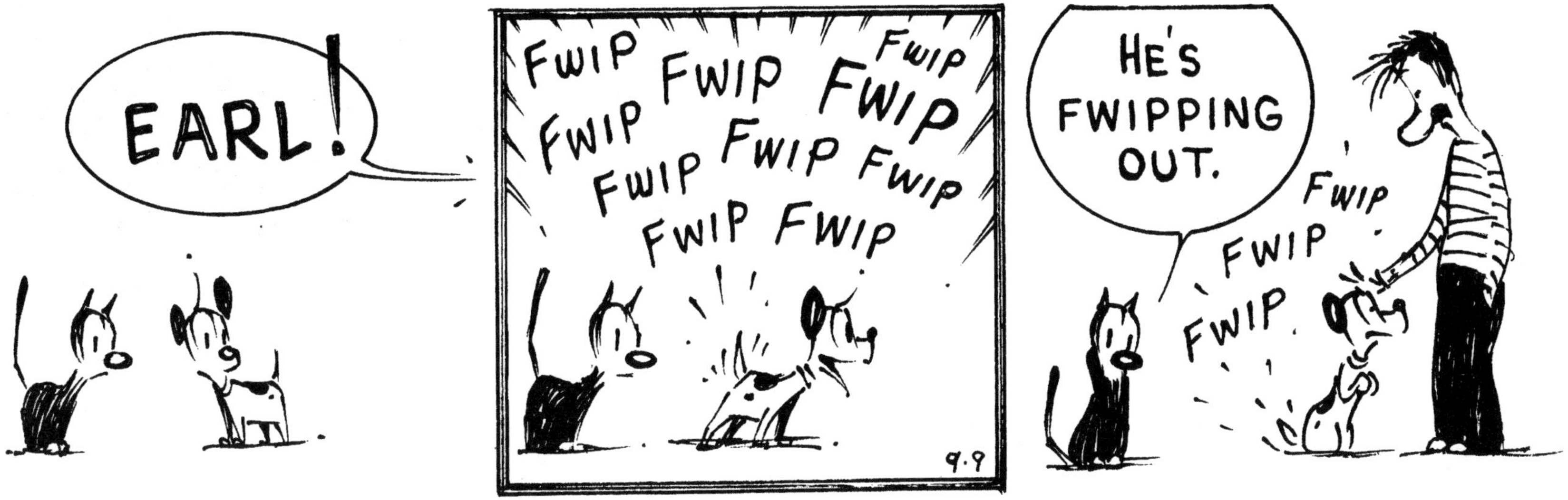
EARL!
FWIP FWIP FWIP FWIP FWIP FWIP FWIP FWIP FWIP FWIP
9.9
HE'S FWIPPING OUT.
FWIP FWIP FWIP

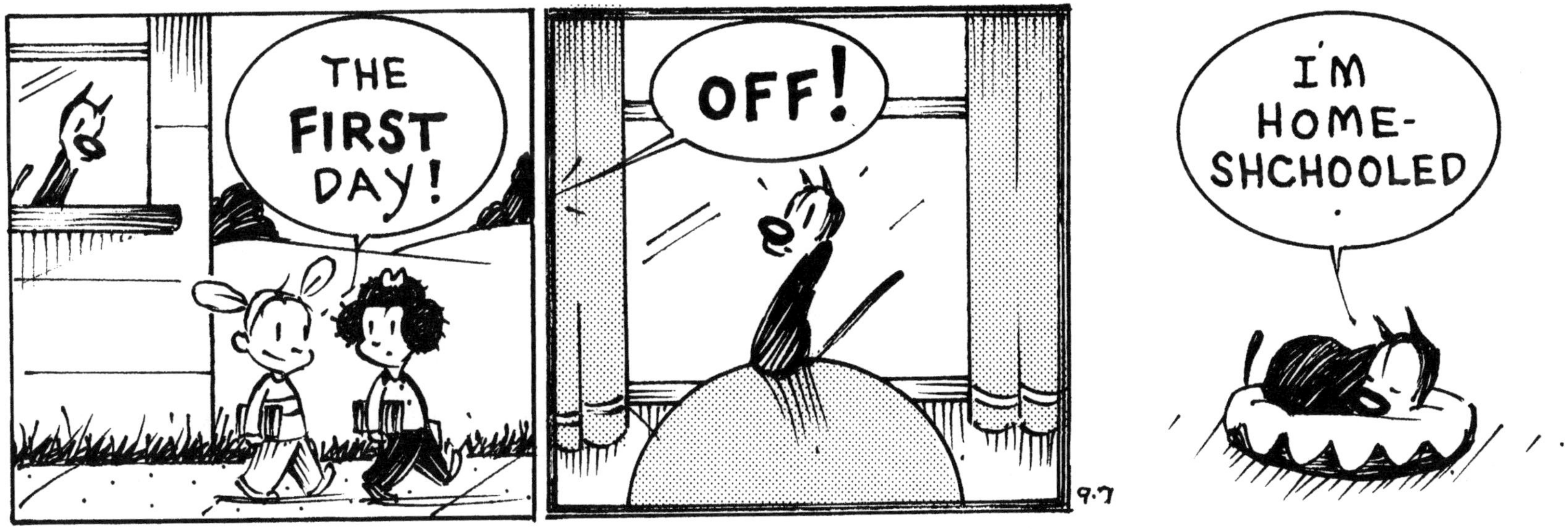
THE FIRST DAY!
OFF!
9.7
I'M HOME-SHCHOOLED

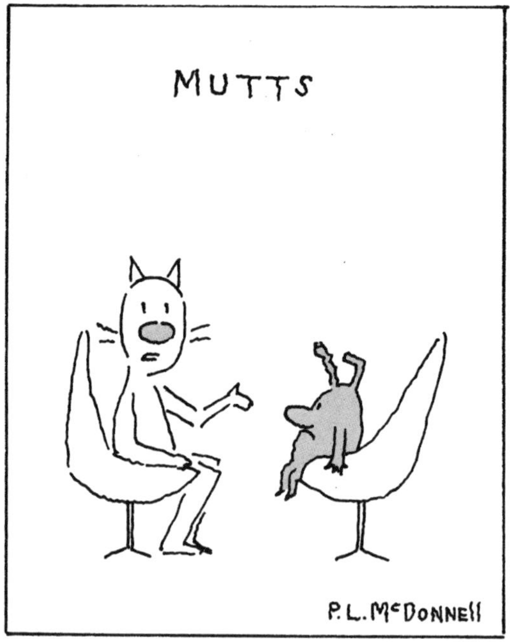
MUTTS
P.L. McDONNELL

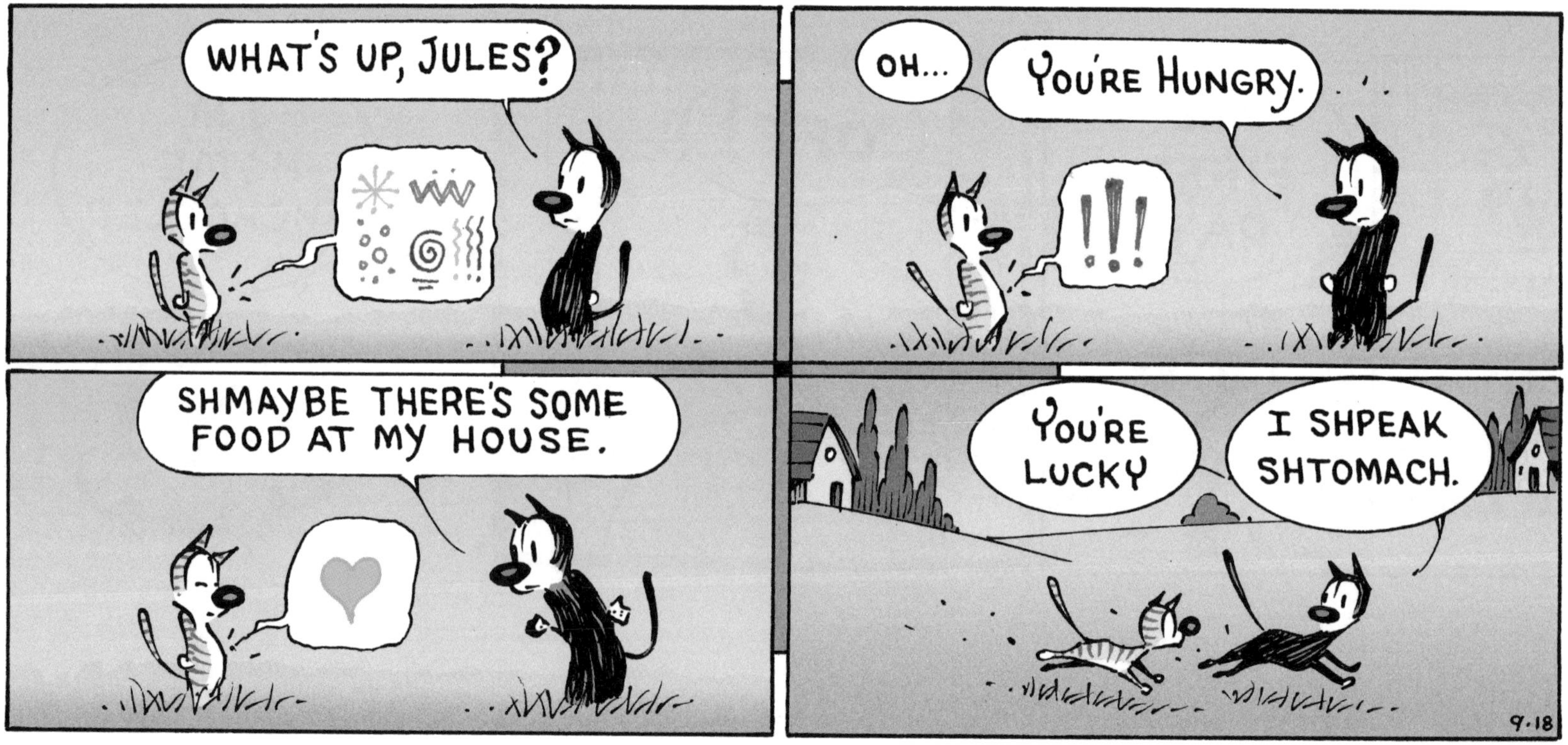
WHAT'S UP, JULES?
OH...
YOU'RE HUNGRY.
SHMAYBE THERE'S SOME FOOD AT MY HOUSE.
YOU'RE LUCKY
I SHPEAK SHTOMACH.
9·18

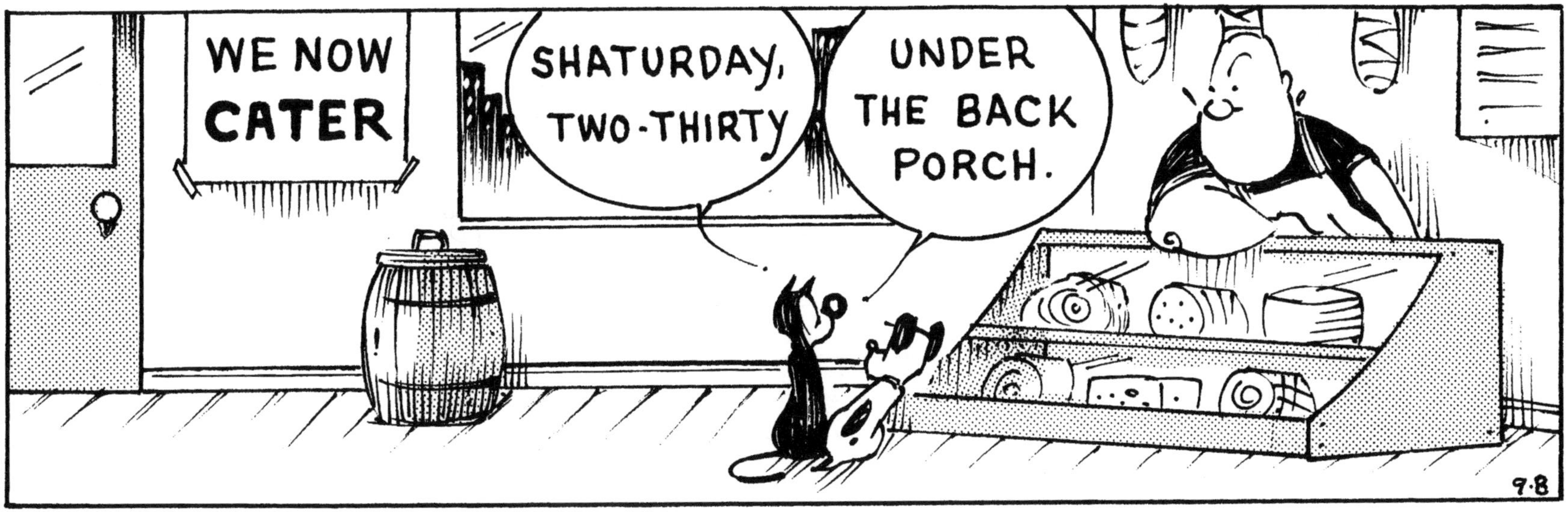
WE NOW CATER
SHATURDAY, TWO-THIRTY
UNDER THE BACK PORCH.
9·8

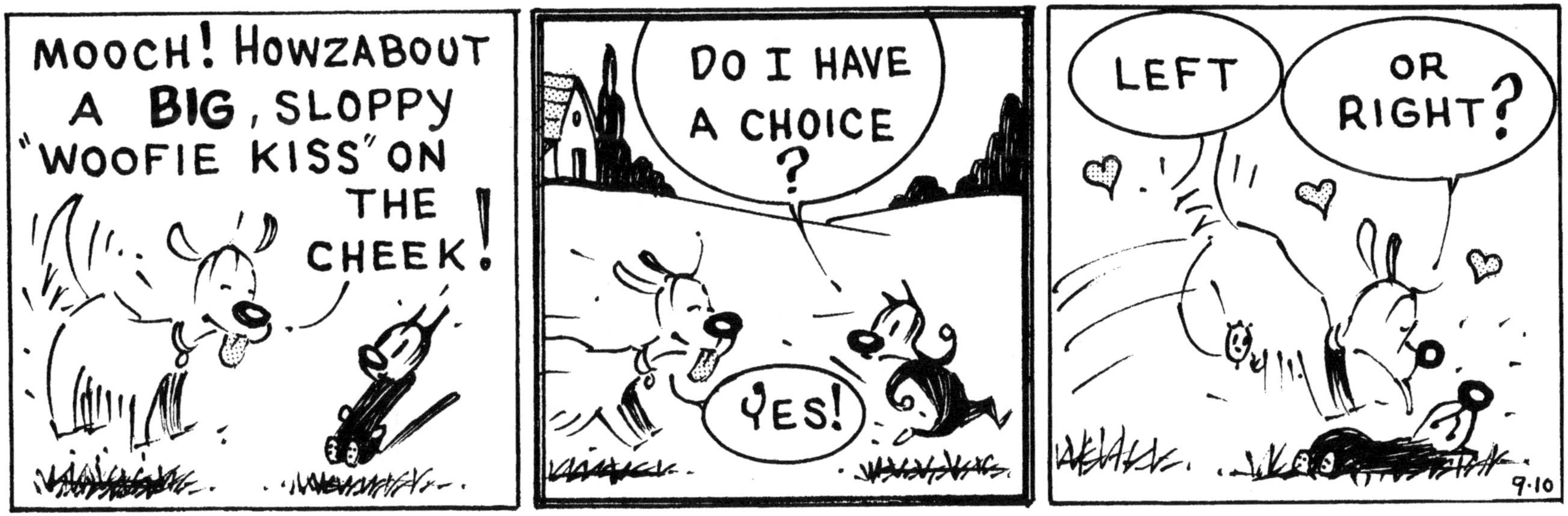
MOOCH! HOWZABOUT A BIG, SLOPPY "WOOFIE KISS" ON THE CHEEK!
DO I HAVE A CHOICE?
YES!
LEFT
OR RIGHT?
9·10

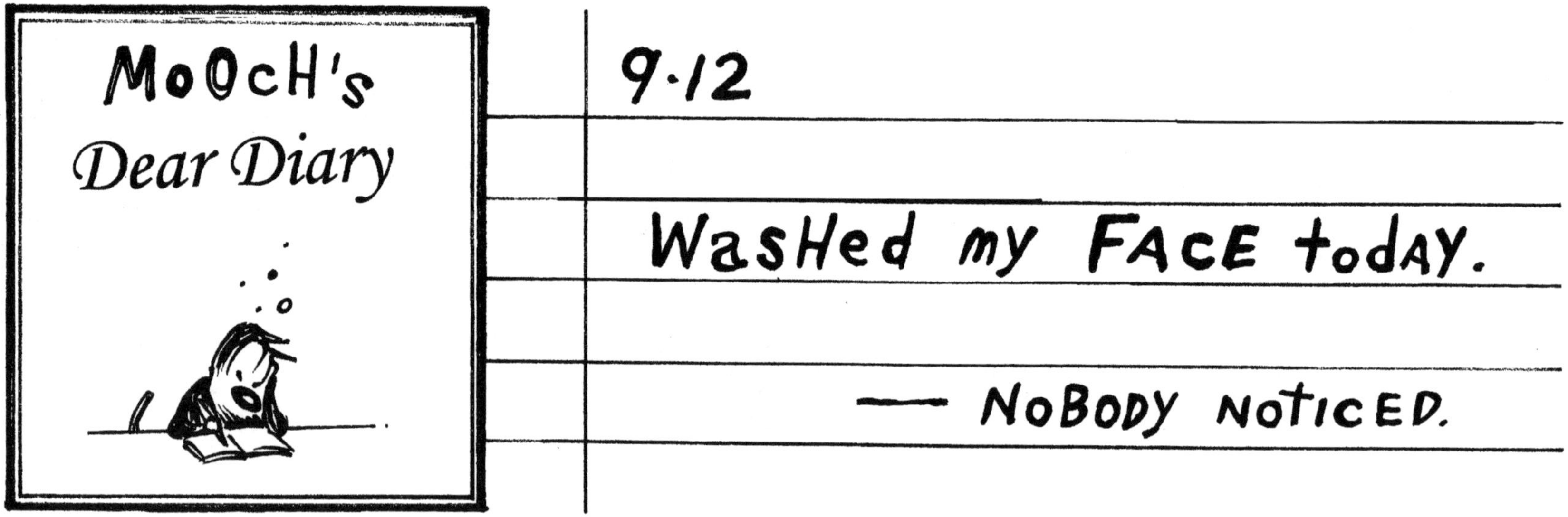
MOOCH'S
Dear Diary
9.12
WASHED MY FACE TODAY.
— NOBODY NOTICED.

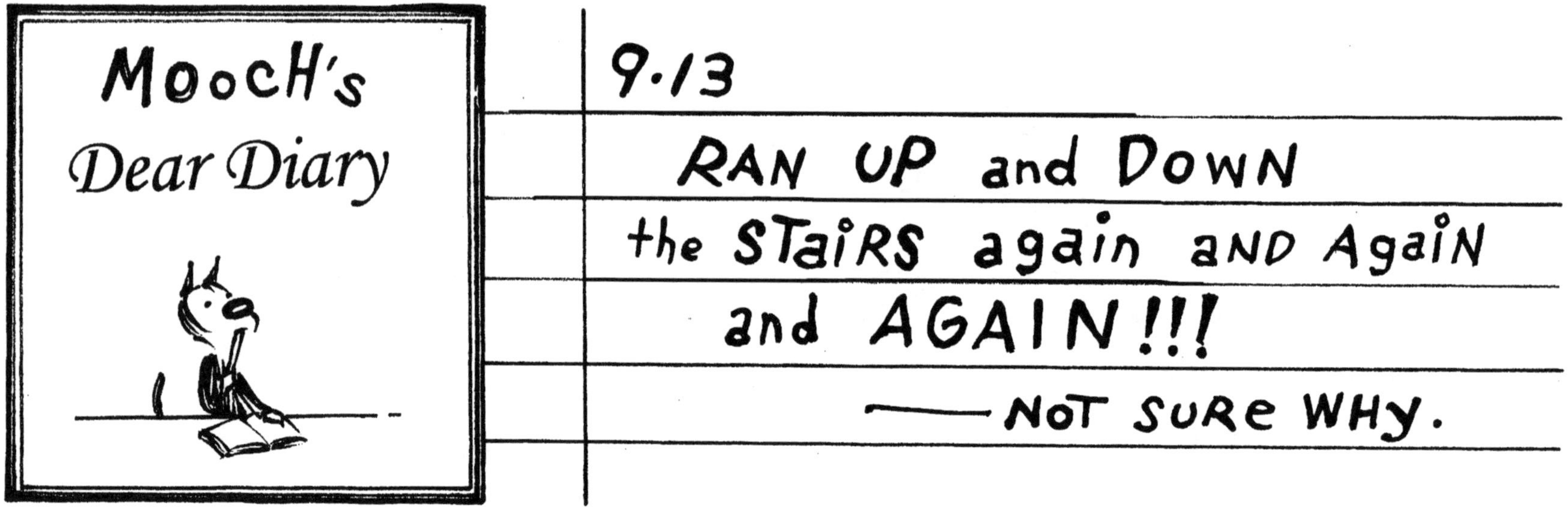
MOOCH'S
Dear Diary
9.13
RAN UP AND DOWN
THE STAIRS AGAIN AND AGAIN
AND AGAIN!!!
— NOT SURE WHY.

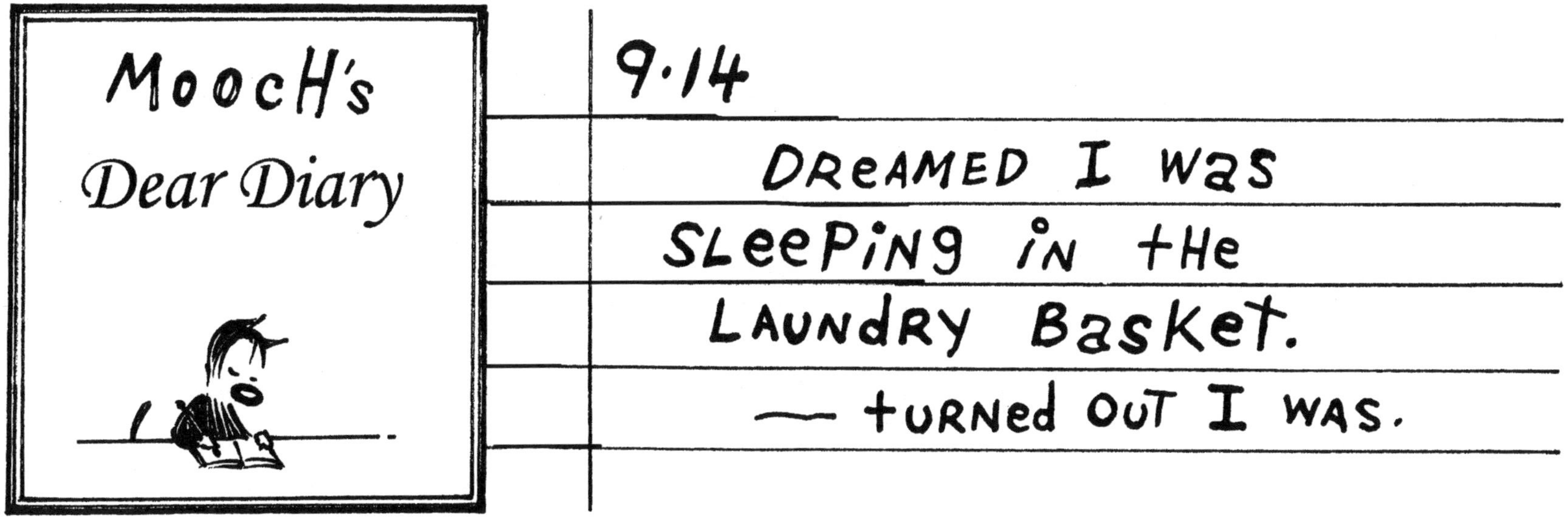
MOOCH'S
Dear Diary
9·14
DREAMED I WAS
SLEEPING IN THE
LAUNDRY BASKET.
— TURNED OUT I WAS.

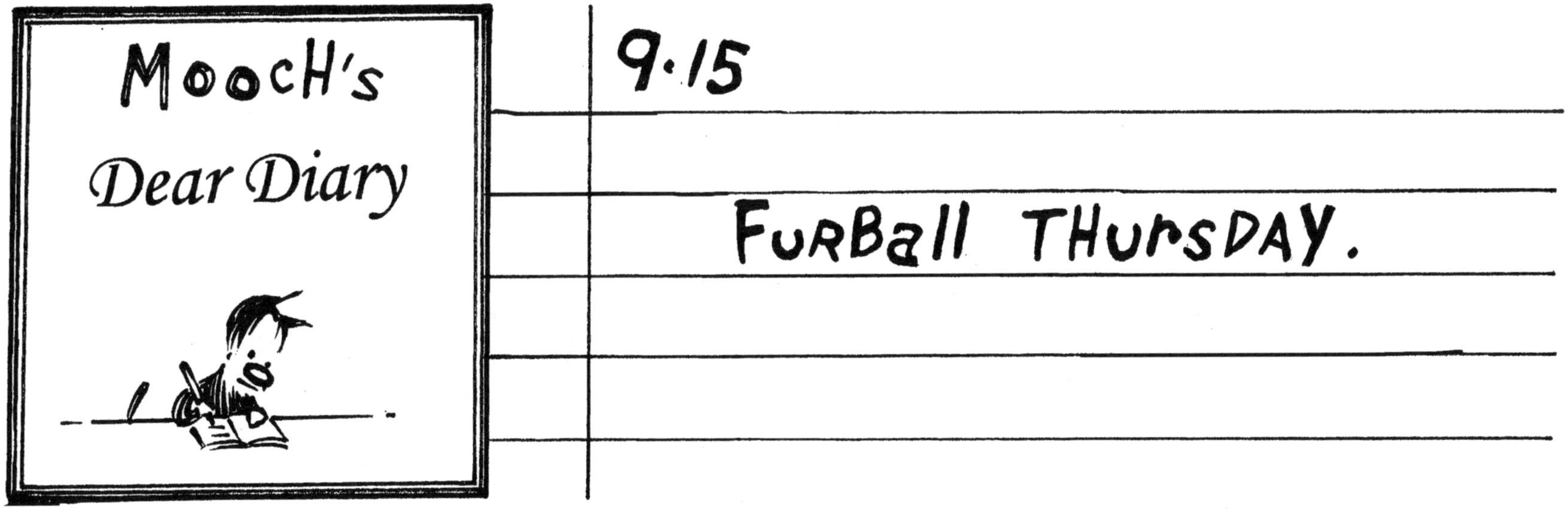
MOOCH'S
Dear Diary
9·15
FURBALL THURSDAY.

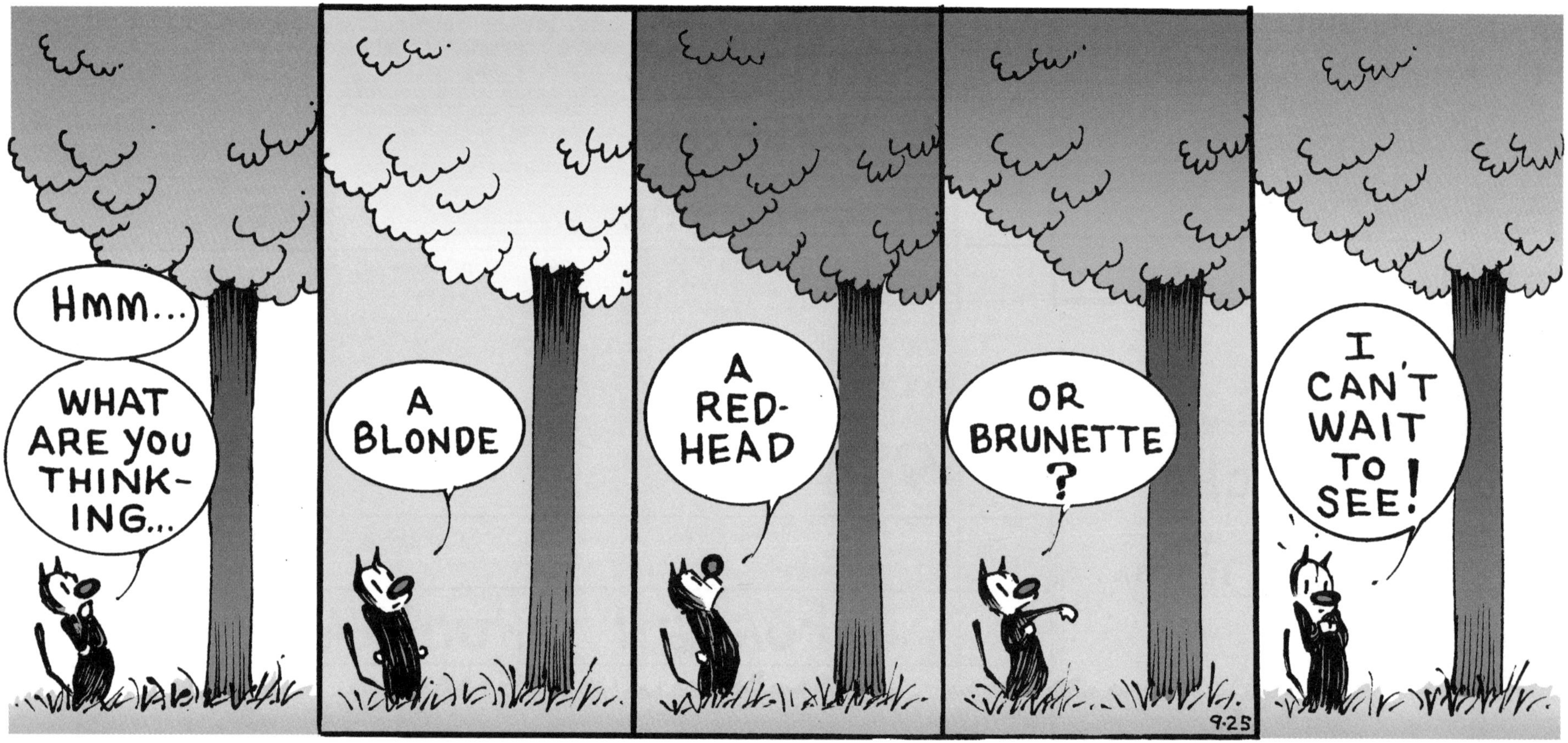
HMM...
WHAT ARE YOU THINKING...
A BLONDE
A RED-HEAD
OR BRUNETTE?
9.25
I CAN'T WAIT TO SEE!

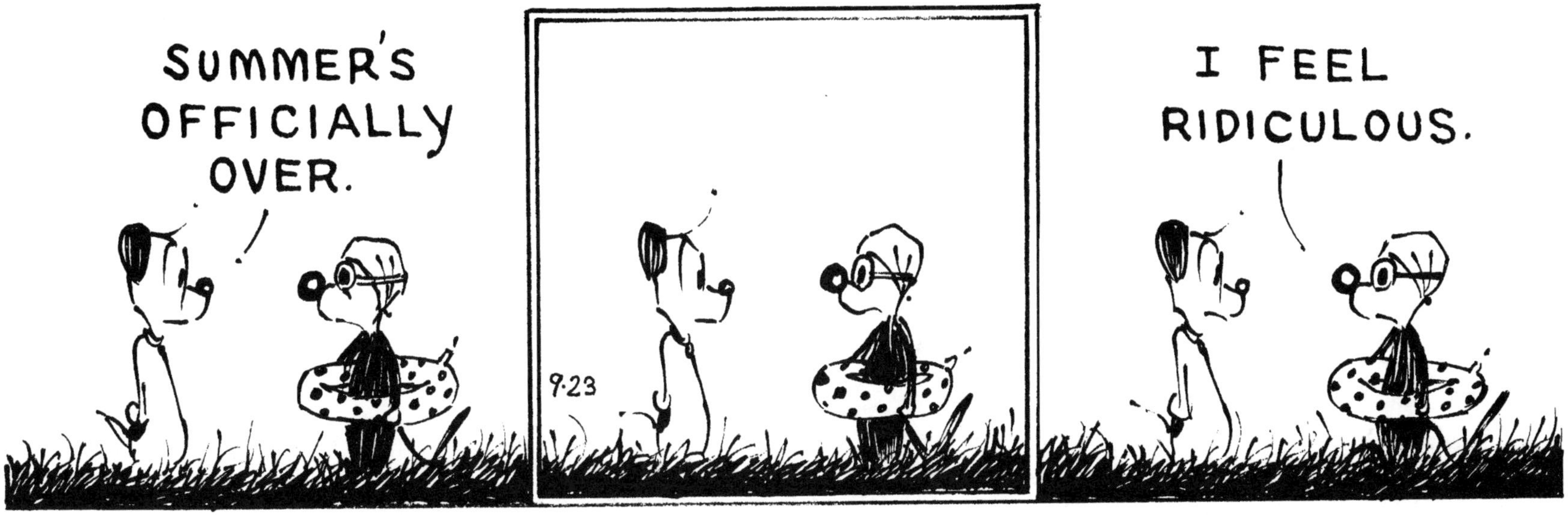
SUMMER'S OFFICIALLY OVER.
9·23
I FEEL RIDICULOUS.

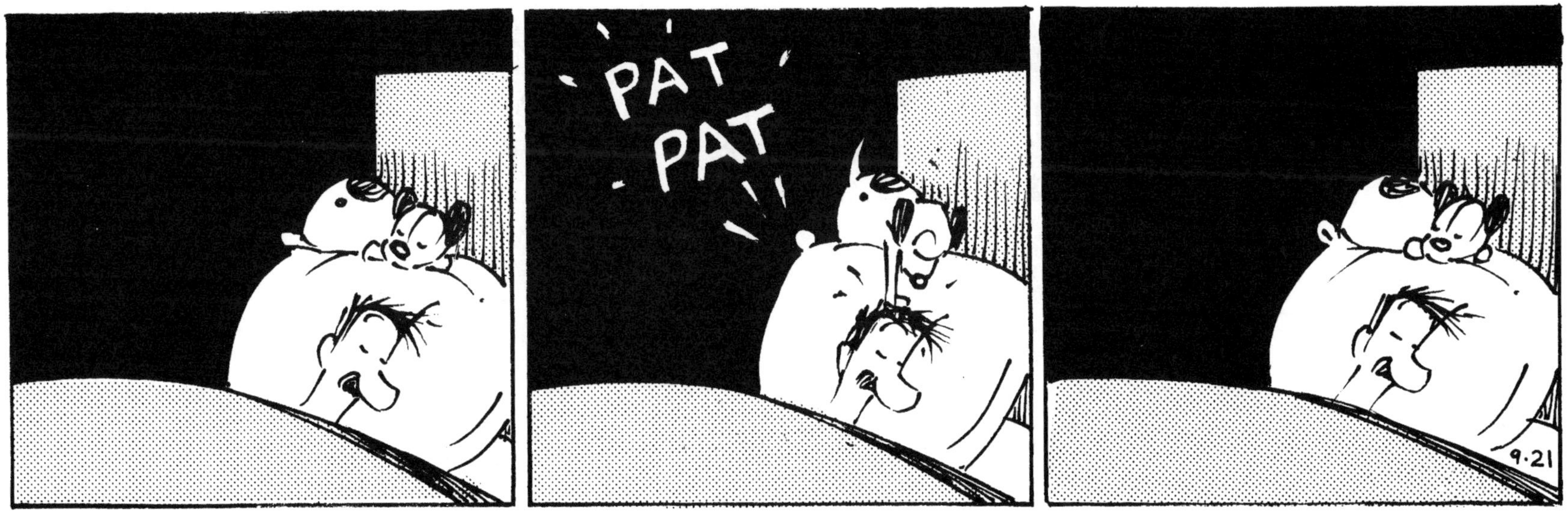
PAT PAT
9·21

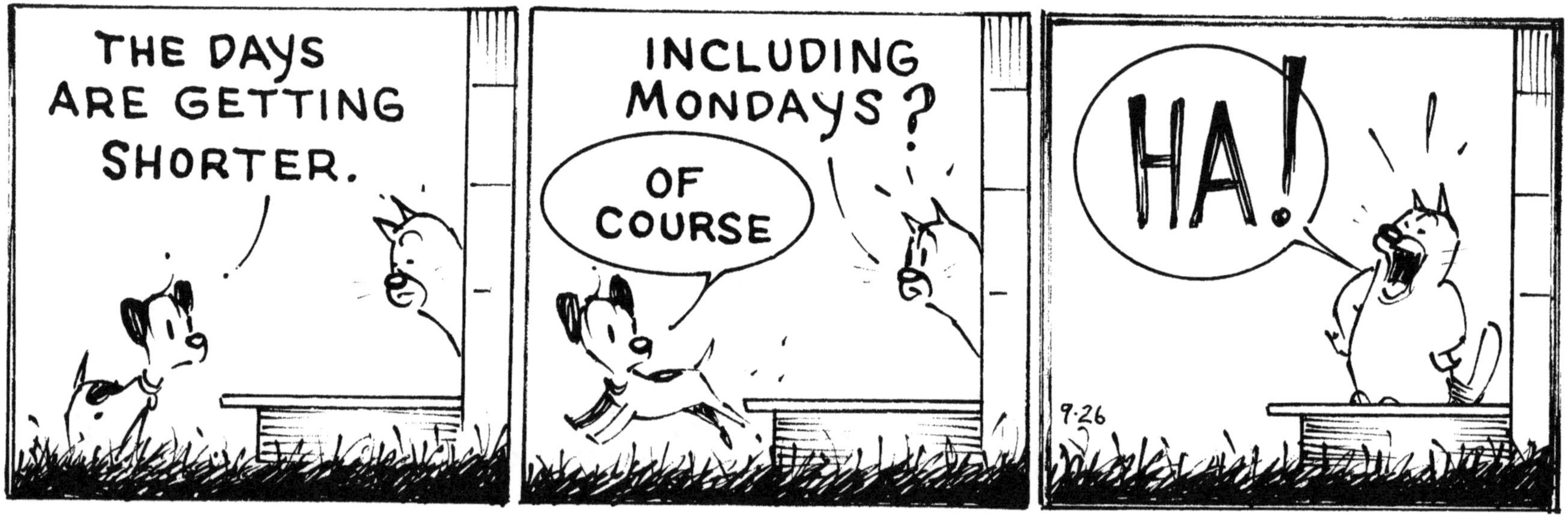
THE DAYS ARE GETTING SHORTER.
INCLUDING MONDAYS?
OF COURSE
HA!
9·26

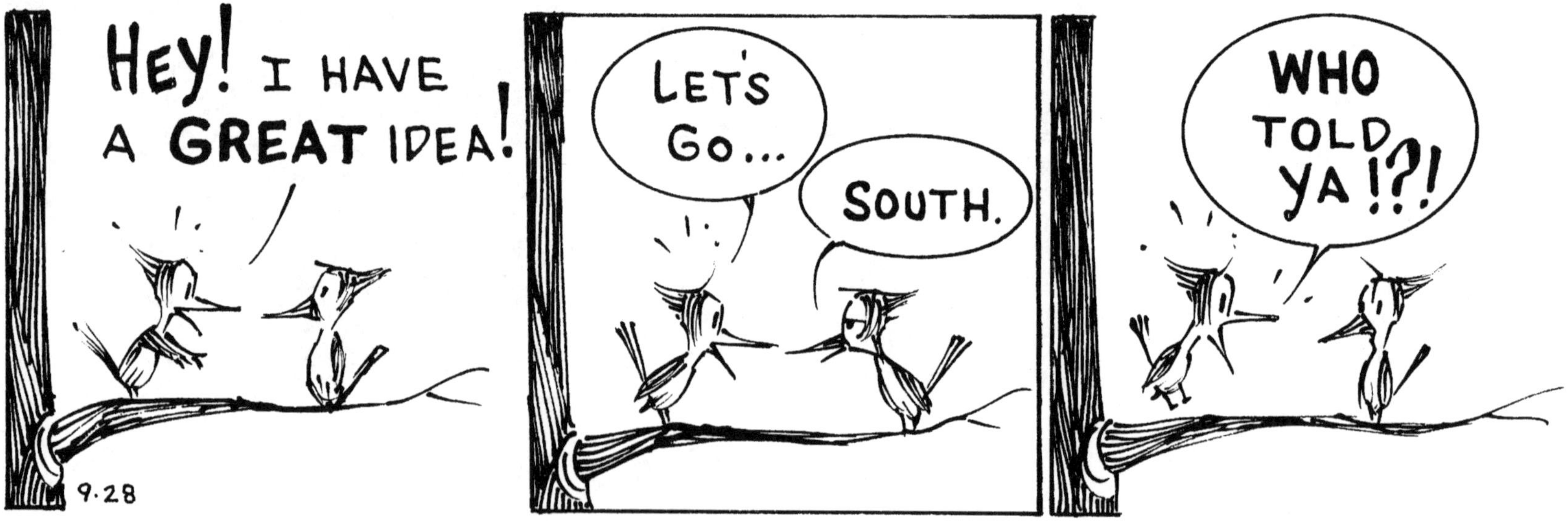
HEY! I HAVE A GREAT IDEA!
9·28
LET'S GO...
SOUTH.
WHO TOLD YA!?!

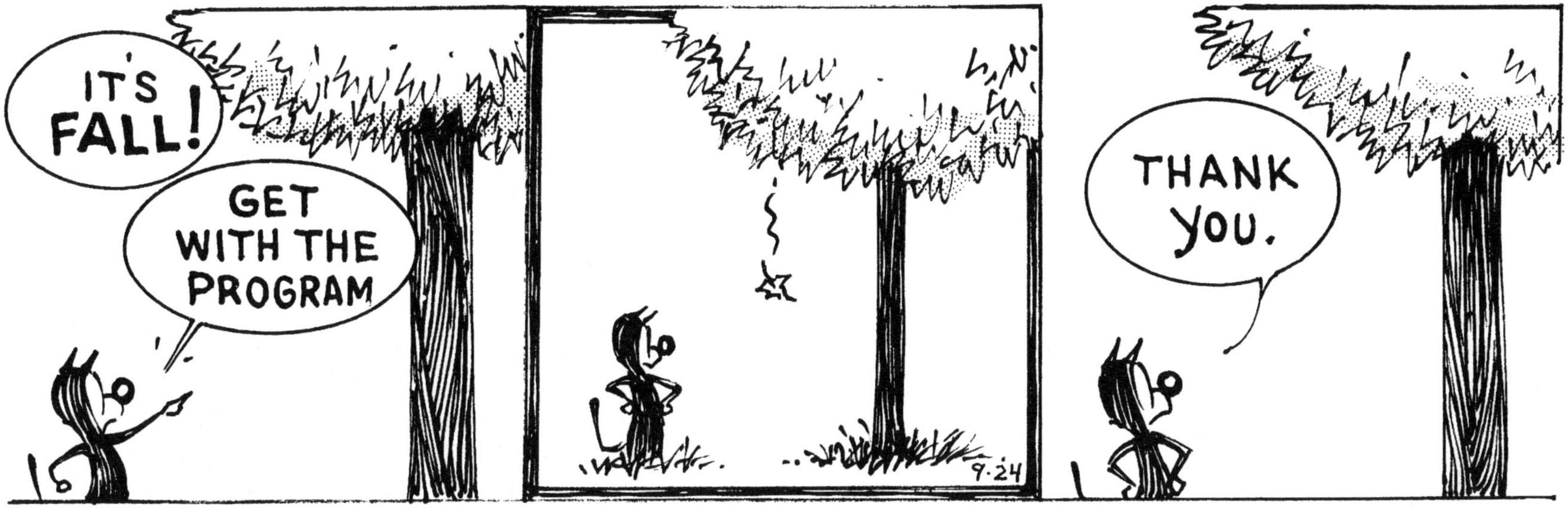
IT'S FALL!
GET WITH THE PROGRAM
9·24
THANK YOU.

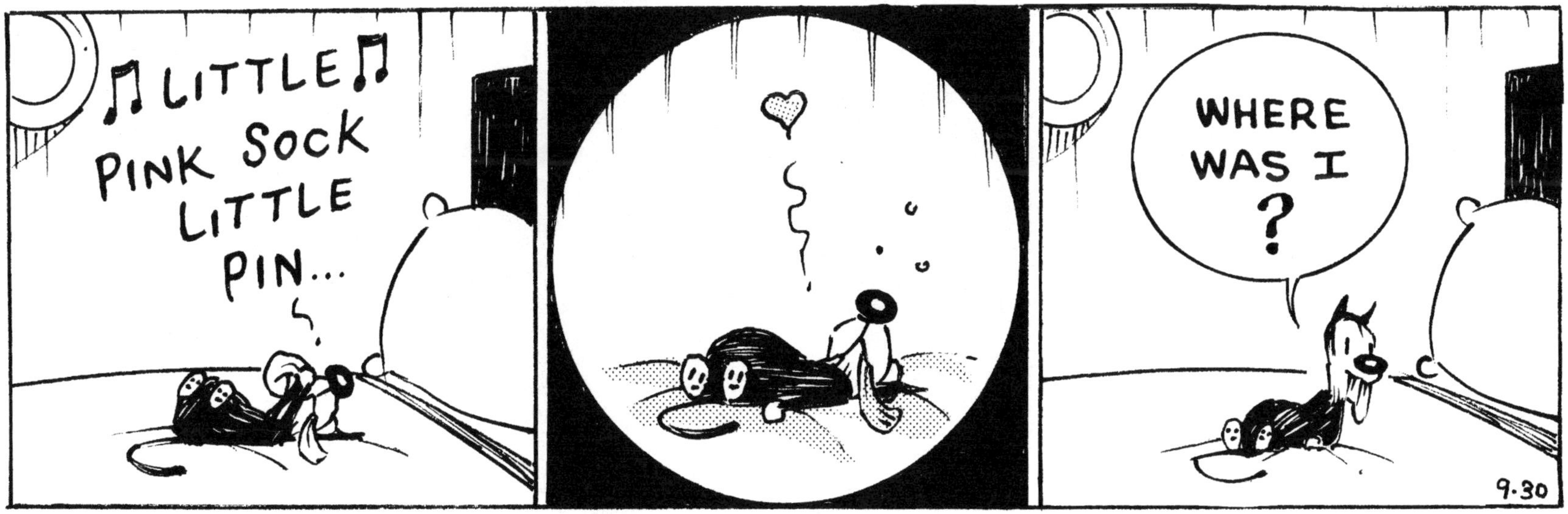
♫ LITTLE ♫ PINK SOCK LITTLE PIN...
WHERE WAS I ?
9·30

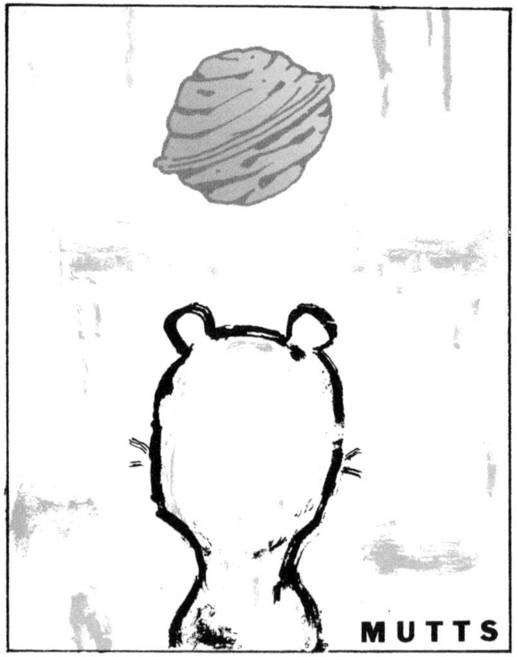
MUTTS

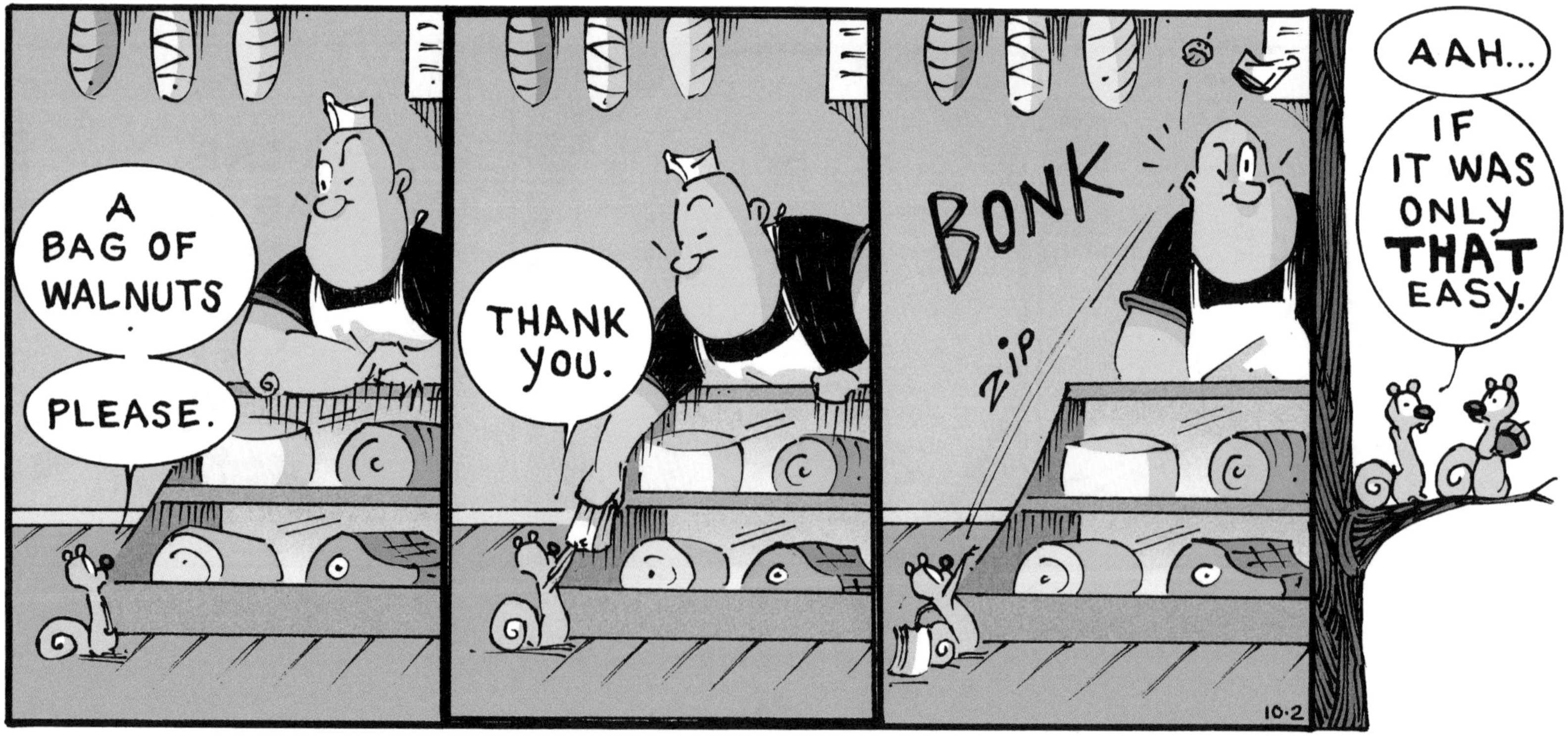
A BAG OF WALNUTS.
PLEASE.
THANK YOU.
BONK
ZIP
AAH...
IF IT WAS ONLY THAT EASY.
10·2

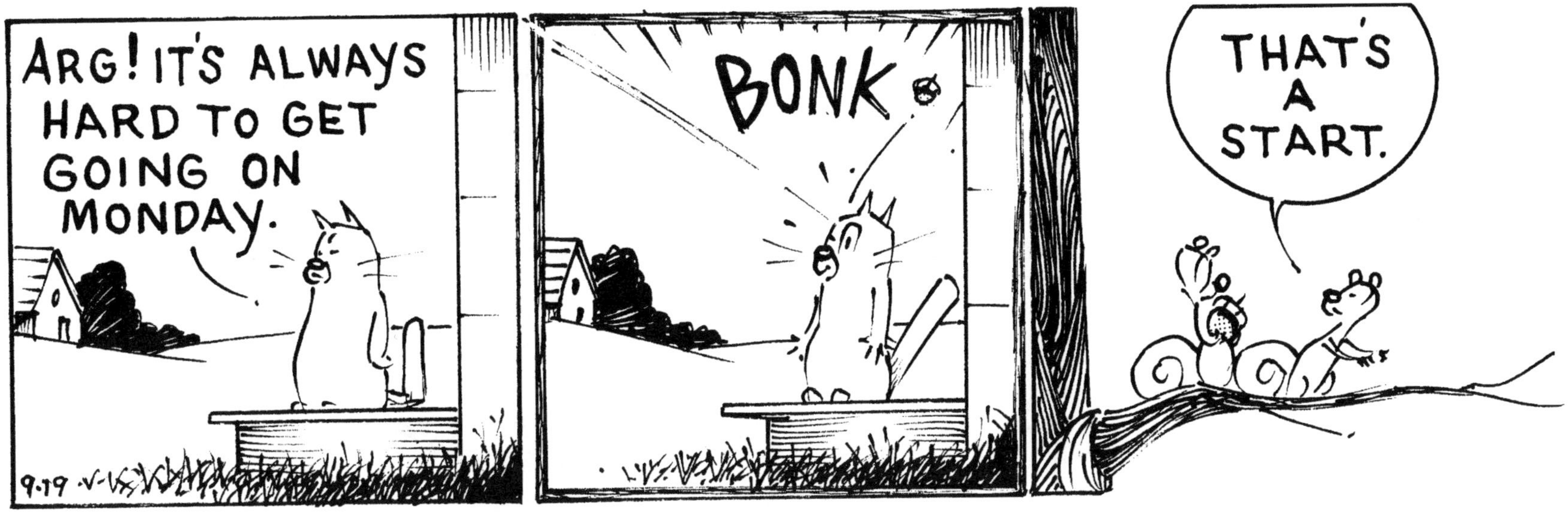
ARG! IT'S ALWAYS HARD TO GET GOING ON MONDAY.
9·19
BONK
THAT'S A START.

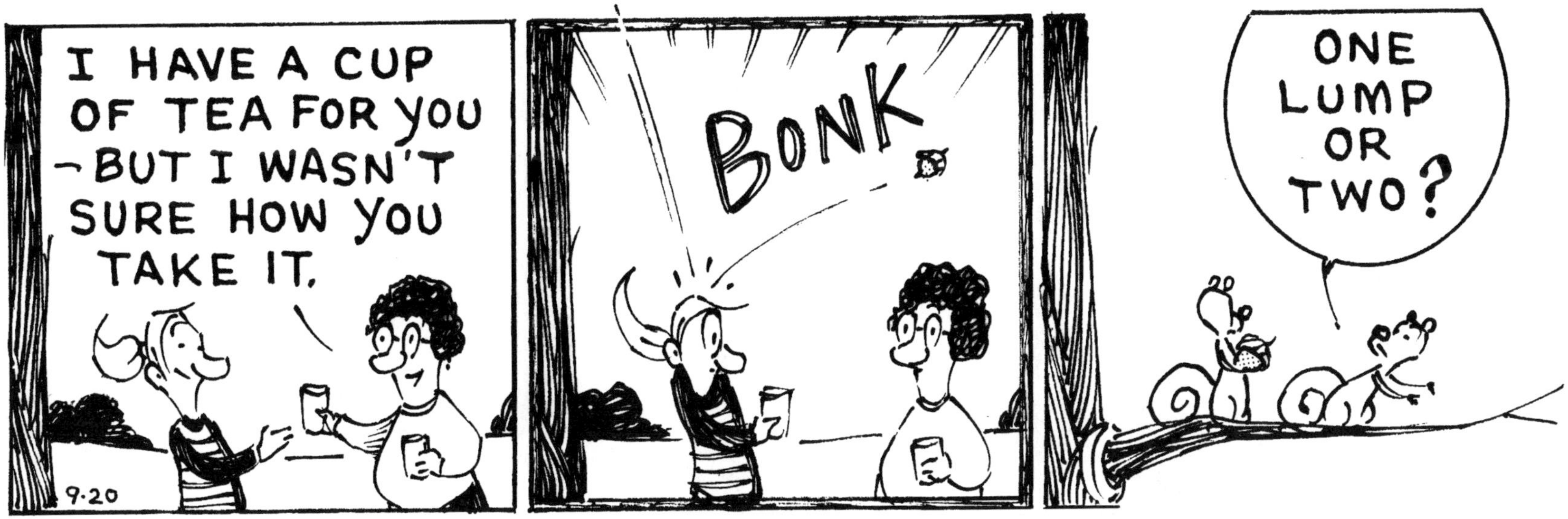
I HAVE A CUP OF TEA FOR YOU – BUT I WASN'T SURE HOW YOU TAKE IT.
9·20
BONK
ONE LUMP OR TWO?

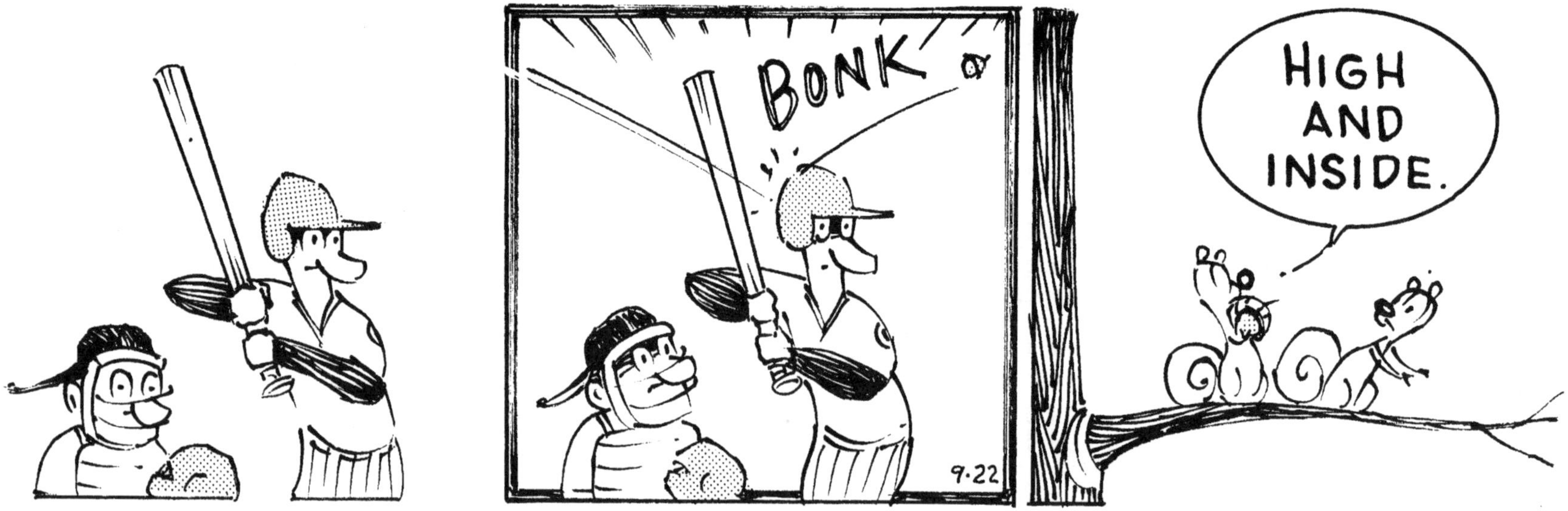
BONK
9·22
HIGH AND INSIDE.

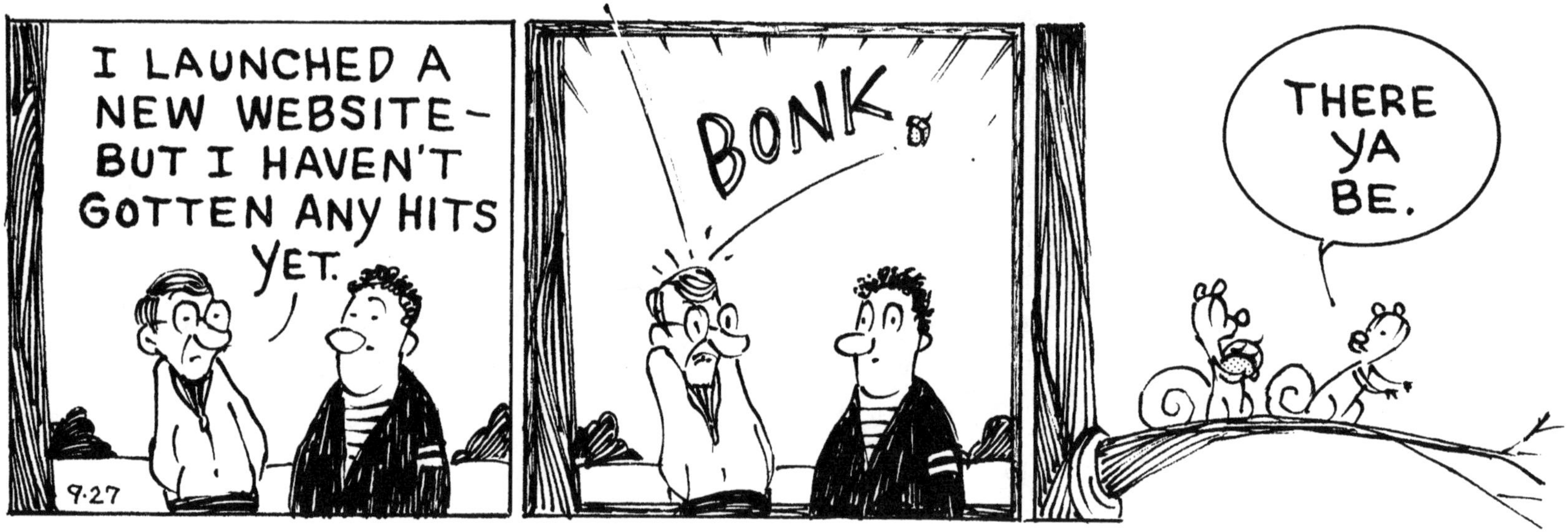
I LAUNCHED A NEW WEBSITE- BUT I HAVEN'T GOTTEN ANY HITS YET.
9·27
BONK
THERE YA BE.

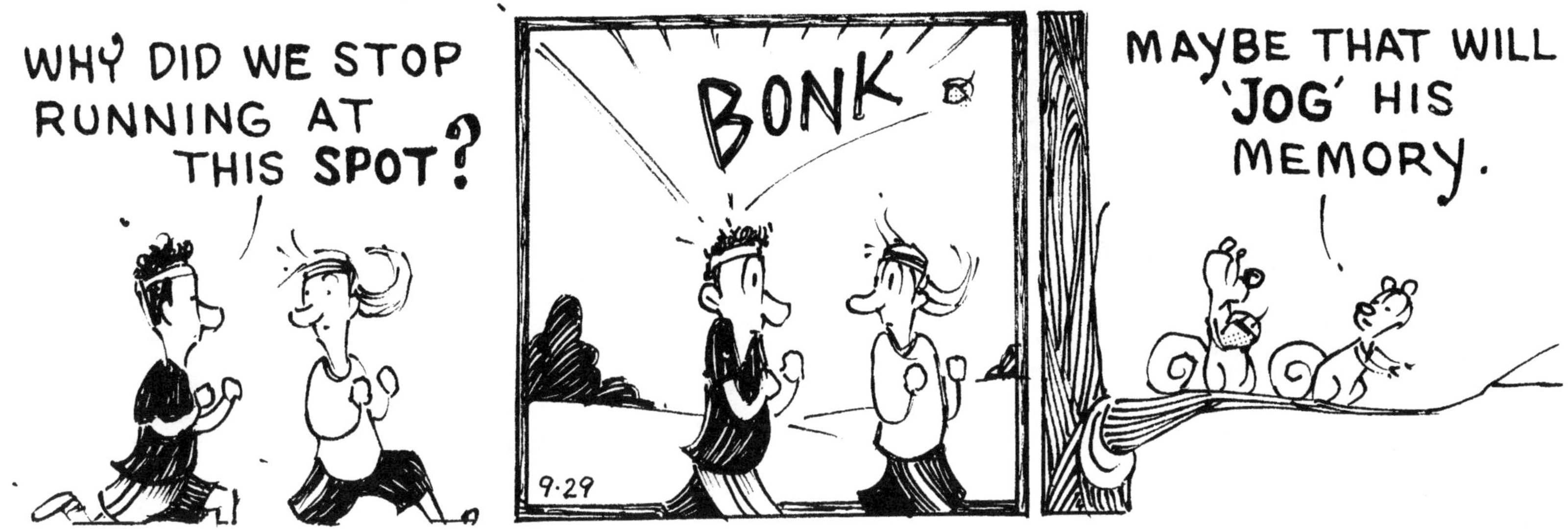
WHY DID WE STOP RUNNING AT THIS SPOT?
BONK
9·29
MAYBE THAT WILL 'JOG' HIS MEMORY.

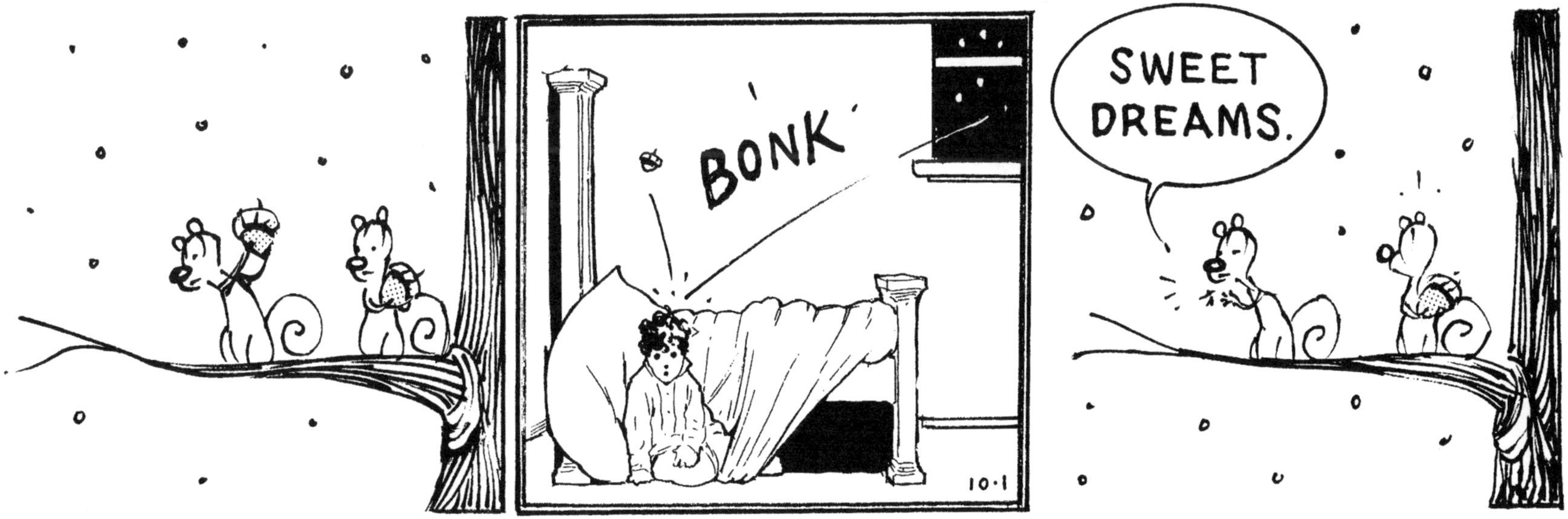
BONK
10·1
SWEET DREAMS.

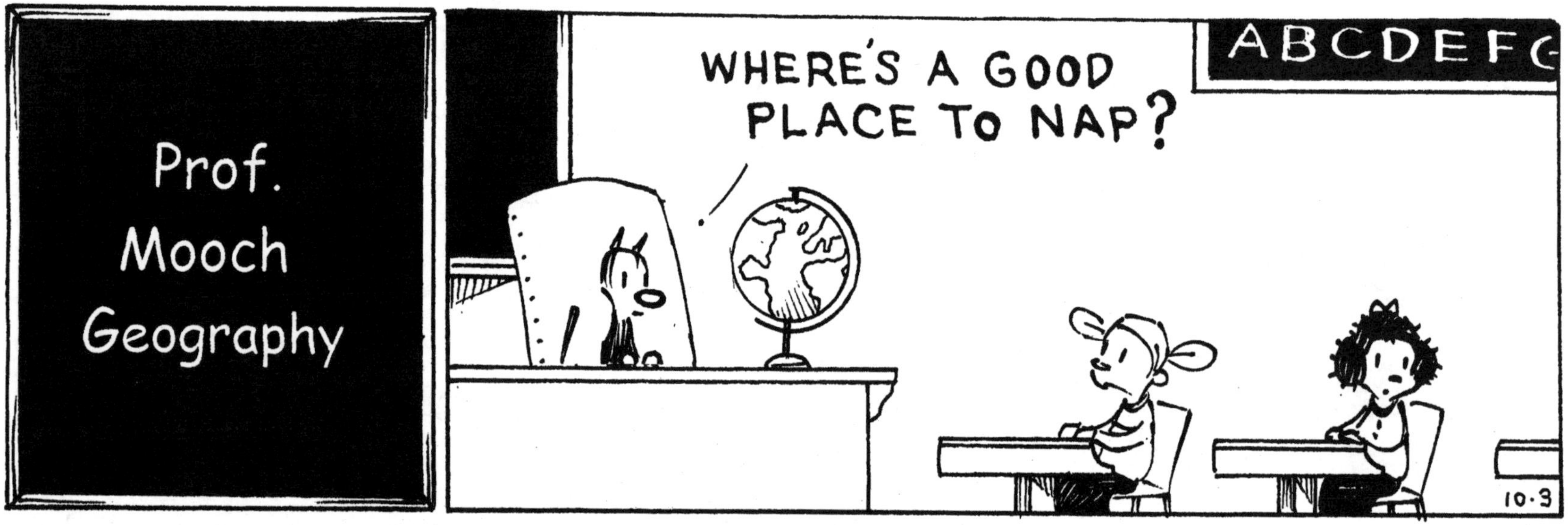
Prof.
Mooch
Geography
WHERE'S A GOOD PLACE TO NAP?
ABCDEFG
10·3

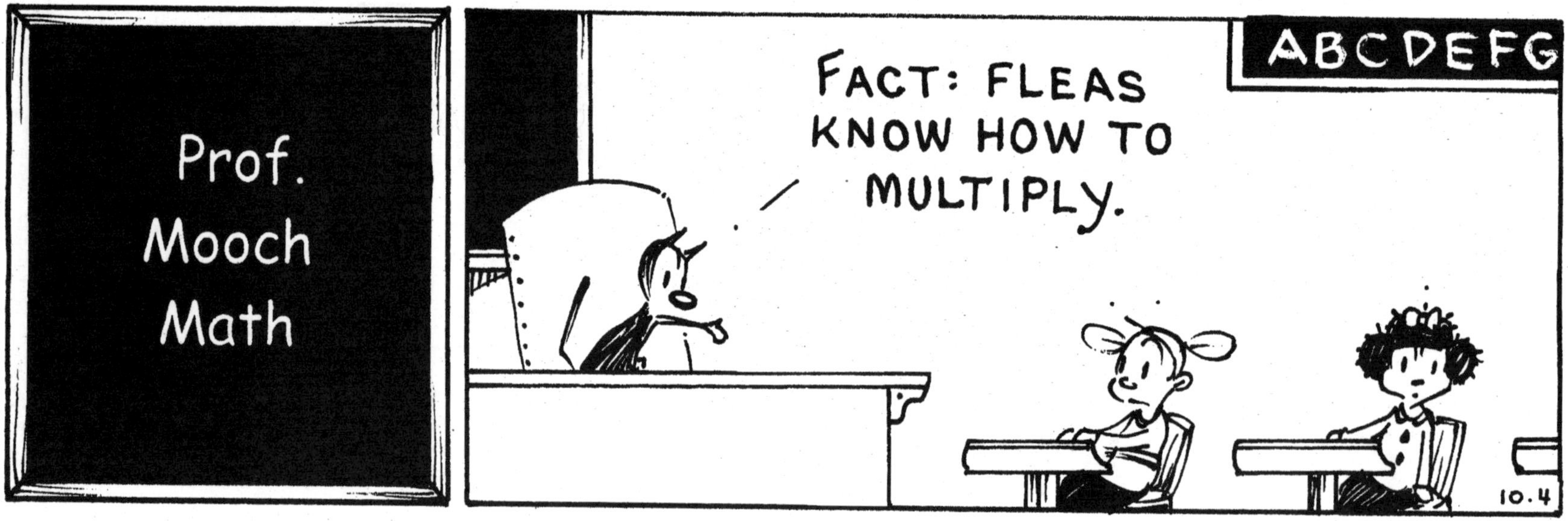
Prof.
Mooch
Math
FACT: FLEAS KNOW HOW TO MULTIPLY.
ABCDEFG
10·4

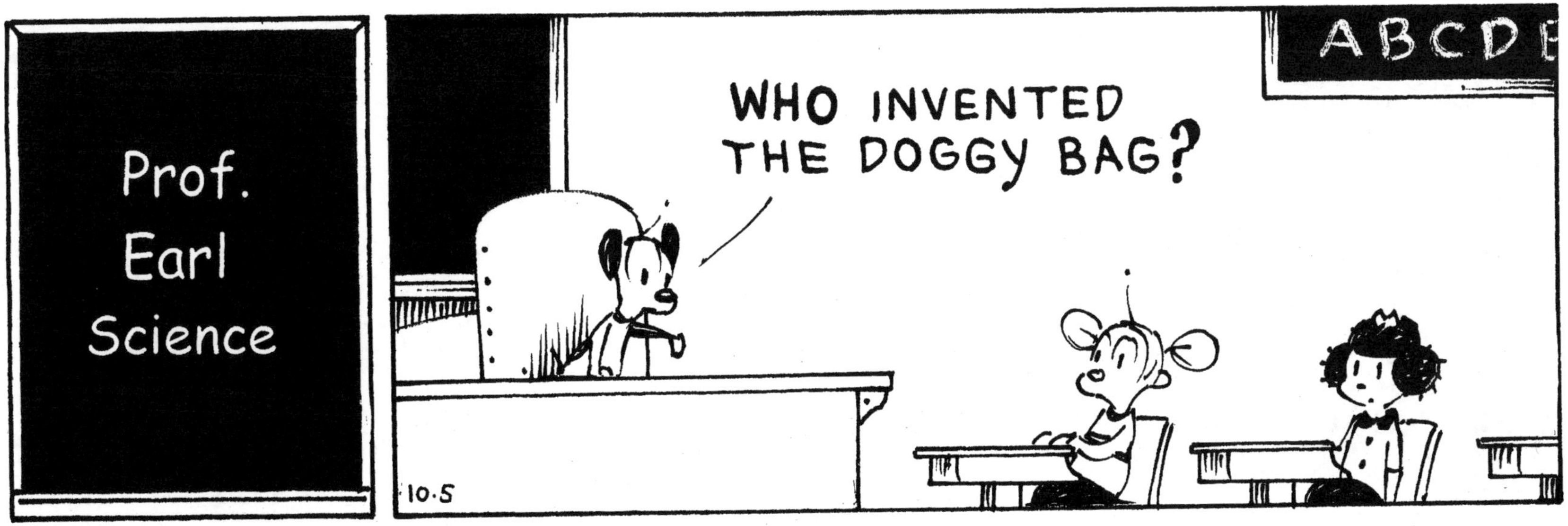
Prof.
Earl
Science
ABCDE
WHO INVENTED THE DOGGY BAG?
10·5

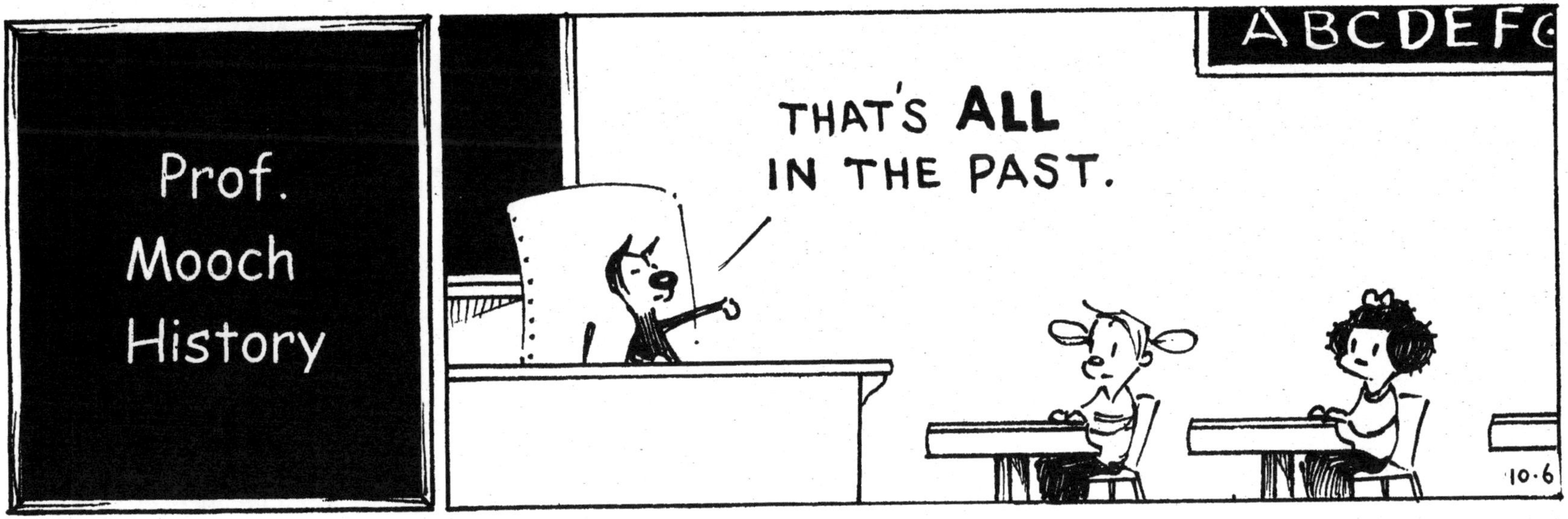
Prof.
Mooch
History
ABCDEFG
THAT'S **ALL** IN THE PAST.
10·6

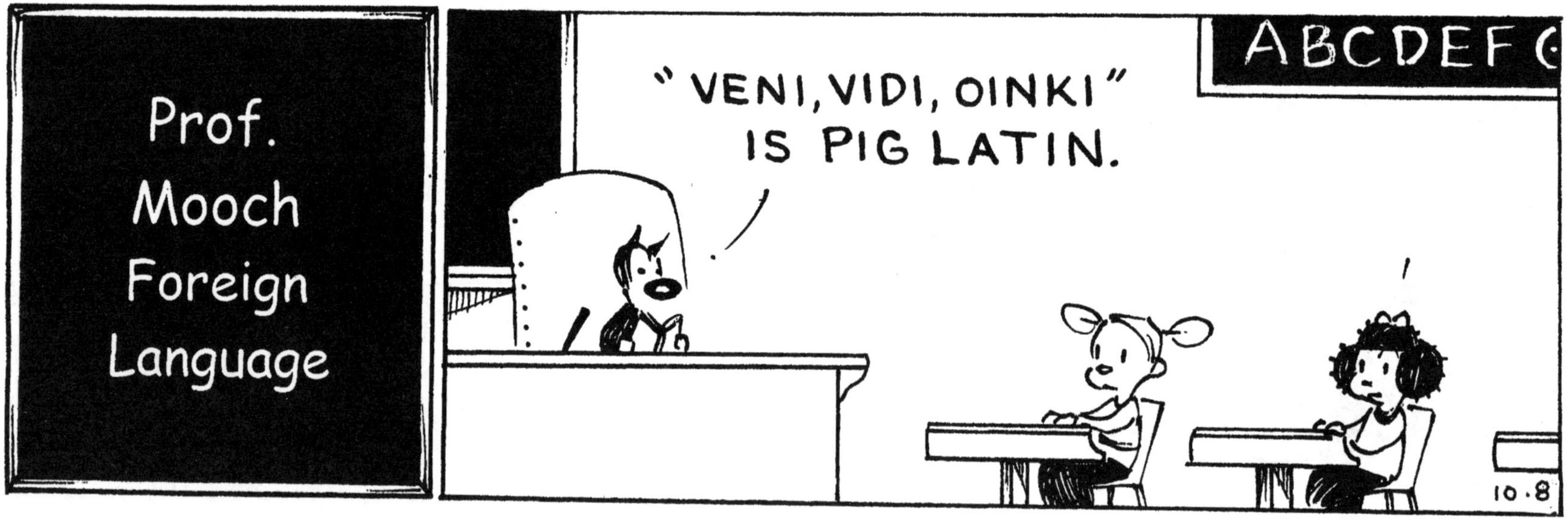
Prof.
Mooch
Foreign
Language
ABCDEF
"VENI, VIDI, OINKI" IS PIG LATIN.
10·8

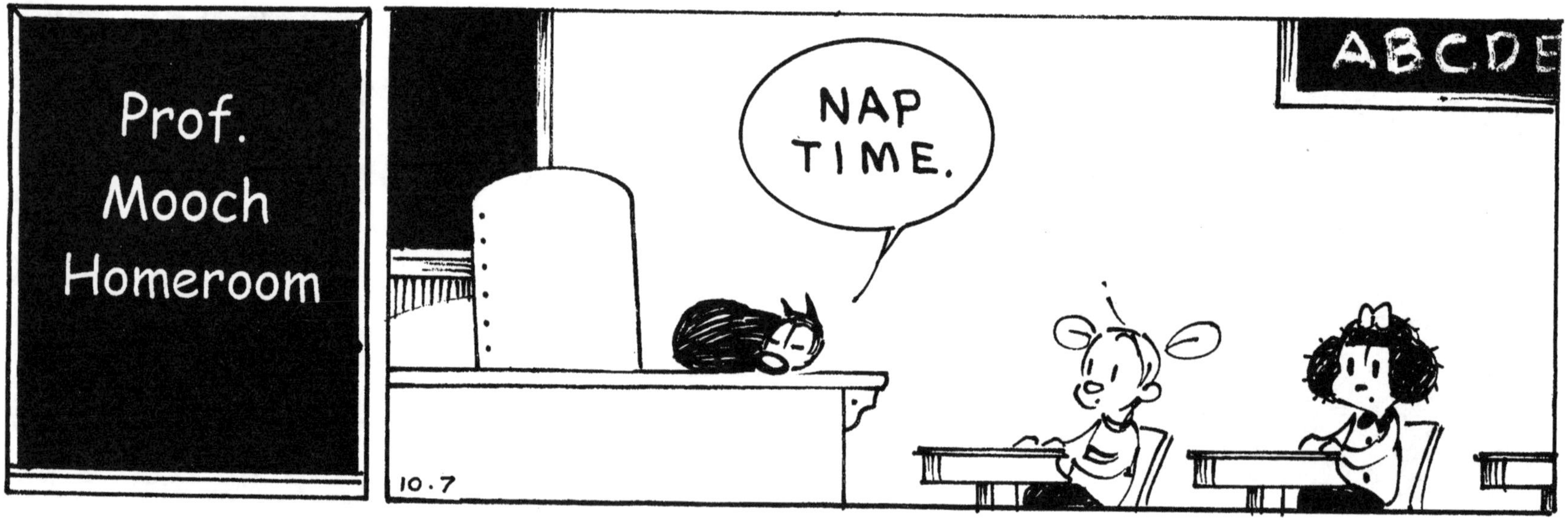
Prof.
Mooch
Homeroom
ABCDE
NAP TIME.
10·7

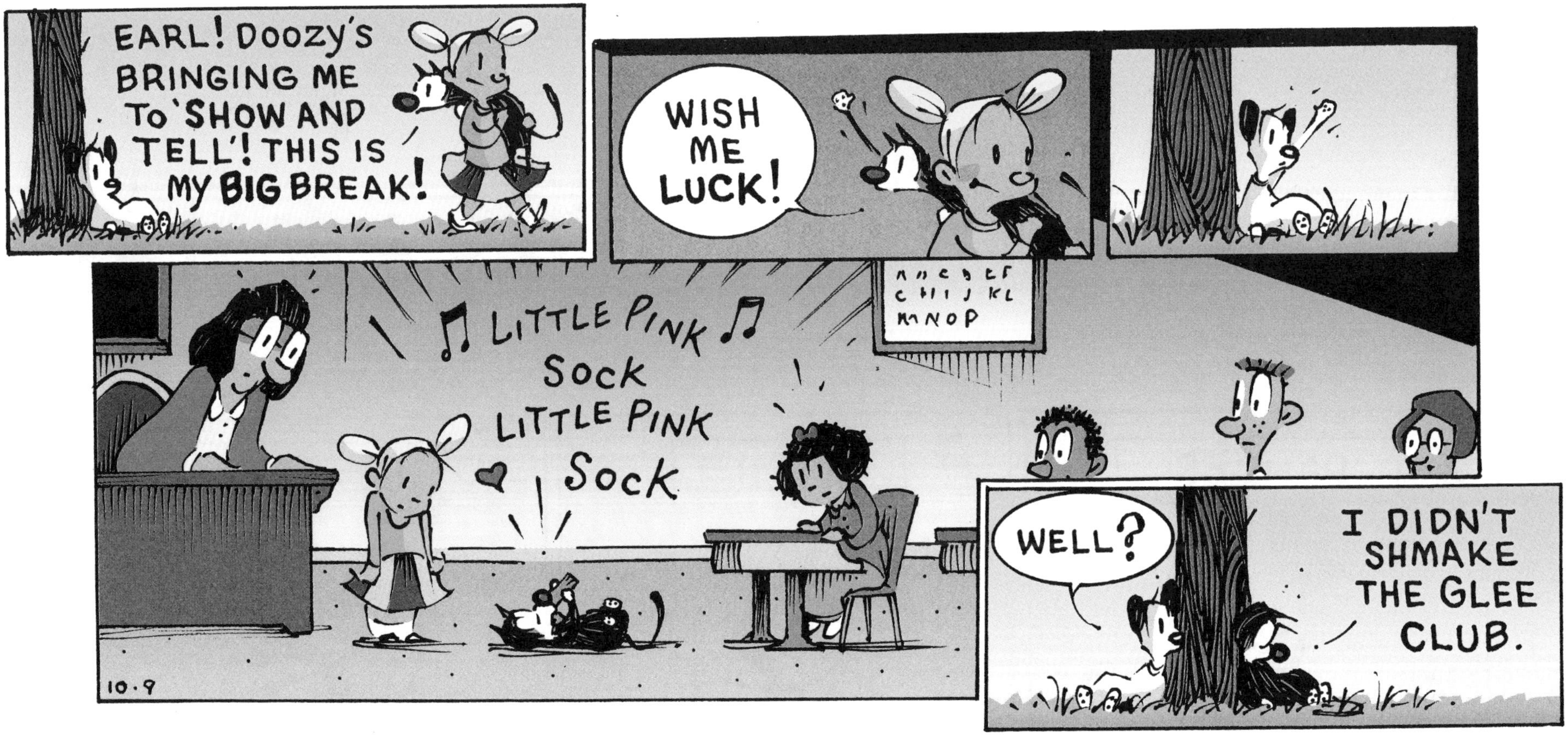
EARL! DOOZY'S BRINGING ME TO 'SHOW AND TELL'! THIS IS MY BIG BREAK!
WISH ME LUCK!
♫ LITTLE PINK ♫ SOCK LITTLE PINK SOCK
WELL?
I DIDN'T SHMAKE THE GLEE CLUB.
10·9

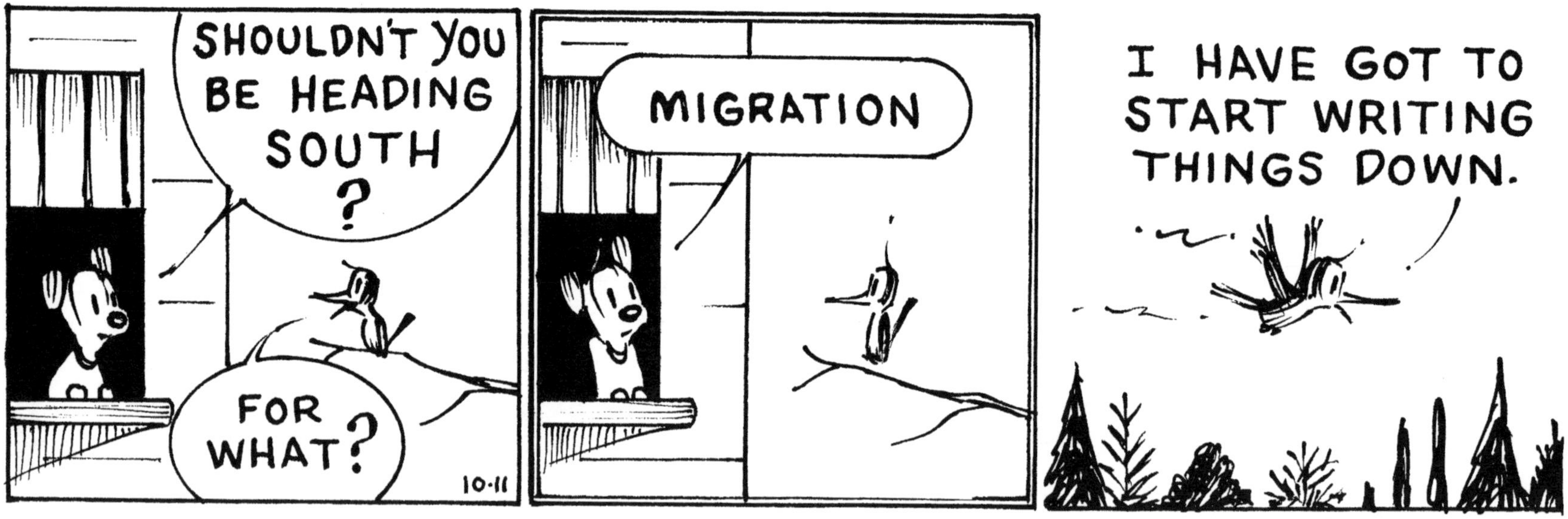
SHOULDN'T YOU BE HEADING SOUTH ?
FOR WHAT?
MIGRATION
I HAVE GOT TO START WRITING THINGS DOWN.
10·11

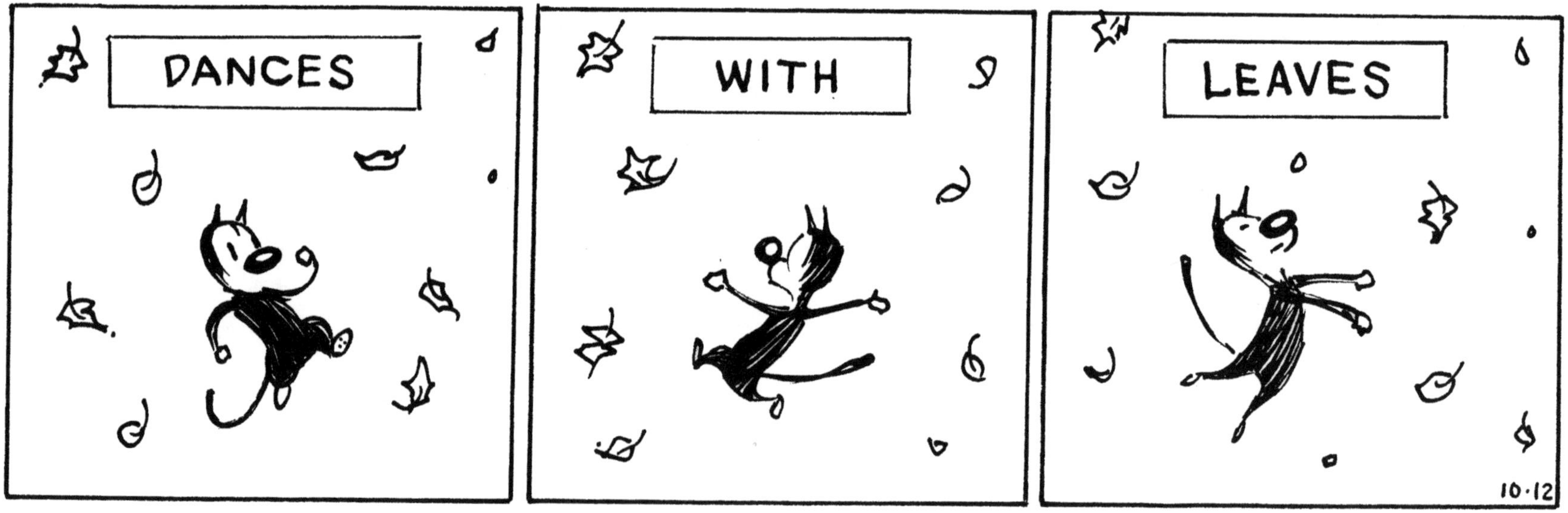
DANCES
WITH
LEAVES
10·12

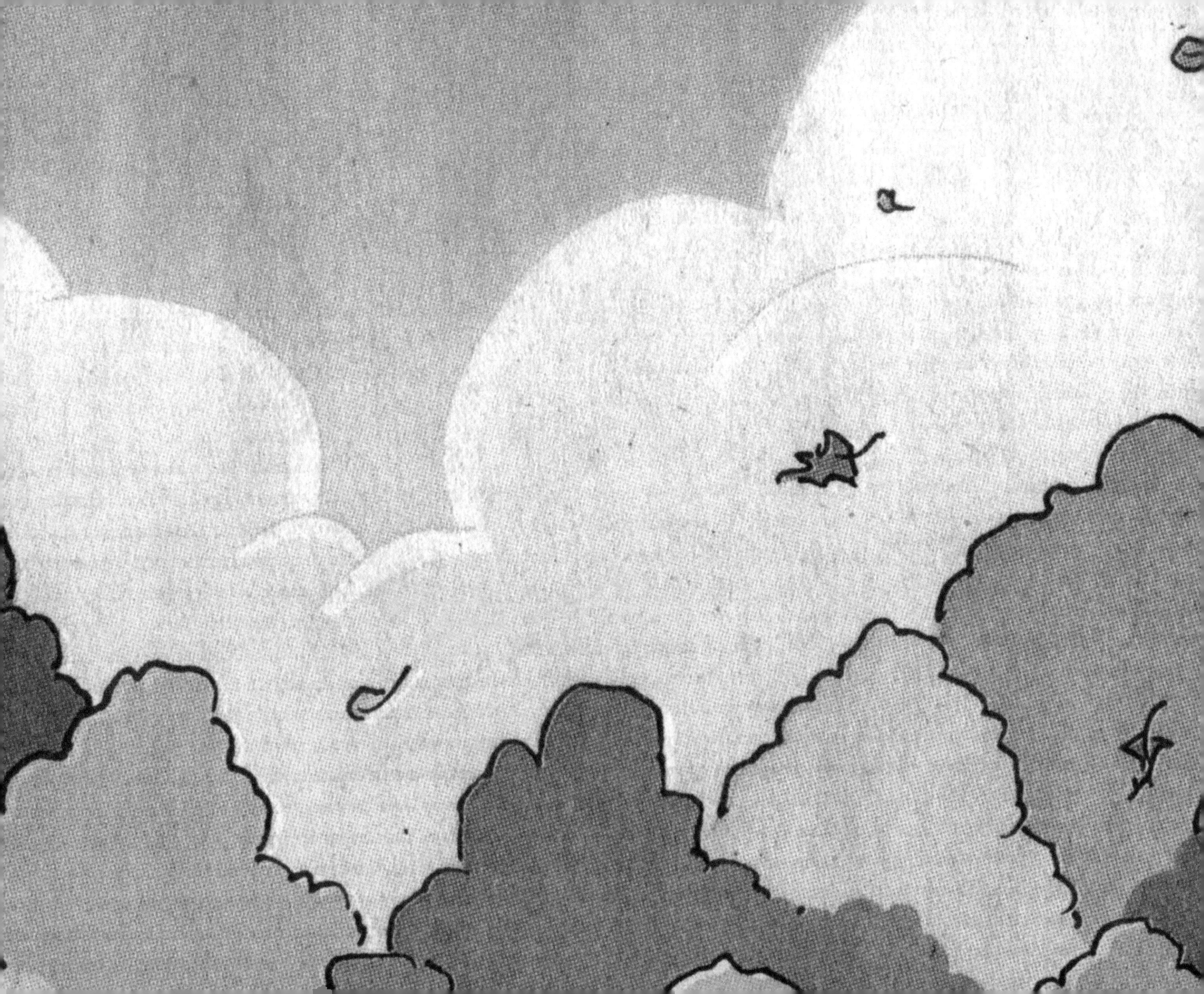

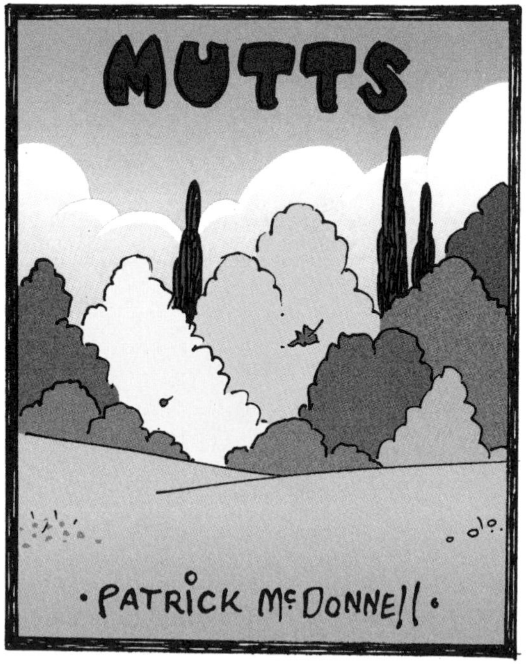
MUTTS
·PATRICK McDONNELL·

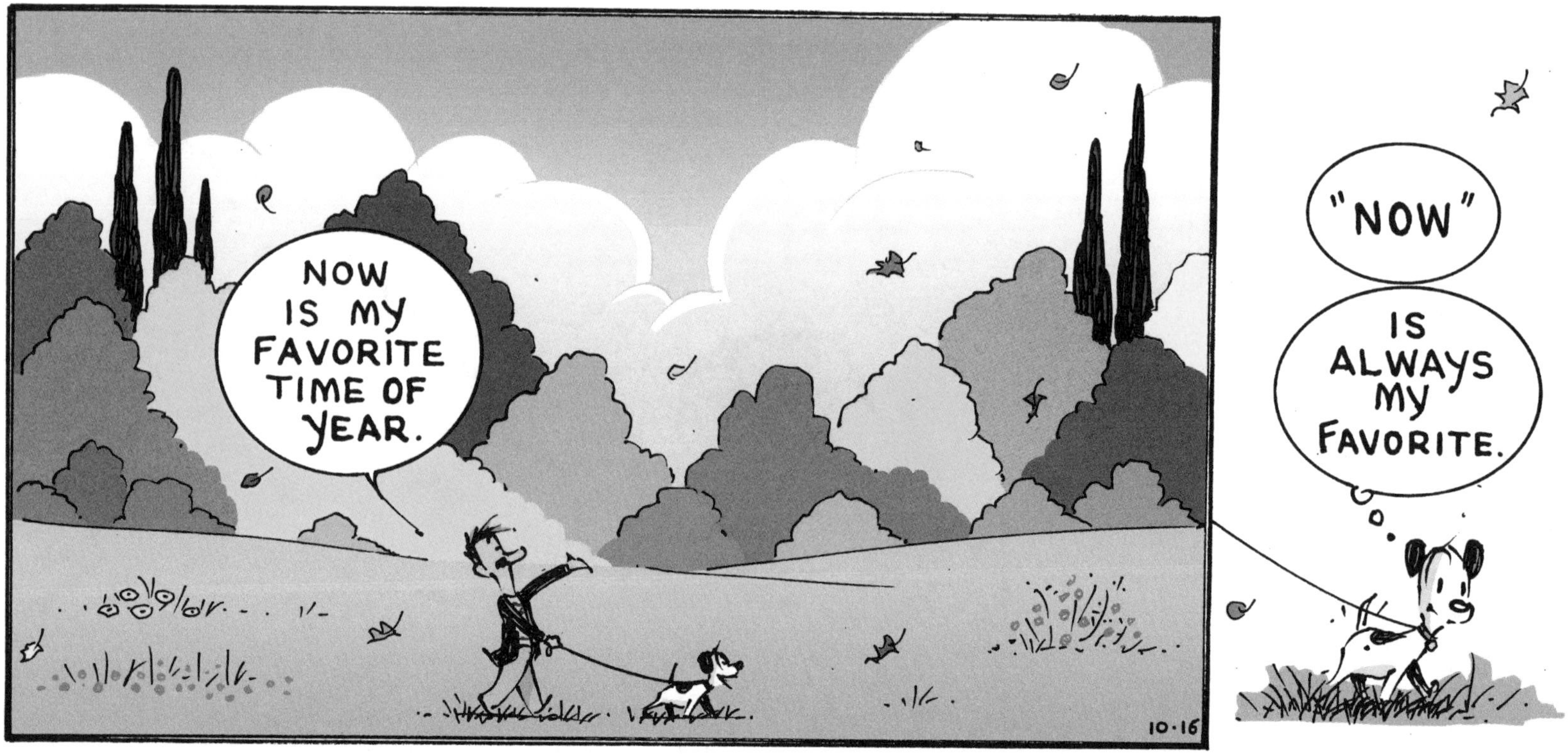
NOW IS MY FAVORITE TIME OF YEAR.
"NOW"
IS ALWAYS MY FAVORITE.
10·16

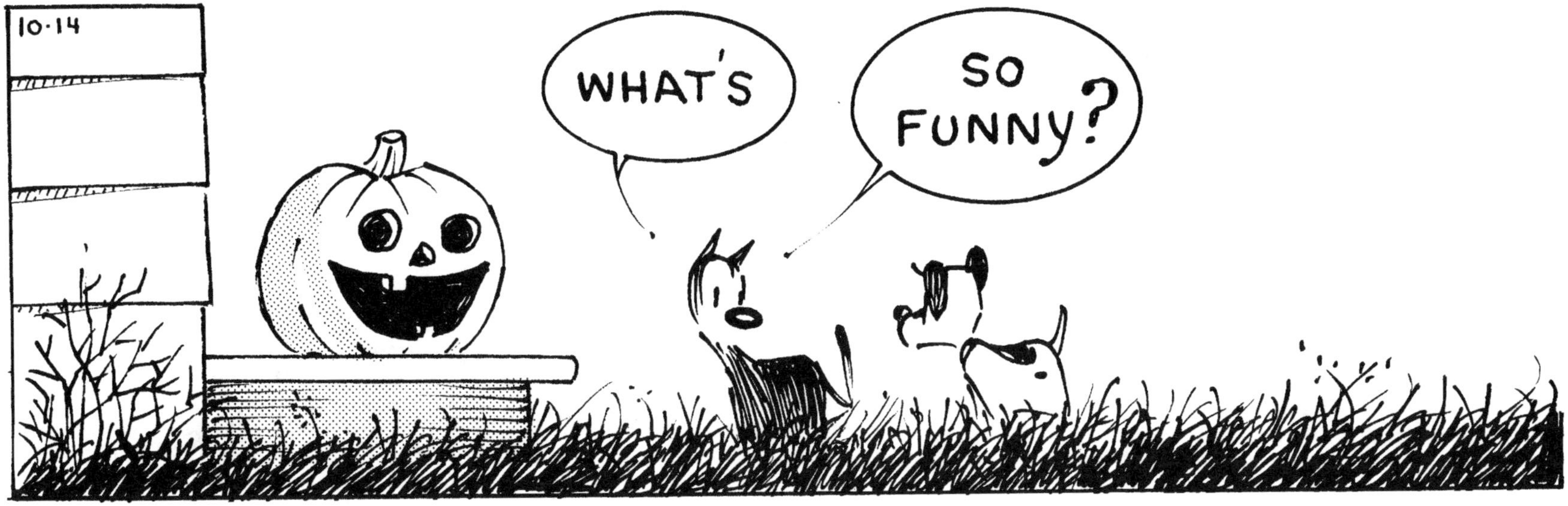
10·14
WHAT'S
SO FUNNY?

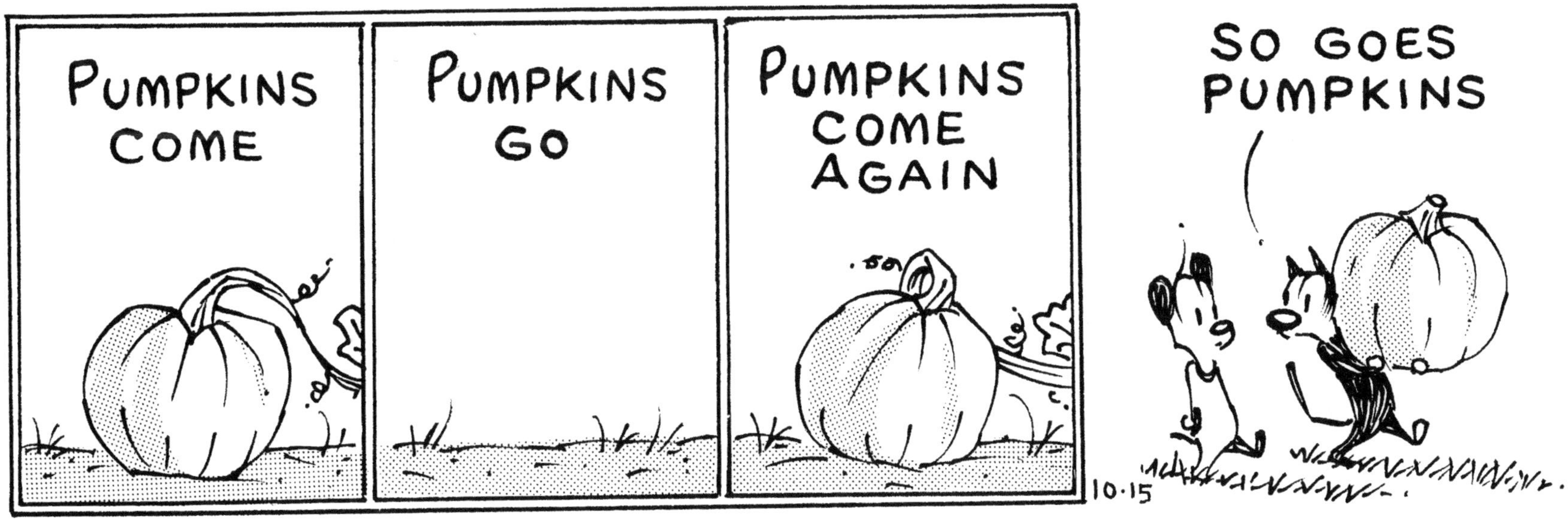
PUMPKINS COME
PUMPKINS GO
PUMPKINS COME AGAIN
SO GOES PUMPKINS
10·15

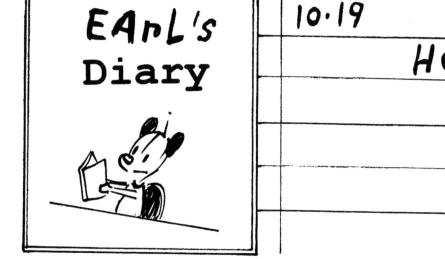

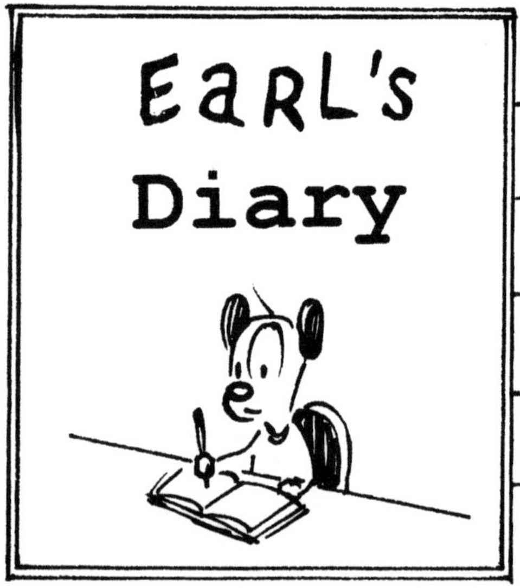
EaRL's
Diary

10·17

PLayed BALL with
my OZZIE

— I THiNK I WON.

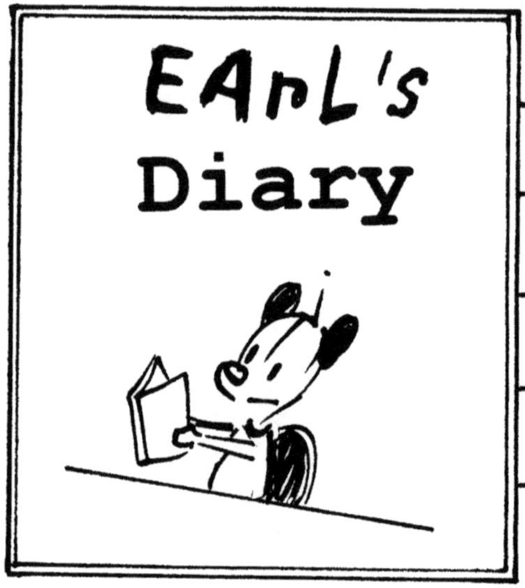
EArL's
Diary

10·19

HOWLed At ThE
MOON.

— felt GooD.

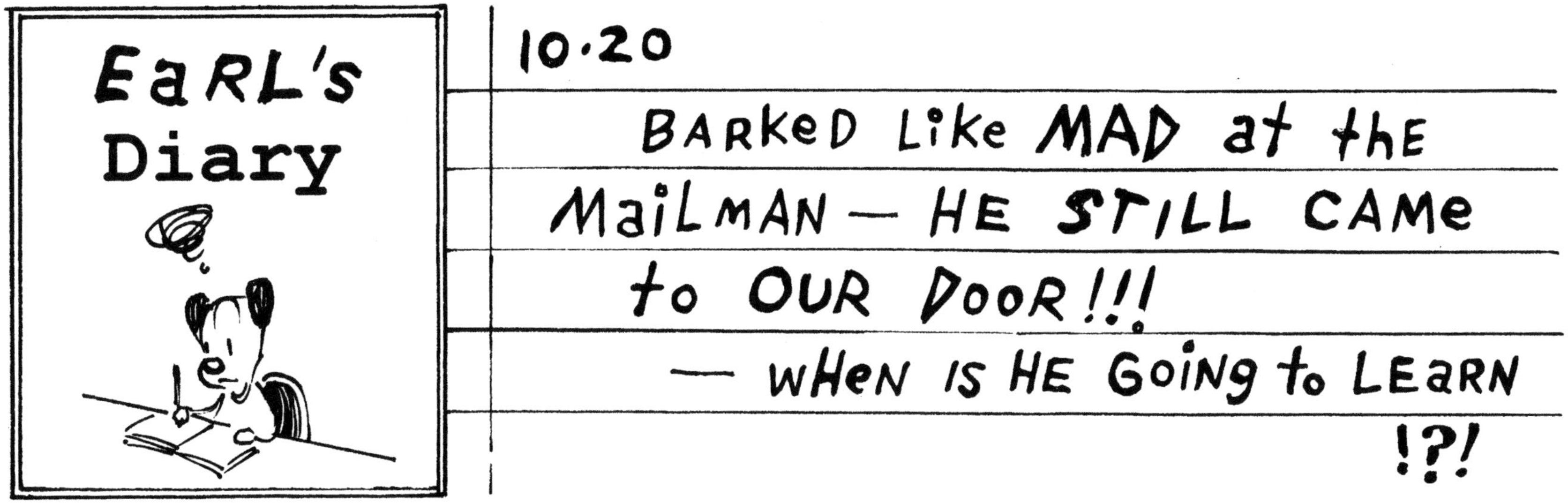
Earl's Diary
10·20
Barked like MAD at the Mailman — He STILL came to our door!!!
— When is he going to learn !?!

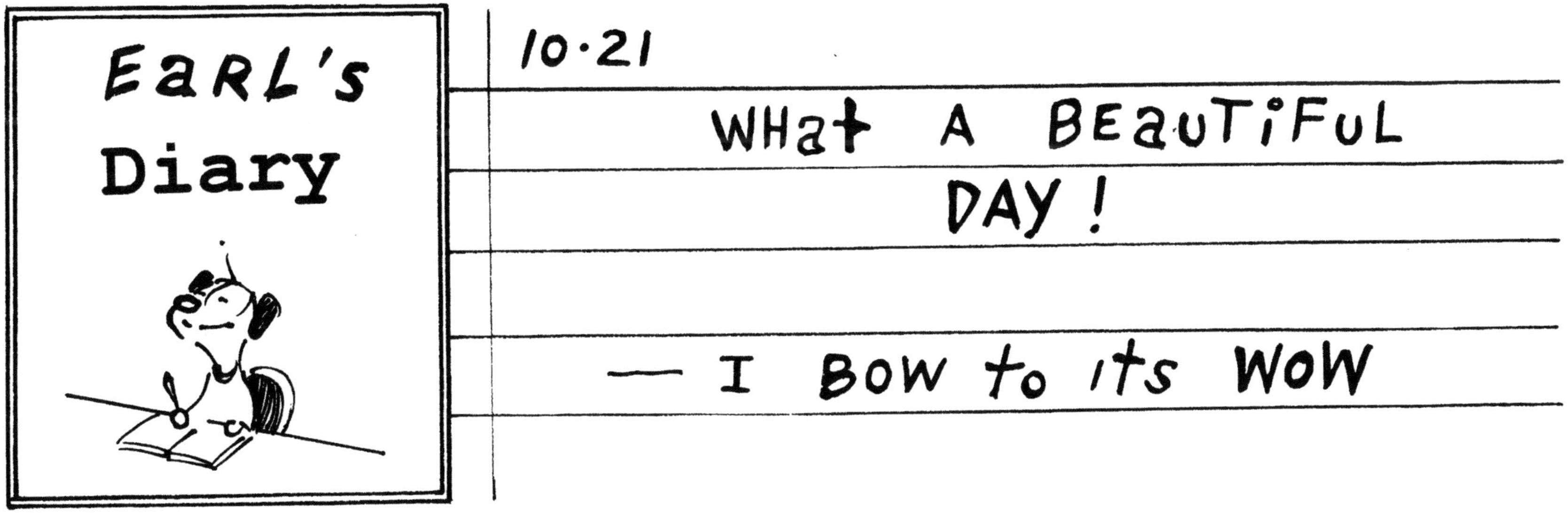
Earl's Diary
10·21
What a beautiful day!
— I bow to its wow

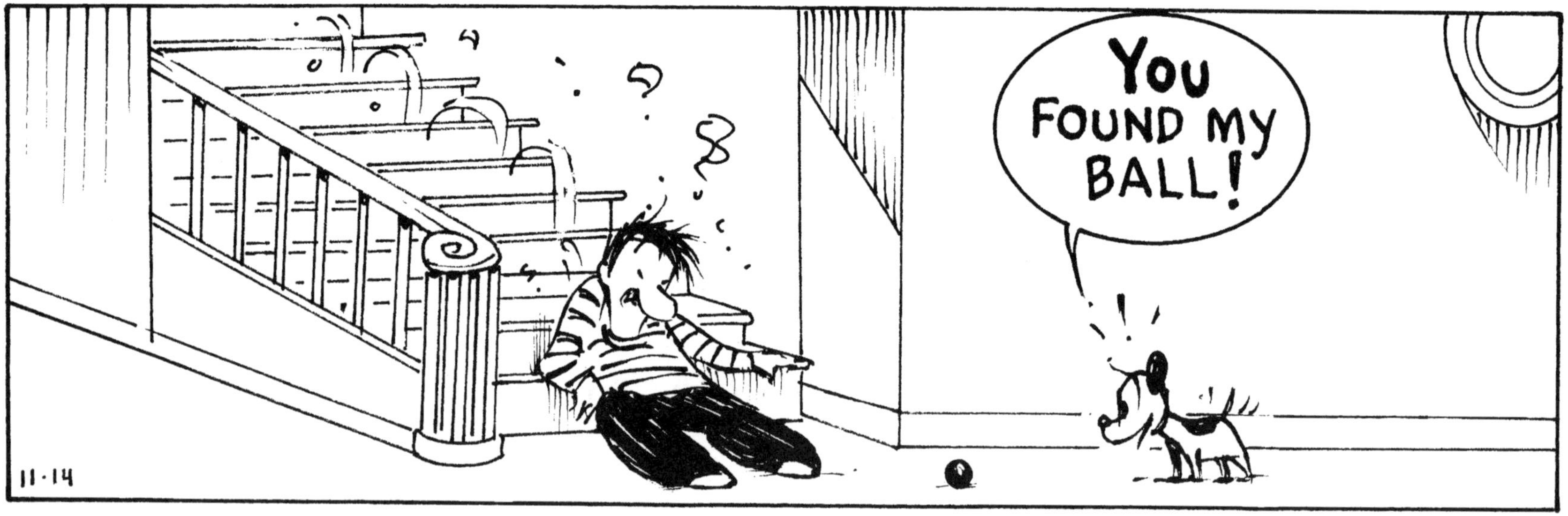
11·14
YOU FOUND MY BALL!

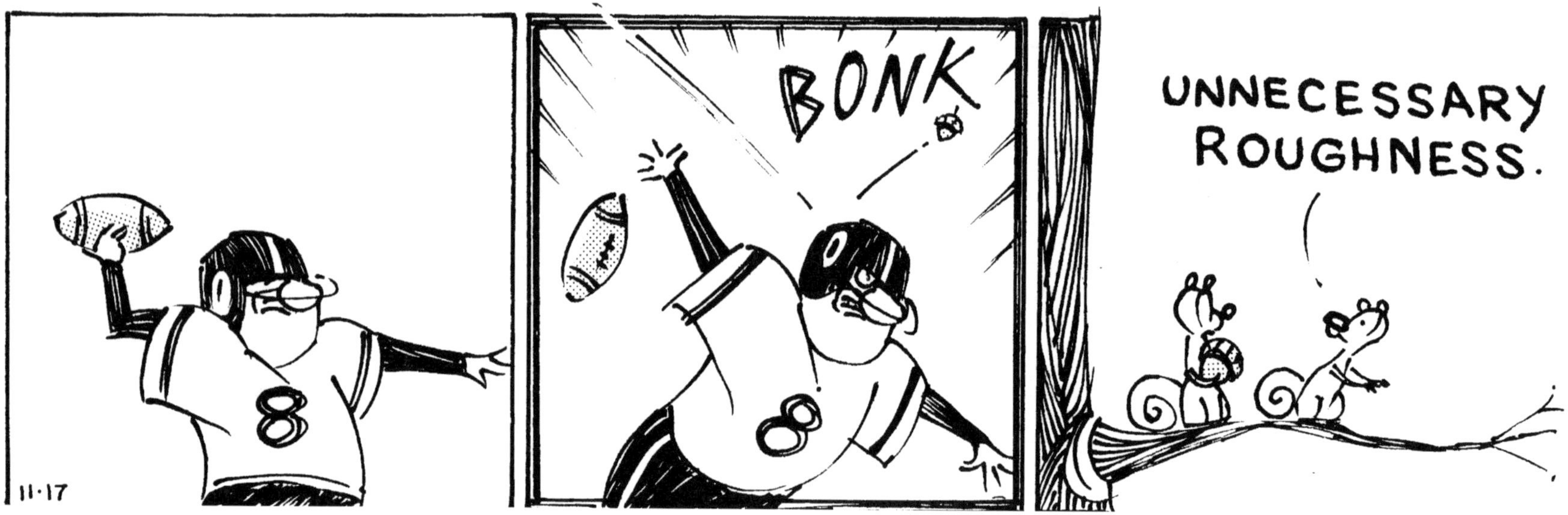
11·17
BONK
UNNECESSARY ROUGHNESS.

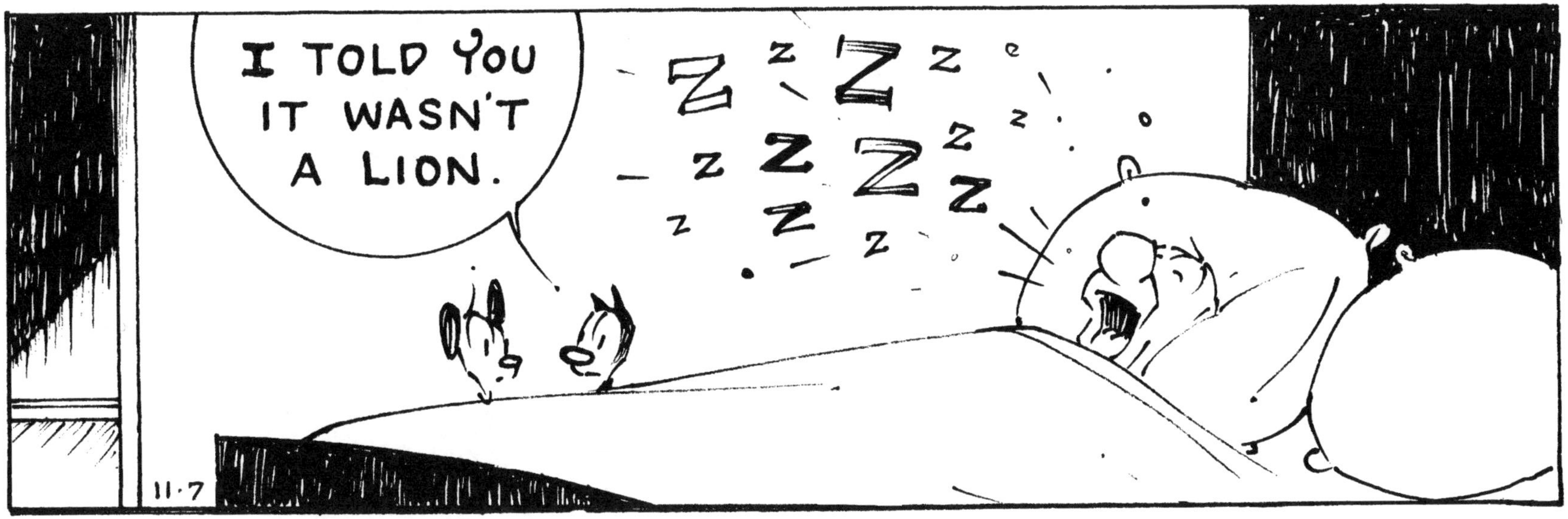
I TOLD YOU IT WASN'T A LION.
11·7

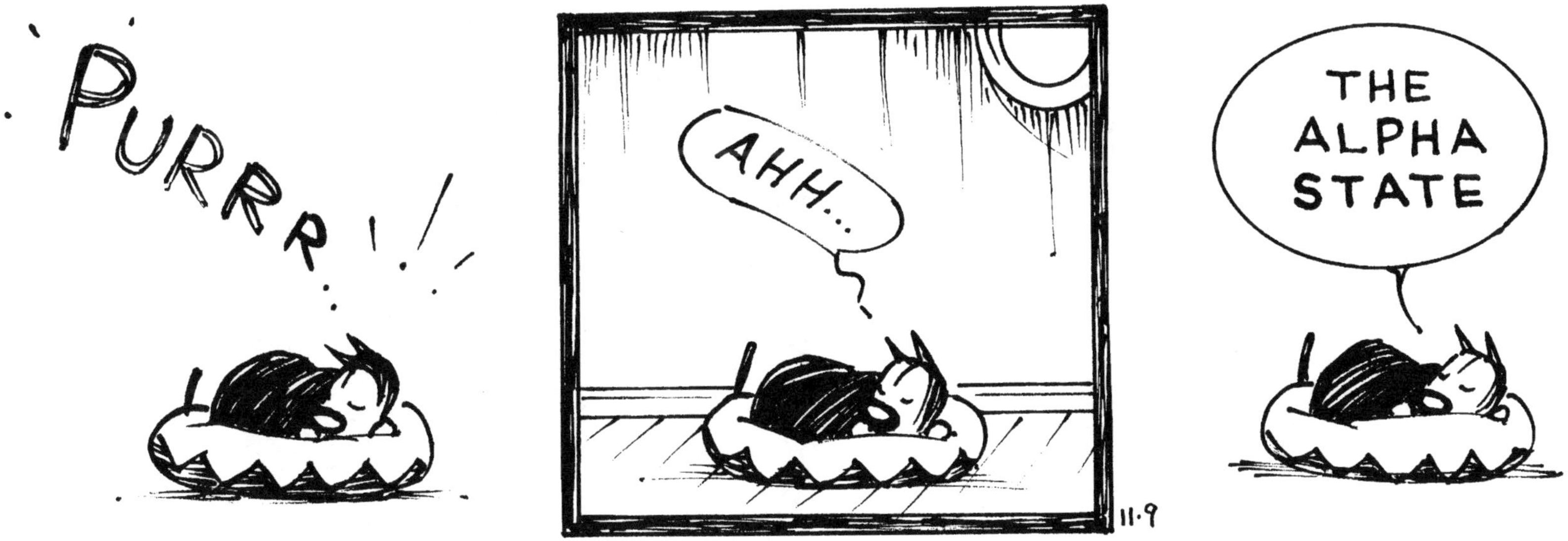
PURRR...
AHH...
11·9
THE ALPHA STATE

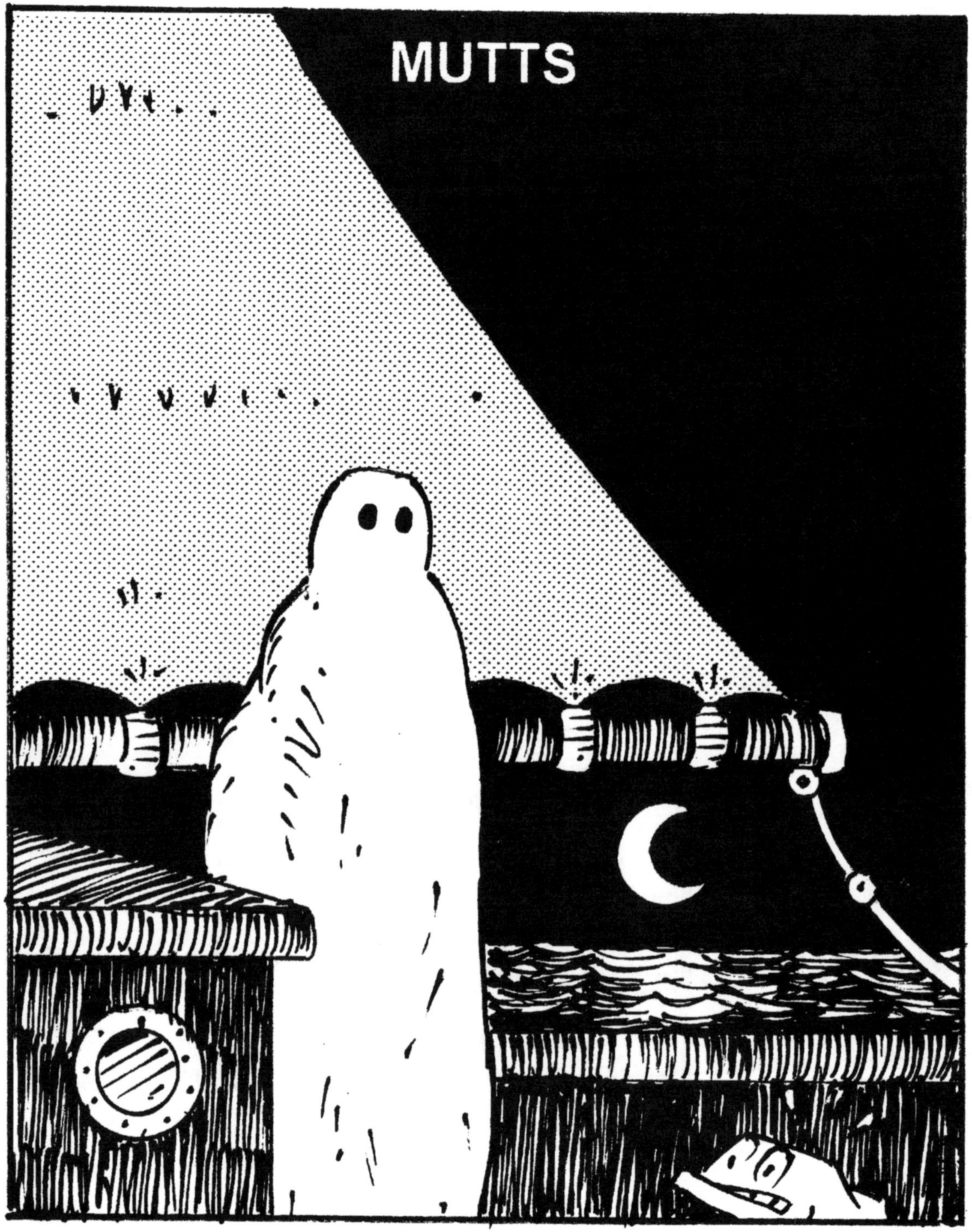
MUTTS

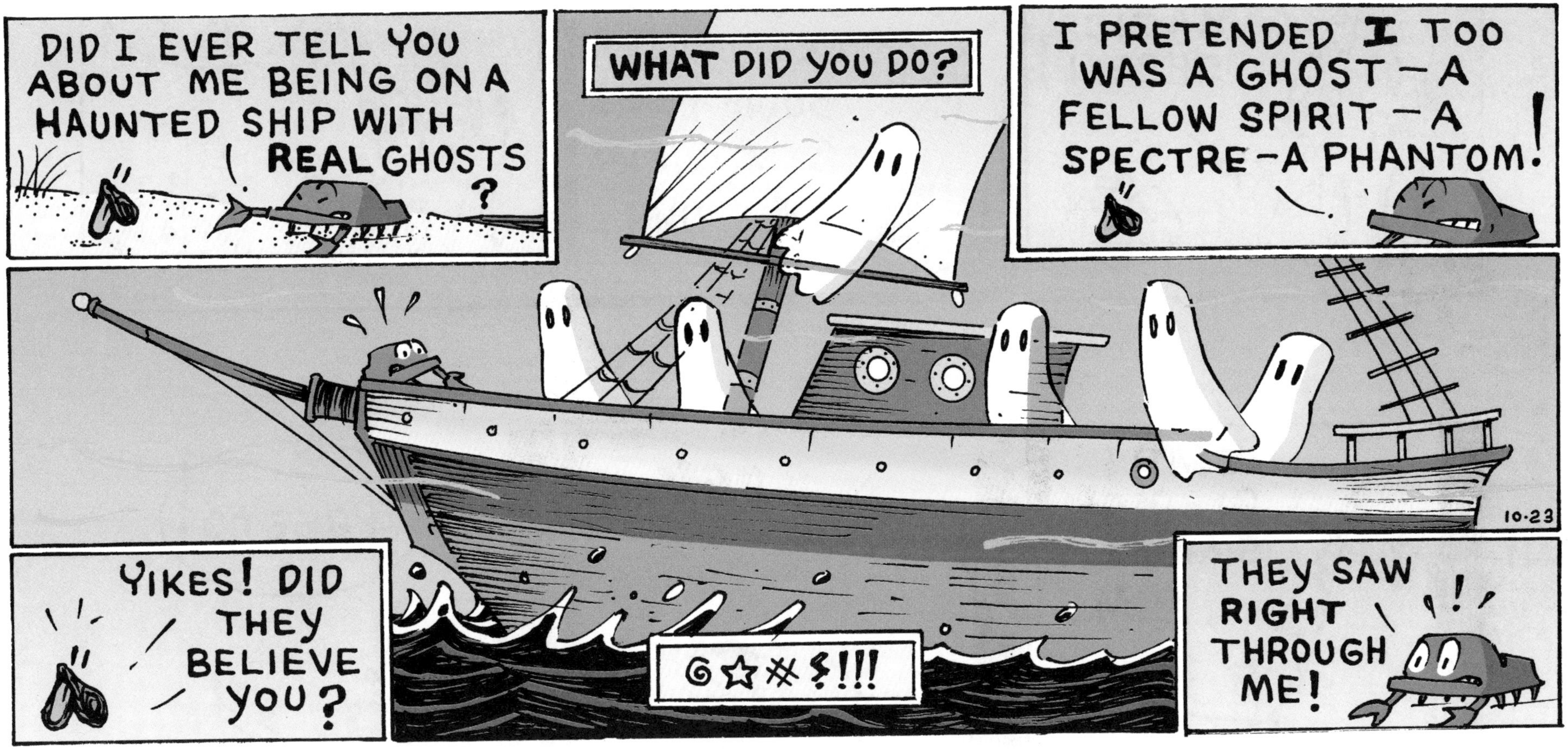

DID I EVER TELL YOU ABOUT ME BEING ON A HAUNTED SHIP WITH REAL GHOSTS?
WHAT DID YOU DO?
I PRETENDED I TOO WAS A GHOST — A FELLOW SPIRIT — A SPECTRE — A PHANTOM!
10·23
YIKES! DID THEY BELIEVE YOU?
G☆#$!!!
THEY SAW RIGHT THROUGH ME!

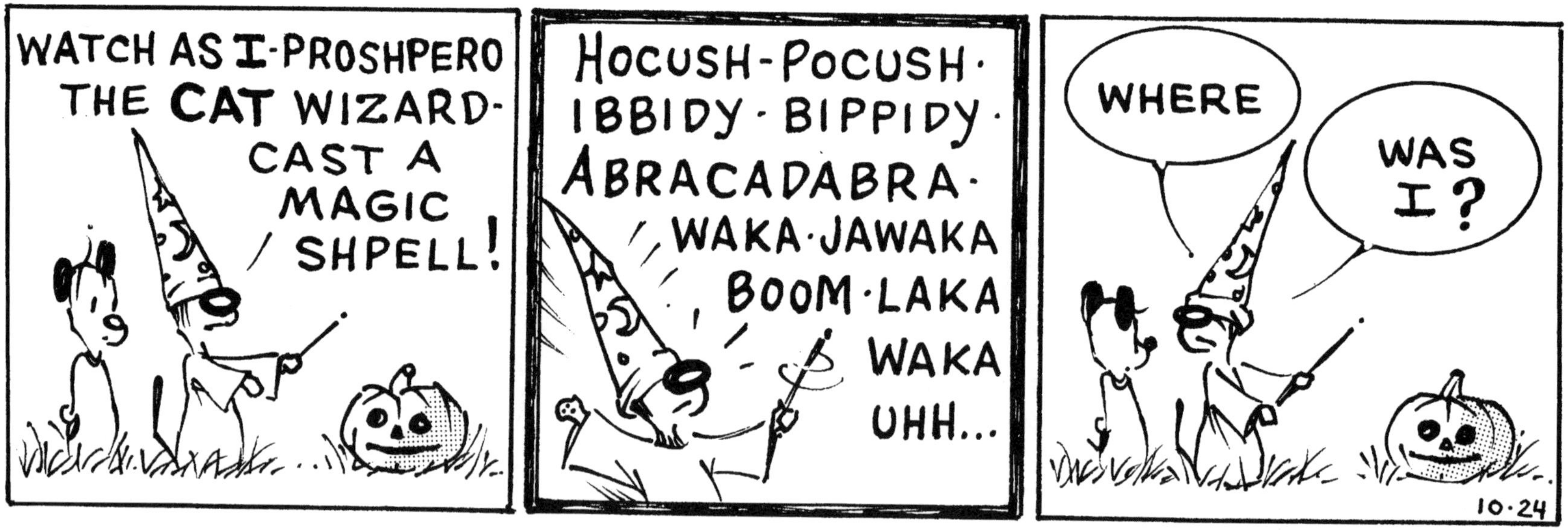
WATCH AS I-PROSHPERO THE CAT WIZARD-CAST A MAGIC SHPELL!
HOCUSH-POCUSH·IBBIDY·BIPPIDY·ABRACADABRA·WAKA·JAWAKA BOOM·LAKA WAKA UHH...
WHERE
WAS I?
10·24

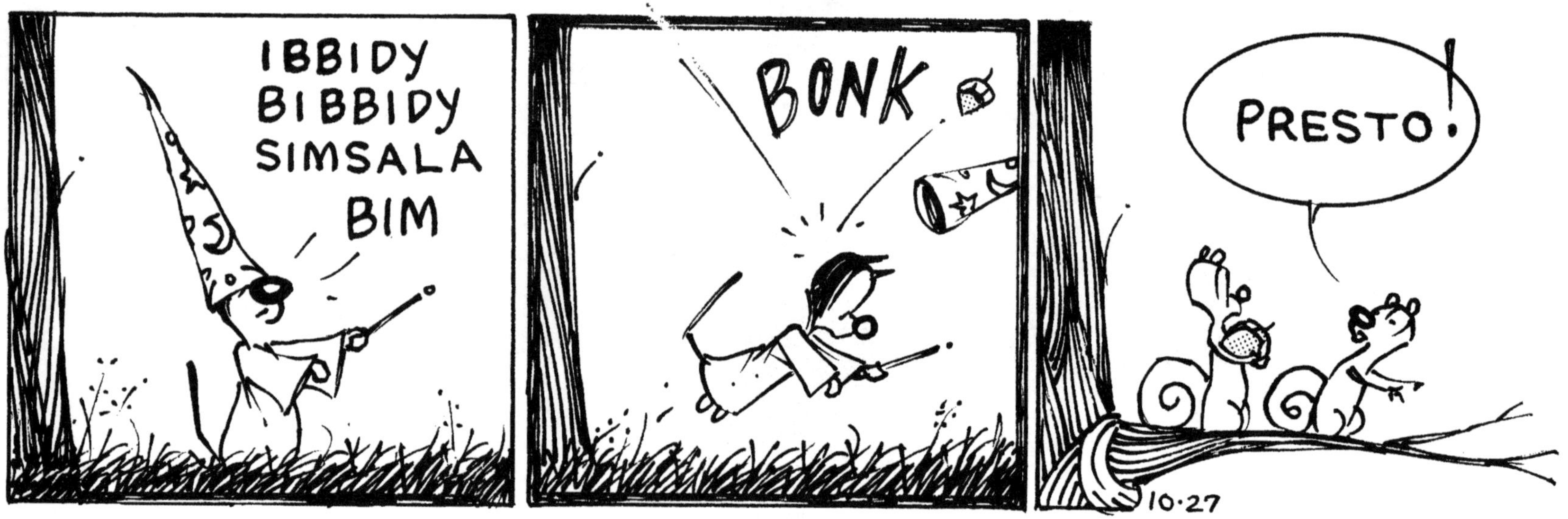
IBBIDY BIBBIDY SIMSALA BIM
BONK
PRESTO!
10·27

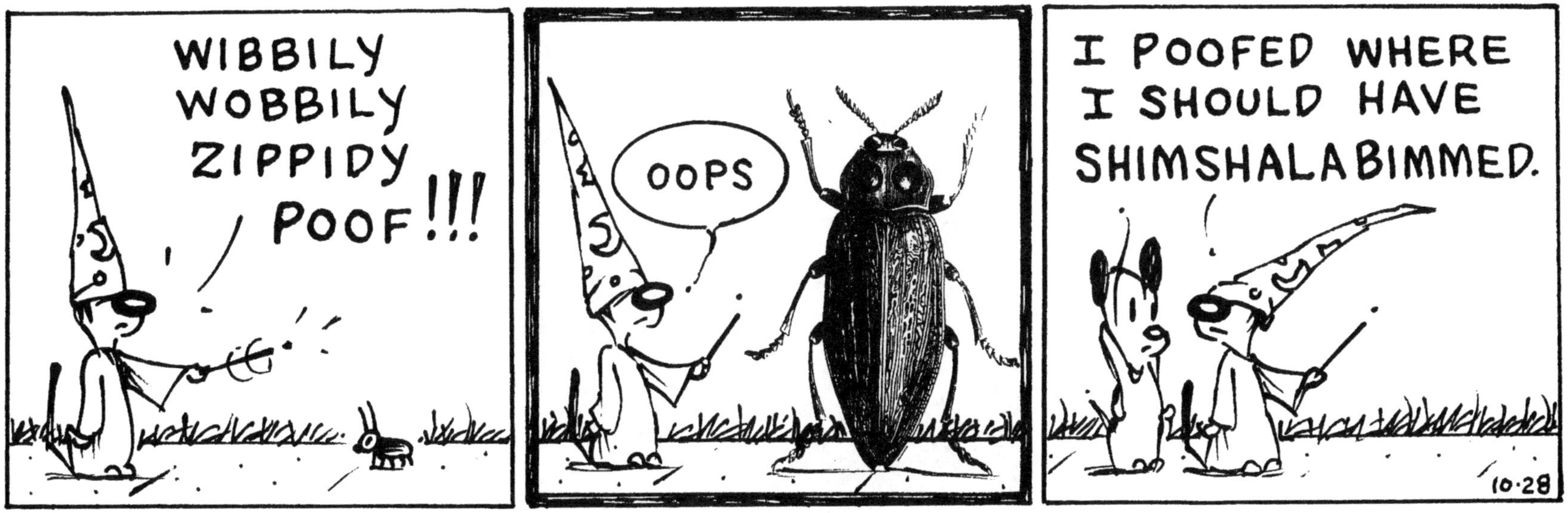
WIBBILY WOBBILY ZIPPIDY POOF!!!
OOPS
I POOFED WHERE I SHOULD HAVE SHIMSHALABIMMED.
10·28

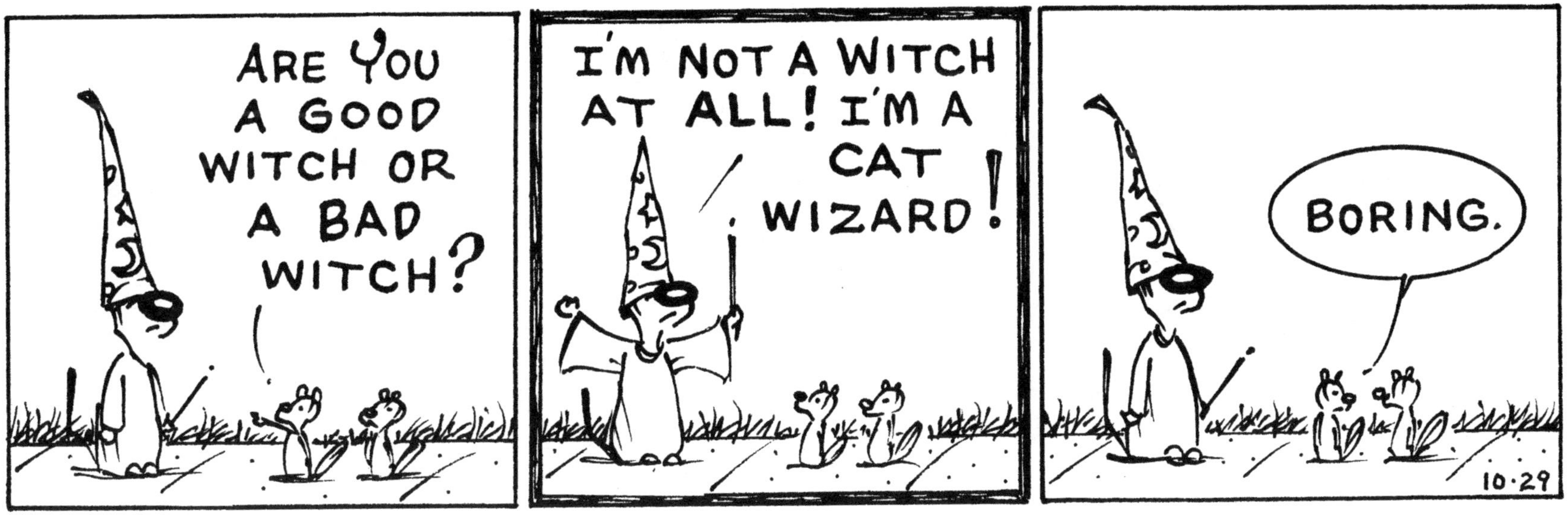
ARE YOU A GOOD WITCH OR A BAD WITCH?
I'M NOT A WITCH AT ALL! I'M A CAT WIZARD!
BORING.
10·29

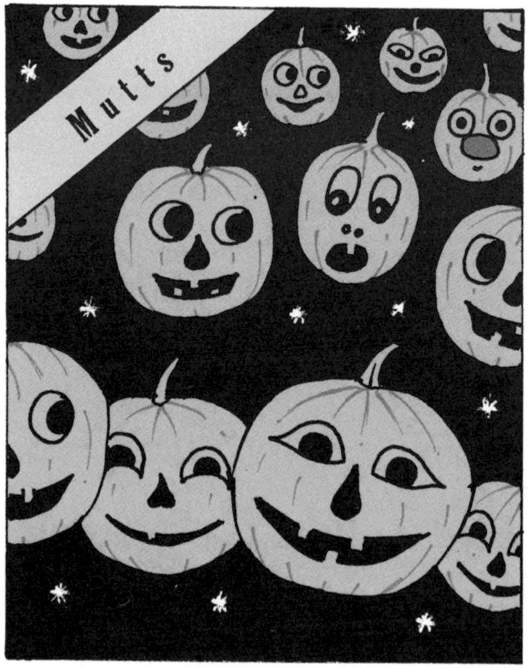
Mutts

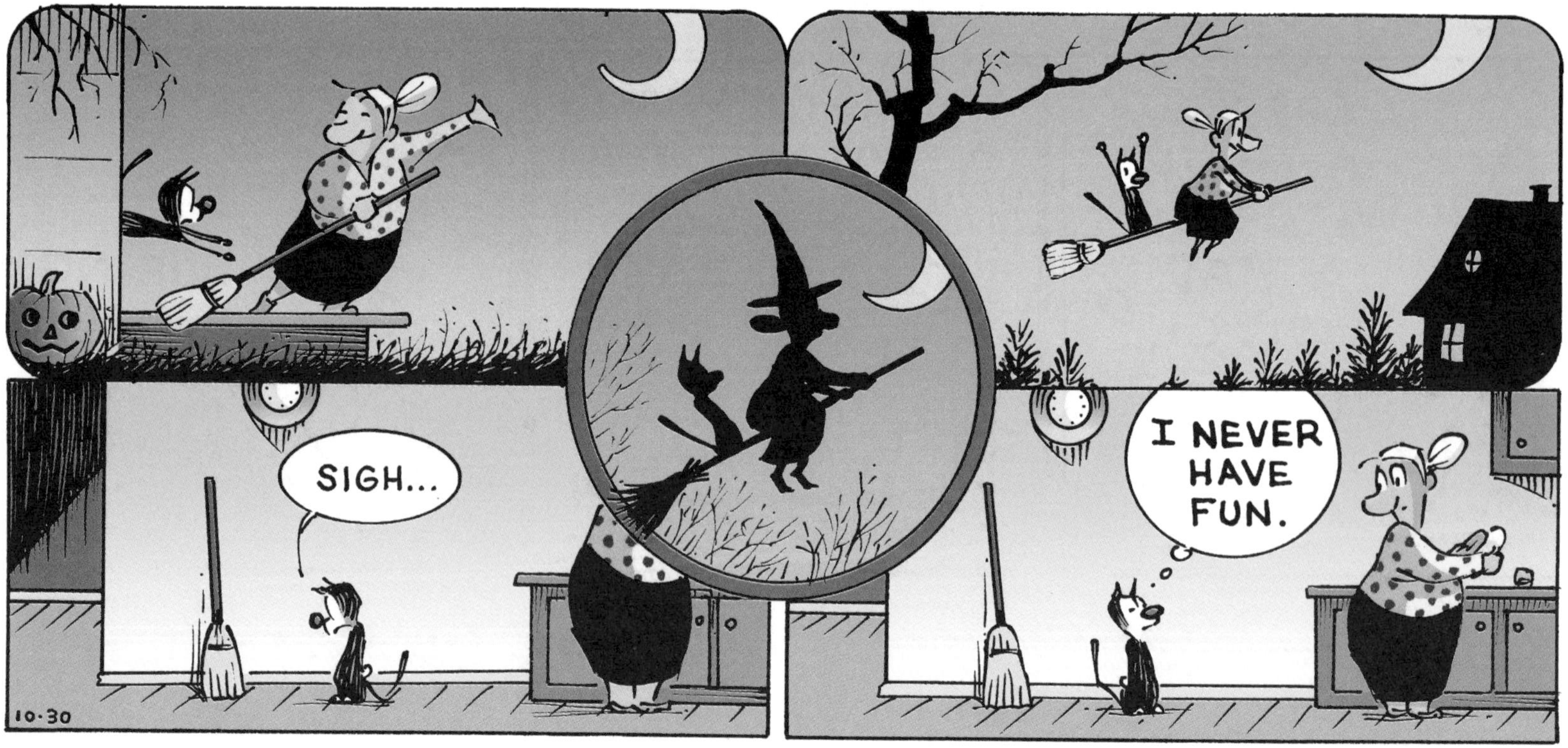
SIGH...
I NEVER HAVE FUN.
10·30

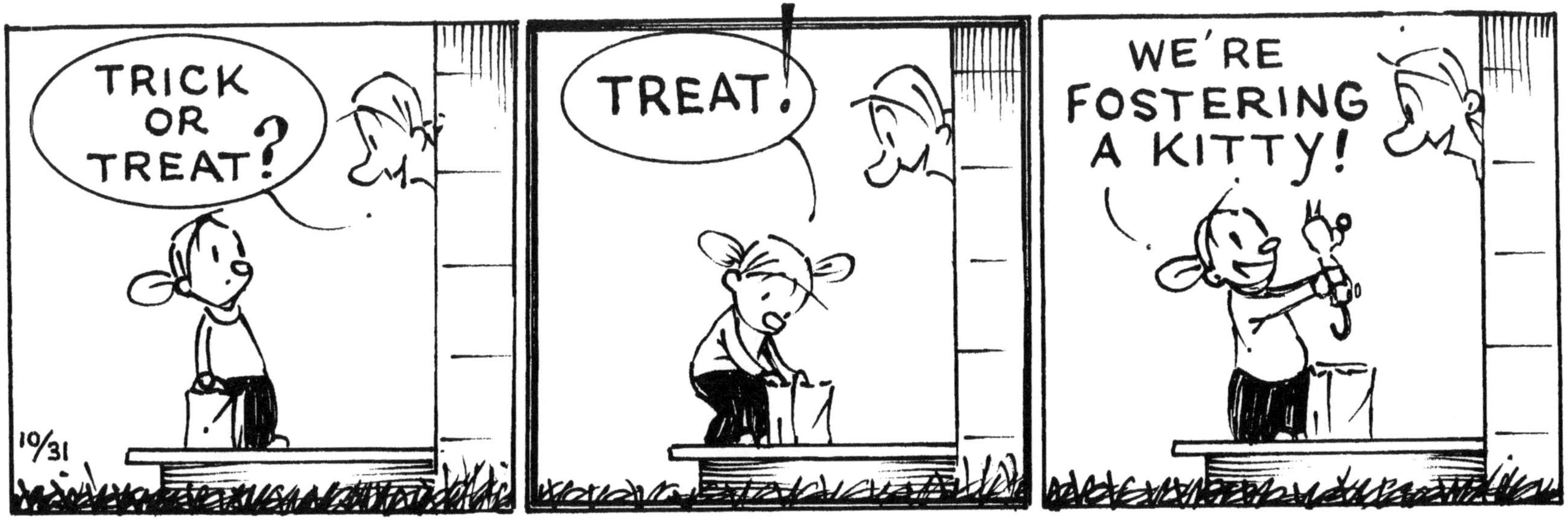
10/31
TRICK OR TREAT?
TREAT!
WE'RE FOSTERING A KITTY!

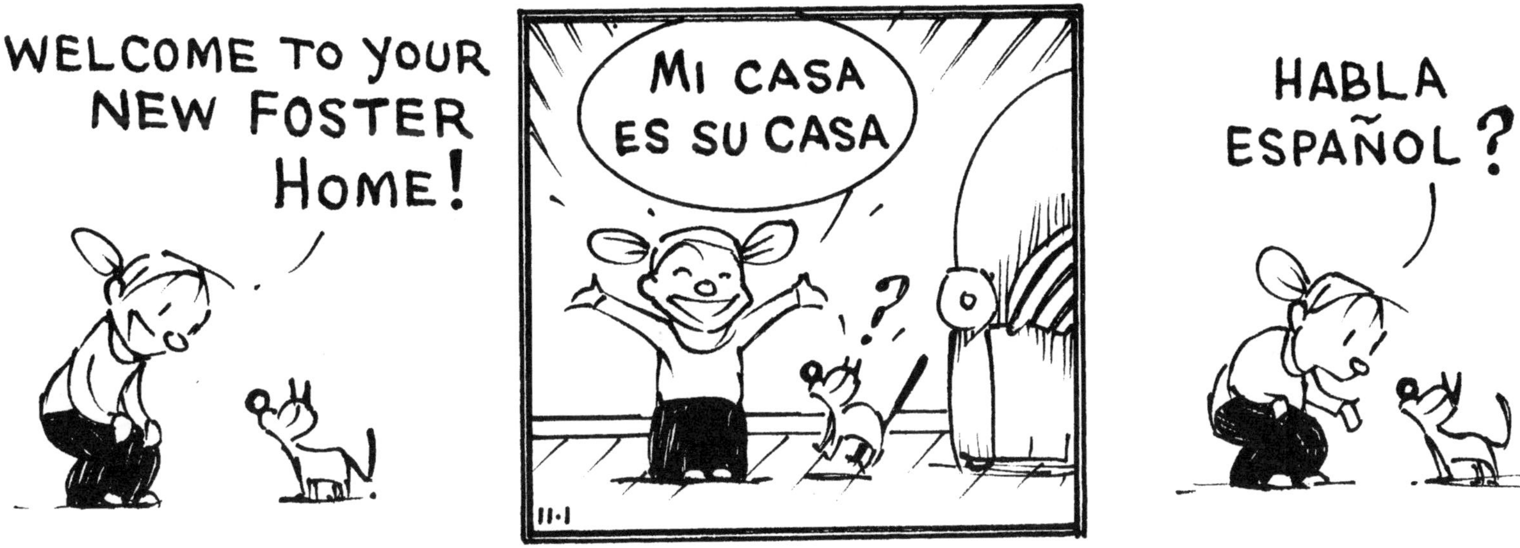
WELCOME TO YOUR NEW FOSTER HOME!
MI CASA ES SU CASA
?
11-1
HABLA ESPAÑOL?

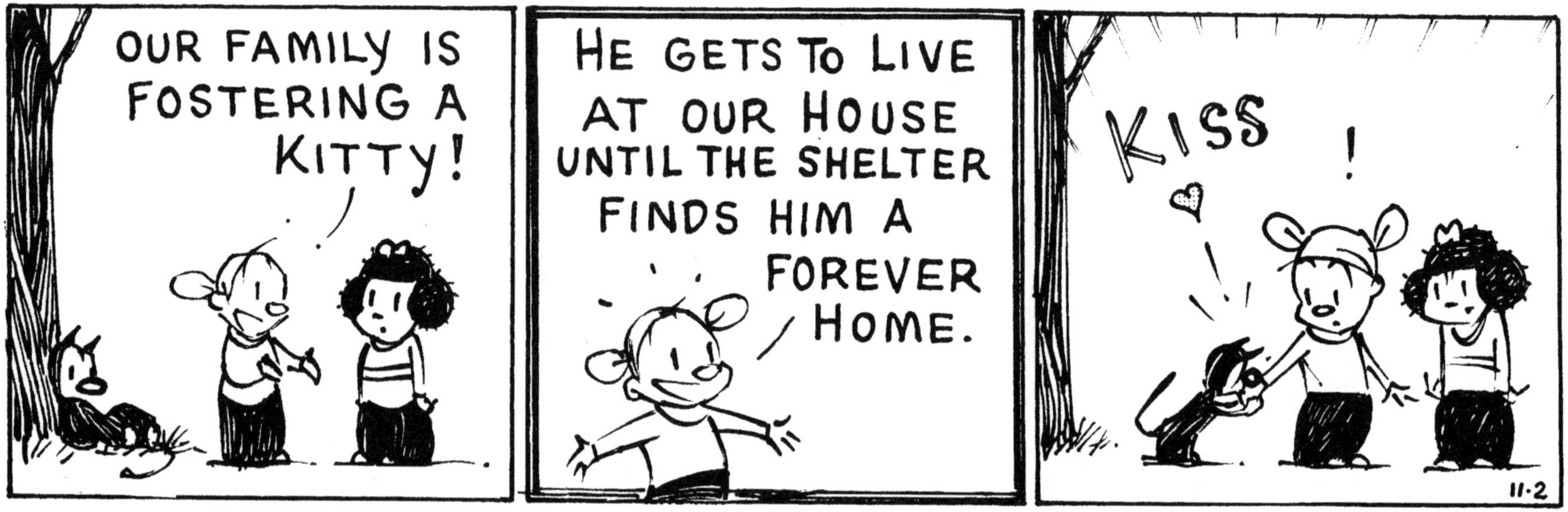
OUR FAMILY IS FOSTERING A KITTY!
HE GETS TO LIVE AT OUR HOUSE UNTIL THE SHELTER FINDS HIM A FOREVER HOME.
KISS
!
11·2

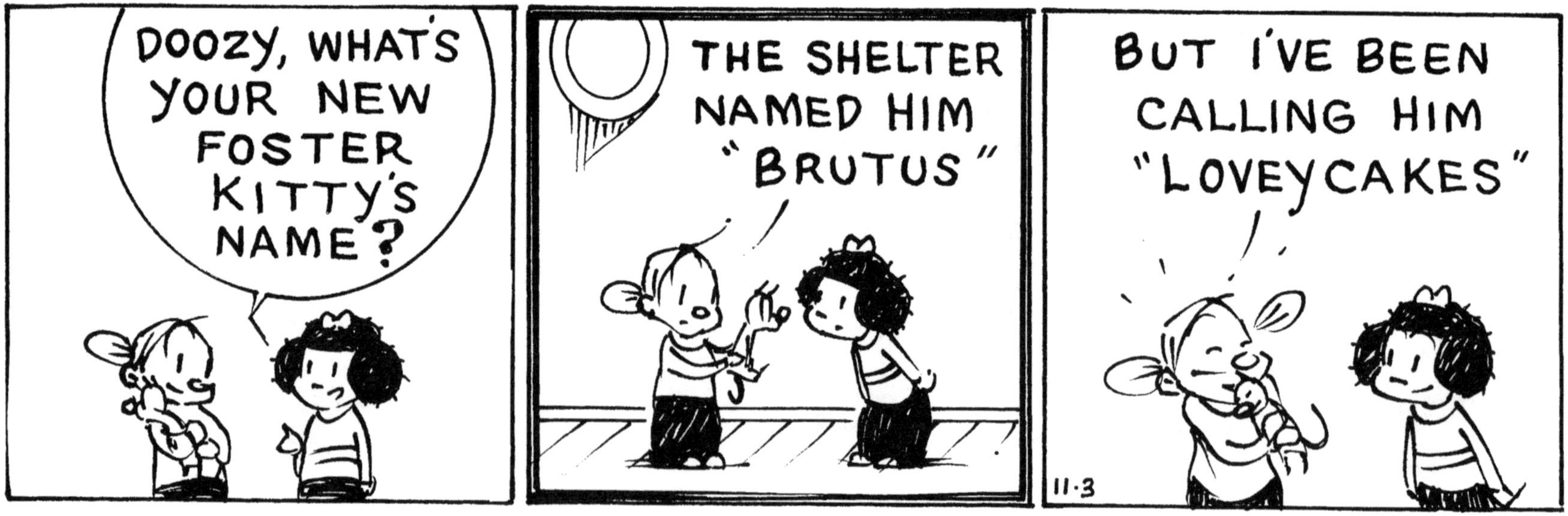
DOOZY, WHAT'S YOUR NEW FOSTER KITTY'S NAME?
THE SHELTER NAMED HIM "BRUTUS"
BUT I'VE BEEN CALLING HIM "LOVEYCAKES"
11·3

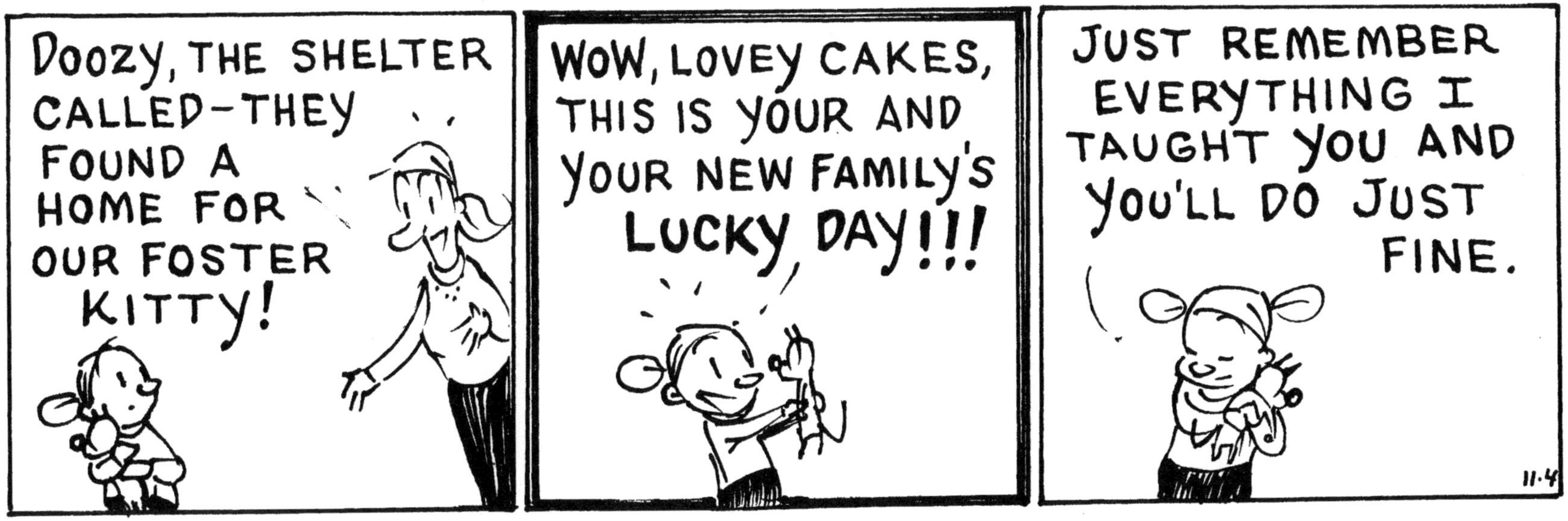
DOOZY, THE SHELTER CALLED-THEY FOUND A HOME FOR OUR FOSTER KITTY!
WOW, LOVEY CAKES, THIS IS YOUR AND YOUR NEW FAMILY'S LUCKY DAY!!!
JUST REMEMBER EVERYTHING I TAUGHT YOU AND YOU'LL DO JUST FINE.
11-4

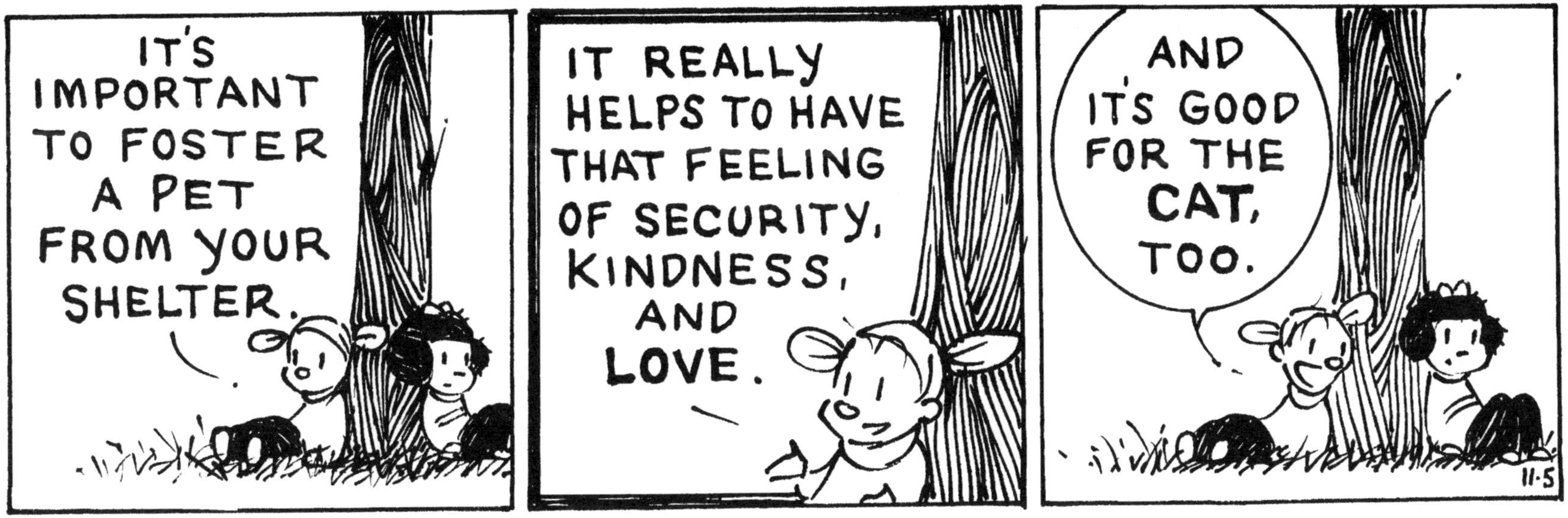
IT'S IMPORTANT TO FOSTER A PET FROM YOUR SHELTER.
IT REALLY HELPS TO HAVE THAT FEELING OF SECURITY, KINDNESS, AND LOVE.
AND IT'S GOOD FOR THE CAT, TOO.
11-5

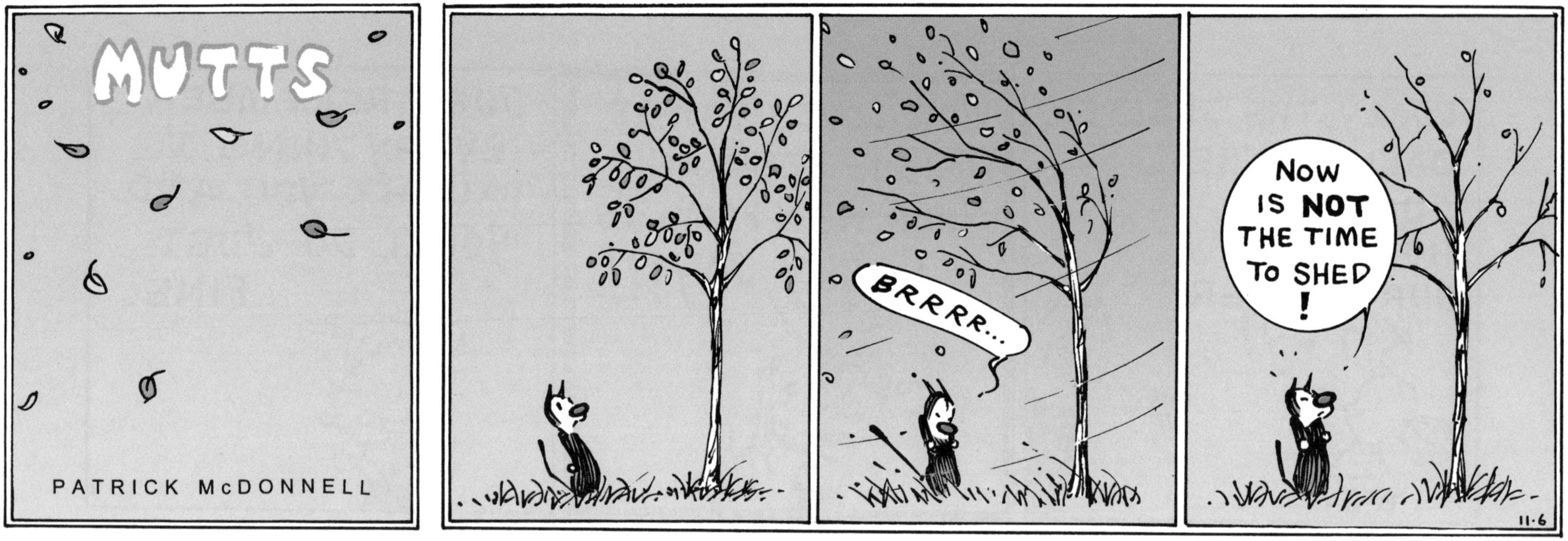
MUTTS
PATRICK McDONNELL
BRRRRR...
NOW IS NOT THE TIME TO SHED!
11·6

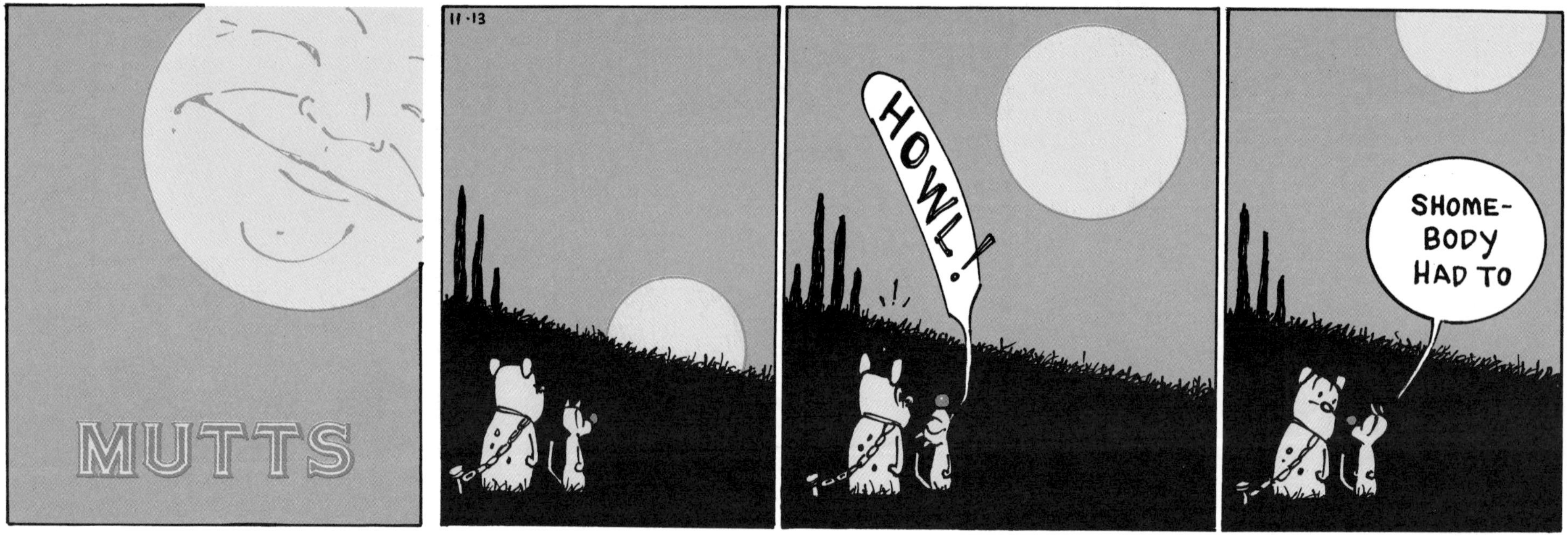
MUTTS
11·13
HOWL!
SHOME-BODY HAD TO

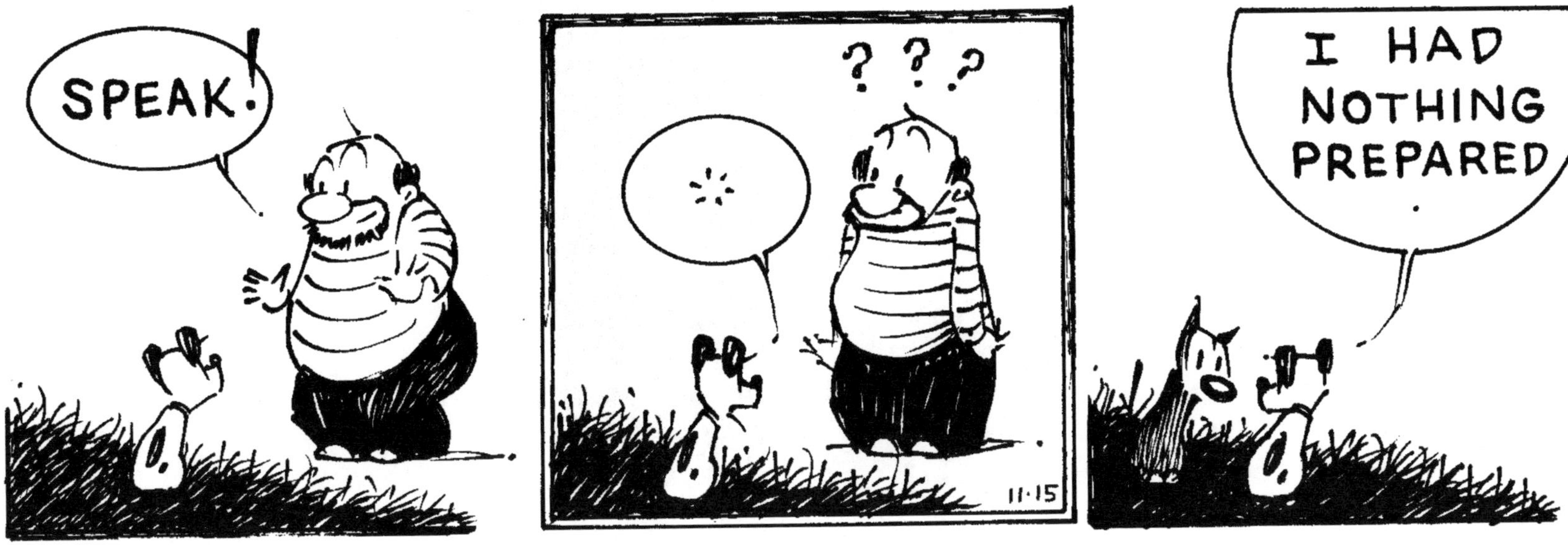
SPEAK!
? ? ?
11·15
I HAD NOTHING PREPARED.

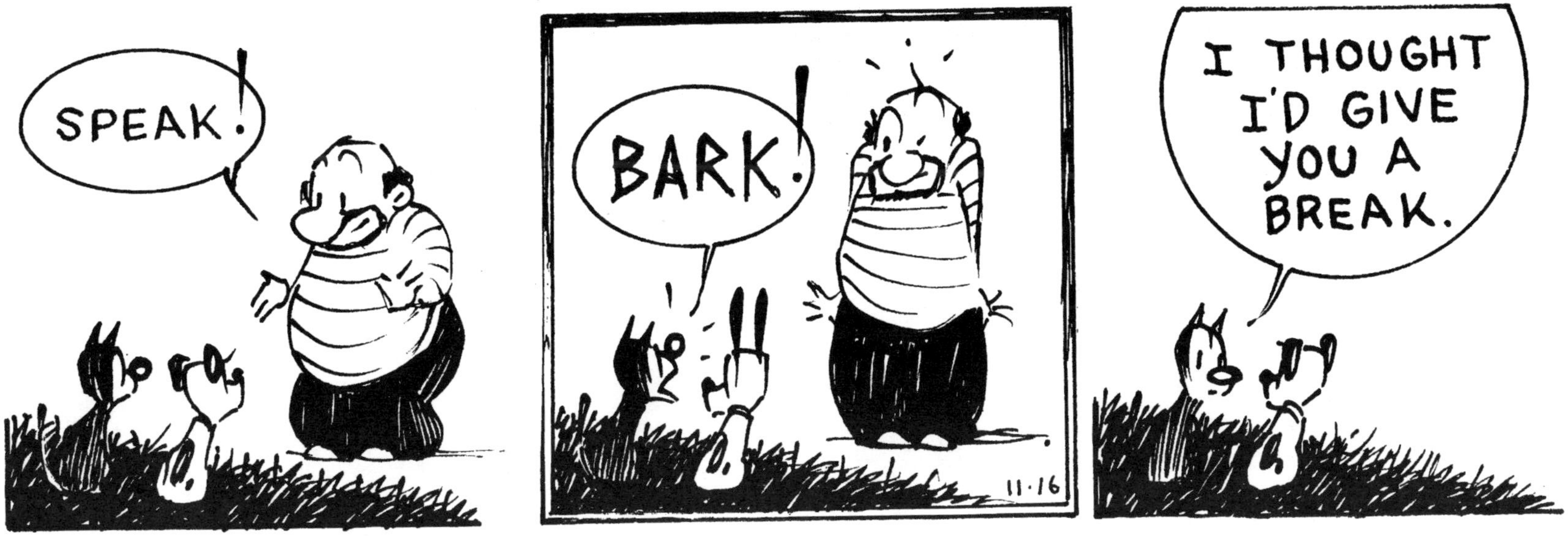
SPEAK!
BARK!
11·16
I THOUGHT I'D GIVE YOU A BREAK.

Mc Donnell's
"Oh…so shweet"
MUTTS

YESH!
I SHMELL PUMPKIN PIE!
ZIP
CRASH
AAAIEE
BAM
I SMELL TROUBLE
11·20

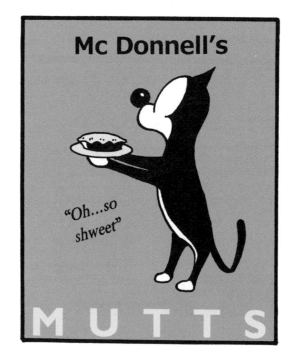

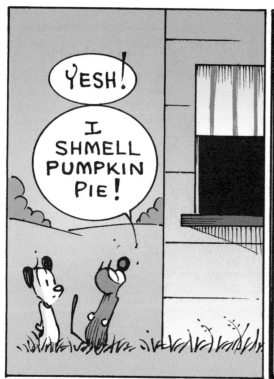

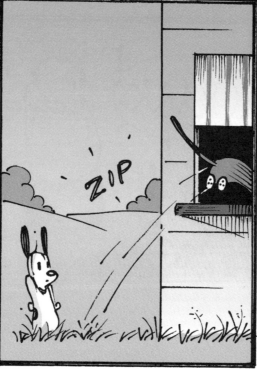

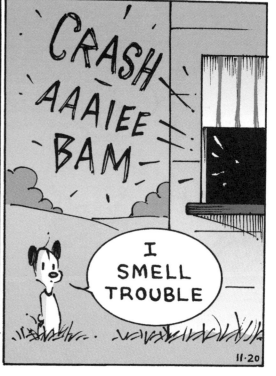

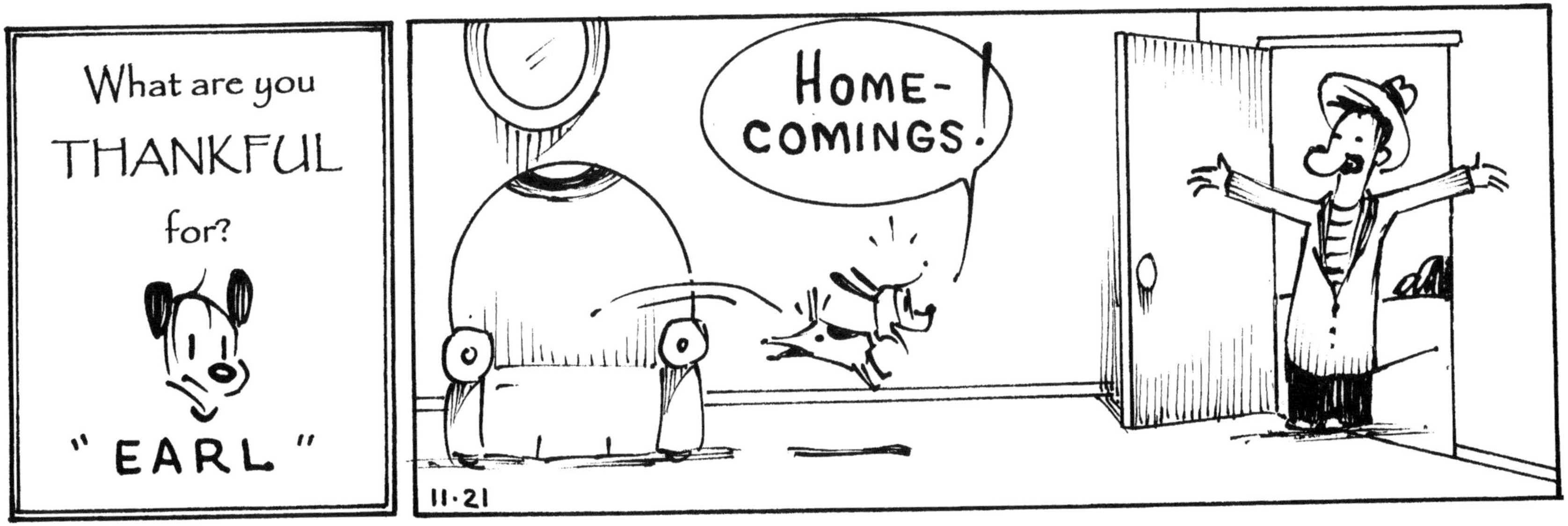
What are you THANKFUL for?
"EARL"
HOME-COMINGS!
11·21

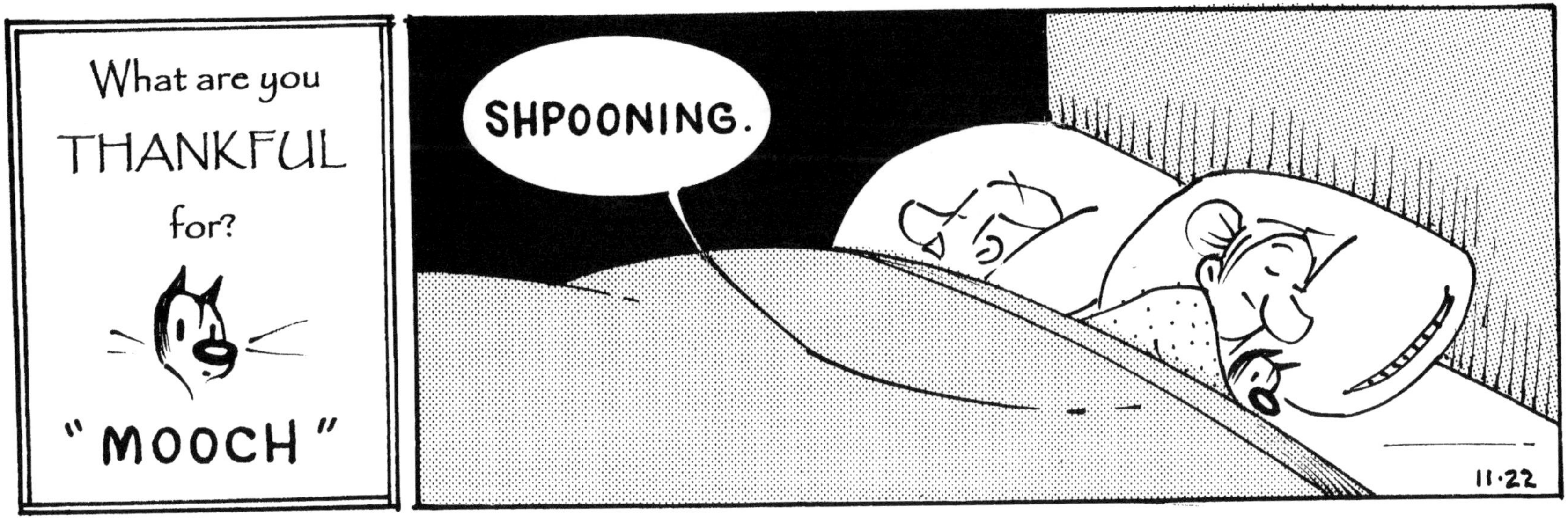
What are you THANKFUL for?
"MOOCH"
SHPOONING.
11·22

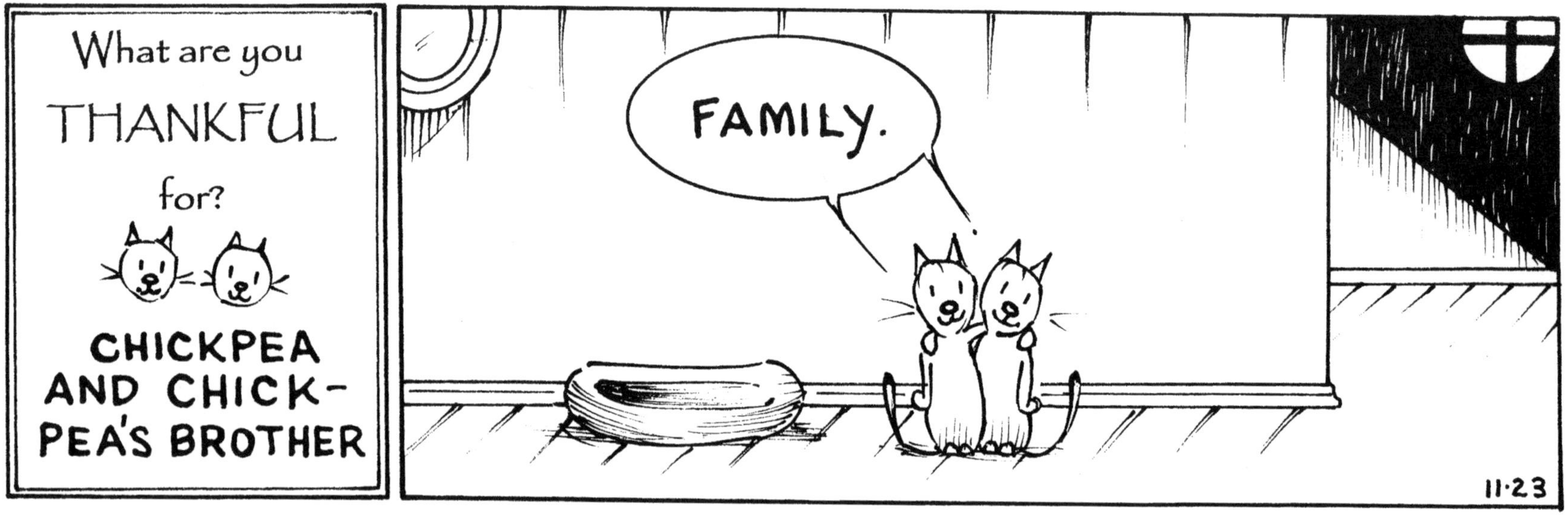
What are you THANKFUL for?
CHICKPEA AND CHICKPEA'S BROTHER
FAMILY.
11·23

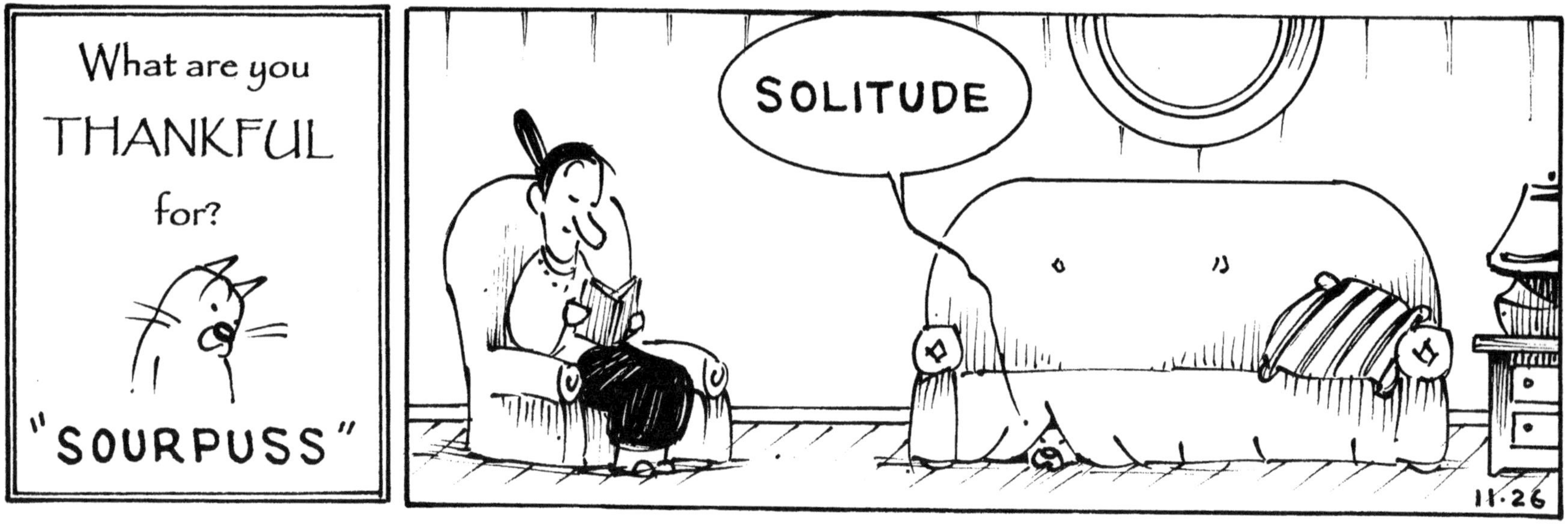
What are you THANKFUL for?
"SOURPUSS"
SOLITUDE
11·26

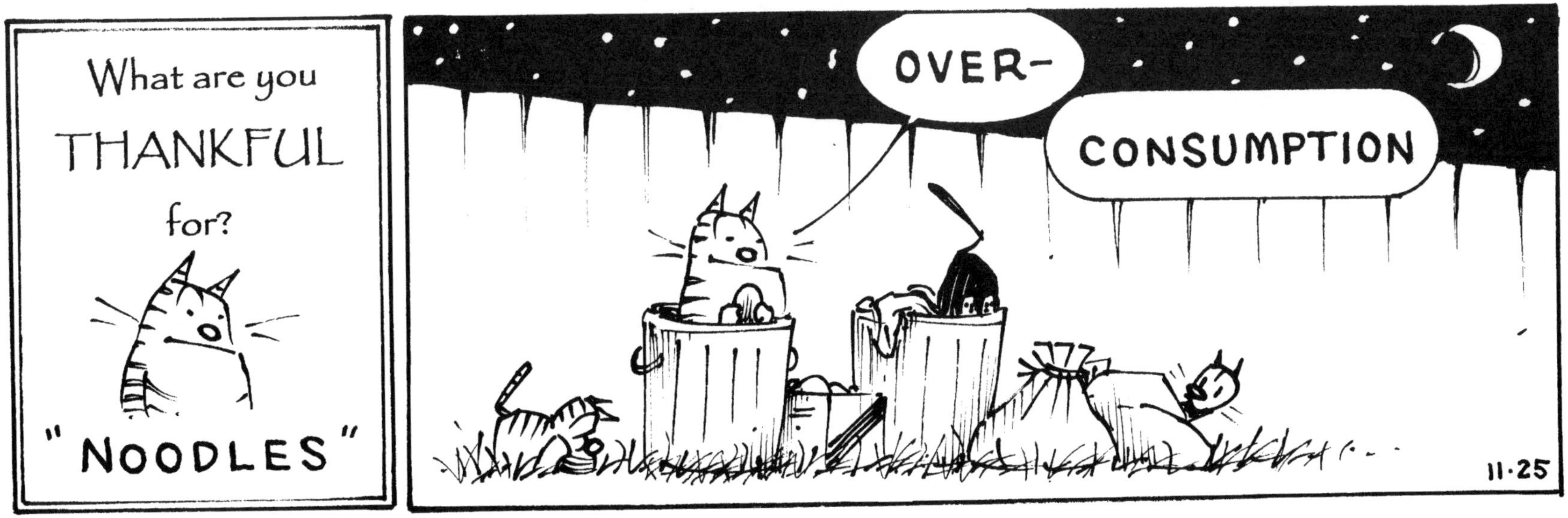
What are you THANKFUL for?
"NOODLES"
OVER-
CONSUMPTION
11·25

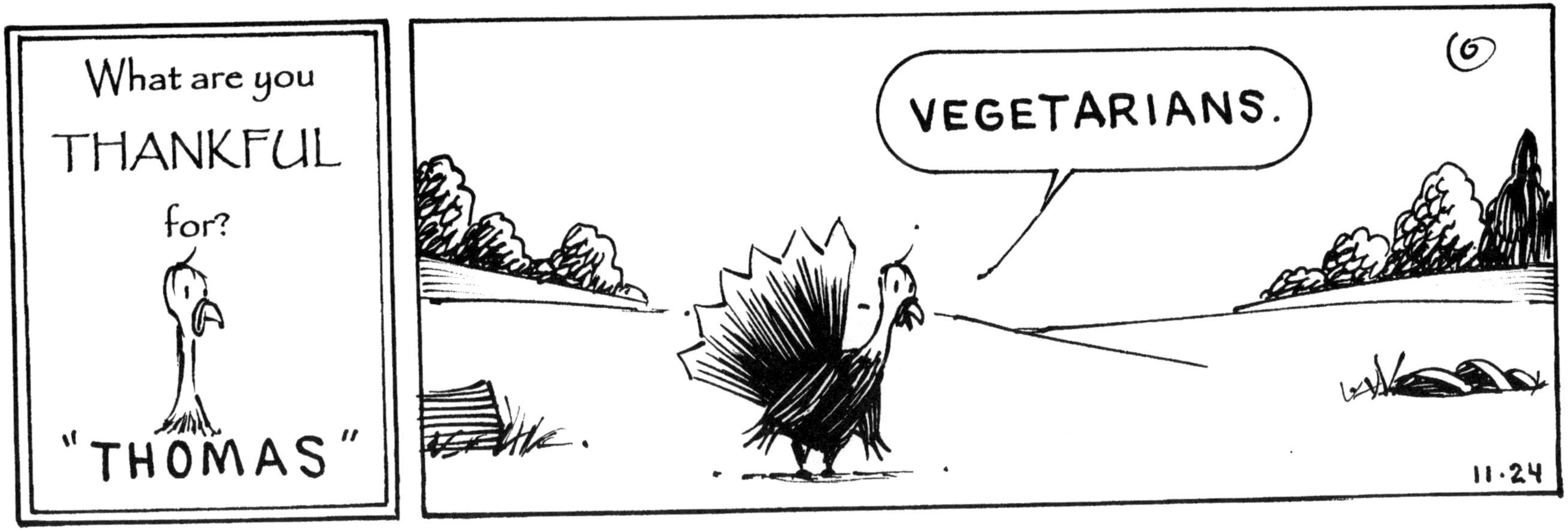
What are you THANKFUL for?
"THOMAS"
VEGETARIANS.
11·24

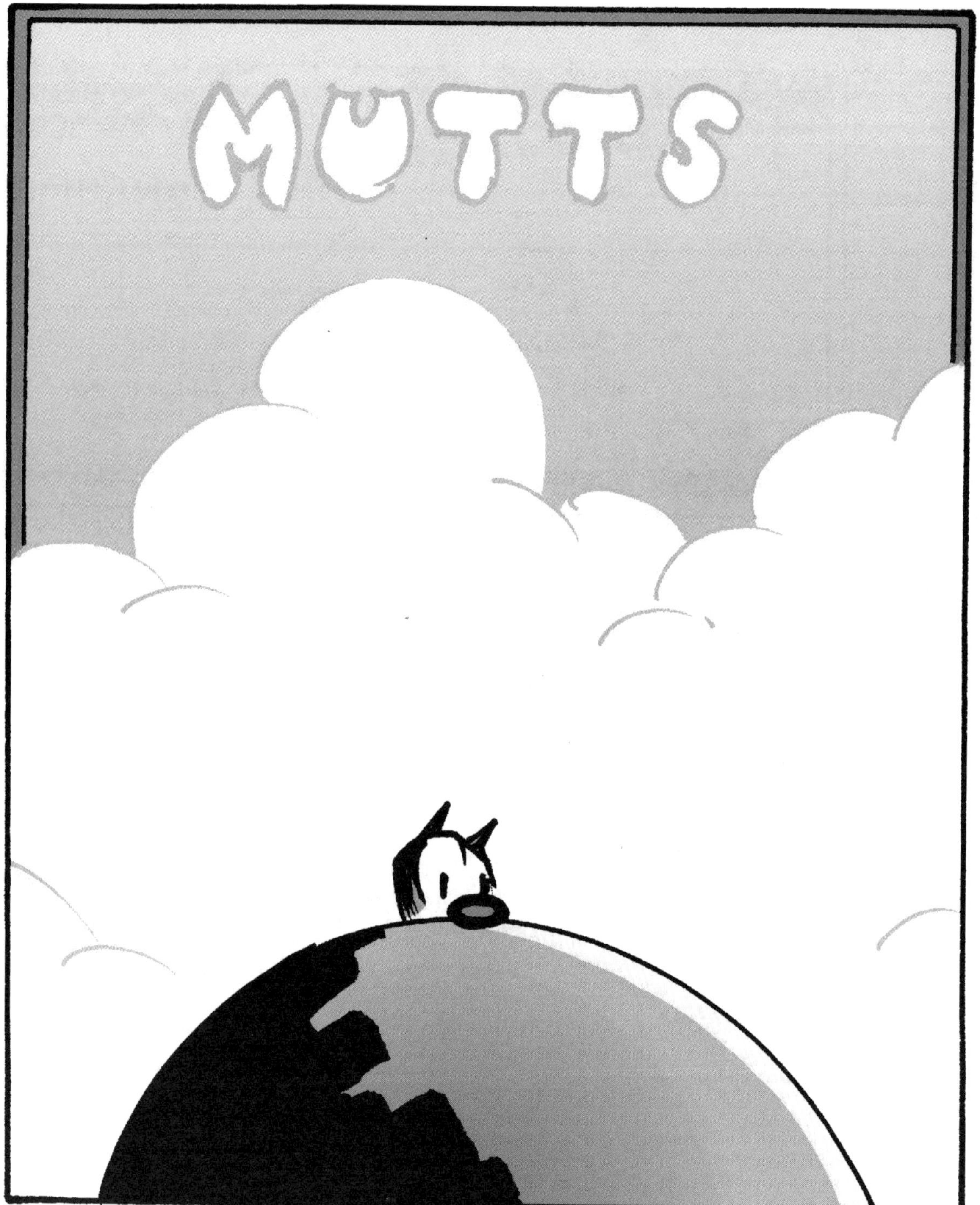
MUTTS

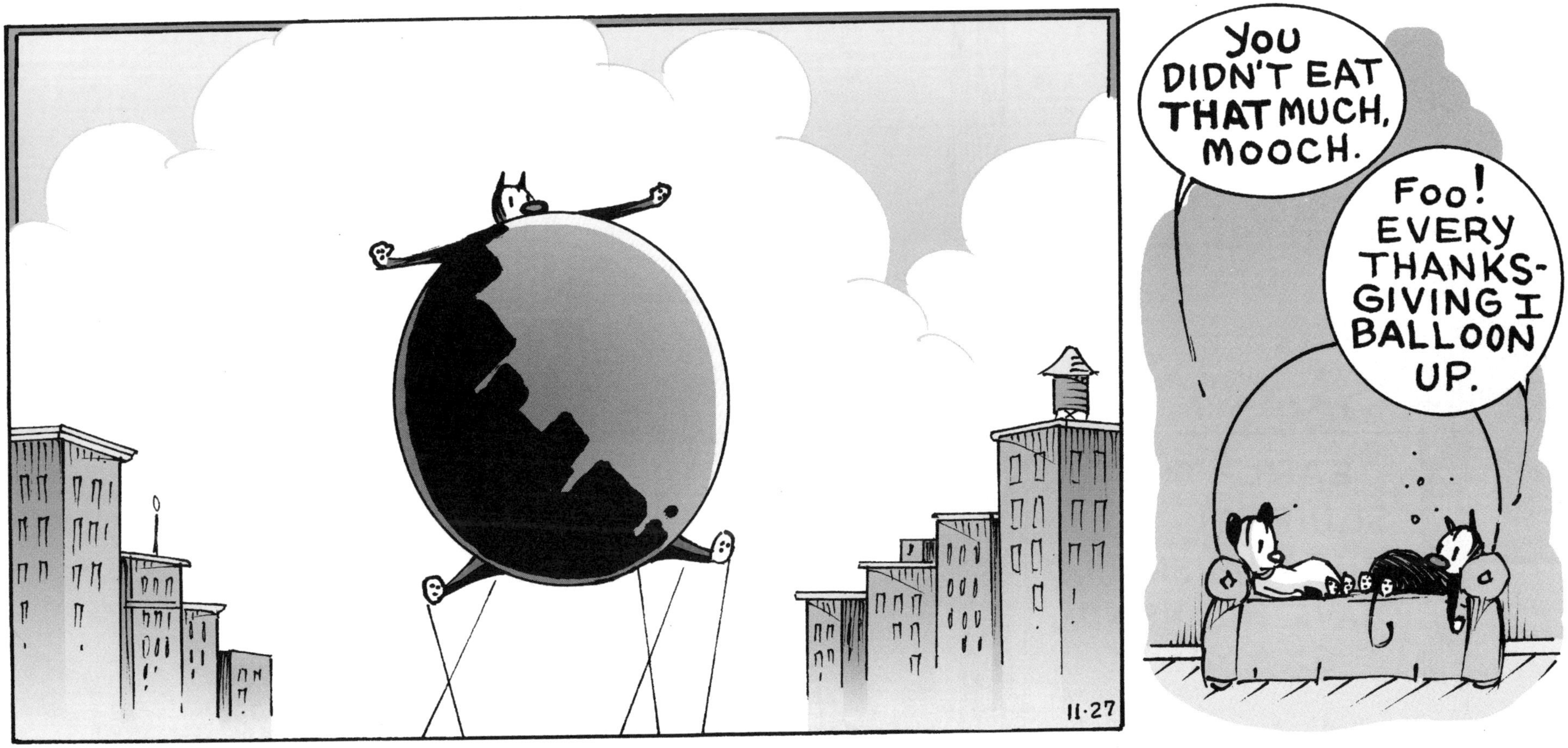
11·27
YOU DIDN'T EAT THAT MUCH, MOOCH.
FOO! EVERY THANKS-GIVING I BALLOON UP.

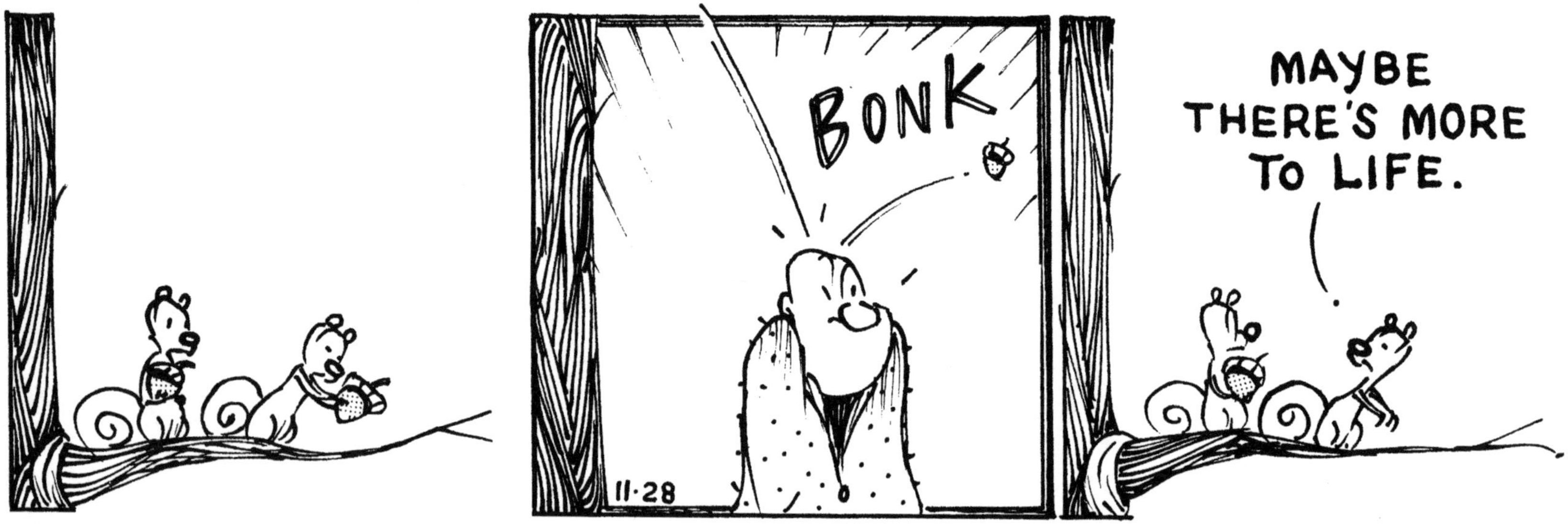
BONK
MAYBE THERE'S MORE TO LIFE.
11·28

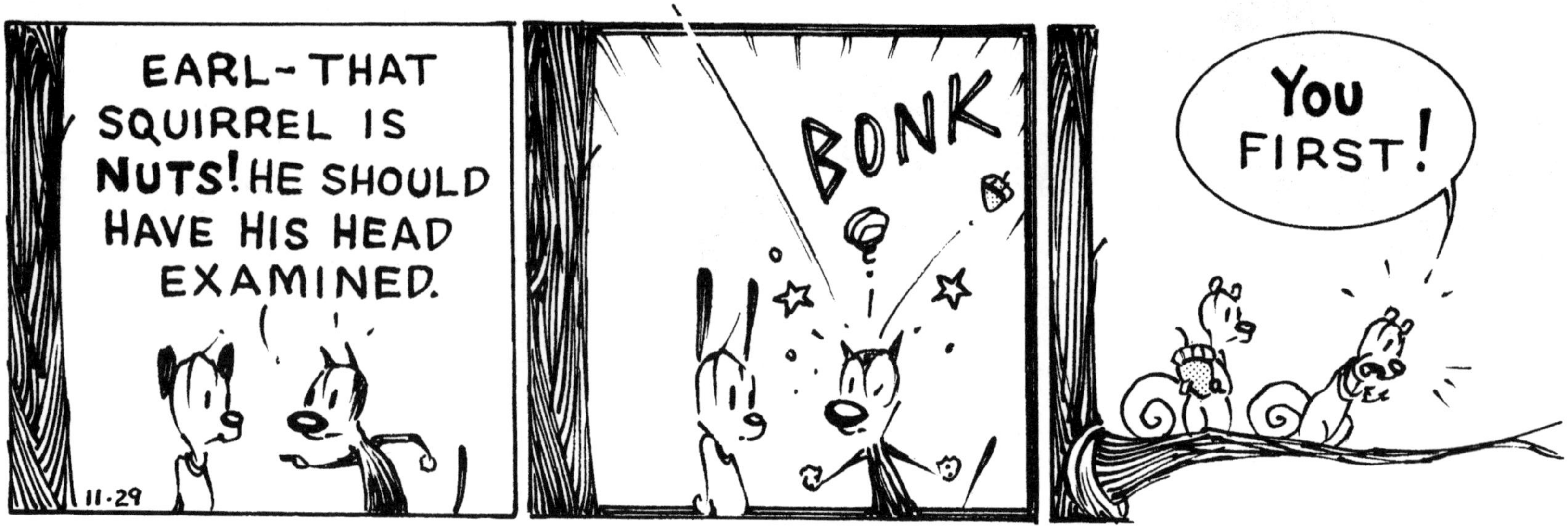
EARL– THAT SQUIRREL IS NUTS! HE SHOULD HAVE HIS HEAD EXAMINED.
11·29
BONK
YOU FIRST!

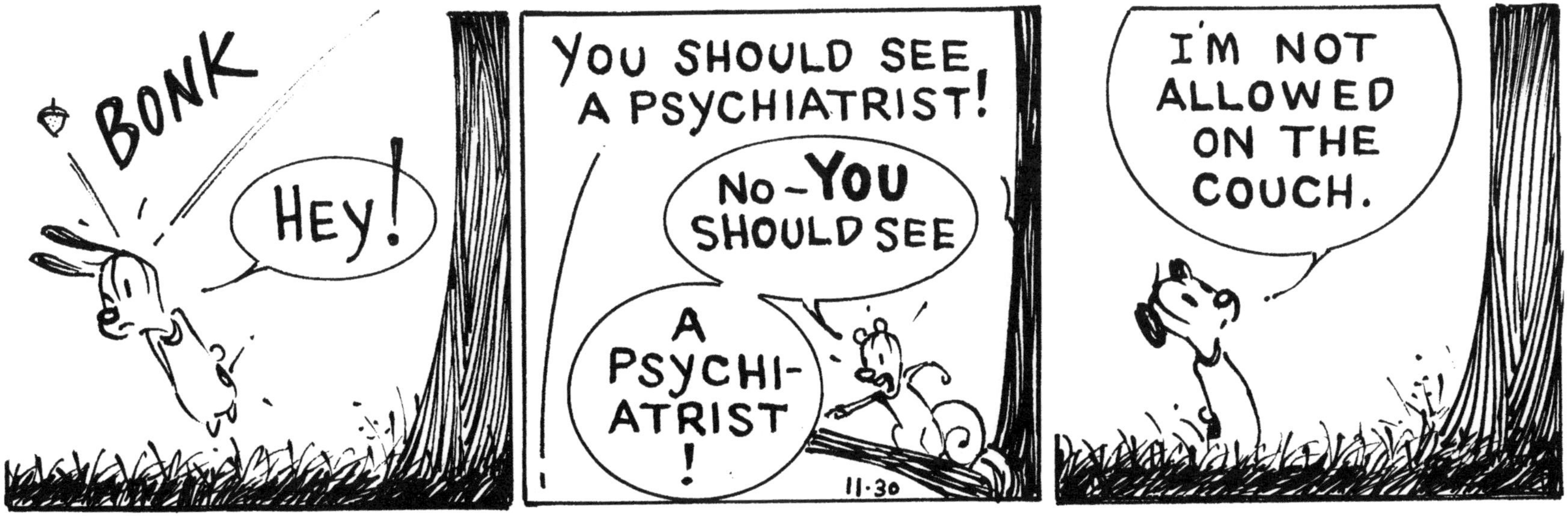
BONK
HEY!
YOU SHOULD SEE A PSYCHIATRIST!
NO-YOU SHOULD SEE
A PSYCHIATRIST!
11·30
I'M NOT ALLOWED ON THE COUCH.

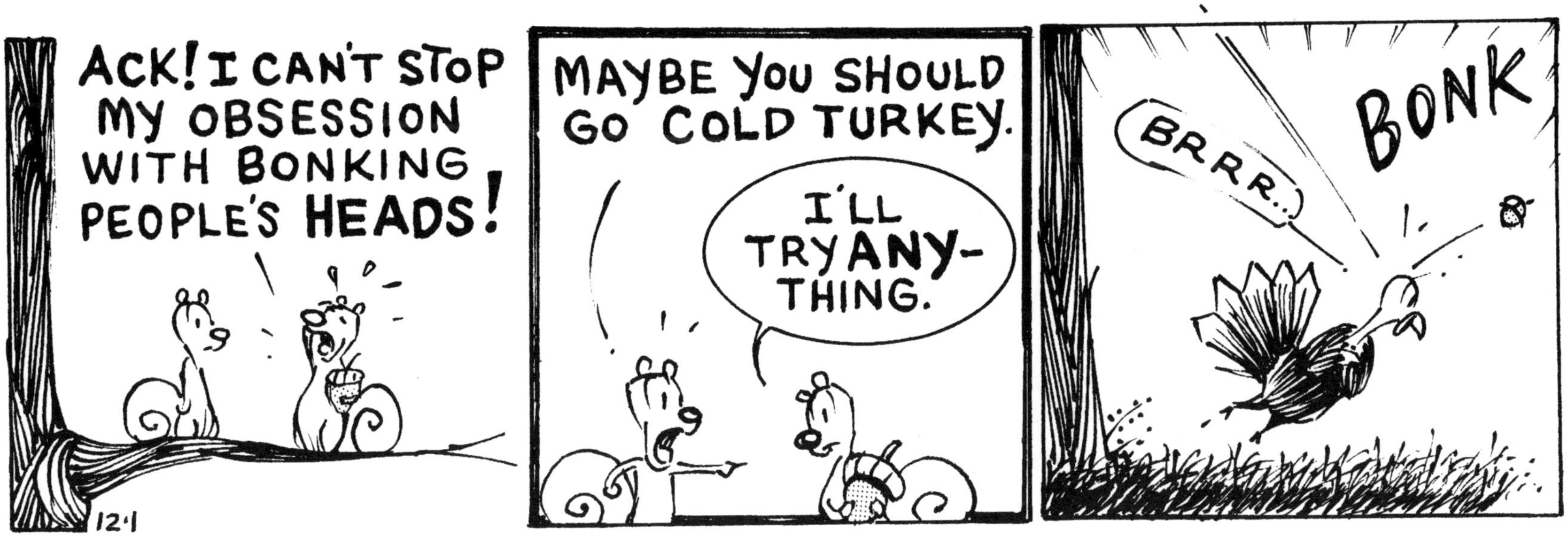
ACK! I CAN'T STOP MY OBSESSION WITH BONKING PEOPLE'S HEADS!
12·1
MAYBE YOU SHOULD GO COLD TURKEY.
I'LL TRY ANYTHING.
BRRRR...
BONK

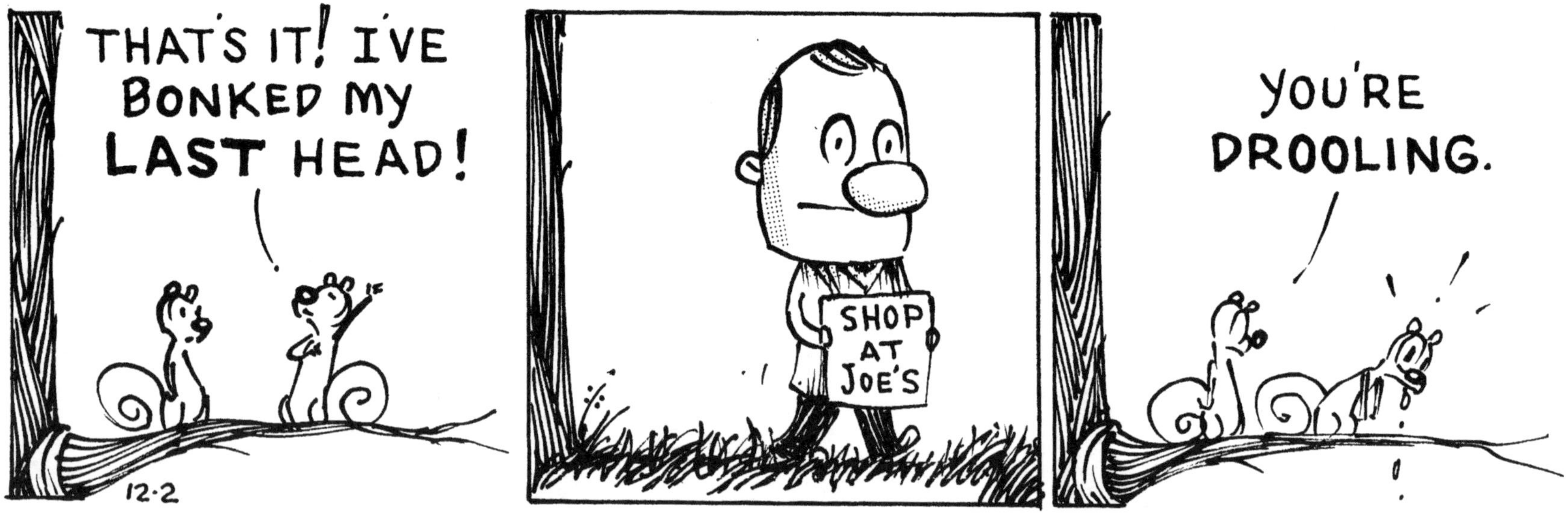

THAT'S IT! I'VE BONKED MY LAST HEAD!
12·2
SHOP AT JOE'S
YOU'RE DROOLING.

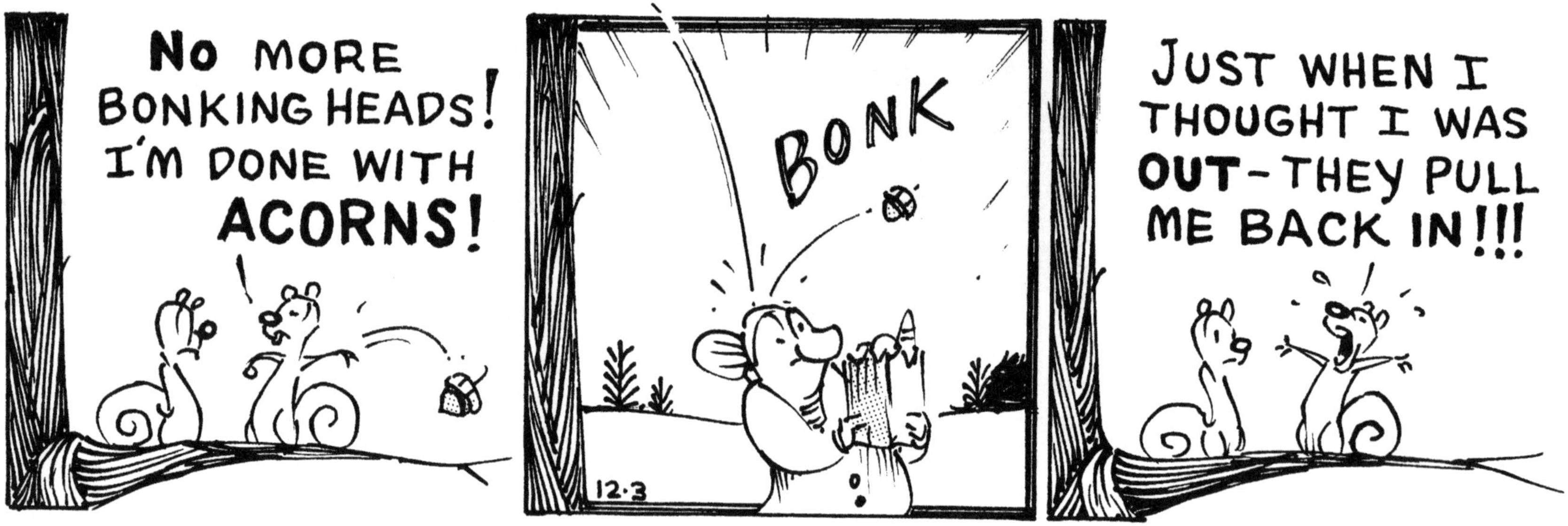

NO MORE BONKING HEADS! I'M DONE WITH ACORNS!
BONK
12·3
JUST WHEN I THOUGHT I WAS OUT–THEY PULL ME BACK IN!!!

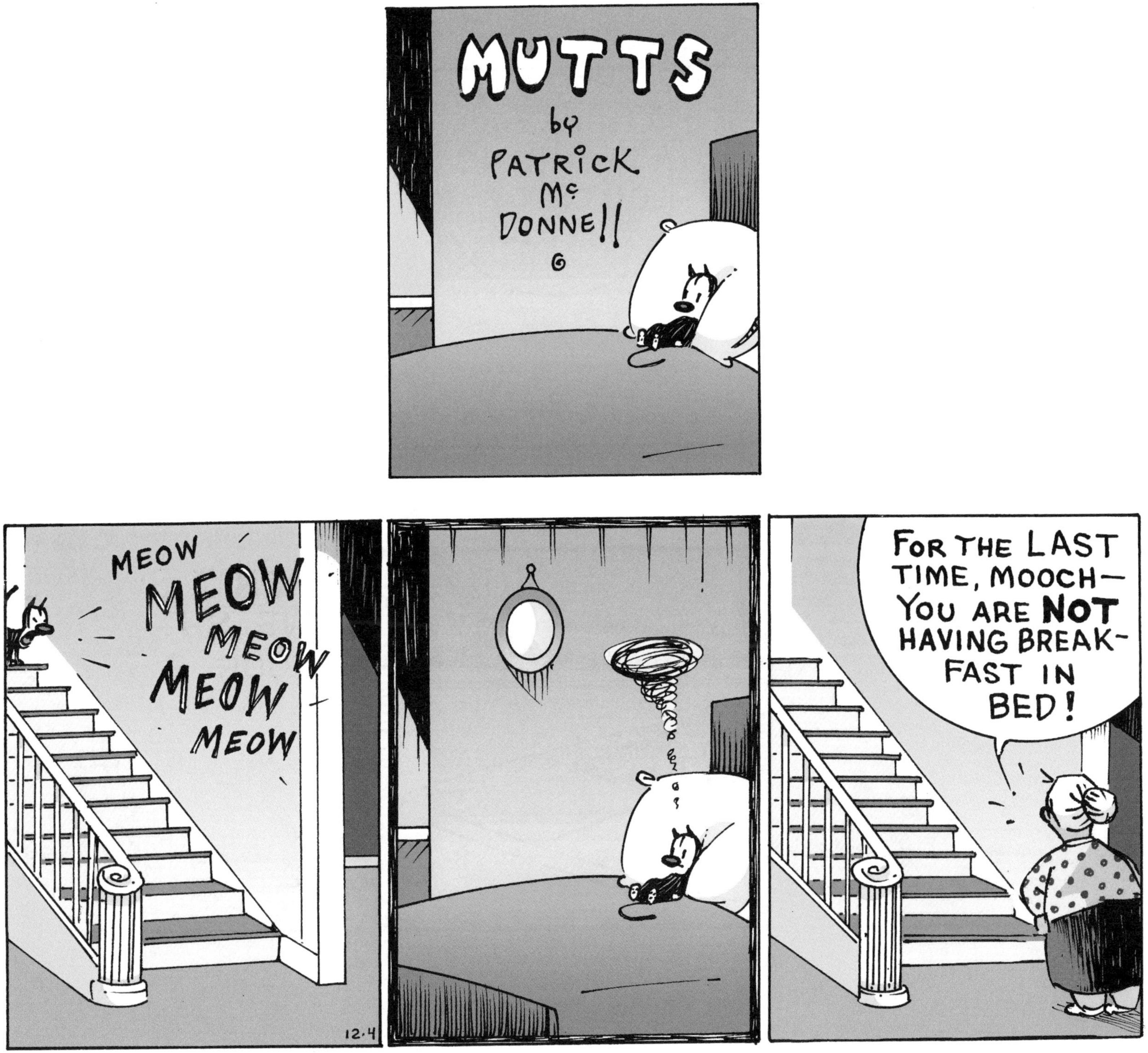
MUTTS
by PATRICK Mc DONNELL
©
MEOW MEOW MEOW MEOW MEOW
12.4
FOR THE LAST TIME, MOOCH— YOU ARE NOT HAVING BREAK-FAST IN BED!

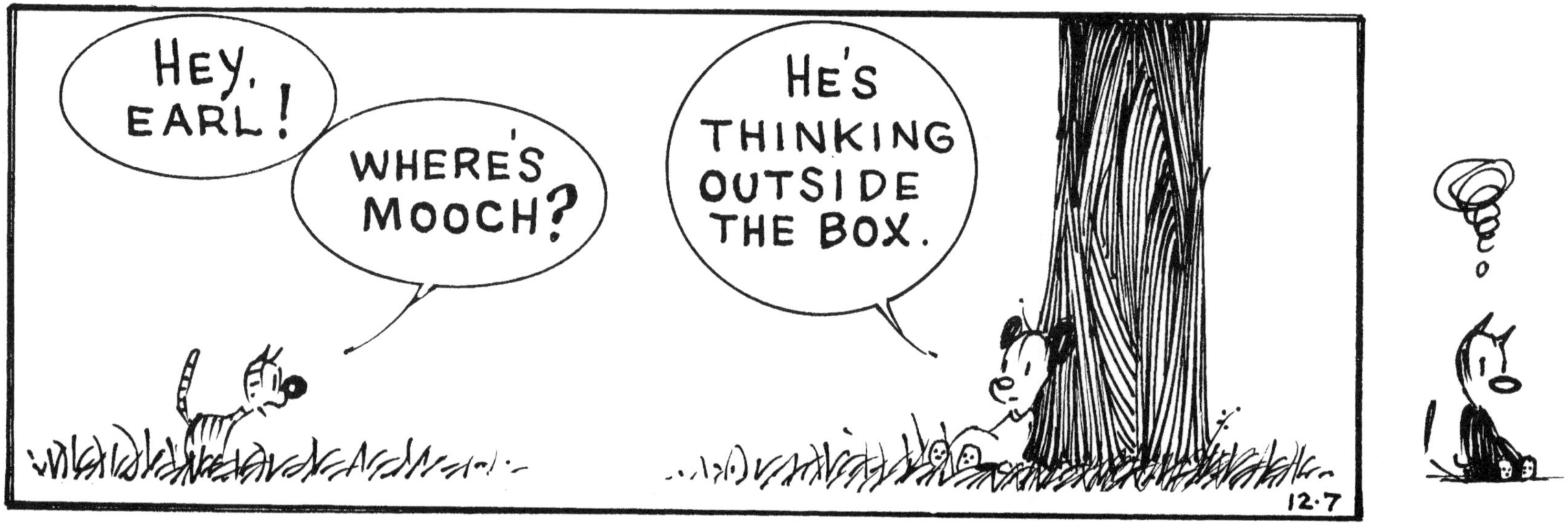
HEY, EARL!
WHERE'S MOOCH?
HE'S THINKING OUTSIDE THE BOX.
12·7

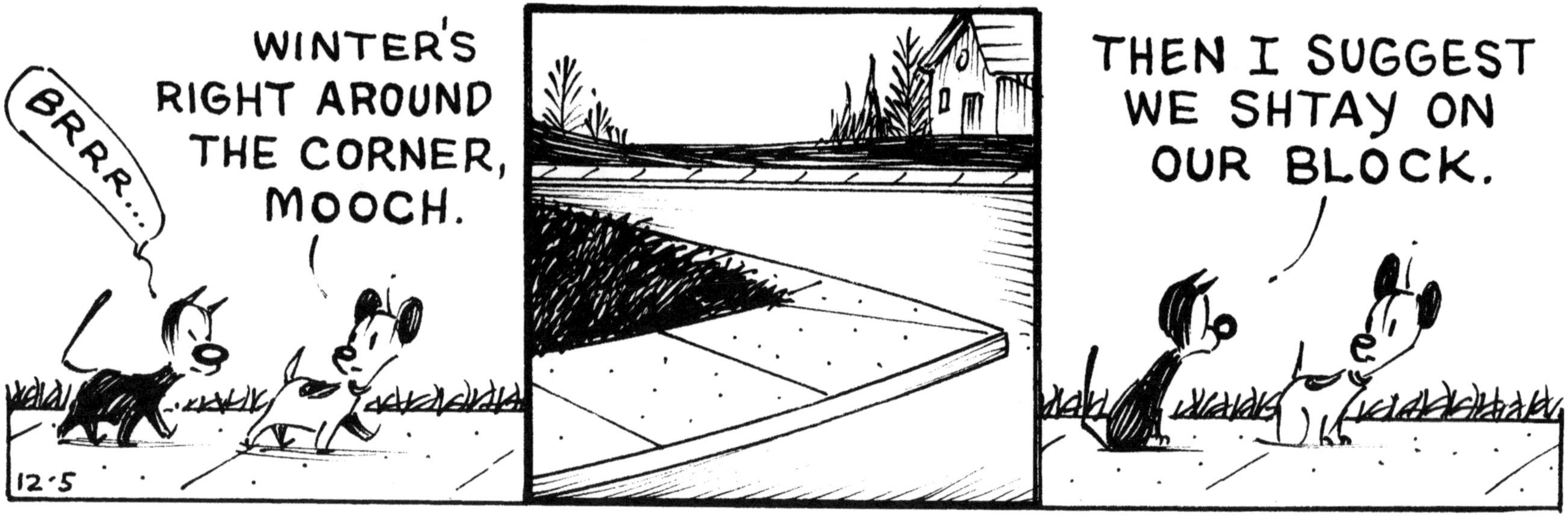
BRRRR...
WINTER'S RIGHT AROUND THE CORNER, MOOCH.
THEN I SUGGEST WE SHTAY ON OUR BLOCK.
12·5

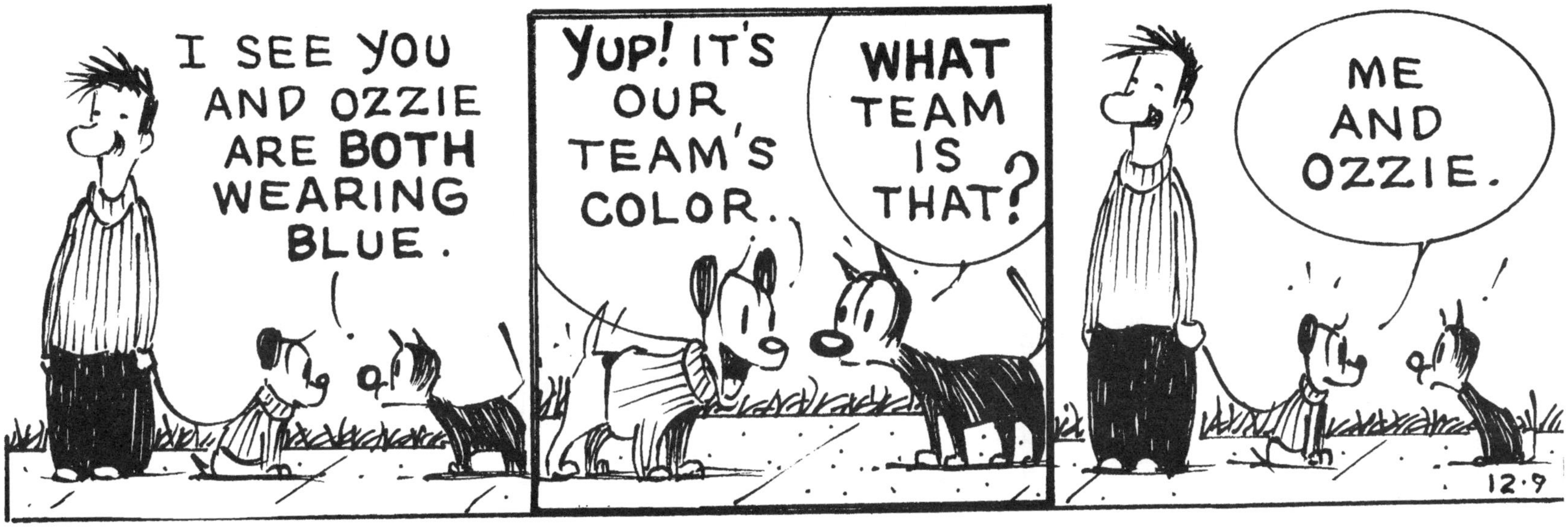
I SEE YOU AND OZZIE ARE BOTH WEARING BLUE.
YUP! IT'S OUR TEAM'S COLOR.
WHAT TEAM IS THAT?
ME AND OZZIE.
12·9

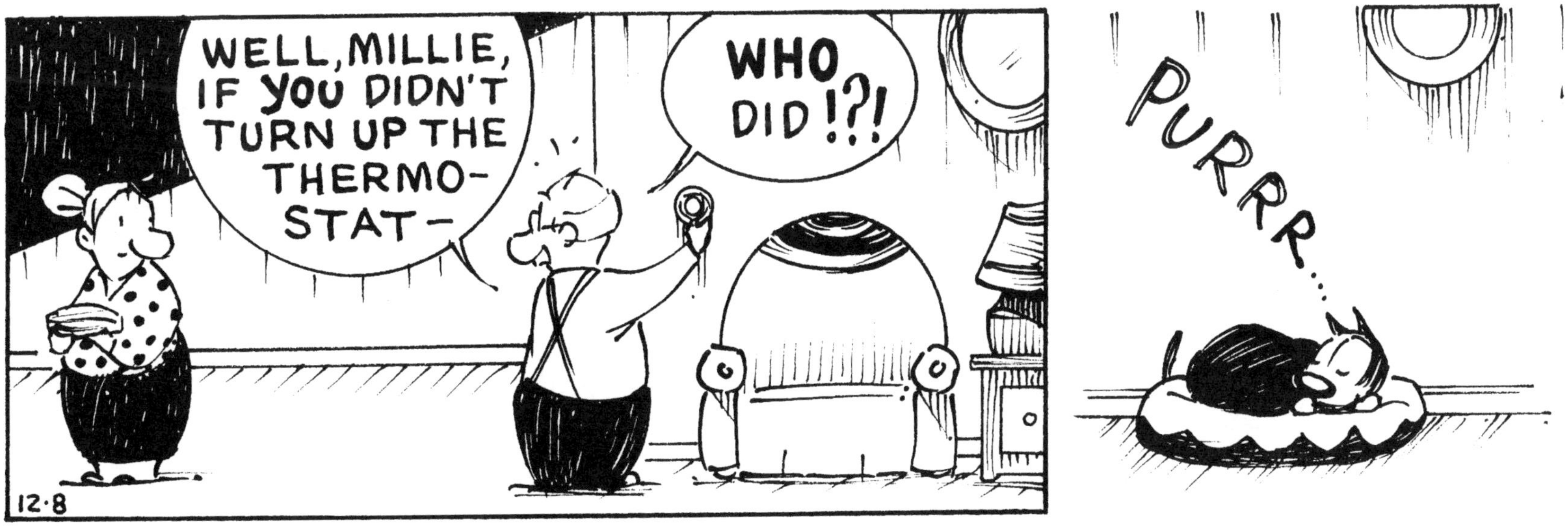
WELL, MILLIE, IF YOU DIDN'T TURN UP THE THERMO-STAT-
WHO DID!?!
12·8
PURRR....

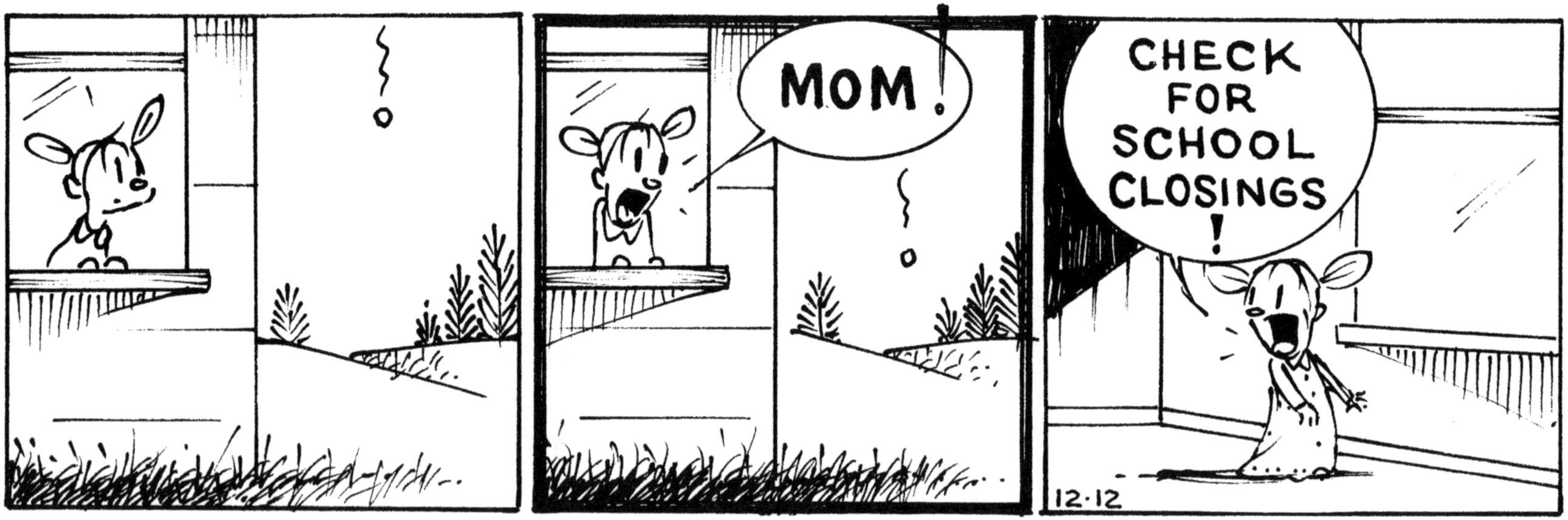
MOM!
CHECK FOR SCHOOL CLOSINGS!
12·12

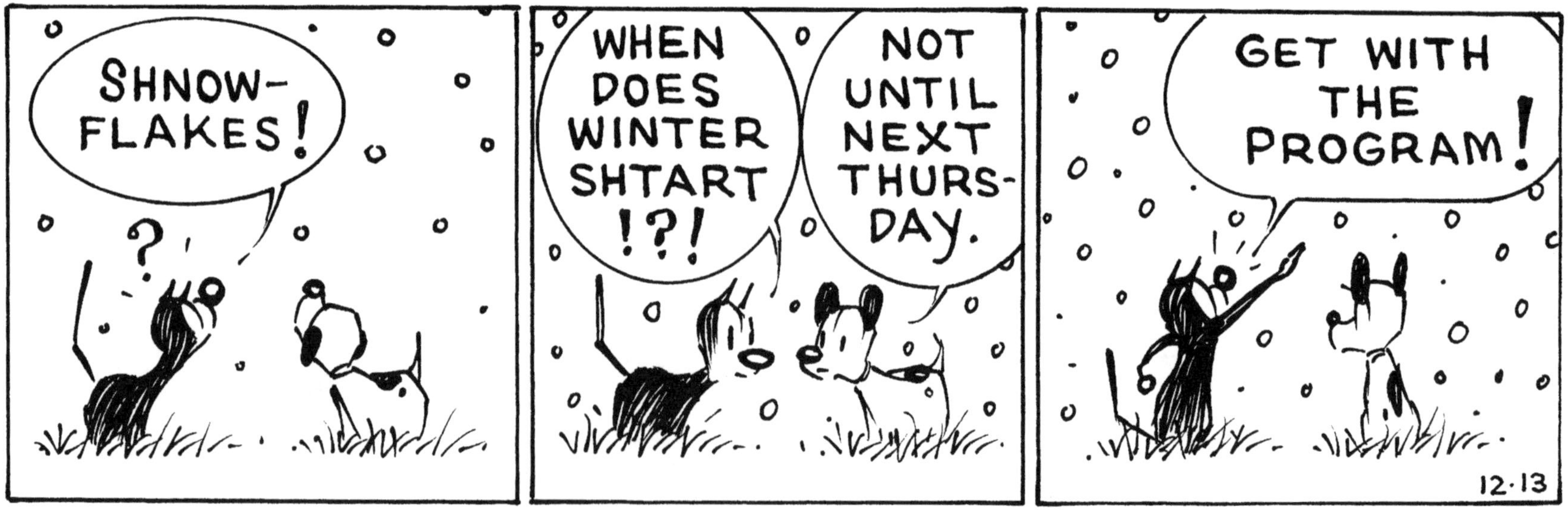
SHNOW-FLAKES!
?
WHEN DOES WINTER SHTART !?!
NOT UNTIL NEXT THURS-DAY.
GET WITH THE PROGRAM!
12·13

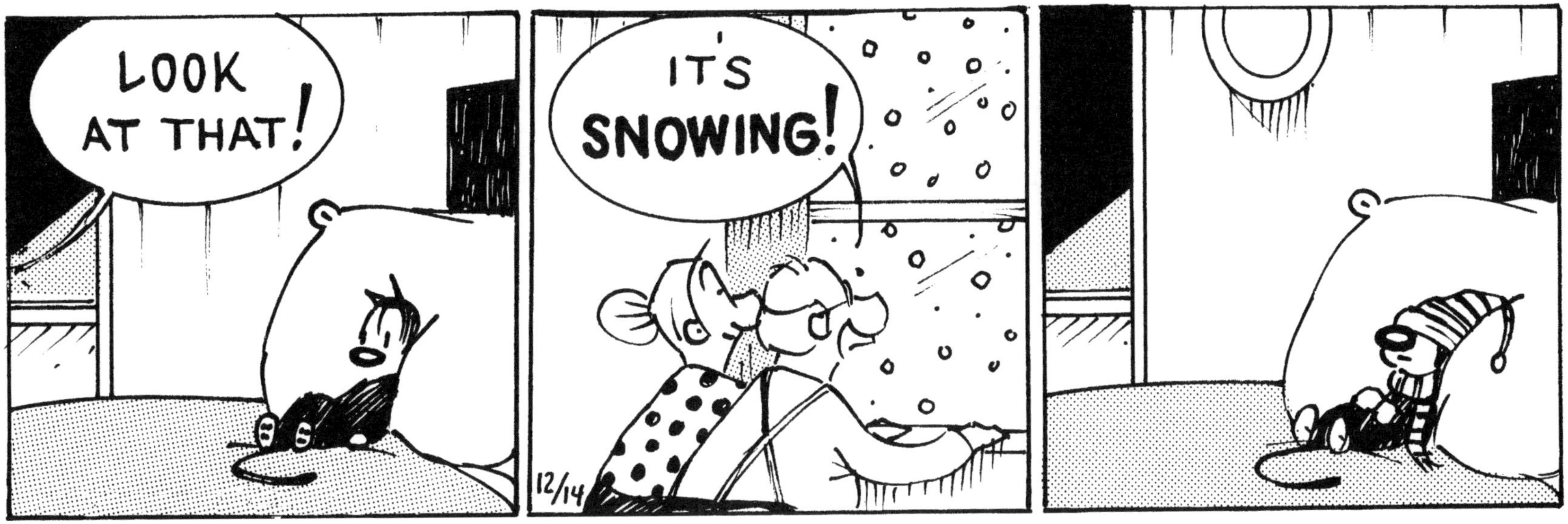
LOOK AT THAT!
IT'S SNOWING!
12/14

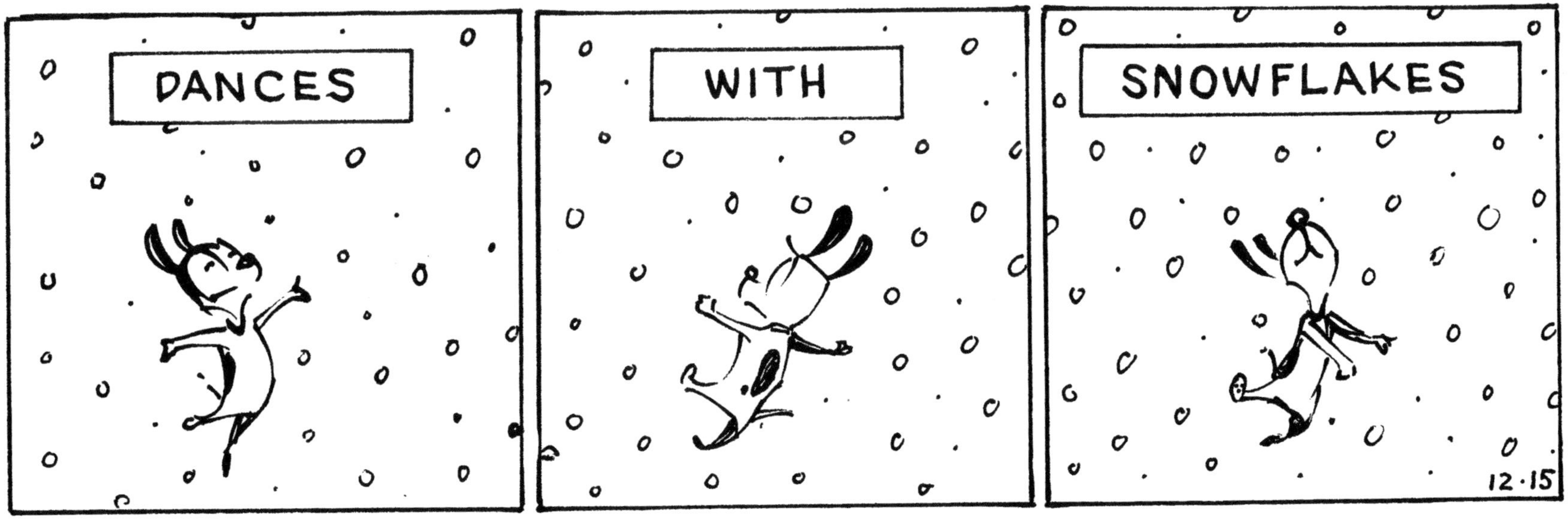
DANCES
WITH
SNOWFLAKES
12·15

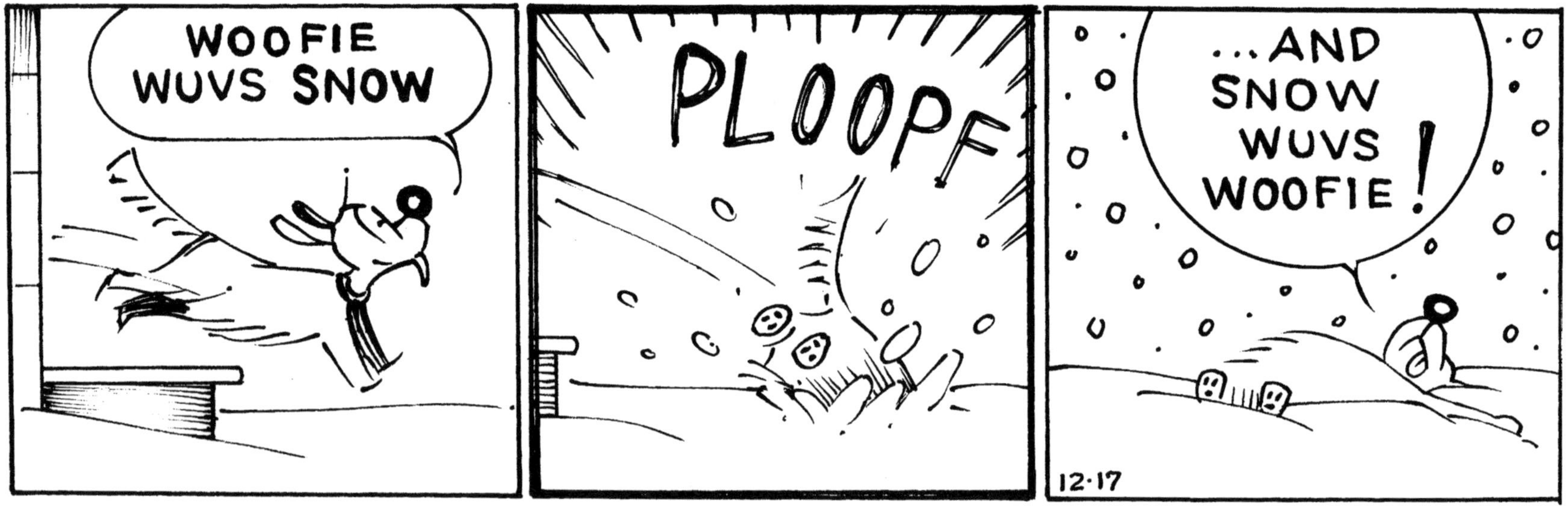
WOOFIE WUVS SNOW
PLOOPF
...AND SNOW WUVS WOOFIE!
12·17

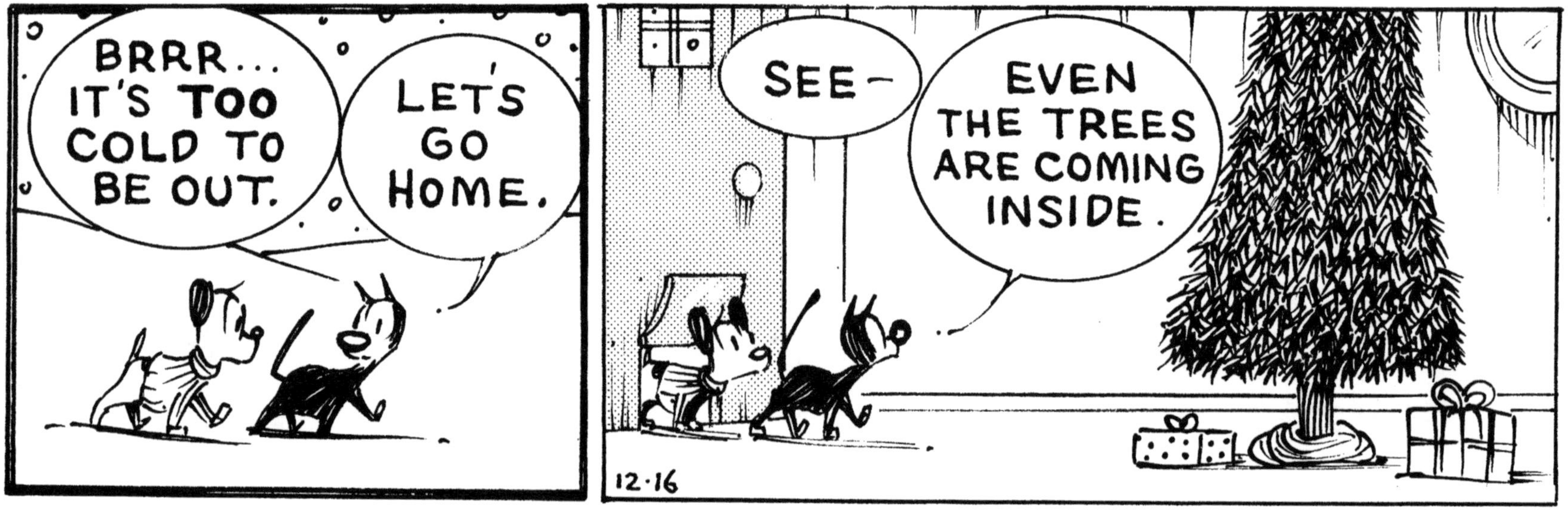
BRRR... IT'S TOO COLD TO BE OUT.
LET'S GO HOME.
SEE-
EVEN THE TREES ARE COMING INSIDE.
12·16

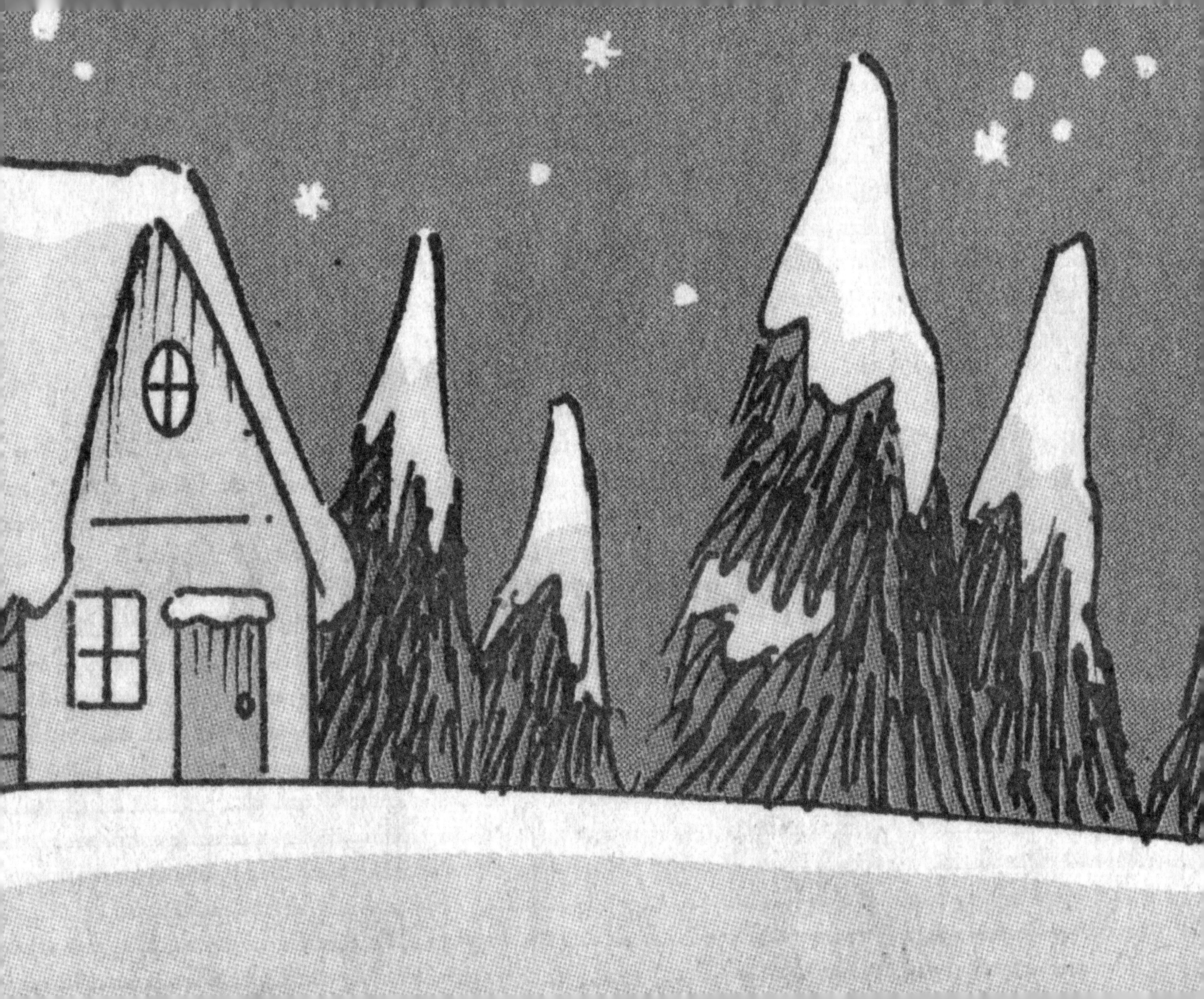

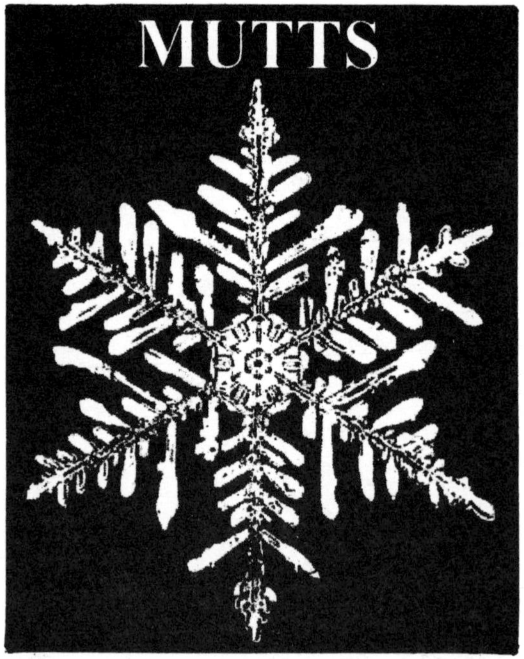
MUTTS

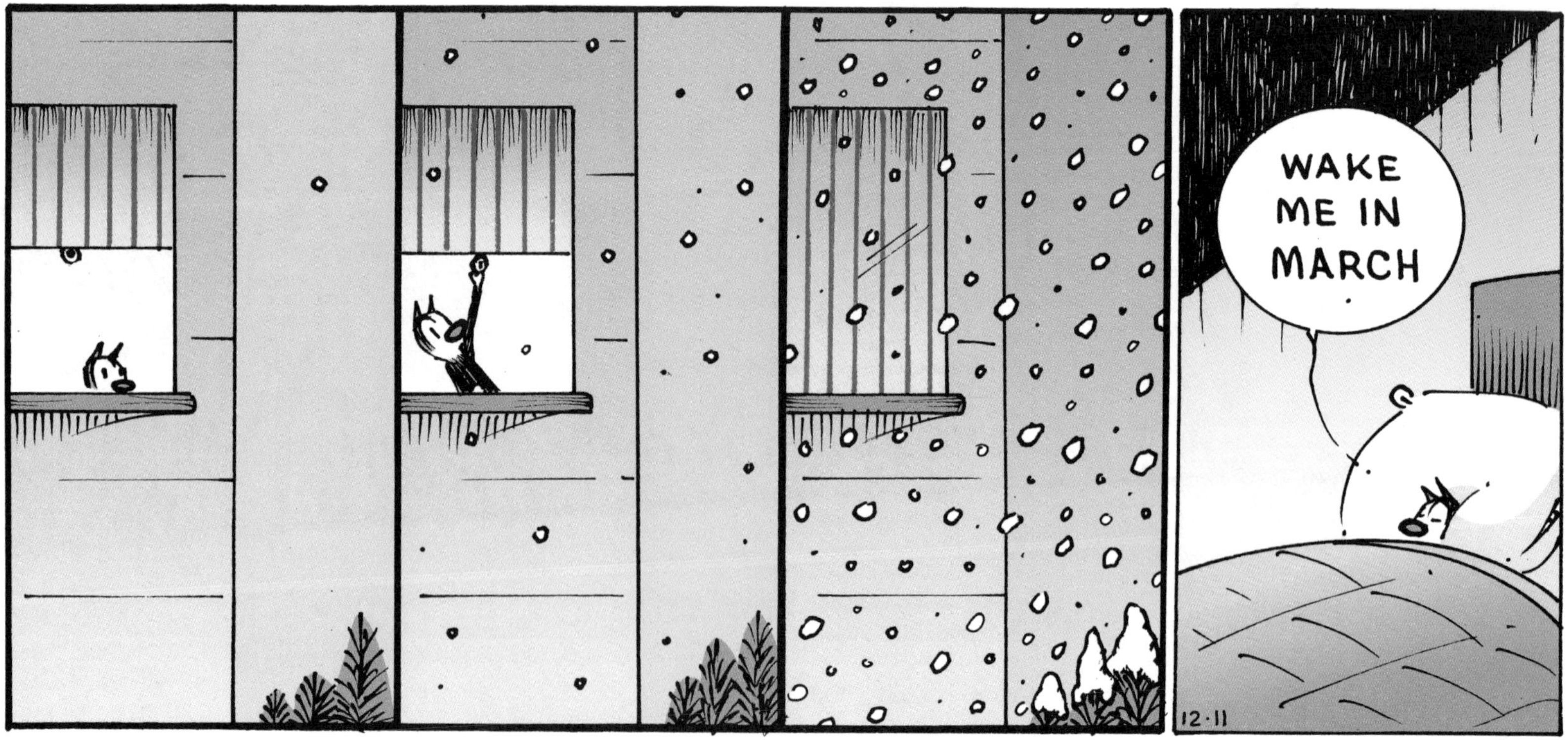
WAKE ME IN MARCH
12·11

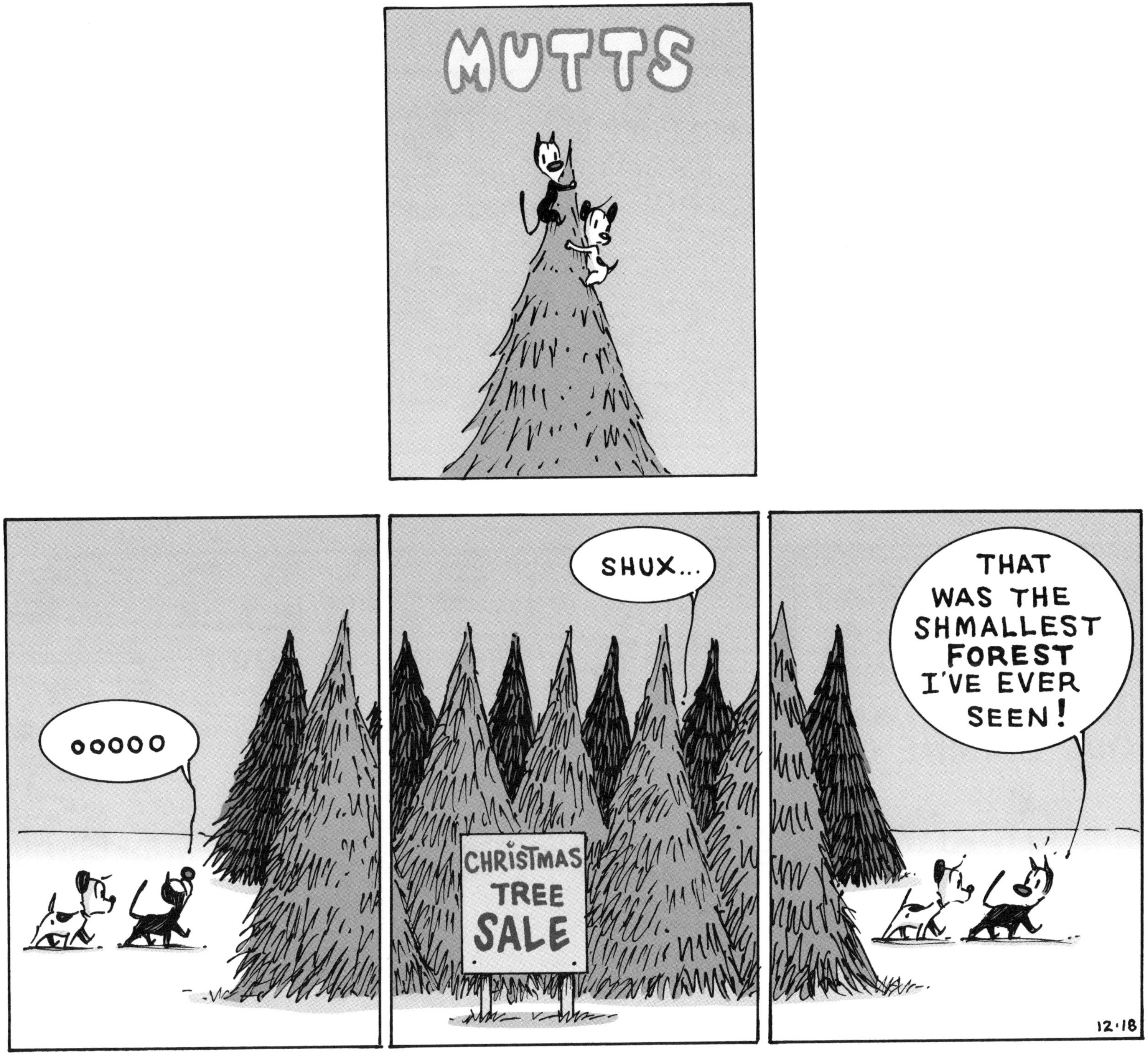
MUTTS
OOOOO
SHUX...
CHRISTMAS TREE SALE
THAT WAS THE SHMALLEST FOREST I'VE EVER SEEN!
12·18

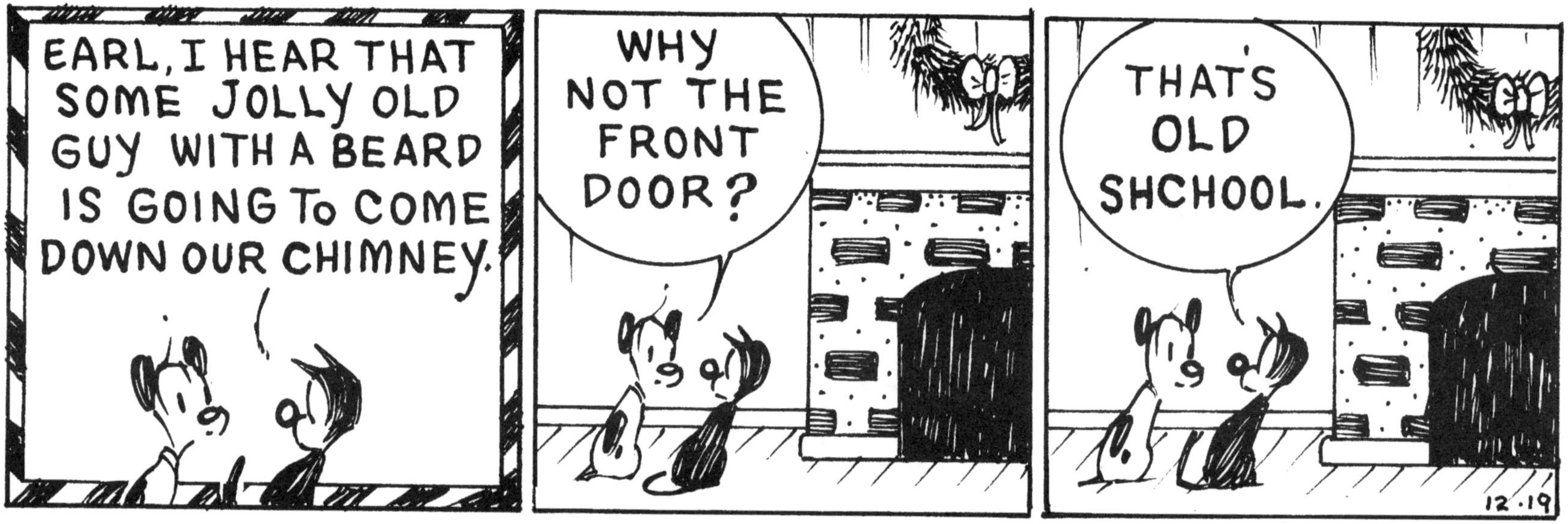
EARL, I HEAR THAT SOME JOLLY OLD GUY WITH A BEARD IS GOING TO COME DOWN OUR CHIMNEY.
WHY NOT THE FRONT DOOR?
THAT'S OLD SHCHOOL.
12·19

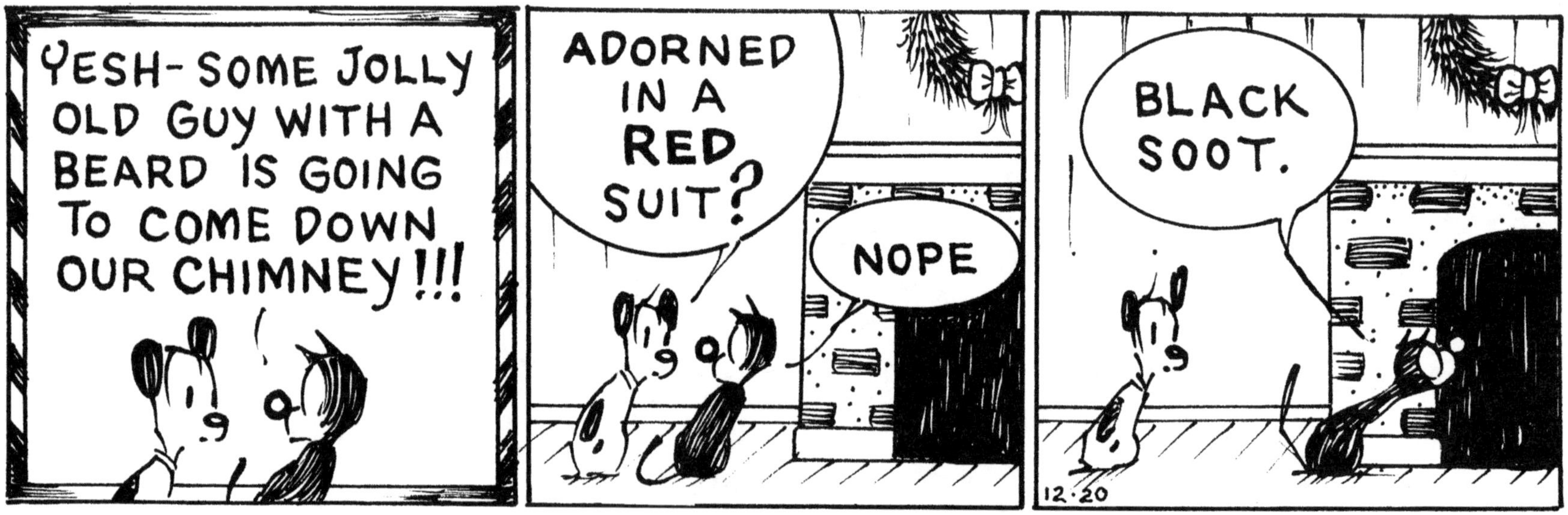
YESH- SOME JOLLY OLD GUY WITH A BEARD IS GOING TO COME DOWN OUR CHIMNEY!!!
ADORNED IN A **RED** SUIT?
NOPE
BLACK SOOT.
12·20

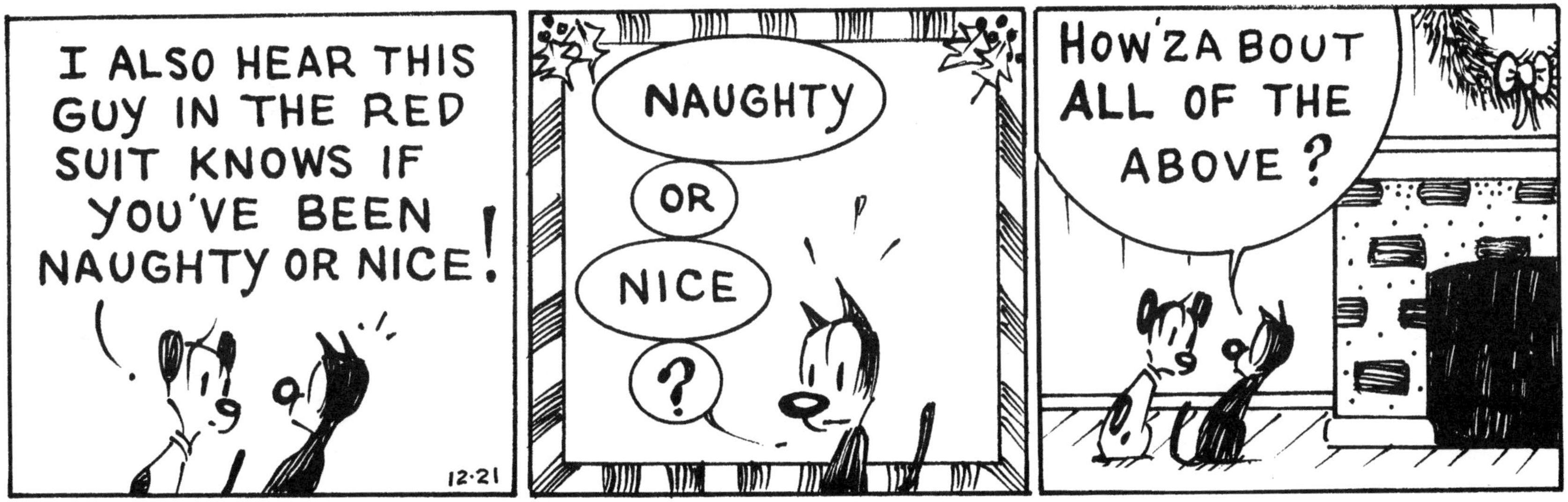
I ALSO HEAR THIS GUY IN THE RED SUIT KNOWS IF YOU'VE BEEN NAUGHTY OR NICE!
12·21
NAUGHTY
OR
NICE
?
HOW'ZA BOUT ALL OF THE ABOVE?

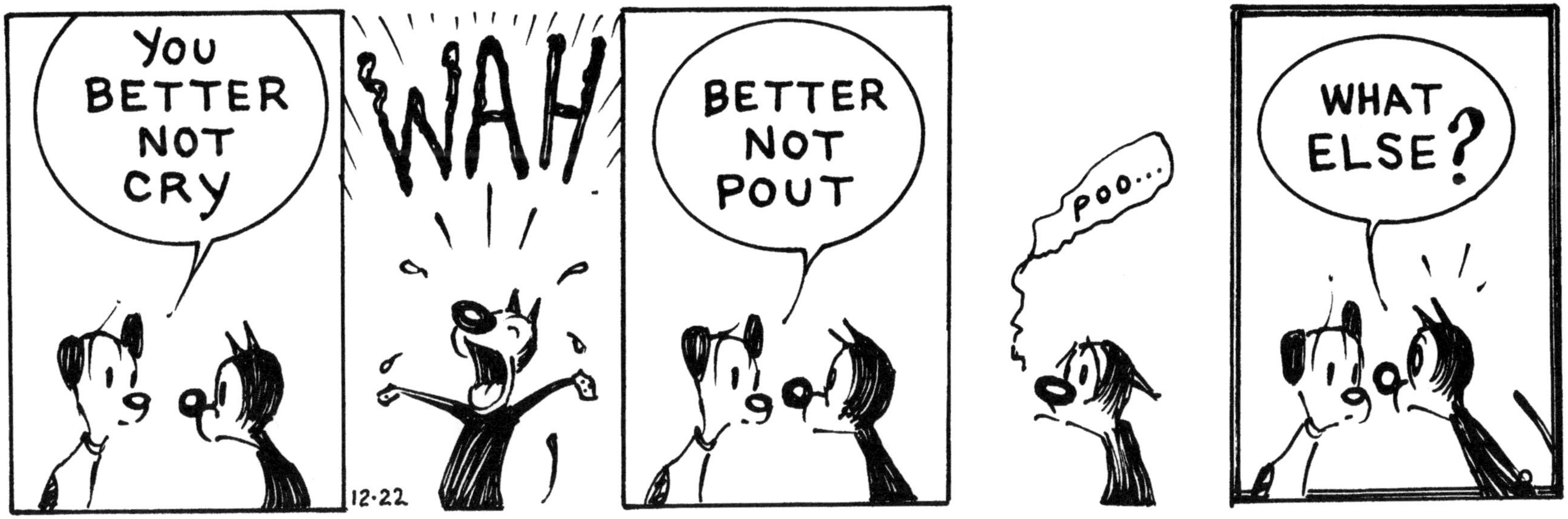
YOU BETTER NOT CRY
WAH
12·22
BETTER NOT POUT
POO...
WHAT ELSE?

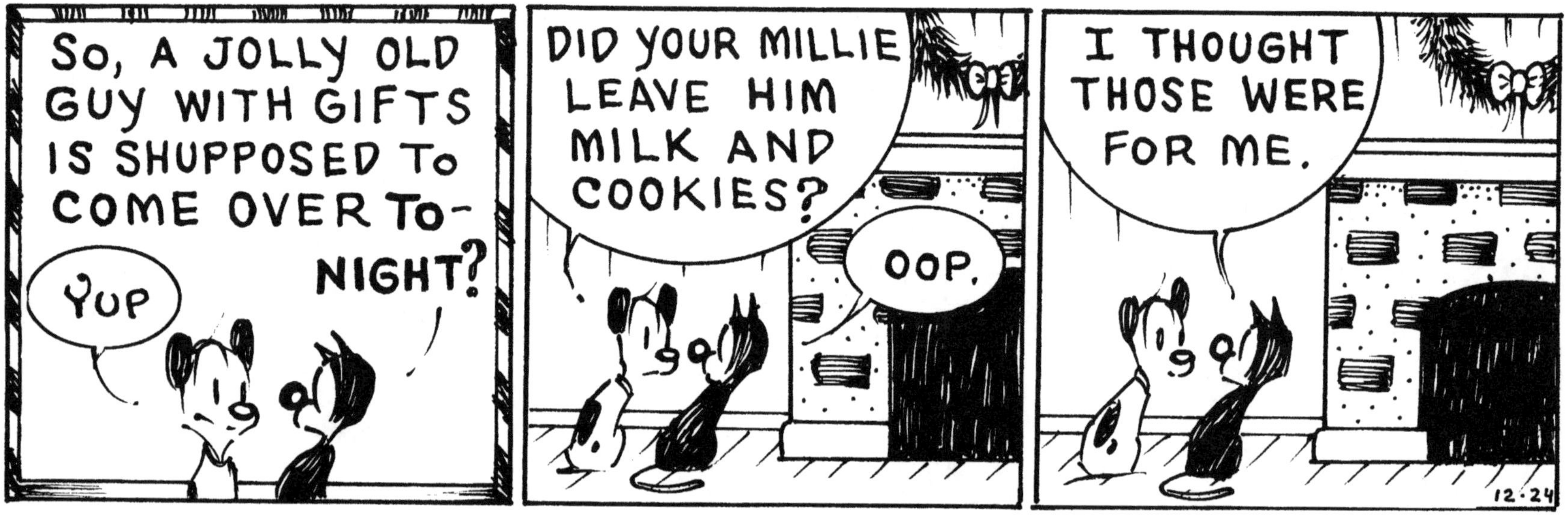
So, A JOLLY OLD GUY WITH GIFTS IS SHUPPOSED To COME OVER TO-
NIGHT?
YUP
DID YOUR MILLIE LEAVE HIM MILK AND COOKIES?
OOP.
I THOUGHT THOSE WERE FOR ME.
12·24

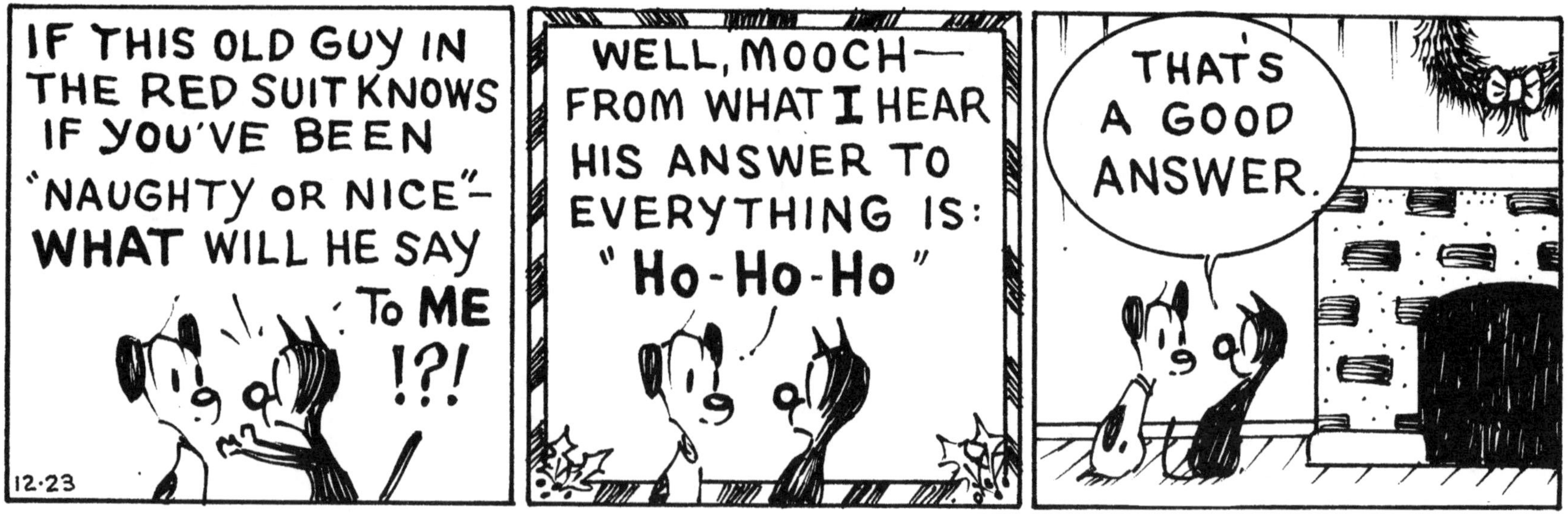
IF THIS OLD GUY IN THE RED SUIT KNOWS IF YOU'VE BEEN "NAUGHTY OR NICE"— WHAT WILL HE SAY
To ME !?!
12·23
WELL, MOOCH— FROM WHAT I HEAR HIS ANSWER TO EVERYTHING IS: "Ho-Ho-Ho"
THAT'S A GOOD ANSWER.

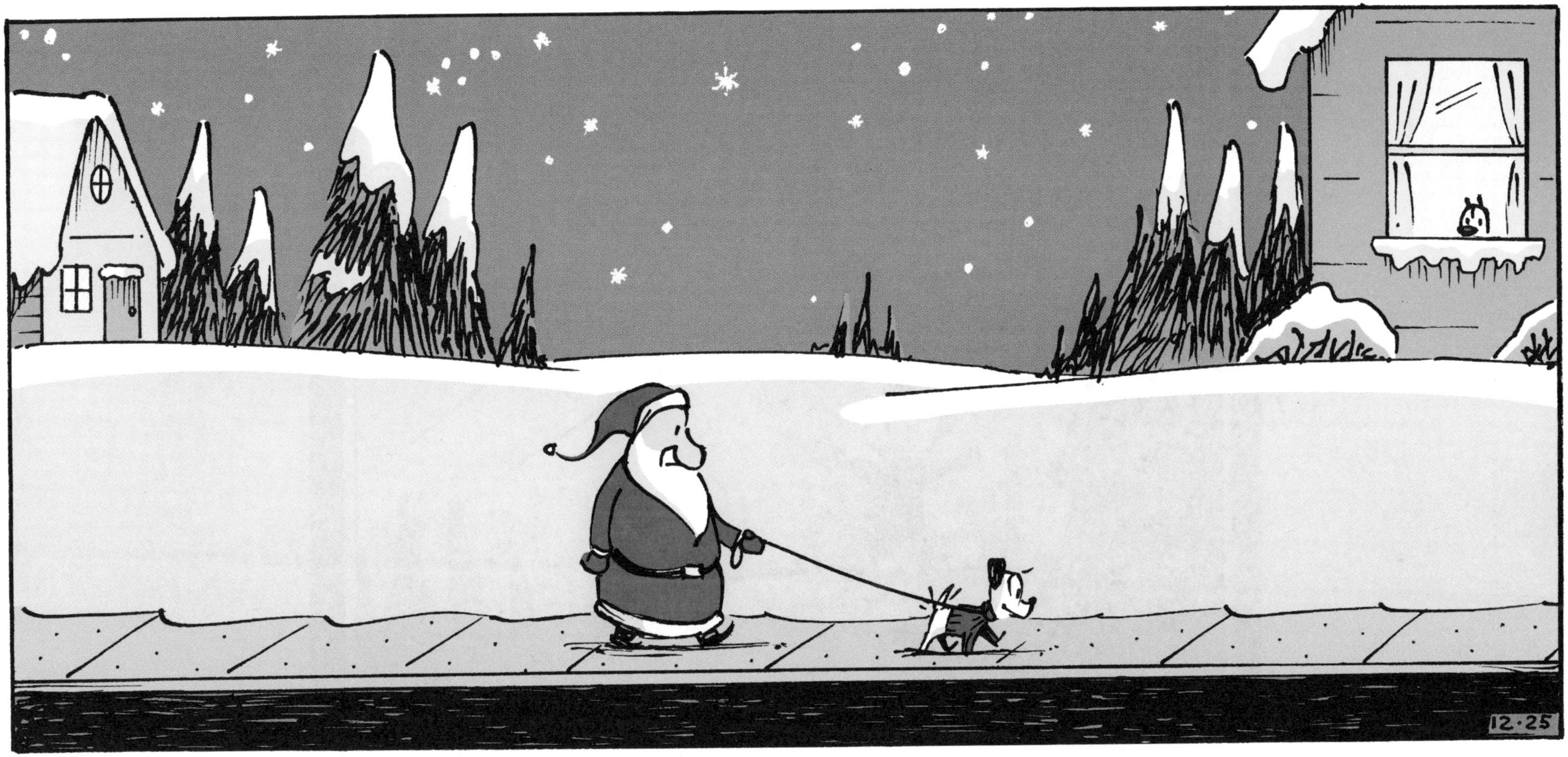
12·25

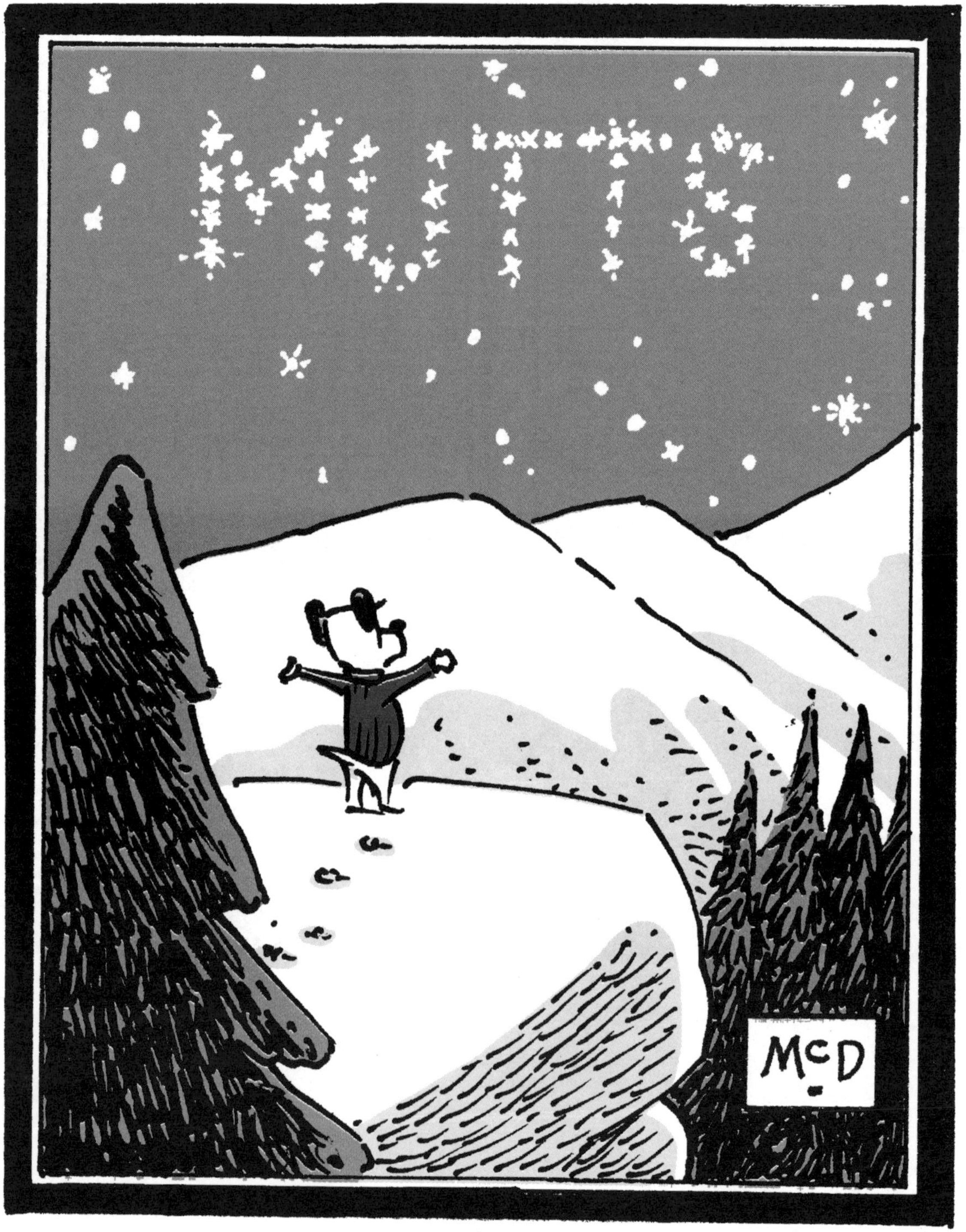
MUTTS
McD